COLORADO S

MW00891993

COLORADO COURT RULES

COLORADO RULES OF

CRIMINAL PROCEDURE

2024 EDITION

3

4

Scope, Purpose, and Construction

Rule 1 - Scope

These Rules govern the procedure in all criminal proceedings in all courts of record with the exceptions stated in Rule 54.

Colo. R. Crim. P. 1

Annotation Law reviews. For article on the Rules of Criminal Procedure, see 34 Rocky Mt. L. Rev. 1 (1961). For article, "1963 Amendments to Colorado Rules of Criminal Procedure", see 35 U. Colo. L. Rev. 303 (1963). Rules of criminal procedure must be read in pari materia. People ex rel. Farina v. District Court, 184 Colo. 406, 521 P.2d 778 (1974).

Rule 2 - Purpose and Construction

These Rules are intended to provide for the just determination of criminal proceedings. They shall be construed to secure simplicity in procedure, fairness in administration, and the elimination of unjustifiable expense and delay.

Colo. R. Crim. P. 2

Initiation of Preliminary Felony Proceedings

Rule 3 - The Felony Complaint

(a) The felony complaint shall be a written statement of the essential facts constituting the offense charged, signed by the prosecutor and filed in the court having jurisdiction over the offense charged.

(b) Repealed.

Colo. R. Crim. P. 3

Source: Amended and adopted September 4, 1997, effective 1/1/1998; a amended and adopted November 22, 2006, effective 1/1/2007.

Annotation Applied in People v. Stoppel, 637 P.2d 384 (Colo. 1981); People v. Abbott, 638 P.2d 781 (Colo. 1981).

Rule 4 - Warrant or Summons Upon Felony Complaint

(a) Issuance.

(1)Request by Prosecution. Upon the filing of a felony complaint in the county court, the prosecuting attorney shall request that the court issue either a warrant for the arrest of the defendant, or a summons to be served on the defendant.

(2)Affidavits or Sworn Testimony. If a warrant is requested, the felony complaint must contain or be accompanied by a sworn statement of facts establishing probable cause to believe that a criminal offense has been committed, and that the offense was committed by the person for whom the warrant is sought. In lieu of such a sworn statement, the felony complaint may be supplemented by sworn testimony of such facts. Such testimony must be transcribed and then signed under oath by the witness giving the testimony.

(3) Summons in Lieu of Warrant. Except in class 1, class 2, and class 3 felonies, level 1 and level 2 drug felonies, and unclassified felonies punishable by a maximum penalty of more than 10 years, whenever a felony complaint has been filed prior to the arrest of the person named as defendant therein, the court shall have power to issue a summons commanding the appearance of the defendant in lieu of an arrest warrant, unless a law enforcement officer presents in writing a basis to believe there is a significant risk of flight or that the victim's or public's safety may be compromised. If empowered to issue a summons under this subsection (a)(3), the court shall issue a summons instead of an arrest warrant when the prosecuting attorney so requests.

(4)Standards Relating to Issuance of Summons. Except in class 1, class 2, and class 3 felonies, level 1 and level 2 drug felonies, and unclassified felonies punishable by a maximum penalty of more than 10 years the general policy shall favor issuance of a summons instead of a warrant for the arrest of the defendant. When an application is made to a court for issuance of an arrest warrant or summons, the court may require the applicant to provide such information as reasonably is available concerning the following:

(I) The defendant's residence;

(II) The defendant's employment;

(III) The defendant's family relationships;

(IV) The defendant's past history of response to legal process; and

7

(V) The defendant's past criminal record.

(5)Failure to Appear. If any person properly summoned pursuant to this Rule fails to appear as commanded by the summons, the court shall forthwith issue a warrant for the arrest of that person.

(6)Corporations. When a corporation is charged with the commission of an offense, the court shall issue a summons setting forth the nature of the offense and commanding the corporation to appear before the court at a certain time and place.

(b) Form.

(1) Warrant. The arrest warrant shall be a written order issued by a judge of a court of record directed to any peace officer and shall:

(I) State the defendant's name or if that is unknown, any name or description by which the defendant can be identified with reasonable certainty;

(II) Command that the defendant be arrested and brought without unnecessary delay before the nearest available judge of a county or district court;

(III) Identify the nature of the offense;

(IV) Have endorsed upon it the amount of bail if the offense is bailable; and

(V) Be signed by the issuing county judge.

(2) Summons. If a summons is issued in lieu of a warrant pursuant to this Rule, the summons shall:

(I) Be in writing;

(II) State the defendant's name and address;

(III) Identify the nature of the offense;

(IV) State the date when issued and the county where issued;

(V) Be signed by the judge or clerk of the court with the title of the office; and

(VI) Command the person to appear before the court at a certain time and place.

(c) Execution or Service and Return.

(1) Warrant.

(I) By Whom. The warrant may be executed by any peace officer.

(II) Territorial Limits. The warrant may be executed anywhere within Colorado.

(III) Manner. The warrant shall be executed by arresting the defendant. The warrant need not be in the officer's possession at the time of the arrest, in which event the officers shall then inform the defendant of the offense and of the fact that a warrant has been issued, and upon request shall show the warrant to the defendant as soon as possible. If the warrant is in the officer's possession at the time of the arrest, then the officer shall show the warrant to the defendant immediately upon request.

(IV) Return. The peace officer executing a warrant shall make return thereof to the issuing court. At the request of the prosecuting attorney any unexecuted warrant shall be returned and cancelled. At the request of the prosecuting attorney, made while a complaint is pending, a warrant returned unexecuted and not cancelled, or a duplicate thereof, may be delivered by the county judge to any peace officer or other authorized person for execution.

(2) Summons.

(I) By Whom. The summons may be served by any person authorized to effect service in a civil action.

(II) Territorial Limits. The summons may be served anywhere within Colorado.

(III) Manner. A summons issued pursuant to this Rule may be served in the same manner as the summons in a civil action or by mailing it to the defendant's last known address, not less than 14 days prior to the time the defendant is required to appear, by registered mail with return receipt requested or certified mail with return receipt requested. Service by mail shall be complete upon the return of the receipt signed by the defendant or signed on behalf of the defendant by one authorized by law to do so. The summons for the appearance of a corporation may be served by a peace officer in the manner provided for service of summons upon a corporation in a civil action.

(IV) Return. At least one business day prior to the return day, the person to whom a summons has been delivered for service shall make return thereof to the county court before whom the summons is returnable. At the request of the prosecuting attorney, made while a complaint is pending, a summons returned unserved, or a duplicate thereof, may be delivered by the county judge to any peace officer or other authorized person for service.

Colo. R. Crim. P. 4

Source: c2III amended and adopted October 15, 2009, effective 1/1/2010; c2III and c2IV amended and adopted December 14, 2011, effective 7/1/2012; amended and Adopted by the Court, En Banc, 9/11/2017, effective immediately.

Annotation I. General Consideration. Applied in People v. Kelderman, 44 Colo. App. 487, 618 P.2d 723 (1980). II. Issuance. Probable cause necessary for issuance of warrant. To support the issuance of an arrest warrant, the complaint must comply with the probable cause requirements of the fourth amendment to the United States constitution, § 7 of art. II, Colo. Const., and this rule. People v. Moreno, 176 Colo. 488, 491 P.2d 575 (1971). And the existence of probable cause must be determined by member of the judiciary, rather than by a law enforcement officer who is employed to apprehend criminals and to bring charges against those who choose to violate the law. People v. Moreno, 176 Colo. 488, 491 P.2d 575 (1971). Judge not to accept mere conclusion of complainant. In determining whether or not probable cause exists, a judge should not accept without question the complainant's mere conclusion that the person whose arrest is sought has committed a crime. People v. Moreno, 176 Colo. 488, 491 P.2d 575 (1971). But should require and examine underlying facts. Before a warrant for arrest can be issued, the judicial officer issuing such a warrant must be supplied with sufficient information to support an independent judgment that probable cause exists for the warrant. People v. Moreno, 176 Colo. 488, 491 P.2d 575 (1971). A complaint standing alone will not support an arrest warrant where no facts are set forth to establish probable cause. Sergent v. People, 177 Colo. 354, 497 P.2d 983 (1972). So judge may require supplemental sworn testimony or amendment of complaint. Should the judge to whom application has been made for the issuance of an arrest warrant determine that the complaint is insufficient, he can require that sworn testimony be offered to supplement the complaint or that the complaint be amended to set forth additional facts if an arrest warrant is to be issued. And under § 7 of art. II, Colo. Const., any testimony taken to supplement the complaint must be reduced to writing and signed by the witness or witnesses who offer the testimony under oath. People v. Moreno, 176 Colo. 488, 491 P.2d 575 (1971). Warrant and supporting affidavits may overcome insufficiency of complaint. Where federal warrants are supported by affidavits which square with all constitutional requirements, they provide a legitimate basis for an arrest, notwithstanding the insufficiency of the complaint to support an arrest warrant. Sergent v. People, 177 Colo. 354, 497 P.2d 983 (1972). III. Execution. There are no constitutional requirements dictating that an arrest warrant be executed at the earliest opportunity. People v. Nisser, 189 Colo. 471, 542 P.2d 84 (1975). Nor does this rule contain limitations regarding the time within which an arrest warrant must be executed. People v. Nisser, 189 Colo. 471, 542 P.2d 84 (1975). No abuse of process where delay in service not prejudicial. Where the record contains no evidence that the delay in the service of an arrest warrant was intended to prejudice the defendant-or that defendant was, in fact, prejudiced by the six-day postponement of her arrest, but on the other hand, uncontroverted evidence indicates that the delay was caused by the perceived need to protect the identity of an undercover agent in a collateral investigation, the delay in the service of the arrest warrant was not an abuse of process. People v. Nisser, 189 Colo. 471, 542 P.2d 84 (1975). Where and by whom execution authorized. Arrest warrants are not territorially limited and, therefore, may be executed anywhere in Colorado by an officer with authority to arrest in the particular jurisdiction in which the person named in the warrant is found. People v. Hamilton, 666 P.2d 152 (Colo. 1983). Arresting officers are not required to have arrest warrants with them at the time of arrest. Sergent v. People, 177 Colo. 354, 497 P.2d 983 (1972). And execution by unauthorized person immaterial if authorized person present. It is immaterial who executes an arrest warrant provided that individuals with lawful authority to make an arrest are actually present at the scene of the arrest and participate in the arrest process. People v. Schultz, 200 Colo. 47, 611 P.2d 977 (1980).

For service of a summons in a civil action, see C.R.C.P. 4.

Rule 4.1 - County Court Procedure-Misdemeanor and Petty Offense-Warrant or Summons Upon Complaint

Where the offense charged is a misdemeanor or petty offense, the action may be commenced in the county court as provided below in this Rule. This Rule shall have no application to misdemeanors or petty offenses prosecuted in other courts or to felonies.

(a) Definitions.

(1) "Complaint" means a written statement charging the commission of a crime by an alleged offender filed in the county court.

(2) Repealed.

9

(3) "Summons" means a written order or notice directing that a person appear before a designated county court at a stated time and place and answer to a charge against him.

(4) "Summons and complaint" means a document combining the functions of both a summons and a complaint.

(b) Initiation of the Prosecution.

(1) Prosecution of a misdemeanor or petty offense may be commenced in the county court by:

    (I) The issuance of a summons and complaint;

    (II) The issuance of a summons following the filing of a complaint;

    (III) The filing of a complaint following an arrest;

    (IV) The filing of a summons and complaint following arrest; or

    (V) In the event that the offense is a class 2 petty offense, by the issuance of a notice of penalty assessment pursuant to statute.

(c) Summons, Summons and Complaint.

(1) Summons. A summons issued by the county court in a prosecution for a misdemeanor or a class 1 petty offense may be served by giving a copy to the defendant personally, or by leaving a copy at the defendant's usual place of abode with some person over the age of eighteen years residing therein, or by mailing a copy to the defendant's last known address not less than 14 days prior to the time the defendant is required to appear by registered mail with return receipt requested or certified mail with return receipt requested. Service by mail shall be complete upon the return of the receipt signed by the defendant or signed on behalf of the defendant by one authorized by law to do so. Personal service shall be made by a peace officer or any disinterested party over the age of eighteen years.

(2) Repealed.

(3) Summons and Complaint. A summons and complaint may be issued by any peace officer for an offense constituting a misdemeanor or a petty offense:

    (I) Committed in his presence; or

    (II) If not committed in his presence, which he has probable cause to believe was committed and probable cause to believe was committed by the person charged. Except for penalty assessment notices which shall be handled according to the procedures set forth in section 16-2-201 and subsection (e) of this Rule, a copy of the summons and complaint shall be filed immediately with the county court before which appearance is required and a second copy shall be given to the district attorney or his deputy for such county.

(4) Content of Summons and Complaint. A summons and complaint issued by a peace officer shall contain the name of the defendant, shall identify the offense charged, including a citation of the statute alleged to have been violated, shall contain a brief statement or description of the offense charged, including the date and approximate location thereof, and shall direct the defendant to appear before a specified county court at a stated time and place.

(d) Arrest followed by a Complaint. If a peace officer makes an arrest without a warrant of a person for a misdemeanor or a petty offense, the arrested person shall be taken without unnecessary delay before the nearest available county or district judge. Thereafter, a complaint shall be filed immediately in the county court having jurisdiction of the offense and a copy thereof given to the defendant at or before the time he is arraigned. The provisions of this Rule are subject to the right of the arresting authority to release the arrested person pursuant to section 16-3-105 .

(e) Penalty Assessment Procedure.

(1) When a person is arrested for a class 2 petty offense, the arresting officer may either give the person a penalty assessment notice and release him upon its terms, or take him before a judge of the county court in the county in which the alleged offense occurred. The choice of procedures shall be based upon circumstances which reasonably persuade the officer that the alleged offender is likely or unlikely to comply with the terms of the penalty assessment notice.

(2) The penalty assessment notice shall be a summons and complaint containing identification of the alleged offender, specification of the offense and applicable fine, a requirement that the alleged offender pay the fine or appear to answer the charge at a specified time and place, that payment of the specified fine without an appearance is an acknowledgment of guilt, and that an appearance must be made or the specified fine paid on or before a certain date or a bench warrant will issue for the offender's arrest. In traffic cases, the penalty assessment notice shall also advise the traffic offender of the immediate consequences of payment of the specified fine without an appearance.

(3) In traffic cases, a duplicate copy of the notice shall be sent by the officer to the Colorado department of revenue, motor vehicle division, Denver, Colorado. In all cases, a duplicate copy shall be sent to the clerk of the county court in the county in which the alleged offense occurred.

(4) If the person given a penalty assessment notice chooses to acknowledge his guilt, he may pay the specified fine in person or by mail at the place and within the time specified in the notice. If he chooses not to acknowledge his guilt, he shall appear as required in the notice. Upon trial, if the alleged offender is found guilty, the fine imposed shall be that specified in the notice for the offense of which he was found guilty, but customary court costs may be assessed against him in addition to such fine.

(f) Failure to Appear. If a person upon whom a summons or summons and complaint has been served pursuant to this Rule fails to appear in person or by counsel at the place and time specified therein, a bench warrant may issue for his arrest. In the case of a penalty assessment notice, if the person to whom a penalty assessment notice has been served pursuant to this Rule fails to appear in person or by counsel, or if he fails to pay the specified fine at a specified time and place, a bench warrant may issue for his arrest.

Colo. R. Crim. P. 4.1

Source: a amended March 15, 1985, effective 7/1/1985; f amended June 9, 1988, effective 1/1/1989; entire rule amended and adopted May 27, 2004, effective 7/1/2004; c1 amended and adopted October 15, 2009, effective 1/1/2010; c1 amended and adopted December 14, 2011, effective 7/1/2012.

Annotation I. General Consideration. Applied in Jeffrey v. District Court, 626 P.2d 631 (Colo. 1981); May v. People, 636 P.2d 672 (Colo. 1981); People v. Abbott, 638 P.2d 781 (Colo. 1981). II. Summons, Summons and Complaint. Minimum requirements of a summons and complaint under this rule are: (1) The name of the defendant, (2) the offense charged, (3) a citation of the statute alleged to have been violated, (4) a brief statement or description of the offense charged, including the date and approximate location thereof, and (5) the direction that the defendant appear before a specified county court at a stated date, time, and place. Francis v. County Court, 175 Colo. 308, 487 P.2d 375 (1971). See Stubert v. County Court, 163 Colo. 535, 433 P.2d 97 (1967). General assembly did not intend that such a summons and complaint be verified. Stubert v. County Court, 163 Colo. 535, 433 P.2d 97 (1967); Francis v. County Court, 175 Colo. 308, 487 P.2d 375 (1971). Only peace officers may sign. The only persons designated as having the authority to sign such a summons and complaint are peace officers. Francis v. County Court, 175 Colo. 308, 487 P.2d 375 (1971). It is sufficient that the summons form alleges that complainant "knows or believes", rather than stating more formally that he "knows or has reason to believe", that the accused committed the offense charged. Francis v. County Court, 175 Colo. 308, 487 P.2d 375 (1971). Prosecution for a misdemeanor charge was properly initiated in accordance with subsection (d) of this rule when the defendant posted bail and executed his appearance bond, thereby waiving service of the complaint on him until his appearance date. This procedure also complies with § 16-2-112 and related rules, which do not require that a person charged with a misdemeanor be given a copy of the complaint until at or before the time he is arraigned. Weld County Court v. Richards, 812 P.2d 650 (Colo. 1991). The statutes and procedural rules do not require that a person charged with a misdemeanor be given a copy of the complaint prior to being released on bail. Weld County Court v. Richards, 812 P.2d 650 (Colo. 1991).

Rule 4.2 - Arrest Warrant Without Information, Felony Complaint, or Complaint

If a warrant for arrest is sought prior to the filing of an information, felony complaint, or complaint, such warrant shall issue only on affidavit sworn to or affirmed before the judge, or a notary public and determined by a judge to relate facts sufficient to establish probable cause that an offense has been committed and probable cause that a particular person committed that offense. A warrant may be obtained by facsimile transmission (FAX) or electronic transmission pursuant to procedures set forth in Rule 41, in which event the procedure in Rule 41 shall be followed. The court shall issue a warrant for the arrest of such person commanding any peace officer to arrest the person so named and to take the person without unnecessary delay before the nearest judge of a court of record.

Colo. R. Crim. P. 4.2

Source: Entire rule amended July 16, 1992, effective 11/1/1992; entire rule amended and effective 9/9/2004; entire rule amended and effective 2/10/2011.

Committee CommentThis rule is intended to facilitate the issuance of warrants by eliminating the need to physically carry the supporting affidavit to the judge (see Section 16-1-106 , C.R.S.).

Annotation This rule is codification of § 7 of art. II, Colo. Const. People v. Kelderman, 44 Colo. App. 487, 618 P.2d 723 (1980). Applied in People v. Schultz, 200 Colo. 47, 611 P.2d 977 (1980).

Rule 5 - Preliminary Proceedings

(a) Felony Proceedings.

(1) Procedure Following Arrest. If a peace officer or any other person makes an arrest, either with or without a warrant, the arrested person shall be taken without unnecessary delay before the nearest available county or district court. Thereafter, a felony complaint, information, or indictment shall be filed, if it has not already been filed, without unnecessary delay in the proper court and a copy thereof given to the defendant.

(2) Appearance Before the Court. At the first appearance of the defendant in court, it is the duty of the court to inform the defendant and make certain that the defendant understands the following:

(I) The defendant need make no statement and any statement made can and may be used against the defendant.

(II) The right to counsel;

(III) If indigent, the defendant has the right to request the appointment of counsel or consult with the public defender before any further proceedings are held;

(IV) Any plea the defendant makes must be voluntary and not the result of undue influence or coercion;

(V) The right to bail, if the offense is bailable, and the amount of bail that has been set by the court;

(VI) The nature of the charges;

(VII) The right to a jury trial;

(VIII) The right to demand and receive a preliminary hearing within a reasonable time to determine whether probable cause exists to believe that the offense charged was committed by the defendant;

(IX) If currently serving in the United States armed forces or if a veteran of such forces, the defendant may be entitled to receive mental health treatment, substance use disorder treatment, or other services as a veteran.

(3) Appearance in the Court not Issuing the Warrant. If the defendant is taken before a court which did not issue the arrest warrant, the court shall inform the defendant of the matters set out in subsection (a)(2) of this Rule and, allowing time for travel, set bail returnable not less than 14 days thereafter before the court which issued the arrest warrant, and shall transmit forthwith all papers in the case to the court which issued the arrest warrant. In the event the defendant does not make bail within forty-eight hours, the sheriff of the county in which the arrest warrant was issued shall return the defendant to the court which issued the warrant.

(4) Preliminary Hearing-County Court Procedures. Every person accused of a class 1, 2, or 3 felony in a felony or a level 1 or 2 drug felony complaint has the right to demand and receive a preliminary hearing to determine whether probable cause exists to believe that the offense charged in the felony complaint was committed by the defendant. In addition, only those persons accused of a class 4, 5, or 6 felony or a level 3 or 4 drug felony by felony complaint which felony requires mandatory sentencing or is a crime of violence as defined in section 18-1.3-406 or is a sexual offense under part 4 of article 3 of title 18, C.R.S., shall have the right to demand and receive a preliminary hearing to determine whether probable cause exists to believe that the offense charged in the felony complaint was committed by the defendant. However, any defendant accused of a class 4, 5, or 6 felony or a level 3 or 4 drug felony who is not otherwise entitled to a preliminary hearing may request a preliminary hearing if the defendant is in custody for the offense for which the preliminary hearing is requested; except that, upon motion of either party, the court shall vacate the preliminary hearing if there is a reasonable showing that the defendant has been released from custody prior to the preliminary hearing. Any person accused of a class 4, 5, or 6 felony or a level 3 or 4 drug felony who is not entitled to a preliminary hearing shall, unless otherwise waived, participate in a dispositional hearing for the purposes of case evaluation and potential resolution. The following procedures shall govern the holding of a preliminary hearing:

(I) Within 7 days after the defendant is brought before the county court for or following the filing of the felony complaint in that court, either the prosecutor or the defendant may request a preliminary hearing. Upon such request, the court forthwith shall set the hearing. The hearing shall be held within 35 days of the day of setting, unless good cause for continuing the hearing beyond that time is shown to the court. The clerk of the court shall prepare and give notice of the hearing, or any continuance thereof, to all parties and their counsel.

(II) The preliminary hearing shall be held before a judge of the county court in which the felony complaint has been filed. The defendant shall not be called upon to plead. The defendant may cross-examine the prosecutor's witnesses and may introduce evidence. The prosecutor shall have the burden of establishing probable cause. The judge presiding at the preliminary hearing may temper the rules of evidence in the exercise of sound judicial discretion.

(III) If the county court determines such probable cause exists or if the case is not otherwise resolved pursuant to a dispositional hearing if no preliminary hearing was held, it shall order the defendant bound over to the appropriate court of record for trial. In appropriate cases, the defendant may be admitted to or continued on bail by the county court, but bond shall be made returnable in the trial court and at a day and time certain. All county court records, except the reporter's transcript notes, or recording, shall be transferred forthwith by the clerk of the county court to the clerk of the appropriate court of record.

(IV) If from the evidence it appears to the county court that there is not probable cause to believe that any or all of the offenses charged were committed by the defendant, the county court shall dismiss those counts from the complaint and, if all counts are dismissed, discharge the defendant. Upon a finding of no probable cause, the prosecution may appeal pursuant to Rule 5(a)(4)(V), file a direct information pursuant to Rule 5(a)(4)(VI) charging the same offense(s), or submit the matter to a grand jury, but may not file a subsequent felony complaint charging the same offenses.

(V) If the prosecutor believes the court erred in its finding of no probable cause, the prosecutor may appeal the ruling to the district court. The appeal of such final order shall be conducted pursuant to the procedures for interlocutory appeals in Rule 37.1 of these rules. Such error, if any, shall not constitute good cause for refiling.

(VI) Upon a finding of no probable cause as to any one or more of the offenses charged in a felony complaint, the prosecution may file a direct information in the district court pursuant to Rule 7(c)(2) charging the same offense(s). If the prosecutor states an intention to proceed in this manner, the bond executed by the defendant shall be continued and returnable in the district court at a day and time certain. If a bond has not been continued, the defendant shall be summoned into court without the necessity of making a new bond.

(VII) If a felony complaint is dismissed prior to a preliminary hearing being held when one is required or, in other cases, prior to being bound over, the prosecution may thereafter file a direct information in the district court pursuant to Rule 7(c)(4) charging the same offense(s), file a felony complaint in the county court charging the same offense(s), or submit the matter to a grand jury. If the prosecution files a subsequent felony complaint charging the defendant with the same offense(s), the felony complaint shall be accompanied by a written statement from the prosecutor providing good cause for dismissing and refiling the charges. Within 21 days of defendant's first appearance following the filing of the new felony complaint the defendant may request an evidentiary hearing at which the prosecutor shall establish the existence of such good cause.

(VIII) If the county court has bound over the defendant to the district court and the case is thereafter dismissed in the district court before jeopardy has attached, the prosecution may file a direct information in the district court pursuant to Rule 7(c)(5) charging the same offense(s), file a felony complaint in county court charging the same offense(s), or submit the matter to a grand jury, and the case shall then proceed as if the previous case had never been filed. The prosecution shall also file with the felony complaint or the direct information a statement showing good cause for dismissing and then refiling the case. Within 21 days of defendant's first appearance following the filing of the new felony complaint or the direct filing of the new information the defendant may request an evidentiary hearing at which the prosecutor shall establish the existence of such good cause.

(4.5) A dispositional hearing is an opportunity for the parties to report to the court on the status of discussions toward disposition, including presenting any resolution pursuant to C.R.S. 16-7-302. The court shall set the dispositional hearing at a time that will afford the parties an opportunity for case evaluation and potential resolution.

(5) **Procedure Upon Failure to Request Preliminary Hearing.** If the defendant or prosecutor fails to request a preliminary hearing within 7 days after the defendant has come before the court, the county court shall forthwith order the defendant bound over to the

appropriate court of record for trial. In no case shall the defendant be bound over for trial to another court until the preliminary hearing has been held, the 7-day period for requesting a preliminary hearing has expired, or the parties have waived their rights to a preliminary hearing. In appropriate cases, the defendant may be admitted to, or continued upon bail by the county court, but bond shall be made returnable in the trial court at a day and time certain. All court records in the case, except the reporter's transcript, notes, or recording shall be transferred forthwith by the clerk to the appropriate court of record.

(b) Bail in Absence of a County Judge. If no county judge is immediately available to set bond in the case of a person in custody for the commission of a bailable felony, any available district judge may set bond, or such person may be admitted to bail pursuant to Rule 46.

(c) Misdemeanor and Petty Offense Proceedings.

(1) Procedure Following Arrest. If a peace officer or any other person makes an arrest, either with or without a warrant, the arrested person shall be taken without unnecessary delay before the nearest available county court. Thereafter a complaint or summons and complaint shall be filed, if it has not already been filed, immediately in the proper court and a copy thereof given to the defendant at or before arraignment. Trial may be held forthwith if the court calendar permits, immediate trial appears proper, and the parties do not request a continuance for good cause. Otherwise the case shall be set for trial as soon as possible.

(2) Appearance Before the Court. At the first appearance in the county court the defendant shall be advised in accordance with the provisions set forth in subparagraphs (a)(2)(I) through (VII) and (IX) of this Rule.

(3) Appearance in the County Court not Issuing the Warrant. If the defendant is taken before a county court which did not issue the arrest warrant, the court shall inform the defendant of the matters set out in subsection (a)(2)(I through VII and (IX) of this Rule and, allowing time for travel, set bail returnable not less than 14 days thereafter before the court which issued the arrest warrant, and shall transmit forthwith a transcript of the proceedings and all papers in the case to the court which issued the arrest warrant. In the event the defendant does not make bail within forty-eight hours, the sheriff of the county in which the arrest warrant was issued shall return the defendant to the court which issued the warrant.

Colo. R. Crim. P. 5

Source: Entire rule amended March 31, 1988, effective 1/1/1989; IPa4 and a4III amended and a4.5 added November 4, 1999, effective 1/1/2000; entire rule amended and adopted September 12, 2000, effective 1/1/2001; a3 amended January 11, 2001, effective 7/1/2001; entire rule amended and adopted June 27, 2002, effective 7/1/2002; a4 amended and effective 1/17/2008; a3, a4I, a4VII, a4VIII, a5, and c3 amended and adopted December 14, 2011, effective 7/1/2012; a4I, a4II, and a5 amended and effective 3/7/2013; c2 amended and adopted October 31, 2013, effective 1/1/2014; amended and adopted September 13, 2018, effective 9/13/2018; amended and adopted January 24, 2019, effective 1/24/2019.

Annotation I. General Consideration. Law reviews. For article, "Police Interrogation in Colorado: The Implementation of Miranda", see 47 Den. L.J. 1 (1970). For article, "Hearsay in Criminal Cases Under the Colorado Rules of Evidence: An Overview", see 50 U. Colo. L. Rev. 277 (1979). For article, "Felony Preliminary Hearings in Colorado", see 17 Colo. Law. 1085 (1988). For article, "The Use of 'No Bond' Holds in Colorado", see 32 Colo. Law. 81 (November 2003). Purpose of this rule is to furnish a prophylaxis against abuses in the detention process and, more importantly, to place the accused in early contact with a judicial officer so that the right to counsel may not only be explained clearly but also be implemented upon the accused's request. People v. Heintze, 200 Colo. 248, 614 P.2d 367 (1980). Limited extraterritorial effect of rule. There is limited extraterritorial effect which the procedural rules of this jurisdiction can generally be given, absent denial of constitutional rights. People v. Robinson, 192 Colo. 48, 556 P.2d 466 (1976). Statements were improperly suppressed when there wasn't an arrest. Defendant was held for the purpose of taking blood samples only. A reasonable person would understand he or she was being detained for that limited purpose and not being arrested. People v. Turtura, 921 P.2d 40 (Colo. 1996). Psychiatric examination of unconsenting party unauthorized. There is no authority in the Rules of Criminal Procedure nor in the statutes for ordering an unconsenting third party to submit to a psychiatric examination. People v. La Plant, 670 P.2d 802 (Colo. App. 1983). Applied in People v. York, 189 Colo. 16, 537 P.2d 294 (1975); People v. Salazar, 189 Colo. 429, 541 P.2d 676 (1975); People v. Lopez, 41 Colo. App. 206, 587 P.2d 792 (1978); People v. District Court, 199 Colo. 398, 610 P.2d 490 (1980); Jeffrey v. District Court, 626 P.2d 631 (Colo. 1981); People v. Boyette, 635 P.2d 552 (Colo. 1981); Corr v. District Court, 661 P.2d 668 (Colo. 1983). II. Procedure Following Arrest. Purpose of subsection (a)(1) is to insure

14

that the defendant is adequately informed of his rights. People v. Casey, 185 Colo. 58, 521 P.2d 1250 (1974). One of the central purposes of restricting unnecessary delay in bringing an arrested person before a judge is to insure that he will be fully informed of the offense involved and of his constitutional rights. People v. Weaver, 179 Colo. 331, 500 P.2d 980 (1972). See People v. Reed, 180 Colo. 16, 502 P.2d 952 (1972). This rule was not designed to prevent incriminating statements willingly made during an unnecessary delay where there were no abuses in the detention process. People v. Roybal, 55 P.3d 144 (Colo. App. 2001). Person arrested must be taken before a county judge within a reasonable time and without unnecessary delay. Washington v. People, 158 Colo. 115, 405 P.2d 735 (1965), cert. denied, 383 U.S. 953, 86 S. Ct. 1217, 16 L. Ed. 2d 215 (1966); England v. People, 175 Colo. 236, 486 P.2d 1055 (1971). "Necessary delay". A "necessary delay" is one reasonably related to the administrative process attendant upon the arrest of the accused, viz., delays associated with fingerprinting, photographing, taking inventory of personal belongings, preparation of necessary charging documents and reports, and other legitimate administrative procedures. People v. Heintze, 200 Colo. 248, 614 P.2d 367 (1980); People v. Raymer, 662 P.2d 1066 (Colo. 1983). Inadvertent delay unnecessary. Where prolonged inadvertence is the only basis for the delay, that delay is unnecessary. People v. Heintze, 200 Colo. 248, 614 P.2d 367 (1980). But where arresting authorities delay the accused's judicial advisement on charges from a foreign jurisdiction until after the local charges are completely resolved, delay is unnecessary. People v. Garcia, 746 P.2d 560 (Colo. 1987). Failure to comply with this rule does not automatically invalidate a confession. Aragon v. People, 166 Colo. 172, 442 P.2d 397 (1968); People v. Weaver, 179 Colo. 331, 500 P.2d 980 (1972); People v. Reed, 180 Colo. 16, 502 P.2d 952 (1972); People v. Litsey, 192 Colo. 19, 555 P.2d 974 (1976). Nor require granting motion to dismiss. A violation of Crim. P. 5(a) and 5(c) does not of itself automatically operate to equire the granting of a motion to dismiss charges. People v. Wiedemer, 180 Colo. 265, 504 P.2d 667 (1972). As each case must be considered on its own facts where a defendant argues that he was not taken before a county judge within the time required by this rule. Aragon v. People, 166 Colo. 172, 442 P.2d 397 (1968); Jaggers v. People, 174 Colo. 430, 484 P.2d 796 (1971); People v. Weaver, 179 Colo. 331, 500 P.2d 980 (1972). Admissibility of confession dependent on compliance with Miranda. If a statement is admissible as being in compliance with "Miranda", it should not be invalidated because of noncompliance with this rule if there was no studied attempt to avoid taking the defendant before a county judge. Jaggers v. People, 174 Colo. 430, 484 P.2d 796 (1971); People v. Weaver, 179 Colo. 331, 500 P.2d 980 (1972). Where defendant was in custody for at least 18 hours before subsection (a)(1) was complied with, and where during this period he was interrogated on two occasions and made incriminating statements during the interrogations, the 18-hour delay neither unfairly prejudiced the defendant nor denied him any basic constitutional right, since prior to both interrogations the defendant was properly advised as required by the Miranda v. Arizona, 384 U.S. 436, 86 S. Ct. 1602, 16 L. Ed. 2d 694, 10 A.L.R.3d 974 (1966) decision, and only thereafter did the defendant choose to give the incriminating statements. People v. Hosier, 186 Colo. 116, 525 P.2d 1161 (1974). Failure to comply with this rule did not result in prejudice to the defendant, where the defendant was properly advised as required by Miranda, and thereafter chose to make incriminating statements rather than to remain silent. People v. Gilmer, 182 Colo. 96, 511 P.2d 494 (1973). Where the statement was voluntarily made and the defendant was several times fully advised of his Miranda rights, any violation of this rule constituted harmless error and the trial court correctly refused to suppress the defendant's statement on this ground. People v. Litsey, 192 Colo. 19, 555 P.2d 974 (1976). And inability of defendant to show prejudice. In the absence of a factual showing of prejudice, the failure to comply with this rule does not require suppression of voluntary statements. People v. Litsey, 192 Colo. 19, 555 P.2d 974 (1976); People v. Robinson, 192 Colo. 48, 556 P.2d 466 (1976). Defendant must prove both unnecessary delay and prejudice to establish a right to relief for a violation of this rule. People v. Johnson, 653 P.2d 737 (Colo. 1982). Violation of subsection (a)(1) does not per se require suppression; rather, the defendant must show prejudice as a result of the delay. People v. La Plant, 670 P.2d 802 (Colo. App. 1983). Showing of prejudice required on motion to dismiss. And before one may prevail on a motion to dismiss charges, he must show that he would be unfairly prejudiced or would be denied some basic rights at trial because of the Crim. P. 5(a)(1) and 5(c) violation. People v. Wiedemer, 180 Colo. 265, 504 P.2d 667 (1972). In the absence of a factual showing of prejudice, the failure to comply with subsection (a)(1) does not require dismissal of a criminal charge. People v. Edwards, 183 Colo. 210, 515 P.2d 1243 (1973). Before a violation of subsection (a)(1) may be grounds for reversal, it must be shown that the defendant was unfairly prejudiced or denied some basic constitutional rights by reason of the failure to comply with the rule. People v. Gilmer, 182 Colo. 96, 511 P.2d 494 (1973); People v. Hosier, 186 Colo. 116, 525 P.2d 1161 (1974). Test for prejudice. In determining the existence of prejudice the proper inquiry is whether the unnecessary delay reasonably contributed to the acquisition of the challenged evidence. People v. Heintze, 200 Colo. 248, 614 P.2d 367 (1980); People v. Raymer, 626 P.2d 705 (Colo. App. 1980). To establish prejudice, a defendant must show a nexus between the unnecessary delay and the challenged evidence. In other words, a defendant must establish that the delay induced, caused, or was used to extract a confession. People v. Roybal, 55 P.3d 144 (Colo. App. 2001). In view of the important role played by this rule in speedily implementing the right to counsel especially for an indigent defendant, some important considerations on the issue of prejudice are: whether an attorney had already been retained by, or had been made available to, the defendant during the period of unnecessary delay; whether that attorney was accessible to the defendant prior to the challenged statement; and whether the defendant freely and knowingly waived the presence of the attorney in making the challenged statement to the police. People v. Heintze, 200 Colo. 248, 614 P.2d 367 (1980). In determining the existence of prejudice, the appropriate inquiry is whether unnecessary delay reasonably contributed to the acquisition of any challenged evidence. The relevant time period which must be examined is the time between the arrest and the acquisition of the challenged evidence. People v. Raymer, 662 P.2d 1066 (Colo. 1983). Sufficiency of evidence showing prejudice and nature of prejudice suffered by defendant should be considered by trial court in fashioning sanction, if any, to be imposed for violation and such drastic sanction as dismissal should be imposed only when violation has rendered accused unable to fairly defend against the charges. People v. Garcia, 746 P.2d 560 (Colo. 1987). Prosecution for a misdemeanor charge was properly initiated in accordance with this rule when the defendant posted bail and executed his appearance bond, thereby waiving service of the complaint on him until his appearance date. This procedure also complies with § 16-2-112 and related rules, which do not require that a person charged with a misdemeanor be given a copy of the complaint until at or before the time he is arraigned. Weld County Court v. Richards, 812 P.2d 650 (Colo. 1991). The statutes and procedural rules do not require that a person charged with a misdemeanor be given a copy of the complaint prior to being released on bail. Weld County Court v. Richards, 812 P.2d 650 (Colo. 1991). No prejudice held shown by delay in presenting defendant before judge. Gottfried v. People, 158 Colo. 510, 408 P.2d 431 (1965); Hubbard v. Patterson, 374 F.2d 856 (10th Cir.), cert. denied, 389 U.S. 868, 88 S. Ct. 142, 19 L. Ed. 2d 144 (1967). Delay to conduct custodial interrogation is not "necessary". Where delay is occasioned by the decision of law enforcement officers to conduct a custodial interrogation of the defendant before presenting him to a judicial officer for a proper advisement of rights, then clearly such a delay is not "necessary". People v. Raymer, 662 P.2d 1066 (Colo. 1983). Presumption of regularity of proceedings. Where it is alleged prejudice resulted from noncompliance with this rule, every presumption is indulged in favor of regularity of the proceedings in the trial court, and the burden of showing error is on the party asserting it. Gottfried v. People, 158 Colo. 510, 408 P.2d 431 (1965). But interview of defendant in sheriff's office over 24 hours after arrest does not fulfill requirements of this rule. People v. Kelley, 172 Colo. 39, 470 P.2d 32 (1970). Confession during six-day delay inadmissible. Where there was a delay of six days between the time a defendant was first questioned and the time he was finally brought before a judge and advised of his rights, any statements made prior to compliance with this rule were inadmissible. Hervey v. People, 178 Colo. 38, 495 P.2d 204 (1972). Where delay not unreasonable. Where the defendant was taken before a judge on the afternoon following the evening of his arrest, this is not an unreasonable delay. People v. Casey, 185 Colo. 58, 521 P.2d 1250 (1974). Where most of delay in taking defendant before a judge was necessitated by treatment of defendant's wounds, such a delay was not unreasonable, particularly since the delay did not appear to result in coercion or in contributing to defendant's desire to talk. People v. Valencia, 181 Colo. 36, 506 P.2d 743 (1973). Noncompliance with rule may be waived by defendant. Washington v. People, 158 Colo. 115, 405 P.2d 735 (1965), cert. denied, 383 U.S. 953, 86 S. Ct. 1217, 16 L. Ed. 2d 215 (1966). Justifiable excuse needed to bring defendant before out-of-county judge. A justifiable excuse must be shown to warrant the removal of defendant to a county seat, other than the one in which the alleged offense was committed, where a county judge is available in that county. Aragon v. People, 166 Colo. 172, 442 P.2d 397 (1968). Prosecution's remedies when case dismissed. The prosecution has one of two remedies available to it when a case is dismissed in the county court. If the case is dismissed before a preliminary hearing is held, the prosecution may appeal the order of dismissal to the district court. If the county court dismisses a charge after holding a preliminary hearing under subsection (a)(4), the exclusive remedy available to the prosecution is

16

*to request leave to file a direct information in the district court. People v. Freiman, 657 P.2d 452
(Colo. 1983). Colorado rule not applicable to defendant arrested in another state by federal
agents, and federal rules of criminal procedure control. People v. Porter, 742 P.2d 922 (Colo.
1987). Posting of officers outside defendant's hospital door for the purpose of effecting an arrest
upon his release from medical care not an arrest requiring compliance with this rule. People v.
MacCallum, 925 P.2d 758 (Colo. 1996). III. Appearance Before Court. Judges' duties upon first
appearance. Subsection (a)(2) of this rule imposes on the judge at the accused's first appearance
the duty to inform him of, and to make certain that he understands, those basic rights applicable
upon the initiation of formal criminal proceedings, especially his privilege against self-
incrimination and his right to the appointment of an attorney at state expense if he is financially
unable to retain one. People v. Heintze, 200 Colo. 248, 614 P.2d 367 (1980); Washington v.
People, 158 Colo. 115, 405 P.2d 735 (1965), cert. denied, 383 U.S. 953, 86 S. Ct. 1217, 16 L. Ed.
2d 215 (1966); England v. People, 175 Colo. 236, 486 P.2d 1055 (1971). Right to counsel need
not be advised where defendant already represented. When accepting a plea of guilty, the trial
court is not necessarily required to advise a defendant of his right to counsel when the defendant
is represented by counsel at the providency hearing. People v. Derrerra, 667 P.2d 1363 (Colo.
1983). Court may properly allow testimony concerning defendant's pre-advisement silence
concerning failure to contact authorities to correct discrepancies in documents if defendant
testified and the evidence of defendant's pre-advisement silence was elicited in the cross-
examination of defendant for credibility purposes. People v. Taylor, 159 P.3d 730 (Colo. App.
2006). IV. Preliminary Hearing. Primary purpose of preliminary hearing is to determine whether
probable cause exists to support the prosecution's charge that the accused committed a specific
crime. People v. Weaver, 182 Colo. 221, 511 P.2d 908 (1973); People v. Quinn, 183 Colo. 245,
516 P.2d 420 (1973); People ex rel. Farina v. District Court, 184 Colo. 406, 521 P.2d 778
(1974). The rules of criminal procedure relating to a preliminary hearing are intended to create
a preliminary screening device by affording a defendant an opportunity, at an early stage of the
criminal proceedings, to challenge the sufficiency of the prosecution's evidence before an
impartial judge. People ex rel. Farina v. District Court, 185 Colo. 118, 522 P.2d 589 (1974);
People v. District Court, 652 P.2d 582 (Colo. 1982). A preliminary hearing provides the accused
with an opportunity to challenge the sufficiency of the people's evidence at an early stage in the
proceedings. The preliminary hearing is designed to weed out groundless or unsupported
charges and to relieve the accused of the degradation and expense of a criminal trial. Holmes v.
District Court, 668 P.2d 11 (Colo. 1983). Level of proof required. It is not necessary to introduce
evidence sufficient to prove defendant's guilt beyond a reasonable doubt but evidence sufficient
to permit a person of ordinary prudence to reasonably believe in defendant's guilt. People v.
Walker, 675 P.2d 304 (Colo. 1984). Preliminary hearing presents forum for the presentation and
assessment of evidence of probable cause and if prosecuting attorney fails to establish probable
cause at a preliminary hearing, the county court is empowered to dismiss the complaint.
Gallagher v. County Court, 759 P.2d 859 (Colo. App. 1988). There is no procedure for
dismissing a felony complaint without prejudice. Once the filing of a felony complaint in county
court is dismissed, the prosecution must either obtain a grand jury indictment or file an
information directly in the district court. People v. Williams, 987 P.2d 232 (Colo. 1999). "The
offense charged," within subsection (a)(4)(IV), encompasses any lesser included offense of the
offense charged. Hunter v. District Court, 184 Colo. 238, 519 P.2d 941 (1974). Defendant's
request for preliminary hearing after indictment has been returned is not authorized where such
a request, or motion, cannot provide a foundation for the trial court's order for delivery of a
requested transcript of the colloquy between the grand jury and the district attorney. People v.
District Court, 199 Colo. 398, 610 P.2d 490 (1980). Demand for hearing to be by written motion.
The statutory right to receive a preliminary hearing is not absolute and requires that either the
defendant or his attorney, or the prosecuting attorney, file a written motion demanding the
preliminary hearing. People v. Moody, 630 P.2d 74 (Colo. 1981). Although oral request may be
treated as written motion. A court may treat a defendant's oral request for a preliminary hearing,
as a written motion as required by this rule. People v. Driscoll, 200 Colo. 410, 615 P.2d 696
(1980). When juvenile entitled to preliminary hearing. Juveniles charged in delinquency
proceedings with crimes (felonies and class 1 misdemeanors) subject to this rule and Crim. P. 7
are entitled to a preliminary hearing. Juveniles held on lesser charges are not granted a right to
a preliminary hearing by statute or by rule. J.T. v. O'Rourke ex rel. Tenth Judicial Dist., 651
P.2d 407 (Colo. 1982). Prosecution not to present all evidences and witnesses. A preliminary
hearing does not require that the prosecution lay out for inspection and for full examination all
witnesses and evidence. People v. Quinn, 183 Colo. 245, 516 P.2d 420 (1973). It is unnecessary*

17

at a preliminary hearing for the prosecution to show beyond a reasonable doubt that the defendant committed the crime, or even the probability of the defendant's conviction. Instead, the trial court is obligated at the preliminary hearing to view the evidence in the light most favorable to the prosecution and the prosecution therefore is accorded latitude at the preliminary hearing to establish probable cause that the defendant committed the crime charged. People v. District Ct., 17th Jud. Dist., 926 P.2d 567 (Colo. 1996); People v. Hall, 999 P.2d 207 (Colo. 2000). Preliminary hearing is not intended to be a mandatory procedural step in every criminal prosecution. People ex rel. Farina v. District Court, 185 Colo. 118, 522 P.2d 589 (1974). And does not alter proposition that accused entitled to trial on merits. Although a preliminary hearing provides the defendant with an early opportunity to question the government's case, it is not designed to alter the basic proposition that an accused is entitled to one trial on the merits of the charge. People v. Quinn, 183 Colo. 245, 516 P.2d 420 (1973). Defendant to appear at requested preliminary hearing. When a defendant requests a preliminary hearing, he has not only the constitutional right to be present, but is under an affirmative obligation and duty to appear at the hearing. People ex rel. Farina v. District Court, 185 Colo. 118, 522 P.2d 589 (1974). Unless court permits defendant to waive his presence. The court may, when a timely request is made, permit the defendant to waive his presence at the preliminary hearing if the ends of justice would not be frustrated, but the tactical ploy of refusing to produce a defendant at the preliminary hearing to frustrate the prosecution's case should not be tolerated. People ex rel. Farina v. District Court, 185 Colo. 118, 522 P.2d 589 (1974). Refusal to appear may constitute implied waiver of hearing. Where the judge of the county court advised counsel that the failure of the defendant to appear would constitute a waiver, the defendant's subsequent refusal to appear constituted an implied waiver and extinguished the defendant's right to a preliminary hearing in the county court. People ex rel. Farina v. District Court, 185 Colo. 118, 522 P.2d 589 (1974); People v. Abbott, 638 P.2d 781 (Colo. 1981). Right to counsel at preliminary hearing reaches constitutional proportions. Schwader v. District Court, 172 Colo. 474, 474 P.2d 607 (1970). Where the case against the defendant is overwhelming, the absence of counsel at the preliminary hearing is harmless error. People v. Gallegos, 680 P.2d 1294 (Colo. App. 1983). Authority to bind over on lesser included offense. The trial court which holds the preliminary hearing has the authority to bind over the defendant on a lesser included offense. People v. Hrapski, 658 P.2d 1367 (Colo. 1983). Hearing may be set beyond 30-day period. The absence of open court dates within 30-day period prescribed by this rule constitute good cause for setting a preliminary hearing for a date outside that period. People v. Hogland, 37 Colo. App. 34, 543 P.2d 1298 (1975). Evidence need not be admissible at trial. Hearsay evidence, and other evidence, which would be incompetent if offered at the time of trial, may be the bulk of evidence at a preliminary hearing. People v. Quinn, 183 Colo. 245, 516 P.2d 420 (1973). Preliminary hearing in district court after such hearing in county court. After the filing of a direct information in the district court, either the people or the defendant may demand a preliminary hearing in that court even where there has been a dismissal of a felony complaint by the county court following a preliminary hearing on the same charge. People v. Burggraf, 36 Colo. App. 137, 536 P.2d 48 (1975). The purpose of a Crim. P. 5 proceeding is to furnish a prophylaxis against abuses in the detention process and, more importantly, to place the accused in early contact with a judicial officer so that the right to counsel may not only be clearly explained but also be implemented upon the accused's request. People v. Heintze, 614 P.2d 367 (Colo. 1980); People v. Vigoa, 841 P.2d 311 (Colo. 1992). Defendant waived showing of good cause necessary to continue preliminary hearing by failing to object to setting of preliminary hearing beyond statutory time requirement. People v. Thompson, 736 P.2d 423 (Colo. App. 1987). Court has jurisdiction to dismiss charges pursuant to this rule after denying continuance where prosecution failed to demonstrate adequate, timely efforts to secure witness' attendance and such dismissal was not an abuse of discretion. Gallagher v. County Court, 759 P.2d 859 (Colo. App. 1988). District court may not review county court's probable cause finding. It is not proper for the district court to review the county court's finding of probable cause. People v. District Court, 652 P.2d 582 (Colo. 1982); People v. Atkin, 680 P.2d 1277 (Colo. App. 1984); White v. MacFarlane, 713 P.2d 366 (Colo. 1986); Blevins v. Tihonovich, 728 P.2d 732 (Colo. 1986). Direct information not available after discharge for failure to gain hearing within 30 days. Crim. P. 7(c), does not allow the filing of a direct information in the district court if the charges, first filed in county court, are dismissed before a preliminary hearing for failure of the prosecution to comply with the 30-day rule in this rule. Chavez v. District Court, 648 P.2d 658 (Colo. 1982). Factors considered when direct filing of information requested. While under Crim. P. 7(c)(2) the district attorney, with the consent of the court, may file a direct information in the district court if a preliminary hearing was held on the same charge in the county court and the accused was discharged, before the district court may properly exercise its discretion, there must be a sufficient evidentiary disclosure by the prosecution to apprise the district court of the earlier dismissal of the identical charges in the county court and the reasons for the requested refiling. When exercising its discretion in deciding whether to permit the direct filing of an information, the district court is required to balance the right of the district attorney to prosecute criminal cases against the need to protect the accused from discrimination and oppression. Holmes v. District Court, 668 P.2d 11 (Colo. 1983). No probable cause necessary to bind over habitual criminal charges. Inasmuch as habitual criminal counts do not constitute "offenses", probable cause need not be established in the preliminary hearing to bind these charges over to the district court. Maestas v. District Court, 189 Colo. 443, 541 P.2d 889 (1975). Where technical difficulties prevented defendant from obtaining a transcript of the preliminary hearing, the judge abused his discretion in denying defendant's motion for a second preliminary hearing. Such motion should have been granted because the testimony presented at the first preliminary hearing was directly relevant and significant to defendant's trial preparation, the prosecution was expected to rely on testimony presented at the preliminary hearing, and there was no alternative method of reconstructing the testimony from the preliminary hearing. Harris v. District Court, 843 P.2d 1316 (Colo. 1993). Prosecution may seek a grand jury indictment after dismissal by a county court on a preliminary hearing for lack of probable cause as an alternative to appealing to or filing a direct information in the district court. People v. Noline, 917 P.2d 1256 (Colo. 1996). Because district court applied a flawed interpretation of the law during the preliminary hearing, assessment of probable cause was in error and review requires the court to determine whether the facts, when viewed in the light most favorable to the prosecution, would induce a reasonably prudent and cautious person to entertain the belief that the defendant committed the crime charged. People v. Hall, 999 P.2d 207 (Colo. 2000). When court applies an erroneous legal standard or bases its ruling on erroneous conclusions of law at preliminary hearing, the proper standard of review is de novo, not abuse of discretion. Reviewing court must review the evidence in the light most favorable to prosecution to determine if a reasonably prudent and cautious person could entertain the belief that defendant committed the crime charged. People v. Beck, 187 P.3d 1125 (Colo. App. 2008). Where district court finds that defendant's waiver of right to preliminary hearing is ineffective, the district court has the authority to restore defendant's right to a preliminary hearing. People v. Nichelson, 219 P.3d 1064 (Colo. 2009). V. Failure to File for Preliminary Hearing. Waiver occurs when defendant fails to request preliminary hearing. People ex rel. Farina v. District Court, 184 Colo. 406, 521 P.2d 778 (1974); People ex rel. Farina v. District Court, 185 Colo. 188, 522 P.2d 589 (1974); People v. Moody, 630 P.2d 74 (Colo. 1981). And affirmative waiver not necessary. Subsection (a)(4)(I), when construed with subsection (a)(5), establishes that an affirmative waiver is not necessary to cause a defendant to lose his right to demand a preliminary hearing. People ex rel. Farina v. District Court, 184 Colo. 406, 521 P.2d 778 (1974). Effect of waiver. If the defendant waives a preliminary hearing in the county court, he must be bound over for trial, and not for a subsequent preliminary hearing in the district court. People ex rel. Farina v. District Court, 184 Colo. 406, 521 P.2d 778 (1974). If the defendant elects to waive the preliminary hearing and to proceed to trial, the waiver operates as an admission by the defendant that sufficient evidence does exist to establish probable cause that the defendant committed the crimes charged. People ex rel. Farina v. District Court, 184 Colo. 406, 521 P.2d 778 (1974); People ex rel. Farina v. District Court, 185 Colo. 118, 522 P.2d 589 (1974). An express written waiver by a defendant of his right to a preliminary hearing operates identically to a failure to file within the time limit prescribed by this rule; both requiring the defendant's case to be bound over for trial. People v. Abbott, 638 P.2d 781 (Colo. 1981). Right not restorable by district court after waiver in county court. A defendant is not entitled to a preliminary hearing in the district court if he has previously waived a preliminary hearing in the county court. People ex rel. Farina v. District Court, 185 Colo. 18, 521 P.2d 780 (1974); People ex rel. Farina v. District Court, 185 Colo. 118, 522 P.2d 589 (1974); People v. Abbott, 638 P.2d 781 (Colo. 1981).

Indictment and Information

Rule 6 - Grand Jury Rules

(a) The chief judge of the district court in each county or a judge designated by him may order a grand jury summoned where authorized by law or required by the public interest.

(b) The grand jury shall hear witnesses as may be determined by the grand jury and may find an indictment on the sworn testimony of one witness only, except in cases of perjury, when at least two witnesses to the same fact shall be necessary. An indictment may also be found upon the information of two of their own body.

(c) The foreman of the grand jury may swear or affirm all witnesses who may come before the grand jury.

Colo. R. Crim. P. 6

Annotation Law reviews. For article, "State Grand Juries in Colorado: Understanding the Process and Attacking Indictments", see 34 Colo. Law. 63 (April 2005). Grand jury proceedings have been traditionally free of technical rules. People ex rel. Dunbar v. District Court, 179 Colo. 321, 500 P.2d 819 (1972). Applied in Thomas v. County Court, 198 Colo. 87, 596 P.2d 768 (1979); People v. District Court, 199 Colo. 398, 610 P.2d 490 (1980). .

Rule 6.1 - Subpoenas-Issuance and Time Limits

Subpoenas and subpoenas duces tecum shall be issued in accordance with the rules of criminal procedure and these rules and shall be served at least forty-eight hours before any appearance is required before the grand jury, unless waived by the witness. The court, for good cause, may shorten the time limit imposed by this rule.

Colo. R. Crim. P. 6.1

Annotation Grand jury dependent on courts for subpoenas. One significant limitation upon the grand jury is that it must rely upon the courts to compel the production of documents or the attendance of witnesses, and, on motion of the witness subpoenaed, the court is given discretion to quash, modify, or order compliance with the subpoena. Losavio v. Robb, 195 Colo. 533, 579 P.2d 1152 (1978). For in camera examination of subpoenaed bank records, see Pignatiello v. District Court, 659 P.2d 683 (Colo. 1983). Applied in People ex rel. Gallagher v. District Court, 198 Colo. 468, 601 P.2d 1380 (1979).

Rule 6.2 - Secrecy of Proceedings-Witness Privacy-Representation by Counsel

(a) All persons associated with a grand jury and its investigations or functions should at all times be aware that a grand jury is an investigative body, the proceedings of which shall be secret. Witnesses or persons under investigation should be dealt with privately to insure fairness. The oath of secrecy shall continue until such time as an indictment is made public, if an indictment is returned, or until a grand jury report dealing with the investigation is issued and made public as provided by law. Nothing in this rule shall prevent a disclosure of the general purpose of the grand jury's investigation by the prosecutor.

(b) Any witness subpoenaed to appear and testify before a grand jury or to produce books, papers, documents, or other objects before such grand jury shall be entitled to assistance of counsel during any time that such witness is being questioned in the presence of said grand jury. If the witness desires legal assistance during his testimony, counsel must be present in the grand jury room with his client during such questioning. However, counsel for the witness shall be permitted only to counsel with the witness and shall not make objections, arguments, or address the grand jury. Such counsel may be retained by the witness or may, for any person financially unable to obtain adequate assistance, be appointed in the same manner as if that person were eligible for appointed counsel. An attorney present in the grand jury room shall take an oath of secrecy. If the court, at an in camera hearing, determines that counsel was disruptive, then the court may order counsel to remain outside the courtroom when advising his client. No attorney shall be permitted to provide counsel in the grand jury room to more than one witness in the same criminal investigation, except with the permission of the grand jury.

Colo. R. Crim. P. 6.2

Source: a amended, effective 11/8/1990.

Annotation Law reviews. For comment, "Reporter's Privilege: Pankratz v. District Court", see 58 Den. L.J. 681 (1981). Grand jury secrecy remains important to safeguard a number of different interests to preserve its proper functioning. Hoffman-Pugh v. Keenan, 338 F.3d 1136 (10th Cir. 2003). Justifications for grand jury secrecy are several: (1) To prevent the escape of those whose indictment may be contemplated; (2) to prevent disclosure of derogatory information presented to the grand jury against someone who has not been indicted; (3) to encourage witnesses to come before the grand jury and speak freely with respect to a commission of crimes; (4) to encourage grand jurors in uninhibited investigation of and deliberation on suspected criminal activity. In re P.R. v. District Court, 637 P.2d 346 (Colo.

1981). Colorado secrecy rules do not violate the first amendment by prohibiting the disclosure of matters a witness learned from her participation in the grand jury process, at least so long as the potential remains for another grand jury to be called to investigate an unsolved murder. Hoffman-Pugh v. Keenan, 338 F.3d 1136 (10th Cir. 2003). Disclosure of grand jury materials to federal prosecutors without prior approval, in violation of § 16-5-204 , did not violate federal constitutional or statutory rights. United States v. Pignatiello, 628 F. Supp. 68 (D. Colo. 1986). Disclosure that testimony of other grand jury witnesses contradicted current witness' testimony did not violate grand jury secrecy rule where identities of witnesses were not disclosed. People v. Rickard, 761 P.2d 188 (Colo. 1988). A line should be drawn between information the witness possessed prior to becoming a witness and information the witness gained through her actual participation in the grand jury process. Hoffman-Pugh v. Keenan, 338 F.3d 1136 (10th Cir. 2003). Disclosure of information the witness already had independently of the grand jury process does not violate this rule. Drawing the line here protects the witness's first amendment right to speak while preserving the state's interest in grand jury secrecy. Hoffman-Pugh v. Keenan, 338 F.3d 1136 (10th Cir. 2003). Breach of secrecy by prosecution does not warrant dismissal of indictment absent factual findings that defendant is prejudiced. People v. Rickard, 761 P.2d (Colo. 1988). Jurors and witnesses should be protected vigorously from outside influences. People v. Zupancic, 192 Colo. 231, 557 P.2d 1195 (1976). Any effort to tamper is reprehensible. Any effort to tamper with or obstruct the due administration of a grand jury's function is reprehensible. People v. Zupancic, 192 Colo. 231, 557 P.2d 1195 (1976). The jury tampering statute, section 18-8-609 , is implemented by this rule. People v. Zupancic, 192 Colo. 231, 557 P.2d 1195 (1976). Despite defendant's contention that unauthorized persons were allowed in grand jury room and proceedings were not kept secret, the alleged violations did not affect defendant's substantial rights. Petit jury's subsequent guilty verdict made alleged error in grand jury proceeding harmless beyond a reasonable doubt. People v. Cerrone, 867 P.2d 143 (Colo. App. 1993), aff'd on other grounds, 900 P.2d 45 (Colo. 1995). Applied in People ex rel. Losavio v. J.L., 195 Colo. 494, 580 P.2d 23 (1978); Pankratz v. District Court, 199 Colo. 411, 609 P.2d 1101 (1980).

Rule 6.3 - Oath of Witnesses

The following oath shall be administered to each witness testifying before the grand jury:
DO YOU SWEAR (AFFIRM), UNDER PENALTY OF PERJURY, THAT THE TESTIMONY YOU ARE TO GIVE IS THE TRUTH, THE WHOLE TRUTH, AND NOTHING BUT THE TRUTH, AND THAT YOU WILL KEEP YOUR TESTIMONY SECRET, EXCEPT TO DISCUSS IT WITH YOUR ATTORNEY, OR THE PROSECUTOR, UNTIL AND UNLESS AN INDICTMENT OR REPORT IS ISSUED?

Colo. R. Crim. P. 6.3

Annotation Applied in People ex rel. Losavio v. J.L., 195 Colo. 494, 580 P.2d 23 (1978); In re P.R. v. District Court, 637 P.2d 346 (Colo. 1981). .

Rule 6.4 - Reporting of Proceedings

A certified or authorized reporter shall be present at all grand jury sessions. All grand jury proceedings and testimony from commencement to adjournment shall be reported. The reporter's notes and any transcripts which may be prepared shall be preserved, sealed, and filed with the court. No release or destruction of the notes or transcripts shall occur without prior court approval.

Colo. R. Crim. P. 6.4

Rule 6.5 - Investigator

(a)Appointment. Upon the written motion of the grand jury, the court shall appoint an investigator or investigators to assist the grand jury in its investigative functions. Said investigator may be an existing investigating law enforcement officer who is presently investigating the subject matter before the grand jury.

(b)Presence. Upon written motion of the grand jury, approved by the prosecutor, the court, for good cause, may allow a grand jury investigator to be present during testimony to advise the prosecutor. No grand jury investigator shall question any witness before the grand jury. A grand jury investigator shall not comment to the grand jury by word or gesture on the evidence or concerning the credibility of any witness but may testify under oath the same as other witnesses.

Colo. R. Crim. P. 6.5

Annotation Despite defendant's contention that unauthorized persons were allowed in grand jury room and proceedings were not kept secret, the alleged violations did not affect defendant's substantial rights. Petit jury's subsequent guilty verdict made alleged error in grand jury proceeding harmless beyond a reasonable doubt. People v. Cerrone, 867 P.2d 143 (Colo. App. 1993), aff'd on other grounds, 900 P.2d 45 (Colo. 1995).

Rule 6.6 - Indictment-Presentation-Sealing

(a) Presentation of an indictment in open court by a grand jury may be accomplished by the foreman of the grand jury, the full grand jury, or by the prosecutor acting under instructions of the grand jury.

(b) Upon motion by the prosecutor, the court shall order the indictment to be sealed and no person may disclose the existence of the indictment until the defendant is in custody or has been admitted to bail, except when necessary for the issuance of a warrant or summons.

Colo. R. Crim. P. 6.6

Source: Entire rule amended and adopted December 19, 1996, effective 3/1/1997.

Annotation It was not essential for all members of a grand jury who issued a true bill to specifically observe the formal charging paper and approve its formal language. People v. Campbell, 194 Colo. 451, 573 P.2d 557 (1978).

Rule 6.7 - Reports

A grand jury report may be prepared and released as permitted by § 16-5-205.5 , C.R.S.

Colo. R. Crim. P. 6.7

Source: Entire rule amended and adopted September 10, 1998, effective 1/1/1999.

Annotation Section 16-5-205 , relating to informations and indictments, applies to the extent of any conflict with this rule. de'Sha v. Reed, 194 Colo. 367, 572 P.2d 821 (1977). Applied in In re 1976 Arapahoe County Statutory Grand Jury, 194 Colo. 308, 572 P.2d 147 (1977); Charnes v. Lilly, 197 Colo. 460, 593 P.2d 967 (1979).

Rule 6.8 - Indictment-Amendment

(a)Matters of Form, Time, Place, Names. At any time before or during trial, the court may, upon application of the people and with notice to the defendant and opportunity for the defendant to be heard, order the amendment of an indictment with respect to defects, errors, or variances from the proof relating to matters of form, time, place, and names of persons when such amendment does not change the substance of the charge, and does not prejudice the defendant on the merits. Upon ordering an amendment, the court, for good cause, may grant a continuance to accord the defendant adequate opportunity to prepare his defense.

(b)Prohibition as to Substance. No indictment may be amended as to the substance of the offense charged.

Colo. R. Crim. P. 6.8

Annotation The policy underlying this rule is to insure that an indictment reflects the will of the grand jury. People v. Campbell, 194 Colo. 451, 573 P.2d 557 (1978). It was not essential for all members of a grand jury who issued a true bill to specifically observe the formal charging paper and approve its formal language. People v. Campbell, 194 Colo. 451, 573 P.2d 557 (1978). Trial court did not violate this rule by allowing the indictment to be amended to add a charge where the defendant entered into an agreement to plead nolo contendere to the added charge in exchange for a dismissal of all other charges in the indictment. People v. Valdez, 928 P.2d 1387 (Colo. App. 1996). Trial court's addition of habitual criminal counts had no effect on the substance of the indictment or the second degree assault charge and did not violate the provision of this rule prohibiting such amendments under this rule. People v. Martinez, 18 P.3d 831 (Colo. App. 2000). An indictment may be amended to fix defects, errors, or variances of proof, if the change is not substantial or an element of the crime. The indictment was amended to change dates and the dates were not a material element of any of the offenses, therefore, the defendant was not prejudiced. People v. James, 40 P.3d 36 (Colo. App. 2001). Applied in People v. Thimmes, 643 P.2d 780 (Colo. App. 1981).

Rule 6.9 - Testimony

(a) Release to Prosecutor. Upon application by the prosecutor, the court, for good cause, may enter an order to furnish to the prosecutor transcripts of grand jury testimony, minutes, reports, or exhibits relating to them.

(b) Release to Witness. Upon application by the prosecutor, or by any witness after notice to the prosecutor, the court, for good cause, may enter an order to furnish to that witness a transcript of his own grand jury testimony, or minutes, reports, or exhibits relating to them.

(c) Limitations on Release. An order to furnish transcripts of grand jury testimony, minutes, reports, or exhibits under this rule shall specify the person or persons who may be granted access to such material upon its release. Such order shall also specify any limitations which the court finds should be imposed on the use to be made of such material by any person or persons, after giving due consideration to the provisions of Rule 6.3. Such order shall also provide that release of such material shall not be made by the clerk of the court until the filing of an oath of affirmation of acceptance by the person receiving such material of the restrictions and limitations which are specified by the court under this paragraph.

(d) Indicted Defendant's Discovery Rights. Nothing herein shall limit the right of an indicted defendant to discovery under the rules of criminal procedure.

Colo. R. Crim. P. 6.9

Annotation Applied in Charnes v. Lilly, 197 Colo. 460, 593 P.2d 967 (1979).

Rule 7 - The Indictment and the Information

(a)The Indictment.

(1) An indictment shall be a written statement presented in open court by a grand jury to the district court which charges the commission of any crime by an alleged offender.

(2) Requisites of the Indictment. Every indictment of the grand jury shall state the crime charged and essential facts which constitute the offense. It also should state:

(I) That it is presented by a grand jury;

(II) That the defendant is identified therein, either by name or by the defendant's patterned chemical structure of genetic information, or described as a person whose name is unknown to the grand jury;

(III) That the offense was committed within the jurisdiction of the court, or is triable therein;

(IV) That it is signed by the foreman of the grand jury, and the prosecutor.

(b)The Information.

(1) An information shall be a written statement, signed by the prosecutor and filed in the court having jurisdiction over the offense charged, alleging that a person committed the criminal offense described therein.

(2)Requisites of the Information. The information shall be deemed technically sufficient and correct if it can be understood therefrom:

(I) That it is presented by the person authorized by law to prosecute the offense;

(II) That the defendant is identified therein, either by name or by the defendant's patterned chemical structure of genetic information, or described as a person whose name is unknown to the informant;

(III) That the offense was committed within the jurisdiction of the court, or is triable therein;

(IV) That the offense charged is set forth with such degree of certainty that the court may pronounce judgment upon a conviction.

(3)Information After Preliminary Hearing Waiver or Dispositional Hearing. An information may be filed, without consent of the trial court having jurisdiction, for any offense against anyone who has either:

(I) Failed to request a preliminary hearing in the county pursuant to Rule 5;

(II) Had a preliminary hearing or dispositional hearing and has been bound over by the county court to appear in the court having trial jurisdiction.

(4) When a defendant has been bound over to the trial court pursuant to Rule 5(a)(4) (III), the felony complaint when transferred to the trial court shall be deemed to be an information if it contains the requirements of an information.

(c)Direct Information. The prosecutor may file a direct information if:

(1) The prosecutor obtains the consent of the court having trial jurisdiction and no complaint was filed against the accused person in the county court pursuant to Rule 5; or

(2) A preliminary hearing was held either in the county court or in the district court and the court found probable cause did not exist as to one or more counts. If the prosecutor states an intention to proceed in this manner, the bond executed by the defendant shall be continued and returnable in the district court at a day and time certain. If a bond has not been continued, the defendant shall be summoned into court without the necessity of making a new bond. The information shall be accompanied by a written statement from the prosecutor alleging facts which establish that evidence exists which for good cause was not presented by the prosecutor at the preliminary hearing. Within 21 days of defendant's first appearance following the direct filing the defendant may request an evidentiary hearing at which the prosecutor shall establish the existence of such good cause; or

(3) The prosecutor obtains the consent of the court having trial jurisdiction and the complaint upon which the preliminary hearing was held and the other records in the case have not been delivered to the clerk of the proper trial court.

(4) The case was dismissed before a preliminary hearing was held in the county court or in the district court, when one is required, or, in other cases, before the defendant was bound over to the trial court or otherwise set for arraignment or trial. The information shall be accompanied by a written statement from the prosecutor stating good cause for dismissing and then refiling the case. Within 21 days after defendant's first appearance following the direct filing the defendant may request a hearing at which the prosecutor shall establish the existence of such good cause. The prosecution may also submit the matter to a grand jury.

(5) The case was dismissed after the district or county court found probable cause at the preliminary hearing if one was required or, in other cases, after the defendant was bound over to the trial court or otherwise set for arraignment or trial, and before jeopardy has attached. If such case was originally filed by direct information in the district court, the prosecution may not file the same offense(s) by a felony complaint in the county court, but the prosecution may charge the same offense(s) by filing a direct information in the district court or may submit the matter to a grand jury, and the case shall then proceed as if the previous case had never been filed. The prosecution shall also file with the direct information or with the felony complaint a statement showing good cause for dismissing and then refiling the case. Within 21 days of defendant's first appearance following the filing of the new felony complaint or the direct filing of the new information the defendant may request an evidentiary hearing at which the prosecutor shall establish the existence of such good cause.

(d) Repealed.

(e)Amendment of Information. The court may permit an information to be amended as to form or substance at any time prior to trial; the court may permit it to be amended as to form at any time before the verdict or finding if no additional or different offense is charged and if substantial rights of the defendant are not prejudiced.

(f)Surplusage. The court, on motion of the defendant or the prosecutor, may strike surplusage from the information or indictment.

(g)Bill of Particulars. The court may direct the filing of a bill of particulars. A motion for a bill of particulars may be made only within 14 days after arraignment or at such other time before or after arraignment as may be prescribed by rule or order. A bill of particulars may be amended at any time subject to such conditions as justice requires.

(h)Preliminary Hearing - District Court Procedures.

(1) In cases in which a direct information was filed pursuant to Rule 7(c), charging: (1) a class 1, 2, or 3 felony; felony; (2) a level 1 or 2 drug felony; or (3) or a class 4, 5, or 6 felony or a level 3 or 4 drug felony if such felony requires mandatory sentencing or is a crime of violence as defined in section 18-1.3-406 or is a sexual offense under part 4 of article 3 of title 18, C.R.S., a preliminary hearing is authorized. Either the defendant or the prosecutor may request a preliminary hearing to determine whether probable cause exists to believe that the offense charged in the information has been committed by the defendant. However, any defendant accused of a class 4, 5, or 6 felony or a level 3 or 4 drug felony who is not otherwise entitled to a preliminary hearing may request a preliminary hearing if the defendant is in custody for the offense for which the preliminary hearing is requested; except that, upon motion of either party, the court shall vacate the preliminary hearing if there is a reasonable showing that the defendant has been released from custody prior to the preliminary hearing. Any person accused of a class 4, 5, or 6 felony or a level 3 or 4 drug felony who may not request a preliminary hearing shall participate in a dispositional hearing unless otherwise waived for the purposes of case evaluation and potential resolution. Except upon a finding of good cause, the request for a preliminary hearing must be made within 7 days after the defendant is brought before the court for or following the filing of the information in that court and prior to a plea. No request for a preliminary hearing may be filed in a case which is to be tried upon indictment.

(2) Upon the making of such a request, or if a dispositional hearing is required, the district court shall set the hearing which shall be held within 35 days of the day of the setting, unless good cause for continuing the hearing beyond that period is shown to the court. The clerk of the court shall prepare and give notice of the hearing, or any continuance thereof, to all parties and their counsel.

(3) The defendant shall not be called upon to plead at the preliminary hearing. The defendant may cross-examine the prosecutor's witnesses and may introduce evidence. The prosecutor shall

24

have the burden of establishing probable cause. The presiding judge at the preliminary hearing may temper the rules of evidence in the exercise of sound judicial discretion.

(4) If, from the evidence, it appears to the district court that no probable cause exists to believe that any or all of the offenses charged were committed by the defendant, the court shall dismiss those counts from the information and, if the court dismisses all counts, discharge the defendant; otherwise, or subsequent to a dispositional hearing, it shall set the case for arraignment or trial. If the prosecutor believes the court erred in its finding of no probable cause, this ruling may be appealed pursuant to Colorado Appellate Rules. Such a ruling shall not constitute good cause for refiling.

(4.5) A dispositional hearing is an opportunity for the parties to report to the court on the status of discussions toward disposition, including presenting any resolution pursuant to C.R.S. 16-7-302. The court shall set the dispositional hearing at a time that will afford the parties an opportunity for case evaluation and potential resolution.

(5) If a request for preliminary hearing has not been filed within the time limitations of subsection (h)(1) of this Rule, such a request shall not thereafter be heard by the court, nor shall the court entertain successive requests for preliminary hearing. The order denying a dismissal of any or all of the counts in the information after a preliminary hearing shall be final and not subject to review on appeal. The granting of such a dismissal or any or all of the counts in an information shall not be a bar to further prosecution of the accused person for the same offenses. Upon a finding of no probable cause, the prosecution may appeal pursuant to Rule 7(h)(4), may file another direct information in the district court pursuant to Rule 7(c)(2) charging the same offense(s) or may submit the matter to a grand jury, but in such cases originally filed by direct information in the district court, the prosecution may not refile the same offense(s) by a felony complaint in the county court.

(i) Motion for Reverse-Transfer Hearing Upon Indictment. In cases commenced by indictment, any motion under section 19-2-517(3)(a), C.R.S., to transfer the case to juvenile court must be filed within 7 days after the defendant is brought before the court for or following the filing of the indictment in that court and prior to a plea, except upon a showing of good cause.

Colo. R. Crim. P. 7

Source: Entire rule amended March 31, 1988, effective 1/1/1989; d repealed September 4, 1997, effective 1/1/1998; b3, h1, h2, and h4 amended and h4.5 added November 4, 1999, effective 1/1/2000; entire rule amended and adopted September 12, 2000, effective 1/1/2001; c and h amended and effective 1/17/2008; c2, c4, c5, g, and h2 amended and adopted December 14, 2011, effective 7/1/2012; amended and adopted September 13, 2018, effective 9/13/2018.

Annotation I. General Consideration. Law reviews. For note, "Preliminary Hearings-The Case for Revival", see U. Colo. L. Rev. 580 (1967). Means by which charges brought by district attorney. A district attorney may bring charges either by filing a complaint or direct information or by presenting a grand jury indictment in open court. Dresner v. County Court, 189 Colo. 374, 540 P.2d 1085 (1975). Applied in Bustos v. People, 158 Colo. 451, 408 P.2d 64 (1965); Lorenz v. People, 159 Colo. 494, 412 P.2d 895 (1966); Tyler v. Russel, 410 F.2d 490 (10th Cir. 1969); Rowse v. District Court, 180 Colo. 44, 502 P.2d 422 (1972); People v. Bergstrom, 190 Colo. 105, 544 P.2d 396 (1975); People v. Shortt, 192 Colo. 183, 557 P.2d 388 (1976); People v. Denn, 192 Colo. 276, 557 P.2d 1200 (1976); People v. Albo, 195 Colo. 102, 575 P.2d 427 (1978); People v. Rice, 40 Colo. App. 374, 579 P.2d 647 (1978); People v. Kreiser, 41 Colo. App. 210, 585 P.2d 301 (1978); People v. Smith, 198 Colo. 120, 597 P.2d 204 (1979); People v. Driscoll, 200 Colo. 410, 615 P.2d 696 (Colo. 1980); Jeffrey v. District Court, 626 P.2d 631 (Colo. 1981); People v. Moody, 630 P.2d 74 (Colo. 1981); People v. Stoppel, 637 P.2d 384 (Colo. 1981); People v. Abbott, 638 P.2d 781 (Colo. 1981); J.T. v. O'Rourke ex rel. Tenth Judicial Dist., 651 P.2d 407 (Colo. 1982); People v. District Court, 652 P.2d 582 (Colo. 1982); People v. Anderson, 659 P.2d 1385 (Colo. 1983); Corr v. District Court, 661 P.2d 668 (Colo. 1983). II. Indictment. It is defendant's right to be informed with reasonable certainty of nature of changes against him by requiring that an indictment answer the questions of "who, what, wheres, and how" in cases where the acts constituting the offense are not adequately described by the statute. People v. Donachy, 196 Colo. 289, 586 P.2d 14 (1978); People v. Gable, 647 P.2d 246 (Colo. App. 1982). Indictment must clearly state essential facts which constitute the offense: Fundamental fairness requires no less. People v. Tucker, 631 P.2d 162 (Colo. 1981). Test of sufficiency of indictment is whether it is sufficiently definite to inform the defendant of the charges against him so as to enable him to prepare a defense and to plead the judgment in bar of any further prosecutions for the same offense. People v. Westendorf, 37 Col. App. 111, 542 P. 2d

1300 (1975); People v. Gable, 647 P.2d 246 (Colo. App. 1982). An indictment is sufficient so long as it is not so indefinite in its statement of a particular charge that it fails to afford defendant a fair opportunity to procure witnesses and prepare for trial. People v. Heller, 698 P.2d 1357 (Colo. App. 1984), rev'd on other grounds, 712 P.2d 1023 (Colo. 1986). When an indictment is procured by or with the assistance of a prosecuting attorney who is disqualified to conduct the prosecution, it is invalid. Once the disqualification of a district attorney is entered and the appointment of a special prosecutor becomes effective, the special prosecutor, and only the special prosecutor, is the authorized prosecuting attorney on the case. People v. Hastings, 903 P.2d 23 (Colo. App. 1994). Orderly sequence of statement of elements of offense should characterize indictment. Johnson v. People, 110 Colo. 283, 133 P.2d 789 (1943). The requirements of a criminal indictment by a grand jury are essentially twofold: First, it must give the defendant sufficient notice of the crime that has allegedly been committed so that a defense may be prepared; second, it must define the acts which constitute the crime with sufficient definiteness so that the defendant may plead the resolution of the indictment as a bar to subsequent proceedings. People v. Tucker, 631 P.2d 162 (Colo. 1981). Insufficient indictment does not legally charge crime or subject defendant to the jurisdiction of the court. People v. Westendorf, 37 Colo. App. 111, 542 P. 2d 1300 (1975). And jeopardy does not attach to indictment defective in substance. An indictment which is defective in substance merely prevents prosecution on the basis of that particular pleading. No jeopardy attaches, and the defendant may be charged be any appropriate and sufficient pleading. People v. Thimmes, 643 P.2d 780 (Colo. App. 1981). Recitation of statute may be insufficient. Where acts constituting an offense are not described by the statute, any indictment merely reciting the statutory words is insufficient. People v. Tucker, 631 P.2d 162 (Colo. 1981). Defendant may raise insufficiency for first time on appeal. Although defendant did not raise the insufficiency of the indictment at trial or in his motion for new trial, he is not thereby precluded from asserting that defect on appeal. People v. Westendorf, 37 Colo. App. 111, 542 P.2d 1300 (1975). Date of offense is material allegation. Allegations specifying the date on which an accused allegedly committed an offense are always material when the offense charged is one which may be barred by an applicable statute of limitations. People v. Thimmes, 643 P.2d 780 (Colo. App. 1981). Because of the veil of secrecy surrounding most conspiracies, considerable latitude is allowed in drafting conspiracy indictment. People v. Gable, 647 P.2d 246 (Colo. App. 1982). III. Information. A. In General. District attorney has the authority to file a complaint or information in derogation of grand jury's true bill. Dresner v. County Court, 189 Colo. 374, 540 P.2d 1085 (1975). Practice of effecting charge through information is not unconstitutionally void as not affording the protection of a grand jury. Falgout v. People, 170 Colo. 32, 459 P.2d 572 (1969); Sergent v. People, 177 Colo. 354, 497 P.2d 983 (1972). But if information fails to charge crime, court acquires no jurisdiction. People v. Moore, 200 Colo. 481, 615 P.2d 726 (1980). If the information is not presented by a person authorized by law to prosecute the offense, it is technically insufficient and incorrect and if it is signed by an unauthorized person, it is invalid. People v. Hastings, 903 P.2d 23 (Colo. App. 1994). When an information is presented by a disqualified prosecuting attorney, it is invalid. Once the disqualification of a district attorney is entered and the appointment of a special prosecutor becomes effective, the special prosecutor, and only the special prosecutor, is the authorized prosecuting attorney on the case. People v. Hastings, 903 P.2d 23 (Colo. App. 1994). Count charged both the crime of sexual assault on a child and the sentence enhancer by clearly identifying each of the elements of both with sufficient particularity. People v. Melillo, 25 P.3d 769 (Colo. 2001). Amendment of information on date of trial was proper since the amendment went to the dates of the offenses and did not prejudice defendant. The date change was not substantive and there was no prejudice to defendant because previous informations had included the dates in the amendment, so defendant was on notice the charges could include those dates. People v. Walker, __ P.3d __ (Colo. App. 2011). Failure to include intent to seek discretionary indeterminate sentencing in information is not plain error. Defendant was aware he was charged with a crime in which indeterminate sentencing was a possibility. People v. Walker, __ P.3d __ (Colo. App. 2011). B. Affidavits. Law reviews. For article, "Confidential Informants To Disclose or Not to Disclose", see 19 Colo. Law. 225 (1990). Verification of an information is required under this rule. Scott v. People, 176 Colo. 289, 490 P.2d 1295 (1971). Technical defects in the form of an information do not require reversal unless substantial rights of the defendant are prejudiced. Information which omitted the words "against the peace and dignity of the People of the State of Colorado ", did not prejudice defendant's substantial rights. People v. Higgins, 874 P.2d 479 (Colo. App. 1994). Affiant's competency presumed. It is unnecessary for the affidavit to recite that affiant is "a competent witness to

26

*testify in the case", as his competency will be presumed until the contrary appears. Walt v.
People, 46 Colo. 136, 104 P.2d 89 (1909), appeal dismissed, 223 U.S. 748, 32 S. Ct. 534, 56 L.
Ed. 640 (1912); Hubbard v. People, 153 Colo. 252, 385 P.2d 419 (1963). As is credibility. An
affiant's credibility as a witness is presumed until the contrary appears. Hubbard v. People, 153
Colo. 252, 385 P.2d 419 (1963). Signing affidavit before reading does not nullify affiant's
credibility. Although it is extremely poor practice to sign without reading, such does not make
affiant an uncredible, where he signed the affidavit as prepared and explained to him, believing
he knew what it said. Williams v. People, 157 Colo. 443, 403 P.2d 436 (1965). Nor does minor
factual discrepancy. A discrepancy in the amount of money taken and charged in the affidavit
does not render affiant incompetent as a witness. Williams v. People, 157 Colo. 443, 403 P.2d
436 (1965). Affidavit complies with rule despite technical error. Where a defendant is charged
with more than one crime, an affidavit which uses the word "offense" rather than "offenses"
substantially complies with this rule. Martinez v. People, 156 Colo. 380, 399 P.2d 415, cert.
denied, 382 U.S. 866, 86 S. Ct. 134, 15 L. Ed. 2d 104 (1965). And evidence adduced at
preliminary hearing may cure defect in affidavit. Where defendants exercised their rights to a
preliminary hearing and had the issue of probable cause determined against them by direct
evidence, which would be sufficient to satisfy the requirements of this rule, the evidence adduced
at the preliminary hearing cured a defect in the affidavit and rendered the issue of personal
knowledge of the affiant on the information moot. People v. Weaver, 182 Colo. 221, 511 P.2d
908 (1973). Affidavit sufficient to meet requirements of this rule. Williams v. People, 157 Colo.
443, 403 P.2d 436 (1965); Coy v. People, 158 Colo. 437, 407 P.2d 345 (1965); Andrews v.
People, 161 Colo. 516, 423 P.2d 322 (1967). Not denial of right of conformation where affiant
does not testify at trial. A defendant is not denied his constitutional right of confrontation
because an individual who verified the information and who was indorsed as a witness does not
testify at the time of trial. Scott v. People, 176 Colo. 289, 490 P.2d 1295 (1971). IV. Direct
Information. Prosecution's remedies upon dismissal in county court. The prosecution has one of
two remedies available to it when a case is dismissed in the county court. If the case is dismissed
before a preliminary hearing is held, the prosecution may appeal the order of dismissal to the
district court. If the county court dismisses a charge after holding a preliminary hearing under
Crim. P. 5(a)(4), the exclusive remedy available to the prosecution is to request leave to file a
direct information in the district court. People v. Freiman, 657 P.2d 452 (Colo. 1983). There is
no procedure for dismissing a felony complaint without prejudice. Once the filing of a felony
complaint in county court is dismissed, the prosecution must either obtain a grand jury
indictment or file an information directly in the district court. People v. Williams, 987 P.2d 232
(Colo. 1999). The purpose to be achieved by the district court consent requirement of subsection
(c)(2) is to insure that the accused is not subject to oppressive and malicious prosecutions.
People v. Elmore, 652 P.2d 571 (Colo. 1982). Consent of court cannot be perfunctory. People v.
Swazo, 191 Colo. 425, 553 P.2d 782 (1976). As informed consent required. The logical
application of section (c), requires informed consent. Otherwise, any real distinction between
subsection (b)(3), and section (c) would be illusory. People v. Swazo, 191 Colo. 425, 553 P.2d
782 (1976). And exercise of discretion. The requirement of court consent implies a real
application of discretion. People v. Swazo, 191 Colo. 425, 553 P.2d 782 (1976); People v.
Elmore, 652 P.2d 571 (Colo. 1982); People v. Sabell, 708 P.2d 463 (Colo. 1985). In exercising
its discretion in deciding whether to permit a direct filing of an information, the district court is
required to balance the right of the district attorney to prosecute criminal cases against the need
to protect the accused from discrimination and oppression. People v. Freiman, 657 P.2d 452
(Colo. 1983). There is no constitutional right to a preliminary hearing when a direct information
is filed. Falgout v. People, 170 Colo. 32, 459 P.2d 572 (1969); Hervey v. People, 178 Colo. 38,
495 P.2d 204 (1972); Sergent v. People, 177 Colo. 354, 497 P.2d 983 (1972); People v. Moreno,
181 Colo. 106, 507 P.2d 857 (1973). As bringing charge by direct information is not in violation
of either state or federal constitution. Habbord v. People, 175 Colo. 417, 488 P.2d 554 (1971).
And whether a preliminary hearing shall be had is a procedural matter. De Baca v. Trujillo, 167
Colo. 311, 447 P.2d 533 (1968). Purpose behind requiring personal knowledge of affiant in
direct information is to assure that there is probable cause to initiate the criminal proceeding, so
as to safeguard the rights of innocent citizens. People v. Weaver, 182 Colo. 221, 511 P.2d 908
(1973). Authority to file direct information charging differently than true bill. Where a true bill
was never filed in district court, the district attorney had the power and authority to file a
complaint or direct information that included charges which were different than those allegedly
set forth in the true bill returned by a grand jury. Dresner v. County Court, 189 Colo. 374, 540
P.2d 1085 (1975). No requirement of new evidence to support direct filing. There is no*

27

requirement that the district attorney establish that there exists new or additional evidence to support the direct filing of an information. The existence of such evidence is only one factor the district court may consider in exercising its discretion to determine whether to allow the direct filing. Holmes v. District Court, 668 P.2d 11 (Colo. 1983). Incompetent evidence acceptable at hearing. Hearsay evidence, and other evidence, which would be incompetent if offered at the time of trial, may be the bulk of evidence at a preliminary hearing. People v. Quinn, 183 Colo. 245, 516 P.2d 420 (1973). Prosecutor must apprise judge of prior dismissal of charges. For consent to be valid, there must be a sufficient evidentiary disclosure by the prosecutor to at least apprise the judge of a prior dismissal of the identical charges in county court and the reasons for the direct filing. People v. Swazo, 191 Colo. 425, 553 P.2d 782 (1976). And hearing in district court may be demanded even though such hearing was held in county court. After the filing of a direct information in the district court either the people or the defendant may demand a preliminary hearing in that court even where there has been a dismissal of a felony complaing by the county court following a preliminary hearing on the same charge. People v. Burggraf, 36 Colo. App. 137, 536 P.2d 48 (1975). Direct information not available after dismissal for failure to prosecute. Section (c) does not allow filing of a direct information in the district court if the charges, first filed in county court, are dismissed before a preliminary hearing for failure of the prosecution to comply with the 30-day rule in Crim. P. 5(a)(4)(I). Chavez v. District Court, 648 P.2d 658 (Colo. 1982). Court's discretion in filing direct information following dismissal. While under subsection (c)(2), the district attorney, with the consent of the court, may file a direct information in the district court if a preliminary hearing was held on the same charge in the county court and the accused was discharged, before the district court may properly exercise its discretion, there must be a sufficient evidentiary disclosure by the prosecution to apprise the district court of the earlier dismissal of the identical charges in the county court and the reasons for the requested refiling. When exercising its discretion in deciding whether to permit the direct filing of an information, the district court is required to balance the right of the district attorney to prosecute criminal cases against the need to protect the accused from discrimination and oppression. Holmes v. District Court, 668 P.2d 11 (Colo. 1983); People v. Sabell, 708 P.2d 463 (Colo. 1985). When the motion under subsection (c)(2) did not identify the county court's error and did not describe testimony at the preliminary hearing in detail, there was not sufficient evidentiary disclosure to allow refiling. Borg v. District Court, 686 P.2d 781 (Colo. 1984). Requirement of district court's consent for filing of direct information implies an exercise of court's discretion which will not be overturned unless there exists abuse of such discretion. People v. Stokes, 812 P.2d 712 (Colo. App. 1991). Trial court's denial of defendant's motion to dismiss, despite failure of prosecution to advise trial court of prior dismissal, was not error where consent by the court was obtained and the dismissed case involved separate and distinct charges. People v. Higgins, 874 P.2d 479 (Colo. App. 1994). Belief that county court erred in finding no probable cause existed for sexual assault charge does not constitute good cause for refiling charges by direct information as issue of adequacy of evidence may be addressed only upon appellate review. People v. Stokes, 812 P.2d 712 (Colo. App. 1991). District court's denial of consent for filing of direct information did not constitute abuse of discretion when prosecution did not present testimony of victim in county court proceedings for tactical reasons. People v. Stokes, 812 P.2d 712 (Colo. App. 1991). District attorney allowed to join offenses arising from criminal episode. This rule allows the district attorney, with the consent of the trial court, to file a direct information joining any or all offenses arising from a criminal episode. People v. District Court, 183 Colo. 101, 515 P.2d 101 (1973). V. Names of Witnesses. Compliance with this rule is mandatory for district attorney. People v. Bailey, 191 Colo. 366, 552 P.2d 1014 (1976). Purpose of supplying names of witnesses with the indictment or information is to advise defendants of the identity of those who might testify against them and to afford counsel an opportunity, where deemed advisable, to interview such witnesses. Reed v. People, 171 Colo. 421, 467 P.2d 809 (1970); People v. Bailey, 191 Colo. 336, 552 P.2d 1014 (1976). Allowance of late endorsements of prosecution witnesses is within discretion of trial court. People v. Muniz, 622 P.2d 100 (Colo. App. 1980); Corbett v. People, 153 Colo. 457, 387 P.2d 409 (1963), cert. denied, 377 U.S. 939, 84 S. Ct. 1346, 12 L. Ed. 2d 302 (1964); People v. Buckner, 180 Colo. 65, 504 P.2d 669 (1972); People v. Wandel, 713 P.2d 398 (Colo. App. 1985). And no error unless defendant prejudiced. In order to constitute reversible error where there is a late endorsement of a witness, the defendant must show that he was prejudiced because the appearance of the witness surprised him and because he did not have adequate opportunity to interview the witness prior to trial. People v. Bailey, 191 Colo. 366, 552 P.2d 1014 (1976). Trial court did not abuse its discretion in allowing prosecution to endorse four witnesses on the day of the trial where defendant was familiar with testimony of three of the witnesses and did not request a continuance for the purpose of interviewing them, and where endorsement of the fourth witness was conditioned upon defendant having access prior to the witness' testimony. People v. Castango, 674 P.2d 978 (Colo. App. 1983). When failure to notify defendant of witness's change of address not reversible error. Failure to notify defendant of a change of address of a witness is not grounds for reversal where no surprise is shown when he testifies at the trial, no continuance has been sought on the grounds that there was no opportunity to interview him prior to trial, and no attempt has been made to ascertain his current address if defendant had sought to locate him for the purpose of interview. Reed v. People, 171 Colo. 421, 467 P.2d 809 (1970). Defense counsel's refusal to request continuance may be waiver of claim of prejudicial error due to late endorsement. People v. Bailey, 191 Colo. 366, 552 P.2d 1014 (1976). VI. Nature and Contents of Information. A specific crime must be alleged in the information. Gomez v. People, 162 Colo. 77, 424 P.2d 387 (1967); Henson v. People, 166 Colo. 428, 444 P.2d 275 (1968). But the name of the crime need not be mentioned in an information, if the crime is adequately described therein. Gallegos v. People, 166 Colo. 409, 444 P.2d 267 (1968). Rather, information is sufficient if it advises a defendant of the offense with which he is charged. Edwards v. People, 176 Colo. 478, 491 P.2d 566 (1971); People v. Ingersoll, 181 Colo. 1, 506 P.2d 364 (1973); People v. Flanders, 183 Colo. 268, 516 P.2d 418 (1973); People v. Gnout, 183 Colo. 366, 517 P.2d 394 (1973); People v. Moore, 200 Colo. 481, 615 P.2d 726 (1980). And can be understood by the jury. An information is sufficient if the charge is in language from which the nature of the offense may be readily understood by the accused and jury. Tracy v. People, 65 Colo. 226, 176 P. 280 (1918); Sarno v. People, 74 Colo. 528, 223 P. 41 (1924); Albert v. People, 90 Colo. 219, 7 P.2d 822 (1932); Johnson v. People, 110 Colo. 283, 133 P.2d 789 (1943); Wright v. People, 116 Colo. 306, 181 P.2d 447 (1947); Ciccarelli v. People, 147 Colo. 413, 364 P.2d 368 (1961); Loggins v. People, 178 Colo. 439, 498 P.2d 1146 (1972); Olguin v. People, 179 Colo. 26, 497 P.2d 1254 (1972). So that defendant can defend against it. An information is sufficient if it advises the accused of the charge he is facing so that he can adequately defend against it. Gallegos v. People, 166 Colo. 409, 444 P.2d 267 (1968); Perez v. People, 176 Colo. 505, 491 P.2d 969 (1971); Loggins v. People, 178 Colo. 439, 498 P.2d 1146 (1972); People v. Flanders, 183 Colo. 268, 516 P.2d 418 (1973); People v. Gnout, 183 Colo. 366, 517 P.2d 394 (1973); People v. Moore, 200 Colo. 481, 615 P.2d 726 (1980); People in Interest of R.G., 630 P.2d 89 (Colo. App. 1981). And be protected from further prosecution for the same offense. An information is sufficient if it advises the defendant of the charges he is facing so that he can adequately defend himself and be protected from further prosecution for the same offense. People v. Warner, 112 Colo. 565, 151 P.2d 975 (1944); Ciccarelli v. People, 147 Colo. 413, 364 P.2d 368 (1961); People v. Allen, 167 Colo. 158, 446 P.2d 223 (1968); Loggins v. People, 178 Colo. 439, 498 P.2d 1146 (1972); Olguin v. People, 179 Colo. 26, 497 P.2d 1254 (1972); People v. Ingersoll, 181 Colo. 1, 506 P.2d 364 (1973). People v. Flanders, 183 Colo. 268, 516 P.2d 418 (1973); People v. Gnout, 183 Colo. 366, 517 P.2d 394 (1973); People v. Moore, 200 Colo. 481, 615 P.2d 726 (1980); People v. Palmer, 87 P.3d 137 (Colo. App. 2003). Although great detail not needed as judgment, not information, constitutes bar. An information need not plead an offense in such detail as to be self-sufficient as a bar to further prosecution for the same offense; for the judgment constitutes a bar, and the extent of the judgment may be determined from an examination of the record as a whole. Mora v. People, 172 Colo. 261, 472 P.2d 142 (1970); Howe v. People, 178 Colo. 248, 496 P.2d 1040 (1972). Jeopardy does not attach if information is insufficient to sustain conviction. People v. Garner, 187 Colo. 294, 530 P.2d 496 (1975). Dimissal if defendant not fairly and reasonably informed of accusations. There must be a variance between the information and the proof to be offered constituting such an imperfection or inaccuracy that the defendant was not fairly and reasonably informed of the nature and cause of the accusations against him in order that a motion of dismissal be granted. People v. Allen, 167 Colo. 158, 446 P.2d 223 (1968). Each count of information must be independent. Absent a clear and specific incorporation by reference, each count of an information to be valid must be independent of the others, and in itself charge the defendant with a distinct and different offense. People v. Moore, 200 Colo. 481, 615 P.2d 726 (1980); People v. Steiner, 640 P.2d 250 (Colo. App. 1981). But clear and specific incorporation by reference permitted. Any count in an information may, by proper reference, incorporate the allegations more fully set forth in another count, such reference must be clear, specific, and leave no doubt as to what provision is intended to be incorporated and this same rule is applicable to incorporating the caption. People v. Steiner, 640 P.2d 250 (Colo. App. 1981). Information is sufficient if it charges crime in the words of the statute. Williams v. People, 26 Colo. 272, 57 P. 701 (1899); Wright v. People, 116 Colo.

306, 181 P.2d 447 (1947); Gallegos v. People, 166 Colo. 409, 444 P.2d 267 (1968); People v. Moreno, 176 Colo. 488, 491 P.2d 575 (1971); Perez v. People, 176 Colo. 505, 491 P.2d 969 (1971); Loggins v. People, 178 Colo. 439, 498 P.2d 1146 (1972); Olguin v. People, 179 Colo. 26, 497 P.2d 1254 (1972); People v. Palmer, 87 P.3d 137 (Colo. App. 2003). However, an information need not follow the exact wording of the statute. Sarno v. People, 74 Colo. 528, 223 P. 41 (1924); Albert v. People, 90 Colo. 219, 7 P.2d 822 (1932); Helser v. People, 100 Colo. 371, 68 P.2d 543 (1937); Ciccarelli v. People, 147 Colo. 413, 364 P.2d 368 (1961); Cortez v. People, 155 Colo. 317, 394 P.2d 346 (1964); Gallegos v. People, 166 Colo. 409, 444 P.2d 267 (1968); Perez v. People, 176 Colo. 505, 491 P.2d 969 (1971); Loggins v. People, 178 Colo. 439, 498 P.2d 1146 (1972); People v. Russell, 36 P.3d 92 (Colo. App. 2001). The charging of a defendant in the conjunctive where a statute defines a crime as being capable of being committed in diverse ways is proper. Rowe v. People, 26 Colo. 542, 59 P. 57 (1899); Hernandez v. People, 156 Colo. 23, 396 P.2d 952 (1964). And statutory reference is not material part of information, and, in the absence of any showing that the defendant is actually misled to his prejudice by such an inaccuracy, no error arises therefrom. Lucero v. People, 164 Colo. 247, 434 P.2d 128 (1967); People v. Marion, 182 Colo. 435, 514 P.2d 327 (1973); People v. Johnson, 644 P.2d 34 (Colo. App. 1980); People in Interest of R.G., 630 P.2d 89 (Colo. App. 1981). Information need not specify lesser included offenses which may have been committed in commission of the described act. People in Interest of R.G., 630 P.2d 89 (Colo. App. 1981). No information is deemed insufficient by any defect which does not tend to prejudice the substantial rights of the defendant on the merits. Albert v. People, 90 Colo. 219, 7 P.2d 822 (1932); Martinez v. People, 156 Colo. 380, 399 P.2d 415, cert. denied, 382 U.S. 866, 86 S. Ct. 134, 15 L. Ed. 2d 104 (1965). Date of offense is not material allegation of information. Marn v. People, 175 Colo. 242, 486 P.2d 424 (1971). Where the defendant made no showing that he was impaired in his defense to the charge at trial or in his ability to plead the judgment as a bar to a subsequent proceeding, a variance between the specific date of the offense as alleged in the information and the date as proved at trial is not fatal. People v. Adler, 629 P.2d 569 (Colo. 1981). The prosecution is not required to specify a precise date of an alleged offense unless that date is a material element of the offense. People v. Salyer, 80 P.3d 831 (Colo. App. 2003). But failure to allege where offense committed makes information insufficient. When an information fails to allege where the offense was committed, and thus, that it occurred within the jurisdiction of the court, it fails to state facts sufficient to confer jurisdiction upon the district court of the county in which it is filed to try the defendant. People v. Steiner, 640 P.2d 250 (Colo. App. 1981). Separate allegation of place where offense was committed, which specifically referred to all previously alleged offenses, clearly advised defendant of claimed location of offenses, and was sufficient. People v. Brinson, 739 P.2d 897 (Colo. App. 1987). If the information is signed by an unauthorized person, it is invalid. People v. Hastings, 903 P.2d 23 (Colo. App. 1994). Information charging offense beyond statute of limitations. The trial court has jurisdiction to entertain a motion to amend an information which charges an offense committed outside of the statute of limitations. People v. Bowen, 658 P.2d 269 (Colo. 1983). When general statement of offense not error. Charging theft of "miscellaneous personal property" in information is sufficient where itemized list is furnished defense. Howe v. People, 178 Colo. 248, 496 P.2d 1040 (1972). And poor writing style not error where nature of charge clear. Where an information could have been written in far better style, but there can be no doubt that its meaning is clear, then defendants are adequately advised of the nature of the crime charged against them, and this is all section (c) requires. Covington v. People, 36 Colo. 183, 85 P. 832 (1906); Petty v. People, 156 Colo. 549, 400 P.2d 666 (1965). Sufficiency of information is matter of jurisdiction. People v. Garner, 187 Colo. 294, 530 P.2d 946 (1975). And such matter may be raised after trial by a motion in arrest of judgment. People v. Garner, 187 Colo. 294, 530 P.2d 496 (1975). VII. Amendment of Information. The purposes served by a criminal information are to advise the defendant of the nature of the charges against him, to enable him to prepare a defense, and to protect him from further prosecution for the same offense, and it is within the discretion of the trial court to allow the information to be amended as to form or substance any time prior to trial. People v. Thomas, 832 P.2d 990 (Colo. App. 1991). When the defendant had actual notice before trial that he was being charged with having committed three prior felonies under § 16-13-101(2) rather than two prior felonies under § 16-13-101(1), an amendment to the information to reflect that state of affairs was a matter of form and not of substance. People v. Butler, 929 P.2d 36 (Colo. App. 1996). Substance should prevail over form and cases generally should not be dismissed for technical irregularities that can be cured through amendment. People v. Hertz, 196 Colo. 259, 586 P.2d 5 (1978); People v. Cervantes, 677 P.2d 403 (Colo. App. 1983), aff'd, 715 P.2d 783 (Colo. 1986). An amended

30

complaint that merely remedies an insufficient list of victims in the original complaint relates back to the date of the original and is not time-barred. People v. Higgins, 868 P.2d 371 (Colo. 1994). Where late amendment of information allowed. Where the court allowed the prosecution to amend the information one week before trial and then denied defendants' motions for continuance, there was no abuse of discretion where defendants' counsel knew of the amendment two weeks before trial, where the trial was reset so as to grant an additional week's continuance, where the amendment added nothing substantial to the original charge, and where there was no showing in the record that defendants were prejudiced by the denial. People v. Buckner, 180 Colo. 65, 504 P.2d 669 (1972). Defendant must request continuance to claim prejudice or surprise. Defendant who did not request continuance when amendments and deletions to information were made has no basis for claiming prejudice or surprise. People v. Marion, 182 Colo. 435, 514 P.2d 327 (1973); People v. Swain, 43 Colo. App. 343, 607 P.2d 396 (1979); People v. Cervantes, 677 P.2d 403 (Colo. App. 1983), aff'd, 715 P.2d 783 (Colo. 1986). No amendment of substance after prosecution presents evidence. An accused person is entitled to be tried on the specific charge contained in the information, and after a plea of not guilty has been entered and the state has submitted all the evidence which the prosecutor desires to present to sustain that charge, no amendment can be made thereto which changes entirely the substance of the crime which defendant is alleged to have committed. Skidmore v. People, 154 Colo. 363, 390 P.2d 944 (1964); People v. Jefferson, 934 P.2d 870 (Colo. App. 1996). A constructive amendment after completion of the evidence is per se reversible error. People v. Madden, 87 P.3d 153 (Colo. App. 2003), rev'd on other grounds, 111 P.3d 452 (Colo. 2005). Prosecution's theory that defendant concealed information to illegally obtain a controlled substance did not effect a constructive amendment to charge involving fraud, deceit, and misrepresentation. People v. Harte, 131 P.3d 1180 (Colo. App. 2005). And no substitution of statute prosecution conducted under. Where an information identifies with particularity the exact section of a statute upon which prosecution is based, no other statute can be substituted for the one actually selected as forming the subject matter of the prosecution. Casadas v. People, 134 Colo. 244, 304 P.2d 626 (1956); Skidmore v. People, 154 Colo. 363, 390 P.2d 944 (1964). Nor amendment to charge more serious offense. Where the amended information would charge a different and more serious offense than that which was originally charged, the amendment should not be permitted. People v. Johnson, 644 P.2d 34 (Colo. App. 1980). Language of information is controlling factor. The language of an information charging an offense is the controlling factor in determining whether the amendment was permissible after trial. People v. Johnson, 644 P.2d 34 (Colo. App. 1980). Section (e) is to be liberally construed to allow amendment of an information "as to form or substance at any time prior to trial", and it is within the trial court's discretion to permit the information to be amended. People v. Wright, 678 P.2d 1072 (Colo. App. 1984). Amendment which does not affect charge permitted prior to verdict. An amendment that does not charge an additional or different offense and does not go to the essence of the charge is one of form rather than substance, and it may be permitted at any time prior to verdict. Collins v. People, 69 Colo. 353, 195 P. 525 (1920); Maraggos v. People, 175 Colo. 130, 486 P.2d 1 (1971). Where an information contains specific language of the offense underlying an habitual criminal count, a defendant is not prejudiced by amendment of the statutory reference thereto. People v. Ybarra, 652 P.2d 182 (Colo. App. 1982); People v. Stephens, 689 P.2d 666 (Colo. App. 1984). No amendment was necessary where the information was sufficient to provide the defendant notice of the charge and defendant's defense was applicable to the offense as stated in the jury instructions. The jury instruction stated that the victim was an at-risk adult, but the count did not specifically refer to § 18-6.5-101, which proscribes crimes against at-risk adults, and the information did not specifically identify the victim as an at-risk adult. However, no amendment was necessary because throughout the trial the prosecution demonstrated its intent to prosecute under the at-risk adult statute and defendant's theory of defense was applicable regardless of how the information stated the elements of the offense. People v. Valdez, 946 P.2d 491 (Colo. App. 1997), aff'd on other grounds, 966 P.2d 587 (Colo. 1998). It was not error to allow amendment of habitual criminal count prior to presentation of evidence but after jury was sworn in. People v. Wandel, 713 P.2d 398 (Colo. App. 1985). No abuse of discretion when court permitted district attorney to amend robbery count to add items taken from victim. The amendment did not result in new charges so there was no prejudice to defendant. People v. Al-Yousif, 206 P.3d 824 (Colo. App. 2006). No error committed by allowing the information to be amended on a matter of form. The amendment reduced the number of victims, thereby reducing the likelihood of criminal liability and benefitting the defendant. People v. Manzanares, 942 P.2d 1235 (Colo. App. 1996). Amendments of form. Changing name of owner of premises in

31

information charging burglary is an amendment of form rather than substance. Maraggos v. People, 175 Colo. 130, 486 P.2d 1 (1971). In prosecutions for larceny, amendments to an information changing the name or description of the owner of the property are of form, not substance, and are allowable during the trial. Collins v. People, 69 Colo. 353, 195 P. 525 (1920); Diebold v. People, 175 Colo. 96, 485 P.2d 900 (1971). An amendment of an information transposing the victim's first and last names is not prejudicial to the defendant, and is one of form rather than substance within the meaning of section (e). McKee v. People, 175 Colo. 410, 487 P.2d 1332 (1971). Amendment of information to add missing words so that defendant could be charged with second degree assault was one of form and was properly allowed by the court. People v. Cervantes, 677 P.2d 403 (Colo. App. 1983), aff'd, 715 P.2d 783 (Colo. 1986). And correction of immaterial errors does not require rearraignment. The mere correction of a clerical or other immaterial error in an indictment does not require a second arraignment and plea. Albritton v. People, 157 Colo. 518, 403 P.2d 772 (1965). Allegations of time are substantive in prosecutions under § 18-4-402(1)(b). Section 18-4-402(1)(b) (theft of rental property) proscribes only conduct which occurs after the expiration of the rental period specified in a rental agreement. In prosecutions commenced under § 18-4-402(1)(b), allegations of time are, therefore, substantive allegations-not mere matters of form which may be altered by amendment at any time prior to the rendering of a verdict in the absence of prejudice to the defendant. People v. Moody, 674 P.2d 366 (Colo. 1984). No abuse of discretion in granting motion to amend information where defendant was served with a copy of the written motion four days before trial, he understood the allegations of the amendment, he failed to request a continuance, and he made no showing of prejudice, misunderstanding, or surprise by reason of the time at which the amendment was made. People v. Thomas, 832 P.2d 990 (Colo. App. 1991). Amendment of information at close of evidence was permissible where amendment related to acts occurring within the statutory limitation period, date of offense was neither a material element nor an issue at trial, and the amendment did not involve an altered accusation or require a different defense strategy from the one defendant had chosen under the initial information. People v. Metcalf, 926 P.2d 133 (Colo. App. 1996). The people's failure actually to file an amended information after filing a written motion containing all of the allegations that would have been contained in any formal amendment to the information did not result in a lack of jurisdiction, nor was it an error so grave as to require a vacation of the conviction. People v. Thomas, 832 P.2d 990 (Colo. App. 1991). Court's decision to submit to the jury a burglary charge based on unlawful sexual contact instead of the underlying offense of sexual assault was not in error. In this case unlawful sexual contact is a lesser included offense of sexual assault based on sexual intrusion. People v. Loyas, 259 P.3d 505 (Colo. App. 2010). VIII. Surplusage. Averments which are not necessary to a sufficient description of the offense may be stricken as surplusage. Specht v. People, 156 Colo. 12, 396 P.2d 838 (1964). IX. Bill of Particulars. Bill not to disclose prosecution's evidence in detail. The purpose of a bill of particulars is not to disclose in detail the evidence upon which the prosecution expects to rely. Balltrip v. People, 157 Colo. 108, 401 P.2d 259 (1965); People v. District Court, 198 Colo. 501, 603 P.2d 127 (1979). Rather, purpose of a bill of particulars is to define more specifically offense charged. Balltrip v. People, 157 Colo. 108, 401 P.2d 259 (1965). A bill of particulars calls for an exposition of the facts that the prosecution intends to prove and limits the proof at trial to those areas described in the bill. People v. District Court, 198 Colo. 501, 603 P.2d 127 (1979). The purpose of a bill of particulars is to enable the defendant to properly prepare his defense in cases where the indictment, although sufficient to advise the defendant of the charges raised against him, is nonetheless so indefinite in its statement of a particular charge that it does not afford the defendant a fair opportunity to procure witnesses and prepare for trial. People v. District Court, 198 Colo. 501, 603 P.2d 127 (1979). A bill of particulars must provide such information requested by defendant as is necessary for the defendant to prepare his defense and to avoid prejudicial surprise. However, a defendant is not necessarily entitled to receive all the information requested for a bill of particulars. The prosecution need not disclose in detail all evidence upon which it intends to rely. People v. Lewis, 671 P.2d 985 (Colo. App. 1983). It is within the trial court's discretion to grant or deny motions for bills of particulars, and its action will not be disturbed on writ of error in the absence of an abuse of discretion. Stewart v. People, 86 Colo. 456, 283 P. 47 (1929); Johnson v. People, 110 Colo. 283, 133 P.2d 789 (1943); Balltrip v. People, 157 Colo. 108, 401 P.2d 259 (1965); Self v. People, 167 Colo. 292, 448 P.2d 619 (1968); Howe v. People, 178 Colo. 248, 496 P.2d 1040 (1972); People v. District Court, 198 Colo. 501, 603 P.2d 127 (1979); People v. Pineda, 40 P.3d 60 (Colo. App. 2001). Considerations in addressing motion for bill. When addressing motions requesting bills of particulars, the trial judge should consider whether the requested information is necessary for the defendant to prepare his defense and to avoid prejudicial surprise. People v. District Court, 198 Colo. 501, 603 P.2d 127 (1979). Bill mandatory where crime charged in words of statute. Where the crime of theft is charged in the words of the statute, an order for a bill of particulars is mandatory upon the defendant's request. People v. District Court, 198 Colo. 501, 603 P.2d 127 (1979). Bill may be denied where information sufficiently advises defendant. There is no abuse of discretion in denying a motion for a bill of particulars where the information sufficiently advises the defendant of the charge he is to meet. Johnson v. People, 110 Colo. 283, 133 P.2d 789 (1943); Balltrip v. People, 157 Colo. 108, 401 P.2d 259 (1965); Self v. People, 167 Colo. 292, 448 P.2d 619 (1968); Howe v. People, 178 Colo. 248, 496 P.2d 1040 (1972). Bill properly denied where, at the time defendant requested a bill of particulars, several preliminary hearings had already been conducted, and the prosecution had provided the defendant with much of the evidence that was later presented at trial. People v. Pineda, 40 P.3d 60 (Colo. App. 2001). Bill cannot aid fundamentally bad indictment. Although the purpose of a bill of particulars is to define more specifically the offense charged, a bill of particulars is not a part of an indictment nor an amendment thereto; it cannot in any way aid an indictment fundamentally bad. People v. Westendorf, 37 Colo. App. 111, 542 P.2d 1300 (1975). A bill of particulars under section (g) cannot save an insufficient indictment. People v. Tucker, 631 P.2d 162 (Colo. 1981). Bill of particulars was sufficient where the defendant was given the specific incidents the prosecution would rely on and the general time frame when the sexual assaults occurred. People v. Graham, 876 P.2d 68 (Colo. App. 1994). X. Preliminary Hearing. Law reviews. For article, "Felony Preliminary Hearings in Colorado", see 17 Colo. Law. 1085 (1988). Primary purpose of the preliminary hearing is to determine whether probable cause exists to support the prosecution's charge that the accused committed a specific crime. People v. Quinn, 183 Colo. 245, 516 P.2d 420 (1973); People ex rel. Farina v. District Court, 184 Colo. 406, 521 P.2d 778 (1974); People v. District Court, 186 Colo. 136, 526 P.2d 289 (1974); McDonald v. District Court, 195 Colo. 159, 576 P.2d 169 (1978); People in Interest of M.V., 742 P.2d 326 (Colo. 1987). Preliminary hearing is a screening device to determine whether probable cause exists. People v. Weaver, 182 Colo. 221, 511 P.2d 908 (1973); People v. Quinn, 183 Colo. 245, 516 P.2d 420 (1973); Hunter v. District Court, 190 Colo. 48, 543 P.2d 1265 (1975); People v. Buhrle, 744 P.2d 747 (Colo. 1987). The preliminary hearing is a screening device, designed to determine whether probable cause exists to support charges that an accused person committed a particular crime or crimes. People v. Treat, 193 Colo. 570, 568 P.2d 473 (1977); People v. Johnson, 618 P.2d 262 (Colo. 1980); Miller v. District Court, 641 P.2d 966 (Colo. 1982). The purpose of a preliminary hearing is to screen out cases in which prosecution is unwarranted by allowing an impartial judge to determine whether there is probable cause to believe that the crime charged may have been committed by the defendant. Rex v. Sullivan, 194 Colo. 568, 575 P.2d 408 (1978); People ex rel. Farina v. District Court, 184 Colo. 406, 521 P.2d 778 (1974). Evidence to support a conviction is not necessary at a preliminary hearing. People v. District Court, 186 Colo. 136, 526 P.2d 289 (1974); People v. Treat, 193 Colo. 570, 568 P.2d 473 (1977); People v. Johnson, 618 P.2d 262 (Colo. 1980); Miller v. District Court, 641 P.2d 966 (Colo. 1982). Result of finding probable cause. A finding by the district court that there is probable cause can only have the result that the court shall set the case for arraignment or trial. People v. District Court, 186 Colo. 136, 526 P.2d 289 (1974). This rule sets forth specific requirements which must be met by a defendant in order to obtain a preliminary hearing. People ex rel. Farina v. District Court, 184 Colo. 406, 521 P.2d 778 (1974). And opening sentence of section (h) limits applicability of that section to those cases which are instituted in the district court by direct information filed under section (c). People ex rel. Farina v. District Court, 184 Colo. 406, 521 P.2d 778 (1974). Proceeding with a preliminary hearing for the sole purpose of preserving the possibility of a direct filing is not good cause for such filing. People v. Stanchieff, 862 P.2d 988 (Colo. App. 1993). The preliminary hearing is not minitrial, but rather is limited to the purpose of determining whether there is probable cause to believe that a crime was committed and that the defendant committed it. Hunter v. District Court, 190 Colo. 48, 543 P.2d 1265 (1975); Johns v. District Court, 192 Colo. 462, 561 P.2d 1 (1977); People v. Cisneros, 193 Colo. 380, 566 P.2d 703 (1977); McDonald v. District Court, 195 Colo. 159, 576 P.2d 169 (1978); Flores v. People, 196 Colo. 565, 593 P.2d 316 (1978); People in Interest of M.V., 742 P.2d 326 (Colo. 1987). The preliminary hearing is not intended to be a minitrial or to afford the defendant an opportunity to effect discovery. Rex v. Sullivan, 194 Colo. 568, 575 P.2d 408 (1978); McDonald v. District Court, 195 Colo. 159, 576 P.2d 169 (1978). And judge not trier of fact. In Colorado, the preliminary hearing is not a "minitrial", and the judge is not a trier of fact; rather, his function is solely to determine the existence or absence of probable cause. Hunter v. District Court, 190 Colo. 48, 543 P.2d 1265 (1975). No consideration of probability of conviction. A preliminary hearing focuses upon a probable cause determination, rather than a consideration of the probability of conviction at the ensuing trial. Hunter v. District Court, 190 Colo. 48, 543 P.2d 1265 (1975). Nor require examination of all prosecution witnesses and evidence. Preliminary hearing does not require that the prosecution lay out for inspection and for full examination all witnesses and evidence. People v. Quinn, 183 Colo. 245, 516 P.2d 420 (1973). Merely quantum necessary to establish probable cause. The prosecution need not produce all of its evidence against the defendant at the preliminary hearing, but only that quantum necessary to establish probable cause. Hunter v. District Court, 190 Colo. 48, 543 P.2d 1265 (1975). The probable cause standard requires evidence sufficient to induce a person of ordinary prudence and caution to entertain a reasonable belief that the defendant committed the crimes charged. People v. Johnson, 618 P.2d 262 (Colo. 1980); People v. Treat, 193 Colo. 570, 568 P.2d 473 (1977); Miller v. District Court, 641 P.2d 966 (Colo. 1982); People in Interest of M.V., 742 P.2d, 326 (Colo. 1987). The prosecution is not required to produce at a preliminary hearing evidence that is sufficient to support a conviction. People in Interest of M.V., 742 P.2d 326 (Colo. 1987). It is not necessary that the prosecution show beyond a reasonable doubt that the defendant committed the crime; nor is it even necessary to show the probability of the defendant's conviction. People in Interest of M.V., 742 P.2d 326 (Colo. 1987). Prosecution may seek a grand jury indictment after dismissal by a county court on a preliminary hearing for lack of probable cause as an alternative to appealing to or filing a direct information in the district court. People v. Noline, 917 P.2d 1256 (Colo. 1996). Under subsection (h)(3), the burden of proof is on the prosecution, and the defendant need not testify, although he has the right to cross-examine the witnesses called by the People. Hunter v. District Court, 190 Colo. 48, 543 P.2d 1265 (1975). Although trial judge may curtail the right to cross-examine and to introduce evidence in the preliminary hearing, he may not completely prevent inquiry into matters relevant to the determination of probable cause or disregard the testimony of a witness favorable to the prosecution unless such testimony is implausible or incredible as a matter of law. People v. Buhrle, 744 P.2d 747 (Colo. 1987). District court may not review county court's probable cause finding. It is not proper for the district court to review the county court's finding of probable cause. Blevins v. Tihonovich, 728 P.2d 732 (Colo. 1986). Rules of evidence and procedure relaxed. In light of its limited purpose, evidentiary and procedural rules in the preliminary hearing in Colorado are relaxed. Hunter v. District Court, 190 Colo. 48, 543 P.2d 1265 (1975). Since the preliminary hearing is not a mini-trial, greater evidentiary and procedural latitude is granted to the prosecution to establish probable cause than would be permqtted at trial to prove the defendant committed the crime. People v. Buhrle, 744 P.2d 747 (Colo. 1987). But may not rely solely on hearsay. While the bulk of testimony at a preliminary hearing may be hearsay, the prosecution may not totally rely on hearsay to establish probable cause where competent evidence is readily available. Hunter v. District Court, 190 Colo. 48, 543 P.2d 1265 (1975); McDonald v. District Court, 195 Colo. 159, 576 P.2d 169 (1978). Consideration of credibility of witnesses limited. A judge in a preliminary hearing has jurisdiction to consider the credibility of witnesses only when, as a matter of law, the testimony is implausible or incredible. Hunter v. District Court, 190 Colo. 48, 543 P.2d 1265 (1975); Johns v. District Court, 192 Colo. 462, 561 P.2d 1 (1977); People in Interest of M.V., 742 P.2d 326 (Colo. 1987). Inferences to be made in favor of prosecution. When there is a mere conflict in the testimony, a question of fact exists for the jury, and the judge in a preliminary hearing must draw the inference favorable to the prosecution. Hunter v. District Court, 190 Colo. 48, 543 P.2d 1265 (1975); Johns v. District Court, 192 Colo. 461, 561 P.2d 1 (1977); People v. Treat, 193 Colo. 570, 568 P.2d 473 (1977); People v. Johnson, 618 P.2d 262 (Colo. 1980); Miller v. District Court, 641 P.2d 966 (Colo. 1982); People in Interest of M.V., 742 P.2d 326 (Colo. 1987). The right to cross-examine and to introduce evidence may be curtailed by the presiding judge consistent with the screening purpose of the preliminary hearing. Rex v. Sullivan, 194 Colo. 568, 575 P.2d 408 (1978). But judge may not completely curtail inquiry into matters relevant to the determination of probable cause. Rex v. Sullivan, 194 Colo. 568, 575 P.2d 408 (1978). When prohibiting defense from calling witness deemed abuse of discretion. Where an eyewitness is available in court during a preliminary hearing and where the prosecution is relying almost completely on hearsay testimony, it is an abuse of discretion to prohibit the defense from calling the witness. McDonald v. District Court, 195 Colo. 159, 576 P.2d 169 (1978). And witness' testimony may be used at trial. Where a defendant cross-examined an adverse witness during a preliminary hearing, that witness' recorded testimony might be used as evidence at trial, although the hearing merely determined the existence of probable cause and witness' credibility was not in issue. People v. Flores, 39 Colo. App. 556, 575 P.2d 11 (1977), rev'd on other grounds, 196 Colo. 565, 593 P.2d 316 (1978). Right to hearing founded in statutes, rules, and constitutions. Defendant in requesting and obtaining a preliminary hearing was exercising a right that was not only guaranteed him by statute and rule of court, but also one that has a constitutional foundation. Lucero v. District Court, 188 Colo. 67, 532 P.2d 955 (1975). Protects accused and benefits judiciary. A preliminary hearing protects the accused by avoiding an embarrassing, costly, and unnecessary trial, and it benefits the interests of judicial economy and efficiency. Hunter v. District Court, 190 Colo. 48, 543 P.2d 1265 (1975). But does not alter proposition that accused entitled to trial on merits. Although a preliminary hearing provides the defendant with an early opportunity to question the government's case, it is not designed to alter the basic proposition that an accused is entitled to one trial on the merits of the charge. People v. Quinn, 183 Colo. 245, 516 P.2d 420 (1973). And deemed to be critical stage. A preliminary hearing is a critical stage in the prosecution of a defendant and should not be conducted in a "perfunctory fashion". McDonald v. District Court, 195 Colo. 159, 576 P.2d 169 (1978). Preliminary hearing is not intended to be mandatory procedural step in every prosecution. People ex rel. Farina v. District Court, 185 Colo. 118, 522 P.2d 589 (1974). When waiver occurs. If a defendant does not request a preliminary hearing, he is deemed to have waived the preliminary hearing and must be bound over for trial. People ex rel. Farina v. District Court, 185 Colo. 118, 522 P.2d 589 (1974). Effect of waiver. If the defendant elects to waive the preliminary hearing and to proceed to trial, the waiver operates as an admission by the defendant that sufficient evidence does exist to establish probable cause that the defendant committed the crimes charged. People ex rel. Farina v. District Court, 184 Colo. 406, 521 P.2d 778 (1974). A defendant requesting preliminary hearing must appear. When a defendant requests a preliminary hearing, he has not only the constitutional right to be present, but is under an affirmative obligation and duty to appear at the hearing. People ex rel. Farina v. District Court, 185 Colo. 118, 522 P.2d 589 (1974). Unless the court permits defendant to waive his presence. The court may, when a timely request is made, permit the defendant to waive his presence at the preliminary hearing if the ends of justice would not be frustrated, but the tactical ploy of refusing to produce a defendant at the preliminary hearing to frustrate the prosecution's case should not be tolerated. People ex rel. Farina v. District Court, 185 Colo. 118, 522 P.2d 589 (1974). Refusal to appear constitutes implied waiver. Where the judge of the county court advised counsel that the failure of the defendant to appear would constitute a waiver, the defendant's subsequent refusal to appear constituted an implied waiver and extinguished the defendant's right to a preliminary hearing in the county court. People ex rel. Farina v. District Court, 185 Colo. 118, 522 P.2d 589 (1974). But application for deferred sentencing does not constitute waiver of the right to a preliminary hearing. Celestine v. District Court, 199 Colo. 514 610 P.2d 1342 (1980). Restoration of right once waived in county court. Under the Colorado Rules of Criminal Procedure and the statutes of this state, a district court is not vested with the power to restore a defendant's statutory right to a preliminary hearing once the defendant had waived that right in county court bind-over proceedings. People ex rel. Farina v. District Court, 184 Colo. 406, 521 P.2d 778 (1974). Once a defendant knowingly waives his right to a preliminary hearing in the county court, the right is extinguished and may not be restored in the subsequent district court proceedings. People ex rel. Farina v. District Court, 185 Colo. 118, 522 P.2d 589 (1974). Authority to bind over on lesser included offense. The trial court which holds the preliminary hearing has the authority to bind over the defendant on a lesser included offense. People v. Hrapski, 658 P.2d 1367 (Colo. 1983). When juvenile not entitled to preliminary hearing in district court. A juvenile who was transferred to the district from the juvenile court, after a transfer hearing where probable cause as to the offenses charged was determined, was not entitled in the district court to another determination of probable cause in the form of a preliminary hearing. People v. Flanigan, 189 Colo. 43, 536 P.2d 41 (1975). Defendant cannot complain if he is committed to a state institution until he is competent to have a preliminary hearing, pursuant to a sanity proceeding, since subsection (h)(2), provides that the preliminary hearing "shall be held within 30 days of the day of the setting, unless good cause for continuing the hearing beyond that time be shown to the court", and the matter of the defendant's sanity is good cause. Schwader v. District Court, 172 Colo. 474, 474 P.2d 607 (1970). The bulk of evidence in a preliminary hearing may consist of hearsay evidence which would be inadmissible at the trial. People v. Buhrle, 744 P.2d 747 (Colo. 1987). Rehearing not provided. There is no provision in this rule for rehearing on, or reconsideration of, a ruling on completion of a preliminary hearing. People v. District Court, 186 Colo. 136, 526 P.2d 289 (1974). Where technical difficulties prevented defendant from obtaining a transcript of the preliminary hearing, the judge abused his discretion in denying defendant's motion for a second preliminary hearing. Such motion should have been granted because the testimony presented at the first preliminary hearing was directly relevant and significant to defendant's trial preparation, the prosecution was expected to rely on testimony presented at the preliminary hearing, and there was no alternative method of reconstructing the testimony from the preliminary hearing. Harris v. District Court, 843 P.2d 1316 (Colo. 1993).

Rule 8 - Joinder of Offenses and of Defendants

(a)Joinder of Offenses.

(1)Mandatory Joinder. If several offenses are actually known to the prosecuting attorney at the time of commencing the prosecution and were committed within his judicial district, all such offenses upon which the prosecuting attorney elects to proceed must be prosecuted by separate counts in a single prosecution if they are based on the same act or series of acts arising from the same criminal episode. Any such offense not thus joined by separate count cannot thereafter be the basis of a subsequent prosecution; except that, if at the time jeopardy attaches with respect to the first prosecution against the defendant, the defendant or counsel for the defendant actually knows of additional pending prosecutions that this subsection (a)(1) requires the prosecuting attorney to charge and the defendant or counsel for the defendant fails to object to the prosecution's failure to join the charges, the defendant waives any claim pursuant to this subsection (a)(1) that a subsequent prosecution is prohibited.

(2)Permissive Joinder. Two or more offenses may be charged in the same indictment or information in a separate count for each offense if the offenses charged, whether felonies or misdemeanors or both, are of the same or similar character or are based on two or more acts or transactions connected together or constituting parts of a common scheme or plan.

(b)Joinder of Defendants. Two or more defendants may be charged in the same indictment, information, or felony complaint if they are alleged to have participated in the same act or series of acts arising from the same criminal episode. Such defendants may be charged in one or more counts together or separately and all of the defendants need not be charged in each count.

Colo. R. Crim. P. 8

Source: a amended December 6, 1990, and effective 3/1/1991; entire rule amended and adopted September 12, 2002, effective 1/1/2003.

Annotation I. General Consideration. Law reviews. For article, "Colorado Felony Sentencing", see 11 Colo. Law. 1478 (1982). Applied in People v. Mendoza, 190 Colo. 519, 549 P.2d 766 (1976); People v. McCrary, 190 Colo. 538, 549 P.2d 1320 (1976); Brutcher v. District Court, 195 Colo. 579, 580 P.2d 396 (1978); Jeffrey v. District Court, 626 P.2d 631 (Colo. 1981); People v. Holder, 632 P.2d 607 (Colo. App. 1981). II. Joinder of Offenses When joinder of offenses permitted. This rule provides that two or more offenses may be charged in the same information, in a separate count for each offense, if the offenses charged are based upon the same act or transaction, or on two or more acts or transactions connected together and that they were properly charged in separate counts for each offense. Ruark v. People, 158 Colo. 287, 406 P.2d 91 (1965). Where the acts involved were committed at the same time or in immediate succession and at the same place, they arose out of the same criminal episode; therefore, it is appropriate to include the separate counts in a single information. People v. McGregor, 635 P.2d 912 (Colo. App. 1981). Purpose of joinder is to prevent vexatious prosecution and harassment of a defendant by a district attorney who initiates successive prosecutions for crimes which stem from the same criminal episode. Ruth v. County Court, 198 Colo. 6, 595 P.2d 237 (1979). "Single prosecution" is a proceeding from the commencement of the criminal action until further prosecution is barred. Ruth v. County Court, 198 Colo. 6, 595 P.2d 237 (1979). Rule 8(a) applies only where prosecution aware of other offenses. Section (a) of this rule and § 18-1-408(2) apply only where the prosecution is aware of other offenses at the time the original action is commenced. People v. Scott, 615 P.2d 680 (Colo. 1980). Jeopardy must attach before there is "subsequent prosecution". The proscription contained in section (a) is against bringing a "subsequent prosecution" based on charges known to the prosecutor at the time he commenced the initial prosecution, and there is no "subsequent prosecution" until jeopardy attaches to the initial prosecution. People v. Freeman, 196 Colo. 238, 583 P.2d 921 (1978). Guilty plea to related charge bars subsequent prosecution. Section (a) and § 18-1-408(2), bar the prosecution of a defendant for two pending charges arising out of the same criminal episode when the defendant has pleaded guilty and has been sentenced for a third related charge. Ruth v. County Court, 198 Colo. 6, 595 P.2d 237 (1979). Effect of dismissal on attachment of jeopardy. Where dismissal of a count occurred prior to trial and the dismissal had nothing to do with the defendant's criminal liability, jeopardy does not attach. People v. Freeman, 196 Colo. 238, 583 P.2d 921 (1978). In joinder of offenses of similar character, prejudice may develop because defendant's statements concerning his involvement in one count would not ordinarily be admissible at a separate trial of the second count, since it is related to the other count only as a crime of a similar nature. People v. McCrary, 190 Colo. 538, 549 P.2d 1320 (1976). Nearness in time, proximity of place and unity of scheme are not indispensable prerequisites to joinder under the "same criminal episode" standard, although multiple offenses characterized by all three components would certainly qualify for joinder under section (a). Corr v. District Court, 661 P.2d 668 (Colo. 1983). Law of joinder and severance dependent on facts in each case. The law relating to joinder and severance and that which permits consolidation of charges depends on the facts in each particular case. Hunter v. District Court, 193 Colo. 308, 565 P.2d 942 (1977). Where joinder permitted in sanity trial. Joinder of a charge of forcible rape with an unrelated deviate sexual intercourse charge committed on a different female on a different date for purposes of trial on the sanity issue was not error. People v. Renfrow, 193 Colo. 131, 564 P.2d 411 (1977). But accessory charge barred if not included in first information. The prosecution is precluded from pursuing a second prosecution where the accessory charge could have been included in the first information. People v. Riddick, 626 P.2d 641 (Colo. 1981). Joinder of offenses permitted. People v. Trujillo, 181 Colo. 350, 509 P.2d 794 (1973). Where two assault counts arose out of the same continuous sequence of events closely related in time and distance, the two counts were "based on two acts connected together", and the trial judge was not obligated to sever them at trial. People v. Walker, 189 Colo. 545, 542 P.2d 1283 (1975). Joinder not sanctioned. Where the alleged victims of the crimes are the same, but the same persons are not charged in each offense and material differences exist as to the date of each offense and the factual transactions specified in each count, joinder under such circumstances is not sanctioned by Crim. P. 8(a). Norman v. People, 178 Colo. 190, 496 P.2d 1029 (1972). To be duplicitous, information must join two or more distinct and separate offenses in the same count of an indictment or information. Marrs v. People, 135 Colo. 458, 312 P.2d 505 (1957); Leyba v. People, 174 Colo. 1, 481 P.2d 417 (1971). Count is not bad for duplicity where it sets forth several overt acts in pursuance of the principal act charged, or where it alleges several acts done by the same person which are only successive stages in the progress of a criminal enterprise, constituting as a whole only one offense, although either, when done alone, might be an offense. Marrs v. People, 135 Colo. 458, 312 P.2d 505 (1957). Rule authorizes the joinder of offenses based on a series of acts arising from the same criminal episode. Joinder of offenses committed at different times and places is permissible provided they are part of a schematic whole. People v. Taylor, 804 P.2d 196 (Colo. App. 1990). Sexual assault offenses may be joined if the evidence of each offense would be admissible in separate trials. People v. Williams, 899 P.2d 306 (Colo. App. 1995). Separate offenses may be joined that are committed at different times and places if they constitute part of a schematic whole. The incident at the grocery store and subsequent shopping spree were a continuous criminal episode and there was no prejudice to the defendant in trying the counts together. People v. Smith, 121 P.3d 243 (Colo. App. 2005). Trial court did not abuse discretion by denying motion to sever when the attempted manslaughter charge (having unprotected intercourse while HIV positive) arose from the same act as the sexual assault charges. People v. Dembry, 91 P.3d 431 (Colo. App. 2003). A defendant does not impliedly waive his right to rely upon the statute and rule by entering a plea of guilty in a county court case with knowledge that the district court case is pending. People v. Robinson, 774 P.2d 884 (Colo. 1989). But the right to compulsory joinder may be waived by raising the issue after jeopardy attaches in the second prosecution. People v. Wilson, 819 P.2d 510 (Colo. App. 1991); People v. Carey, 198 P.3d 1223 (Colo. App. 2008). III. Joinder of Defendants. Law reviews. For article, "Pronouncements of the U. S. Supreme Court Relating to the Criminal Law Field: 1985-1986", which discusses a recent case relating to misjoinder of defendants, see 15 Colo. Law. 1615 (1986). By consenting to a joint trial defendant waives any right to urge a later objection thereto based solely on the joinder. Pineda v. People, 152 Colo. 545, 383 P.2d 793 (1963). Considerations in granting motion for severance. When deciding whether to grant a motion for severance, the trial court should consider whether evidence inadmissible against one defendant will be considered against the other defendant, despite the issuance by the trial court of the proper admonitory instructions. An additional consideration is whether the defendants plan to offer antagonistic defenses. People v. Gonzales, 198 Colo. 450, 601 P.2d 1366 (1979). Severance required if joinder prevents fair trial. When joint prosecution would prevent a fair trial of one or more of the defendants, the trial court must grant a motion for severance. People v. Magoon, 645 P.2d 286 (Colo. App. 1982). Motion for severance is addressed to the sound discretion of trial court. People v. Magoon, 645 P.2d 286 (Colo. App. 1982). And not disturbed on appeal absent prejudice. A ruling on a motion for severance will not be disturbed on appeal in the absence of a showing that the denial of such motion prejudiced a defendant. People v. Magoon, 645 P.2d 286 (Colo. App. 1982).

Rule 9 - Warrant or Summons Upon Indictment or Information

(a)**Issuance.**

(1)**Request by Prosecution.** Upon the return of an indictment by a grand jury, or the filing of an information, the prosecuting attorney shall request that the court issue either a warrant for the arrest of the defendant or a summons to be served on the defendant.

(2)**Affidavits or Sworn Testimony.** If a warrant is requested upon an information, the information must contain or be accompanied by a sworn written statement of facts establishing probable cause to believe that a criminal offense has been committed and that the offense was committed by the person for whom the warrant is sought. In lieu of such sworn statement, the information may be supplemented by sworn testimony of such facts. Such testimony must be transcribed and then signed under oath or affirmation by the witness giving the testimony.

(3)**Summons in Lieu of Warrant.** Except in class 1, class 2, and class 3 felonies, level 1 and level 2 drug felonies, and unclassified felonies punishable by a maximum penalty of more than 10 years, whenever an indictment is returned or an information has been filed prior to the arrest of the person named as defendant therein, the court shall have power to issue a summons commanding the appearance of the defendant in lieu of a warrant for his arrest, unless a law enforcement officer presents in writing a basis to believe there is a significant risk of flight or that the victim's or public's safety may be compromised. If empowered to issue a summons under this subsection (a)(3), the court shall issue a summons instead of an arrest warrant when the prosecuting attorney so recommends.

(4)**Standards Relating to Issuance of Summons.** Except in class 1, class 2, and class 3 felonies, level 1 and level 2 drug felonies, and unclassified felonies punishable by a maximum penalty of more than 10 years, the general policy shall favor issuance of a summons instead of a warrant for the arrest of the defendant. When an application is made to a court for issuance of an arrest warrant or summons, the court may require the applicant to provide such information as reasonably is available concerning the following:

(I) The defendant's residence;

(II) The defendant's employment;

(III) The defendant's family relationships;

(IV) The defendant's past history of response to legal process; and

(V) The defendant's past criminal record.

(5)**Failure to Appear.** If any person properly summoned pursuant to this Rule fails to appear as commanded by the summons, the court shall forthwith issue a warrant for the arrest of that person.

(6)**Corporations.** When a corporation is charged with the commission of an offense, the court shall issue a summons setting forth the nature of the offense and commanding the corporation to appear before the court at a certain time and place.

(b)**Form.**

(1)**Warrant.** The form of the warrant shall be as provided in Rule 4(b)(1), except that it shall be signed by the clerk, it shall identify the nature of the offense charged in the indictment or information, and it shall command that the defendant be arrested and brought before the court unless he shall be admitted to bail as otherwise provided in these Rules.

(2)**Summons.** The summons shall be in the same form as provided in Rule 4(b)(2).

(c)**Execution or Service and Return.**

(1)**Execution or Service.** The warrant shall be executed or the summons served as provided in Rule 4(c). The officer executing the warrant shall bring the arrested person before the court without unnecessary delay, or for the purposes of admission to bail, before the clerk of the court, the sheriff of the county where the arrest occurs, or any other officer authorized to admit to bail.

(2)**Return.** The peace officer executing a warrant shall make a return thereof to the court. At the request of the prosecuting attorney, any unexecuted warrant shall be returned and cancelled. At least one day prior to the return day, the person to whom a summons was delivered for service shall make return thereof. At the request of the prosecuting attorney made at any time while the indictment or information is pending, a warrant returned unexecuted and not cancelled or a summons returned unserved, or a duplicate thereof may be delivered by the clerk to any peace officer or other authorized person for execution or service.

38

Amended and Adopted by the Court, En Banc, 9/11/2017, effective immediately.

Arraignment and Preparation for Trial

Rule 10 - Arraignment

Following preliminary proceedings pursuant to the provisions of Rules 5, 7, and 12, the arraignment shall be conducted in open court, informing the defendant of the offense with which he is charged, and requiring him to enter a plea to the charge. The defendant shall be arraigned in the court having trial jurisdiction in which the indictment, information, or complaint is filed, unless before arraignment the cause has been removed to another court, in which case he shall be arraigned in that court.

(a) If the offense charged is a felony or a class 1 misdemeanor, or if the maximum penalty for the offense charged is more than one year's imprisonment, the defendant must be personally present for arraignment, except that the court for good cause shown may accept a plea of not guilty made by an attorney representing the defendant without requiring the defendant to be personally present.

(b) In all other cases the court may permit arraignment without the presence of the defendant. If a plea of guilty or nolo contendere is entered by counsel in the absence of the defendant, the court may command the appearance of the defendant in person for the imposition of sentence.

(c) Upon arraignment, the defendant or his counsel shall be furnished with a copy of the indictment or information, complaint, or summons and complaint if one has not been previously served.

(d) A record shall be made of the proceedings at every arraignment.

(e) If the defendant appears without counsel at an arraignment, the information, indictment, or complaint shall be read to him by the court or the clerk thereof. If the defendant appears with counsel, the information or indictment need not be read and no waiver of said reading is necessary.

(f) As soon as the jury panel is drawn which will try the case, a list of the names and addresses of the jurors on the panel shall be made available by the clerk of the court to defendant's counsel, and if the defendant has no counsel, the list shall be served on him personally or by certified mail. It shall not be necessary to serve a list of jurors upon the defendant at the time of arraignment.

Colo. R. Crim. P. 10

Annotation No arraignment required in certain criminal contempts. In criminal contempt cases, no arraignment is required, at least with respect to those criminal contempts which are analogous to petty offenses. Robran v. People ex rel. Smith, 173 Colo. 378, 479 P.2d 976 (1971). Correction of immaterial error in indictment does not require rearraignment. The mere correction of a clerical or other immaterial error in an indictment does not require a second arraignment and plea. Albritton v. People, 157 Colo. 518, 403 P.2d 772 (1965). The denial of a motion to dismiss for failure to rearraign on an amended information is not error where the amendment is not one of substance, and where, when counsel calls the court's attention to it during the course of the trial, the trial court follows the provision of Rule 11(d), C. R. Crim. P., and enters a plea of not guilty and, thereupon, the trial proceeds. People v. Buckner, 180 Colo. 65, 504 P.2d 669 (1972). It is essential that the record show affirmatively an arraignment. Wright v. People, 22 Colo. 143, 43 P. 1021 (1896).

Rule 11 - Pleas

(a) **Generally**. A defendant personally or by counsel may plead guilty, not guilty, not guilty by reason of insanity (in which event a not guilty plea may also be entered), or with the consent of the court, nolo contendere.

(b) **Pleas of Guilty and Nolo Contendere**. The court shall not accept a plea of guilty or a plea of nolo contendere without first determining that the defendant has been advised of all the rights set forth in Rule 5(a)(2) and also determining:

(1) That the defendant understands the nature of the charge and the elements of the offense to which he is pleading and the effect of his plea;

(2) That the plea is voluntary on defendant's part and is not the result of undue influence or coercion on the part of anyone;

(3) That he understands the right to trial by jury and that he waives his right to trial by jury on all issues;

(4) That he understands the possible penalty or penalties;

(5) That the defendant understands that the court will not be bound by any representations made to the defendant by anyone concerning the penalty to be imposed or the granting or the denial of probation, unless such representations are included in a formal plea agreement approved by the court and supported by the findings of the presentence report, if any;

(6) That there is a factual basis for the plea. If the plea is entered as a result of a plea agreement, the court shall explain to the defendant, and satisfy itself that the defendant understands, the basis for the plea agreement, and the defendant may then waive the establishment of a factual basis for the particular charge to which he pleads;

(7) That in class 1 felonies, or where the plea of guilty is to a lesser included offense, a written consent shall have been filed with the court by the district attorney.

(c) Misdemeanor Cases. In all misdemeanor cases except class 1, the court may accept, in the absence of the defendant, any plea entered in writing by the defendant or orally made by his counsel.

(d) Failure or Refusal to Plead. If a defendant refuses to plead, or if the court refuses to accept a plea of guilty, or a plea of nolo contendere, or if a corporation fails to appear, the court shall enter a plea of not guilty. If for any reason the arraignment here provided for has not been had, the case shall for all purposes be considered as one in which a plea of not guilty has been entered.

(e) Defense of Insanity.

(1) The defense of insanity must be pleaded at the time of arraignment, except that the court for good cause shown may permit such plea to be entered at any time before trial. It must be pleaded orally, either by the defendant or by his counsel, in the form, "not guilty by reason of insanity". A defendant who does not thus plead not guilty by reason of insanity shall not be permitted to rely on insanity as a defense as to any accusation of any crime; provided, however, that evidence of mental condition may be offered in a proper case as bearing upon the capacity of the accused to form specific intent essential to the commission of a crime. The plea of not guilty by reason of insanity includes the plea of not guilty.

(2) If counsel for the defendant believes that a plea of not guilty by reason of insanity should be entered on behalf of the defendant, but the defendant refuses to permit the entry of such plea, counsel may so inform the court. The court shall then conduct such investigation as it deems proper, which may include the appointment of psychiatrists or psychologists to assist a psychiatrist to examine the defendant and advise the court. After its investigation the court shall conduct a hearing to determine whether the plea should be entered. If the court finds that the entry of a plea of not guilty by reason of insanity is necessary for a just determination of the charge against the defendant, it shall enter such plea on behalf of the defendant, and the plea so entered shall have the same effect as though it had been voluntarily entered by the defendant himself.

(3) If there has been no grand jury indictment or preliminary hearing prior to the entry of the plea of not guilty by reason of insanity, the court shall hold a preliminary hearing prior to the trial of the insanity issue. If probable cause is not established the case shall be dismissed, but the court may order the district attorney to institute civil commitment proceedings if it appears that the protection of the public or the accused requires it.

(f) Plea Discussions and Plea Agreements.

(1) Where it appears that the effective administration of criminal justice will thereby be served, the district attorney may engage in plea discussions for the purpose of reaching a plea agreement. He should engage in plea discussions or reach plea agreements with the defendant only through or in the presence of defense counsel except where the defendant is not eligible for or refuses appointment of counsel and has not retained counsel.

(2) The district attorney may agree to one of the following depending upon the circumstances of the individual case:

(I) To make or not to oppose favorable recommendations concerning the sentence to be imposed if the defendant enters a plea of guilty or nolo contendere;

(II) To seek or not to oppose the dismissal of an offense charged if the defendant enters a plea of guilty or nolo contendere to another offense reasonably related to the defendant's conduct;

(III) To seek or not to oppose the dismissal of other charges or not to prosecute other potential charges against the defendant if the defendant enters a plea of guilty or nolo contendere.

(3) Defendants whose situations are similar should be afforded similar opportunities for plea agreement.

(4) The trial judge shall not participate in plea discussions.

(5) Notwithstanding the reaching of a plea agreement between the district attorney and defense counsel or defendant, the judge in every case should exercise an independent judgment in deciding whether to grant charge and sentence concessions.

(6) Except as to proceedings resulting from a plea of guilty or nolo contendere which is not withdrawn, the fact that the defendant or his defense counsel and the district attorney engaged in plea discussions or made a plea agreement shall not be received in evidence against or in favor of the defendant in any criminal or civil action or administrative proceeding.

Colo. R. Crim. P. 11

Annotation I. General Consideration. Law reviews. For article, "Attacking Prior Convictions in Habitual Criminal Cases: Avoiding the Third Strike", see 11 Colo. Law. 1225 (1982). Prosecutor should discuss pleas with defense counsel. A prosecutor should make known a general policy of willingness to consult with defense counsel concerning disposition of charges by pleas. Dabbs v. People, 175 Colo. 273, 486 P.2d 1053 (1971). And court should allow changes of, and additions to, pleas. Where good cause is shown, it is incumbent upon the trial court to allow changes of plea or additional pleas to accomplish the fair and just determination of criminal charges. Perez v. People, 176 Colo. 505, 491 P.2d 969 (1971). Through a plea agreement accepted by the trial court, a defendant may preserve the right to appeal a suppression ruling while entering a conditional plea of guilty. People v. Bachofer, 85 P.3d 615 (Colo. App. 2003); People v. Hoffman, __ P.3d __ (Colo. App. 2010). Neither the Colorado statutes nor the Colorado rules of criminal procedure prohibit conditional pleas. The obvious advantages of a conditional plea procedure are not outweighed by any significant or compelling disadvantages. A conditional plea is particularly effective when the issue preserved for appeal is dispositive of the case. People v. Hoffman, __ P.3d __ (Colo. App. 2010). It is essential that the record show a plea. Wright v. People, 22 Colo. 143, 43 P. 1021 (1896). The decision to enter a guilty plea or withdraw a guilty plea is one of the few fundamental choices that must be decided by the defendant alone. People v. Davis, 2012 COA 1, __ P.3d __. Applied in McClendon v. People, 175 Colo. 451, 488 P.2d 556 (1971); Romero v. District Court, 178 Colo. 200, 496 P.2d 1049 (1972); People v. Baca, 179 Colo. 156, 499 P.2d 317 (1972); Hyde v. Hinton, 180 Colo. 324, 505 P.2d 376 (1973); People v. Kelly, 189 Colo. 31, 536, P.2d 39 (1975); People v. Taylor, 190 Colo. 144, 544 P.2d 392 (1975); People v. Breazeale, 190 Colo. 17, 544 P.2d 970 (1975); People v. Arnold, 190 Colo. 193, 544 P.2d 968 (1976); People v. Banks, 190 Colo. 295, 545 P.2d 1356 (1976); People v. Smith, 190 Colo. 449, 548 P.2d 603 (1976); People v. Worsley, 191 Colo. 351, 553 P.2d 73 (1976); People v. Carino, 193 Colo. 412, 566 P.2d 1061 (1977); People v. Cole, 39 Colo. App. 323, 570 P.2d 8 (1977); People v. Smith, 195 Colo. 404, 579 P.2d 1129 (1978); Gelfand v. People, 196 Colo. 487, 586 P.2d 1331 (1978); People v. Palmer, 42 Colo. App. 460, 595 P.2d 1060 (1979); People v. Weber, 199 Colo. 25, 604 P.2d 30 (1979); People v. Baca, 44 Colo. App. 167, 610 P.2d 1083 (1980); People v. Adargo, 622 P.2d 593 (Colo. App. 1980); People v. Horton, 628 P.2d 117 (Colo. App. 1980); People v. Shaver, 630 P.2d 600 (Colo. 1981); State v. Laughlin, 634 P.2d 49 (Colo. 1981); People v. Marquez, 644 P.2d 59 (Colo. App. 1981); People v. Velasquez, 641 P.2d 943 (Colo. 1982); Crocker v. Colo. Dept. of Rev., 652 P.2d 1067 (Colo. 1982); People v. Vollentine, 643 P.2d 800 (Colo. App. 1982); People v. M.A.W., 651 P.2d 433 (Colo. App. 1982); People v. Ramirez, 652 P.2d 1077 (Colo. App. 1982); People in Interest of J.F.C., 660 P.2d 7 (Colo. App. 1982); Flower v. People, 658 P.2d 266 (Colo. 1983); People v. Akins, 662 P.2d 486 (Colo. 1983). II. Pleas of Guilty and Nolo Contendere. Law reviews. For article, "Collateral Effects of a Criminal Conviction in Colorado", see 35 Colo. Law. 39 (June 2006). For comment, "Ineffective Assistance of Counsel Under People v. Pozo: Advising Non-Citizen Criminal Defendants of Possible Immigration Consequences in Criminal Plea Agreements", see 80 Colo. L. Rev. 793 (2009). Defendant's guilty plea was unconstitutional since he was illiterate, was told by the interpreter to sign the plea advisement form without having it read to him, had difficulty hearing the interpreter during the plea hearing, was pro se, and lacked the knowledge or understanding of the criminal justice system and process. The guilty plea was not made based on a voluntary and intelligent choice among alternative courses of action. Sanchez-Martinez v. People, 250 P.3d 1248 (Colo. 2011). This rule sets forth required guidelines for the entry of a plea upon arraignment. People v. Marsh, 183 Colo. 258, 516 P.2d 431 (1973). This rule itemizes certain requirements which must be followed by a court before it may accept a plea of guilty or one of nolo contendere. People v. Van Hook, 36 Colo. App. 226, 539 P.2d 507 (1975). Purpose of section (b). Section (b) contemplates that the transcribed colloquy between the court and the defendant will eliminate the need to resort to a subsequent fact-finding proceeding in order to determine whether a guilty plea was voluntarily and understandingly made. People v. Quintana, 634 P.2d 413 (Colo. 1981).

Judge to determine fulfillment of certain conditions before accepting plea. Section 16-7-207 and section (b) of this rule require that a trial court must make certain determinations before it accepts a plea of guilty or a plea of nolo contendere. People v. Lambert, 189 Colo. 264, 539 P.2d 1238 (1975); People v. Gleason, 180 Colo. 71, 502 P.2d 69 (1972); Laughlin v. State, 44 Colo. App. 341, 618 P.2d 689 (1980), rev'd on other grounds, 634 P.2d 49 (Colo. 1981). Trial courts must adhere strictly to the requirements of this rule when pleas of guilty are being considered. People v. Sandoval, 188 Colo. 431, 535 P.2d 1120 (1975). As a valid plea of guilty waives substantially all the fundamental procedural rights afforded an accused in a criminal proceeding, such as his rights to the assistance of counsel, confrontation of witnesses, and trial by jury. People v. Harrington, 179 Colo. 312, 500 P.2d 360 (1972). But compliance not shown by use of printed form. Compliance with this rule cannot be demonstrated solely by reliance upon a printed form. People v. Van Hook, 36 Colo. App. 226, 539 P.2d 507 (1975). And formal ritual is not required by this rule. People v. Duran, 183 Colo. 180, 515 P.2d 1117 (1973); People v. Marsh, 183 Colo. 258, 516 P.2d 431 (1973). Satisfaction of this rule does not require that a prescribed ritual or wording be employed, but rather the substance of the circumstances surrounding the plea should prevail over form. People v. Edwards, 186 Colo. 129, 526 P.2d 144 (1974); People v. Cushon, 650 P.2d 527 (Colo. 1982). The overriding consideration in analyzing a record pertaining to a guilty plea or a plea of nolo contendere is that a set ritual is not required. People v. Lambert, 189 Colo. 264, 539 P.2d 1238 (1975). A trial court is not required to follow any particular formula for advising a defendant at a preliminary hearing. People v. Thimmes, 643 P.2d 778 (Colo. App. 1981). So that reading charge may be sufficient. Where the language of a charge is not highly technical, the reading of the charge is sufficient explanation. People v. Wright, 662 P.2d 489 (Colo. App. 1982), aff'd, 690 P.2d 1257 (Colo. 1984); People v. Muniz, 667 P.2d 1377(Colo. 1983); People v. Cabral, 698 P.2d 234 (Colo. 1985); People v. Wilson, 708 P.2d 792 (Colo. 1985) (term "feloniously" sufficiently informed defendant of mens rea element of the offense of rape); People v. Trujillo, 731 P.2d 649 (Colo. 1986). Effect of noncompliance with rule. Where rule is not complied with, the defendant's conviction will be reversed and the cause will be remanded to the trial court to set aside the plea and to rearraign the defendant. People v. Golden, 184 Colo. 311, 520 P.2d 127 (1974); People v. Baca, 186 Colo. 95, 525 P.2d 1146 (1974). Failure of trial court to advise or to make a proper inquiry precludes treating the defendant's plea of guilty as a voluntary and intelligent waiver of his constitutional rights, so defendant may withdraw his plea of guilty and be permitted to plea anew. People v. Harrington, 179 Colo. 312, 500 P.2d 360 (1972); People v. Gleason, 180 Colo. 71, 502 P.2d 69 (1972). Failure of the trial court to comply with each requirement of this rule affords defendants the opportunity to later challenge the trial court's refusal to permit a withdrawal of a guilty plea. People v. Sandoval, 188 Colo. 431, 535 P.2d 1120 (1975). Without showing of compliance, guilty plea not acceptable. Without an affirmative showing of compliance with the mandatory provisions of this rule, a plea of guilty cannot be accepted, and any judgment and sentence which is entered following the plea is void. Martinez v. People, 152 Colo. 521, 382 P.2d 990 (1963); Lamb v. People, 174 Colo. 441, 484 P.2d 798 (1971); People v. Randolph, 175 Colo. 454, 488 P.2d 203 (1971). Thus, conduct of proceedings to appear in record. The conduct of proceedings under this rule must affirmatively appear in the record, since an appellate court cannot presume a waiver of constitutional rights from a silent record. People v. Brewer, 648 P.2d 167 (Colo. App. 1982). But lack of precise language not grounds for reversal. If the record reflects that the trial court had assured itself that defendant's plea was voluntary and intelligently entered with full knowledge of the nature and elements of the offense and of the waiver of his rights as an accused person, then lack of precise language in the record expressing these things is not of itself a valid reason to reverse acceptance of a plea of nolo contendere. People v. Lambert, 189 Colo. 264, 539 P.2d 1238 (1975). Test for proper plea advisement. In deciding if a plea advisement was proper, the dispositive issue is whether the constitutional requirements of voluntariness then in effect were met. People v. Wright, 662 P.2d 489 (Colo. App. 1982), aff'd, 690 P.2d 1257 (Colo. 1984). Record must show factual basis for plea. A guilty plea cannot be accepted if the record lacks an affirmative showing of a factual basis. People v. Cushon, 631 P.2d 1164 (Colo. App. 1981), rev'd on other grounds, 650 P.2d 527 (Colo. 1982). As guilty plea cannot stand if it lacks a factual basis and is not voluntary and accurate. People v. Alvarez, 181 Colo. 213, 508 P.2d 1267 (1973); People v. Hutton, 183 Colo. 388, 517 P.2d 392 (1973). Nor may nolo contendere plea. Nolo contendere plea that is voluntarily and understandingly made, with a factual basis that appears in the record, should be upheld. People v. Canino, 181 Colo. 207, 508 P.2d 1273 (1973). Although court not required to ascertain factual basis for nolo contendere plea. There is no requirement that a court ascertain that there is a factual basis for a plea of nolo contendere when such a plea is permitted. People v. Canino, 181 Colo. 207, 508 P.2d 1273 (1973). Entering of guilty plea to lesser charge does not automatically waive factual basis requirement of subsection (b)(6). People v. Cushon, 631 P.2d 1164 (Colo. App. 1981), rev'd on other grounds, 650 P.2d 527 (Colo. 1982). Record must affirmatively show that accused understandingly and voluntarily waived his constitutional rights. People v. Harrington, 179 Colo. 312, 500 P.2d 360 (1972). Compliance with this rule requires that there be an adequate basis in the record to support a determination by the court that the defendant understands the nature of the charge to which he is pleading guilty. People v. Montoya, 667 P.2d 1377 (Colo. 1983). Compliance with this rule creates an adequate record to support a determination by both the arraigning court and a reviewing court of the defendant's understanding of the crime to which a plea is tendered. People v. Leonard, 673 P.2d 37 (Colo. 1983). Even when the defendant or his attorney waives the formal reading of the information, such waiver does not serve to dispense with the express mandate of this rule that the court not accept the plea of guilty without first determining that the defendant understands the nature of the charge. People v. Montoya, 667 P.2d 1377 (Colo. 1983). Silent record insufficient. Where there are no facts in the record to establish the defendant's complete understanding of the nature of the offense with which he is charged, then, when the state attempts to prove waiver of such knowledge, it bears a heavy burden, and a silent record will not suffice. People v. Colosacco, 177 Colo. 219, 493 P.2d 650 (1972). Application of Boykin v. Alabama. Boykin v. Alabama, 395 U.S. 238, 89 S. Ct. 1709, 23 L. Ed. 2d 274 (1969), holding that waiver of the privilege against self-incrimination, of the right to trial by jury, and of the right to confrontation cannot be presumed by a silent record, is given only prospective application. People v. Crater, 182 Colo. 248, 512 P.2d 623 (1973); People v. Edwards, 186 Colo. 129, 526 P.2d 144 (1974); People v. Malouff, 721 P.2d 159 (Colo. App. 1986). Record held to show defendant's knowing and intelligent waiver of rights. People v. Chavez, 650 P.2d 1310 (Colo. App. 1982); People v. Chavez, 730 P.2d 321 (Colo. 1986); People v. Campbell, 174 P.3d 860 (Colo. App. 2007). Trial court's failure to explain elements of second degree burglary was cured by evidence in record showing defendant understood and had knowledge of elements of second degree burglary. Wieder v. People, 722 P.2d 396 (Colo. 1986). While the court gave a proper advisement under this rule, it did not specifically evaluate the totality of the circumstances surrounding juvenile defendant's waiver of critical constitutional rights. After applying the totality of circumstances standard, defendant did not knowingly and voluntarily waive his constitutional rights when he entered a guilty plea. People v. Simpson, 51 P.3d 1022 (Colo. App. 2001), rev'd on other grounds, 69 P.3d 79 (Colo. 2003). Guilty plea must be voluntarily and intelligently given. In order for a court to accept a plea of guilty, there must be an affirmative showing that it was given voluntarily and intelligently. Martinez v. Ricketts, 498 F. Supp. 893 (D. Colo. 1980); People v. Drake, 785 P.2d 1257 (1990). A plea of guilty, to be valid, must be intelligently made. Hampton v. Tinsley, 240 F. Supp. 213 (D. Colo. 1965), rev'd on other grounds, 355 F.2d 470 (10th Cir. 1966). For a waiver of such the fundamental rights which results from the acceptance of a guilty plea, a defendant must voluntarily, knowingly, and intentionally relinquish those rights. People v. Harrington, 179 Colo. 312, 500 P.2d 360 (1972). A plea of guilty must be entered voluntarily and with full understanding of the essential elements of the offense to withstand constitutional scrutiny. People v. Cisneros, 665 P.2d 145 (Colo. App. 1983). Defendant who is subject to sentencing act must be informed of the penalties under such act prior to acceptance of guilty plea or else the plea cannot be voluntarily and understandingly entered. People v. Sutka, 713 P.2d 1326 (Colo. App. 1985). Defendant entered a guilty plea without being informed that he could receive an aggravated range sentence. Consequently, defendant's plea was not given voluntarily and intelligently and did not satisfy due process. People v. Corral, 179 P.3d 837 (Colo. App. 2007). Due process of law mandates that a guilty plea must be voluntary and understandingly made before a valid judgment can be entered thereon. People v. Chavez, 730 P.2d 321 (Colo. 1986). Test whether plea intelligently and voluntarily made. When determining whether pleas of guilty were intelligently and voluntarily entered, the test to be applied is that a plea of guilty entered by one fully aware of the direct consequences, including the actual value of any commitments made to him by the court, prosecutor, or his own counsel, must stand unless induced by threats (or promises to discontinue improper harassment), misrepresentation (including unfulfilled or unfulfillable promises), or perhaps by promises that are by their nature improper as having no proper relationship to the prosecutor's business (e.g. bribes). Ward v. People, 172 Colo. 244, 472 P.2d 673 (1970); England v. People, 175 Colo. 236, 486 P.2d 1055 (1971); Bresnahan v. People, 175 Colo. 286, 487 P.2d 551 (1971); People v. Mason, 176 Colo. 544, 491 P.2d 1383 (1971); People v. Cumby, 178 Colo. 31, 495 P.2d 223 (1972); Bresnahan v. Patterson, 352 F. Supp. 1180 (D. Colo. 1973);

People v. Musser, 187 Colo. 198, 529 P.2d 626 (1974). However, every relevant factor need not be correctly assessed. The rule that a plea must be intelligently made to be valid does not require that a plea be vulnerable to later attack if the defendant did not correctly assess every relevant factor entering into his decision. Simms v. People, 175 Colo. 191, 486 P.2d 22 (1971). Defendant must understand elements of offense and his rights. Rather than any ritualistic formalism, this rule requires only that a defendant be aware of the elements of the offense and that he voluntarily and understandingly acknowledge his guilt after being made aware of his various rights. People v. Marsh, 183 Colo. 258, 516 P.2d 431 (1973). The constitution requires that the defendant be aware of the elements of the offense and that he voluntarily and understandingly acknowledge his guilt when pleading guilty, but a formalistic recitation by the trial judge at a providency hearing is not a constitutional requisite. People v. Canino, 181 Colo. 207, 508 P.2d 1273 (1973); People v. Duran, 183 Colo. 180, 515 P.2d 1117 (1973); People v. Keenan, 185 Colo. 317, 524 P.2d 604 (1974). No guilty plea can be deemed valid unless a defendant understands the nature and elements of the crime with which he stands charged. People v. Colosacco, 177 Colo. 219, 493 P.2d 650 (1972); People v. Hubbard, 184 Colo. 243, 519 P.2d 945 (1974); People v. Keenan, 185 Colo. 317, 524 P.2d 604 (1974); People v. Sanders, 185 Colo. 356, 524 P.2d 299 (1974); People v. Brown, 187 Colo. 244, 529 P.2d 1338 (1974); People v. Murdock, 187 Colo. 418, 532 P.2d 43 (1975); Harshfield v. People, 697 P.2d 391 (Colo. 1985); People v. Wade, 708 P.2d 1366 (Colo. 1985); People v. Cisneros, 824 P.2d 16 (Colo. App. 1991). A guilty plea cannot stand as voluntarily and knowingly entered unless the defendant understands the nature of the crime charged, and this requirement is not met unless the critical elements of the crime charged are explained in terms which are understandable to the defendant. People v. Gorniak, 197 Colo. 289, 593 P.2d 349 (1979). As well as consequences of guilty plea. Every defendant that stands at the bar of justice charged with a crime must be advised and must know what the possible consequences are of his tendered plea of guilty. People v. Jones, 176 Colo. 61, 489 P.2d 596 (1971). A plea of guilty must be a genuine one by a defendant who is guilty and who understands his situation, his rights, and the consequences of his plea, and is neither deceived nor coerced. Westendorf v. People, 171 Colo. 123, 464 P.2d 866 (1970). A defendant must be advised of the pertinent fundamental constitutional rights and must understand the consequences of a guilty plea for him to voluntarily and understandingly enter such a plea and waive the right to a jury trial. People v. Weed, 830 P.2d 1095 (Colo. App. 1991). And trial judge must determine that defendant understands nature of offense with which he stands charged. People v. Riney, 176 Colo. 221, 489 P.2d 1304 (1971); People v. Colosacco, 177 Colo. 219, 493 P.2d 650 (1972); People v. Keenan, 185 Colo. 317, 524 P.2d 604 (1974); People v. Sanders, 185 Colo. 356, 524 P.2d 299 (1974). And consequences of act. Prior to the acceptance of a guilty plea the trial court must be assured that the defendant is fully aware of the consequences of his act. People v. Brown, 187 Colo. 244, 529 P.2d 1338 (1974). Colorado law does not contemplate an increase in the statutory maximum sentence to which a defendant has subjected himself by pleading guilty, based on subsequent jury findings, which are the functional equivalent of elements of a greater offense than the one to which he pled. People v. Lopez, 148 P.3d 121 (Colo. 2006). Violation of requirement that defendant understand the effects of his plea occurs if consideration of subsequent jury findings is allowed to increase defendant's maximum sentence. People v. Lopez, 148 P.3d 121 (Colo. 2006). Court's determination may be implied. Where the trial judge advises the defendant that his plea has to be voluntary and that any promises which have been made are not binding on the court, but judge fails to ask the defendant whether any such promises or coercion were involved in his decision to plead guilty, implicit in the court's acceptance of the guilty plea is its determination that the plea was intelligently and voluntarily entered. People v. Derrerra, 667 P.2d 1363 (Colo. 1983). Mere assertion of understanding of charge does not satisfy rule. The mere assertion of understanding of a charge by the defendant does not satisfy either the letter or spirit of this rule, but it must be clear, in fact, that the defendant understands the elements of the charge. People v. Sanders, 185 Colo. 356, 524 P.2d 299 (1974). Court to explain elements of crime and meaning of guilty plea. The requirement of understanding is not met unless critical elements of crime charged are explained in terms understandable to the defendant and unless meaning of guilty plea is explained in relation to each of such elements. People v. Gleason, 180 Colo. 71, 502 P.2d 69 (1972); People v. Brown, 187 Colo. 244, 529 P.2d 1338 (1974); People v. Van Hook, 36 Colo. App. 226, 539 P.2d 507 (1975); People v. Steelman, 200 Colo. 177, 613 P.2d 334 (1980); People v. Wieghard, 709 P.2d 81 (Colo. App. 1985); Waits v. People, 724 P.2d 1329 (Colo. 1986). And reading simply worded information may suffice. By reading an information, which is couched in language which is easily understandable to a person with ordinary intelligence and by inquiring into the

44

defendant's understanding of the charge before a plea of guilty was accepted, the trial judge satisfied the requirements of this rule. People v. Lottie, 183 Colo. 308, 516 P.2d 430 (1973). In explaining the critical elements of the charge to the defendant, unless the language of the charge is highly technical, no more full explanation of the substantive crime could be given than the charge itself. People v. Gorniak, 197 Colo. 289, 593 P.2d 349 (1979); People v. Moore, 636 P.2d 1290 (Colo. App. 1981); People v. Wieghard, 709 P.2d 81 (Colo. App. 1985). Where language was readily understandable by person of average intelligence and defendant affirmatively acknowledged he understood nature of charge, reading of information was sufficient. Wilson v. People, 708 P.2d 792 (Colo. 1985). The court is not required to advise a non-English speaking defendant that an official interpreter may be utilized for communication with the defendant's attorney. People v. Ochoa-Magana, 36 P.3d 141 (Colo. App. 2001). If defendant enters guilty plea under mistaken assurance that defendant's immigration status would not be affected by guilty plea, then plea may not have been made knowingly, voluntarily, and intelligently. People v. Nguyen, 80 P.3d 903 (Colo. App. 2003). Explanation of "unlawful act" more properly described burglary than the trespass with which the defendant was charged but the court concluded that it adequately apprised the defendant of the necessary elements of first degree criminal trespass. People v. Wood, 844 P.2d 1299 (Colo. App. 1992). Court must also explain attendant waiver of rights. In accordance with this rule, the trial court must make certain, by inquiry of the defendant, that he understands that the guilty plea stands as a waiver of nearly all of his rights as guaranteed by the fifth and sixth amendments to the United States Constitution. People v. Sandoval, 188 Colo. 431, 535 P.2d 1120 (1975). However, trial court is not required to advise defendant, before accepting his guilty plea, of the right to testify on his own behalf. People v. Malouff, 721 P.2d 159 (Colo. App. 1986). And definite, immediate, and automatic consequences of plea. The judge who accepts a plea of guilty is required to inform the defendant only of those consequences which have a definite, immediate and largely automatic effect on the range of a defendant's punishment. People v. Heinz, 197 Colo. 102, 589 P.2d 931 (1979). Where consequence of guilty plea to a crime of moral turpitude subjected defendant to mandatory deportation proceeding, defendant was denied effective assistance of counsel since counsel was unaware of deportation consequence and therefore defendant was entitled to withdraw plea and plead anew. People v. Pozo, 712 P.2d 1044 (Colo. App. 1985), rev'd on other grounds, 746 P.2d 523 (Colo. 1987). A mandatory parole term is such a consequence because parole imposes a significant limitation on a defendant's freedom during the term of parole. People v. Tyus, 776 P.2d 1143 (Colo. App. 1989); People v. Sandoval, 809 P.2d 1058 (Colo. App. 1990), overruled in Craig v. People, 986 P.2d 951 (Colo. 1999). Trial court, therefore, must advise the defendant of mandatory parole even if a plea agreement contemplates a sentence to probation or community corrections. The only exception is if the parties stipulate to a sentence to probation or to community corrections, the judge explicitly accepts and agrees to be bound by the stipulation, and the judge so advises the defendant. Dawson v. People, 30 P.3d 213 (Colo. 2001). Mandatory sentencing of defendant on parole status under § 18-1-105 is a definite, immediate, and automatic consequence of plea which defendant must understand. People v. Chippewa, 713 P.2d 1311 (Colo. App. 1985). A proper advisement on the subject of mandatory parole requires that a defendant be informed that he or she is subject to a period of mandatory parole, the maximum possible length of that period, and the fact that mandatory parole is a consequence distinct from imprisonment. People v. Laurson, 70 P.3d 564 (Colo. App. 2002). The proper inquiry is whether the record as a whole demonstrates that a defendant was given sufficient notice of the issue. When a defendant indicates at the providency hearing that he or she understood the matters contained in a written guilty plea advisement form, the burden of proof is on the defendant to show that the apparent waiver was not effective. People v. Laurson, 70 P.3d 564 (Colo. App. 2002). Failure to properly advise of the term of mandatory parole is harmless if the length of parole and imprisonment together does not exceed the total term of imprisonment to which the defendant was advised. Craig v. People, 986 P.2d 951 (Colo. 1999) (overruling People v. Sandoval, 809 P.2d 1058 (Colo. App. 1990)). Thus, it was harmless error where the defendant received an inadequate mandatory advisement but was sentenced to a total sentence of 11 years, plus three years of mandatory parole, when he could have been sentenced to a maximum of 24 years. Dawson v. People, 30 P.3d 213 (Colo. 2001). No script or formula is required so long as the advisement adequately informs defendant of the mandatory parole requirement. People v. Flagg, 18 P.3d 792 (Colo. App. 2000). Where defendant was advised that his sentence would include a term of parole in addition to a stipulated maximum term of incarceration, it is not reasonable to hold that the full range of penalties that the defendant risked receiving is limited to the term of incarceration specified in the plea agreement or the Crim. P. 11 advisement. If defendant was advised of mandatory parole but not its duration, his sentence cannot be modified and the only available remedy under the facts is withdrawal of the guilty plea. Clark v. People, 7 P.3d 163 (Colo. 2000). An agreement that is silent as to parole should not be construed as containing a promise to eliminate or reduce the mandatory period of parole. A plea agreement to reduce or modify the statutorily mandated period of parole calls for an illegal sentence. Craig v. People, 986 P.2d 951 (Colo. 1999) (overruling People v. Sandoval, 809 P.2d 1058 (Colo. App. 1990)). Defendant's understanding of the mandatory parole requirement and the lack of indication in the record that the parties' negotiations included the issue of mandatory parole supported trial court's conclusion that the parties' agreement to a "ten year cap" pertained only to the imprisonment component and did not include the five-year mandatory parole period. People v. Wright, 53 P.3d 730 (Colo. App. 2002). A mittimus that does not specify the mandatory parole period should be read as including the appropriate mandatory parole period and must be corrected. Craig v. People, 986 P.2d 951 (Colo. 1999) (overruling People v. Sandoval, 809 P.2d 1058 (Colo. App. 1990)). A trial court is not generally required to inform a defendant of the collateral consequences of his guilty plea. People v. Moore, 841 P.2d 320 (Colo. App. 1992). To satisfy due process, a defendant must be informed only of the direct consequences of his guilty plea, which include those which have a definite, immediate, and largely automatic effect on the range of possible punishment. People v. Moore, 841 P.2d 320 (Colo. App. 1992). Accordingly, a guilty plea is not invalid for failure of a trial court to warn a defendant of its possible effect on future criminal liability. People v. Heinz, 589 P.2d 931 (Colo. 1979); People v. Moore, 841 P.2d 320 (Colo. App. 1992). Although the defendant's sentence to imprisonment and mandatory parole was not inevitable at the time of his pleas and, in fact, could not have been lawfully imposed prior to his subsequent breach of the terms of his deferred sentencing agreement, it was a direct consequence of his plea to burglary and, therefore, the defendant should have been advised of the mandatory parole. People v. Marez, 39 P.3d 1190 (Colo. 2002). Defendant cannot be lawfully sentenced for a crime to which he has pled guilty to a term longer than that of which he was advised when it was still within his power to reject the plea. People v. Marez, 39 P.3d 1190 (Colo. 2002). Case must be remanded to allow defendant the opportunity to affirm or withdraw his guilty plea where the trial court's rejection of the sentence recommendation contained in the plea agreement calls into question the voluntariness of that plea and the defendant had no opportunity to affirm or withdraw that plea. People v. Walker, 46 P.3d 495 (Colo. App. 2002). Case must be remanded to allow defendant to reaffirm or withdraw guilty plea after advisement of the proper sentencing range, including the possibility of sentencing in the aggravated range. Because defendant's plea was not induced by prosecutor's promise, the proper remedy was not to resentence defendant based upon the providency hearing advisement, but to allow defendant to reaffirm or withdraw the plea after advisement of the proper sentencing range. People v. Corral, 179 P.3d 837 (Colo. App. 2007). Possibility that required counseling cannot be completed if the defendant does not admit guilt and that probation may therefore be revoked is a collateral consequence of a guilty plea. Person who entered an Alford plea and could not complete required counseling because of failure to admit guilt could have his or her probation revoked. People v. Birdsong, 958 P.2d 1124 (Colo. 1998). Due process requires compliance only with the mandatory provisions of this rule which inform an accused of the constitutional protection and the critical elements of the charge he faces, and not the factual basis of the plea or the possible defenses to the charge. People v. Moore, 841 P.2d 320 (Colo. App. 1992). However, the appropriate remedy is not to allow withdrawal of the plea, but reduce the sentence to the maximum that the defendant could receive under the plea agreement. People v. Sandoval, 809 P.2d 1058 (Colo. App. 1990). And waiver of previously raised defenses. Where the defendant previously filed a notice of alibi defense, the trial court, in accepting a later guilty plea, should have assiduously adhered to the requirements of this rule and should have even made a more detailed inquiry of the defendant to make certain that he was fully aware that by pleading guilty, he was, in effect, making a judicial statement that he was guilty of the offense charged and that his alibi defense was in fact baseless. People v. Sandoval, 188 Colo. 431, 535 P.2d 1120 (1975), overruled in Craig v. People, 986 P.2d 951 (Colo. 1999). But judge not required to point out available affirmative defenses. Absent from the provisions of section (b) is any requirement that the trial judge in accepting a guilty plea explain to the defendant possible affirmative defenses to the crime charged; the rationale is that such advice is properly the role of counsel. People v. Gorniak, 197 Colo. 289, 593 P.2d 349 (1979); People v. Nieto, 715 P.2d 1262 (Colo. App. 1985). And need not be informed of possible future operation of habitual criminal statutes. It is not required that an adult, before he enters an otherwise uncoerced guilty plea, be informed of the operation of the habitual criminal statutes in the event he should in the future be

46

convicted of illegal acts. People v. District Court, 191 Colo. 298, 552 P.2d 297 (1976). Trial court's oversight may be cured. An oversight on the part of the trial court in a providency hearing may be cured if the record, as a whole, discloses evidence of understanding and knowledge. People v. Moore, 636 P.2d 1290 (Colo. App. 1981). The degree of explanation that a court is required to provide a defendant at a providency hearing is dependent upon the nature and complexity of the crime. People v. Muniz, 667 P.2d 1377 (Colo. 1983); Ramirez v. People, 682 P.2d 1181 (Colo. 1984); People v. Cabral, 698 P.2d 234 (Colo. 1985); People v. District Court, Arapahoe County, 868 P.2d 400 (Colo. 1994). And mere reading of a charge may be sufficient if the charge itself is readily understandable to persons of ordinary intelligence. People v. Muniz, 667 P.2d 1377 (Colo. 1983); People v. Cabral, 698 P.2d 234 (Colo. 1985). By reading the charges, which were couched in language easily understandable to a person of ordinary intelligence, by briefly explaining the mens rea necessary, and by inquiring into the defendant's understanding of the charges, the trial judge adequately advised the defendant and provided a fully sufficient basis for the court's determination that the pleas were freely, voluntarily, and intelligently given. People v. District Court, Arapahoe County, 868 P.2d 400 (Colo. 1994). Defining "attempt" as conduct constituting a substantial step toward the commission of the crime is sufficient for the purpose of providing a defendant with the necessary understanding of the crime charged. People v. District Court, Arapahoe County, 868 P.2d 400 (Colo. 1994). A defendant need not be advised of the right to appeal before a guilty plea may be said to be knowingly and voluntarily given. People v. District Court, Arapahoe County, 868 P.2d 400 (Colo. 1994). Court need not advise defendant of the prosecution's burden to prove his guilt beyond a reasonable doubt as long as defendant is advised that the prosecution has the burden of proof. People v. Wells, 734 P.2d 655 (Colo. App. 1986). Guilty plea of defendant who was not aware of possibility of consecutive sentencing when he entered plea is constitutionally deficient. People v. Peters, 738 P.2d 395 (Colo. App. 1987). Defendant adequately advised regarding the special offender sentence enhancer where the sentences defendant received were within the range of sentences he or she was advised of and were on the low end of the range required by the special offender statute. Thus, defendant was not prejudiced by the erroneous advisements, and the fact that they understated the maximum allowable sentence did not undermine the validity of his or her guilty plea. People v. Zuniga, 80 P.3d 965 (Colo. App. 2003). Failure to advise defendant of a mandatory parole obligation did not invalidate his guilty plea since defendant was correctly advised that he could be incarcerated for a term of from six months to four years and defendant's sentence of one year plus one year parole fell below the four-year maximum. People v. Coleman, 844 P.2d 1215 (Colo. App. 1992). To understand the "possible penalty or penalties", the court must advise the defendant of mandatory parole for all class 2 through class 6 felony convictions that involve a sentence of imprisonment. Young v. People, 30 P.3d 202 (Colo. 2001). Record of providency hearing helpful in satisfying rule. A record of a providency hearing demonstrating compliance with this rule should be deemed supportive of the conclusion that the defendant did enter his or her guilty plea voluntarily and understandingly. People v. Wade, 708 P.2d 1366 (Colo. 1985). The proper basis for analyzing the constitutional validity of a guilty plea should include not only the statements made during the providency hearing but also those statements made by both defendant and defendant's attorney in the petition to plead guilty. People v. Weed, 830 P.2d 1095 (Colo. App. 1991). Evidence in record that defendant understood nature and elements of crime. People v. Marsh, 183 Colo. 258, 516 P.2d 431 (1973); People v. Waits, 695 P.2d 1176 (Colo. App. 1984), aff'd in part and rev'd in part on other grounds, 724 P.2d 1329 (Colo. 1986). Validity of guilty plea should not be based solely on the colloquy during the providency hearing. The proper basis for determining the validity of a guilty plea should include not only the statements made during a providency hearing but also the statements made by the defendant and the defendant's attorney in the petition to plead guilty. People v. Weed, 830 P.2d 1095 (Colo. App. 1991). Upon entry of a guilty plea, suppression issues become moot. People v. Waits, 695 P.2d 1176 (Colo. App. 1984), aff'd in part and rev'd in part on other grounds, 724 P.2d 1329 (Colo. 1986). Trial court to determine defendant's capacity to plead, where appropriate. If there is any question, the trial court has the duty to determine the defendant's mental capacity to understand the nature and effect of such a plea before accepting it. Hampton v. Tinsley, 240 F. Supp. 213 (D. Colo. 1965), rev'd on other grounds, 355 F.2d 470 (10th Cir. 1966). Where the trial court was aware of the possible mental infirmities of the defendant, it should have made sure he clearly, voluntarily, and knowingly entered his guilty plea. People v. Brown, 187 Colo. 244, 529 P.2d 1338 (1974). And if a defendant is insane, plea of guilty should be stricken, and the sentence vacated. Gallegos v. People, 166 Colo. 409, 444 P.2d 267 (1968); Simms v. People, 175 Colo. 191, 486 P.2d 22 (1971); Moneyhun v. People, 175

Colo. 220, 486 P.2d 434 (1971). As guilty plea not acceptable from legally insane. As a plea of guilty cannot be accepted where the evidence before the judge suggests that the accused may be legally insane, until his sanity is finally determined; if the plea is accepted prior to such a determination, the judgment is potentially void, depending on whether the accused had the capacity to enter a plea. Martinez v. Tinsley, 241 F. Supp. 730 (D. Colo. 1965). Sixteen-year old competent to enter guilty plea. Although a trial court should act with great caution in accepting a guilty plea from a 16-year old, such a defendant is competent. Bresnahan v. Patterson, 352 F. Supp. 1180 (D. Colo. 1973). Although restraints may be one circumstance that affects defendant's decision to plead guilty, the constitutionality of a defendant's restraints at the time of entry of his pleas is not relevant to determine whether he entered the plea voluntarily. People v. Kyler, 991 P.2d 810 (Colo. 2000). When bargain upon which plea based not honored. If plea of guilty results from plea bargaining and bargain is not honored, the judgment must be vacated. People v. McClellan, 183 Colo. 176, 515 P.2d 1127 (1973). Effect of invalid plea upon bargain. When an invalid guilty plea is a result of plea bargaining, vacation of the plea results in an abrogation of the bargain, and there is no impediment to the reinstatement of the charges dismissed as a result of the bargain. People v. Mason, 176 Colo. 544, 491 P.2d 1383 (1971); People v. Keenan, 185 Colo. 317, 524 P.2d 604 (1974). Plea bargaining per se does not invalidate a guilty plea. Smith v. People, 162 Colo. 558, 428 P.2d 69 (1967); Lucero v. People, 164 Colo. 247, 434 P.2d 128 (1967); Maes v. People, 164 Colo. 481, 435 P.2d 893 (1968); Brewer v. People, 168 Colo. 505, 452 P.2d 370 (1969). Purpose of subsection (b)(5). Subsection (b)(5) of this rule is specifically designed to insure that a criminal defendant voluntarily pleads to a charge unfettered by promises of a light sentence or of probation, and is in addition to the inquiry concerning coercion or threats. People v. Golden, 184 Colo. 311, 520 P.2d 127 (1974). Subsection (b)(5) applies to representations and promises by defendant's own counsel. People v. Golden, 184 Colo. 311, 520 P.2d 127 (1974). Pleas of guilty induced by threats or promises are not valid. Normand v. People, 165 Colo. 509, 440 P.2d 282 (1968). As such pleas involuntary. A plea of guilty is clearly involuntary if it is induced by threats or by a promise of lenient sentence. People v. McClellan, 183 Colo. 176, 515 P.2d 1127 (1973). And involuntary guilty plea violates due process. A guilty plea which is not entered voluntarily and knowingly is obtained in violation of due process guarantees. People v. Moore, 636 P.2d 1290 (Colo. App. 1981). Defendant's burden to set aside plea. Upon postconviction procedures to set aside an involuntary plea, it becomes the burden of the defendant to establish that the plea was entered because of coercion. Normand v. People, 165 Colo. 509, 440 P.2d 282 (1968). With evidence to overcome presumption of valid plea. The burden is upon the defendant to produce sufficient evidence to overcome the presumption of validity and regularity surrounding entry of his plea of guilty. Hampton v. Tinsley, 240 F. Supp. 213 (D. Colo. 1965), rev'd on other grounds, 355 F.2d 470 (10th Cir. 1966). And every reasonable presumption against waiver must be indulged. People v. Harrington, 179 Colo. 312, 500 P.2d 360 (1972). Withdrawal of guilty plea generally should not be denied. The withdrawal of a plea of guilty should not be denied in any case where it is the least evident that the ends of justice would be subserved by permitting not guilty to be pleaded in its place. Burman v. People, 172 Colo. 247, 472 P.2d 121 (1970). Denial of motion to withdraw guilty pleas was not an abuse of discretion by the trial court where the pleas were entered in accordance with due process of law and this rule. People v. Chavez, 730 P.2d 321 (Colo. 1986). Defendant was properly advised of his right to a jury trial and knowingly and voluntarily waived that right where the record shows that he executed a five-page "Petition to Enter Plea of Guilty", the trial court held a providency hearing and ascertained that the defendant had read and discussed the petition with his attorney and understood the petition, and the petition was signed by the defense attorney who certified that he had fully discussed the matter with the defendant, the attorney considered the defendant to be competent to understand the effect of the guilty plea, and the attorney recommended the court accept the plea. People v. Weed, 830 P.2d 1095 (Colo. App. 1991). Requirement that defendant understand the possible penalty when pleading guilty met where defendant signed a "Petition to Enter Plea of Guilty" that recited the possible years of incarceration in both the presumptive and extraordinary ranges in addition to the possible fines to which the defendant would be subject, the possibility of consecutive sentencing, mandatory sentencing in the aggravated range, the factors precluding grant of probation, and incarceration as a condition of probation, the plea was entered with an express stipulation that defendant receive a three-year sentence, the trial court at the providency hearing advised the defendant of the stipulation and further advised him that, if at the sentencing hearing, the court rejected the stipulation, defendant would be allowed to withdraw the plea, and defendant responded that he understood. People v. Weed, 830 P.2d 1095 (Colo. App. 1991). Denial of motion to withdraw guilty plea was not an abuse of discretion where the court held a fact hearing before denying defendant's motion, the judge had also conducted the advisement, the court found that defendant's plea had been voluntarily entered, and justice would not be subverted by denying defendant's request. People v. Weed, 830 P.2d 1095 (Colo. App. 1991). Valid guilty plea requires that defendant understand the possible penalty or penalties which could be imposed. People v. Chavez, 902 P.2d 891 (Colo. App. 1995). Subsection (b)(4) requires that defendant be advised, prior to the entry of a guilty plea, of the maximum possible sentence to which that plea will subject him or her, including the maximum that may result if the sentences are ordered to be served consecutively. People v. Peters, 738 P.2d 395 (Colo. App. 1987); People v. Phillips, 964 P.2d 628 (Colo. App. 1998). Court not required to advise defendant of the possibility of consecutive sentences that might result from crimes not yet committed or sentences or charges not pending. People v. Phillips, 964 P.2d 628 (Colo. App. 1998). Fact that defense counsel may not have advised client of maximum penalty defendant might be sentenced to does not form the basis for vacating a guilty plea where court gave defendant a complete advisement with respect to the possible penalties, including presumptive and aggravated range penalties for each conviction and the difference between concurrent and consecutive sentences. People v. Chavez, 902 P.2d 891 (Colo. App. 1995). And showing of reason for plea change within discretion of court. Whether a showing of "fair and just reason" for a change of plea was made is a matter within the discretion of the trial court, and the Colorado supreme court will intervene only if the court has abused its discretion. People v. Gutierrez, 622 P.2d 547 (Colo. 1981). In determining whether defendant received a proper advisement under the rule, the court looks to whether the record as a whole shows defendant received sufficient information as to be fairly placed on notice of the matter in question. Young v. People, 30 P.3d 202 (Colo. 2001). If an advisement indicates an affirmative waiver, the defendant has the burden to prove, by a preponderance of the evidence, the ineffectiveness of his apparent waiver. Young v. People, 30 P.3d 202 (Colo. 2001). Defendant was entitled to a hearing on motion to withdraw guilty plea where court understated minimum sentence that could be imposed and defendant's plea agreement was not in evidence. On remand, defendant must establish that his asserted belief that he would receive a sentence below the minimum sentence stated by the court was objectively reasonable. People v. Hodge, 205 P.3d 481 (Colo. App. 2008). Burden on defendant. The burden of demonstrating a "fair and just reason" for a change of plea rests on the defendant. People v. Gutierrez, 622 P.2d 547 (Colo. 1981). If the advisement is infirm, the court determines if it can correct the error. If the error cannot be corrected, the defendant can withdraw his plea. Young v. People, 30 P.3d 202 (Colo. 2001). The trial court is not bound by the plea agreement, and has an independent duty to examine the appropriate sentence prior to issuance of that sentence. On review, the court looks at the maximum statutory exposure recited by the trial court or included in the documentation. Young v. People, 30 P.3d 202 (Colo. 2001). Except when the trial court explicitly states at the providency hearing that it will accept and agree to be bound by the plea agreement, and so advises the defendant. Young v. People, 30 P.3d 202 (Colo. 2001). Who must show that denial would subvert justice. To warrant a change of plea before entry of a sentence, there must be some showing that denial of the request will subvert justice. People v. Gutierrez, 622 P.2d 547 (Colo. 1981). Gutierrez distinguished where the defendant acknowledged his own guilt rather than an independent trier of fact that determined defendant's guilt based on sworn trial testimony. People v. Schneider, 25 P.3d 755 (Colo. 2001). Use of statements made in conjunction with withdrawn or rejected guilty plea. A defendant who challenges the voluntariness or reliability of statements made in the course of tendering a guilty plea which is subsequently withdrawn or rejected and is later sought to be used against him at trial for impeachment purposes is entitled to a hearing which provides the safeguards set forth in Jackson v. Denno, 378 U.S. 368, 84 S. Ct. 1774, 12 L. Ed. 2d 908 (1964), before those statements may be used against him. People v. Cole, 195 Colo. 483, 584 P.2d 71 (1978). The prosecution has the right to cure a deficient record by offering evidence at a rule 35(c) hearing which establishes that the defendant's plea was constitutionally obtained. People v. Lesh, 668 P.2d 1362 (Colo. 1983). Jurisdictional defects not waived by plea. Jurisdictional defects, such as insufficiency of a charging instrument, are not waived by a plea of nolo contendere. People v. Roberts, 668 P.2d 977 (Colo. App. 1983). Limitation on use of plea accepted in violation of rule. Conviction based on plea accepted in violation of this rule cannot be used in a later proceeding to support the imposition of statutory liabilities. People v. Heinz, 197 Colo. 102, 589 P.2d 931 (1979). Conditional guilty pleas are not authorized in Colorado by statute or court rule. People v. Neuhaus, 240 P.3d 391 (Colo. App. 2009). A plea accepted in violation of this rule may not be used to support a conviction for purposes of the habitual traffic offender statute. People v.

Roybal, 618 P.2d 1121 (Colo. 1980). Substantial compliance with subsection (b)(7). District attorney's oral consent to entry of a guilty plea, made on the record at the providency hearing, substantially complies with the requirements of subsection (b)(7). People v. Mascarenas, 643 P.2d 786 (Colo. App. 1981). Evidence that requirements of rules not complied with. People v. Van Hook, 36 Colo. App. 226, 539 P.2d 507 (1975). **III. Misdemeanor Cases.** More simplified procedures can properly be used for minor offenses than those required to be followed in receiving a plea of guilty in serious criminal cases. Cave v. Colo. Dept. of Rev., 31 Colo. App. 185, 501 P.2d 479 (1972). Procedure for plea to misdemeanor or traffic offense. Before accepting a plea of guilty or nolo contendere to a misdemeanor or traffic offense, the trial court must be satisfied that the defendant's decision to acknowledge guilt has been made knowingly and understandingly. People v. Lesh, 668 P.2d 1362 (Colo. 1983). **IV. Failure or Refusal to Plead.** When court may enter plea. Where a trial court denies a motion to dismiss for failure to rearraign on an amended information because the amendment is not one of substance, when counsel calls the court's attention to the amended information during the course of the trial, the court may follow the provisions of Crim. P. 11(d) and enter a plea of not guilty, allowing the trial to proceed. People v. Buckner, 180 Colo. 65, 504 P.2d 669 (1972). **V. Defense of Insanity.** Fact that defendant is insane does not conclusively render him incompetent to proceed or enter a plea of guilty. People v. Blehm, 791 P.2d 1177 (Colo. App. 1989), aff'd in part and rev'd in part, 817 P.2d 988 (Colo. 1991). Plea of not guilty by reason of insanity includes a not guilty plea. Sanchez v. District Court, 200 Colo. 33, 612 P.2d 519 (1980). Section (e) is to be liberally construed in favor of defendants. Martinez v. People, 179 Colo. 197, 499 P.2d 611 (1972); Ellis v. District Court, 189 Colo. 123, 538 P.2d 107 (1975); Labor v. Gibson, 195 Colo. 416, 578 P.2d 1059 (1978). Common-law bar on pleading and trial of mentally ill. It has long been the rule of the common law that a person cannot be required to plead to an indictment or be tried for a crime while he is so mentally disordered as to be incapable of making a rational defense, and he cannot be adjudged to punishment or executed while he is so disordered as to be incapable of stating any reasons that may exist why judgment should not be pronounced or executed. Hampton v. Tinsley, 240 F. Supp. 213 (D. Colo. 1965), rev'd on other grounds, 355 F.2d 470 (10th Cir. 1966). Plea at arraignment or before trial upon good cause showing. Section (e) sets forth in unequivocal terms that the insanity defense must be interposed at the time of arraignment, except when the court, for good cause shown, permits the plea to be interposed prior to trial. Ellis v. District Court, 189 Colo. 123, 538 P.2d 107 (1975). Determination of good cause in discretion of trial court. Whether good cause is shown to permit a plea of insanity rests within discretion of trial court. Taylor v. District Court, 182 Colo. 406, 514 P.2d 309 (1973). Not disturbed on appeal absent clear abuse. The question of good cause is one addressed to the sound discretion of the trial judge and, absent a clear abuse of discretion, the trial judge's ruling will not be disturbed on appeal. Martinez v. People, 179 Colo. 197, 499 P.2d 611 (1972); Taylor v. District Court, 182 Colo. 406, 514 P.2d 309 (1973); Garza v. People, 200 Colo. 62, 612 P.2d 85 (1980). Showing required to prove good cause. Good cause in section (e) of this rule is shown when it is demonstrated that fairness and justice are best subserved by permitting the additional plea. Ellis v. District Court, 189 Colo. 123, 538 P.2d 107 (1975). Good cause in section (e) of this rule is satisfied if the accused establishes that the plea was not entered at the time of arraignment due to mistake, ignorance, or inadvertence. Ellis v. District Court, 189 Colo. 123, 538 P.2d 107 (1975). Good cause not established. Garza v. People, 200 Colo. 62, 612 P.2d 85 (1980). Abuse of discretion in not allowing insanity plea. Taylor v. District Court, 182 Colo. 406, 514 P.2d 309 (1973); Ellis v. District Court, 189 Colo. 123, 538 P.2d 107 (1975). Right to have jury solve dispute as to sanity. Where there is a disputed question as to the defendant's sanity, he is entitled to have a jury pass on it. Abad v. People, 168 Colo. 202, 450 P.2d 327 (1969). Choice of entering plea is defendant's. The tactical choice of whether to enter a plea of not guilty by reason of insanity by a defendant found "mentally competent" is left to the defendant and his counsel. People v. Lopez, 640 P.2d 275 (Colo. App. 1982). And court not authorized to enter insanity plea unless defendant requests. Neither section (e) nor § 16-8-103 , gives a trial court the authority to enter a plea of not guilty by reason of insanity when it has not been requested by the defendant or his counsel. Labor v. Gibson, 195 Colo. 416, 578 P.2d 1059 (1978); People v. Lopez, 640 P.2d 275 (Colo. App. 1982). Insanity inquiry at any time during trial. If a court, at any of the stages of a trial, has a reasonable doubt whether a defendant is mentally disordered, it should suspend the criminal proceedings and hold an inquiry on the matter. Hampton v. Tinsley, 240 F. Supp. 213 (D. Colo. 1965), rev'd on other grounds, 355 F.2d 470 (10th Cir. 1966). Otherwise due process is violated. It is fundamental that a proceeding against an insane person in a criminal matter is a violation of his rights under the due process clause of the fourteenth *amendment. Hampton v. Tinsley, 240 F. Supp. 213 (D. Colo. 1965), rev'd on other grounds, 355 F.2d 470 (10th Cir. 1966). VI. Plea Bargaining. Law reviews. For article, "Felony Plea Bargaining in Six Colorado Judicial Districts: A Limited Inquiry into the Nature of the Process", see 66 Den. U. L. Rev. 243 (1989). Plea agreements, or plea bargainings, are approved. Dabbs v. People, 175 Colo. 273, 486 P.2d 1053 (1971); People v. White, 182 Colo. 417, 514 P.2d 69 (1973). But it may not be utilized to subvert truth or as means of forcing plea to an uncommitted crime. People v. White, 182 Colo. 417, 514 P.2d 69 (1973). Plea bargain may not be hidden and must be brought to the surface for scrutiny. DeLuzio v. People, 177 Colo. 389, 494 P.2d 589 (1972). And defense lawyer must first obtain permission and the consent of his client before plea bargaining. Dabbs v. People, 175 Colo. 273, 486 P.2d 1053 (1971). Coercion. Negotiation regarding charges against a loved one does not necessarily render a plea bargain the product of coercion, because such a plea can be voluntary. People v. Duran, 179 Colo. 129, 498 P.2d 937 (1972). Judge not to participate in bargaining. Participation by trial judge in the plea bargaining process must be condemned. People v. Clark, 183 Colo. 201, 515 P.2d 1242 (1973). Court may involve itself in plea discussions if such involvement merely involves observations regarding the evolving legal posture of the case or inquiries as to whether the parties still wish to consummate the agreement. People v. Venzor, 121 P.3d 260 (Colo. App. 2005). Section (f)(4) makes it clear that a trial judge shall not participate in plea discussions. This prohibition is designed to prevent coercion by the court in shaping a bargain. People v. Roy, 109 P.3d 993 (Colo. App. 2004). When rejecting a plea agreement, a trial court must demonstrate on the record that it has actually exercised its discretion. A court's failure to make such showing is an abuse of discretion. People v. Copenhaver, 21 P.3d 413 (Colo. App. 2000). Court has discretion to reject a plea agreement, separately from the merits, on the basis that the parties tendered it in an untimely fashion. The trial court must provide adequate notice to the parties of the plea bargain cutoff date and must permit an exception to the rule for good cause. If a court rejects a plea for failure to conform to plea deadline, court need not necessarily consider the terms of the plea agreement proffered by the parties. People v. Jasper, 17 P.3d 807 (Colo. 2001). Court is not bound by a recommendation; in its discretion it may refuse to grant the district attorney's sentence concession. People v. Wright, 38 Colo. App. 271, 559 P.2d 249 (1976), aff'd, 194 Colo. 448, 573 P.2d 551 (1978); People v. McGhee, 677 P.2d 419 (Colo. App. 1983); People v. Smith, 827 P.2d 577 (Colo. App. 1991). A prosecutor can only make sentence recommendations, not promises, and sentencing determinations remain within the discretion of the trial court regardless of plea agreements between the prosecution and the defense. People v. Smith, 827 P.2d 577 (Colo. App. 1991). Subsection (f)(2)(I) clearly contemplates that a defendant should be permitted to withdraw his guilty plea where the trial court chooses not to follow the prosecutor's sentence recommendation, regardless of whether the prosecution has promised that the court will follow the recommendation. People v. Wright, 194 Colo. 448. 573 P.2d 551 (1978); People v. Smith, 827 P.2d 577 (Colo. App. 1991). But court must comply with Rule 32(e). The provision in subsection (b)(5) of this rule and § 16-7-207(2)(e), that the court will not be bound by representations made to the defendant "unless the representations are included in a formal plea agreement approved by the court and supported by the findings of the presentence report . . .", does not free the court from complying with Crim. P. 32(e), which states, that if the court decides that the final disposition should not include the charge or sentence concessions contemplated by the plea agreement, the judge must so advise the defendant and call upon the defendant to affirm or withdraw his plea of guilty or nolo contendere. People v. Wright, 38 Colo. App. 271, 559 P.2d 249 (1976), aff'd, 194 Colo. 448, 573 P.2d 551 (1978). Although district judges are barred from the plea negotiation process by this rule, once they have given unqualified approval to a plea agreement they, like the parties, become bound by the terms of that agreement. Were courts free to re-examine the wisdom of plea bargains with the benefit of hindsight, the agreements themselves would lack finality, and the benefits that encourage the government and defendants to enter into pleas might prove illusory. People v. Roy, 109 P.3d 993 (Colo. App. 2004). Application of C.R.E. 410, when read in light of this rule and § 16-7-303 , requires the exclusion of evidence of statements made by defendant during plea bargaining process only in regard to plea discussions with the attorney for the government. People v. Rollins, 759 P.2d 816 (Colo. App. 1988). Sentence recommendation is a sentence concession whether or not the court approves or concurs. People v. Wright, 38 Colo. App. 271, 559 P.2d 249 (1976), aff'd, 194 Colo. 448, 573 P.2d 551 (1978). Offers of identical concessions for similarly situated defendants not required. Section 16-7-301(3) and subsection (f)(3) of this rule do not require that similarly situated defendants must be offered identical concessions. People v. Lewis, 671 P.2d 985 (Colo. App. 1983). District attorneys have the power to refuse to recommend sentence or probation.*

People v. Wright, 38 Colo. App. 271, 559 P.2d 249 (1976), aff'd, 194 Colo. 448, 573 P.2d 551 (1978). Failure to object at time of acceptance of bargain bars later appeal of sentence. Where the trial court repeatedly reminded the defendant of what the sentence would be when it advised him at the time of the acceptance of his plea of guilty, pursuant to this rule, and where at no time did the defendant or his counsel protest the sentence nor raise an objection that the trial court was not properly exercising its discretion in imposing the sentence, the defendant could not, after benefiting from the plea bargain, claim on appeal that he has been unjustly sentenced. People v. Cunningham, 200 Colo. 303, 614 P.2d 886 (1980); People v. Campbell, 174 P.3d 860 (Colo. App. 2007). The proper standard for evaluating whether a prosecution remains bound by its obligations under a plea agreement is whether a defendant has materially and substantially breached his obligation to perform under the plea agreement. People v. McCormick, 859 P.2d 946 (Colo. 1993). A plea agreement is more than merely a contract between two parties and must be attended by constitutional safeguards to ensure that a defendant receives the performance that he is due. People v. McCormick, 856 P.2d 846 (Colo. 1993). Once the court chose to engage in the bargaining process and agreed to terms, it became obligated to comply with those terms, just as any other party to the agreement. The court's faithful observance of the terms of the bargain was just as vital to the fairness and efficiency of the process as was the prosecutor's compliance. Once the court committed to the plea agreement, it became bound by the terms of the agreement and could not, absent proof of fraud or breach of the plea bargain, set the agreement aside. People v. Roy, 109 P.3d 993 (Colo. App. 2004). Partial performance not enough. A defendant who materially and substantially breaches a plea agreement cannot enforce the agreement, regardless of whether the defendant has partially performed some of his obligations under it. People v. McCormick, 859 P.2d 846 (Colo. 1993).

Rule 12 - Pleadings, Motions Before Trial, Defenses, and Objections

(a) Pleadings and Motions. Pleadings shall consist of the indictment or information or complaint, or summons and complaint, and the pleas of guilty, not guilty, not guilty by reason of insanity, and nolo contendere. All other pleas, demurrers, and motions to quash are abolished and defenses and objections raised before trial which heretofore could have been raised by one or more of them shall be raised only by motion to dismiss or to grant appropriate relief, as provided in these Rules.

(b) The Motion Raising Defenses and Objections.

(1) Defenses and Objections Which May Be Raised. Any defense or objection which is capable of determination without the trial of the general issue may be raised by motion.

(2) Defenses and Objections Which Must Be Raised. Defenses and objections based on defects in the institution of the prosecution or in the indictment or information or complaint, or summons and complaint, other than that it fails to show jurisdiction in the court or to charge an offense, may be raised only by motion. The motion shall include all such defenses and objections then available to the defendant. Failure to present any such defense or objection constitutes a waiver of it, but the court for cause shown may grant relief from the waiver. Lack of jurisdiction or the failure of the indictment or information to charge an offense shall be noticed by the court at any time during the proceeding. When a motion challenging the constitutionality of the statute upon which the charge is based or asserting lack of jurisdiction is made after the commencement of the trial, the court shall reserve its ruling on that motion until the conclusion of the trial.

(3) Time of Making Motion. The motion shall be made within 21 days following arraignment.

(4) Hearing on Motion. A motion before trial raising defenses or objections shall be determined before the trial unless the court orders that it be deferred for determination at the trial of the general issue except as provided in Rule 41. An issue of fact shall be tried by a jury if a jury trial is required by the Constitution or by statute. All other issues of fact shall be determined by the court with or without a jury or on affidavits or in such other manner as the court may direct.

(5) Effect of Determination. If a motion is determined adversely to the defendant, he shall be permitted to plead if he has not previously pleaded. A plea previously entered shall stand.

Colo. R. Crim. P. 12

Source: (b)(3) amended and adopted December 14, 2011, effective 7/1/2012.

Annotation I. General Consideration. Technical noncompliance with Crim. P. 16 that does not cause prejudice to defendant will not constitute reversible error. People v. Hernandez, 695 P.2d 308 (Colo. App. 1984). Applied in Stapleton v. District Court, 179 Colo. 187, 499 P.2d 310

(1972); People v. McCabe, 37 Colo. App. 181, 546 P.2d 1289 (1975); People v. Davis, 194 Colo. 466, 573 P.2d 543 (1978); People v. Dickinson, 197 Colo. 338, 592 P.2d 807 (1979); People v. Velasquez, 641 P.2d 943 (Colo. 1982); People v. Peterson, 656 P.2d 1301 (Colo. 1983). II. Pleading and Motions. Legal effect of present nomenclature for old procedures is the same. Although the granting of motions to quash, demurrers, pleas in bar, pleas in abatement, motions in arrest of judgment, and the declarations of a statute unconstitutional have been abolished by Crim. P. 12(a) and Crim. P. 29(a) the legal effect of the present nomenclature for those procedures is the same, that is, a ruling adverse to the state effectively terminates its prosecution of the defendant and results in a "final judgment". People v. Cochran, 176 Colo. 364, 490 P.2d 684 (1971). III. Motion Raising Defenses and Objections. A. Defenses and Objections Which May be Raised. Motion to suppress a lineup identification is within the scope of this subsection (b)(1). People v. Renfrow, 172 Colo. 399, 473 P.2d 957 (1970). B. Defenses and Objections Which Must be Raised. Waiver of defenses and objections by failure to raise. Failure to raise defenses and objections referred to in subsection (b)(2) by motion constitutes waiver of the defenses and objections. Mora v. People, 172 Colo. 261, 472 P.2d 142 (1970). Motions not within scope of subsection (b)(2). A motion for the return of property and to suppress evidence is not a defense or objection based on defects in the institution of the prosecution or in the indictment, information, or complaint, and, thus, does not fall within the scope of subsection (b)(2). Adargo v. People, 173 Colo. 323, 478 P.2d 308 (1970). A motion to suppress is not a "defense or objection" based on defects listed in this section. People v. Robertson, 40 Colo. App. 386, 577 P.2d 314 (1978). Trial court should entertain motion to dismiss for lack of jurisdiction at whatever stage of the proceedings the question is raised. Maddox v. People, 178 Colo. 366, 497 P.2d 1263 (1972). Absence of verification on information is not jurisdictional. Quintana v. People, 168 Colo. 308, 451 P.2d 286 (1969). Rather, it is for benefit of defendant and is waived unless timely objection is made thereto. Quintana v. People, 168 Colo. 308, 451 P.2d 286 (1969); Bergdahl v. People, 27 Colo. 302, 61 P. 228 (1900); Curl v. People, 53 Colo. 578, 127 P. 951 (1912); Harris v. Municipal Court, 123 Colo. 539, 234 P.2d 1055 (1951); Bustamante v. People, 136 Colo. 362, 317 P.2d 885 (1957); Mora v. People, 172 Colo. 261, 472 P.2d 142 (1970); Workman v. People, 174 Colo. 194, 483 P.2d 213 (1971); Maraggos v. People, 175 Colo. 130, 486 P.2d 1 (1971); Scott v. People, 176 Colo. 289, 490 P.2d 1295 (1971). C. Time of Making Motion. Defects raisable in motion in arrest of judgment or for new trial. When objections to the want of a verifying affidavit and to the competency and credibility of the affiant are raised by the defendant for the first time in a motion in arrest of judgment or in the alternative for a new trial, and the record does not reveal that any objections were raised prior to that time, although the opportunity existed, then the objections come too late. Maraggos v. People, 175 Colo. 130, 486 P.2d 1 (1971). Insufficiency of indictment assertable on appeal. Although defendant did not raise the insufficiency of the indictment at trial or in his motion for new trial, he is not thereby precluded from asserting that defect on appeal. People v. Westendorf, 37 Colo. App. 111, 542 P.2d 1300 (1975). Selective prosecution claim must be raised prior to trial. A selective prosecution claim is an objection based upon a defect in the institution of the prosecution, and, therefore, a defendant's failure to raise the objection in a timely motion constitutes a waiver of the objection. People v. Gallegos, 226 P.3d 1112 (Colo. App. 2009). Motion made after trial but before sentencing. A motion challenging the constitutionality of a statute preserves the issue on appeal where the motion is made after oral argument on motion for judgment of acquittal or for new trial, but before sentencing. People v. Cagle, 751 P.2d 614 (Colo. 1988). A substantive defect in an information may be raised at any time during the proceedings. People v. Williams, 961 P.2d 533 (Colo. App. 1997), aff'd in part and rev'd in part on other grounds, 984 P.2d 56 (Colo. 1999). Exceptions to duplicitous count must be made before trial. A duplicitous count in a criminal information is only a matter of form, and exceptions which go merely to form must be made before trial. Russell v. People, 155 Colo. 422, 395 P.2d 16 (1964); Specht v. People, 156 Colo. 12, 396 P.2d 838 (1964). Compulsory joinder defense not waived. Where compulsory joinder defense was not available when prosecution of felony charge was instituted because second charge had not been filed, defendant did not waive compulsory joinder claim when he failed to raise issue within twenty days after his arraignment on felony charge and, therefore, claim was not based on a defect in institution of prosecution and, thus, this rule did not prevent defendant from moving to dismiss. People v. Rogers, 742 P.2d 912 (Colo. 1987). Waiver of objection to legality of arrest. A defendant who fails to object to his arrest before trial waives his right to challenge the legality of his arrest. Massey v. People, 179 Colo. 167, 498 P.2d 953 (1972); People v. Hernandez, 695 P.2d 308 (Colo. App. 1984). Admissibility of alibi evidence. While a showing by a defendant of good cause for noncompliance

with this rule is a proper factor to be considered by a trial court in deciding whether alibi evidence should be admitted, justification for noncompliance is not the sole determinant of admissibility. People v. Moore, 36 Colo. App. 328, 539 P.2d 489 (1975). The critical consideration for admissibility of alibi evidence is whether the proffered alibi evidence should be admitted in order to assure the defendant a fair trial. People v. Moore, 36 Colo. App. 328, 539 P.2d 489 (1975). D. Hearing. Defendant's burden on motion to dismiss for want of due prosecution. A motion for discharge or for dismissal for want of due prosecution of a charge of crime must be sustained by the accused; he has the burden of showing that he was not afforded a speedy trial. Jordan v. People, 155 Colo. 224, 393 P.2d 745 (1964).

Rule 12.1 - Notice of Alibi

Colo. R. Crim. P. 12.1

Repealed March 15, 1985, effective 7/1/1985.

For present provisions on notice of alibi, see Crim. P. 16 part II(d).

Rule 13 - Trial Together of Indictments, Informations, Complaints, Summons and Complaints

Subject to the provisions of Rule 14, the court may order two or more indictments, informations, complaints, or summons and complaints to be tried together if the offenses, and the defendants, if there are more than one, could have been joined in a single indictment, information, complaint, or summons and complaint. The procedure shall be the same as if the prosecution were under such single indictment, information, complaint, or summons and complaint.

Colo. R. Crim. P. 13

Annotation Law dependent on facts of each case. The law relating to joinder and severance, and that which permits consolidation of charges, depends on the facts in each particular case. Hunter v. District Court, 193 Colo. 308, 565 P.2d 942 (1977). Evidence sufficient to justify consolidation of informations. Brown v. District Court, 197 Colo. 219, 591 P.2d 99 (1979). When defendant uses a common scheme to commit highly similar crimes, consolidation is not an abuse of discretion. People v. Gross, 39 P.3d 1279 (Colo. App. 2001); People v. Gregg, __ P.3d __ (Colo. App. 2011). Sexual assault offenses may be joined if the evidence of each offense would be admissible in separate trials. People v. Williams, 899 P.2d 306 (Colo. App. 1995). Joint trial of defendants permitted. People v. Trujillo, 181 Colo. 350, 509 P.2d 794 (1973). Joinder of unrelated charges allowed for trial on sanity issue. Joinder of a charge of forcible rape with an unrelated deviate sexual intercourse charge committed on a different female on a different date for purposes of trial on the sanity issue was not error. People v. Renfrow, 193 Colo. 131, 564 P.2d 411 (1977). Applied in People v. Lyons, 185 Colo. 112, 521 P.2d 1265 (1974); People v. Gonzales, 198 Colo. 450, 601 P.2d 1366 (1979); Jeffrey v. District Court, 626 P.2d 631 (Colo. App. 1981); Gimmy v. People, 645 P.2d 262 (Colo. 1982); Corr v. District Court, 661 P.2d 668 (Colo. 1983).

Rule 14 - Relief from Prejudicial Joinder

If it appears that a defendant or the prosecution is prejudiced by a joinder of offenses or of defendants in any indictment or information, or by such joinder for trial together, the court may order an election or separate trials of counts, grant a severance of defendants, or provide whatever other relief justice requires. However, upon motion any defendant shall be granted a separate trial as of right if the court finds that the prosecution probably will present against a joint defendant evidence, other than reputation or character testimony, which would not be admissible in a separate trial of the moving defendant, and that such evidence would be prejudicial to those against whom it is not admissible. In ruling on a motion by a defendant for severance, the court may order the prosecuting attorney to deliver to the court for inspection in camera any statements or confessions made by the defendants which the prosecution intends to introduce in evidence at the trial.

Colo. R. Crim. P. 14

Annotation Duty of trial judge. The trial judge has a duty to safeguard the rights of the accused and to ensure the fair conduct of the trial, and, in furtherance of that duty, he has broad discretion to order a separate trial of counts when their joinder would result in prejudice. People v. Fullerton, 186 Colo. 97, 525 P.2d 1166 (1974). Consolidation of trials, when the defendant uses a common scheme to commit highly similar crimes, is not an abuse of discretion. People v. Gross, 39 P.3d 1279 (Colo. App. 2001). Purpose of severance is to promote a fair determination of guilt or innocence of one or more defendants. People v. Horne, 619 P.2d 53 (Colo. 1980). Matter of election is within the sound discretion of trial court. People v. Mayfield, 184 Colo. 399,

520 P.2d 748 (1974). And motion for separate trial is addressed to sound discretion of trial court. People v. Maestas, 183 Colo. 378, 517 P.2d 461 (1973); Ruark v. People, 158 Colo. 287, 406 P.2d 91 (1965); Small v. People, 173 Colo. 304, 479 P.2d 386 (1970); Kurtz v. People, 177 Colo. 306, 494 P.2d 97 (1972); People v. Trujillo, 181 Colo. 350, 509 P.2d 794 (1973); People v. Robles, 183 Colo. 4, 514 P.2d 630 (1973); People v. Walker, 189 Colo. 545, 542 P.2d 1283 (1975); People v. Martinez, 190 Colo. 507, 549 P.2d 758 (1976); People v. McCrary, 190 Colo. 538, 549 P.2d 1320 (1976); People v. Pickett, 194 Colo. 178, 571 P.2d 1078 (1977); People v. Horne, 619 P.2d 53 (Colo. 1980); People v. Wortham, 690 P.2d 876 (Colo. App. 1984). A motion for severance is directed to the sound discretion of the trial court, and, absent an abuse of that discretion resulting in prejudice to the moving defendant, denial of the motion will not be disturbed on appeal. People v. Warren, 196 Colo. 75, 582 P.2d 663 (1978); People v. Allen, 42 Colo. App. 345, 599 P.2d 264 (1979); People v. Horne, 619 P.2d 53 (Colo. 1980); People v. Martinez, 652 P.2d 174 (Colo. App. 1981); People v. Early, 692 P.2d 1116 (Colo. App. 1984); People v. Hoefer, 961 P.2d 563 (Colo. App. 1998). And what constitutes abuse of discretion depends upon facts of each particular case. People v. Trujillo, 181 Colo. 350, 509 P.2d 794 (1973); Hunter v. District Court, 193 Colo. 308, 565 P.2d 942 (1977). To show abuse of discretion with respect to the denial of a motion to sever counts, a defendant must demonstrate that joinder caused actual prejudice and that trier of fact was unable to separate the facts and legal principles applicable to each offense. People v. Knight, 167 P.3d 141 (Colo. App. 2006); People v. Cousins, 181 P.3d 365 (Colo. App. 2007). And court granted discretion in determining prejudicial circumstances. Although this rule specifies one situation in which separate trials of joint defendants are mandatory, it leaves to the trial court's discretion the determination of what circumstances may prejudice a sole defendant if multiple counts against him are joined in a single trial. People v. Gallagher, 194 Colo. 121, 570 P.2d 236 (1977). There must be actual prejudice to the defendant and not just differences that are inherent in any trial of different offenses. People v. Pickett, 194 Colo. 178, 571 P.2d 1078 (1977); People v. Early, 692 P.2d 1116 (Colo. App. 1984); People v. Guffie, 749 P.2d 976 (Colo. App. 1987). Joinder requiring disclosure of prior conviction denies fair trial. Joinder of counts, one of which requires the disclosure of the defendant's prior conviction to the jury panel at the inception of a case, so taints the trial with the defendant's prior criminality that a fair trial on the other counts is impossible. People v. Peterson, 633 P.2d 1088 (Colo. App. 1981). And unfairness to deny defendant favorable inferences of codefendant's silence. There is a distinct element of unfairness, albeit not always prejudicial, in denying one codefendant any favorable inference to be drawn from the other's silence, for it prohibits him from urging upon the jury every point favorable to his case. People v. Warren, 196 Colo. 75, 582 P.2d 663 (1978). When denial of severance disturbed on appeal. Absent an abuse of discretion resulting in prejudice to the moving defendant, a denial of a motion for severance will not be disturbed on appeal. People v. Robles, 183 Colo. 4, 514 P.2d 630 (1973). And inartfully raised motion to sever is sufficient to preserve issue for appeal. People v. Peterson, 633 P.2d 1088 (Colo. App. 1981). Factors to be considered on motion for severance. Motion for severance will be granted when grounded on the presence of four factors: (1) The defenses of the defendants were antagonistic; (2) one defendant took the stand and his attorney could not comment on the other defendant's silence; (3) one defendant, if tried first, could conceivably testify on behalf of the other at the later trial; (4) the evidence was largely circumstantial and stronger against one defendant. People v. Robles, 183 Colo. 4, 514 P.2d 630 (1973). Necessity of severance is tested by the standard that it must be "deemed appropriate to promote a fair determination of the guilt or innocence of a defendant", and that standard, in turn, is tested by the following: (1) Whether the number of defendants or the complexity of the evidence is such that the jury will probably confuse the evidence and law applicable to each defendant; (2) whether evidence inadmissible against one defendant will be considered against the other defendant despite admonitory instructions; (3) whether there are antagonistic defenses. People v. Maestas, 183 Colo. 378, 517 P.2d 461 (1973); People v. Warren, 196 Colo. 75, 582 P.2d 663 (1978). When deciding whether to grant a motion for severance, the trial court should consider whether evidence inadmissible against one defendant will be considered against the other defendant, despite the issuance by the trial court of the proper admonitory instructions. An additional consideration is whether the defendants plan to offer antagonistic defenses. People v. Gonzales, 198 Colo. 450, 601 P.2d 1366 (1979). Important inquiry is whether the trier of fact will be able to separate the facts and legal theories applicable to each offense. People v. Pickett, 194 Colo. 178, 571 P.2d 1078 (1977); People v. Taylor, 804 P.2d 196 (Colo. App. 1990). Joinder of offenses permissible to show common elements. Joinder of sexual assault offenses is permissible where the evidence tending to prove each offense would be admissible in separate trials to show common plan, scheme, design, identity, modus operandi, motive, guilty knowledge, or intent. People v. Allen, 42 Colo. App. 345, 599 P.2d 264 (1979). Desire to testify on one count does not entitle defendant to separate trial. The mere fact that defendant wishes to testify on one count and not on the other does not automatically entitle one to severance. People v. Walker, 189 Colo. 545, 542 P.2d 1283 (1975); People v. Early, 692 P.2d 1116 (Colo. App. 1984). And fact of antagonistic defenses may not always demand severance, but certainly it justifies separate trials in many instances. Eder v. People, 179 Colo. 122, 498 P.2d 945 (1972). When separate trial not required. Where references to a defendant are carefully and completely deleted from a codefendant's written statement which also implicates the defendant and the jury is instructed that such written statement is to be considered solely for the purpose of determining the guilt or innocence of the codefendant, then, in a separate trial of the defendant as an accessory, the questioned statement, under such a limiting instruction, would be admissible on the issue of the guilt of the codefendant, and, accordingly, this rule, by its very terms, does not require a separate trial. Stewart v. People, 161 Colo. 1, 419 P.2d 650, 26 A.L.R.3d 943 (1966). Bifurcated trial before single jury did not result in defendant being denied his right to a fair trial on previous offender charges or abuse of court's discretion in denying motion for separate trials before different juries. People v. Robinson, 187 P.3d 1166 (Colo. App. 2008). When separate trial to be granted as of right. Upon motion, any defendant must be granted a separate trial as of right if the court finds that the prosecution probably will present, against a joint defendant, evidence, other than reputation or character testimony, which would not be admissible in a separate trial of the moving defendant. Ruark v. People, 158 Colo. 287, 406 P.2d 91 (1965); Kurtz v. People, 177 Colo. 306, 494 P.2d 97 (1972); People v. Horne, 619 P.2d 53 (Colo. 1980). Severance not mandatory where one codefendant testifies while other does not. The fact that one codefendant testifies while the other does not, does not mandate severance. People v. Toomer, 43 Colo. App. 182, 604 P.2d 1180 (1979). But if defendant fails to move for severance, he cannot raise question on appeal. Pineda v. People, 152 Colo. 545, 383 P.2d 793 (1963); Reed v. People, 174 Colo. 43, 482 P.2d 110 (1971); People v. Barker, 180 Colo. 28, 501 P.2d 1041 (1972). Failure to renew pretrial motion to sever waives right to challenge trial court's denial on appeal. People v. Aalbu, 696 P.2d 796 (Colo. 1985). Nor where defendant accedes to limitation on admissibility of evidence. Where the trial court rules that certain evidence is admissible only as to a codefendant and the defendant accedes to this ruling, he waives any further objection. Maes v. People, 169 Colo. 200, 454 P.2d 792 (1969). And motion need not detail specific objectionable evidence. Where the court has no basis for concluding that the defendant was aware of objectionable testimony relied on in a motion for severance of trials until after the trial commenced, and the defendant rightfully filed his motion before the evidence was presented, it is not necessary for the motion to make reference to the specific evidence being relied upon. People v. Gonzales, 43 Colo. App. 312, 602 P.2d 6 (1978), rev'd on other grounds, 198 Colo. 450, 601 P.2d 1366 (1979). But motion for severance must contain evidence which is claimed to be incompetent toward the moving party, so that the court will be given the opportunity to determine whether the one requesting a severance may be prejudiced by testimony admissible against the codefendant, but not admissible as to him. Padilla v. People, 171 Colo. 521, 470 P.2d 846 (1970); People v. Gonzales, 43 Colo. App. 312, 602 P.2d 6 (1978), rev'd on other grounds, 198 Colo. 450, 601 P.2d 1366 (1979). Applied in People v. Story, 182 Colo. 122, 511 P.2d 492 (1973); People v. Lyons, 185 Colo. 112, 521 P.2d 1265 (1974); People v. Ciari, 189 Colo. 325, 540 P.2d 1094 (1975); People v. Renfrow, 193 Colo. 131, 564 P.2d 411 (1977); People v. McGregor, 635 P.2d 912 (Colo. App. 1981); People v. Peterson, 656 P.2d 1301 (Colo. 1983); People v. Gregory, 691 P.2d 357 (Colo. App. 1984). .

Rule 15 - Depositions

(a)**Motion and Order.** The prosecutor or the defendant may file a motion supported by an affidavit any time after an indictment, information, complaint, or summons and complaint is filed requesting that the deposition of a prospective witness be taken before the court. The court may order that a deposition be taken before the court if a prospective witness may be unable to attend a trial or hearing and it is necessary to take that person's deposition to prevent injustice. The court shall identify the witness and fix the date and time for the deposition in the order and shall give every party reasonable notice of the time and place for taking the deposition. For good cause shown, the court may reschedule the date and time for the deposition.

(a.5) **Deposition by Stipulation Permitted.** The prosecution and defense may take a deposition before a judge by stipulation.

(b) Subpoena of Witness. Upon entering an order for the taking of a deposition, the court shall direct that a subpoena issue for each person named in the order and may require that any designated books, papers, documents, photographs, or other tangible objects, not privileged, be produced at the deposition. If it appears, however, that the witness will disregard a subpoena, the court may direct the sheriff to produce the prospective witness in court where the witness may be released upon personal recognizance or upon reasonable bail conditioned upon the witness's appearance at the time and place fixed for the taking of deposition. If the witness fails to give bail, the court shall remand him to custody until the deposition can be taken but in no event for longer than forty-eight hours. If the deposition be not taken within forty-eight hours, the witness shall be discharged.

(c) Presence of Defendant. The defendant shall be present at the deposition unless the defendant voluntarily fails to appear after receiving notice of the date, time, and place of the deposition.

(d) Taking and Preserving Depositions. Depositions shall be taken as directed by the court. All depositions shall be preserved by video recording at the expense of the requesting party. A copy of the video recording shall be filed with the clerk of the court and provided to the opposing party.

(e) Use. At the trial, or at any hearing, a part or all of a deposition may be used, so far as otherwise allowed by law or by stipulation.

(f) Transcripts of Depositions. The requesting party shall file a transcript of the deposition with the clerk of the court and provide a copy to the opposing party without cost.

Colo. R. Crim. P. 15

Source: Entire rule amended and adopted May 25, 2006, effective 7/1/2006; amended September 6, 2018, effective 9/6/2018.

Annotation Law reviews. For article, "Hearsay in Criminal Cases Under the Colorado Rules of Evidence: An Overview", see 50 U. Colo. L. Rev. 277 (1979). This rule limits taking of depositions in a criminal proceeding to those situations where the prospective witness "may be unable to attend a trial or hearing". Bresnahan v. District Court, 164 Colo. 263, 434 P.2d 419 (1967). Primary purpose of subdivision (e) is to safeguard the confrontation rights of the criminally accused by limiting the use of deposition testimony to narrowly defined situations of unavailability. People ex rel. Faulk v. District Court, 667 P.2d 1384 (Colo. 1983). Trial court has great discretion in determining whether to allow the taking of deposition testimony under this rule. People v. Hernandez, 899 P.2d 297 (Colo. App. 1995). A Colorado court does not have authority under this rule to order a deposition of a person outside of its jurisdiction. Trial court was in error in granting a motion to depose a witness residing in Mexico. The rule specifically provides that the deposition must be taken in the court's presence. It also logically follows that, since the rule requires the court to subpoena the witness who is to be deposed, the court may not order a deposition of any person who may not be legally served a subpoena. The provisions of the Uniform Act to Secure the Attendance of Witnesses from Without a State in Criminal Proceedings, which extends a court's jurisdiction to persons in other states, applies only within the United States and only to other states that have enacted the same law. Thus, in ordering the deposition of a person in Mexico, the district court was proceeding without jurisdiction. People v. Arellano-Avila, 20 P.3d 1191 (Colo. 2001). This rule does not allow taking of depositions for purely discovery purposes, be it in-state or out-of-state. Bresnahan v. District Court, 164 Colo. 263, 434 P.2d 419 (1967). "Unavailability" determined at time of trial. Unavailability within the context of subdivision (e) is to be determined at the time of trial in light of the circumstances then existing. The mere granting of a pretrial motion to depose a witness accords no presumption of unavailability at the time of trial. People ex rel. Faulk v. District Court, 667 P.2d 1384 (Colo. 1983); People v. Hernandez, 899 P.2d 297 (Colo. App. 1995). Showing required before deposition admitted. Before a deposition is admitted into evidence, the proponent of the deposition must make some showing, by evidence or stipulation, that the witness's inability to testify at trial is due to sickness or infirmity. Mere inconvenience or passing discomfort does not satisfy the unambiguous provisions of the rule. People ex rel. Faulk v. District Court, 667 P.2d 1384 (Colo. 1983). Affidavit not essential to motion. The purpose of the affidavit requirement in section (a) is to ensure that the court has sufficient information to decide the merits of the motion, i.e., whether a witness might be unable to attend the trial. Where the court is thoroughly informed of the facts supporting the motion by other means, and defendant does not dispute these assertions, the lack of an affidavit is not fatal. People v. Hernandez, 899 P.2d 297 (Colo. App. 1995). Lack of finding of unavailability may not constitute deprivation of rights. Where prosecution uses depositions of witnesses at trial, and the defendant was present with counsel and granted full rights of cross-examination at the time of the taking of the depositions before a judge, the defendant is not deprived of his right to confront the witnesses at the trial where the depositions are used without a finding of unavailability of the deponents when it is a matter of his counsel's trial strategy. Morse v. People, 180 Colo. 49, 501 P.2d 1328 (1972). Applied in People v. Mann, 646 P.2d 352 (Colo. 1982).

For depositions in specific circumstances, see § 18-6.5-103.5 (victims or witnesses who are at-risk adults), § 18-6-401.3 (victims of child abuse), and § 18-3-413 (children who are victims of sexual offenses), C.R.S.

Rule 16 - Discovery and Procedure Before Trial

Definitions.

(1) "Defense", as used in this rule, means an attorney for the defendant, or a defendant if pro se.

Part I. Disclosure to the Defense

(a) Prosecutor's Obligations.

(1) The prosecuting attorney shall make available to the defense the following material and information which is within the possession or control of the prosecuting attorney, and shall provide duplicates upon request, and concerning the pending case:

(I) Police, arrest and crime or offense reports, including statements of all witnesses;

(II) With consent of the judge supervising the grand jury, all transcripts of grand jury testimony and all tangible evidence presented to the grand jury in connection with the case;

(III) Any reports or statements of experts made in connection with the particular case, including results of physical or mental examinations and of scientific tests, experiments, or comparisons;

(IV) Any books, papers, documents, photographs or tangible objects held as evidence in connection with the case;

(V) Any record of prior criminal convictions of the accused, any codefendant or any person the prosecuting attorney intends to call as a witness in the case;

(VI) All tapes and transcripts of any electronic surveillance (including wiretaps) of conversations involving the accused, any codefendant or witness in the case;

(VII) A written list of the names and addresses of the witnesses then known to the district attorney whom he or she intends to call at trial;

(VIII) Any written or recorded statements of the accused or of a codefendant, and the substance of any oral statements made to the police or prosecution by the accused or by a codefendant, if the trial is to be a joint one.

(2) The prosecuting attorney shall disclose to the defense any material or information within his or her possession or control which tends to negate the guilt of the accused as to the offense charged or would tend to reduce the punishment therefor.

(3) The prosecuting attorney's obligations under this section (a) extend to material and information in the possession or control of members of his or her staff and of any others who have participated in the investigation or evaluation of the case and who either regularly report, or with reference to the particular case have reported, to his or her office.

(b) Prosecutor's Performance of Obligations.

(1) The prosecuting attorney shall perform his or her obligations under subsections (a)(1)(I), (IV), (VII), and with regard to written or recorded statements of the accused or a codefendant under (VIII) as soon as practicable but not later than 21 days after the defendant's first appearance at the time of or following the filing of charges, except that portions of such reports claimed to be nondiscoverable may be withheld pending a determination and ruling of the court under Part III but the defense must be notified in writing that information has not been disclosed.

(2) The prosecuting attorney shall request court consent and provide the defense with all grand jury transcripts made in connection with the case as soon as practicable but not later than 35 days after indictment.

(3) The prosecuting attorney shall perform all other obligations under subsection (a)(1) as soon as practicable but not later than 35 days before trial.

(4) The prosecuting attorney shall ensure that a flow of information is maintained between the various investigative personnel and his or her office sufficient to place within his or her possession or control all material and information relevant to the accused and the offense charged.

(c) Material Held by Other Governmental Personnel.

(1) Upon the defense's request and designation of material or information which would be discoverable if in the possession or control of the prosecuting attorney and which is in the possession or control of other governmental personnel, the prosecuting attorney shall use diligent good faith efforts to cause such material to be made available to the defense.

(2) The court shall issue suitable subpoenas or orders to cause such material to be made available to the defense, if the prosecuting attorney's efforts are unsuccessful and such material or other governmental personnel are subject to the jurisdiction of the court.

(d) Discretionary Disclosures.

(1) The court in its discretion may, upon motion, require disclosure to the defense of relevant material and information not covered by Parts I (a), (b), and (c), upon a showing by the defense that the request is reasonable.

(2) The court may deny disclosure authorized by this section if it finds that there is substantial risk to any person of physical harm, intimidation, bribery, economic reprisals, or unnecessary annoyance or embarrassment, resulting from such disclosure, which outweighs any usefulness of the disclosure to the defense.

(3) Where the interests of justice would be served, the court may order the prosecution to disclose the underlying facts or data supporting the opinion in that particular case of an expert endorsed as a witness. If a report has not been prepared by that expert to aid in compliance with other discovery obligations of this rule, the court may order the party calling that expert to provide a written summary of the testimony describing the witness's opinions and the bases and reasons therefor, including results of physical or mental examination and of scientific tests, experiments, or comparisons. The intent of this section is to allow the defense sufficient meaningful information to conduct effective cross- examination under CRE 705.

(e) Matters not Subject to Disclosure.

(1) Work Product. Disclosure shall not be required of legal research or of records, correspondence, reports, or memoranda to the extent that they contain the opinions, theories, or conclusions of the prosecuting attorney or members of his legal staff.

(2) Informants. Disclosure shall not be required of an informant's identity where his or her identity is a prosecution secret and a failure to disclose will not infringe the constitutional rights of the accused. Disclosure shall not be denied hereunder of the identity of witnesses to be produced at a hearing or trial.

Part II. Disclosure to Prosecution

(a) The Person of the Accused.

(1) Notwithstanding the initiation of judicial proceedings, and subject to constitutional limitations, upon request of the prosecuting attorney, the court may require the accused to give any nontestimonial identification as provided in Rule 41.1(h)(2).

(2) Whenever the personal appearance of the accused is required for the foregoing purposes, reasonable notice of the time and place of such appearance shall be given by the prosecuting attorney to the accused and his or her counsel. Provision may be made for appearance for such purposes in an order admitting the accused to bail or providing for his or her release.

(b) Medical and Scientific Reports.

(1) Subject to constitutional limitations, the trial court may require that the prosecuting attorney be informed of and permitted to inspect and copy or photograph any reports or statements of experts, made in connection with the particular case, including results of physical or mental examinations and of scientific tests, experiments, or comparisons.

(2) Subject to constitutional limitations, and where the interests of justice would be served, the court may order the defense to disclose the underlying facts or data supporting the opinion in that particular case of an expert endorsed as a witness. If a report has not been prepared by that expert to aid in compliance with other discovery obligations of this rule, the court may order the party calling that expert to provide a written summary of the testimony describing the witness's opinions and the bases and reasons therefor, including results of physical or mental examinations and of scientific tests, experiments, or comparisons. The intent of this section is to allow the prosecution sufficient meaningful information to conduct effective cross-examination under CRE 705.

(c) Nature of Defense. Subject to constitutional limitations, the defense shall disclose to the prosecution the nature of any defense, other than alibi, which the defense intends to use at trial. The defense shall also disclose the names and addresses of persons whom the defense intends to call as witnesses at trial. At the entry of the not guilty plea, the court shall set a deadline for such disclosure. In no case shall such disclosure be less than 35 days before trial for a felony trial, or 7 days before trial for a non-felony trial, except for good cause shown. Upon receipt of the information required by this subsection (c), the prosecuting attorney shall notify the defense of any additional witnesses which the prosecution intends to call to rebut such defense within a reasonable time after their identity becomes known.

(d) **Notice of Alibi**. The defense, if it intends to introduce evidence that the defendant was at a place other than the location of the offense, shall serve upon the prosecuting attorney as soon as practicable but not later than 35 days before trial a statement in writing specifying the place where he or she claims to have been and the names and addresses of the witnesses he or she will call to support the defense of alibi. Upon receiving this statement, the prosecuting attorney shall advise the defense of the names and addresses of any additional witnesses who may be called to refute such alibi as soon as practicable after their names become known. Neither the prosecuting attorney nor the defense shall be permitted at the trial to introduce evidence inconsistent with the specification, unless the court for good cause and upon just terms permits the specification to be amended. If the defense fails to make the specification required by this section, the court shall exclude evidence in his behalf that he or she was at a place other than that specified by the prosecuting attorney unless the court is satisfied upon good cause shown that such evidence should be admitted.

Part III. Regulation of Discovery

(a) **Investigation Not to be Impeded**. Subject to the provisions of Parts I (d) and III (d), neither the prosecuting attorney, the defense counsel, the defendant nor other prosecution or defense personnel shall advise persons having relevant material or information (except the defendant) to refrain from discussing the case or with showing any relevant material to any party, counsel or their agent, nor shall they otherwise impede counsel's investigation of the case. The court shall determine that the parties are aware of the provision.

(b) **Continuing Duty to Disclose**. If, subsequent to compliance with these standards or orders pursuant thereto, a party discovers additional material or information which is subject to disclosure, including the names and addresses of any additional witnesses who have become known or the materiality of whose testimony has become known to the district attorney after making available the written list required in part I (a)(1)(VII), he or she shall promptly notify the other party or his or her counsel of the existence of such additional material, and if the additional material or information is discovered during trial, the court shall also be notified.

(c) **Custody of Materials**. Materials furnished in discovery pursuant to this rule may only be used for purposes of preparation and trial of the case and may only be provided to others and used by them for purposes of preparation and trial of the case, and shall be subject to such other terms, conditions or restrictions as the court, statutes or rules may provide. Defense counsel is not required to provide actual copies of discovery to his or her client if defense counsel reasonably believes that it would not be in the client's interest, and other methods of having the client review discovery are available. An attorney may also use materials he or she receives in discovery for the purposes of educational presentations if all identifying information is first removed.

(d) **Protective Orders**. With regard to all matters of discovery under this rule, upon a showing of cause, the court may at any time order that specified disclosures be restricted or deferred, or make such other order as is appropriate, provided that all material and information to which a party is entitled must be disclosed in time to permit the party to make beneficial use thereof.

(e) **Excision**.

(1) When some parts of certain material are discoverable under the provisions of these court rules, and other parts are not discoverable, the nondiscoverable material may be excised and the remainder made available in accordance with the applicable provisions of these rules.

(2) Material excised pursuant to judicial order shall be sealed and preserved in the records of the court, to be made available to the appellate court in the event of an appeal.

(f) **In Camera Proceedings**. Upon request of any person, the court may permit any showing of cause for denial or regulation of disclosures, or portion of such showing, to be made in camera. A record shall be made of such proceedings. If the court enters an order granting relief following a showing in camera, the entire record of such showing shall be sealed and preserved in the records of the court, to be made available to the appellate court in the event of an appeal.

(g) **Failure to Comply; Sanctions**. If at any time during the course of the proceedings it is brought to the attention of the court that a party has failed to comply with this rule or with an order issued pursuant to this rule, the court may order such party to permit the discovery or inspection of materials not previously disclosed, grant a continuance, prohibit the party from

60

introducing in evidence the material not disclosed or enter such other order as it deems just under the circumstances.

Part IV. Procedure

(a) General Procedural Requirements.

(1) In all criminal cases, in procedures prior to trial, there may be a need for one or more of the following three stages:

(I) An exploratory stage, initiated by the parties and conducted without court supervision to implement discovery required or authorized under this rule;

(II) An omnibus stage, when ordered by the court, supervised by the trial court and court appearance required when necessary;

(III) A trial planning stage, requiring pretrial conferences when necessary.

(2) These stages shall be adapted to the needs of the particular case and may be modified or eliminated as appropriate.

(b) Setting of Omnibus Hearing.

(1) If a plea of not guilty or not guilty by reason of insanity is entered at the time the accused is arraigned, the court may set a time for and hold an omnibus hearing in all felony and misdemeanor cases.

(2) In determining the date for the omnibus hearing, the court shall allow counsel sufficient time:

(I) To initiate and complete discovery required or authorized under this rule;

(II) To conduct further investigation necessary to the defendant's case;

(III) To continue plea discussion.

(3) The hearing shall be no later than 35 days after arraignment.

(c) Omnibus Hearing.

(1) If an omnibus hearing is held, the court on its own initiative, utilizing an appropriate checklist form, should:

(I) Ensure that there has been compliance with the rule regarding obligations of the parties;

(II) Ascertain whether the parties have completed the discovery required in Part I (a), and if not, make orders appropriate to expedite completion;

(III) Ascertain whether there are requests for additional disclosures under Part I (d);

(IV) Make rulings on any motions or other requests then pending, and ascertain whether any additional motions or requests will be made at the hearing or continued portions thereof;

(V) Ascertain whether there are any procedural or constitutional issues which should be considered; and

(VI) Upon agreement of the parties, or upon a finding that the trial is likely to be protracted or otherwise unusually complicated, set a time for a pretrial conference.

(2) Unless the court otherwise directs, all motions and other requests prior to trial should be reserved for and presented orally or in writing at the omnibus hearing. All issues presented at the omnibus hearing may be raised without prior notice by either party or by the court. If discovery, investigation, preparation, and evidentiary hearing, or a formal presentation is necessary for a fair determination of any issue, the omnibus hearing should be continued until all matters are properly disposed of.

(3) Any pretrial motion, request, or issue which is not raised at the omnibus hearing shall be deemed waived, unless the party concerned did not have the information necessary to make the motion or request or raise the issue.

(4) Stipulations by any party or his or her counsel should be binding upon the parties at trial unless set aside or modified by the court in the interests of justice.

(5) A verbatim record of the omnibus hearing shall be made. This record shall include the disclosures made, all rulings and orders of the court, stipulations of the parties, and an identification of other matter determined or pending.

(d) Omnibus Hearing Forms.

(1) The forms set out in the Appendix to Chapter 29 shall be utilized by the court in conducting the omnibus hearing. These forms shall be made available to the parties at the time of the defendant's first appearance.

(2) Nothing in the forms shall be construed to make substantive changes of these rules.

(e) Pretrial Conference.

(1) Whenever a trial is likely to be protracted or otherwise unusually complicated, or upon request by agreement of the parties, the trial court may (in addition to the omnibus hearing) hold one or more pretrial conferences, with trial counsel present, to consider such matters as will promote a fair and expeditious trial. Matters which might be considered include:

(I) Making stipulations as to facts about which there can be no dispute;

(II) Marking for identification various documents and other exhibits of the parties;

(III) Excerpting or highlighting exhibits;

(IV) Waivers of foundation as to such documents;

(V) Issues relating to codefendant statements;

(VI) Severance of defendants or offenses for trial;

(VII) Seating arrangements for defendants and counsel;

(VIII) Conduct of jury examination, including any issues relating to confidentiality of juror locating information;

(IX) Number and use of peremptory challenges;

(X) Procedure on objections where there are multiple counsel or defendants;

(XI) Order of presentation of evidence and arguments when there are multiple counsel or defendants;

(XII) Order of cross-examination where there are multiple defendants;

(XIII) Temporary absence of defense counsel during trial;

(XIV) Resolution of any motions or evidentiary issues in a manner least likely to inconvenience jurors to the extent possible; and

(XV) Submission of items to be included in a juror notebook.

(2) At the conclusion of the pretrial conference, a memorandum of the matters agreed upon should be signed by the parties, approved by the court, and filed. Such memorandum shall be binding upon the parties at trial, on appeal and in postconviction proceedings unless set aside or modified by the court in the interests of justice. However, admissions of fact by an accused if present should bind the accused only if included in the pretrial order and signed by the accused as well as his or her attorney.

(f) Juror Notebooks. Juror notebooks shall be available during all felony trials and deliberations to aid jurors in the performance of their duties. The parties shall confer about the items to be included in juror notebooks and, by the pre-trial conference or other date set by the court, shall make a joint submission to the court of items to be included in a juror notebook. In non-felony trials, juror notebooks shall be optional.

Part V. Time Schedules and Discovery Procedures

(a) Mandatory Discovery. The furnishing of the items discoverable, referred to in Part I (a), (b) and (c) and Part II (b)(1), (c) and (d) herein, is mandatory and no motions for discovery with respect to such items may be filed.

(b) Time Schedule.

(1) In the event the defendant enters a plea of not guilty or not guilty by reason of insanity, or asserts the defense of impaired mental condition, the court shall set a deadline for such disclosure to the prosecuting attorney of those items referred to in Parts II (b) (1) and (c) herein, subject to objections which may be raised by the defense within that period pursuant to Part III (d) of this rule. In no case shall such disclosure be less than 35 days before trial for a felony trial, or 7 days before trial for a non-felony trial, except for good cause shown.

(2) Regarding the use and timing of electronic discovery.

(i) The prosecutor may perform his or her obligations by use of a statewide discovery sharing system as established pursuant to 16-9-702, C.R.S.

(ii) When utilizing such system the prosecutor's obligations to make discovery available to the defense as required by Part I are fulfilled when any such material or information is made available for electronic download to defense counsel, defense counsel's designee, or, in the case of a public defender, to the central administrative office of the Office of the State Public Defender.

(3) If either the prosecuting attorney or the defense claims that discoverable material under this rule was not furnished, was incomplete, was illegible or otherwise failed to satisfy this rule, or if claim is made that discretionary disclosures pursuant to Part I (d) should be made, the prosecuting attorney or the defense may file a motion concerning these matters and the motion shall be promptly heard by the court.

(4) For good cause, the court may, on motion of either party or its own motion, alter the time for all matters relating to discovery under this rule.

(c) Cost and Location of Discovery.

(1) The prosecution's costs of providing any discoverable material electronically to the defense shall be funded as set forth in section 16-9-702(2), C.R.S. The prosecution shall not charge for discovery. For any materials provided to the prosecution as part of the defense discovery obligation, the cost shall be borne by the prosecution based on the actual cost of duplication. Copies of any discovery provided to a defendant by court appointed counsel shall be paid for by the defendant.

(1) The place of discovery for materials not capable of being provided electronically shall be at the office of the party furnishing it, or at a mutually agreeable location.

(d) Compliance Certificate.

(1) When deemed necessary by the trial court, the prosecuting attorney and the defense shall furnish to the court a compliance certificate signed by all counsel listing specifically each item furnished to the other party. The court may, in its discretion, refuse to admit into evidence items not disclosed to the other party if such evidence was required to be disclosed under Parts I and II of this rule.

(2) If discoverable matters are obtained after the compliance certificate is filed, copies thereof shall be furnished forthwith to the opposing party and, upon application to the court, the court may either permit such evidence to be offered at trial or grant a continuance in its discretion.

Colo. R. Crim. P. 16

Source: Entire rule repealed and readopted March 15, 1985, effective 7/1/1985; Part I IP(a)(1), (a)(1)(I), and (b)(1) and Part V (d)(1) amended September 9, 1985, effective 1/1/1986; Part I (a)(1) and (b)(1) and Part III (b) amended and adopted September 4, 1997, effective 1/1/1998; Part IV (e) amended and Part IV (f) added June 25, 1998, effective 1/1/1999; Part IV (f) corrected, effective 1/7/1999; Part I (a)(1)(VI) corrected, effective 3/2/1999; Part I (a)(1)(I) and (a)(1)(VII), Part II (c), and Part V (a) and (b)(1) amended and Part I (a)(1)(VIII) and (d)(3) and Part II (b)(2) added November 4, 1999, effective 1/1/2000; entire rule amended and adopted May 17, 2001, effective 7/1/2001; entire rule amended and effective 1/17/2008; Part III (c) amended and effective 4/6/2009; Part I (b)(1), (b)(2), and (b)(3), Part II (c) and (d), Part IV (b)(3), and Part V (b)(1) amended and adopted December 14, 2011, effective 7/1/2012; amended and Adopted by the Court, En Banc, 8/24/2017, effective immediately; amended and Adopted by the Court, En Banc, 5/14/2020, effective immediately.

Annotation I. General Consideration. Law reviews. For case note, "A Proposed Rule of Criminal Pretrial Discovery", see 49 U. Colo. L. Rev. 443 (1978). For article, "Attacking the Seizure-Over-coming Good Faith", see 11 Colo. Law. 2395 (1982). For article, "Governmental Loss or Destruction of Exculpatory Evidence: A Due Process Violation", see 12 Colo. Law. 77 (1983). For article, "Discovery and Admissibility of Police Internal Investigation Reports", see 12 Colo. Law. 1745 (1983). For comment, "'Twenty Questions' Doesn't Yield Due Process: Chaney v. Brown and the Continued Need to Open Prosecutor's Files in Criminal Proceeding", see 62 Den. U. L. Rev. 193 (1985). For comment, "Limiting Prosecutorial Discovery Under the Sixth Amendment Right to Effective Assistance of Counsel: Hutchinson v. People", see 66 Den. U. L. Rev. 123 (1988). Trial court must rule on motion for disclosure of the names of confidential informants. A trial court cannot delay ruling on a defendant's motion for disclosure of the names of confidential informants, notwithstanding the agreement of the parties, on the theory that the motion would be moot if the court were to deny defendant's motion to suppress evidence because reasonable suspicion justified an investigatory stop even absent the information obtained from the confidential informants. The court must rule on the disclosure motion so that the basis for the investigatory detention can be considered in light of the totality of the circumstances. People v. Saint-Veltri, 945 P.2d 1339 (Colo. 1997). Right to pretrial discovery was nonexistent under the common law. People ex rel. Shinn v. District Court, 172 Colo. 23, 469 P.2d 732 (1970); Roybal v. People, 177 Colo. 144, 493 P.2d 9 (1972); Sergent v. People, 177 Colo. 354, 497 P.2d 983 (1972). Trial court's authority to grant discovery is limited to the categories expressly set forth in this rule. Richardson v. District Court, 632 P.2d 595 (Colo. 1981). Scope of discovery prior to preliminary hearing is specifically limited by this rule. People v. Kingsley, 187 Colo. 258, 530 P.2d 501 (1975). Categories of discoverable material do not include compelled physical examination of child victim of sexual abuse. People v. Chard, 808 P.2d 351 (Colo. 1991); People v. Melendez, 80 P.3d 883 (Colo. App. 2003), aff'd on other grounds, 102 P.3d 315 (Colo. 2004). But rule is not designed to convert preliminary hearing into a mini trial. People v. Kingsley, 187 Colo. 258, 530 P.2d 501 (1975). Defendant and prosecution granted independent rights. This rule is not conditional, but rather grants independent discovery rights to both the prosecution and the defendant. People v. District Court, 187 Colo. 333, 531 P.2d 626 (1975). Exemption from discovery under the attorney work-product doctrine is intended to ensure the privacy of a party's attorney from unnecessary intrusion by opposing parties and counsel, but this privilege is not absolute; it is not personal to the client, and it can be waived by an attorney's course of conduct. People v. Small, 631 P.2d 148 (Colo. 1981). The decision of whether to order disclosure is committed to the sound discretion of the trial court, and the court's exercise of that discretion is entitled to strong deference. People v. Vigil, 729 P.2d 360 (Colo. 1986). Technical non-compliance with rule does not constitute reversible error, and evidence is generally not improperly withheld if the defense has knowledge of it. People v. Graham, 678 P.2d 1043 (Colo. App. 1983), cert denied, 467 U.S. 1216, 104 S. Ct. 2660, 81 L. Ed. 2d 366 (1984); People v. Rivers, 727 P.2d 394 (Colo. App. 1986). Although prosecution violated this rule by the untimely disclosure of expert's report to defendant, it did not necessarily follow that the trial court's denial of defendant's motion for a continuance was reversible error, since failure to comply with discovery rules is not reversible error absent a demonstration of prejudice to the defendant. Salazar v. People, 870 P.2d 1215 (Colo. 1994). The work product doctrine, although most frequently asserted as a bar to discovery in civil litigation, applies with equal, if not greater, force in criminal prosecutions. People v. District Court, 790 P.2d 332 (Colo. 1990); People v. Ullery, 964 P.2d 539 (Colo. App. 1997), aff'd in part and rev'd in part on other grounds, 984 P.2d 586 (Colo. 1999). Witness statements in prosecutor's notes and work sheets of the prosecuting attorney or members of the prosecutor's staff are ordinarily considered non-discoverable work product because they are prepared for litigation. People v. District Court, 790 P.2d 332 (Colo. 1990). Report of an interview of a witness by a lay investigator is not prosecutor's work product and, hence, is automatically discoverable under subsection (I)(a)(1)(I). People v. Alberico, 817 P.2d 573 (Colo. App. 1991). Section 19-1-307(2) does not provide equal access to social services records in a criminal case, and it changes the automatic disclosure process contemplated by subsection (I)(a)(1) of this rule. People v. Jowell, 199 P.3d 38 (Colo. App. 2008). Section 19-1-307(2)(f) limits defendant's access to items that the court, after an in camera review, determines necessary for the resolution of an issue. Therefore, defendant cannot expect automatic disclosure of records within the possession and control of prosecuting attorney. Instead, defendant must request an in camera review, identify the information sought, and explain why disclosure is necessary for resolution of an issue. To achieve the broadest possible disclosure, defendant should explain the relevance and materiality of the information sought. People v. Jowell, 199 P.3d 38 (Colo. App. 2008). Prosecutor has full access to records while investigating a report of known or suspected incident of child abuse or neglect. Section 19-1-307(2)(f) does not suspend prosecutor's obligation to disclose information that is materially favorable to defendant, but it does change it. The duty to disclose is subject to the in camera review process in § 19-1-307(2)(f). Therefore, if the prosecutor believes a social services record contains information it must disclose, the prosecutor must ask the trial court to conduct an in camera review of the information to determine if disclosure is necessary for the resolution of an issue. If the trial court determines the information is necessary, then it is disclosed to the defendant. The prosecutor does not have the right to offer the material into evidence without first obtaining the trial court's approval. People v. Jowell, 199 P.3d 38 (Colo. App. 2008). Section 19-1-307(2)(f) places the trial court in the middle of a procedural issue that normally would have been handled by counsel through the automatic disclosure requirements under subsection (I)(a)(1) of this rule. The trial court must review the records to determine whether the records are necessary for the resolution of an issue. Although the determination of whether the records should be disclosed must be made on case-specific circumstances, there are three principles that apply generally. First, under due process considerations, the trial court must disclose any information that is materially favorable to defendant because it is either exculpatory or impeaching. Second, the trial court should disclose inculpatory information when the information would materially assist in preparing the defense. Finally, it may be significant, although not determinative, that the information would be otherwise subject to automatic disclosure under subsection (I)(a)(1) of this rule. People v. Jowell, 199 P.3d 38 (Colo. App. 2008). For history of this rule, see People v. Adams County Court, 767 P.2d 802 (Colo. App. 1988). Applied in Oaks v. People, 161 Colo. 561, 424 P.2d 115 (1967); People v. Couch, 179 Colo. 324, 500 P.2d 967 (1972); People v. Smith, 179 Colo. 413, 500 P.2d 1177 (1972); People v. Manier, 184 Colo. 44, 518 P.2d 811 (1974); People v. Smith, 185 Colo. 369, 524 P.2d 607 (1974); People v. Steed, 189 Colo. 212, 540 P.2d 323 (1975); People v. Pearson, 190 Colo. 313, 546 P.2d 1259 (1976); People v. Henderson, 38 Colo. App. 308, 559 P.2d 1108 (1976); People v. Bloom, 195 Colo. 246, 577 P.2d 288 (1978); Goodwin v. District Court, 196 Colo. 246, 588

P.2d 874 (1979); People v. Davenport, 43 Colo. App. 41, 602 P.2d 871 (1979); People v. Schlegel, 622 P.2d 98 (Colo. App. 1980); People v. Callis, 666 P.2d 1100 (Colo. App. 1982), aff'd in part and rev'd in part, 692 P.2d 1045 (Colo. 1984); Denbow v. Williams, 672 P.2d 1011 (Colo. 1983); People v. Aalbu, 696 P.2d 796 (Colo. 1985); People v. Madsen, 743 P.2d 437 (Colo. App. 1987). II. Disclosure to Defendant. Remedial purpose of automatic disclosure requirement in subsection (I)(a)(1) is broader than merely to ensure disclosure of evidence known to prosecution but unknown to defense. Disclosure of evidence within scope of rule is required whether or not material to the case, whether or not requested by defense, and whether or not it pertains to witnesses endorsed by the defense or who would be called by prosecution only for rebuttal purposes. Rule is designed to avoid loss of defendants' rights through inadvertent failure to make timely requests and to minimize court's supervisory role in basic discovery process, and to this end disclosure must be automatic unless prosecution takes specified action. People v. Alberico, 817 P.2d 573 (Colo. App. 1991). Written notification expressly required if prosecutor deems material not discoverable. People v. Alberico, 817 P.2d 573 (Colo. App. 1991). This rule governs the obligation of the prosecutor to cooperate with the defendant in the securing of evidence. Thus the prosecutor is obligated to give the names and addresses of witnesses as well as reports, statements, etc., of experts it intends to use. People v. Diefenderfer, 784 P.2d 741 (Colo. 1989). Duty of prosecution and courts to disclose evidence favorable to defendant. It is the duty of both the prosecution and the courts to see that no known evidence in the possession of the state which might tend to prove a defendant's innocence is withheld from the defense before or during trial. Cheatwood v. People, 164 Colo. 334, 435 P.2d 402 (1967); People v. Millitello, 705 P.2d 514 (Colo. 1985); People v. Terry, 720 P.2d 125 (Colo. 1986). The prosecution is obligated to disclose to the defendant evidence favorable to the accused. People v. Austin, 185 Colo. 229, 523 P.2d 989 (1974). This rule does not conflict with § 18-6-403(3)(b). Therefore the prosecution was required to provide the defense an opportunity to examine photographs under the same conditions as the prosecution. People v. Arapahoe County Court, 74 P.3d 429 (Colo. App. 2003). Scope of discovery includes names, photographs, and statements. Where the defense seeks discovery, the defense should be given access to the names of those whose prints have been compared, photographs of the crime scene, and statements which the defendant has made prior to the time he testifies at trial. Hervey v. People, 178 Colo. 38, 495 P.2d 204 (1972). This rule clearly grants defense counsel the right to obtain names of witnesses and any statements which they might have given prior to the preliminary hearing. People v. Kingsley, 187 Colo. 258, 530 P.2d 501 (1975). This rule requires that every statement made by the accused which is in the possession or control of the district attorney and which relates in any way to the series of events from which the charges pending against the accused arose must be disclosed to the defense upon an appropriate motion. People v. McKnight, 626 P.2d 678 (Colo. 1981). And appropriate portions of grand jury minutes. A prosecuting attorney shall disclose to defense counsel those portions of grand jury minutes containing testimony of the accused and relevant testimony of persons whom the prosecuting attorney intends to call as witnesses at the hearing or trial. Parlapiano v. District Court, 176 Colo. 521, 491 P.2d 965 (1971). This rule permits discovery of grand jury testimony of a party. Robles v. People, 178 Colo. 181, 496 P.2d 1003 (1972). Even where trial is upon a direct information. Examination of the grand jury testimony of a witness testifying at the trial is to be permitted whether the trial is upon an indictment or upon a direct information when the grand jury has not returned any indictment. Norman v. People, 178 Colo. 190, 496 P.2d 1029 (1972). Disclosure not dependent on showing of particularized need. A disclosure of grand jury testimony should be granted without a showing of a particularized need. Parlapiano v. District Court, 176 Colo. 521, 491 P.2d 965 (1971); McNulty v. People, 180 Colo. 246, 504 P.2d 335 (1972). Although automatic disclosure of grand jury testimony not required. The liberal discovery rights which have been granted to a defendant in this state do not guarantee automatic access to everything that transpires before the grand jury. Parlapiano v. District Court, 176 Colo. 521, 491 P.2d 965 (1971); People v. District Court, 199 Colo. 398, 610 P.2d 490 (1980). Refusal to allow examination of grand jury testimony held not error. Robles v. People, 178 Colo. 181, 496 P.2d 1003 (1972). Generally, defendant has no constitutional right to compel disclosure of a confidential informant, but consideration of fundamental fairness sometimes requires that identity of such informant be revealed. People v. Dailey, 639 P.2d 1068 (Colo. 1982); People v. Vigil, 729 P.2d 360 (Colo. 1986). In determining whether the government's privilege of not disclosing informants should yield in a particular case, court must balance the public's interest in protecting the flow of information to law enforcement officials about criminal activity against the defendant's need to obtain evidence necessary for the preparation of a defense. People v.

Bueno, 646 P.2d 931 (Colo. 1982); People v. Vigil, 729 P.2d 360 (Colo. 1986). Defendant not entitled to the disclosure of informant based on assertion that his defense requires it, but such disclosure may be ordered only where the defendant has established a reasonable basis in fact to believe the informant is a likely source of relevant and helpful evidence to the accused. People v. Bueno, 646 P.2d 931 (Colo. 1982); People v. Vigil, 729 P.2d 360 (Colo. 1986). A defendant is presumptively entitled to cross-examine a prosecution witness as to the witness's address and place of employment. Absent sufficient justification for withholding this information, a defendant's right to it is unqualified, and the defendant is under no obligation to provide reasons for seeking it. People ex. rel Dunbar v. District Court, 177 Colo. 429, 494 P.2d 841 (1972); People v. Thurman, 787 P.2d 646 (Colo. 1990). The trial court, in exercising its sound discretion, is in the best position to assess the basis for and seriousness of the witness's apprehension. When such apprehension is expressed, the key consideration for a trial court in assessing a defendant's constitutional claim to a witness's identity, address or place of employment is whether in absence of that information the defendant will have sufficient opportunity to place the witness in his proper setting. People v. Thurman, 787 P.2d 646 (Colo. 1990). The rule that an adequate showing by the prosecution that the witness legitimately fears for his safety requires some showing in turn by the defendant that the disclosure is so material as to outweigh the matter of the safety of the witness followed by a balancing of interests by the trial court should not be interpreted as requiring a threshold demonstration by the defendant that the information to be developed from learning the witness's identity, address and place of employment would prove highly material. The defendant's burden extends only to showing that the confidential informant is a material witness on the issue of guilt and that nondisclosure would deprive the defendant of a fair opportunity to test the witness's credibility. People v. Thurman, 787 P.2d 646 (Colo. 1990); People v. Turley, 870 P.2d 498 (Colo. App. 1993). A witness's assertion of concern for personal safety does not have a talismanic quality automatically giving the witness the right to withhold information about identity, address and place of employment. Rather, the proper resolution of such issues requires careful attention to the facts of each case and application of the law concerning the right of an accused to confront adverse witnesses. People v. Thurman, 787 P.2d 646 (Colo. 1990). Witnesses' personal safety outweighs defendant's confrontation right, as evidenced by the delay in the disclosure of their identities until they had been placed under witness protection. Witnesses' former addresses and telephone numbers should not be disclosed. People v. District Court, 933 P.2d 22 (Colo. 1997). Dismissal of an action may be ordered in proper circumstances if the government declines to disclose a confidential informant in accordance with the court's order. People v. Martinez, 658 P.2d 260 (Colo. 1983); People v. Vigil, 729 P.2d 360 (Colo. 1986). Dismissal was not warranted where the evidence that the prosecution failed to disclose was not exculpatory to the defendant, and the trial court's proposed remedy was a continuance conditioned on defendant's waiver of speedy trial until the date of the continuance. People v. Loggins, 981 P.2d 630 (Colo. App. 1998). Trial court properly granted defendant additional time at trial to review previously undisclosed bank records for which summaries had been provided. Material was not exculpatory to defendant, there was no prejudice to defendant, and the information was relevant to show what defendant did with the victim's money. People v. Pagan, 165 P.3d 724 (Colo. App. 2006). The decision to order disclosure of a witness's address and place of employment was committed to the sound discretion of the trial court. If there is evidence in the record to support the trial court's order compelling disclosure despite the witness's apprehension, the prosecution's willful refusal to comply with that order was properly sanctioned by the trial court under subsection (III)(g). People v. Thurman, 787 P.2d 646 (Colo. 1990). The trial court acted within the bounds of its discretion in dismissing an information against the defendants where no actual threat was made against a witness, the trial court attempted to accommodate all parties by limiting disclosure to defense counsel alone, both the witness's and place of employment were withheld, and without the sought-after information the defense could not place the witness in her proper setting. People v. Thurman, 787 P.2d 646 (Colo. 1990). Dismissal was appropriate sanction where disclosure of investigator's report of interview of victim was not made until after victim had testified, defense was in the midst of presenting its case, and alternative sanction of striking victim's testimony would have been tantamount to dismissal. People v. Alberico, 817 P.2d 573 (Colo. App. 1991). Written statements outside possession and control of prosecution cannot be discovered pursuant to this rule. Dickerson v. People, 179 Colo. 146, 499 P.2d 1196 (1972); People v. Garcia, 690 P.2d 869 (Colo. App. 1984). However, statements in possession of police are within "possession or control" of the prosecuting attorney so as to meet the requirement of this rule. Ortega v. People, 162 Colo. 358, 426 P.2d 180 (1967). Material in possession of the

66

police is constructively in the possession of the prosecution. People v. Lucero, 623 P.2d 424 (Colo. App. 1980). Offense report not within scope of discovery. An offense report, although signed by a complaining witness, is not within the scope of a pretrial discovery order as it is not a statement of a witness; it is, in fact, a compilation of information relating to the commission of crimes. People v. Morgan, 189 Colo. 256, 539 P.2d 130 (1975). As internal police documents are not within purview of pretrial discovery order. People v. Morgan, 189 Colo. 256, 539 P.2d 130 (1975); Losavio v. Mayber, 178 Colo. 184, 496 P.2d 1032 (1972). When contents of police records discoverable. Where the district attorney's office regularly receives information from police records, defense attorneys, including public defenders, are entitled to obtain such information in possession of prosecution. Losavio v. Mayber, 178 Colo. 184, 496 P.2d 1032 (1972). Prosecution's failure to provide defendant with a written police incident report violated this section, but a new trial was not required because the report was either cumulative to information provided to the defense or was immaterial to the outcome of the trial, and the judge allowed defendant a continuance to study the document and the opportunity to examine witnesses as to its contents. People v. Banuelos, 674 P.2d 964 (Colo. App. 1983). Failure by prosecution to provide defendant statement codefendant made to federal drug enforcement administration agent harmless error because defendant was not tried jointly with codefendant who had already pled guilty and been sentenced prior to defendant's trial and because defendant knew of the statement and its contents but failed to request it. People v. Montalvo-Lopez, 215 P.3d 1139 (Colo. App. 2008). Discovery costs. Prior to requiring the public defender's office to pay costs of copying a police officer's file for an in camera review by the court, the court should make the following specific findings: Was the defendant's subpoena unreasonable or oppressive and were the city's proffered concerns as to use and possible loss justified? The court should consider whether adequate safeguards could be provided for an initial in camera review of the original documents and whether any payment should be limited to actual costs. In doing so, the court must balance the government's interests against defendant's interests in disclosure. People v. Trujillo, 62 P.3d 1034 (Colo. App. 2002), rev'd on other grounds, 83 P.3d 642 (Colo. 2004). Where defendant received forensics report linking him to tire slashing incident prior to trial and the court allowed the defendant to interview the report's introducing witness prior to testifying, court's admission of the evidence in an arson prosecution was not reversible error even though defendant claimed the evidence had not been disclosed to him. People v. Copeland, 976 P.2d 334 (Colo. App. 1998), aff'd on other grounds, 2 P.3d 1283 (Colo. 2000). Notes of interviews with witnesses discoverable. This rule includes not only materials which have been signed or adopted by the government's witness, but also notes taken by officers when talking to the witness. Ortega v. People, 162 Colo. 358, 426 P.2d 180 (1967). Defendant's right to discovery of a witness's statement includes the right to examine notes which are substantial recitals of the statement and were reduced to writing contemporaneously with the making of the statement. People v. Shaw, 646 P.2d 375 (Colo. 1982). All that is required is that notes be substantially verbatim recitals of the oral statement. Ortega v. People, 162 Colo. 358, 426 P.2d 180 (1967); People v. Thatcher, 638 P.2d 760 (Colo. 1981). Notes must not contain the interpretations, impressions, comments, ideas, opinions, conclusions, evaluations, or summaries of the person transcribing the notes. Ortega v. People, 162 Colo. 358, 426 P.2d 180 (1967). Destruction of notes not necessarily violation of rule. Destruction of written notes made by a government agent during the taping of a phone conversation is not a violation of this rule when the substance of that conversation is set forth in the agent's formal report and made available to the defendant. People v. Alonzi, 40 Colo. App. 507, 580 P.2d 1263 (1978), aff'd, 198 Colo. 160, 597 P.2d 560 (1979). Failure to disclose prosecutor's notes of an interview with a defense expert witness before the prosecutor relied on the notes when cross-examining the witness was harmless error, even if assumed to be a discovery violation, where the notes were provided to defense counsel during the cross-examination in time for redirect examination of the witness the next day. People v. Pasillas-Sanchez, 214 P.3d 520 (Colo. App. 2009). Right to discover statements of prosecution witnesses not absolute. The defendant does not have an absolute right to discover statements of prosecution witnesses under any and all circumstances. People v. Smith, 185 Colo. 369, 524 P.2d 607 (1974). Witness statements included in prosecution's notes and emails are not automatically discoverable. Those statements are only provided to the defense if they contain exculpatory information or if the trial court, exercising its discretion, finds the information is relevant, unavailable from any other source, and request is reasonable. People v. Vlassis, 247 P.3d 196 (Colo. 2011). Court granted discretion to require disclosure. This rule vests in the trial court discretion to require disclosure prior to trial of any relevant material and information. People ex rel. Shinn v. District Court, 172 Colo. 23, 469 P.2d 732 (1970). Trial court must exercise sound discretion in permitting discovery under part I (e)(1) (now (d)(1)), guided by the standards suggested in part I (e)(2) (now (d)(2)). People v. Maestas, 183 Colo. 378, 517 P.2d 461 (1973); People v. Smith, 185 Colo. 369, 524 P.2d 607 (1974). And in granting discovery, court may enter appropriate protective orders under part III (d). People v. Smith, 185 Colo. 369, 524 P.2d 607 (1974). And trial court's discovery ruling may consider judicial economy as long as constitutional rights are not violated. People v. Thatcher, 638 P.2d 760 (Colo. 1981). Defendant must prove prejudice to show abuse of discretion. To show an abuse of discretion in not permitting discovery, the facts must reveal that the defendant was prejudiced. People v. Maestas, 183 Colo. 378, 517 P.2d 461 (1973). When court may refuse discovery of relevant testimony. It is within the sound discretion of the court to refuse to compel discovery of what may be relevant testimony where defense counsel had the opportunity and failed to institute timely discovery. People v. Thatcher, 638 P.2d 760 (Colo. 1981). But discovery compelled when information of material importance to defense. Where the defense has made a specific request for certain information in the possession or control of the prosecution, discovery of that information is constitutionally compelled, not only when it is exculpatory, but also when it is of material importance to the defense. People v. Thatcher, 638 P.2d 760 (Colo. 1981); Chambers v. People, 682 P.2d 1173 (Colo. 1984). Discovery material used for impeachment purposes is of material importance. The use of discovery material for impeachment purposes implicates the due process rights of the defendant and is of material importance to the defense. People v. Thatcher, 638 P.2d 760 (Colo. 1981); People v. Hamer, 689 P.2d 1147 (Colo. App. 1984). Material to be used for impeachment purposes is subject to the discovery provisions of this rule. People v. Rivers, 727 P.2d 394 (Colo. App. 1986). "Material" defined. In the context of a completed trial, "material," constitutionally, means evidence which, when evaluated in light of the entire record, likely would have affected the outcome of the trial. People v. Shaw, 646 P.2d 375 (Colo. 1982); People v. Hamer, 689 P.2d 1147 (Colo. App. 1984); People v. Wilson, 841 P.2d 337 (Colo. App. 1992). And refusal to disclose such evidence mandates reversal. Where information sought on discovery by a defendant might have affected the outcome of the trial, failure to disclose that information mandates reversal of trial court's guilty verdict. People v. Thatcher, 638 P.2d 760 (Colo. 1981). Minimal showing of necessity required of defendant. A defendant seeking disclosure must make a minimal showing of necessity, and mere speculation concerning the need for disclosure will not suffice. People v. McLean, 633 P.2d 513 (Colo. App. 1981). Defense counsel to determine relevance and usefulness of statement to defense. Generally, defense counsel is the appropriate party to make the determination that a statement is relevant to the conduct of the defense. People v. Gallegos, 644 P.2d 920 (Colo. 1982). Determination of usefulness of evidence under part I (e) (now (d)) is a defense function, not a prosecutorial function, as only the defense can determine what will be material and helpful to its case. People v. Smith, 185 Colo. 369, 524 P.2d 607 (1974). And statement need not be admissible to be relevant. A witness' statement, to be relevant, need not contain information admissible at trial, as long as the contents of the statement are relevant to the conduct of the defense. People v. Gallegos, 644 P.2d 920 (Colo. 1982). But must tend to prove or disprove fact of consequence. Information which would not tend to prove or disprove any fact that is of consequence to the defendant's guilt or innocence is not relevant and need not be disclosed under part I (a)(1)(I). People v. Gallegos, 644 P.2d 920 (Colo. 1982). Whether nondisclosure is erroneous depends on all circumstances of case, the nature of the crime charged, and possible defenses, as well as the possible significance of the informant's testimony. People v. Peterson, 40 Colo. App. 102, 576 P.2d 175 (1977). Prosecution not required to furnish statements of anticipated witnesses. A discovery order does not impose an affirmative obligation on the prosecution to reduce the oral statements of anticipated witnesses to writing and to furnish the substance of their testimony to the defense. People v. Garcia, 627 P.2d 255 (Colo. App. 1980). Subsection (a)(1) of part I specifically requires disclosure only of the substance of oral statements made by the accused, or, if a joint trial is to be held, by a codefendant, and, aside from these specified situations, additional disclosure of oral statements is not mandated. People v. Garcia, 627 P.2d 255 (Colo. App. 1980). Prosecution fulfilled its discovery obligations by providing notice that officer would testify and providing officer's written report. Prosecution was not required to reduce the substance of the officer's anticipated testimony to writing and furnish it to the defense before trial. People v. Knight, 167 P.3d 141 (Colo. App. 2006). Subsection (I)(a)(1)(I) requires the prosecution to provide the defense only with the written statements of witnesses or any written reports that quote or summarize oral statements made by witnesses. If the supreme court had intended the disclosure of unrecorded oral statements, then it would have so specified. People v. Denton, 91 P.3d 388 (Colo. App. 2003). No abuse of discretion where trial court found

68

prosecution had not committed a discovery violation by failing to disclose certain oral statements that the victim made to a police officer and to the prosecutor. The victim's statements were not exculpatory, and nothing in the record suggests that the prosecutor or the police officer deliberately refrained from reducing the victim's statements to writing in order to avoid a discovery obligation. People v. Denton, 91 P.3d 388 (Colo. App. 2003). When disclosure of rebuttal witness unnecessary. The requirement, contained in part (II)(c), that the prosecution disclose the identity of its rebuttal witnesses under certain circumstances, is inapplicable where the rebuttal testimony is not introduced to refute a defense, but is introduced solely to impeach the credibility of a defense witness. People v. Vollentine, 643 P.2d 800 (Colo. App. 1982). The disclosure requirements of this rule are not applicable to impeachment testimony which does not contradict alibi evidence but does attack the credibility of defense witnesses on matters collateral to the alibi defense. People v. Muniz, 622 P.2d 100 (Colo. 1980). And prosecution not required to disclose which witnesses will be called for rebuttal. Neither this rule nor § 16-5-203 specifically requires the prosecution to endorse or to disclose which of the endorsed witnesses it will call for rebuttal. People v. Hamrick, 624 P.2d 1333 (Colo. App. 1979), aff'd, 624 P.2d 1320 (Colo. 1981); People v. Avila, 944 P.2d 673 (Colo. App. 1997). Disclosure of identity of confidential informant. The prosecution's privilege to refuse to disclose the identity of a confidential informant is subject to a defendant's right to disclosure of the identity of an informant when the informant's testimony or identity is relevant or helpful to the defense of the accused or is necessary to a fair determination of the cause. People v. McLean, 633 P.2d 513 (Colo. App. 1981). When determining whether the identity of a confidential informant should be disclosed, the trial court must balance the needs of law enforcement officials to preserve the anonymity of the informant with the defendant's right to obtain evidence necessary for the preparation of his defense. People v. Gable, 647 P.2d 246 (Colo. App. 1982). When informant's identity to be disclosed. The interests of a fair trial require disclosure of the informant's identity if the facts reveal that he is "so closely related" to the defendant as to make his testimony highly material. People v. Peterson, 40 Colo. App. 102, 576 P.2d 175 (1977). When informant's identity not be disclosed. There was no prejudicial error in the denial of appellant's motion to disclose the informer's identity where the trial judge concluded that the public's and the informer's interest in preserving his anonymity outweighed appellant's interest in disclosure. People v. Mulligan, 193 Colo. 509, 568 P.2d 449 (1977). This rule does not require the prosecution to specifically identify that a witness is an expert witness, although that is the better practice. People v. Greer, 262 P.3d 920 (Colo. App. 2011). Under reciprocal discovery order, defendant was not entitled to disclosure of police interview with witness which concerned crime other than that with which the defendant was charged. People v. Green, 759 P.2d 814 (Colo. App. 1988). Prosecution's duty is to keep in contact with witness to offense. The prosecution is under a duty to make reasonable and good faith efforts to keep in contact with an eye and ear witness to an alleged criminal offense from the time the decision to file charges is made. People v. Velasquez, 645 P.2d 850 (Colo. 1982); People v. Rodriguez, 645 P.2d 851 (Colo. 1982); People v. Wandel, 696 P.2d 288 (Colo. 1985), cert. denied, 474 U.S. 1032, 106 S. Ct. 592, 88 L. Ed. 2d 572 (1985). However, this duty does not include the obligation to establish and employ a regularized method of maintaining contact with the informant. People v. Wandel, 696 P.2d 288 (Colo. 1985), cert. denied, 474 U.S. 1032, 106 S. Ct. 592, 88 L. Ed. 2d 572 (1985). Lack of full name or current address not violation of disclosure obligation. Although the prosecution is obligated to provide all pertinent information in its possession which might assist the defense in locating the informant, if such information does not contain the informant's full name or current address, the disclosure obligation may, nonetheless, still be satisfied. People v. Velasquez, 645 P.2d 850 (Colo. 1982); People v. Rodriguez, 645 P.2d 851 (Colo. 1982). Charges dismissed for failure to disclose informant's address. People v. Velasquez, 645 P.2d 850 (Colo. 1982); People v. Rodriguez, 645 P.2d 851 (Colo. 1982). Prosecution must disclose to the defense any evidence within the prosecution's possession or control that tends to negate the guilt of the accused as to the offense charged, or tends to reduce the punishment therefor. People v. Bradley, 25 P.3d 1271 (Colo. App. 2001). Tangible evidence must be preserved and made available to defendant, where it may assist defense. People v. Morgan, 199 Colo. 237, 606 P.2d 1296 (1980). Requirements of part I (a)(1)(IV) (now (a)(1)(III)) met. Where the trial court denied a defense motion to allow the defense's expert to examine a sample of the alleged cocaine in the expert's lab, but did allow the defense expert to examine a sample of cocaine in the forensic laboratory at the Denver general hospital and also ordered the disclosure of the test results of the people's expert, this met the requirements of part I (a)(1)(IV) (now (a)(1)(III)). People v. Brown, 185 Colo. 272, 523 P.2d 986 (1974). Test to determine whether destruction of evidence violates due process. There is a three-

prong test to determine whether the loss or destruction of evidence by the state, with the result that the defendant is denied access to that evidence, violates a defendant's right to due process of law: (1) Whether the evidence was suppressed or destroyed by the prosecution; (2) whether the evidence is exculpatory; and (3) whether the evidence is material to the defendant's case. People v. Garries, 645 P.2d 1306 (Colo. 1982). For the imposition of a judicial sanction in connection with a defendant's due process claim based upon the loss or destruction of evidence, the record must show that the destroyed evidence is constitutionally material. People v. Shaw, 646 P.2d 375 (Colo. 1982). (See note above, with the catchline "'Material' defined.") No due process violation where mere claim that evidentiary material could have been subjected to tests and a failure to preserve that evidence, unless an accused can show bad faith on the part of the police. People v. Wyman, 788 P.2d 1278 (Colo. 1990); People v. Apodaca, 998 P.2d 25 (Colo. App. 1999).

Failure to comply with this rule is not reversible error unless the withheld evidence was material to guilt or punishment. No due process violation unless the accused can show bad faith by the police or the prosecution. People v. Bradley, 25 P.3d 1271 (Colo. App. 2001). Where testimony about destroyed evidence suppressed, defendant not entitled to dismissal of complaint. Where all physical evidence collected by law enforcement officers in the investigation of a crime was destroyed or released prior to the defendant's arrest, so it was unavailable to him at trial, and the defendant is granted an order suppressing testimony by officers about the missing evidence, he is not entitled to a dismissal of the complaint against him. People v. Archuleta, 43 Colo. App. 474, 607 P.2d 1032 (1979). Discovery during trial of prior out-of-court statement. Under this rule defense counsel is provided with access to a witness' out-of-court statements immediately after the witness testifies on direct examination. Robles v. People, 178 Colo. 181, 496 P.2d 1003 (1972). Notes of district attorney are not within ambit of this rule and are not to be furnished to defense counsel. Hopper v. People, 152 Colo. 405, 382 P.2d 540 (1963); Rapue v. People, 171 Colo. 324, 466 P.2d 925 (1970); Norman v. People, 178 Colo. 190, 496 P.2d 1029 (1972). Prosecution's notes on voir dire are protected by the work product doctrine even under a Batson challenge. People v. Trujillo, 15 P.3d 1104 (Colo. App. 2000). Record of witnesses' oral statement not protected as work product. Where the majority of notes are in substance a record of oral statements made by witnesses, such notes are not protected by the work-product exception. People v. Thatcher, 638 P.2d 760 (Colo. 1981). Finding of denial of fair trial because of violation of rule. People v. Edgar, 40 Colo. App. 377, 578 P.2d 666 (1978). Where district attorney learned of physician's opinion in an oral interview, and it appeared that the interview was not recorded in any manner, and the defense learned of physician's opinion before trial and did not request a continuance, the district attorney was under no duty to furnish the opinion to the defendant, and there was no prejudice to defendant. People v. Graham, 678 P.2d 1043 (Colo. App. 1983), cert. denied, 467 U.S. 1216, 104 S. Ct. 2660, 81 L. Ed. 2d 366 (1984). A compelling reason or need for an involuntary psychological examination of a victim must be shown before the trial court will grant such a motion by the defense. The defendant's right to a fair trial must be balanced against the victim's privacy interests. People v. Chard, 808 P.2d 351 (Colo. 1991); People v. Turley, 870 P.2d 498 (Colo. App. 1993). Defendant failed to show he was prejudiced by the late disclosure of the prosecution's expert's report where, at the time the report was disclosed, defendant had already obtained the services of an expert witness to examine evidence and 25 days still remained to review prosecution's expert's report and perform additional tests if desired. Salazar v. People, 870 P.2d 1215 (Colo. 1994). Defendant's failure to move for continuance, after admission of incriminating evidence at trial, discredited any claim of prejudice arising from alleged discovery violation. People v. Wieghard, 727 P.2d 383 (Colo. App. 1986). Mere speculation regarding the court's disposition of a motion for a continuance or to recall a witness does not obviate the defendant's duty to seek such procedures if the defendant is to base his claim of prejudice on the inability to prepare new theories of defense or to cross-examine past witnesses in light of previously undisclosed evidence. Salazar v. People, 870 P.2d 1215 (Colo. 1994). Information in possession of detective concerning drug use and crimes of prosecution witness is covered by this rule, and failure of prosecution to disclose such information violates this rule even if prosecutor had no actual knowledge of the information. People v. District Court, 793 P.2d 163 (Colo. 1990). Trial court's refusal to order the prosecution to obtain and disclose the criminal histories of all prosecution witnesses, including police officers, was not in error. Trial court's order requiring the prosecution to disclose any criminal history of a police officer witness of which it is aware was held to not be in error. People v. Fox, 862 P.2d 1000 (Colo. App. 1993). The sanction for nondisclosure applies only against the prosecution and not against a co-defendant; a co-defendant in a joint trial should be able to use prior felony convictions to impeach the testimony of a defendant who chooses to testify. People v. Lesney, 855 P.2d 1364 (Colo. 1993). No mistrial resulted when the prosecution refused to provide defendant with the readouts printed by the instruments used to reach the test results. This rule requires only that the expert's report and the results be provided, and defendant had the results for four months before trial and did not file a motion indicating the results were incomplete or inadequate. People v. Evans, 886 P.2d 288 (Colo. App. 1994). Defendant's statement was not subject to the mandatory disclosure provisions of subsection (I)(a)(2), or the constitutional obligation to disclose exculpatory information where the trial court found defendant's testimony implausible and essentially made a finding of fact that the statement was not made. Salazar v. People, 870 P.2d 1215 (Colo. 1994). Prosecution not required to disclose derivative trial exhibits of identical content that prosecution prepared from disclosed material. People v. Armijo, 179 P.3d 134 (Colo. App. 2007). Applied in People v. Shannon, 683 P.2d 792 (Colo. 1984); People v. Doss, 782 P.2d 1198 (Colo. App. 1989); People v. Cobb, 962 P.2d 944 (Colo. 1998). III. Disclosure to Prosecution. Part II (b) is constitutional on its face, as it does not violate the privilege against self-incrimination. People v. District Court, 187 Colo. 333, 531 P.2d 626 (1975). Part II (c) is constitutional on its face, as it does not violate the privilege against self-incrimination. People v. District Court, 187 Colo. 333, 531 P.2d 626 (1975). Trial court to determine whether discovery will violate defendant's constitutional rights. The trial court, in ruling on the prosecution's motions under this rule, must first determine whether discovery which has been objected to will constitute a violation of the defendant's constitutional rights. People v. District Court, 187 Colo. 333, 531 P.2d 626 (1975); People v. Castro, 854 P.2d 1262 (Colo. 1993). A balancing approach may be used to measure the state's interest in enforcing discovery rules against the defendant's right to call witnesses in his favor. The factors considered in such approach include: (1) Whether the discovery violation was willful or in bad faith; (2) the materiality of the evidence excluded; (3) the extent to which the prosecution will be surprised or prejudiced; (4) the effectiveness of less severe sanctions; and (5) whether the defendant himself knew of or cooperated in the discovery violation. People v. Pronovost, 756 P.2d 387 (Colo. App. 1987). Balancing approach applied in People v. Pronovost, 756 P.2d 387 (Colo. App. 1987). Discovery of statements of nonexpert defense witnesses not authorized. Part II (c) neither explicitly nor implicitly authorizes trial courts to grant prosecution motions for pretrial discovery of statements of nonexpert defense witnesses. Richardson v. District Court, 632 P.2d 595 (Colo. 1981). Scope of part II (c) does not purport to extend to work product. People v. District Court, 187 Colo. 333, 531 P.2d 626 (1975). But discovery of defense theories and names of supporting witnesses permitted upon condition. By its direct and uncontradicted terms, part II (c) permits discovery of defense theories and the names of supporting witnesses only when the defendant intends to introduce them at trial. People v. District Court, 187 Colo. 333, 531 P.2d 626 (1975). Demonstrative, nontestimonial evidence. While the privilege against self-incrimination does not extend to demonstrative evidence obtained from a defendant or from a witness, demonstrative evidence is limited to nontestimonial evidence such as fingerprints, blood specimens, handwriting examples, photographs and other evidence of similar character. Richardson v. District Court, 632 P.2d 595 (Colo. 1981). When request for disclosure by prosecution invalid. The request for disclosure by the prosecution under this rule may be overbroad and, therefore, invalid if it seeks information which might serve as an unconstitutional link in a chain of evidence tending to establish the accused's guilt of a criminal offense. People v. District Court, 187 Colo. 333, 531 P.2d 626 (1975); Richardson v. District Court, 632 P.2d 595 (Colo. 1981). This rule governs a prosecution request for nontestimonial identification once judicial proceedings against a defendant have been initiated. People v. Angel, 701 P.2d 149 (Colo. App. 1985). A prosecuting attorney has both a statutory and a constitutional obligation to disclose to the defense any material, exculpatory evidence he possesses; however, failure to disclose information helpful to the accused results in a violation of due process only where the evidence is "material" either to guilt or punishment. Salazar v. People, 870 P.2d 1215 (Colo. 1994). More specifically, there must be a reasonable probability that, had the evidence been disclosed to the defense, the result of the proceeding would have been different. Salazar v. People, 870 P.2d 1215 (Colo. 1994). "Reasonable time" requirement of rule violated when defendant failed to respond to prosecution's specification for several months or until actual commencement of trial unless there is a showing of unusual circumstances. People v. Hampton, 696 P.2d 765 (Colo. 1985) (decided under former Crim. P. 12.1). Factors for determining when exclusion of alibi testimony is proper are discussed in People v. Hampton, 696 P.2d 765 (Colo. 1985) (decided under former Crim. P. 12.1). The trial court, after applying the factors for determining when exclusion of alibi testimony is proper, determined that the exclusion of the alibi evidence was appropriate under the facts of the case and the trial court's exercise of its

71

discretionary authority will not be overturned on appeal because the trial court did not abuse its discretion. People v. Hampton, 758 P.2d 1344 (Colo. 1988) (decided under former Crim. P. 12.1). No abuse of discretion when court prohibited defense witness from testifying when the defense did not disclose the witness within the time period in the rule and failed to articulate why the disclosure was made late. In addition, the witness was not a key witness, and the evidence that the witness was going to rebut was rebutted by another defense witness. People v. Carmichael, 179 P.3d 47 (Colo. App. 2007), rev'd on other grounds, 206 P.3d 800 (Colo. 2009). Although a prosecutor's duty to disclose potentially exculpatory evidence is not limited by the circumstances of known defense theories or considerations of relevancy, reversible error did not exist since the only evidence linking gun to the shooting in question was its discovery in the back seat of the suspects' vehicle and there was no reasonable probability that had the evidence been disclosed, the result of the trial would have been different. Salazar v. People, 870 P.2d 1215 (Colo. 1994). Although an alibi defense not an affirmative defense so as to place on the People the burden of proof to rebut, and trial court did not err by refusing a theory of case instruction treating alibi as an affirmative defense, defendant was entitled to a properly worded instruction setting forth his theory of the case. People v. Nunez, 824 P.2d 54 (Colo. App. 1991). Notice of alibi is admissible as a prior inconsistent statement when a defendant testifies at trial in a manner inconsistent with such notice. People v. Lowe, 969 P.2d 746 (Colo. App. 1998). Defendant's statement to psychiatrist that was provided to the prosecution under this rule loses its confidential nature and cross-examination of the defendant concerning such statements as prior inconsistent statements is proper impeachment, even if the psychiatrist did not testify at the defendant's trial. Use of such statements do not violate the attorney-client privilege or the right to effective assistance of counsel. People v. Lanari, 811 P.2d 399 (Colo. App. 1989), aff'd, 827 P.2d 495 (Colo. 1992). Purpose of the rule is fulfilled by the entry of a not guilty plea followed by no further disclosure of defenses, which operates to inform the prosecution that the defense is a general denial. People v. Castro, 835 P.2d 561 (Colo. App. 1992), aff'd, 854 P.2d 1262 (Colo. 1993). Nor does the rule require disclosure of intent to cross-examine prosecution witnesses. People v. Castro, 835 P.2d 561 (Colo. App. 1992), aff'd, 854 P.2d 1262 (Colo. 1993). Exclusion of a defense witness by the court as a sanction against the defense attorney, for failing to disclose such witness to the prosecution in violation of this rule, was excessive and violated defendant's right to challenge a prosecution witness's credibility through cross-examination based on testimony that would have been given by the excluded witness. People v. Cobb, 962 P.2d 944 (Colo. 1998). Although the trial court has broad discretion in deciding the appropriate course of action in response to a violation of this rule by the defense, it must consider: (1) The reason for and degree of culpability associated with the violation; (2) the extent of resulting prejudice to the other party; (3) any events after the violation that mitigate such prejudice; (4) reasonable and less drastic alternatives to exclusion; and (5) any other relevant facts. People v. Cobb, 962 P.2d 944 (Colo. 1998). Because the error violated the defendant's right under the sixth amendment to confront the witnesses against him and caused material prejudice to his defense, the error was not harmless beyond a reasonable doubt and required a new trial. People v. Cobb, 962 P.2d 944 (Colo. 1998). Prosecution could not be sanctioned for police conduct in which it did not participate. Trial court may not preclude prosecution from applying for and obtaining order for nontestimonial identification evidence though blood and hair samples obtained by police through a warrantless search were suppressed. People v. Diaz, 55 P.3d 1171 (Colo. 2002). IV. Regulation. Rule relates only to pretrial discovery and not to posttrial discovery. Roybal v. People, 177 Colo. 144, 493 P.2d 9 (1972). Preservation of evidence upon motion for protective order. If the government seeks a protective order regarding grand jury testimony, the court should first examine "in camera" the material sought to be protected before making its ruling, and if material is withheld from the defendant under such an order, it should be sealed by the court and preserved for consideration on appeal. Parlapiano v. District Court, 176 Colo. 521, 491 P.2d 965 (1971). Introduction of identification testimony within court's discretion. But where a trial judge, after considering the totality of the circumstances at an "in camera" hearing, permits the introduction of identification testimony, he does not abuse his discretion, and a reviewing court will not substitute its judgment for that of the trial court. People v. Knapp, 180 Colo. 280, 505 P.2d 7 (1973). Trial court properly allowed witness endorsed as a perceiving witness to testify as an expert witness after defense raised the issue related to the expertise at trial. People v. Jowell, 199 P.3d 38 (Colo. App. 2008). In camera review of documents obtained only by showings of necessity and undue hardship. Although subsection (f) of part III allows for in camera review of documents to determine whether they are covered by attorney work-product doctrine, the party seeking inspection in camera of confidential portions of the attorney's documents must show necessity and that obtaining the information through other means would cause undue hardship. *People v. Madera, 112 P.3d 688 (Colo. 2005). If, however, parties in a discovery dispute must resort to court intervention, the moving party must show that other means of resolving the dispute have been exhausted and that the requested relief is narrowly tailored to fit the implied waiver of the attorney-client privilege involved. People v. Madera, 112 P.3d 688 (Colo. 2005). Sanction within discretion of trial court. Whether the sanction imposed by the trial court for failure to comply with section (c) of part II is appropriate, under the facts and circumstances of a case, is a matter which is within the sound discretion of the trial court. People v. Lyle, 200 Colo. 236, 613 P.2d 896 (1980); People v. Madsen, 743 P.2d 437 (Colo. App. 1987). A trial judge has broad discretion in considering motions to endorse additional witnesses and fashioning remedies for violations of a discovery order under this rule. People v. District Court, 664 P.2d 247 (Colo. 1983). Trial court need not prevent district attorney from using evidence that was not disclosed to defendant when the court recessed for the day to permit defense time to investigate evidence and the substance of the evidence was similar to other statements which had been disclosed. People v. Hammons, 771 P.2d 1 (Colo. App. 1988). When exercising its discretion in fashioning remedies for violations of this rule, the trial court should impose the least severe sanction that will ensure full compliance with the court's discovery orders. People v. District Court, 793 P.2d 163 (Colo. 1990); People v. Castro, 854 P.2d 1262 (Colo. 1993); People v. Lee, 18 P.3d 192 (Colo. 2001). The trial court should also take into account the reason why disclosure was not made, the extent of the prejudice, if any, to the opposing party, the feasibility of rectifying that prejudice by a continuance, and any other relevant circumstances. People v. District Court, 793 P.2d 163 (Colo. 1990); People v. Castro, 854 P.2d 1262 (Colo. 1993); People v. Lee, 18 P.3d 192 (Colo. 2001). Sanction held to abridge right to fair trial. Discovery sanction which substantially prevents the negation of the prosecution's direct testimony, abridges defendant's right to a fair trial and constitutes an abuse of discretion. People v. Willis, 667 P.2d 246 (Colo. App. 1983). Sanction held not to be abuse of discretion. An order preventing the district attorney from using certain evidence is a harsh sanction, but it is not necessarily an abuse of discretion. People v. District Court, 664 P.2d 247 (Colo. 1983). Sanction of excluding presentation of evidence by a defendant is a matter of judicial discretion to be preceded by adequate inquiry into circumstances of defendant's noncompliance with court's discovery order and effect of exclusion. People v. Reger, 731 P.2d 752 (Colo. App. 1986). Factors pertinent to sanction of excluding evidence for noncompliance with a discovery order include reason for and degree of culpability associated with failure to timely respond to prosecution's request for discovery, whether and to what extent nondisclosure prejudiced prosecution's opportunity effectively to prepare for trial, whether events occurring subsequent to noncompliance mitigate prejudice to prosecution, whether there is a reasonable and less drastic alternative to preclusion of evidence, and any other relevant factors arising out of circumstances of the case. People v. Reger, 731 P.2d 752 (Colo. App. 1986). Monetary sanction payable from public funds for violation of discovery rules is beyond authority of district court. People v. District Court, 808 P.2d 831 (Colo. 1991). Preclusion is proper method to assure compliance with discovery order. People v. Patterson, 189 Colo. 451, 541 P.2d 894 (1975). Sanction of a continuance held to be abuse of discretion where delay was not attributable to the defendant and he was thereby denied his right to a speedy trial. People v. Castro, 835 P.2d 561 (Colo. App. 1992), aff'd, 854 P.2d 1262 (Colo. 1993). Decision whether to continue trial is within court's sound discretion, even when a defendant asserts a need to prepare to meet unexpected or newly discovered evidence or testimony. Trial court properly denied defense motion for continuance where prosecution's toxicologist had been endorsed two months before trial and materials used by toxicologist during his testimony were made during trial. People v. Scarlett, 985 P.2d 36 (Colo. App. 1998). A balancing approach may be used to measure the state's interest in enforcing discovery rules against the defendant's right to call witnesses in his favor. The factors considered in such approach include: (1) The reason for and the degree of culpability associated with the failure to timely respond to the prosecution's specification of time and place; (2) whether and to what extent the nondisclosure prejudiced the prosecution's opportunity to effectively prepare for trial; (3) whether events occurring subsequent to the defendant's noncompliance mitigate the prejudice to the prosecution; (4) whether there is a reasonable and less drastic alternative to the preclusion of alibi (or other defense) evidence; (5) and any other relevant factors arising out of the circumstances of the case. People v. Hampton, 696 P.2d 765 (Colo. 1985); People v. Pronovost, 773 P.2d 555 (Colo. 1989); cert. denied, 785 P.2d 611 (Colo. 1990). Exclusion or suppression of exculpatory evidence which should have been disclosed by prosecution to defense does not further search for truth and is not merited by the possible deterrence of prosecutorial misconduct, where the prosecutor had no actual knowledge of the evidence, where the evidence is crucial to the case, where a continuance would cure any prejudice suffered by the defendant because of the violation of the rule, and where the prosecutor did not willfully act in bad faith. People v. District court, 793 P.2d 163 (Colo. 1990). No prosecutorial misconduct exists where the prosecutor leaves it to the discretion of the potential witness as to whether the witness talks to the defendant's investigator. People v. Antunes, 680 P.2d 1321 (Colo. App. 1984). It was an abuse of discretion to exclude DNA evidence when record supported prosecutor's explanation that she was complying with court's earlier directives, when such exclusion could have a potentially distorting effect on truth finding, and when record shows that continuance may have been adequate to cure any prejudice suffered by defendant. People v. Lee, 18 P.3d 192 (Colo. 2001). It was an abuse of discretion to impose sanctions that were tantamount to dismissal of the charges where trial court had found no bad faith or willful violation of this rule and determined that dismissal would be inappropriate. People v. Daley, 97 P.3d 295 (Colo. App. 2004). V. Procedure. Discovery rules not applicable to extradition proceedings. Allowing full discovery in extradition proceedings would defeat the limited purpose of the habeas corpus hearing. Temen v. Barry, 695 P.2d 745 (Colo. 1984). Evidentiary hearing on disclosure. Once a defendant has made an initial showing of the necessity for disclosure, the issue becomes an evidentiary matter for resolution by the trial court and an evidentiary hearing normally will be required. People v. McLean, 633 P.2d 513 (Colo. App. 1981). Rule not guide as to when discovery to take place. This rule is only intended to create a cut-off time for the filing of discovery motions, and offers no guidance as to when the discovery should take place. People v. Quinn, 183 Colo. 245, 516 P.2d 420 (1973). Procedure for exchange of statements from prosecution to defense counsel established. Howe v. People, 178 Colo. 248, 496 P.2d 1040 (1972). Informally or through in camera proceedings, the trial court should have examined the requested medical files to determine which portions, if any, were defense counsel's work product and therefore entitled to protection from discovery. On completing the examination, the trial court should have protected confidential or privileged material, only allowing disclosure of the files after defense counsel had an opportunity to excise any confidential or privileged material. People v. Ullery, 984 P.2d 506 (Colo. 1999). The court erred by allowing the jurors to take juror notebooks home, but the error was not a structural error requiring reversal. The error was not a fundamentally serious error that would prevasively prejudice the entire of the proceedings. People v. Willcoxon, 80 P.3d 817 (Colo. App. 2002). Failure to allow defense counsel to review juror notebooks prior to trial is harmless error if counsel is allowed to review the notebook during trial and make objections. People v. Baird, 66 P.3d 183 (Colo. App. 2002). Jury notebooks are not to supplant the requirement of Crim. P. 30 that jurors be orally instructed prior to closing arguments. People v. Baenziger, 97 P.3d 271 (Colo. App. 2004). Part V (c) applies only to materials that are discoverable and actually received by the requesting party. Any other reading would require a requesting party to pay for materials that requesting party might not be allowed to review. People v. Trujillo, 114 P.3d 27 (Colo. App. 2004). .*

For a limitation on the disclosure of names and addresses of witnesses, see § 16-5-203 , C.R.S.

Rule 17 - Subpoena

In every criminal case, the prosecuting attorneys and the defendant have the right to compel the attendance of witnesses and the production of tangible evidence by service upon them of a subpoena to appear for examination as a witness upon the trial or other hearing.

(a) For Attendance of Witnesses-Form-Issuance. A subpoena shall be issued either by the clerk of the court in which case is filed or by one of counsel whose appearance has been entered in the particular case in which the subpoena is sought. It shall state the name of the court and the title, if any, of the proceedings, and shall command each person to whom it is directed to attend and give testimony at the time and place specified therein.

(b) Pro Se Defendants. Subpoenas shall be issued at the request of a pro se defendant, as hereinafter provided. The court or a judge thereof, in its discretion in any case involving a pro se defendant, may order at any time that a subpoena be issued only upon motion or request of a pro se defendant and upon order entered thereon. The motion or request shall be supported by an affidavit stating facts supporting the contention that the witness or the items sought to be subpoenaed are material and relevant and that the defendant cannot safely go to trial without the witness or items which are sought by subpoena. If the court is satisfied with the affidavit it shall direct that the subpoena be issued.

(c) For Production of Documentary Evidence and of Objects. A subpoena may also command the person to whom it is directed to produce the books, papers, documents, photographs, or other objects designated therein. The subpoenaing party shall forthwith provide a copy of the subpoena to opposing counsel (or directly to the defendant if unrepresented) upon issuance. The court on motion made promptly may quash or modify the subpoena if compliance would be unreasonable or oppressive. The court may direct that books, papers, documents, photographs, or objects designated in the subpoena be produced before the court at a time prior to the trial or prior to the time when they are to be offered in evidence and may upon their production permit the books, papers, documents, photographs, or objects or portions thereof to be inspected by the parties and their attorneys.

(d) Service on a Minor. Service of a subpoena upon a parent or legal guardian who has physical care of an unemancipated minor that contains wording commanding said parent or legal guardian to produce the unemancipated minor for the purpose of testifying before the court shall be valid service compelling the attendance of both said parent or legal guardian and the unemancipated minor for examination as witnesses. In addition, service of a subpoena as described in this subsection shall compel said parent or legal guardian either to make all necessary arrangements to ensure that the unemancipated minor is available before the court to testify or to appear in court and show good cause for the unemancipated minor's failure to appear.

(e) Service. Unless service is admitted or waived, a subpoena may be served by the sheriff, by his deputy, or by any other person who is not a party and who is not less than eighteen years of age. Service of a subpoena may be made by delivering a copy thereof to the person named. Service may also be made in accordance with Section 24-30-2104(3), C.R.S.. Service is also valid if the person named has signed a written admission or waiver of personal service, including an admission or waiver signed using a scanned or electronic signature. If ordered by the court, a fee for one day's attendance and mileage allowed by law shall be tendered to the person named if the person named resides outside the county of trial.

(f) Place of Service.

(1) **In Colorado.** A subpoena requiring the attendance of a witness at a hearing or trial may be served anywhere within Colorado.

(2) **Witness from Another State.** Service on a witness outside this state shall be made only as provided by law.

(g) For Taking Deposition-Issuance. A court order to take a deposition authorizes the issuance by the clerk of the court of subpoenas for the persons named or described in the order.

(h) Failure to Obey Subpoena.

(1) **Contempt.** Failure by any person without adequate excuse to obey a duly served subpoena may be deemed a contempt of the court from which the subpoena issued. Such contempt is indirect contempt within the meaning of C.R.C.P. 107. The trial court may issue a contempt citation under this subsection (1) whether or not it also issues a bench warrant under subsection (2) below.

(2) **Trial Witness-Bench Warrant.**

(A) When it appears to the court that a person has failed without adequate excuse to obey a duly served subpoena commanding appearance at a trial, the court, upon request of the subpoenaing party, shall issue a bench warrant directing that any peace officer apprehend the person and produce the person in court immediately upon apprehension or, if the court is not then in session, as soon as court reconvenes. Such bench warrant shall expire upon the earliest of:

(i) submission of the case to the jury; or

(ii) cancellation or termination of the trial.

(B) Upon the person's production in court, the court shall set bond.

Colo. R. Crim. P. 17

Source: (d) amended June 19, 1986, effective 1/1/1987; (c) amended and effective 10/31/1996; (d) to (h) amended November 4, 1999, effective 1/1/2000; entire rule amended and effective 9/4/2003; (e) amended and adopted October 15, 2009, effective 1/1/2010; (h) amended and adopted April 23, 2012, effective 7/1/2012.

Annotation A defendant is not entitled to issue ex parte subpoenas duces tecum by leave of the court. The fifth and sixth amendments to the federal constitution do not give the defendant the right to engage in this type of discovery without providing the information to the prosecution. People v. Baltazar, 241 P.3d 941 (Colo. 2010). Effect of failure of subpoenaed witness to appear. Under some circumstances, failure of court to grant continuance or to order mistrial when witness who has been subpoenaed fails to appear requires reversal. People v. Lee, 180 Colo. 376, 506 P.2d 136 (1973). A trial court does not abuse its discretion in denying a continuance because the defendant's psychiatric witness who had not been served with a subpoena failed to appear. People v. Mann, 646 P.2d 352 (Colo. 1982). Order of court should be required before a subpoena duces tecum is issued. Digiallonardo v. People, 175 Colo. 560, 488 P.2d 1109 (1971). During the course of a criminal prosecution, the prosecution may compel production of telephone and bank records through the use of a subpoena duces tecum so long as the defendant has the opportunity to challenge the subpoena for lack of probable cause. Use of a subpoena duces tecum for such records is not an unreasonable search and seizure provided that it is supported by probable cause and is properly defined and executed. People v. Mason, 989 P.2d 757 (Colo. 1999). Probable cause for issuance of a subpoena duces tecum for obtaining telephone and bank records exists if there is a reasonable likelihood that the evidence sought exists and that it would link the defendant to the crime charged. People v. Mason, 989 P.2d 757 (Colo. 1999). District attorney has standing to challenge defense subpoena of third party. As the prosecuting party, the district attorney has an independent interest in ensuring the propriety of third-party subpoenas as part of the management of the case and the prevention of complainant or witness harassment through improper discovery. People v. Spykstra, 234 P.3d 662 (Colo. 2010). To withstand challenge to criminal pretrial third-party subpoena, defendant must demonstrate: (1) A reasonable likelihood that the subpoenaed materials exist, by setting forth a specific factual basis; (2) that the materials are evidentiary and relevant; (3) that the materials are not otherwise procurable reasonably in advance of trial by the exercise of due diligence; (4) that the party cannot properly prepare for trial without such production and inspection in advance of trial and that the failure to obtain such inspection may tend unreasonably to delay the trial; and (5) that the application is made in good faith and is not intended as a general fishing expedition. People v. Spykstra, 234 P.3d 662 (Colo. 2010). In addition to this basic test, for subpoenas issued for materials that may be protected by privilege or a right to confidentiality, a balancing of interests is necessary and the defendant must make a greater showing of need. In camera review may be necessary in some instances, but is not mandated. People v. Spykstra, 234 P.3d 662 (Colo. 2010). Witnesses for indigent defendants. The expenses of obtaining the testimony of witnesses for an indigent defendant must be paid by the state. People v. McCabe, 37 Colo. App. 181, 546 P.2d 1289 (1975). Defendant must establish indigency to satisfaction of court. People v. McCabe, 37 Colo. App. 181, 546 P.2d 1289 (1975). No authority to quash properly issued subpoena. There is no authority under this rule to quash a subpoena if the district attorney has complied with the technical requirements. People v. Ensor, 632 P.2d 641 (Colo. App. 1981). Mailing a subpoena to a witness, without more, does not comply with the requirements in section (e). The record does not indicate that the prosecution exercised diligence in trying to obtain the witness' presence. People v. Stanchieff, 862 P.2d 988 (Colo. App. 1993). Subpoena served by mail insufficient to invoke contempt. A subpoena served by mail, pursuant to an administrative order, is insufficient to invoke the sanction of contempt under section (h). People v. Mann, 646 P.2d 352 (Colo. 1982). For in camera examination of subpoenaed bank records, see Pignatiello v. District Court, 659 P.2d 683 (Colo. 1983). Discovery costs. Prior to requiring the public defender's office to pay costs of copying a police officer's file for an in camera review by the court, the court should make the following specific findings: Was the defendant's subpoena unreasonable or oppressive and were the city's proffered concerns as to use and possible loss justified? The court should consider whether adequate safeguards could be provided for an initial in camera review of the original documents and whether any payment should be limited to actual costs. In doing so, the court must balance the government's interests against defendant's interests in disclosure. People v. Trujillo, 62 P.3d 1034 (Colo. App. 2002), rev'd on other grounds, 83 P.3d 642 (Colo. 2004). Applied in People v. Duncan, 179 Colo. 253, 500 P.2d 137 (1972); A v. District Court, 191 Colo. 10, 550 P.2d 315 (1976); Losavio v. Robb, 195 Colo. 533, 579 P.2d 1152 (1978).

For fees of witnesses, see §§ 13-33-102 and 13-33-103 , C.R.S.

Venue

Rule 18 - Venue

Comment. The place for trying criminal cases is governed by applicable statutes or rules, such as section 18-1-202 (general venue statute), section 13-73-107 and section 13-74-107 (on statewide and judicial district grand jury indictments), section 18-2-202(2) (a) (conspiracy), section 18-3-304(4) (violation of custody orders), and section 19-2-105 (juvenile cases), as well as section 16-6-101 et seq. and Crim. P. 21 (change of venue), or the state or federal constitutions.

Colo. R. Crim. P. 18

Source: Entire rule amended and adopted May 17, 2001, effective 7/1/2001; entire rule amended and adopted March 4, 2004, effective 7/1/2004.

Annotation I. General Consideration. Applied in People v. Gould, 193 Colo. 176, 563 P.2d 945 (1977); People v. Freeman, 668 P.2d 1371 (Colo. 1983). II. Place of Trial. Burden is on the state to prove venue in a criminal prosecution. Stout v. People, 171 Colo. 142, 464 P.2d 872 (1970). But venue is a matter which may be proved by positive testimony or inferred from proof of other facts. Stout v. People, 171 Colo. 142, 464 P.2d 872 (1970). For venue is a matter to be determined from all evidence in the case. Fernandez v. People, 176 Colo. 346, 490 P.2d 690 (1971). Venue may be established by circumstantial evidence. People v. Bd., 656 P.2d 712 (Colo. App. 1982). Waiver of error related to venue. Any error relating to venue, not mentioned during trial, in motion for acquittal, or in motion for a new trial, is waived, and cannot be raised on appeal. People v. Jones, 184 Colo. 96, 518 P.2d 819 (1974). Failure of county resident to pay taxes constitutes act in that county. Failure of a Pueblo county resident to pay taxes or file a return constitutes an act in Pueblo county in furtherance of the crimes charged, within the meaning of this rule. People v. Vickers, 199 Colo. 305, 608 P.2d 808 (1980).

Rule 19 - No Colorado Rule
Colo. R. Crim. P. 19

Rule 20 - No Colorado Rule
Colo. R. Crim. P. 20

Rule 21 - Change of Venue or Judge

(a) Change of Venue.

(1) For Fair or Expeditious Trial. The place of trial may be changed when the court in its sound discretion determines that a fair or expeditious trial cannot take place in the county or district in which the trial is pending.

(2) The Motion for Change of Venue.

(I) A motion for a change of venue shall be in writing and accompanied by one or more affidavits setting forth the facts upon which the moving party relies, or in lieu of such affidavits the motion, with approval of the court, may contain a stipulation of the parties to a change of venue.

(II) The written motion and the affidavits shall be served upon the opposing party 7 days before the hearing; the nonmoving party may submit a written brief or affidavit or both in opposition to the motion.

(III) As soon as practicable, the court may hold a hearing on the motion.

(3) Effect of Motions. After a motion for a change of venue has been denied, the applicant may renew his motion for good cause shown, if since denial he has learned of new grounds for a change of venue. All questions concerning the regularity of the proceedings in obtaining changes of venue or the right of the court to which the change is made to try the case and execute the judgment, and all grounds for a change of venue, shall be considered waived if not raised before trial.

(4) Order of Change. Every order for a change of venue shall be in writing, signed by the judge, and filed by the clerk with the motion as a part of the record in the case. The order shall state the court to which venue has been changed and the date and time at which the defendant shall appear at said court. The bond made, if any, shall remain in force and effect.

(5) Disposition of Confined Defendant. When the defendant is in custody, the court shall order the sheriff, or other officer having custody of the defendant, to remove him not less than 7 days before trial to the jail of the county to which the venue is changed and there deliver him together with the warrant under which he is held, to the jailer. The sheriff or other officers shall endorse on the warrant of commitment the reason for the change of custody, and deliver the warrant, with the prisoner, to the jailer of the proper county, who shall give the sheriff or other officer a receipt and keep the prisoner in the same manner as if he had originally been committed to his custody.

(6) Transcript of Record. When a change of venue is granted, the clerk of the court from which the change is granted shall immediately make a full transcript of the record and proceedings in the case, and of the motion and order for the change of venue, and shall transmit the same, together with all papers filed in the case, including the indictment or information, complaint, or summons and complaint, and bonds of the defendant and of all witnesses, to the proper court. When the change is granted to one or more, but not of several defendants, a certified copy of the indictment or information, and of each other paper in the case, shall be transmitted to the court to which the change of venue is ordered. Such certified copies shall stand as the originals, and the defendant shall be tried upon them. The transcript and papers may be transmitted by mail, or in any other way the court may direct. The clerk of the court to which the venue is changed shall file the transcript and papers transmitted to him, and docket the case; and the case shall proceed before and after judgment, as if it had originated in that court.

(7) Imprisonment. When after a change of venue the defendant is convicted and sentenced to imprisonment in the county jail, the sheriff shall transport him at once to the county where the crime was committed if that county has a jail or other place of confinement.

(b) Substitution of Judges.

(1) Within 14 days after a case has been assigned to a court, a motion, verified and supported by affidavits of at least two credible persons not related to the defendant, may be filed with the court and served on the opposing party to have a substitution of the judge. Said motion may be filed after the 14-day period only if good cause is shown to the court why it was not filed within the original 14-day period. The motion shall be based on the following grounds:

(I) The judge is related to the defendant or to any attorney of record or attorney otherwise engaged in the case; or

(II) The offense charged is alleged to have been committed against the person or property of the judge, or of some person related to him; or

(III) The judge has been of counsel in the case; or

(IV) The judge is in any way interested or prejudiced with respect to the case, the parties, or counsel.

(2) Any judge who knows of circumstances which disqualify him in a case shall, on his own motion, disqualify himself.

(3) Upon the filing of a motion under this section (b), all other proceedings in the case shall be suspended until a ruling is made thereon. If the motion and supporting affidavits state facts showing grounds for disqualification, the judge shall immediately enter an order disqualifying himself or herself. Upon disqualifying himself or herself, the judge shall notify forthwith the chief judge of the district, who shall assign another judge in the district to hear the action. If no other judge in the district is available or qualified, the chief judge shall notify forthwith the state court administrator, who shall obtain from the Chief Justice the assignment of a replacement judge.

Colo. R. Crim. P. 21

Source: (a)(2)(II), (a)(5), and IP(b)(1) amended and adopted December 14, 2011, effective 7/1/2012.

Annotation I. Change of Venue. Right to fair and impartial jury is a constitutional right which can never be abrogated. Brisbin v. Schauer, 176 Colo. 550, 492 P.2d 835 (1971). Change of venue subject to judicial discretion. Motion for change of venue due to local prejudice is a matter of judicial discretion. People v. Simmons, 183 Colo. 253, 516 P.2d 117 (1973). Trial court has inherent power to change venue on its own motion if such action is necessary to provide a fair trial and, in appropriate circumstances, may do so over the defendant's objections. Wafai v. People, 750 P.2d 37 (Colo. 1988). Question of prejudice one of fact. The question as to the existence of prejudice such as would dictate the granting of a motion for a change of venue is one of fact and rests within the sound discretion of the trial court. Nowels v. People, 166 Colo. 140, 442 P.2d 410 (1968); Kurtz v. People, 177 Colo. 306, 494 P.2d 97 (1972). Inquiry on review relating to fair trial. Regardless of the means imposed by the trial judge to insure the accused's constitutional right to a fair trial by a panel of impartial jurors, the critical inquiry on appellate review is whether the chosen means did in fact preserve the accused's right to a fair trial. People v. Botham, 629 P.2d 589 (Colo. 1981). When change of venue must be granted. If a community is prejudiced against a citizen, or if other circumstances are likely to deny him a fair and impartial jury trial, then a change of venue must be granted. Brisbin v. Schauer, 176 Colo. 550, 492 P.2d 835 (1971); Sergent v. People, 177 Colo. 354, 497 P.2d 983 (1972); Sollitt v. District Court, 180 Colo. 114, 502 P.2d 1108 (1972). Denial of fair trial may be presumed when pretrial publicity is massive, pervasive, and prejudicial. People v. Simmons, 183 Colo. 253, 516 P.2d 117 (1973). Showing required when pretrial publicity not presumptively prejudicial. Where a defendant has not demonstrated the existence of massive, pervasive, and prejudicial publicity, which would create a presumption that he was denied a fair trial, he must establish the denial of a fair trial based upon a nexus between extensive pretrial publicity and the jury panel. People v. Botham, 629 P.2d 589 (Colo. 1981). If prejudice exists, it should show up in the voir dire examination. Nowels v. People, 166 Colo. 140, 442 P.2d 410 (1968). Burden of showing partiality of jurors met. Where it is shown that a significant number of jurors entertained an opinion of the defendant's guilt, had been exposed to pretrial publicity, and had knowledge of the details of the crime, the defendant has met his burden of showing the existence of an opinion in the minds of the jurors which raises a presumption of partiality. People v. Botham, 629 P.2d 589 (Colo. 1981). Failure to grant change of venue not error. People v. Trujillo, 181 Colo. 350, 509 P.2d 794 (1973); People v. Medina, 185 Colo. 101, 521 P.2d 1257 (1974). Change of venue is available pursuant to writ of habeas corpus. Brisbin v. Schauer, 176 Colo. 550, 492 P.2d 835 (1971). II. Substitution of Judges. Law reviews. For article, "Pronouncements of the U.S. Supreme Court Relating to the Criminal Law Field: 1985-1986", which discusses a recent case relating to the personal interest of judge in case, see 15 Colo. Law. 1609 (1986). Rule to be strictly applied. This rule and its statutory counterpart on change of judge must be strictly applied. People in Interest of A.L.C., 660 P.2d 917 (Colo. App. 1982). Purpose of section (b) is to guarantee that no person is forced to stand trial before a judge with a bent of mind. People v. Botham, 629 P.2d 589 (Colo. 1981). Judge's duty to sit on case unless prejudiced. Unless a reasonable person could infer that the judge would in all probability be prejudiced against the petitioner, the judge's duty is to sit on the case. Smith v. District Court, 629 P.2d 1055 (Colo. 1981). Prejudice is mental condition or status, a certain bent of mind, which cannot be demonstrated, ordinarily, by direct proof. Smith v. District Court, 629 P.2d 1055 (Colo. 1981). To be distinguished from normal personal opinions. Prejudice must be distinguished from the sort of personal opinions that as a matter of course arise during a judge's hearing of a cause. Smith v. District Court, 629 P.2d 1055 (Colo. 1981). Discourteousness or rudeness do not dictate disqualification. It does not comport with sound judicial policy or the intent of either section (b) or § 16-6-201 to require disqualification of a judge solely on the basis of subjective conclusions that he was discourteous or rude. Carr v. Barnes, 196 Colo. 70, 580 P.2d 803 (1978). But appearance of possible prejudice can dictate disqualification. People v. District Court, 192 Colo. 503, 560 P.2d 828 (1977). In reviewing the motion and affidavits, both the actuality and appearance of fairness must be considered. Even where the trial judge is convinced of his own impartiality, the integrity of the judicial system is impugned when it appears to the public that the judge is partial. People v. Botham, 629 P.2d 589 (Colo. 1981). Section (b) of this rule has uniformly been applied in disqualification cases. People v. District Court, 192 Colo. 503, 560 P.2d 828 (1977). Rule measures timeliness of motion to disqualify. One apparent purpose of section (b) of this rule was to provide a standard by which to measure timeliness of a motion for disqualification, whether filed pursuant to § 16-6-201 , or to this rule. People v. District Court, 192 Colo. 503, 560 P.2d 828 (1977). Later discovered or occurring disqualifying facts. When disqualifying facts do not occur or are not discovered by the moving party until after expiration of the time within which the motion and affidavits normally must be presented, application for a change of judge is timely if made as soon as possible after occurrence or discovery of those facts. People v. District Court, 192 Colo. 503, 560 P.2d 828 (1977); People v. Botham, 629 P.2d 589 (Colo. 1981). Good cause for delay in filing shown. People v. District Court, 192 Colo. 503, 560 P.2d 828 (1977). Because prosecutor did not argue to the trial court that the motion was untimely and court did not consider the timeliness issue and further because the motion to recuse was triggered by comments the trial judge made at sentencing, good cause existed for the late filing. People v. Barton, 121 P.3d 230 (Colo. App. 2004). Timeliness and sufficiency of motion and affidavit deemed questions of law. Whether the motion is timely and whether it sufficiently states grounds for disqualification are questions of law subject to plenary review. People v. District Court, 192 Colo. 503, 560 P.2d 828 (1977). A motion for recusal must be verified and supported by affidavits of at least two credible witnesses not related to defendant. People v. Grenemyer, 827 P.2d 603 (Colo. App. 1992). Whether recusal is required will depend on whether defendant's motion and supporting affidavits set forth legally sufficient facts upon which bias or prejudice may be implied. James v. People, 727 P.2d 850 (Colo. 1986); People v. Grenemyer, 827 P.2d 603 (Colo. App. 1992). And facts in affidavits and motion taken as true. As a matter of judicial policy courts must take as true, for purposes of a motion to disqualify, facts stated in the affidavits and motion. People v. District Court, 192 Colo. 503, 560 P.2d 828 (1977); People v. Botham, 629 P.2d 589 (Colo. 1981). The facts set forth in affidavits supporting a motion to disqualify a judge are not subject to a trial court's inquiry, but are presumed to be true. Smith v. District Court, 629 P.2d 1055 (Colo. 1981); People v. Cook, 22 P.3d 947 (Colo. App. 2000); Kane v. County Court Jefferson County, 192 P.3d 443 (Colo. App. 2008). Thus, the trial judge engaging in this inquiry cannot pass upon the truth or falsity of statements of fact in the motion and supporting affidavits. Estep v. Hardeman, 705 P.2d 523 (Colo. 1985); S.S. v. Wakefield, 764 P.2d 70 (Colo. 1988); Brewster v. District Court, 811 P.2d 812 (Colo. 1991). The judge must confine the analysis to the four corners of the motion and supporting affidavits, and then determine as a matter of law whether they allege legally sufficient facts for disqualification. Klinck v. District Court, 876 P.2d 1270 (Colo. 1994). Recusal not discretionary where affidavits sufficiently allege prejudice. The trial judge has no discretion in the matter of recusing himself upon finding the affidavits sufficient under the rule to allege prejudice. He immediately loses all jurisdiction in the matter except to grant the change. People v. District Court, 192 Colo. 503, 560 P.2d 828 (1977); Brewster v. District Court, 811 P.2d 812 (Colo. 1991). Test of sufficiency of motion and affidavit. The test of the legal sufficiency of a motion to disqualify a judge is whether the motion and affidavits state facts from which it may reasonably be inferred that the respondent judge has a bias or prejudice that will in all probability prevent him or her from dealing fairly with the petitioner. People v. Botham, 629 P.2d 589 (Colo. 1981); Smith v. District Court, 629 P.2d 1055 (Colo. 1981); People v. Baca, 633 P.2d 528 (Colo. App. 1981); People v. Hrapski, 718 P.2d 1050 (Colo. 1986). To be sufficient, the affidavits must state facts from which the respondent judge's prejudice may reasonably be inferred. People v. District Court, 192 Colo. 503, 560 P.2d 828 (1977). Test is applied in Estep v. Hardeman, 705 P.2d 523 (Colo. 1985). There can be no presumption that a judge is intimidated by the outrage of the community in which the judge serves. Thus, motion for disqualification properly denied where there was no allegation that the judge was in fact intimidated by the community's animosity toward the defendant. People v. Vecchio, 819 P.2d 533 (Colo. App. 1991). Prejudgments regarding the quality of evidence to be heard are not consistent with the duty of a trial court to reach an unbiased decision after weighing all the evidence. Estep v. Hardeman, 705 P.2d 523 (Colo. 1985). Subjective conclusion of party not sufficient. Neither § 16-6-201 nor section (b) of this rule requires disqualification of a judge on the basis of a party's subjective conclusion that the judge is not impartial because of acts or statements made by the party. Smith v. District Court, 629 P.2d 1055 (Colo. 1981). And motion without supporting affidavits or facts insufficient. Where defendant filed no affidavits and alleged no facts which would reasonably indicate that the judge was interested or prejudiced with respect to the case, the parties, or counsel, the defendant's motion to disqualify the judge was insufficient as a matter of law. People v. Johnson, 634 P.2d 407 (Colo. 1981). The mere allegation that a trial judge engaged in an ex parte communication with a doctor who would testify as an expert witness is not alone sufficient to require recusal of the trial judge. Comiskey v. District Ct., 926 P.2d 539 (Colo. 1996). Recusal not required where the trial court's statements merely consisted of comments about a second co-defendant as part of the consideration of mitigating factors during sentencing of first co-defendant, and not statements expressing bias or prejudice about the second co-defendant, especially when judge specifically refused at the co-defendant's sentencing hearing to speculate as to co-defendant's role in the crimes charged. People v. Cook, 22 P.3d 947 (Colo. App. 2000). An appearance of impropriety cannot be inferred simply because the judge was a member of the general public that witnessed the fire started by defendant or because the judge assisted in general relief efforts. People v. Barton, 121 P.3d 230 (Colo. App. 2004). However, numerous other allegations of the judge's personal involvement and comments made by the judge during the sentencing hearing about his or her personal experience presented legally sufficient basis to create the appearance of prejudice that could have prevented the judge from dealing fairly with the defendant. People v. Barton, 121 P.3d 230 (Colo. App. 2004). Trial judge's presence in courtroom in which defendant allegedly threatened a witness did not require recusal. A mere order for an investigation of threat did not create a potential conflict of interest or indicate that the judge might become a witness. People v. Hagos, 250 P.3d 596 (Colo. App. 2009). Defendant's attorney may file affidavit in support of motion for substitution of judge where the attorney-affiant is not related to the defendant within the third degree by blood, adoption, or marriage. People v. Botham, 629 P.2d 589 (Colo. 1981). To disqualify, suit against judge must be probably successful. To create an adverse interest sufficient to disqualify a trial judge from presiding over a criminal trial, a suit brought against him by the accused person must have some probability of success. Watson v. People, 155 Colo. 357, 394 P.2d 737 (1964), cert. denied, 380 U.S. 966, 85 S. Ct. 1111, 14 L. Ed. 2d 156 (1965). Challenged judge may request hearing before another judge. A challenged judge in juvenile delinquency matters may, after self-disqualification, request a hearing before another judge on the issues raised in respondent's motion and affidavits. People in Interest of A.L.C., 660 P.2d 917 (Colo. App. 1982). Referring a motion for substitution to another judge for decision is not reversible error, even if it is not the procedure contemplated by this rule. Comiskey v. District Ct., 926 P.2d 539 (Colo. 1996). Disqualification where court only determining matters of law. It is unnecessary to determine whether a trial judge errs in not disqualifying himself where the error committed by him is not prejudicial error in that there is no disagreement over the facts and the sole material determinations to be made by the trial court are matters of law, in which case an appellate court is to determine whether the trial court correctly ruled on such matters. Robran v. People ex rel. Smith, 173 Colo. 378, 479 P.2d 976 (1971). A judge's bias or prejudice against defense counsel, while not generally requiring recusal, may so require when the judge's manifestation of hostility or ill will is apparent from the motion and affidavits and indicates the absence of the impartiality required for a fair trial. Brewster v. District Court, 811 P.2d 812 (Colo. 1991). A government attorney is not an "attorney otherwise engaged in the case" unless he has worked on it directly. While a partner in a law firm is said to be "engaged" in every case in which a member of his firm represents a party because he has a financial interest in the case's outcome, a government lawyer's compensation and clientele are set, and the prestige of the office as a whole is not greatly affected by the outcome of a particular case. Smith v. Beckman, 683 P.2d 1214 (Colo. App. 1984). Judges are not disqualified solely on the basis that they were formerly employed by the prosecutor's office. Instead, when employed by that office, the judge to be disqualified must have performed some role in the case or have obtained actual knowledge of disputed evidentiary facts of the case. People v. Julien, 47 P.3d 1194 (Colo. 2002). Where defendant failed to submit affidavits in accordance with requirements of § 16-2-201 and section (b) of this rule, and supplied allegations himself that record did not verify, there were insufficient grounds for disqualification. People v. Grenemyer, 827 P.2d 603 (Colo. App. 1992). Where defendant failed to present evidence to substantiate his claim that the judge knew of circumstances that would disqualify him from presiding in case and improperly filed a motion for case transfer with another trial court judge but failed to inform presiding judge of defendant's motion or to seek a decision on such motion, there were insufficient grounds for disqualification. People v. Harmon, 3 P.3d 480 (Colo. App. 2000). Mere filing of complaint with the judicial performance commission, without more, does not establish sufficient grounds for recusal. Further, county court judge's decision to recuse herself in seven prior cases does not lead to the conclusion that she should permanently recuse herself in all cases involving the attorneys. Kane v. County Court Jefferson County, 192 P.3d 443 (Colo. App. 2008). .

Rule 22 - Time of Motion to Transfer

A motion for a change of venue or for a change of judge under these Rules may be made at or before arraignment or, for good cause shown for a late filing, at any time before trial.

Colo. R. Crim. P. 22

Annotation Am. Jur.2d. See 5 Am. Jur.2d, Arrest, §§ 10, 12, 25, 27, 29-33.

Trial

Rule 23 - Trial by Jury or to the Court

(a)

(1) Every person accused of a felony has the right to be tried by a jury of twelve. Before the jury is sworn, the defendant may, except in class 1 felonies, elect a jury of less than twelve but no fewer than six, with the consent of the court.

(2) Every person accused of a misdemeanor has the right to be tried by a jury of six. Before the jury is sworn, the defendant may elect a jury of less than six but no fewer than three, with the consent of the court.

(3) Every person accused of a class 1 or class 2 petty offense has the right to be tried by a jury of three, if he or she:

(I) Files a written jury demand within 21 days after entry of a plea;

(II) Tenders twenty-five dollars to the court within 21 days after entry of a plea, unless such fee is waived by the judge because of the indigence of the defendant. If the charge is dismissed or the defendant is acquitted of the charge, or if the defendant, having paid the jury fee, files with the court, at least 7 days before the scheduled trial date a written waiver of jury trial, the jury fee shall be returned to the defendant.

(4) The jury, in matters involving class 1 and class 2 petty offenses, shall consist of a greater number than three, not to exceed six, if requested by the defendant in the jury demand.

(5)

(I) The person accused of a felony or misdemeanor may, with the consent of the prosecution, waive a trial by jury in writing or orally in court. Trial shall then be to the court.

(II) The court shall not proceed with a trial to the court after waiver of jury trial without first determining:

(a) That the defendant's waiver is voluntary;

(b) That the defendant understands that:

(i) The waiver would apply to all issues that might otherwise need to be determined by a jury including those issues requiring factual findings at sentencing;

(ii) The jury would be composed of a certain number of people;

(iii) A jury verdict must be unanimous;

(iv) In a trial to the court, the judge alone would decide the verdict;

(v) The choice to waive a jury trial is the defendant's alone and may be made contrary to counsel's advice.

(III) In a proceeding where the waiver of a jury trial is part of a determination preceding the entry of a guilty or nolo contendere plea, the court need only make the determinations required by Rule 11(b) and not those required by this rule.

(6) A defendant may not withdraw a voluntary and knowing waiver of trial by jury as a matter of right, but the court, with the consent of the prosecution, may permit withdrawal of the waiver prior to the commencement of the trial.

(7) In any case in which a jury has been sworn to try a case, and any juror by reason of illness or other cause becomes unable to continue until a verdict is reached, the court may excuse such juror. Except in class 1 felonies, if no alternate juror is available to replace such juror, the defendant and the prosecution, at any time before verdict, may stipulate in writing or on the record in open court, with approval of the court, that the jury shall consist of less than twelve but no fewer than six in felony cases, and less than six but no fewer than three in misdemeanor cases, and the jurors thus remaining shall proceed to try the case and determine the issues.

(8) All jury verdicts must be unanimous.

Colo. R. Crim. P. 23

Source: a1 and a2 amended June 9, 1988, effective 1/1/1989; headnote a repealed and a5 amended July 16, 1992, effective 11/1/1992; a5 amended and adopted September 7, 2006, effective 1/1/2007; entire rule amended and effective 4/17/2008; entire rule corrected July 16, 2008, effective nunc pro tunc 4/17/2008; a3 amended and adopted December 14, 2011, effective 7/1/2012.

Committee CommentAmended Rule 23(a)(5) reflects the legislature's 1989 decision to condition a defendant's waiver of a jury trial upon the consent of the prosecution. See 1989 S.B. 246, Section 35, amending Section 16-10-101 , C.R.S. See also People v. District Court, 731 P.2d 720, 722 (Colo. 1987). Also, consistent with Colorado caselaw, the amended rule would permit the waiver of a jury trial even in a class 1 felony case. See People v. Davis, 794 P.2d 159, 209-12 (Colo. 1990). .

Annotation Annotator's note. For other annotations concerning the right to trial by jury, see § 23 of art. II, Colo. Const., and § 18-1-406 . Section 18-1-406(1) and this rule, which provide for six jurors in misdemeanor cases, are constitutional under § 23 of art. II of the Colorado Constitution. People v. Rodriguez, 112 P.3d 693 (Colo. 2005). Right to waive trial by jury is substantive in nature. Garcia v. People, 200 Colo. 413, 615 P.2d 698 (1980). Rule conflicts with § 18-1-406 . Subsection (a)(5) of this rule and § 18-1-406(2) are not reconcilable and are in direct conflict with each other. Garcia v. People, 200 Colo. 413, 615 P.2d 698 (1980). And section 18-1-406(2) controls over subsection (a)(5) of this rule, so that the consent of the prosecuting attorney cannot be imposed as a condition on right to waive trail by jury. Garcia v. People, 200 Colo. 413, 615 P.2d 698 (1980). Defendant must personally waive right to jury. The plain meaning of subsection (a)(5) requires that a defendant personally waive his right to a jury trial and that a statement by his counsel does not operate as a waiver. Rice v. People, 193 Colo. 270, 565 P.2d 940 (1977); People v. Evans, 44 Colo. App. 288, 612 P.2d 1153 (1980); Moore v. People, 707 P.2d 990 (Colo. 1985). A waiver must be understandingly, voluntarily, and deliberately made. A defendant in a criminal case may waive his right to a jury trial; however, that waiver must be understandingly, voluntarily, and deliberately made, and a determination of waiver must be a matter of certainty and not implication. People v. Evans, 44 Colo. App. 288, 612 P.2d 1153 (1980); Moore v. People, 707 P.2d 990 (Colo. 1985). Presumption accorded waiver of jury trial. Where, when the jury was assembled in the courtroom ready for trial, defendants' counsel orally announced that defendants had decided to waive their right to a jury trial, and the court inquired of each defendant if that was their desire and both indicated in the affirmative, and as a further precaution, the court then insisted that a written waiver of jury trial be prepared and be signed by each defendant and their counsel, which was done, it will be presumed that defendants understandingly, voluntarily, and deliberately decided to waive the jury. People v. Fowler, 183 Colo. 300, 516 P.2d 428 (1973). Advisement by court did not substantially comply with this rule, however the remedy is not an automatic new trial. The proper remedy is a postconviction evidentiary hearing. People v. Walker, __ P.3d __ (Colo. App.

2011). Waiver not constitutional right. The defendant in a criminal case does not have a constitutional right to waive a jury and be tried by the court. People v. Linton, 193 Colo. 64, 565 P.2d 919 (1977). Effect of waiver. Where the defendant voluntarily and with advice of counsel waived a jury trial, defendant in such circumstances cannot be heard to complain when he creates a situation which necessarily makes the trial judge both the one who decides the admissibility of evidence and the one who renders the verdict. People v. Thompson, 182 Colo. 198, 511 P.2d 909 (1973). Waiver is effective where defendant fails to present evidence from which it could be reasonably inferred that the waiver was not voluntary, knowing, and intentional. People v. Porterfield, 772 P.2d 638 (Colo. App. 1988). Jury to be sworn. While there is no explicit statute or rule requiring the administration of an oath to a jury in this state, subsection (a)(7) of this rule and subsection (b)(2) and section (e) of Crim. P. 24, implicitly require that a jury will be sworn to try a case. Hollis v. People, 630 P.2d 68 (Colo. 1981). But delayed swearing not error. Where no prejudice is shown by the delayed swearing of the jury, no objection is made, and the oath is administered before the jury retires to begin its deliberations, the error is harmless. Hollis v. People, 630 P.2d 68 (Colo. 1981). Juror properly dismissed and replaced. A juror, after being sequestered for eight days, was properly dismissed and replaced with an alternative when the juror was shown to be quite nervous and upset, and no evidence of prejudice against the defendant was shown by the dismissal and replacement of the juror. People v. Evans, 674 P.2d 975 (Colo. App. 1983). Requirement of written stipulation to jury of less than 12 met. Where defense counsel stipulates to a jury of less than 12 in open court and on the record, the requirement of section (a)(7) that the stipulation be in writing is met. People v. Waters, 641 P.2d 292 (Colo. App. 1981). Unanimity is required only with respect to the ultimate issue of the defendant's guilt or innocence of the crime charged, and not with respect to alternative means by which the crime was committed. People v. Taggart, 621 P.2d 1375 (Colo. 1981). Although there is a statutory right to a unanimous verdict in criminal cases in Colorado, the state constitution does not explicitly guarantee the right to a unanimous verdict. Nevertheless, there are some cases in which the jury may return a general verdict of guilty when instructed on alternative theories of principal and complicitor liability and in which the state constitution has provided a criminal defendant the right to a unanimous jury verdict. People v. Hall, 60 P.3d 728 (Colo. App. 2002). Subsection (a)(5)(II) is intended to require that trial courts conduct on-the-record advisements to defendants, informing them of specific elements of their right to a trial by jury and of certain consequences if they waive that right. People v. Montoya, 251 P.3d 35 (Colo. App. 2010). Trial court did not substantially comply with subsection (a)(5)(II)(b) due to omissions in the court's advisement to defendant about the waiver. Nor did the omissions in the advisement merely constitute a "slip-up" by the trial court. People v. Montoya, 251 P.3d 35 (Colo. App. 2010). Advisement regarding waiver was not deficient simply because trial court did not advise defendant of the possible penalties upon conviction. Such an advisement is neither required nor necessary. People v. Montoya, 251 P.3d 35 (Colo. App. 2010). Where advisement is deficient under subsection (a)(5)(II), the appropriate remedy is to remand the case to the trial court for an evidentiary hearing to resolve defendant's challenge to the validity of the waiver of a jury trial. People v. Montoya, 251 P.3d 35 (Colo. App. 2010). The right to a 12-person jury is purely statutory. The sixth and fourteenth amendments to the U.S. Constitution guarantee the right to trial by jury, but do not, nor does the Colorado Constitution guarantee the right to a 12-person jury. People v. Chavez, 791 P.2d 1210 (Colo. App. 1990). Constitutional right to a jury of 12 lies only with felony cases and does not extend to misdemeanor cases. A defendant in a misdemeanor case does not have a constitutional right under art. II, § 23, of the Colorado Constitution to demand a 12-person jury. People v. Rodriguez, 112 P.3d 693 (Colo. 2005). The statutory right to a 12-person jury could be waived by counsel's statements. The requirement that a defendant must make a written or oral "announcement" of his intention to waive a jury does not extend to a reduction in the number of jurors. People v. Chavez, 791 P.2d 1210 (Colo. App. 1990). Defense counsel stipulation to a jury of less than 12 in open court and on the record satisfies the statutory requirement that the stipulation must be in writing. People v. Baird, 66 P.3d 183 (Colo. App. 2002). Applied in Hawkins v. Superior Court, 196 Colo. 86, 580 P.2d 811 (1978); People v. Ledman, 622 P.2d 534 (Colo. 1981); People v. Andrews, 632 P.2d 1012 (Colo. 1981); People v. Norman, 703 P.2d 1261 (Colo. 1985).

Rule 24 - Trial Jurors

(a) Orientation And Examination Of Jurors. An orientation and examination shall be conducted to inform prospective jurors about their duties and service and to obtain information about prospective jurors to faciliate an intelligent exercise of challenges for cause and peremptory challenges.

(1) The jury commissioner is authorized to examine and, when appropriate, excuse prospective jurors who do not satisfy the statutory qualifications for jury service, or who are entitled to a postponement, or as otherwise authorized by appropriate court order.

(2) When prospective jurors have reported to the courtroom, the judge shall explain to them in plain and clear language:

(i) The grounds for challenge for cause;

(ii) Each juror's duty to volunteer information that would constitute a disqualification or give rise to a challenge for cause;

(iii) The identities of the parties and their counsel;

(iv) The nature of the case using applicable instructions if available or, alternatively a joint statement of factual information intended to provide a relevant context for the prospective jurors to respond to questions asked of them. Alternatively, at the request of counsel and in the discretion of the judge, counsel may present such information through brief non-argumentative statements;

(v) General legal principles applicable to the case including the presumption of innocence, burden of proof, definition of reasonable doubt, elements of charged offenses and other matters that jurors will be required to consider and apply in deciding the issues.

(3) The judge shall ask prospective jurors questions concerning their qualifications to serve as jurors. The parties or their counsel shall be permitted to ask the prospective jurors additional questions. In the discretion of the judge, juror questionnaires, posterboards and other methods may be used. In order to minimize delay, the judge may reasonably limit the time available to the parties or their counsel for juror examination. The court may limit or terminate repetitious, irrelevant, unreasonably lengthy, abusive or otherwise improper examination.

(4) Jurors shall not be required to disclose personal locating information, such as address or place of business in open court and such information shall not be maintained in files open to the public. The trial judge shall assure that parties and counsel have access to appropriate and necessary locating information.

(5) Once the jury is impaneled, the judge shall again explain in more detail the general principles of law applicable to criminal cases, the procedural guidelines regarding conduct by jurors during the trial, case specific legal principles and definitions of technical or special terms expected to be used during the presentation of the case.

(b) **Challenges for Cause.**

(1) The court shall sustain a challenge for cause on one or more of the following grounds:

(I) Absence of any qualification prescribed by statute to render a person competent as a juror;

(II) Relationship within the third degree, by blood, adoption, or marriage, to a defendant or to any attorney of record or attorney engaged in the trial of the case;

(III) Standing in the relation of guardian and ward, employer and employee, landlord and tenant, debtor and creditor, or principal and agent to, or being a member of the household of, or associated in business with, or surety on any bond or obligation for, any defendant;

(IV) The juror is or has been a party adverse to the defendant in a civil action, or has complained against or been accused by him in a criminal prosecution;

(V) The juror has served on the grand jury which returned the indictment or on a coroner's jury which inquired into the death of a person whose death is the subject of the indictment or the information, or on any other investigatory body which inquired into the facts of the crime charged;

(VI) The juror was a juror at a former trial arising out of the same factual situation or involving the same defendant;

(VII) The juror was a juror in a civil action against the defendant arising out of the act charged as a crime;

(VIII) The juror was a witness to any matter related to the crime or its prosecution;

(IX) The juror occupies a fiduciary relationship to the defendant or a person alleged to have been injured by the crime or the person on whose complaint the prosecution was instituted;

(X) The existence of a state of mind in a juror manifesting a bias for or against the defendant, or for or against the prosecution, or the acknowledgement of a previously formed or expressed opinion regarding the guilt or innocence of the defendant shall be grounds for disqualification of the juror, unless the court is satisfied that the juror will render an impartial verdict based solely upon the evidence and the instructions of the court;

(XI) Reserved

(XII) The juror is an employee of a public law enforcement agency or public defender's office.

(2) If either party desires to introduce evidence, other than the sworn responses of the prospective juror, for the purpose of establishing grounds to disqualify or challenge the juror for cause, such evidence shall be heard and all issues related thereto shall be determined by the court out of the presence of the other prospective jurors. All matters pertaining to the qualifications and competency of the prospective jurors shall be deemed waived by the parties if not raised prior to the swearing in of the jury to try the case, except that the court for good cause shown or upon a motion for mistrial or other relief may hear such evidence during the trial out of the presence of the jury and enter such orders as are appropriate.

(c) Challenge to Pool.

(1) Upon the request of the defendant or the prosecution in advance of the commencement of the trial, the defendant or the prosecution shall be furnished with a list of prospective jurors who will be subject to call in the trial.

(2) Either the prosecution or the defendant may challenge the pool on the ground that there has been a substantial failure to comply with the requirements of the law governing the selection of jurors. Such challenge must be made in writing setting forth the particular ground upon which it is based and shall be accompanied by one or more affidavits specifying the supporting facts and demographic data. The challenge must be filed prior to the swearing in of the jury selected to try the case.

(3) If the court finds the affidavit or affidavits filed under subsection (2) of this section, if true, demonstrate a substantial failure to comply with the "Uniform Jury Selection and Service Act", the moving party is entitled to present in support of the motion the testimony of any person responsible for the implementation of the "Uniform Jury Selection and Service Act." Any party may present any records used in the selection and summoning of jurors for service, and any other relevant evidence. If the court determines, by a preponderance of the evidence, that in selecting either a grand jury or a petit jury there has been a substantial failure to comply with the "Uniform Jury Selection and Service Act", the court shall discharge the jury panel and stay the proceedings pending the summoning of a new juror pool or dismiss an indictment, information, or complaint, or grant other appropriate relief.

(4) At any time before trial, upon motion by a party or on its own motion, the court may declare a mistrial in a case on the ground that a fair jury pool cannot be safely assembled in that particular case due to a public health crisis or limitations brought about by such crisis. A declaration of a mistrial under this paragraph must be supported by specific findings.

(d) Peremptory Challenges.

(1) For purposes of Rule 24 a capital case is a case in which a class 1 felony is charged.

(2) In capital cases the state and the defendant, when there is one defendant, shall each be entitled to ten peremptory challenges. In all other cases where there is one defendant and the punishment may be by imprisonment in a correctional facility, the state and the defendant shall each be entitled to five peremptory challenges, and in all other cases, to three peremptory challenges. If there is more than one defendant, each side shall be entitled to an additional three peremptory challenges for every defendant after the first in capital cases, but not exceeding twenty peremptory challenges to each side; in all other cases, where the punishment may be by imprisonment in a correctional facility, to two additional peremptory challenges for every defendant after the first, not exceeding fifteen peremptory challenges to each side; and in all other cases to one additional peremptory challenge for every defendant after the first, not exceeding ten peremptory challenges to each side. In any case where there are multiple defendants, every peremptory challenge shall be made and considered as the joint peremptory challenge of all defendants. In case of the consolidation of any indictments, informations, complaints, or summons and complaints for trial, such consolidated cases shall be considered, for all purposes concerning peremptory challenges, as though the defendants had been joined in the same indictment, information, complaint, or summons and complaint. When trial is held on a plea of not guilty by reason of insanity, the number of peremptory challenges shall be the same as if trial were on the issue of substantive guilt.

(3) For good cause shown, the court at any time may add peremptory challenges to either or both sides.

(4) Peremptory challenges shall be exercised by counsel, alternately, the first challenge to be exercised by the prosecution. A prospective juror so challenged shall be excused, and another juror from the panel shall replace the juror excused. Counsel waiving the exercise of further peremptory challenges as to those jurors then in the jury box may thereafter exercise peremptory challenges only as to jurors subsequently called into the jury box without, however, reducing the total number of peremptory challenges available to either side.

(e) Alternate Jurors. The court may direct that a sufficient number of jurors in addition to the regular jury be called and impaneled to sit as alternate jurors. Alternate jurors in the order in which they are called shall replace jurors who become unable or disqualified to perform their duties. Alternate jurors shall be drawn in the same manner, shall have the same qualifications, shall be subject to the same examination and challenges, shall take the same oath, and shall have the same functions, powers, facilities, and privileges as the regular jurors. An alternate juror shall not be discharged until the jury renders its verdict or until such time as determined by the court. When alternate jurors are impaneled, each side is entitled to one peremptory challenge for each alternate to be selected, and such additional peremptory challenges may be exercised as to any prospective jurors. In a case in which a class 1, 2 or 3 felony is charged and in any case in which a felony listed in Section 24-4.1-302(1), C.R.S. is charged, the court, at the request of the defendant or the prosecution, shall impanel at least one alternate juror.

(f) Custody of Jury.

(1) The court should only sequester jurors in extraordinary cases. Otherwise, (J)urors should be permitted to separate during all trial recesses, both before and after the case has been submitted to the jury for deliberation. Cautionary instructions as to their conduct during all recesses shall be given to the jurors by the court.

(2) The jurors shall be in the custody of the bailiff whenever they are deliberating and at any other time as ordered by the court.

(3) If the jurors are permitted to separate during any recess of the court, the court shall order them to return at a day and hour appointed by the court for the purpose of continuing the trial, or for resuming their deliberations if the case has been submitted to the jury.

(g) Juror Questions. Jurors shall be allowed to submit written questions to the court for the court to ask of witnesses during trial, in compliance with procedures established by the trial court. The trial court shall have the discretion to prohibit or limit questioning in a particular trial for reasons related to the severity of the charges, the presence of significant suppressed evidence or for other good cause. After giving the parties notice and an opportunity to be heard on each question, the court shall determine whether to ask the submitted question. The trial court shall permit appropriate follow-up questions from the parties within the scope of the jurors' questions.

Colo. R. Crim. P. 24

Source: e amended September 20, 1984, effective 1/1/1985; d4 amended June 9, 1988, effective 1/1/1989; the introductory portion to c, c2, and c3 amended July 16, 1992, effective 11/1/1992; e amended February 4, 1993, effective 4/1/1993; a repealed and readopted and f1 amended June 25, 1998, effective 1/1/1999; b1XI repealed and reserved March 11, 1999, effective 7/1/1999; g added and adopted February 19, 2003, effective 7/1/2004; amended September 6, 2018, effective 9/6/2018; amended and adopted April 7, 2020, effective 4/7/2020; amended and adopted July 22, 2020, effective 7/22/2020.

Committee Comment to (c)These changes were made in order to conform Rule 24 to the legislative changes in the Colorado Uniform Jury Selection and Service Act, Sections 13-71-101 to 13-71-145 , C.R.S. which became effective January 1, 1990.Committee Comment to (d)The rule is changed to permit, but not to require, the court to allow the simultaneous questioning of more than 12 potential jurors and one or two alternate jurors at one time. Further, the rule permits, but does not require, the court to allow the exercise of peremptory challenges, in writing, in its discretion, as is done in civil cases. This rule change is intended to apply to both district and county court criminal cases.

Annotation I. General Consideration. Law reviews. For article, "Challenges for Cause in Criminal Trials", see 12 Colo. Law. 1799 (1983). For article, "Criminal Procedure", which discusses a recent Tenth Circuit decision dealing with co-conspirators and voir dire, see 61 Den. L.J. 310 (1984). For article, "Curbing the Prosecutor's Abuse of the Peremptory Challenge", see 14 Colo. Law. 1629 (1985). For article, "Pronouncements of the U.S. Supreme Court Relating to the Criminal Law Field: 1985-1986", which discusses recent cases relating to peremptory challenges on the basis of race, see 15 Colo. Law. 1609 (1986). Standard of review is "abuse of discretion". Phrases used in prior case law such as "clear abuse of discretion" and "gross abuse of discretion" are deemed to express this standard and have the same meaning. Carrillo v. People, 974 P.2d 478 (Colo. 1999). Defendant entitled to impartial jury. It is fundamental to the right to a fair trial that a defendant be provided with an impartial jury. Nailor v. People, 200 Colo. 30, 612 P.2d 79 (1980); People v. Gurule, 628 P.2d 99 (Colo. 1981); People v. Collins,

730 P.2d 293 (Colo. 1986). Although a defendant is entitled to a trial by a fair and impartial jury, he is not entitled to any particular juror. People v. Johnson, 757 P.2d 1098 (Colo. App. 1988). The right to an impartial jury does not require counsel be granted unlimited voir dire examination. People v. O'Neill, 803 P.2d 164 (Colo. 1990). And discrimination in summoning of jurors may be ground for reversal. Counsel may request, in the presence of the presiding judge, or the judge himself may direct, that only good and lawful men be summoned as jurors; but to discriminate in favor of or against any class of citizens eligible for jury duty would be a grievous wrong. Whether such intermeddling would be ground for reversal depends upon the circumstances of the case. Babcock v. People, 13 Colo. 515, 22 P. 817 (1889). Qualified person should not be excused except for statutory reason. Jury service being an obligation of citizenship, the court should not excuse a person otherwise qualified for jury service for any reason short of the statutory criteria of "undue hardship, extreme inconvenience, or public necessity" set out in § 13-71-112(2). People ex rel. Faulk v. District Court, 667 P.2d 1384 (Colo. 1983). Jury to be sworn. While there is no explicit statute or rule requiring the administration of an oath to a jury in this state, subsection (b)(2) and section (e) of this rule and Crim. P. 23(a)(7) implicitly require that a jury will be sworn to try a case. Hollis v. People, 630 P.2d 68 (Colo. 1981). And delayed swearing not necessarily error. Where no prejudice is shown by the delayed swearing of the jury, no objection is made, and the oath is administered before the jury retires to begin its deliberations, the error is harmless. Hollis v. People, 630 P.2d 68 (Colo. 1981). A ruling by the trial court which calls an alternative juror to replace a juror who becomes "disqualified" to perform his duties is a matter within the discretion of the trial court and will not be disturbed on review unless an abuse of discretion is shown. People v. Johnson, 757 P.2d 1098 (Colo. App. 1988). It is within the trial court's prerogative to give considerable weight to a potential juror's statement that he or she can fairly and impartially serve on the case. People v. Montoya, 942 P.2d 1287 (Colo. App. 1996). This rule is not in agreement with § 16-10-105 because that section requires that jurors may be replaced with alternate jurors before deliberations begin and not after. Since the court rules govern practice and procedure in civil and criminal cases while the statute affects the substantive right to a fair trial, § 16-10-105 is the operative provision in deciding that the trial court erred by applying section (e) of this rule and allowing the replacement of a regular juror with an alternate juror after the jury had begun its deliberations People v. Montoya, 942 P.2d 1287 (Colo. App. 1996). Trial court's use of random selection to choose alternate juror was error, but, in the absence of any prejudice demonstrated against the defendant, it was harmless error. People v. Tippett, 733 P.2d 1183 (Colo. 1987). The purpose of seating an alternate juror is to have available another juror when, through unforeseen circumstances, a juror is unable to continue to serve and the trial court is in the best position to evaluate whether a juror is unable to serve, and its decision to excuse a juror will not be disturbed absent a gross abuse of discretion. People v. Abbott, 690 P.2d 1263 (Colo. 1984); People v. Christopher, 896 P.2d 876 (Colo. 1995). Applied in Raullerson v. People, 157 Colo. 462, 404 P.2d 149 (1965); Reed v. People, 171 Colo. 421, 467 P.2d 809 (1970); People v. Bercillio, 179 Colo. 383, 500 P.2d 975 (1972); People v. Fink, 41 Colo. App. 47, 579 P.2d 659 (1978); Kaltenbach v. Julesburg Sch. Dist. Re-1, 43 Colo. App. 150, 603 P.2d 955 (1979); People v. Velarde, 200 Colo. 374, 616 P.2d 104 (1980); People v. Gonzales, 631 P.2d 1170 (Colo. App. 1981); People v. Rivers, 727 P.2d 394 (Colo. App. 1986). II. Examination. Purpose of voir dire examination is to enable counsel to determine whether any prospective jurors are possessed of beliefs which would cause them to be biased in such a manner as to prevent his client from obtaining a fair and impartial trial. People v. Mackey, 185 Colo. 24, 521 P.2d 910 (1974); People v. Heller, 698 P.2d 1357 (Colo. App. 1984), rev'd on other grounds, 712 P.2d 1023 (Colo. 1986); People v. Collins, 730 P.2d 293 (Colo. 1986). While a defendant does not have a constitutional right to voir dire a prospective jury panel, such right is expressly granted under rules of criminal procedure. People v. Lefebre, 981 P.2d 650 (Colo. App. 1998), aff'd on other grounds, 5 P.3d 295 (Colo. 2000). Court may limit, but may not deny, the defendant's right to voir dire. People v. Lefebre, 981 P.2d 650 (Colo. App. 1998), aff'd on other grounds, 5 P.3d 295 (Colo. 2000). The court's error in denying defense counsel the right to question a prospective juror who was excused by the court does not constitute prejudice requiring a reversal of the conviction where defendant does not allege that the jury that was seated was unfair or partial and where the prosecution did not exhaust its peremptory challenges and thus could have removed the prospective juror even if the court had not excused him. People v. Evans, 987 P.2d 845 (Colo. App. 1998). The knowledge or ignorance of prospective jurors concerning questions of law is generally not a proper subject of inquiry for voir dire. People v. Collins, 730 P.2d 293 (Colo. 1986). Restrictions within court's discretion. Restrictions on the scope of the voir dire examination are within the trial court's discretion, and will not be reversed on appeal absent an abuse of that discretion. People v. Saiz, 660 P.2d 2 (Colo. App. 1982); People v. Rivers, 727 P.2d 394 (Colo. App. 1986); People v. Reaud, 821 P.2d 870 (Colo. App. 1991). If there is firm and clear evidence that a potential juror holds an actual bias that is unlikely to change through education concerning the trial process, exposure to basic principles governing criminal trials, or questioning by the court or the parties, the judge is permitted to excuse that juror without additional questioning. Under subsection (a)(3) of this rule, a trial judge must ordinarily permit voir dire of jurors in circumstances that could involve actual bias. Such questioning is useful to determine whether the juror can set aside bias and decide the case based on the evidence presented and the court's instructions. However, the trial need not waste time on further questioning where there is firm and clear evidence that a juror is unfit to serve under subparagraph (b)(1)(X) of this rule or if there is implied bias under subparagraphs (b)(1)(I) through (IX) or (b)(1)(XII) of this rule. People v. Lefebre, 5 P.3d 295 (Colo. 2000). Trial court abused its discretion in dismissing jurors without allowing the defense to question them where the record did not contain firm and clear evidence that the jurors removed for cause held actual biases that they could not set aside. The following responses on a written questionnaire were insufficient to support dismissal for cause without further questioning: Juror's assertion that he could not be fair because his brother had been convicted of the same offense with which defendant was charged; juror's assertion that a prior criminal background would prevent him from being fair; and juror's statement that he could not be fair because his sister serves as an expert witness and he had not liked the district attorney's treatment of her on the witness stand. People v. Lefebre, 5 P.3d 295 (Colo. 2000). Propriety of questions within discretion of trial court. The propriety of questions to potential jurors on voir dire is within the discretion of the trial court, and its ruling thereon will not be disturbed on appeal unless an abuse of that discretion is shown. People v. Buckner, 180 Colo. 65, 504 P.2d 669 (1972); People v. Collins, 730 P.2d 293 (Colo. 1986); People v. Shipman, 747 P.2d 1 (Colo. App. 1987). Trial court did not abuse its discretion in disallowing one of defense counsel's questions that went to the defendant's theory of the case. The court permitted other questions that allowed the defendant to determine whether potential jurors held certain attitudes toward the defendant's affirmative defense. People v. Lybarger, 790 P.2d 855 (Colo. App. 1989), rev'd on other grounds, 807 P.2d 570 (Colo. 1991). Rule expressly authorizes counsel to directly question prospective jurors and the judge cannot require counsel to submit questions to prospective jurors through the judge. The judge may, however, limit counsel's questions if they are unduly repetitious, irrelevant, or otherwise improper. People v. Reaud, 821 P.2d 870 (Colo. App. 1991). The court's blanket prohibition against questions regarding a prospective juror's understanding of an instruction is an abuse of discretion where the court makes no inquiry as to the nature of the questions. People v. Reaud, 821 P.2d 870 (Colo. App. 1991). Trial court's failure to conduct examination not plain error. Trial court's failure to explain to potential jurors the qualifications for jury service, the grounds for challenges for cause, and juror's duty to inform the court of anything that would disqualify them from service was not plain error when no party objected. People v. Page, 907 P.2d 624 (Colo. App. 1995). Court's questioning and "rehabilitation" of prospective jurors was not improper where the questions were directed to eliciting information on the subject of the prospective jurors' possible bias and were no more leading than necessary. People v. James, 981 P.2d 637 (Colo. App. 1998). III. Challenges for Cause. A. In General. Distinguishing between challenges. Courts distinguish between challenges "propter affectum", those relating to a juror's bias, prejudice, interest, etc., and challenges "propter defectum", those relating to the absence of some purely statutory qualification such as residence, citizenship, property owning, taxpaying, etc., holding that disregard of the former constitutes reversible error but not disregard of the latter. Also, in case of the former, prejudice to the litigant may be assumed; in case of the latter, it must be shown. Exceptions to this rule are not wanting, but these rest generally upon special facts and are supported by sound reason. Harris v. People, 113 Colo. 511, 160 P.2d 372 (1945). Examination and disposal of challenges within discretion of court. The method and order of procedure in ascertaining the qualifications of veniremen and in disposing of challenges for cause are commonly in the discretion of the court. Denver City Tramway Co. v. Carson, 21 Colo. App. 604, 123 P. 680 (1912). But discretion is not an arbitrary one, and a party is not to be unreasonably denied a challenge to which he shows himself entitled, because his right in such case is a substantial right which it is not within the discretion of the court to take away. Denver City Tramway Co. v. Carson, 21 Colo. App. 604, 123 P. 680 (1912). Determination of the trial court upon a question of fact is not subject to review in challenges to jurors. Union Gold Mining Co. v. Rocky Mt. Nat'l Bank, 2 Colo. 565 (1875), aff'd, 96 U.S. 640, 24 L. Ed. 648 (1877).

Challenge need not be made immediately when grounds become apparent. The challenge of a particular juror for cause need not be made at the very time when the ground of challenge becomes apparent and before proceeding to the examination of another juror. Denver City Tramway Co. v. Carson, 21 Colo. App. 604, 123 P. 680 (1912). Improper for court to require challenge for cause, and subsequent argument, in the presence of potential jurors. However, not plain error requiring reversal of conviction where there is no evidence in record supporting assertion that the challenged jurors were biased by hearing the challenges for cause nor were the challenges so obviously inflammatory to raise the presumption that bias resulted. People v. Flockhart, __ P.3d __ (Colo. App. 2009). No dismissal if juror will render impartial verdict. No juror can be dismissed for cause if the trial court is satisfied the juror will render an impartial verdict. People v. Romero, 42 Colo. App. 20, 593 P.2d 365 (1978). No abuse of discretion to deny challenge for cause where trial court conducted inquiry of juror who was related to sheriff's posse members and was satisfied with juror's specific assurances that she could render a fair and impartial verdict. People v. Goodpaster, 742 P.2d 965 (Colo. App. 1987). No abuse of discretion to deny challenge for cause where trial court concluded that prospective juror, who was a neighbor of police officer who would be testifying, specifically stated that he would not give more or less credibility to the officer's testimony as a result. People v. Loggins, 981 P.2d 630 (Colo. App. 1998). No abuse of discretion in denying challenge for cause where trial court determined that first cousin of investigating police department's chief of police who indicated that while her relationship with the mother of the chief could create a hardship for her she could nonetheless be impartial. People v. Pasillas-Sanchez, 214 P.3d 520 (Colo. App. 2009). Missing portion of transcript of voir dire proceedings does not automatically require reversal. Where trial court held a hearing to reconstruct, to the extent possible, the relevant portion of voir dire, the court's denial of the challenge for cause was upheld. People v. Loggins, 981 P.2d 630 (Colo. App. 1998). Prejudice is shown if defendant exhausts all of his peremptory challenges and one of those challenges is expended on a juror who should have been removed for cause. A defendant is not required to request an additional peremptory challenge to preserve this issue on appeal. People v. Prator, 833 P.2d 819 (Colo. App. 1992). Court properly denied challenge for cause of a prospective juror because, although the juror stated that she basically believed children to be honest, she also indicated she would apply the principles of law given by the court to their testimony. People v. Howard, 886 P.2d 296 (Colo. App. 1994). Defendant must exercise reasonable diligence to determine whether a prospective juror should have been excused. If defendant fails to do so, he or she is considered to have waived his or her opportunity to raise any matters pertaining to the qualifications and competency of the excluded juror on appeal. People v. Asberry, 172 P.3d 927 (Colo. App. 2007). B. Effect of Juror's Opinion or Interest. Subparagraph (b)(1)(X) of this rule does not conflict with the sixth amendment to the United States Constitution, which secures to persons charged with crime the right to be tried by an impartial jury. Jones v. People, 2 Colo. 351 (1874). Defendant has right to ask questions to show existence of grounds for challenge. The defendant has a right to propound questions to the proposed jurors, to show not only that there exists proper grounds for a challenge for cause but also to elicit facts to enable him to decide whether or not he would make a peremptory challenge. Union Pac. Ry. v. Jones, 21 Colo. 340, 40 P. 891 (1895); Jones v. People, 23 Colo. 276, 47 P. 275 (1896); Zancannelli v. People, 63 Colo. 252, 165 P. 612 (1917). The mere expression of some concern by a prospective juror regarding a certain aspect or issue of a case should not result in automatic dismissal of that prospective juror for cause. Likewise, dismissal for cause is not required merely because a prospective juror answers questions in a way that might indicate some bias, prejudice, or preconceived notion. The decisive question is whether it is possible for the prospective juror to set aside his or her preconceived notions and decide the case based on the evidence and the court's instructions. In determining whether a prospective juror can do so, the trial court should consider all available facts, including the prospective juror's assurances of fairness and impartiality. People v. Arko, 159 P.3d 713 (Colo. App. 2006), rev'd on other grounds, 183 P.3d 555 (Colo. 2008). Challenge for cause should be granted where prospective juror is unwilling or unable to accept the basic principles of law applicable to the case and to render a fair and impartial verdict based upon the trial. People v. Russo, 713 P.2d 356 (Colo. 1986); People v. Esch, 786 P.2d 462 (Colo. App. 1989). Juror who is not impartial should be dismissed. If there is sufficient reason to question the impartiality of the juror, the trial court should grant a challenge for cause if the trial court is satisfied the juror will render an impartial verdict. People v. Romero, 42 Colo. App. 20, 593 P.2d 365 (1978). No abuse of discretion to deny challenge for cause where trial court conducted inquiry of juror who was related to should grant a challenge for cause and dismiss the juror. Nailor v. People, 200 Colo. 30, 612 P.2d 79 (1980); People v. Russo, 677 P.2d 386 (Colo. App. 1983). To ensure that the right to a fair trial is protected, the trial court must excuse prejudiced or biased persons from the jury. Nailor v. People, 200 Colo. 30, 612 P.2d 79 (1980); People v. Gurule, 628 P.2d 99 (Colo. 1981).

If the trial court has genuine doubt about the juror's ability to be impartial, it should resolve the doubt by sustaining the challenge. People v. Russo, 713 P.2d 356 (Colo. 1986). Or who will not follow court's instructions. A prospective juror should be excused if it appears doubtful that he will be governed by the instructions of the court as to the law of the case. Morgan v. People, 624 P.2d 1331 (Colo. 1981). And failure to excuse prejudiced juror is abuse of discretion. Where a juror repeatedly indicated that he would have difficulty applying the principles that the burden of proof rests solely upon the prosecution to establish the guilt of the accused, the trial court abused its discretion by failing to excuse him. Morgan v. People, 624 P.2d 1331 (Colo. 1981). Where the prospective juror patently demonstrates a fixed prejudgment about the merits of the case and an unwillingness to accept and apply those principles that form the bedrock of a fair trial, the trial court errs in refusing to excuse that juror when casually challenged. People v. Gurule, 628 P.2d 99 (Colo. 1981). But denying challenge to juror with bias against handguns not abuse. In a prosecution for armed robbery, the court does not abuse its discretion in denying a challenge for cause to potential juror who admits his long-standing bias against handguns, where the juror is questioned extensively by the court and defendant's counsel on his opinions concerning handguns and the probable effect of his opinions and experiences on his evaluation of the evidence, where the juror reveals no enmity or bias toward the defendant or the state, and where he expresses an understanding of the principles upon which a fair trial is based. People v. Ward, 673 P.2d 47 (Colo. App. 1983). General prejudice against crime does not disqualify. Under this rule a general prejudice against crime, or prejudice against the particular crime with which the accused stands charged, does not disqualify a juror. Smith v. People, 39 Colo. 202, 88 P. 1072 (1907); Ausmus v. People, 47 Colo. 167, 107 P. 204 (1910); Forte v. People, 57 Colo. 450, 140 P. 789 (1914); McGonigal v. People, 74 Colo. 270, 220 P. 1003 (1923); Shank v. People, 79 Colo. 576, 247 P. 559 (1926); Fleagle v. People, 87 Colo. 532, 289 P. 1078 (1930). Nor does a financial interest not directly affected. Where, in a prosecution of bank officers for a conspiracy to defraud the bank, certain jurors, though creditors of the bank or financially interested therein at the time of its failure, testified that they had no bias or prejudice against the defendants, and any interest they might have in the bank's affairs could not be affected in any way by the litigation, they were not disqualified. Imboden v. People, 40 Colo. 142, 90 P. 608 (1907). And fact that jurors have read newspaper articles relating to a case does not disqualify them as jurors. Kurtz v. People, 177 Colo. 306, 494 P.2d 97 (1972). Even though juror may have preconceived notion as to the guilt or innocence of an accused he may not be automatically disqualified from serving. Kurtz v. People, 177 Colo. 306, 494 P.2d 97 (1972). That a person has an opinion or impression concerning the guilt or innocence of the accused which can only be removed by evidence is by no means conclusive of his disqualification to serve as a juror. Solander v. People, 2 Colo. 48 (1873); Union Gold Mining Co. v. Rocky Mt. Nat'l Bank, 2 Colo. 565 (1875), aff'd, 96 U.S. 640, 24 L. Ed. 648 (1877); Jones v. People, 6 Colo. 452, 45 Am. R. 526 (1882); Denver, S. P. & P. R. R. v. Driscoll, 12 Colo. 520, 21 P. 708, 13 Am. St. R. 243 (1889); Babcock v. People, 13 Colo. 515, 22 P. 817 (1889); Carroll v. People, 177 Colo. 288, 494 P.2d 80 (1972); Kurtz v. People, 177 Colo. 306, 494 P.2d 97 (1972); People v. Buckner, 180 Colo. 65, 504 P.2d 669 (1972). On the theory that news report will not control judgment. As a rule, citizens who are fit to try criminal cases will not allow previous opinions based upon unofficial reports to control their judgment against the sworn evidence in a case. Babcock v. People, 13 Colo. 515, 22 P. 817 (1889); Power v. People, 17 Colo. 178, 28 P. 1121 (1892). Where the voir dire amply demonstrates the absence of prejudice and the ability of the jurors to set aside any opinions that they may have received from the news media to the end that the case could be determined on the law and on the evidence, reversal is not called for. Sergent v. People, 177 Colo. 354, 497 P.2d 983 (1972). Where the record contained no evidence that any juror was prejudiced by having read anything in the newspapers, the denial of a challenge for cause was clearly within the trial court's discretion. People v. McKay, 191 Colo. 381, 553 P.2d 380 (1976). The fact that a juror entertains an opinion as to the guilt or innocence of a defendant does not disqualify him, if the court believes that he can and will disregard that opinion and return a verdict based solely upon the evidence. McGonigal v. People, 74 Colo. 270, 220 P. 1003 (1923); Johns v. Shinall, 103 Colo. 381, 86 P.2d 605 (1939); Goldsberry v. People, 149 Colo. 431, 369 P.2d 787 (1962); People v. Buckner, 180 Colo. 65, 504 P.2d 669 (1972). So long as the court is satisfied, from an examination of the prospective juror or from other evidence, that the juror will render an impartial verdict according to the evidence admitted at trial and the court's instructions of law, the court may permit the juror to serve. People v. Gurule, 628 P.2d 99 (Colo. 1981). The proper test under this rule when a juror states he has "partially" formed an opinion is, can and will the juror render a verdict according to the evidence heard upon the trial impartially and fairly under his oath so to do, regardless of his preconceived opinions. If the juror declares upon his voir dire oath that he can and will so decide, there is no cause for sustaining a challenge on the ground of such previously formed opinion. Solander v. People, 2 Colo. 48 (1873); Jones v. People, 6 Colo. 452, 45 Am. R. 526 (1882). General discussions of crime and possible punishments by a prospective juror do not show sufficient bias or prejudice to disqualify him from serving where he clearly states to the court that he has not arrived at any conclusions and that his mind is free and open. Fleagle v. People, 87 Colo. 532, 289 P. 1078 (1930); Abshier v. People, 87 Colo. 507, 289 P. 1081 (1930). Trial courts have considerable discretion in ruling on challenges for cause, because the trial judge is in the best position to assess the credibility, demeanor, and sincerity of the potential juror's responses, including statements that linguistically may appear to be inconsistent. People v. Richardson, 58 P.3d 1039 (Colo. App. 2002). Trial court did not abuse its discretion in denying challenge for cause to juror who admitted familiarity with murder case from press accounts, but who stated she would attempt to be fair and impartial despite such knowledge. People v. Brown, 731 P.2d 763 (Colo. App. 1986). Nor did trial court abuse its discretion in denying challenge for cause to juror who admitted that she had read about the case involving felony child abuse that resulted in death and may have formed an opinion about the defendant's affirmative defense. Juror, upon sufficient questioning by the court, said she would listen to the evidence presented and would apply the court's instruction on the law in reaching a verdict. People v. Lybarger, 790 P.2d 855 (Colo. App. 1989), rev'd on other grounds, 807 P.2d 570 (Colo. 1991). Test as to whether prospective juror has been unduly affected by pretrial publicity is whether the nature and strength of the opinion formed or of the information learned from that publicity are such as necessarily raise the presumption of partiality or of the inability of the potential juror to block out the information from his consideration. People v. Romero, 42 Colo. App. 20, 593 P.2d 365 (1978); People v. Bashara, 677 P.2d 1376 (Colo. App. 1983). Neither the department of social services nor the equal employment opportunity commission constitute a "law enforcement agency", and therefore trial court did not err by refusing defendant's challenge for cause of jurors employed by such entities. People v. Zurenko, 833 P.2d 794 (Colo. App. 1991). Exclusion of unconscious influence of preconceptions cannot be assumed. One cannot assume that the average juror is so endowed with a sense of detachment, so clear in his introspective perception of his own mental processes, that he may exclude even the unconscious influence of his preconceptions. Beeman v. People, 193 Colo. 337, 565 P.2d 1340 (1977). Belief that failure to testify indicates guilt does not disqualify. Notwithstanding a juror expressed belief that failure of defendant to testify would be an indication of guilt, where such juror acknowledges a willingness to lay aside any personal belief and follow the law as instructed by the court, a challenge for cause is properly overruled. Goldsberry v. People, 149 Colo. 431, 369 P.2d 787 (1962). Trial court did not abuse its discretion in denying defendant's challenge for cause where defense counsel asked during voir dire whether anyone believed it would be impossible to be fair if defendant did not testify and juror stated that it would and that it might upset her, but not so much as to affect her decision making. The trial court found that the juror indicated she would do what the court instructed her to do even though she might not like it. People v. Frantz, 114 P.3d 34 (Colo. App. 2004). Informing jurors of mandatory sentence for crime not proper purpose for voir dire. The trial court did not err in refusing to allow defense counsel to conduct voir dire for the purpose of informing potential jurors of the mandatory sentence for a crime of violence. People v. Swain, 43 Colo. App. 343, 607 P.2d 396 (1979). Voir dire examination concerning capital punishment. Carroll v. People, 177 Colo. 288, 494 P.2d 80 (1972); Segura v. District Court, 179 Colo. 20, 498 P.2d 926 (1972); People v. District Court, 190 Colo. 342, 546 P.2d 1268 (1976). Knowledge of jurors concerning questions of law not proper subject for voir dire. The knowledge or ignorance of prospective jurors concerning questions of law is generally not a proper subject of inquiry for voir dire, for it is presumed that jurors will be adequately informed as to the applicable law by the instructions of the court. People v. Swain, 43 Colo. App. 343, 607 P.2d 396 (1979). Juror with tenuous relationship with law enforcement agency should be excused. To insure that a jury is impartial in both fact and appearance, a prospective juror who has even a tenuous relationship with any prosecutorial or law enforcement arm of the state should be excused from jury duty in a criminal case. People in Interest of R.A.D., 196 Colo. 430, 586 P.2d 46 (1978). Challenge for cause valid. Juror's close association with the law enforcement establishment, the crime scene, and the co-employee who attended the murder victim required dismissal for cause. People v. Rogers, 690 P.2d 886 (Colo. App. 1984). The trial court did not abuse its discretion in denying defendant's challenge for cause to a juror that had multiple associations with law enforcement. The juror understood that the defense had no burden of

91

proof, that the prosecution had the burden of proving every element, and that both sides would get a fair trial from said juror. People v. Richardson, 58 P.3d 1039 (Colo. App. 2002). The trial court did not abuse its discretion in denying defendant's challenge for cause to a juror based on said juror's views regarding the death penalty and previous traumatic experiences. The juror did not express any partiality for or bias in favor of or against either side. People v. Richardson, 58 P.3d 1039 (Colo. App. 2002). State penitentiary deemed law enforcement agency. The state penitentiary, as a state "institution" within the department of institutions, is a law enforcement agency for the purposes of determining the eligibility of employees thereof to serve as jurors. People v. Scott, 41 Colo. App. 66, 583 P.2d 939 (1978). Showing of bias not required. Under § 16-10-103 and subsection (b)(XII), the actual bias of a law enforcement employee need not be shown to sustain a challenge for cause. People in Interest of R.A.D., 196 Colo. 430, 586 P.2d 46 (1978). But disqualification not applicable to former employees. As § 16-10-103 and this rule do not purport to disqualify former employees of a public law enforcement agency challenged for cause, a defendant's challenge of a retired guard member of the jury panel should be denied. People v. Scott, 41 Colo. App. 66, 583 P.2d 939 (1978). Prospective juror clearly was not an "employee" under subparagraph (b)(1)(XII) of this rule or § 16-10-103 where she volunteered to serve on an on-call basis to work with victims, at the time of trial had been an advocate for a brief period, had been called only approximately six times, and had only a casual limited time commitment. People v. Gilbert, 12 P.3d 331 (Colo. App. 2000). Defendants were not prejudiced by having the wife of the deputy sheriff on jury where voir dire questions revealed that her husband was a police officer, but where she was not asked whether he was a deputy sheriff nor did she disclose the information, because it would have added nothing material to counsel's decision as to whether to challenge for bias. Ray v. People, 147 Colo. 587, 364 P.2d 578 (1961). Noncitizen properly excused from jury. It is proper to excuse from the jury a person who is not a citizen of the United States. Babcock v. People, 13 Colo. 515, 22 P. 817 (1889). A county official whose office, by statutory mandate, is represented by the prosecutor need not automatically be excluded from serving on a jury on the grounds that the county official is implicitly biased. The relationship between the offices of the clerk and county recorder and of the district attorney, standing alone, does not provide sufficient grounds to justify a challenge for cause. People v. Rhodus, 870 P.2d 470 (Colo. 1994). C. Public Law Enforcement Agency or Public Defender's Office Employee as Juror. While § 16-10-103(1)(k) and subparagraph (b)(1)(XII) of this rule require a trial court to grant a party's challenge for cause to a juror who is employed by a public law enforcement agency, neither expressly requires the court to excuse a juror sua sponte. People v. Hinojos-Mendoza, 140 P.3d 30 (Colo. App. 2005), aff'd in part and rev'd in part on other grounds, 169 P.3d 662 (Colo. 2007). For purposes of § 16-10-103(1)(k) or subparagraph (b)(1)(XII) of this rule, the environmental protection agency is properly characterized as an investigatory and rulemaking body, and not a law enforcement agency. People v. Simon, 100 P.3d 487 (Colo. App. 2004). Division of youth corrections (DYC) within the department of human services is a public law enforcement agency within the meaning of § 16-10-103(1)(k) and subparagraph (b)(1)(XII) of this rule. The court erroneously denied defendant's challenge for cause to a prospective juror employed by the DYC. People v. Sommerfeld, 214 P.3d 570 (Colo. App. 2009). An employee of a community corrections facility is an employee of a public law enforcement agency within the meaning of § 16-10-103(1)(k) and subparagraph (b)(1)(XII) of this rule. People v. Romero, 197 P.3d 302 (Colo. App. 2008). The office of the state attorney general is a law enforcement agency for purposes of § 16-10-103(1)(k). People v. Novotny, __ P.3d __ (Colo. App. 2010). D. Determination of Juror's Fitness. Court is trier of qualifications of jurors. Babcock v. People, 13 Colo. 515, 22 P. 817 (1889). Extent of examination by trial judge. The trial judge may examine prospective jurors on any matter relevant to their competence as jurors. People v. Mackey, 185 Colo. 24, 521 P.2d 910 (1974). Court to determine if juror indifferent. This rule makes the trial court the trier of the qualifications of the jurors when challenged on the ground of having formed opinions, and it is for that court to determine, as a matter of fact, whether the juror stands indifferent. Thompson v. People, 26 Colo. 496, 59 P. 51 (1899); Solander v. People, 2 Colo. 48 (1873); Jones v. People, 6 Colo. 452, 45 Am. R. 526 (1882); Babcock v. People, 13 Colo. 515, 22 P. 817 (1889); Power v. People, 17 Colo. 178, 28 P. 1121 (1892); Leick v. People, 136 Colo. 535, 322 P.2d 674, cert. denied, 357 U.S. 922, 78 S. Ct. 1363, 2 L. Ed. 2d 1366 (1958). While a challenge based upon the interest or bias or prejudice of a juror is somewhat different from that based upon the grounds of having formed an opinion, so far as the determination of his qualifications is concerned, the principle is the same; and as this rule makes the trial court trier of the qualifications of jurors when challenged upon the grounds of having formed opinions, it is for that court to determine as a matter of fact whether the juror stands indifferent. Imboden v. People, 40 Colo. 142, 90 P. 608 (1907); Minich v. People, 8 Colo. 440, 9 P. 4 (1885); Babcock v. People, 13 Colo. 515, 22 P. 817 (1889); Thompson v. People, 26 Colo. 496, 59 P. 51 (1899). "Undue hardship" may include financial burden. What constitutes "undue hardship" sufficient to excuse a juror lies within the discretion of the trial court, and includes one for whom jury service would impose an undue financial burden. People v. Reese, 670 P.2d 11 (Colo. App. 1983). Trial judge determines as a fact the fitness of the jurors to hear and determine an issue. Leick v. People, 136 Colo. 535, 322 P.2d 674, cert. denied, 357 U.S. 922, 78 S. Ct. 1363, 2 L. Ed. 2d 1366 (1958). And appellate court to review trial judge's determination. The placing of discretion in the trial judge in jury selection procedures does not permit appellate courts to abdicate their responsibility to ensure that the requirements of fairness are fulfilled. Morgan v. People, 624 P.2d 1331 (Colo. 1981). But trial court's determination will not be disturbed on review. Where a trial court is satisfied that a juror can lay aside a previously formed opinion and decide a case upon its evidence, the court's decision will not be disturbed on review. Fleagle v. People, 87 Colo. 532, 289 P. 1078 (1930); Babcock v. People, 13 Colo. 515, 22 P. 817 (1889); Hillen v. People, 59 Colo. 280, 149 P. 250 (1915); Shank v. People, 79 Colo. 576, 247 P. 559 (1926); People v. Nunez, 698 P.2d 1376 (Colo. App. 1984), aff'd, 737 P.2d 422 (Colo. 1987). The trial court is in the best position to view the demeanor of a juror claiming impartiality, and the record must affirmatively demonstrate that the trial court abused its discretion before its decision can be disturbed on appeal. People v. Russo, 713 P.2d 356 (Colo. 1986); People v. Christopher, 896 P.2d 876 (Colo. 1995). A new trial may be required where a juror deliberately misrepresents or knowingly conceals information relevant to a challenge for cause or a preemptory challenge; however, where the juror's nondisclosure was inadvertent, the defendant must show that the nondisclosed fact was such as to create an actual bias either in favor of the prosecution or against the defendant. People v. Christopher, 896 P.2d 876 (Colo. 1995). Absent abuse of discretion. If the trial judge is persuaded that a juror would fairly and impartially try the issues, his denial of a challenge for cause should not be disturbed, except where such denial is clearly an abuse of discretion. Leick v. People, 136 Colo. 535, 322 P.2d 674, cert. denied, 357 U.S. 922, 78 S. Ct. 1363, 2 L. Ed. 2d 1366 (1958); Solander v. People, 2 Colo. 48 (1873); Jones v. People, 2 Colo. 351 (1874); Jones v. People, 6 Colo. 452, 45 Am. R. 526 (1882); Babcock v. People, 13 Colo. 515, 22 P. 817 (1889); Thompson v. People, 26 Colo. 496, 59 P. 51 (1899); McGonigal v. People, 74 Colo. 270, 220 P. 1003 (1923); Shank v. People, 79 Colo. 576, 247 P. 559 (1926). Since trial judge in best position to observe. While a trial judge hears the questions put to a juror and the answers given, observes a juror's demeanor while being interrogated, and discerns through the use of his eyes, ears, and intelligence wherein truth and credit should be given, a reviewing court does not have the benefit of this personal observation which is so important in judging the credibility of a juror. Leick v. People, 136 Colo. 535, 322 P.2d 674, cert. denied, 357 U.S. 922, 78 S. Ct. 1363, 2 L. Ed. 2d 1366 (1958). The ultimate decision of whether or not to grant a challenge for cause is one for the trial court's sound discretion, since the factors of credibility and appearance which are determinative of bias are best observed at the trial court level. Nailor v. People, 200 Colo. 30, 612 P.2d 79 (1980). The need for a careful evaluation of the competence of potential jurors to assess the defendant's guilt or innocence solely on the evidence admitted at trial, and the serious practical problems involved with these assessments, are sound reasons for placing great discretion in the trial court in the jury selection procedures. Morgan v. People, 624 P.2d 1331 (Colo. 1981). IV. Peremptory Challenges. Section 16-10-104 controls over section (d). Peremptory challenges, while not constitutionally required, are deemed to be an effective means of securing a more impartial and better qualified jury and, as such, are an important right of an accused. While also having an incidental effect on trial procedure, § 16-10-104 , is primarily an expression of policy concerning this right of the accused, a substantive matter, and, thus, controls over section (d) of this rule. People v. Hollis, 670 P.2d 441 (Colo. App. 1983). Although § 16-10-104 refers to the number of challenges in capital cases, it does not define "capital case". By contrast, subsection (d)(1) of this rule does define the term. The rule and the statute, therefore, do not "conflict" in the sense of being irreconcilable or necessarily incompatible with each other, and the rule can be given effect without producing a result irreconcilable with the plain language of the statute. People v. Reynolds, 159 P.3d 684 (Colo. App. 2006). The time for determining the number of peremptory challenges is the time voir dire is commenced. People v. Hollis, 670 P.2d 441 (Colo. App. 1983). Number of peremptory challenges allowed is governed by the statute and rule in effect at the time voir dire is conducted. People v. Priest, 672 P.2d 539 (Colo. App. 1983). Party has absolute right to use all peremptory challenges granted him by this rule, and any frustration thereof, whether by erroneous ruling, false information, or concealment constitutes reversible error. Harris v. People, 113 Colo. 511, 160 P.2d 372 (1945). And unnecessary use of peremptory challenges not error where not fatal. Where a challenge by the accused to a juror for cause should have been sustained, but the objectionable juror was subsequently peremptorily challenged by defendant, and, at the time of going to trial, defendant had left unused seven peremptory challenges, the error was not fatal to the judgment. Minich v. People, 8 Colo. 440, 9 P. 4 (1885); Solander v. People, 2 Colo. 48 (1873); Jones v. People, 2 Colo. 351 (1874). But error where peremptory challenges exhausted unnecessarily. Where a challenge is properly made, but is overruled by the court, and the challenging party afterwards exhausted his peremptory challenges, using one of them on the disqualified juror, the action of the court in denying the challenge is error to the substantial prejudice of the party who made the challenge. Denver City Tramway Co. v. Carson, 21 Colo. App. 604, 123 P. 680 (1912); Denver City Tramway Co. v. Kennedy, 50 Colo. 418, 117 P. 167 (1911); People v. Maes, 43 Colo. App. 365, 609 P.2d 1105 (1979); People v. Russo, 677 P.2d 386 (Colo. App. 1983). Prejudice is shown if defendant exhausts all of his peremptory challenges and one of those challenges is expended on a juror who should have been removed for cause. A defendant is not required to request an additional peremptory challenge to preserve this issue on appeal. People v. Prator, 833 P.2d 819 (Colo. App. 1992). However, defendant must show exhaustion on appeal. Where defendant claims error in denial of his challenge of a juror for cause who was later excused by peremptory challenge, but makes no showing that all of the peremptory challenges to which defendant was entitled were exercised, nor is it shown that he was deprived of the right to challenge any other prospective juror because he was forced to exhaust his peremptory challenges, even assuming that the court should have sustained the challenge for cause, there can be no prejudice to the rights of the defendant resulting from the denial of such challenge. Skeels v. People, 145 Colo. 281, 358 P.2d 605 (1961). Where the trial court improperly removed jurors for cause and the prosecution subsequently used all of its peremptory challenges, the prosecution enjoyed an unfair tactical advantage in determining the makeup of the jury, detrimentally affecting the rights of the defendant and requiring a new trial. Improperly dismissing some jurors for cause had the effect of granting additional peremptory challenges to the prosecution. It was irrelevant that the defendant had full ability to use his peremptory challenges. The prosecution's relatively greater ability to remove jurors it viewed as objectionable was independently prejudicial to the defendant's rights, and the court presumed prejudice to the defendant. People v. Lefebre, 5 P.3d 295 (Colo. 2000). Defendant must object to the use of excess peremptory challenges. Right to object to prosecution's use of more than statutorily allowed number of peremptory challenges is waived unless there is timely objection by the defendant. Righi v. People, 145 Colo. 457, 359 P.2d 656 (1961). Judge may grant peremptory challenge of juror after his acceptance. Although there is no provision in section (d), for the trial judge to exercise his discretion, in a proper case the trial judge may properly exercise his discretion, upon a showing of good cause, and grant a peremptory challenge even after the juror has been accepted. Simms v. People, 174 Colo. 85, 482 P.2d 974 (1971). Subsection (d)(3) of this rule allows the court to add peremptory challenges to either or both sides, but does not require the court to do so. People v. Heller, 698 P.2d 1357 (Colo. App. 1984), rev'd on other grounds, 712 P.2d 1023 (Colo. 1986). Applicability of right of 10 peremptory challenges to adjudicative stage of a juvenile proceeding. People in Interest of T.A.W., 38 Colo. App. 175, 556 P.2d 1225 (1976). V. Custody of Jury. This rule implements traditional practice of trial courts in this state. Segura v. People, 159 Colo. 371, 412 P.2d 227 (1966). Colorado permits the separation of jurors even in capital cases where assented to by the attorneys for the parties, although the supreme court has expressed its disapproval of the practice in serious criminal cases. Segura v. People, 159 Colo. 371, 412 P.2d 227 (1966). But rule requires sequestration of jurors in first-degree murder case unless requirement waived by the accused. Tribe v. District Court, 197 Colo. 433, 593 P.2d 1369 (1979); Segura v. People, 159 Colo. 371, 412 P.2d 227 (1966). Defendant's personal assent as opposed to counsel's alone is not mandatory for such waiver in capital cases. Segura v. People, 159 Colo. 371, 412 P.2d 227 (1966). Showing of prejudice necessary for error where counsel agrees to separation. Where defense counsel expressly agrees to separation of the jury in a capital case, error cannot be predicated on that procedure in the absence of a showing of prejudice to the defendant. Segura v. People, 159 Colo. 371, 412 P.2d 227 (1966). And, in such a case, the defendant has burden of proof. Segura v. People, 159 Colo. 371, 412 P.2d 227 (1966). Burden of showing prejudice from separation of a deliberating jury in a noncapital case also rests upon the defendant. People v. Maestas, 187 Colo. 107, 528 P.2d 916 (1974). And absent a showing of prejudice, separation is not grounds for reversal. People v. Maestas, 187 Colo. 107, 528 P.2d 916 (1974). Determination of whether prejudice has occurred during jury sequestration is within the sound discretion of the trial court and only where that discretion has been abused will a new trial be ordered. People v. Mackey, 185 Colo. 24, 521 P.2d 910 (1974). Trial of a first-degree murder charge is a "capital case" for purposes of jury sequestration under section (f), even though the district attorney does not intend to qualify the jury for consideration of the death penalty or to seek the imposition of the death penalty in the event of a conviction. People ex rel. Faulk v. District Court, 667 P.2d 1384 (Colo. 1983) (decided prior to 1983 amendment of this rule); People v. Jones, 677 P.2d 383 (Colo. App. 1983), aff'd in part and rev'd in part on other grounds, 711 P.2d 1270 (Colo. 1986). While the rule does not expressly forbid a trial court from allowing jurors to predeliberate, those juror discussions are not allowed in criminal cases in Colorado. People v. Preciado-Flores, 66 P.3d 155 (Colo. App. 2002). VI. Alternate Jurors. Alternate jurors must be discharged at the time the jury retires to deliberate; any replacement of a regular juror by an alternate must occur prior to such time. People v. Burnette, 753 P.2d 773 (Colo. App. 1987), aff'd, 775 P.2d 583 (Colo. 1989) (decided prior to 1993 amendment). Section 16-10-105 controls over section (e) of this rule because the statute provides substantive, in addition to procedural, direction to the trial court. Carrillo v. People, 974 P.2d 478 (Colo. 1999). Trial court has the authority under both § 16-10-105 and section (e) of this rule to replace a juror with an alternate after jury deliberations have commenced. Carrillo v. People, 974 P.2d 478 (Colo. 1999). If a trial court interrupts deliberations of a jury and suspends the jury's fact finding functions to investigate allegations of juror misconduct, the court's inquiry must not intrude into the deliberative process. In the exercise of judicial discretion, before a juror is dismissed from a deliberating jury due to an allegation of juror misconduct, the court must make findings supporting a conclusion that the allegedly offending juror will not follow the court's instructions. Garcia v. People, 997 P.2d 1 (Colo. 2000). Prejudice is presumed when alternate juror replaces regular juror during deliberations. People v. Burnette, 775 P.2d 583 (Colo. 1989); Carrillo v. People, 974 P.2d 478 (Colo. 1999). Presence of alternate juror during jury's deliberations sufficiently impinges upon defendant's constitutional right to a jury that renders its verdict in secret as to create a presumption of prejudice that requires reversal if not rebutted, and, where it is unclear from the record whether the alternate juror was actually present during the jury deliberations, the issue should be remanded for an evidentiary hearing. People v. Boulies, 690 P.2d 1253 (Colo. 1984). Presumption of prejudice held sufficiently rebutted where juror was replaced for an obvious and bona fide hearing impairment, court carefully instructed remaining jurors and the alternate juror to start their deliberations anew, the jury physically tore up and discarded their notes from the earlier deliberations, and the second set of deliberations took two hours longer than the first. Carrillo v. People, 974 P.2d 478 (Colo. 1999). Presumption of prejudice may be rebutted only by a showing that trial court took extraordinary precautions to ensure that defendant would not be prejudiced and that, under the circumstances of the case, such precautions were adequate to achieve that result. People v. Burnette, 775 P.2d 583 (Colo. 1989). Procedures instituted by the trial court did not meet the People v. Burnette standard. People v. Patterson, 832 P.2d 1083 (Colo. App. 1992). Reversible error. Where trial court replaced regular juror with alternate juror during jury deliberations but did not ask regular jurors if they were capable of disregarding their previous deliberations or if they would be receptive to an alternate juror's attempt to assert a non-conforming view and did not ask alternate juror about his activities after being discharged or his present ability to serve on the jury, trial court did not take extraordinary measures to ensure that defendant would not be prejudiced by such mid-deliberation replacement and, as a result thereof, defendant's conviction required reversal. People v. Burnette, 753 P.2d 773 (Colo. App. 1987), aff'd, 775 P.2d 583 (Colo. 1989). Absent a showing of prejudice, a defendant's failure to timely object to the separation of the jury during a trial constitutes a waiver of sequestration. Jones v. People, 711 P.2d 1270 (Colo. 1986). Defendant did not waive right to challenge the procedure followed in accomplishing substitution of juror by consenting to the fact of substitution. People v. Patterson, 832 P.2d 1083 (Colo. App. 1992). Applied in People v. Avery, 736 P.2d 1233 (Colo. App. 1986). VII. Juror Questions. Juror questioning in a criminal trial does not, in and of itself, violate a defendant's constitutional rights to a fair and impartial jury. Medina v. People, 114 P.3d 845 (Colo. 2005). Where the court errs by asking an improper question from the jury, the impact of the question should be reviewed for harmless error. Medina v. People, 114 P.3d 845 (Colo. 2005). Trial court did not commit reversible error by posing jury's questions to witnesses without first consulting defense counsel. When an improper question from the jury is asked of a witness, the proper course is not to apply structural error but to review the impact of the trial court's ruling for harmless error. People v. Zamarippa-Diaz, 187 P.3d 1120 (Colo. App. 2008).

Rule 25 - Disability of Judge

If by reason of absence from the district, death, sickness, or other disability, the judge before whom the defendant was tried is unable to perform the duties to be performed by the court after a verdict or finding, any other judge regularly sitting in or assigned to the court may perform those duties. If the substitute judge is satisfied that he cannot perform those duties because he did not preside at the trial, or for any other reason, he may, in his discretion, grant a new trial.

Colo. R. Crim. P. 25

Annotation Substitution of judges is permitted so long as a justifiable reason for the substitution appears in the record. Substitution need not be required by an emergency or other situation beyond the control of the original judge to be justifiable. People v. Little, 813 P.2d 816 (Colo. App. 1991). Where the reason for substituting judges does not appear in the record, the case must be remanded for statement of the reason. The sentence will only be affirmed thereafter if the reason is one specified in the rule. If the reason is not one of those specified in the rule, the sentence will be vacated and the defendant will be resentenced by the original judge. People v. Little, 813 P.2d 816 (Colo. App. 1991). Case remanded to trial court for the judge who tried the case to explain on the record why he recused himself before sentencing. People v. Brewster, 240 P.3d 291 (Colo. App. 2009). Rule does not apply where conviction was the result of a guilty plea and not a trial and because a revocation hearing on a deferred judgment is not a trial. People v. Rivera-Bottzeck, 119 P.3d 546 (Colo. App. 2004). The requirement that the same judge impose sentence after a trial, except for justifiable reasons to substitute another judge, does not apply to resentencing proceedings. People v. Holwuttle, 155 P.3d 447 (Colo. App. 2006).

Rule 26 - Evidence

In all trials the testimony of witnesses shall be taken orally in open court, unless otherwise provided by law.

Colo. R. Crim. P. 26

Source: Entire rule amended and adopted November 9, 2006, effective 1/1/2007.

Annotation I. General Consideration. Law reviews. For comment, "Reporter's Privilege: Pankratz v. District Court", see 58 Den. L.J. 681 (1981). For article, "Good-Faith Exception to the Exclusionary Rule: The Fourth Amendment is Not a Technicality", see 11 Colo. Law. 704 (1982). For article, "People v. Mitchell: The Good Faith Exception in Colorado", see 62 Den. U. L. Rev. 841 (1985). Opening statements and arguments of lawyers are not evidence. People v. Jacobs, 179 Colo. 182, 499 P.2d 615 (1972). Such arguments are designed only to sway findings. Arguments to the court are not matters of evidence, have no probative value, and are designed only to sway the court's findings and conclusions. People In Interest of B. L. M. v. B. L. M., 31 Colo. App. 106, 500 P.2d 146 (1972). II. Function of Judge and Jury. Order of proof and presentation of witnesses is within sound discretion of the trial court, and error may not be predicated thereon in the absence of a showing of prejudice. Martinez v. People, 177 Colo. 272, 493 P.2d 1350 (1972). Allowing prosecution to recall witnesses for further cross-examination after defense rests its case is matter pertaining to proof and is within sound discretion of trial judge. People v. Lewis, 180 Colo. 423, 506 P.2d 125 (1973). Jury is permitted to draw any and all reasonable inferences of guilt from the evidence before it. Huser v. People, 178 Colo. 300, 496 P.2d 1035 (1972). Effect of waiving jury trial. Where the defendant voluntarily waived a jury trial, the trial judge had no recourse but to examine the evidence and rule on its admissibility, and the defendant cannot be heard to complain, when he voluntarily, and with advice of counsel, created a situation which by necessity made the trial judge both the one who decides if evidence is admissible and the one who renders the verdict. People v. Mascarenas, 181 Colo. 268, 509 P.2d 303 (1973). The credibility of witnesses, including experts, is within the province of the jury as the fact finder and the jury's obvious acceptance of the testimony by the prosecution's experts is not subject to reversal. People v. Moore, 841 P.2d 320 (Colo. App. 1992). III. Witnesses. A. Testimony. It is axiomatic that witnesses should relate facts and not conclusions. Elliott v. People, 176 Colo. 373, 490 P.2d 687 (1971). But exception when witness must summarize impressions of senses. An exception to the rule that a witness may only relate facts exists when a witness has personally observed the physical activity of another and summarizes his sensory impressions thereof because they can hardly be described in any other manner. Elliott v. People, 176 Colo. 373, 490 P.2d 687 (1971). Especially where witness qualifies conclusionary statement. Where a witness qualifies his conclusion immediately subsequent to defendant's objection by stating that defendant "looked like" he was going to do a certain act, the trial court commits no error in overruling defendant's objection to such testimony. Elliott v. People, 176 Colo. 373, 490

P.2d 687 (1971). Admission of unresponsive testimony not per se wrong. There is nothing per se wrong with the admission into evidence of testimony which may be unresponsive, provided that it is relevant for some purpose. People v. Maestas, 183 Colo. 378, 517 P.2d 461 (1973). Testimony as to possible places of incarceration is not to be placed before a jury. People v. Scheidt, 186 Colo. 142, 526 P.2d 300 (1974). The trial court did not commit plain error in allowing the prosecution to elicit testimony during its case-in-chief showing the victim's character for peacefulness. Defense counsel raised self-defense as an affirmative defense during opening statements and elicited testimony to support the affirmative defense during cross examination of a prosecution witness. People v. Baca, 852 P.2d 1302 (Colo. App. 1992). B. Corroboration. Defendant may be convicted upon uncorroborated testimony of accomplice. Davis v. People, 176 Colo. 378, 490 P.2d 948 (1971). Corroborating evidence defined. Corroborating evidence is evidence, either directly or by proof of surrounding facts and circumstances, that tends to establish the participation of the defendant in the commission of the offense. Davis v. People, 176 Colo. 378, 490 P.2d 948 (1971). IV. Admissibility. A. In General. Trial court did not err by admitting gun where there was conflicting testimony concerning the gun's origin since the lack of a positive identification of the gun affected the weight to be given the evidence, not the admissibility. People v. Rodriguez, 888 P.2d 278 (Colo. App. 1994). All facts proving crime charged admissible. All the facts which are necessary to prove the crime charged, when linked to the chain of events which supports that crime, are admissible. People v. Anderson, 184 Colo. 32, 518 P.2d 828 (1974). Weakness in chain of evidence addresses weight of evidence. Where the chain of evidence is complete, any weakness in the chain goes merely to the weight of the evidence and not to its admissibility. People v. Sanchez, 184 Colo. 25, 518 P.2d 818 (1974). Admission of cumulative evidence is within the discretion of the trial court and its ruling will not be overturned unless a clear abuse of discretion appears. People v. Manier, 184 Colo. 44, 518 P.2d 811 (1974). On rebuttal, party may introduce any competent evidence to explain, refute, counteract, or disprove proof of other party, even if evidence also tends to support the party's case in chief. People v. Lewis, 180 Colo. 423, 506 P.2d 125 (1973); People v. Knight, 167 P.3d 141 (Colo. App. 2006). Propriety of permitting surrebuttal evidence is within discretion of trial court. People v. Hutto, 181 Colo. 279, 509 P.2d 298 (1973). Where defendant seeks to discuss on surrebuttal matters that are not a reply to new evidence of prosecution, but have been specifically covered in earlier testimony, the trial court does not commit an abuse of discretion in denying defendant's request. People v. Martinez, 181 Colo. 27, 506 P.2d 744 (1973). Except where defendant meeting matter introduced by prosecution on rebuttal. Defendants should always be permitted to introduce, as surrebuttal, evidence which tends to meet any new matter introduced by prosecution on rebuttal; otherwise, it is within discretion of trial court to allow or deny surrebuttal. People v. Martinez, 181 Colo. 27, 506 P.2d 744 (1973). When error in admission of evidence not curable by instructions to jury. Error in admitting evidence may be cured by instructing the jury to disregard it, unless such evidence is so prejudicial that it is unlikely that the jury will be able to erase it from their minds; if it is so prejudicial, a mistrial should be ordered. Edmisten v. People, 176 Colo. 262, 490 P.2d 58 (1971). An error in exposing to the jury certain inadmissible evidence may be cured by instructing the jury to disregard it; however, when such evidence is highly prejudicial, it is conceivable that, but for its exposure, the jury may not have found the defendant guilty, and the trial court's cautionary instruction to disregard it will not suffice. People v. Goldsberry, 181 Colo. 406, 509 P.2d 801 (1973). Remarks by judge may not constitute reversible error. Casual remarks of the trial judge, made while passing upon objections to testimony, although ill-advised, do not constitute reversible error when not so couched as to especially reflect upon defendant. McCune v. People, 179 Colo. 262, 499 P.2d 1184 (1972). Nor correct comments by district attorney on evidence. Where the record shows beyond a doubt that the testimony implicated the companions of defendant as accomplices, any statement by the district attorney with regard to those persons as accomplices, after such a showing, is within the boundaries of proper comment. Fernandez v. People, 176 Colo. 346, 490 P.2d 690 (1971). Trial court's curative instruction, which directed jurors not to consider evidence relating to other transactions allegedly involving defendant, cured any errors resulting from admission of such evidence in "theft by receiving" prosecution where evidence of defendant's "theft by receiving" was overwhelming. Vigil v. People, 731 P.2d 713 (Colo. 1987). B. Confessions and Admissions. Admissibility of defendant's statement to be determined at trial. Where a defendant is given a full "Miranda" warning following his arrest, the admissibility of the statements he made as evidence must be determined by the court at the time of trial rather than on interlocutory appeal under Rule 41.2, Crim. P. People v. Vaughns, 175 Colo. 369, 489 P.2d 591 (1971). Outside presence of jury. The trial court must make a determination of the

*admissibility of a confession, which entails a determination of the propriety of the "Miranda"
warning, outside of the presence of the jury, at an in camera hearing. Perez v. people, 176 Colo.
505, 491 P.2d 969 (1971). Including issue of voluntariness. Whenever voluntariness in an issue
in a trial, there must be a hearing before the trial judge and a determination made on that issue.
People v. Sanchez, 180 Colo. 119, 503 P.2d 619 (1972). As to be admissible, confession must be
free and voluntary; that is, it must not be extracted by any sort of threats or violence, nor
obtained by any direct or implied promises, however slight. People v. Pineda, 182 Colo. 385,
513 P.2d 452 (1973). Where the defendant makes a voluntary, knowing, and intelligent waiver of
his constitutional rights, the trial court's ruling that an oral statement of the defendant is
admissible is not error. Dyett v. People, 177 Colo. 370, 494 P.2d 94 (1972). Two-step procedure
is proper to resolve issue of voluntariness of confession: First, the trial judge must determine
whether the confession is voluntary; and, second, if the confession is voluntary and is admitted
into evidence, the trial judge should instruct the jury on the weight to be given the confession.
People v. Shearer, 181 Colo. 237, 508 P.2d 1249 (1973). Admissibility need only be established
by preponderance of evidence. People v. Shearer, 181 Colo. 237, 508 P.2d 1249 (1973). A trial
judge only has to find that a defendant's statement is voluntary by a preponderance of the
evidence to justify submission of the statement to the jury. People v. Smith, 179 Colo. 413, 500
P.2d 1177 (1972). Although waiver of rights must be found beyond a reasonable doubt. Before a
criminal defendant's extrajudicial statement is admissible as evidence against him, a trial court
must find beyond a reasonable doubt that the defendant was fully informed of his constitutional
rights and that he intelligently and expressly waived them. People v. Vigil, 175 Colo. 373, 489
P.2d 588 (1971). And the burden is upon the state to show attendant circumstances sufficient
from which a knowing and intelligent waiver may be implied. Roybal v. People, 178 Colo. 259,
496 P.2d 1019 (1972). Or testimony inadmissible. Where the state does not meet its burden of
showing by clear and convincing evidence that defendant was represented by counsel at a lineup,
lineup testimony is properly excluded. Fresquez v. People, 178 Colo. 220, 497 P.2d 1246 (1972).
Total circumstances and conduct of accused must be considered. In passing on whether a
statement is voluntary and whether the accused waived his rights, the court must consider and
examine the totality of the facts and circumstances of the case, as well as the conduct of the
accused. Duncan v. People, 178 Colo. 314, 497 P.2d 1029 (1972). Findings must be supported
by evidence. Where the findings of the court entered after an in camera hearing are that the
statements were understandingly and voluntarily given, that defendant at the time had full
knowledge of his rights, and the findings are supported by the evidence, it is not error to admit
defendant's statements with evidence. People v. Gallegos, 180 Colo. 238, 504 P.2d 343 (1972).
Appellate review. An appellate court is bound to accept the trial court's findings and ruling on
the admissibility of a confession, if the evidence is sufficient to support the trial court's
determination. Redmond v. People, 180 Colo. 24, 501 P.2d 1051 (1972). Where trial court's
finding that accused's confession was voluntary and admissible is supported by competent
evidence, it will not be disturbed on appeal. People v. Shearer, 181 Colo. 237, 508 P.2d 1249
(1973). Trial court's findings of facts on the voluntariness of a confession will be upheld on
review if supported by adequate evidence in the record. People v. Pineda, 182 Colo. 385, 513
P.2d 452 (1973); People v. McIntyre, 789 P.2d 1108 (Colo. 1990). Evidence held sufficient to
show intelligent waiver of rights. Jorgensen v. People, 178 Colo. 8, 495 P.2d 1130 (1972);
McClain v. People, 178 Colo. 103, 495 P.2d 542 (1972). Prior refusal does not make subsequent
voluntary statement inadmissible. When the police fully honor a defendant's refusal to make a
statement, the fact of a prior refusal to make any statement should not taint a statement
subsequently given voluntarily and with full advisement of rights. Dyett v. People, 177 Colo. 370,
494 P.2d 94 (1972). When Miranda warning not necessary. Where defendant is not in custody
nor deprived of his freedom when a police officer asks a question and the investigation has not
focused upon any individual, then the Miranda warning is not necessary, since the defendant is
not in custody, and no error is committed in admitting a statement into evidence. Walker v.
People, 175 Colo. 173, 489 P.2d 584 (1971). Effect of intoxication on admissibility of statement.
See Carroll v. People, 177 Colo. 288, 494 P.2d 80 (1972). Police testimony as to defendant's
oral confession was proper and permissible in all its aspects, where the record indicates that
before being questioned the defendant was advised of her complete rights; that she read and
signed a rights advisement form; that she understood her rights; that she indicated a willingness
to talk; and that she freely and voluntarily told the police about her involvement in the crime.
People v. Gallegos, 181 Colo. 264, 509 P.2d 596 (1973). Admonition to jury does not cure
erroneous admission of incriminating statements. An admonition or an instruction to the jury to
disregard involuntary incriminating statements does not cure the erroneous admission of such*

statements. Edmisten v. People, 176 Colo. 262, 490 P.2d 58 (1971). Entire statement is admissible if any portion thereof is admissible. McCune v. People, 179 Colo. 262, 499 P.2d 1184 (1972). But burden of showing continuity or relevance in series of statements, or among various parts of a single statement, is on the party seeking to have the entire series or statement admitted. McCune v. People, 179 Colo. 262, 499 P.2d 1184 (1972). Consequently, admission of only the relevant portions of a statement is not error where there is no showing of continuity or relevance between the admitted portions of the statement and the remainder of the statement. McCune v. People, 179 Colo. 262, 499 P.2d 1184 (1972). Moreover, when the trial court admits into evidence a duplicate copy in addition to the original copy of a formal statement, which has been likewise corrected and signed by the defendant, the evidence is merely cumulative, and there is no abuse of discretion in its admission. Jorgensen v. People, 178 Colo. 8, 495 P.2d 1130 (1972). Independent proof of corpus delicti required. An accused's extra-judicial confession or statement is not sufficient to sustain a conviction without proof of the corpus delicti independent of the statement or confession. People v. Maestas, 181 Colo. 180, 508 P.2d 782 (1973); People v. Applegate, 181 Colo. 339, 509 P.2d 1238 (1973); People v. Smith, 182 Colo. 31, 510 P.2d 893 (1973). Use of evidence from uncounseled witness against third party. No reason exists for exclusion of evidence obtained from an uncounseled witness, so long as the evidence obtained is not offered against that witness. People v. Knapp, 180 Colo. 280, 505 P.2d 7 (1973). When reference to defendant's silence is reversible error. Not every reference to defendant's exercise of his fifth amendment right to remain silent mandates automatic reversal; the relevant inquiry is whether the prosecution "utilized defendant's silence as a means of creating an inference of guilt". People v. Key, 185 Colo. 72, 522 P.2d 719 (1974); People v. Benevidez, 679 P.2d 125 (Colo. App. 1984). Defendant's statement held to be voluntary when given in a hospital five hours after a serious accident when he was alert, resting, and not under the effects of medication. Defendant willingly participated, no threats were made to secure his cooperation. People v. Miller, 829 P.2d 443 (Colo. App. 1991). Defendant was not in custody when he was in the hospital for medical treatment. Confinement to a hospital bed is insufficient alone to constitute custody. People v. Miller, 829 P.2d 443 (Colo. App. 1991). There was a valid waiver of defendant's Miranda rights when the defendant nodded his head in response to an officer's question concerning whether he understood his rights. A valid waiver need not be express, but may be inferred from actions and words. People v. Miller, 829 P.2d 443 (Colo. App. 1991). Defendant was not in custody when she was in the hospital even though she had been given morphine prior to her making certain incriminating statements. Expert testimony indicated that the morphine she had been given would not have affected her ability to think, speak, and understand the situation. People v. DeBoer, 829 P.2d 447 (Colo. App. 1991). C. Exclusionary Rule. Annotator's note. For further annotations concerning search and seizure, see § 7 of art. II, Colo. Const., part 3 of article 3 of title 16, and Crim. P. 41. Exclusionary rule has traditionally barred from trial physical, tangible materials obtained either during, or as the direct result of, an unlawful invasion of a defendant's rights by the police. People v. Vigil, 175 Colo. 373, 489 P.2d 588 (1971). Applicability of "fruit of the poisonous tree" doctrine. To apply the "fruit of the poisonous tree" doctrine, the fruit of the search must have been obtained as the direct result of a violation of the defendant's constitutional rights-such a violation is said to taint the tree and, in turn, the fruit. People v. Vigil, 175 Colo. 373, 489 P.2d 588 (1971); People v. Potter, 176 Colo. 510, 491 P.2d 974 (1971). Standing to object to illegal seizure. A person who is only aggrieved by the admission of evidence illegally seized from a third person lacks standing to object. People v. Knapp, 180 Colo. 280, 505 P.2d 7 (1973). Test of admissibility of evidence seized in lawful search following an unlawful search is whether, granting establishment of the primary illegality, the evidence to which instant objection is made has been arrived at by exploitation of that illegality, or instead by means sufficiently distinguishable to be purged of the primary taint. People v. Hannah, 183 Colo. 9, 514 P.2d 320 (1973). Defendant's allegedly criminal acts were sufficiently attenuated from any illegal conduct of sheriff's deputies so that exclusion of evidence was not appropriate. Evidence of a new crime committed in response to an unlawful trespass is admissible. People v. Doke, 171 P.3d 237 (Colo. 2007). Information in sheriff deputy's affidavit, when considered separately and as a whole, failed to establish a substantial basis for the magistrate's determination that probable cause existed to issue the warrant. People v. Hoffman, __ P.3d __ (Colo. App. 2010). Deputy who conducted the search and who was the same officer who prepared the deficient affidavit either knew or should have known that the warrant he obtained based on his own affidavit was lacking in probable cause, and thus it was objectively unreasonable for him to rely on it. People v. Hoffman, __ P.3d __ (Colo. App. 2010). Trial court erred when it concluded that (1) probable cause existed to issue the search warrant, and, (2)

99

even absent probable cause, the officers acted in good faith in executing the warrant. *People v. Hoffman, __ P.3d __ (Colo. App. 2010).* **D. In-Court Identification.** *Admissibility of in-court identification after illegal lineup.* Where evidence is presented showing that an in-court identification of the defendant has an independent origin other than an illegal lineup and the trial court so finds, the in-court identification is admissible. *People v. Bowen, 176 Colo. 302, 490 P.2d 295 (1971).* *Determination of independent basis at "in camera hearing".* A trial judge's determination at an "in camera hearing" that an independent basis exists for in-court identification of defendant provides a proper foundation for admission of identification testimony before the jury. *People v. Marion, 182 Colo. 435, 514 P.2d 327 (1973).* *And reviewing court will not substitute its judgment.* Where trial judge, after considering the totality of the circumstances at an "in camera hearing", permits the introduction of identification testimony, he does not abuse his discretion, and reviewing court will not substitute its judgment for that of the trial court. *People v. Knapp, 180 Colo. 280, 505 P.2d 7 (1973).* *Burden of proof is on prosecution.* Where there is a violative lineup identification of a defendant, the burden of proof is on the prosecution to show an untainted identification of the defendant at trial. *People v. Bowen, 176 Colo. 302, 490 P.2d 295 (1971).* *Clear and convincing evidence required that identification from witness' own recollection.* It is the burden of the prosecution to show by clear and convincing evidence that any suggestion was not present and that the identification of the defendant is the product of the witness's own recollection. *Constantine v. People, 178 Colo. 16, 495 P.2d 208 (1972); Sandoval v. People, 180 Colo. 180, 503 P.2d 1020 (1972).* *Suggestive circumstances do not necessitate reversal.* Suggestive circumstances at an out-court identification will not by themselves necessitate reversal of a conviction. The concern of court is to prevent extrajudicial identification so unduly suggestive that, as matter of law, it results in substantial likelihood of mistaken in-court identification. *People v. Pacheco, 180 Colo. 39, 502 P.2d 70 (1972).* *Nor merely cumulative identification.* Even if extrajudicial identifications were inadmissible hearsay, where, in light of the other material evidence relating defendants to the crime, such identification is clearly cumulative and any error harmless. *Kurtz v. People, 177 Colo. 306, 494 P.2d 97 (1972).* *Behavior of witness at confrontation with defendant bears on credibility of the witness's identification of the defendant at the trial. People v. Bugarin, 181 Colo. 57, 507 P.2d 879 (1973).* *Independent in-court identification of defendant held sufficient to admit into evidence. McGregor v. People 176 Colo. 309, 490 P.2d 287 (1971).* **E. Codefendants.** *Testimony of accomplice must be scrutinized and acted upon with great caution. People v. Gomez, 189 Colo. 91, 537 P.2d 297 (1975). Evidence admissible in separate trial also admissible in joint trial.* Where evidence would be admissible against defendant in a separate trial, there is no prejudice as a result of the admission of that evidence in a joint trial. *Kurtz v. People, 177 Colo. 306, 494 P.2d 97 (1972). And evidence inadmissible in separate trial admissible in joint trial with limiting instruction.* It is not reversible error to admit a statement into evidence which would not be admissible against one of the defendants in a separate trial where the court gives a limiting instruction and the evidence of that defendant's involvement is overwhelming, even though it would be better trial procedure not to admit the statement. *Kurtz v. People, 177 Colo. 306, 494 P.2d 97 (1972). Articles in possession of codefendant may be admitted.* Where defendant and his codefendant jointly participated in the criminal venture, they acted in concert in furtherance of a common illegal purpose, and each, as to the other, was an accomplice; hence, admitting in evidence as against defendant, the articles found in the possession of his codefendant is not error where they were a part of the state's case against both defendants. *Miller v. People, 141 Colo. 576, 349 P.2d 685, cert. denied, 364 U.S. 851, 81 S. Ct. 97, 5 L. Ed. 2d 75 (1960). Codefendant cannot object to evidence of the history of the joint undertaking, even though it involves the commission of a crime by one or more of the other codefendants, if the history of the enterprise might throw light on the motive he or his codefendants might have had for committing another crime and which history constitutes a chain of circumstances throwing some light on the probability of their having jointly undertaken to commit the crime charged. Kurtz v. People, 177 Colo. 306, 494 P.2d 97 (1972). Examination of coconspirator concerning guilty plea arising out of same events. People v. Craig, 179 Colo. 115, 498 P.2d 942, cert. denied, 409 U.S. 1077, 93 S. Ct. 690, 34 L. Ed. 2d 666 (1972).* **F. Circumstantial.** *Circumstantial evidence is not relegated to secondary status but is to be considered under the same criteria as direct evidence. People v. Durbin, 187 Colo. 230, 529 P.2d 630 (1974). Conviction of crime may be based upon circumstantial evidence. Diebold v. People, 175 Colo. 96, 485 P.2d 900 (1971). Circumstantial evidence, when viewed in the light most favorable to the prosecution, can provide proof of guilt beyond a reasonable doubt. People v. Salas, 189 Colo. 111, 538 P.2d 437 (1975). And quantum of proof required same as for direct evidence. The quantum of proof where guilt is founded upon* *circumstantial evidence is the same as where it is based on direct evidence. Diebold v. People, 175 Colo. 96, 485 P.2d 900 (1971). So that evidence not compatible with hypothesis of innocence. Where a conviction is sought on circumstantial evidence alone, the prosecution must not only show beyond a reasonable doubt that the alleged facts and circumstances are true, but the facts and circumstances must be such as are incompatible, upon any reasonable hypothesis, with the innocence of the defendant and incapable of explanation upon any reasonable hypothesis other than that of the guilt of the defendant. People v. Calise, 179 Colo. 162, 498 P.2d 1154 (1972). In a circumstantial evidence case, the evidence must be consistent with guilt and inconsistent with any reasonable hypothesis of innocence. Roybal v. People, 178 Colo. 259, 496 P.2d 1019 (1972); People v. Vigil, 180 Colo. 104, 502 P.2d 418 (1972); People v. Larsen, 180 Colo. 140, 503 P.2d 343 (1972). And exclusion of every possible theory other than guilt is not required, when referring to the sufficiency of circumstantial evidence. People v. Florez, 179 Colo. 176, 498 P.2d 1162 (1972). Test is exclusion of every rational hypothesis, which means reasonable hypothesis. People v. Florez, 179 Colo. 176, 498 P.2d 1162 (1972). Where sufficient question is raised by circumstantial evidence, the finding of the jury is conclusive. Elliott v. People, 176 Colo. 373, 490 P.2d 687 (1971). Specific intent proved by circumstantial evidence. Specific intent is ordinarily inferable from the facts, and proof thereof is necessarily by circumstantial evidence. Elliott v. People, 176 Colo. 373, 490 P.2d 687 (1971). Circumstantial evidence held sufficient to justify inference of criminal intent. Evans v. People, 175 Colo. 269, 486 P.2d 1062 (1971). Fingerprint evidence may in some instances be sufficient to support conviction where that evidence is tied directly to the commission of the crime and no explanation other than guilt exists. Solis v. People, 175 Colo. 127, 485 P.2d 903 (1971). Fingerprints warrant a conviction when the fingerprints clearly and unequivocally establish that the accused committed the crime. Hervey v. People, 178 Colo. 38, 495 P.2d 204 (1972). G. Documentary. Use of photographs. Photographs may be used to graphically portray the appearance and condition of a deceased and the extent of existing wounds and injuries and are competent evidence of any relevant matters which a witness may describe in words. Gass v. People, 177 Colo. 232, 493 P.2d 654 (1972). Photographs may be used to graphically portray, among other things, the scene of a crime, the identification of a victim, the appearance and condition of the deceased, and the location, nature, and extent of the wounds or injuries, all of which matters are relevant. People v. Jones, 184 Colo. 96, 518 P.2d 819 (1974). Photographs are competent evidence of any relevant matter which is competent for a witness to describe in words. People v. Jones, 184 Colo. 96, 518 P.2d 819 (1974). Test for admissibility of photographs rests on whether the probative value of the photographs is "far outweighed" by their potential inflammatory effect on the jury. People v. White, 199 Colo. 82, 606 P.2d 847 (1980). Test for admissibility applied in People v. Franklin, 683 P.2d 775 (Colo. 1984); People v. Marquiz, 685 P.2d 242 (Colo. App. 1984), aff'd, 726 P.2d 1105 (Colo. 1986). Not inadmissible because of shocking content. That shocking details of a crime may be revealed by photographs does not render them inadmissible if they are otherwise relevant. Gass v. People, 177 Colo. 232, 493 P.2d 654 (1972); People v. Jones, 184 Colo. 96, 518 P.2d 819 (1974). Rather, admissibility discretionary with trial court. The trial court has discretion to determine whether a photographic exhibit is unnecessarily gruesome and inflammatory. People v. Jones, 184 Colo. 96, 518 P.2d 819 (1974). Decision not disturbed absent abuse. Unless an abuse of discretion is shown, a trial court's decision as to admissibility of a photograph will not be disturbed on review. People v. Jones, 184 Colo. 96, 518 P.2d 819 (1974). Standard for review of admission of pictures into evidence is whether they were without probative value and they served only to incite the jurors to passion, prejudice, vengeance, hatred, disgust, nausea, revolt, and all of the human emotions that are supposed to be omitted from the jury's deliberations. Carroll v. People, 177 Colo. 288, 494 P.2d 80 (1972). Photographs which should not be used. Photographs such as mug shots which necessarily import prior criminality to the defendant should not be used as evidence at trial. People v. Bugarin, 181 Colo. 57, 507 P.2d 879 (1973). Although no prejudice in use of mugshot of confederate. Mugshot of defendant's confederate, used by the district attorney for identification purposes, where codefendant was tried separately and the mugshot was taken as a result of the charges in the present case, did not import prior criminal conduct on the defendant's part; no prejudice to defendant resulted by the use of the photograph of his confederate and codefendant for identification purposes in defendant's trial. People v. York, 189 Colo. 16, 537 P.2d 294 (1975). Pretrial photographic identification. Where the pretrial photographic identification was not, as a matter of law, tainted with impermissible suggestiveness, it is not incumbent upon the prosecution to establish at trial an independent basis for the in-court identification. People v. Opson, 632 P.2d 602 (Colo. App. 1980). Out-of-court identification by photographic array held unduly suggestive. People v. Stevens, 642 P.2d 39 (Colo. App. 1981). Waiver of error regarding admission of photographs. Where no question as to the admission of a photographic exhibit has been raised on appeal, any error has been waived. People v. Jones, 184 Colo. 96, 518 P.2d 819 (1974). Weight to be given fingerprint evidence for trier of fact. Where a proper foundation was laid for the admission of a fingerprint, the weight to be afforded the fingerprint evidence was for the trier of the fact. People v. Gomez, 189 Colo. 191, 537 P.2d 297 (1975). Generally, old fingerprint card inadmissible. In the usual case, where other sample prints are available, a fingerprint card made in connection with prior criminal activity should not be admitted because of the danger of disclosing a past criminal record. Serratore v. People, 178 Colo. 341, 497 P.2d 1018 (1972). Admissibility of tape recording in discretion of trial court. The decision as to the admissibility of a tape recording is one that rests in the sound discretion of the trial court. People v. Quintana, 189 Colo. 330, 540 P.2d 1097 (1975). H. Exhibits. Use of exhibits from earlier trial not prejudicial. Fact that certain exhibits used in defendant's trial had court reporter's identification marks on them remaining from their use in the codefendant's trial did not result in any prejudice, and at most, the marks constituted harmless error which is not ground for reversal. People v. Gallegos, 181 Colo. 264, 509 P.2d 596 (1973). Exhibits of doubtful admissibility to be kept from view of jury. Matters of evidence which are of doubtful admissibility should not be placed on counsel's table where they may readily be seen by a trial jury. Zamora v. People, 175 Colo. 340, 487 P.2d 1116 (1971). Proper admission of exhibits presumed where not certified as part of appellate record. Where appellate court is unable to appraise the alleged prejudicial effect of exhibits because none are certified as a part of the record on review, the reviewing court may presume that the trial court did not abuse its discretion in admitting them into evidence. Gass v. People, 177 Colo. 232, 493 P.2d 654 (1972). Reconstructed scene inadmissible where accuracy disputed. Where an exhibit has been arranged simply to portray a scene and thereby support testimonial contentions, and when other witnesses dispute the accuracy or correctness of the reconstructed scene, trial court should not admit the evidence. People v. Wright, 182 Colo. 87, 511 P.2d 460 (1973). V. On Review. Waiver of right to appeal admission of testimony. Where defendant does not move the trial court to strike testimony complained of, such is a waiver of his right to appeal. Larkin v. People, 177 Colo. 156, 493 P.2d 1 (1972). Absent serious prejudicial error. Where contemporaneous objection to the admission of evidence on the grounds offered for reversal is not made, then, absent serious prejudicial error, the court will not review the issue. Duncan v. People, 178 Colo. 314, 497 P.2d 1029 (1972). Lack of contemporaneous objection at trial constitutes waiver of objections to admission of evidence, and such issues may not be raised on appeal; if they are, they will not be considered unless errors are so fundamental as to seriously prejudice basic rights of defendant. Larkin v. People, 177 Colo. 156, 493 P.2d 1 (1972); People v. Vigil, 180 Colo. 104, 502 P.2d 418 (1972). On review, evidence is viewed in light most favorable to the jury's verdict. People v. Lankford, 185 Colo. 445, 524 P.2d 1382 (1974). On the issue of sufficiency of the evidence to sustain a jury's verdict, the evidence, which includes all reasonable inferences which may be drawn therefrom, must be viewed in the light which most favors the jury's verdict. People v. Trujillo, 184 Colo. 387, 524 P.2d 1379 (1974). Reviewing court is required to view the evidence in the light most supportive of the jury's verdict, for purposes of appeal. People v. Eades, 187 Colo. 74, 528 P.2d 382 (1974). Where there is an overwhelming amount of evidence in the record that supports the jury's verdict, that verdict cannot be set aside on review. People v. Barker, 189 Colo. 148, 538 P.2d 109 (1975). Because the jury is presumed to have adopted that evidence which supports its verdict. People v. Lankford, 185 Colo. 445, 524 P.2d 1382 (1974). Reversal not to be predicated on admission of own evidence. A defendant cannot predicate reversible error on the admission of evidence he offered as a part of his defense. Roybal v. People, 177 Colo. 144, 493 P.2d 9 (1972). Appellate court will not review weight of evidence jury found sufficient. Where the jury has found the guilt of an accused to have been proven beyond a reasonable doubt, a court on review will not weigh the evidence. Schermerhorn v. People, 175 Colo. 256, 486 P.2d 428 (1971). A reviewing court cannot invade the province of the jury by making a redetermination on conflicting evidence. People v. Elliston, 181 Colo. 118, 508 P.2d 379 (1973). The supreme court will not substitute its judgment for that of the jury in resolving conflicts in the evidence. People v. Saavedra, 184 Colo. 90, 518 P.2d 283 (1974); People v. O'Donnell, 184 Colo. 434, 521 P.2d 771 (1974). Nor reassess credibility of witnesses. The supreme court will not substitute its judgment for that of the jury in assessing the credibility of witnesses. People v. Saavedra, 184 Colo. 90, 518 P.2d 283 (1974); People v. O'Donnell, 184 Colo. 434, 521 P.2d 771 (1974). Appellate court must look at evidence in state's favor after conviction. Where the evidence was conflicting in many particulars, the court on appeal must look at it in the light most favorable to the state in*

102

*determining whether there is substantial evidence to support the verdict against defendant.
People v. Focht, 180 Colo. 259, 504 P.2d 1096 (1972). When reviewing the sufficiency of the
evidence to sustain a conviction, it must be examined in the light most favorable to the
prosecution. People v. Scheidt, 182 Colo. 374, 513 P.2d 446 (1973). Evidence sufficient to
sustain judgment. Martin v. People, 178 Colo. 94, 495 P.2d 537 (1972). For reversal,
questionable evidence must substantially influence verdict. To constitute reversible error, the
questionable evidence must have had a substantial influence on the verdict. People v. Thomas,
189 Colo. 490, 542 P.2d 387 (1975). The trial court did not commit plain error in allowing the
prosecution to elicit testimony during its case-in-chief showing the victim's character for
peacefulness. During opening statements, the defense counsel raised the affirmative defense of
self-defense. In addition, defense counsel elicited testimony to support the affirmative defense
during cross examination of a prosecution witness. People v. Baca, 852 P.2d 1302 (Colo. App.
1992). In addition, the court did not abuse its discretion in denying the defendant's motion for a
mistrial on the basis that the court improperly allowed cumulative evidence of the defendant's
flight to be admitted into evidence. Even though the prosecution elicited testimony during cross-
examination that the defendant was living under an assumed name, without establishing the
relevance of the evidence as instructed by the court, the court issued a curative instruction to
counter any unfair prejudice to the defendant. People v. Baca, 852 P.2d 1302 (Colo. App. 1992).*

Rule 26.1 - Determination of Foreign Law

A party who intends to raise an issue concerning the law of a foreign country shall give
reasonable written notice. The court, in determining foreign law, may consider any relevant
material or source, including testimony, whether or not submitted by a party. The court's
determination shall be treated as a ruling on a question of law.

Colo. R. Crim. P. 26.1

Annotation Am. Jur.2d. See 29 Am. Jur.2d, Evidence, §§ 109, 110.

Rule 26.2 - Written Records

Colo. R. Crim. P. 26.2

Deleted by amendment November 9, 2006, effective 1/1/2007.

Rule 27 - Proof of Official Record

Colo. R. Crim. P. 27

Deleted by amendment November 9, 2006, effective 1/1/2007.

Rule 28 - No Colorado Rule

Colo. R. Crim. P. 28

Rule 29 - Motion for Acquittal

(a) Motion for Judgment of Acquittal. Motions for directed verdict are abolished and motions
for judgment of acquittal shall be used in their place. The court on motion of a defendant or of its
own motion shall order the entry of a judgment of acquittal of one or more offenses charged in
the indictment or information, or complaint, or summons and complaint after the evidence on
either side is closed, if the evidence is insufficient to sustain a conviction of such offense or
offenses. If a defendant's motion for judgment of acquittal at the close of the evidence offered by
the prosecution is not granted, the defendant may offer evidence without having reserved the
right. The court may not reserve ruling on a motion for judgment of acquittal made at the close of
the People's case.

(b) Reservation of Decision on Motion. If a motion for a judgment of acquittal is made at the
close of all the evidence, the court may reserve decision on the motion, submit the case to the
jury, and decide the motion either before the jury returns a verdict or after it returns a verdict of
guilty or is discharged without having returned a verdict.

(c) Motion After Verdict or Discharge of Jury. If the jury returns a verdict of guilty or is
discharged without having returned a verdict, a motion for judgment of acquittal may be made or
renewed within 14 days after the jury is discharged or within such further time as the court may
fix during the 14-day period. If a verdict of guilty is returned, the court may on such motion set
aside the verdict and enter judgment of acquittal. If no verdict is returned, the court may enter
judgment of acquittal. It shall not be necessary to the making of such a motion that such a similar
motion has been made prior to the submission of the case to the jury.

Colo. R. Crim. P. 29

Source: c amended and adopted December 14, 2011, effective 7/1/2012.

*Annotation I. General Consideration. Judge has more leeway in granting in trial to court. In
a trial to the court, the judge sits also as the trier of fact, and, thus, he has considerably more*

leeway in granting a motion for judgment of acquittal than if the case were tried before a jury. People v. Kirkland, 174 Colo. 362, 483 P.2d 1349 (1971). Rule as basis for jurisdiction. Edwards v. People, 176 Colo. 478, 491 P.2d 566 (1971); People v. Ware, 187 Colo. 28, 528 P.2d 224 (1974); People v. Gould, 193 Colo. 176, 563 P.2d 945 (1977). Applied in People v. Berry, 191 Colo. 125, 550 P.2d 332 (1976); People v. Maestas, 196 Colo. 245, 586 P.2d 4 (1978); People v. Paulsen, 198 Colo. 458, 601 P.2d 634 (1979); People in Interest of G.L., 631 P.2d 1118 (Colo. 1981); People v. Hoffman, 655 P.2d 393 (Colo. 1982). II. Motion for Judgment of Acquittal. Prosecution's burden to withstand motion. To withstand a motion for a judgment of acquittal, the prosecution has the burden of establishing a prima facie case of guilt and must introduce sufficient evidence to establish guilt beyond a reasonable doubt. People v. Bennett, 183 Colo. 125, 515 P.2d 466 (1973); People v. Ramos, 708 P.2d 1347 (Colo. 1985); People v. Hollenbeck, 944 P.2d 537 (Colo. App. 1996). The prosecution is given the benefit of every reasonable inference which might fairly be drawn from the evidence as long as there is a logical and convincing connection between the facts established and the conclusion inferred. People v. Hollenbeck, 944 P.2d 537 (Colo. App. 1996). The proper standard to be applied to a defendant's motion for acquittal is whether the relevant admissible evidence, both direct and circumstantial, when viewed in the light most favorable to the prosecution, is substantial and sufficient to support a conclusion by a reasonable mind that the defendant is guilty of the charge beyond a reasonable doubt. People v. Gonzales, 666 P.2d 123 (Colo. 1983); People v. Newton, 940 P.2d 1065 (Colo. App. 1996), aff'd on other grounds, 966 P.2d 563 (Colo. 1998); People v. Madison, 176 P.3d 793 (Colo. App. 2007). Prima facie case against defendant required. The primary question for determining the merits of a motion under this rule is: Did the prosecution establish a prima facie case against the defendant? People v. Gomez, 189 Colo. 91, 537 P.2d 297 (1975). When the state introduces evidence on its case in chief from which the jury may properly infer the essential elements of the crime, the state has then made out a "prima facie" case impregnable against a motion for acquittal. People v. Chavez, 182 Colo. 216, 511 P.2d 883 (1973); People v. Rivera, 37 Colo. App. 4, 542 P.2d 90 (1975). Or questions for jury's determination. A court properly denies a defendant's motion for acquittal at the conclusion of all of the evidence where the question of credibility of the witnesses and the ultimate guilt of defendant remain, for such matters are for the jury's determination. Roybal v. People, 177 Colo. 144, 493 P.2d 9 (1972). Where record contains ample evidence to sustain a conviction, the trial court is correct in denying the defendant's motion for judgment of acquittal. People v. Small, Jr., 177 Colo. 118, 493 P.2d 15 (1972); People v. Adams, 678 P.2d 572 (Colo. App. 1984). Standard is same for trial to court or to jury. The standard for determining the merits of a motion for a judgment of acquittal is the same whether the trial is to the court or to a jury. People v. Gomez, 189 Colo. 91, 537 P.2d 297 (1975). When refusal of motion at end of state's case may be reviewed. When an accused moves for acquittal at the close of the state's case, he is not entitled to have an adverse ruling on the motion reviewed unless he stands on the motion. Silcott v. People, 176 Colo. 442, 492 P.2d 70 (1971); People v. Olinger, 180 Colo. 58, 502 P.2d 79 (1972); People v. Becker, 181 Colo. 384, 509 P.2d 799 (1973). If defendant introduces evidence following denial of a motion for acquittal made at the close of the state's case, the correctness of the ruling is determined from the state of the evidence at the end of the trial. Silcott v. People, 176 Colo. 442, 492 P.2d 70 (1971); People v. Becker, 181 Colo. 384, 509 P.2d 799 (1973). But review not on state's evidence alone. Where, upon trial court's denial of a defendant's motion for acquittal at close of the state's case, the defendant proceeds to offer evidence warranting submission of case to jury, defendant cannot assert error on the state's evidence alone. People v. Olinger, 180 Colo. 58, 502 P.2d 79 (1972). Effect of denial of motion. When a trial court denies a defendant's motion for acquittal, it in effect rules that the evidence presented by the state is entirely consistent with the defendant's guilt and that, upon any reasonable hypothesis, this evidence is not also consistent with the defendant's innocence. Nunn v. People, 177 Colo. 87, 493 P.2d 6 (1972); People v. Hankin, 179 Colo. 70, 498 P.2d 1116 (1972). Role of trial judge in passing upon motion. In passing upon a motion for judgment of acquittal, the trial judge is required to give full consideration to the right of the jury to determine the credibility of witnesses and the weight to be afforded evidence, as well as the right to draw all justifiable inferences of fact from the evidence. People v. Bennett, 183 Colo. 125, 515 P.2d 466 (1973). When a trial judge is confronted with a motion for a judgment of acquittal at either the close of the prosecution's case, or the close of all of the evidence, he must determine whether the evidence before the jury is sufficient in both quantity and quality to submit the issue of the defendant's guilt or innocence to the jury. People v. Bennett, 183 Colo. 125, 515 P.2d 466 (1973); People v. Franklin, 645 P.2d 1 (Colo. 1982). The issue before the trial judge in passing upon a motion for judgment of acquittal is whether the relevant evidence, both direct and circumstantial, when viewed as a whole and in the light most favorable to the prosecution, is substantial and sufficient to support a conclusion by a reasonable mind that the defendant is guilty of the charge beyond a reasonable doubt. People v. Bennett, 183 Colo. 125, 515 P.2d 466 (1973); People v. Waggoner, 196 Colo. 578, 595 P.2d 217 (1979); People v. Botham, 629 P.2d 589 (Colo. 1981); People v. Gomez, 632 P.2d 586 (Colo. 1981); People v. Andrews, 632 P.2d 1012 (Colo. 1981); People v. Franklin, 645 P.2d 1 (Colo. 1982); People v. Brassfield, 652 P.2d 588 (Colo. 1982); People v. Renstrom, 657 P.2d 461 (Colo. App. 1982); People v. Bartowsheski, 661 P.2d 235 (Colo. 1983); People v. Graham, 678 P.2d 1043 (Colo. App. 1983), cert. denied, 467 U.S. 1216, 104 S. Ct. 2660, 81 L. Ed. 2d 366 (1984); People v. Paiva, 765 P.2d 581 (Colo. 1988); People v. Williams, 827 P.2d 612 (Colo. App. 1992); People v. Ramirez, 30 P.3d 807 (Colo. App. 2001). When ruling on a motion for judgment of acquittal, the trial court must consider both the prosecution and the defense evidence. In performing this function, the court is bound by five well-established principles of law. First, the court must give the prosecution the benefit of every reasonable inference, which might be fairly drawn from the evidence. Second, the determination of the credibility of witnesses is solely within the province of the jury. Third, the trial court may not serve as a thirteenth juror and determine what specific weight should be accorded to various pieces of evidence or by resolving conflicts in the evidence. Fourth, a modicum of relevant evidence will not rationally support a conviction beyond a reasonable doubt. Finally, verdicts in criminal cases may not be based on guessing, speculation, or conjecture. People v. Sprouse, 983 P.2d 771 (Colo. 1999); People v. Beatty, 80 P.3d 847 (Colo. App. 2003). Judge not to invade province of jury. In passing upon a motion for judgment of acquittal, the trial judge should not attempt to serve as a thirteenth juror or invade the province of the jury, but should prevent a case from being submitted to the jury when the prosecution has failed to meet its burden of proof. People v. Bennett, 183 Colo. 125, 515 P.2d 466 (1973); People v. Ramirez, 30 P.3d 807 (Colo. App. 2001). The determination of the credibility of witnesses is a matter solely within the province of the jury. Only when the testimony of a witness is so palpably incredible and so totally unbelievable as to be rejected as a matter of law can a court properly take this function from a jury. People v. Franklin, 645 P.2d 1 (Colo. 1982); People v. Ramirez, 30 P.3d 807 (Colo. App. 2001). Testimony is "incredible as a matter of law" if it is in conflict with nature or fully established or conceded facts. People v. Ramirez, 30 P.3d 807 (Colo. App. 2001). Testimony that is merely biased, inconsistent, or conflicting is not incredible as a matter of law. People v. Ramirez, 30 P.3d 807 (Colo. App. 2001). Evidence must be viewed favorably to state. In ruling on a motion for judgment of acquittal, the court must view the evidence in the light most favorable to the people. People v. Chavez, 182 Colo. 216, 511 P.2d 883 (1973). The trial court must give the prosecution the benefit of every reasonable inference which might be fairly drawn from the evidence. People v. Bartowsheski, 661 P.2d 235 (Colo. 1983). Where prosecution's evidence is insufficient to support conviction in that it does not prove all the elements of the offense charged, the court should enter a judgment of acquittal. People v. Rutt, 179 Colo. 180, 500 P.2d 362 (1972). Juvenile court erred when it denied motion for acquittal where there was a constructive amendment variance between the charge and the evidence presented at trial. People ex rel. H.W., III, 226 P.3d 1134 (Colo. App. 2009). Or fails to establish guilt beyond a reasonable doubt. Where the testimony is not sufficiently clear and convincing, standing alone, to establish guilt beyond a reasonable doubt, the trial court should grant a defendant's motion for acquittal at the end of all the evidence. Davis v. People, 176 Colo. 378, 490 P.2d 948 (1971). When viewing the evidence upon a motion for acquittal, the trial judge must determine whether a reasonable mind would conclude that the defendant's guilt as to each material element of the offense was proven beyond a reasonable doubt. People v. Bennett, 183 Colo. 125, 515 P.2d 466 (1973); People v. Ramos, 708 P.2d 1347 (Colo. 1985). Test for denial of motion where guilt proven by circumstantial evidence. Where the guilt of the defendant is proven by circumstantial evidence, the test for denial of a motion for judgment of acquittal is whether there is evidence in the record from which a jury can find beyond a reasonable doubt that the circumstances are such as to exclude every reasonable hypothesis of innocence. People v. Naranjo, 181 Colo. 273, 509 P.2d 1235 (1973). Substantial evidence test affords same status to circumstantial evidence as to direct evidence, and an exclusively circumstantial case need not exclude every reasonable hypothesis other than guilt to withstand a motion for a judgment of acquittal. People v. Andrews, 632 P.2d 1012 (Colo. 1981). In passing upon a motion for judgment of acquittal, the same test for measuring the sufficiency of evidence should apply, whether the evidence is direct or circumstantial. People v. Bennett, 183 Colo. 125, 515 P.2d 466 (1973). A motion for judgment of acquittal does not preserve a challenge to the foundation for expert testimony that was admitted without objection. Insofar as defendant relied solely on the purported lack of an adequate foundation for the expert opinion, defendant waived the insufficiency of evidence argument. People v. Wheeler, 170 P.3d 817 (Colo. App. 2007). Ruling against the state is a "final judgment". Although the granting of motions to quash, demurrers, pleas in bar, pleas in abatement, motions in arrest of judgment, and the declaration of a statute unconstitutional have been abolished by Crim. P. 12(a) and Crim. P. 29(a), the legal effect of the present nomenclature for these procedures is the same, that is, a ruling adverse to the state effectively terminates its prosecution of the defendant and results in a "final judgment". People v. Cochran, 176 Colo. 364, 490 P.2d 684 (1971). A trial court's ruling granting a defendant's motion for judgment of acquittal at the close of the prosecution's evidence is not a final order unless and until the court terminates the trial by dismissing the jury. Before that time, the trial court retains authority to reconsider its ruling. Thus, the court could submit the case to the jury on a lesser included offense. People v. Scott, 10 P.3d 686 (Colo. App. 2000). Defendants in Colorado are on notice that a midtrial order granting a motion for judgment of acquittal is not final and is subject to change until the jury is dismissed. People v. Madison, 176 P.3d 793 (Colo. App. 2007). District attorney may appeal. Since the issue of sufficiency of the evidence as postured where the trial court has granted a defendant's motion for judgment of acquittal, involves a question of law, the district attorney is given authority to appeal. People v. Kirkland, 174 Colo. 362, 483 P.2d 1349 (1971). Though such an appeal is in most instances nonproductive. An appeal after the trial judge has granted a motion for judgment of acquittal upon the completion of the state's evidence on the ground that the evidence is insufficient is, in most instances, a completely nonproductive exercise. People v. Kirkland, 174 Colo. 362, 483 P.2d 1349 (1971). Trial court's decision not set aside where adequately supported. Upon appeal of the denial of motion for judgment of acquittal, where the trial court is the trier of fact, its decision will not be set aside when adequately supported by the evidence, even though a portion of that evidence may be in conflict. Stewart v. People, 175 Colo. 304, 487 P.2d 371 (1971). Denial of motion for acquittal upheld. White v. People, 175 Colo. 119, 486 P.2d 4 (1971); Marn v. People, 175 Colo. 242, 486 P.2d 424 (1971); Kurtz v. People, 177 Colo. 306, 494 P.2d 971 (1972); Sergent v. People, 177 Colo. 354, 497 P.2d 983 (1972); Hervey v. People, 178 Colo. 38, 495 P.2d 204 (1972); People In Interest of B. L. M. v. B. L. M., 31 Colo. App. 106, 500 P.2d 146 (1972); People v. Olona, 180 Colo. 299, 505 P.2d 372 (1973); People v. Thomas, 181 Colo. 317, 509 P.2d 592 (1973). Denial of motion for judgment of acquittal held error. Johns v. People, 179 Colo. 8, 497 P.2d 1253 (1972); Velarde v. People, 179 Colo. 207, 500 P.2d 125 (1972). Granting of motion for judgment of acquittal disapproved. People v. Franklin, 645 P.2d 1 (Colo. 1982); People v. Gonzales, 666 P.2d 123 (Colo. 1983); People v. Madison, 176 P.3d 793 (Colo. App. 2007). Judgment of acquittal upheld. People v. Emeson, 179 Colo. 308, 500 P.2d 368 (1972); People v. Theel, 180 Colo. 348, 505 P.2d 964 (1973). III. Motion After Verdict or Discharge of Jury. Standard applicable to motions for acquittal made before a case goes to the jury also applies to motions made after verdict or discharge. The court shall order the entry of a judgment of acquittal if the evidence is insufficient to sustain a conviction of such offense. People v. Waggoner, 196 Colo. 578, 595 P.2d 217 (1979). Motion may be renewed after verdict. When a motion for judgment of acquittal is made at the close of all the evidence and denied, the motion may be renewed after verdict. People v. Chapman, 174 Colo. 545, 484 P.2d 1234 (1971). Motion satisfies requirement of motion for new trial. The filing of a motion for acquittal satisfies the purpose of a required motion for a new trial, since the only purpose of requiring a motion for new trial is to afford a fair opportunity to the trial court to correct its own errors, and, thus, where a defendant who does not want a new trial repeatedly asserts a motion for acquittal throughout the trial, the denial of the motion puts the defendant in a position to seek review of the judgment. Haas v. People, 155 Colo. 371, 394 P.2d 845 (1964). Court cannot modify jury verdict under this rule. Where there were no instructions tendered, given, or refused on any offense other than the offense charged in the information, but the trial court modified the verdict of the jury, Rule 29(c), Crim. P., delineates the power and discretion of the court under the circumstances, and, accordingly, the cause will be remanded to the trial court with directions to reinstate the verdict of the jury and to rule on defendant's combined motion for judgment of acquittal or, in the alternative, for a new trial. People v. Chapman, 174 Colo. 545, 484 P.2d 1234 (1971). If the evidence, although conflicting, supports the jury's verdict of guilty, the verdict must be upheld. People v. Emeson, 179 Colo. 308, 500 P.2d 368 (1972). Jury verdicts shall not be reversed for inconsistency if the crimes charged required different elements of proof and the jury could find from the very same evidence that the element of one crime was present while finding that the element of another crime was absent. People v. Strachan, 775 P.2d 37 (Colo. 1989). When a trial judge detects a material deficiency in the evidence after a careful examination of it and expresses a strong and abiding belief that the jury's verdict of guilty cannot stand, it becomes his responsibility to vacate the verdict. People v. Emeson, 179 Colo. 308, 500 P.2d 368 (1972). Court may not sua sponte order a judgment of acquittal after the date it has "fixed" pursuant to section (c), and any extension of time after that date is a nullity for purposes of entertaining a motion for judgment of acquittal. People v. Darland, 200 Colo. 276, 613 P.2d 1310 (1980). Even if victim was grossly inaccurate or confused about the incidents, it was not physically impossible for assaults to have occurred as she testified they did, and victim's therapist testified that inconsistencies and contradictions in her story were normal for a child of recurrent abuse. Thus, child victim's testimony was not incredible as a matter of law, and it was error for trial court to grant defendant's motion for judgment of acquittal notwithstanding the verdict on that basis. People v. Ramirez, 30 P.3d 807 (Colo. App. 2001).

Rule 30 - Instructions

A party who desires instructions shall tender his proposed instructions to the court in duplicate, the original being unsigned. All instructions shall be submitted to the parties, who shall make all objections thereto before they are given to the jury. Only the grounds so specified shall be considered on motion for a new trial or on review. Before argument the court shall read its instructions to the jury, but shall not comment upon the evidence. Such instructions may be read to the jury and commented upon by counsel during the argument, and they shall be taken by the jury when it retires. All instructions offered by the parties, or given by court, shall be filed with the clerk and, with the endorsement thereon indicating the action of the court, shall be taken as a part of the record of the case.

Colo. R. Crim. P. 30

Annotation I. General Consideration. Law reviews. For article, "Limitations of the Power of Courts in Instructing Juries", see 6 Dicta 23 (March 1929). For article, "Criminal Procedure", which discusses a recent Tenth Circuit decision dealing with the failure to instruct on lesser included offense, see 62 Den. U. L. Rev. 191 (1985). For article, "Pronouncements of the U.S. Supreme Court Relating to the Criminal Law Field: 1985-1986", which discusses a recent case relating to jury instructions, see 15 Colo. Law. 1616 (1986). "Instruction" construed. An instruction is an exposition of the principles of law applicable to a case, or to some branch or phase of a case, which the jury is bound to apply in order to render the verdict, establishing the rights of the parties in accordance with the facts proved. Kolkman v. People, 89 Colo. 8, 300 P. 575 (1931). Jury presumed to understand and heed. In the absence of a showing to the contrary, it is presumed that the jury understands instructions and heeds them. People v. Motley, 179 Colo. 77, 498 P.2d 339 (1972); People v. Jacobs, 179 Colo. 182, 499 P.2d 615 (1972); People v. Knapp, 180 Colo. 280, 505 P.2d 7 (1973). Applied in Brasher v. People, 81 Colo. 113, 253 P.827 (1927); Marshall v. People, 160 Colo. 323, 417 P.2d 491 (1966); People v. Butcher, 180 Colo. 429, 506 P.2d 362 (1973); People v. Thorpe, 40 Colo. App. 159, 570 P.2d 1311 (1977); People v. Padilla, 638 P.2d 15 (Colo. 1981); People v. Swanson, 638 P.2d 45 (Colo. 1981); People v. Mack, 638 P.2d 257 (Colo. 1981); People v. Founds, 631 P.2d 1166 (Colo. App. 1981); People v. Dillon, 633 P.2d 504 (Colo. App. 1981); Massey v. People, 649 P.2d 1070 (Colo. 1982); People v. Handy, 657 P.2d 963 (Colo. App. 1982); People v. Jones, 665 P.2d 127 (Colo. App. 1982). II. Duty to Instruct. A. In General. Law reviews. For article, "Jury Nullification and the Rule of Law", see 17 Colo. Law. 2151 (1988). Purpose of this rule is to enable the trial judge to prevent error from occurring and to correct an error if an improper instruction is tendered. People v. Barker, 180 Colo. 28, 501 P.2d 1041 (1972). The procedure set forth in this rule affords counsel the opportunity to structure closing arguments based on the instructions which will govern the jury's deliberations. People v. Bastin, 937 P.2d 761 (Colo. App. 1996). Court has a duty to instruct the jury properly on all of the elements of the offenses charged. People v. Bastin, 937 P.2d 761 (Colo. App. 1996). Court has a corresponding duty to correct erroneous instructions. People v. Bastin, 937 P.2d 761 (Colo. App. 1996). Counsel has a duty to assist the court by objecting to erroneous instructions and by tendering correct instructions. Arellano v. People, 177 Colo. 286, 493 P.2d 1362 (1972); Fresquez v. People, 178 Colo. 220, 497 P.2d 1246 (1972); People v. Zapata, 759 P.2d 754 (Colo. App. 1988). It is incumbent on counsel to object to the court's proposed instruction, if defective or deficient, and to request and tender correct instructions, or instructions that have been overlooked or omitted by the court. People v. Sharpe, 183 Colo. 64, 514 P.2d 1138 (1973). And to request instruction. It is the responsibility of a party's counsel to request an instruction if he believed circumstances warranted, and, having failed to do so, the party cannot afterwards complain that such instruction was not given.

Edwards v. People, 73 Colo. 377, 215 P. 855 (1923); Rhodus v. People, 158 Colo. 264, 406 P.2d 679 (1965). All objections must be made prior to submission to jury. Defendant must make all objections which he has to instructions prior to their submission to the jury. People v. O'Donnell, 184 Colo. 104, 518 P.2d 945 (1974); People v. Tilley, 184 Colo. 424, 520 P.2d 1046 (1974). In determining the propriety of any one instruction, the instructions must be considered as a whole, and, if the instructions as a whole properly instruct a jury, then there is no error. People v. Kurts, 721 P.2d 1201 (Colo. App. 1986). Failure to instruct the jury properly with respect to an essential element of the offense charged generally constitutes reversible error. People v. Williams, 707 P.2d 1023 (Colo. App. 1985); People v. Gracey, 940 P.2d 1050 (Colo. App. 1996). The trial court's failure to re-instruct the jury on the presumption of innocence and the burden of proof prior to closing arguments did not constitute structural or plain error. The court instructed the jury on these matters before the trial and reminded the jury of these instructions before closing arguments. The court also pointed jurors to their handbooks that included the instruction. This was enough to indicate that jurors were aware of the proper standard of review. People v. Baenziger, 97 P.3d 271 (Colo. App. 2004). Jury notebooks are not to supplant the requirement of Crim. P. 30 that jurors be orally instructed prior to closing arguments. People v. Baenziger, 97 P.3d 271 (Colo. App. 2004). The practice of instructing the jurors immediately prior to closing arguments has many benefits, including ensuring that the jury hears and considers all the applicable law before deliberations and aiding the overall comprehension of the jury. Because the presumption of innocence and the burden of proof beyond a reasonable doubt are so critical in a criminal case, it is especially important to instruct the jury on those points at the close of the case. People v. Baenziger, 97 P.3d 271 (Colo. App. 2004). B. Law of the Case. Duty to instruct on all issues. The trial court has a duty to properly instruct the jury on every issue presented, and the failure to do so with respect to the essential elements of the crime charged constitutes plain error. People v. Archuleta, 180 Colo. 156, 503 P.2d 346 (1972). Ingrained in the law is the right of an accused to insist that the court instruct the jury on all legal questions in order to reach a true verdict. People v. Woods, 179 Colo. 441, 501 P.2d 117 (1972). It is the trial court's duty to instruct the jury on all matters of law which it may consider. People v. Alvarez, 187 Colo. 290, 530 P.2d 506 (1975). Trial court has duty to instruct the jury on the law, properly, plainly, and accurately, on every issue presented. People v. Zapata, 759 P.2d 754 (Colo. App. 1988), aff'd on other grounds, 779 P.2d 1307 (Colo. 1989). Instruction directing the jury to accept as fact any portion of a witness' testimony invades the province of the jury. People v. Roybal, 775 P.2d 67 (Colo. App. 1989). Thus, in a felony child abuse case where the defendant raised the affirmative defense of religious healing, the defendant's tendered instruction asking the court to instruct the jury that the court had determined as a matter of law that the defendant was acting in good faith and that the defendant was a duly accredited practitioner of a recognized church or religion would have invaded the province of the jury, and therefor was properly denied. People v. Lybarger, 790 P.2d 855 (Colo. App. 1989), rev'd on other grounds, 807 P.2d 570 (Colo. 1991). Whether or not requested to do so. The court has a duty to fully instruct the jury on every issue presented, whether requested to do so or not. People v. Mackey, 185 Colo. 24, 521 P.2d 910 (1974). Instructions to the jury should be confined to the law of the case, leaving the facts to be determined by the jury. Sopris v. Truax, 1 Colo. 89 (1868); Rumley v. People, 149 Colo. 132, 368 P.2d 197 (1962); People v. Bercillio, 179 Colo. 383, 500 P.2d 975 (1972). And to issues for which evidence has been presented. Instructions should relate to and be confined to issues concerning which evidence has been presented. Rumley v. People, 149 Colo. 132, 368 P.2d 197 (1962). Including presumptions of fact. It is the duty of the court to draw the attention of the jury to the points in the case and to presumptions of fact, which the law authorizes them to deduce from the evidence. Hill v. People, 1 Colo. 436 (1872). As well as issues presented by pleadings. No instruction should be given by the court, either on its own motion or at the request of counsel, which tenders an issue that is not presented by the pleadings or supported by the evidence or which deviates therefrom in any material respect. Martinez v. People, 166 Colo. 524, 444 P.2d 641 (1968); Luna v. People, 170 Colo. 1, 461 P.2d 724 (1969). Instructions must be plain and accurate. It is the duty of the trial court to instruct the jury so plainly and accurately on the law of the case that they may comprehend the principles involved. Rumley v. People, 149 Colo. 132, 368 P.2d 197 (1962); People v. Garcia, 690 P.2d 869 (Colo. App. 1984). It is bad practice to give to the jury instruction on abstract propositions of law not called for by the evidence even though the instruction is harmless. Nilan v. People, 27 Colo. 206, 60 P. 485 (1900). The trial court should instruct on a principle of law when there is some evidence to support it, but should not instruct on abstract principles of law unrelated to the issues in controversy. People v. Kurts, 721 P.2d 1201 (Colo. App. 1986). Or excerpts from court opinions. Mere abstract statements of law or excerpts from court opinions generally should not be given as instructions. Rumley v. People, 149 Colo. 132, 368 P.2d 197 (1962). Or law review article. To allow counsel to read an opinion from a law review article on the credibility of eyewitness identifications would have substituted the writer for the judge, and usurped the trial court's duty to instruct on the law. People v. Alvarez, 187 Colo. 290, 530 P.2d 506 (1975). Sufficiency of instruction determined by facts of case. The question of the sufficiency of instructions must be determined always by the facts of each case. Rumley v. People, 149 Colo. 132, 368 P.2d 197 (1962). Requested instruction not justified by the evidence is properly refused. Morletti v. People, 72 Colo. 7, 209 P. 796 (1922); Kinselle v. People, 75 Colo. 579, 227 P. 823 (1924); Dickson v. People, 82 Colo. 233, 259 P. 1038 (1927); Rumley v. People, 149 Colo. 132, 368 P.2d 197 (1962). And refusal is not error. Where the court finds that there is no evidence of a certain matter, it is not error to refuse to instruct thereon. McCune v. People, 179 Colo. 262, 499 P.2d 1184 (1972). C. Defendant's Theory. Accused in a criminal case is entitled to an instruction based on his theory of the case. Martinez v. People, 166 Colo. 524, 444 P.2d 641 (1968); Roybal v. People, 177 Colo. 144, 493 P.2d 9 (1972); People v. Montague, 181 Colo. 143, 508 P.2d 388 (1973); People v. Griego, 183 Colo. 419, 517 P.2d 460 (1973); People v. White, 632 P.2d 609 (Colo. App. 1981); People v. Anaya, 732 P.2d 1241 (Colo. App. 1986), rev'd on other grounds, 764 P.2d 779 (Colo. 1988); People v. Banks, 804 P.2d 203 (Colo. App. 1990). An instruction embodying a defendant's theory of the case must be given by the trial court if the record contains any evidence to support the theory, the rationale being the belief that it is for the jury and not the court to determine the truth of the defendant's theory. People v. Nunez, 841 P.2d 261 (Colo. 1992). A trial court has an affirmative obligation to cooperate with counsel to either correct the tendered theory of the case instruction or to incorporate the substance of such in an instruction drafted by the court. People v. Nunez, 841 P.2d 261 (Colo. 1992). Although an alibi defense not an affirmative defense so as to place on the People the burden of proof to rebut, and trial court did not err by refusing a theory of case instruction treating alibi as an affirmative defense, defendant was entitled to a properly worded instruction setting forth his theory of the case. People v. Nunez, 824 P.2d 54 (Colo. App. 1991). As constitutional right. A defendant has a constitutional right to have a lucid, accurate, and comprehensive statement by the court to the jury of the law on the subject from his standpoint. Bustamonte v. People, 157 Colo. 146, 401 P.2d 597 (1965). No matter how improbable or unreasonable the contention, a defendant is entitled to an appropriate instruction upon the hypothesis that it might be true. Johnson v. People, 145 Colo. 314, 358 P.2d 873 (1961); People v. Moya, 182 Colo. 290, 512 P.2d 1155 (1973); People v. Banks, 804 P.2d 203 (Colo. App. 1990); People v. Nunez, 841 P.2d 261 (Colo. 1992); People v. Gordon, 32 P.3d 575 (Colo. App. 2001). Or poorly drafted. The fact that an instruction on the defendant's theory may be ineptly worded, grammatically incorrect, or inaccurate in some particular does not excuse the trial court from properly instructing on the theory of defense, assuming there is evidence to support such an instruction. People v. Moya, 182 Colo. 290, 512 P.2d 1155 (1973). Failure to give instruction requires new trial. Where no instruction is given by the trial court embodying the theory of defendant, a new trial must be had. Johnson v. People, 145 Colo. 314, 358 P.2d 873 (1961). Because the determination of the truth of defendant's theory is a jury function, it is error for the court to refuse to give defendant's instruction on the theory of his defense. People v. Moya, 182 Colo. 290, 512 P.2d 1155 (1973); Nora v. People, 176 Colo. 454, 491 P.2d 62 (1971). No new trial required if erroneous instruction causes no prejudice. Where instruction implied that one nonessential factor was an element of the crime, but jury's finding on that point was immaterial to the verdict and defense counsel was not unfairly misled in formulating closing argument or prevented from arguing any meritorious defense, denial of defense's motion for mistrial was not an abuse of discretion. People v. Bastin, 937 P.2d 761 (Colo. App. 1996). The failure to give a jury instruction on a defendant's theory of the case constitutes reversible error. People v. Nunez, 841 P.2d 261 (Colo. 1992). Instruction must be grounded upon evidence and in proper form. A defendant under certain circumstances is entitled to an instruction based on his theory of the case, but it must be grounded upon the evidence and not a mere fanciful invention of counsel nor one involving an impossibility, and it must be in proper form. Marn v. People, 175 Colo. 242, 486 P.2d 424 (1971); Kurtz v. People, 177 Colo. 306, 494 P.2d 97 (1972). Defendant is entitled to an instruction on his theory of the case subject to two conditions: The instruction must be in proper form, and must be supported by evidence in the record. People v. Duran, 185 Colo. 359, 524 P.2d 296 (1974). Defendant's jury instruction on his theory of the case must be in proper form and based on evidence in the record. People v. Griego, 183 Colo. 419, 517 P.2d 460 (1973). A defendant is entitled to an instruction on his theory of the case, provided it is grounded in the

109

evidence. People v. Mackey, 185 Colo. 24, 521 P.2d 910 (1974). A defendant is entitled to instructions consistent with his theory of the case if there is evidence to support it. People v. Nace, 182 Colo. 127, 511 P.2d 501 (1973); People v. Travis, 183 Colo. 255, 516 P.2d 121 (1973); People v. Meller, 185 Colo. 389, 524 P.2d 1366 (1974); People v. Shearer, 650 P.2d 1293 (Colo. App. 1982); People v. Banks, 804 P.2d 203 (Colo. App. 1990). General instruction should be adapted to defendant's theory. When a general instruction does not particularly direct the jury's attention to defendant's theory, it is the duty of the court either to correct the tendered instruction or to give the substance of it in an instruction drafted by the court. Nora v. People, 176 Colo. 454, 491 P.2d 62 (1971). Or supplementary instruction given. If a statutory instruction does not fit a particular case, or if it is given and yet other supplementary instructions are needed to state a defendant's position, then such, when properly worded and tendered, should be submitted to the jury. Bustamonte v. People, 157 Colo. 146, 401 P.2d 597 (1965). No instruction where no theory other than denial set forth. When a tendered instruction does not set forth any theory of the case other than a general denial, is merely a restatement of defendant's evidence without any resultant theory, and is merely another attempt to reargue the case, the defendant is not entitled to have it reiterated in instructions given by the court. Marn v. People, 175 Colo. 242, 486 P.2d 424 (1971); People v. Cole, 926 P.2d 164 (Colo. App. 1996). A defendant is not entitled to an instruction on a theory of the case that is simply a denial of the charges and a trial court may also refuse to give a tendered theory of the case instruction which contains argumentative matter or which is merely a restatement of the defendant's evidence. People v. Gracey, 940 P.2d 1050 (Colo. App. 1996). Defendant not entitled to different instructions concerning same subject. Though a defendant is entitled to an instruction on his theory of the case, he is not entitled to different instructions, all concerning the same general subject, and each couched in only slightly different verbiage. Bennett v. People, 168 Colo. 360, 451 P.2d 443 (1969). A properly worded instruction setting forth defendant's theory, when supported by the evidence, should always be given by a trial court unless the defendant's theory is encompassed in other instructions to the jury. People v. Moya, 182 Colo. 290, 512 P.2d 1155 (1973); People v. Meller, 185 Colo. 389, 524 P.2d 1366 (1974). All that is required is that the theory of the case be accurately embodied in the instructions given by the court. McCune v. People, 179 Colo. 262, 499 P.2d 1184 (1972); People v. Montague, 181 Colo. 143, 508 P.2d 388 (1973). The trial court properly rejected defendant's theory of defense instruction on the grounds that it was argumentative, did little more than summarize defendant's version of the incident, and was encompassed within the other instructions. People v. Lee, 18 P.3d 192 (Colo. App. 2000). Once a principle is covered it is not error to refuse to repeat the instruction in other language. McCune v. People, 179 Colo. 262, 499 P.2d 1184 (1972); People v. Montague, 181 Colo. 143, 508 P.2d 388 (1973). Instruction may be refused where jury otherwise adequately instructed. Where the jury is adequately instructed by the court and defendant's instructions would add nothing, it is not error to refuse to give instructions tendered by the defendant. Yerby v. People, 176 Colo. 115, 489 P.2d 1308 (1971); People v. Focht, 180 Colo. 259, 504 P.2d 1096 (1972); People v. Shearer, 650 P.2d 1293 (Colo. App. (1982); People v. Cole, 926 P.2d 164 (Colo. App. 1996); People v. Gordon, 32 P.3d 575 (Colo. App. 2001). No error occurred when trial court refused to give instruction requested by defendant which merely restated points covered by other instructions and reiterated a general denial of guilt. People v. Anaya, 732 P.2d 1241 (Colo. App. 1986), rev'd on other grounds, 764 P.2d 779 (Colo. 1988); People v. Lybarger, 790 P.2d 855 (Colo. App. 1989), rev'd on other grounds, 807 P.2d 570 (Colo. 1991). No abuse of discretion by court in refusal to give defendant's proposed misidentification instructions when such instructions were repetitive, were substantially included in stock instructions, and placed undue emphasis on a single issue presented by the evidence. People v. Zapata, 759 P.2d 754 (Colo. App. 1988), aff'd on other grounds, 779 P.2d 1307 (Colo. 1989); People v. Harte, 131 P.3d 1180 (Colo. App. 2005). Where tendered instructions do not contain a correct statement of the law, and the instructions given by the court adequately advise the jury of the refusal to submit defendant's tendered instructions, which are covered by those given by the trial court, is not error. Quintana v. People, 178 Colo. 213, 496 P.2d 1009 (1972). Evidence of affirmative defense of "treatment by spiritual means" in criminal child abuse case was sufficient to require trial court to instruct the jury on such defense. Lybarger v. People, 807 P.2d 570 (Colo. 1991). Where the trial record contained substantial evidence to support the defendant's alibi theory of defense and the jury instructions set forth only the elements of the offense and the burden of proof and did not encompass or embody the defendant's defense of alibi, it was reversible error for the trial court to fail to correct the tendered alibi instruction or to incorporate an alibi instruction in the other jury instructions. People v. Nunez, 841 P.2d 261 (Colo. 1992). III. Form. Object of rule.

One object of this rule is that the jury may have all the instructions before them when they retire to consider their verdict, and in that view it can make but little difference whether instructions are given orally or read from a book, for, in either case, they would be equally liable to forget them. Gile v. People, 1 Colo. 60 (1867). All instructions must be submitted to the jury in writing. Dorsett v. Crew, 1 Colo. 18 (1864); Gile v. People, 1 Colo. 60 (1867); Nieto v. People, 160 Colo. 179, 415 P.2d 531 (1966). Failure to do so is error. Failure to submit instructions to the jury in writing has always been held to be an error. Dorsett v. Crew, 1 Colo. 18 (1864); Gile v. People, 1 Colo. 60 (1867); Nieto v. People, 160 Colo. 179, 415 P.2d 531 (1966). Giving instructions orally not error if without prejudice. If a statement can be considered as an instruction as to the law, it being in favor of the plaintiff in error, giving it orally is at most an error without prejudice, and one that does not constitute a ground for reversal. Irving v. People, 43 Colo. 260, 95 P. 940 (1908); Martinez v. People, 124 Colo. 170, 235 P.2d 810 (1951). Instructions cannot be orally qualified or modified. Dorsett v. Crew, 1 Colo. 18 (1864). But failure of counsel to object to oral clarifying comments made by the trial court in response to a request by the jury, particularly where counsel is a more or less active participant in this further instructing of the jury, amounts to a waiver of any rights afforded by this rule. Valley v. People, 165 Colo. 555, 441 P.2d 14, cert. denied, 393 U.S. 925, 89 S. Ct. 256, 21 L. Ed. 2d 260 (1968). There is no restriction to the giving of additional written instructions to the jury by the court, in a proper case, after they have retired to consider their verdict. Davis v. People, 83 Colo. 295, 264 P. 658 (1928). But should be given in presence of counsel. Good practice requires that the court, before giving such an instruction, should call the jury into the courtroom and read it to them in the presence of counsel for both sides, unless they waive this formality, inasmuch as trial courts should not communicate with the jury on matters affecting the rights of the parties except in open court and in the presence of counsel. Ray v. People, 147 Colo. 587, 364 P.2d 578 (1961). If not, there must be prejudice for reversible error. While the giving of an additional instruction outside of the presence of counsel is bad procedure, it is not reversible error where it does not appear that it in any manner prejudices the rights of the defendant. Ray v. People, 147 Colo. 587, 364 P.2d 578 (1961). Comments to jury are not instructions. Comments to the jury are advisory and in no respect binding upon the jury, hence they are not instructions, and therefore they need not precede the arguments nor be reduced to writing as provided in this rule. Kolkman v. People, 89 Colo. 8, 300 P. 575 (1931). Provided they do not modify or qualify instructions. The remarks of the trial court do not constitute an instruction within this rule where they are merely an oral direction which in no way modifies or qualifies an instruction given. Irving v. People, 43 Colo. 260, 95 P. 940 (1908). "Instructions" to jury to revise verdicts not within rule. Where, upon verdict, the judge "instructs" the jury that the accused cannot be convicted of more than one offense and directs them to revise their verdict, these remarks are not instructions within the meaning of this rule. Bush v. People, 68 Colo. 75, 187 P. 528 (1920). Nor court's answer to jury on what is charged. When the jury asks the court whether defendant is charged with a certain offense only or with that offense and another, the court's answer to the jury's question is not an instruction to the jury within the meaning of the provisions of this rule. Wiseman v. People, 179 Colo. 101, 498 P.2d 930 (1972). Trial court's response to jury's question concerning instructions outside the presence of defense counsel was reversible error because it was a denial of the constitutional right to counsel. Such error is harmless only if so demonstrated beyond a reasonable doubt. If jury's question shows a fundamental misunderstanding of the instructions, it is prejudicial to the defendant. Leonardo v. People, 728 P.2d 1252 (Colo. 1986). Three instructions on one page not error. Where trial court instructed jury by placing three instructions on one sheet of paper-instructions related to the burden of proof, the presumption of innocence, and reasonable doubt-and defendant contends the jury was thereby confused, but no contention is made that the instructions did not properly set forth the law, and defendant has totally failed to suggest how these three instructions, if given on three separate sheets of paper, would have resulted in greater clarity, nor does he explain how the placing of the instructions on one sheet of paper would confuse the jury, this claim of error is totally without merit. People v. Romero, 182 Colo. 50, 511 P.2d 466 (1973). The court committed harmless error in failing to give the jury cautionary hearsay instructions after each hearsay witnesses' testimony. Three hearsay witnesses testified in sequence, the court gave the cautionary instruction following the testimony of the last hearsay witness and during the general charge to the jury, and the hearsay testimony corroborated the testimony of other witnesses. People v. Valdez, 874 P.2d 415 (Colo. App. 1994). IV. Content. A. In General. No instruction which is contradictory in itself is good. Magwire v. People, 77 Colo. 149, 235 P. 339 (1925). Irreconcilable instructions require reversal. Where instructions given by the court are irreconcilable, and it is impossible to say *which the jury followed or what the verdict would have been but for the error, a reversal is imperative. Clair v. People, 9 Colo. 122, 10 P. 799 (1886); White v. People, 76 Colo. 208, 230 P. 614 (1924). Erroneous instruction is not cured by another covering the same point which is correct. Mackey v. People, 2 Colo. 13 (1873); Lybarger v. People, 807 P.2d 570 (Colo. 1991). Cumulative effect of improper instruction with proper instruction was to provide the jury with mixed messages and did not dispel the potential for harm created by erroneous instruction. Lybarger v. People, 807 P.2d 570 (Colo. 1991). All instructions are to be taken together, and what might mislead, when considered by itself, may be corrected by another passage of the charge. Forte v. People, 57 Colo. 450, 140 P. 789 (1914); Clarke v. People, 64 Colo. 164, 171 P. 69 (1918); Taylor v. People, 21 Colo. 426, 42 P. 652 (1895); Ausmus v. People, 47 Colo. 167, 107 P. 204 (1910). Instructions in a case must be read and considered as a whole. McCune v. People, 179 Colo. 262, 499 P.2d 1184 (1972); People v. Casey, 185 Colo. 58, 521 P.2d 1250 (1974). In determining the effect of a particular instruction, it must be read in conjunction with the other instructions. People v. Manier, 184 Colo. 44, 518 P.2d 811 (1974). Not error if jury adequately informed. Where the instructions, when read together, adequately inform the jury of the applicable law, there is no error. Blincoe v. People, 178 Colo. 34, 494 P.2d 1285 (1972). If, taken as a whole, the instructions adequately inform the jury of the law, there is no reversible error. People v. Manier, 184 Colo. 44, 518 P.2d 811 (1974). Even though one instruction is not proper. Where one instruction is not entirely proper, its use does not constitute reversible error when the instructions read as a whole adequately inform the jury on the law. People v. Olona, 180 Colo. 299, 505 P.2d 372 (1973). Where the law of the case is clearly and explicitly set forth in one point of the charge, the effect of equivocal language elsewhere is thereby eliminated. LeMaster v. People, 54 Colo. 416, 131 P. 269 (1913). An inadequate instruction is not deemed to constitute fundamental error although it does not fully instruct the jury as to the definition of the crime, nor follows the statutory definition, where, when it is read in conjunction with the other instructions, it appears that in substance the jury is told of the elements of the crime. Morehead v. People, 167 Colo. 287, 447 P.2d 215 (1968). The omission from one instruction of the words "from the evidence" does not constitute reversible error when, by other instructions, the jury is told that its findings must be based upon the evidence, and that alone. Gorman v. People, 7 Colo. 596, 31 P. 335, 31 Am. St. R. 350 (1884); Boykin v. People, 22 Colo. 496, 45 P. 419 (1896). Improper jury instructions not grounds for reversal on appeal where defendant did not object to such instructions at trial and failed to raise such issue in motion for new trial. People v. Quintana, 701 P.2d 1264 (Colo. App. 1985). When reversal not required despite failure to instruct on element. Where the court fails to give an instruction on one element of a crime, reversal is not called for when the prima facie case established by the state stands unrebutted, the defendant offers no defense of which he is deprived by the failure to give the instruction, and he does not object to the instructions given nor request other instructions. Ruark v. People, 164 Colo. 257, 434 P.2d 124 (1967), cert. denied, 390 U.S. 1044, 88 S. Ct. 1644, 20 L. Ed. 2d 306 (1968). It is not error to refuse cumulative instructions. Minich v. People, 8 Colo. 440, 9 P. 4 (1885). Since requested instructions need not be given when covered by other instructions. It is not error for a trial court to fail to give a tendered instruction covering the same matter already dealt with in other instructions. People v. Mackey, 185 Colo. 24, 521 P.2d 910 (1974); People v. Lee, 199 Colo. 301, 607 P.2d 998 (1980); People v. Garcia, 690 P.2d 869 (Colo. App. 1984). Perhaps no point of law is more amply substantiated in Colorado than the rule that requested instructions which are covered by instructions given by the court are properly refused. Dougherty v. People, 1 Colo. 514 (1872); May v. People, 8 Colo. 210, 6 P. 816 (1885); Van Houton v. People, 22 Colo. 53, 43 P. 137 (1895); Benedict v. People, 23 Colo. 126, 46 P. 637 (1896); Thompson v. People, 26 Colo. 496, 59 P. 51 (1899); Covington v. People, 36 Colo. 183, 85 P. 832 (1960); O'Grady v. People, 42 Colo. 312, 95 P. 346 (1908); Campbell v. People, 55 Colo. 302, 133 P. 1043 (1913); De Rinzie v. People, 56 Colo. 249, 138 P. 1009 (1914); McKee v. People, 72 Colo. 55, 209 P. 632 (1922); Brindisi v. People, 76 Colo. 244, 230 P. 797 (1924); Roll v. People, 78 Colo. 589, 243 P. 641 (1926); Wilder v. People, 86 Colo. 35, 278 P. 594, 65 A.L.R. 1260 (1929); Abshier v. People, 87 Colo. 507, 289 P. 1081 (1930); Gould v. People, 89 Colo. 596, 5 P.2d 580 (1931); Farmer v. People, 90 Colo. 250, 7 P.2d 947 (1932); Jagger Prod. Co. v. Gylling, 90 Colo. 517, 10 P.2d 942 (1932); Updike v. People, 92 Colo. 125, 18 P.2d 472 (1933); Militello v. People, 95 Colo. 519, 37 P.2d 527 (1934). Instructions for multiple offenses. It is error for court to instruct jury that it could convict if evidence showed crime occurred within 3 years prior to filing of information. Such instruction is only proper if evidence proves one act, but date of incident is in question. Woertman v. People, 804 P.2d 188 (Colo. 1991). Because they tend to confuse jury. When a proposition of law is once clearly stated in the charge, a repetition thereof in the same or different language only tends to confuse the jury. Minich v. People, 8 Colo. 440, 9 P. 4 (1885). Combining instructions not abuse of discretion. Combining in one instruction the instructions on presumption of innocence, burden of proof, and reasonable doubt does not amount to an abuse of discretion, where no prejudice is shown. People v. Sharpe, 183 Colo. 64, 514 P.2d 1138 (1973). Particular portions of evidence should not be singled out and emphasized by special instructions. Gallegos v. People, 166 Colo. 409, 444 P.2d 267 (1968). Special instruction unfair if not warranted by the evidence. Where the evidence does not warrant it, a special instruction is unfair and a basis for reversible error. Gallegos v. People, 166 Colo. 409, 444 P.2d 267 (1968). When an instruction conceivably could be improved by rephrasing in certain particulars, yet it adequately states the basic requirements, then the jury is properly charged. Jorgensen v. People, 178 Colo. 8, 495 P.2d 1130 (1972). Although an instruction may be unduly prolix, if it properly advises the jury it is not in error. Yerby v. People, 176 Colo. 115, 489 P.2d 1308 (1971). Instruction interfering with jurors' deliberation is error. Where there is little doubt that the giving of an additional instruction interferes with the free and unbiased deliberation of the jurors, the trial court errs in acting, abusing its discretion. Mogan v. People, 157 Colo. 395, 402 P.2d 928 (1965). A defendant's due process rights are violated when a trial court intrudes on the jury's deliberative process and deprives the jury of its fact-finding duty. People v. Gracey, 940 P.2d 1050 (Colo. App. 1996). The court's response to the jurors' question effectively amounted to an impermissible directed verdict, where the primary contested issue at trial was the defendant's authority to borrow money from victim's account and that response left the jury with no alternative but to determine that defendant had no such authority. People v. Gracey, 940 P.2d 1050 (Colo. App. 1996). Instruction may assume commission of a crime. In a prosecution where there was no dispute at all that a crime was committed and the only defense made is that it was done by another, that the defendants had no part in it, and that instead of encouraging or assisting the criminal they came to the rescue of the injured party, and instruction that "if you believe beyond a reasonable doubt from all the facts and circumstances and evidence in the case that these men aided, abetted and encouraged the offense then you may find them guilty as charged in this information", is not reversible error because it assumes the commission of the crime instead of requiring the jury to find such fact beyond a reasonable doubt from the evidence. Komrs v. People, 31 Colo. 212, 73 P. 25 (1903). B. Statutory Language. Instruction based on statute upheld. In a felony child abuse case, the court properly instructed the jury that if the prosecution proved beyond a reasonable doubt that a reason other than spiritual treatment existed demonstrating that the child was endangered, the defendant was not entitled to the affirmative defense of spiritual healing. In addition, an instruction referring to the statutory duty of a parent to provide medical care was proper. People v. Lybarger, 790 P.2d 855 (Colo. App. 1989), rev'd on other grounds, 807 P.2d 570 (Colo. 1991). Trial court's decision to use instruction tracking deadly physical force language in § 18-1-704 instead of instruction containing specific language requested by defendant was not erroneous. People v. Phillips, 91 P.3d 476 (Colo. App. 2004). It is a good rule to couch instructions in the language of a statute. Bustamonte v. People, 157 Colo. 146, 401 P.2d 597 (1965). Objection to such instruction is not tenable. The objection that instructions in a criminal case are given in the language of a statute is not tenable. Kent v. People, 8 Colo. 563, 9 P. 852 (1885). If the language is clear. Where an instruction is worded substantially in the language of the statute, no more is required if the language is clear. People v. Dago, 179 Colo. 1, 497 P.2d 1261 (1972); People v. Pahlavan, 83 P.3d 1138 (Colo. App. 2003). Other instructions may be proper. An instruction couched in the language of a statute is not the only type of instruction that is proper. Bustamonte v. People, 157 Colo. 146, 401 P.2d 597 (1965). Inclusion of inapplicable provisions not necessarily error. Even in cases where the inclusion verbatim of inapplicable subsections of statutes in instructions to the jury are said to be improper, the giving of such an instruction does not, in itself, constitute reversible error. Bodhaine v. People, 175 Colo. 14, 485 P.2d 116 (1971). Instruction based on statute upheld. Where instructions on specific intent are phrased in the language of a statute, such instructions are proper and will be upheld on review. Blincoe v. People, 178 Colo. 34, 494 P.2d 1285 (1972). Jury instruction which is in conflict with the legislative intent of § 18-1-407 concerning affirmative defenses should not be used. People v. Rex, 689 P.2d 669 (Colo. App. 1984). In instructing the jury on the issue of the voluntariness of a confession, the court need not define the term since the general understanding of the word is clear. Kwiatkowski v. People, 706 P.2d 407 (Colo. 1985). Jury instruction providing supplemental definition of "knowing" for the purposes of second degree murder was unnecessary, but was not reversible error. The trial court's instruction did not pose a barrier to the jury in considering fully the defendant's affirmative defense. People v. Baca, 852 P.2d 1302 (Colo. App. 1992). C. Particular*

113

Instructions. Giving or refusal of cautionary instructions rests largely in the sound discretion of the trial court, and in the absence of a showing of an abuse of discretion and resulting prejudice to the defendant the trial court's ruling will not be disturbed. Luna v. People, 170 Colo. 1, 461 P.2d 724 (1969). Such as on weighing testimony of private detectives. The giving of instructions as to the caution to be observed in weighing testimony of private detectives or persons employed to find evidence is based upon rules of practice rather than of law and rests largely in the discretion of the trial judge. O'Grady v. People, 42 Colo. 312, 95 P. 346 (1908). Where the jury has been instructed to disregard tendered evidence, it must be presumed that the jury in the performance of its duty did so. People v. Goff, 187 Colo. 103, 530 P.2d 514 (1974). Credibility of defendant's testimony. The jury may be instructed that in determining the credibility of the defendant in a criminal case testifying in his own behalf, they have a right to take into consideration the fact that he is interested in the result of the prosecution, as well as his demeanor and conduct during the trial. Minich v. People, 8 Colo. 440, 9 P. 4 (1884); Boykin v. People, 22 Colo. 496, 45 P. 419 (1896); O'Brien v. People, 42 Colo. 40, 94 P. 284 (1908). Or of witness who has wilfully testified falsely. An instruction directing the jury that they are at liberty to disregard the entire testimony of a witness who has wilfully testified falsely to a material point is good. Minich v. People, 8 Colo. 440, 9 P. 4 (1885). Only one instruction on credibility of witnesses necessary. The practice of giving two instructions on the creditibility of witnesses is not necessary, and is not the modern trend, for it is the better practice to give only one instruction as to credibility of witnesses. Fernandez v. People, 176 Colo. 346, 490 P.2d 690 (1971). It is not error to deny a special instruction on credibility of eyewitnesses where a general instruction on credibility is given. People v. Ross, 179 Colo. 293, 500 P.2d 127 (1972); People v. Lopez, 182 Colo. 152, 511 P.2d 889 (1973). Where the stock instruction on credibility includes language of caution to the jury applicable to the witnesses' testimony, it is not an abuse of the trial court's discretion to refuse another cautionary instruction. Luna v. People, 170 Colo. 1, 461, P.2d 724 (1969). The failure of the court sua sponte to specially instruct the jury on an identification issue is not patently prejudicial where the jury is given an instruction concerning the credibility of witnesses which details the factors to be considered by them such as means of knowledge, strength of memory, and opportunities for observation. Fresquez v. People, 178 Colo. 220, 497 P.2d 1246 (1972). But separate instruction on defendant's credibility not error. While it is unnecessary and poor practice to give the jury a separate instruction on the credibility of a defendant as a witness, the giving of such an instruction does not constitute reversible error. People v. Hankin, 179 Colo. 70, 498 P.2d 1116 (1972). The giving of separate instruction dealing with the credibility of defendant as witness was not reversible error, although the better procedure is to give only one integrated credibility instruction. Lamb v. People, 181 Colo. 446, 509 P.2d 1267 (1973). Including in sanity trial. In a sanity trial, the court does not commit prejudicial error by instructing the jury specifically concerning the test of defendant's credibility as a witness, while a general instruction on the credibility of witnesses is also given. Elliott v. People, 176 Colo. 373, 490 P.2d 687 (1971). Where the evidence in a criminal case is wholly circumstantial, it is error to instruct the jury that they need not be satisfied beyond a reasonable doubt of each link in the chain of circumstances relied upon to establish the defendant's guilt. Clair v. People, 9 Colo. 122, 10 P. 799, 97 Am. St. R. 780 (1886). If in ruling upon the sufficiency or insufficiency of evidence in circumstantial evidence cases judges must follow the rule that the evidence must be consistent with guilt and inconsistent with innocence, it follows that the better practice is to so advise the jury. People v. Calise, 179 Colo. 162, 498 P.2d 1154 (1972). No error if defendant is not prejudiced. Where an instruction conveys the essence of the law to be applied in regard to circumstantial evidence and when all the instructions are read as a whole the defendant is not prejudiced by this instruction which does not include the language that "the circumstances relied upon must be consistent with guilt and inconsistent with any reasonable hypothesis of innocence", there is no error. People v. Hankin, 179 Colo. 70, 498 P.2d 1116 (1972). Circumstantial evidence held sufficient basis for instruction. Yerby v. People, 176 Colo. 115, 489 P.2d 1308 (1971). Stock instruction on presumption of innocence held inappropriate. Renfrow v. People, 176 Colo. 160, 489 P.2d 582 (1971); Brown v. People, 177 Colo. 397, 494 P.2d 587 (1972). For instruction on presumption of innocence recommended by supreme court, see Martinez v. People, 172 Colo. 82, 470 P.2d 26 (1970). Trial court need not instruct jury to exclude every reasonable hypothesis of innocence where the evidence of defendant's guilt was primarily direct. People v. Lopez, 182 Colo. 152, 511 P.2d 889 (1973). A court does not err in instructing the jury that they are "not to search for a doubt". People v. Sharpe, 183 Colo. 64, 514 P.2d 1138 (1973). Where instruction on presumption of innocence was given prior to recommendation of supreme court that it be reworded to exclude objectionable language, giving of such instruction was not reversible error. People v. Pacheco, 180 Colo. 39, 502 P.2d 70 (1972). The giving of a stock instruction on the presumption of innocence does not constitute reversible error just because of its historical use. Jorgensen v. People, 178 Colo. 8, 495 P.2d 1130 (1972). Submitting erroneous instruction on presumption of innocence would ordinarily require reversal, but only if the defendant objected to the instruction. People v. Simmons, 182 Colo. 350, 513 P.2d 193 (1973). Instruction that defendant not compelled to testify. It is error to refuse a tendered instruction that the defendant is not compelled to testify, and that the fact that he does not testify cannot be used as an inference of guilt and should not prejudice him in any way. People v. Crawford, 632 P.2d 626 (Colo. App. 1981). Limiting instruction on prior convictions. When defendant's prior felony convictions are elicited during his testimony, a limiting instruction is required. People v. Goldsberry, 181 Colo. 406, 509 P.2d 801 (1973). Instructions where evidence of other crimes is used. When evidence from other crimes is used: First, the prosecutor should advise the trial court of the purpose for which he offers the evidence; secondly, if the court admits such evidence, it should then and there instruct the jury as to the limited purpose for which the evidence is being received and for which the jury may consider it; thirdly, the general charge should contain a renewal of the instruction on the limited purpose of such evidence; lastly, the offer of the prosecutor and the instructions of the court should be in carefully couched terms-they should refer to "other transactions", "other acts", or "other conduct" and should eschew such designations as "similar offenses", "other offenses", "similar crimes", and so forth. Kurtz v. People, 177 Colo. 306, 494 P.2d 97 (1972); Howe v. People, 178 Colo. 248, 496 P.2d 1040 (1972). Where evidence relating to other prior incidents of a similar nature between the defendant and the prosecuting witness is admitted, and the court gives an oral cautionary instruction to the jury on the limited relevance of similar act testimony at the conclusion of the prosecuting witness's testimony as well as a similar written instruction when the case is submitted to the jury, there is no reversible error. People v. Elliston, 181 Colo. 118, 508 P.2d 379 (1973). Even when defendant has not requested such. Where the trial judge instructs the jury on the limited purposes for which evidence of prior felony convictions is admitted when the defendant has not requested such an instruction, such action is proper inasmuch as the judge has a duty to instruct the jury on the limited purpose for which such evidence is admissible in his general instructions. Lee v. People, 170 Colo. 268, 460 P.2d 796 (1969). Evidence of former convictions used to attack credibility. Where testimony as to former convictions is elicited for the purpose of attacking the defendant's credibility, the court acts properly in so instructing the jury. Candelaria v. People, 177 Colo. 136, 493 P.2d 355 (1972). When instructing a deadlocked jury deliberating a charge involving lesser offenses, the court should first ask whether there is a likelihood of progress towards a unanimous verdict upon further deliberation. If the jury indicates that a unanimous verdict is unlikely, the court should then inquire whether the jury is divided over guilt as to any one of the offenses and nonguilt as to all offenses or, instead, whether the division centers only on the particular degree of guilt. People v. Lewis, 676 P.2d 682 (Colo. 1984); People v. Hayward, 55 P.3d 803 (Colo. App. 2002). When a lesser offense involves elements that are not necessarily included in a greater offense, the additional instruction should set forth the nonincluded elements of the offense and should advise the jury that before the defendant can be found guilty of that particular offense each of the jurors must be satisfied beyond a reasonable doubt that the defendant acted in such a manner so as to satisfy all of the nonincluded elements. People v. Lewis, 676 P.2d 682 (Colo. 1984). Instruction on lesser included offense limited. The rule that an instruction on a lesser included offense is required when requested is limited to those cases where there is evidence to support such instruction. People v. Ross, 179 Colo. 293, 500 P.2d 127 (1972). A defendant is entitled to an instruction on a lesser included offense, unless it is clear from the evidence that the defendant is guilty of the greater offense or nothing at all. Ortega v. People, 178 Colo. 419, 498 P.2d 1121 (1972). Mere chance of the jury's rejection of uncontroverted testimony and conviction on a lesser charge does not necessitate an instruction on the lesser charge. People v. Campbell, 678 P.2d 1035 (Colo. App. 1983). The giving of such instruction is not mandatory. Where the court already knew that a juror disagreed with the other jurors and felt pressured to issue a verdict against her conscience, court had reasonable concern that such an instruction could be perceived as coercive. People v. Barnard, 12 P.3d 290 (Colo. App. 2000). Defendant was not entitled to special instruction concerning testimony of immunized witnesses where, considering circumstances of case, the standard credibility instruction given by trial court was sufficient. People v. Loggins, 709 P.2d 25 (Colo. App. 1985). There must be evidence tending to establish lower grade. In a prosecution for a crime which includes within the charge lower grades of crime, where there is any evidence tending to establish a lower grade, the jury should be instructed as to such lower grade; but, where there is no evidence tending to establish a lower grade, such lower grade should not be submitted to the jury. Carpenter v. People, 31 Colo. 284, 72 P.1072 (1903). Lesser nonincluded offense. A defendant is entitled to an instruction on a lesser nonincluded offense when he requests such an instruction and there is evidence to support it. People v. Best, 665 P.2d 644 (Colo. App. 1983). Trial court's refusal to give a lesser nonincluded offense instruction does not justify reversal if the court instructed on a comparable lesser nonincluded offense. People v. Rubio, 222 P.3d 355 (Colo. App. 2009). The decision whether to request a lesser offense instruction is a matter to be decided by counsel after consultation with the defendant. Arko v. People, 183 P.3d 555 (Colo. 2008). Instruction on reasonable doubt upheld. Minich v. People, 8 Colo. 440, 9 P. 4 (1885); People v. Couch, 179 Colo. 324, 500 P.2d 967 (1972); People v. Focht, 180 Colo. 259, 504 P.2d 1096 (1972); People v. Rubio, 222 P.3d 355 (Colo. App. 2009). An instruction to the jury that a reasonable doubt must be grounded upon irreconcilable evidence is incorrect, because the evidence may be insufficient to prove the charge. Mackey v. People, 2 Colo. 13 (1873). Instruction on general intent upheld. People v. Couch, 179 Colo. 324, 500 P.2d 967 (1972). But inadequate for specific intent crime. An instruction on general intent is inadequate guidance for a jury deliberating specific intent crime. People v. Mingo, 181 Colo. 390, 509 P.2d 800 (1973). Instruction on specific intent read in context with other instructions which made specific reference to specific intent, requiring proof of each element beyond a reasonable doubt, adequately informs the jury of the law. People v. Couch, 179 Colo. 324, 500 P.2d 967 (1972). Instruction omitting specific "animus" improper. An instruction which makes the question of guilt depend solely upon the intentional doing of an unlawful act constitutes prejudicial error in cases where the specific "animus" as a material element of the crime for which the accused is convicted is omitted. Gonzales v. People, 166 Colo. 557, 445 P.2d 74 (1968). Instruction dealing with the effect of defendant's statement does not require for its submission that the defendant's statement reached the level of a confession or a direct admission of a crime. People v. Naranjo, 181 Colo. 273, 509 P.2d 1235 (1973). Instruction on definition of confession held properly denied. Roybal v. People, 177 Colo. 144, 493 P.2d 9 (1972). Instruction on weight given confession is improper comment on evidence. An instruction that tells a jury that a confession may be entitled to great weight is an improper comment upon the weight of the evidence. Fincher v. People, 26 Colo. 169, 56 P. 902 (1899). Admonition does not cure erroneous admission of incriminating statement. An admonition or an instruction to the jury to disregard involuntary incriminating statements does not cure the erroneous admission of such statements. Edmisten v. People, 176 Colo. 262, 490 P.2d 58 (1971). Unless such is not an issue of significance. Where the admissions of the defendant in the nature of either extrajudicial statements or a confession is not an issue of significance, the giving of an instruction on them is not grounds for relief. Yerby v. People, 176 Colo. 115, 489 P.2d 1308 (1971). Instruction held not to be judicial comment on the evidence. People v. Olona, 180 Colo. 299, 505 P.2d 372 (1973). Comments of counsel. Where the trial judge instructed the jury that comments of counsel were not evidence and should not be considered as such, in the absence of a showing to the contrary, it is presumed that the jury understood the instructions and heeded them. People v. Becker, 187 Colo. 344, 531 P.2d 386 (1975). Instruction defining accomplice held not fatally erroneous. Komrs v. People, 31 Colo. 212, 73 P. 25 (1903). Instruction on accomplice's testimony held proper. Wisdom v. People, 11 Colo. 170, 17 P. 519 (1887); People v. Small, 177 Colo. 118, 493 P.2d 15 (1972). nstruction on evidence showing plan, scheme, and design held proper. Mays v. People, 177 Colo. 92, 493 P.2d 4 (1972). Instruction on flight. Where there is evidence of flight as a deliberate attempt to avoid detection or arrest for a crime just committed, an instruction on flight is proper. Gallegos v. People, 166 Colo. 409, 444 P.2d 267 (1968); Nunn v. People, 177 Colo. 87, 493 P.2d 6 (1972). Instruction on alibi held sufficient. McGregor v. People, 176 Colo. 309, 490 P.2d 287 (1971). Instruction on alibi held liable to mislead jury and was therefore grounds for new trial. Wisdom v. People, 11 Colo. 170, 17 P. 519 (1887). Instruction on negligence held valid. People v. Olona, 180 Colo. 299, 505 P.2d 372 (1973). Instruction on complicity appropriate where evidence was sufficient to show that two or more persons were jointly engaged in the commission of a crime. People v. Phillips, 732 P.2d 1226 (Colo. App. 1986). Instruction on defendant's denials and theory of case held error. Trial court's instruction that defendant's denials of charges and theory of case were issues but not evidence held incorrect statement of law and reversible error. People v. Herbison, 761 P.2d 263 (Colo. App. 1988). State's pattern reasonable doubt jury instruction accurately describes proof beyond a reasonable doubt. People v. Alvarado-Juarez, 252 P.3d 1135 (Colo. App. 2010). Where trial court should have given an additional clarifying instruction, its failure to do so did not constitute prejudicial error where conviction could not have been affected by the lack of response to jurors' inquiry. People v. Fell, 832 P.2d 1015 (Colo. App. 1991). Trial court's comment regarding whether defendant was the initial aggressor did not violate this rule and did not constitute error, much less plain error. With respect to a trial court's comments, questions, and demeanor, more than mere speculation concerning the possibility of prejudice must be demonstrated to warrant a reversal. The record must clearly establish bias, and the test is whether the trial judge's conduct so departed from the required impartiality as to deny the defendant a fair trial. People v. Martinez, 224 P.3d 1026 (Colo. App. 2009), aff'd on other grounds, 244 P.3d 135 (Colo. 2010). Court responded to defendant's objection to prosecutor's closing argument about self-defense by finding there was "some evidence" defendant was initial aggressor. Its ruling was on a matter of law, it did not invade the fact-finding province of the jury, and court immediately instructed jurors that they were to decide the facts. People v. Martinez, 224 P.3d 1026 (Colo. App. 2009), aff'd on other grounds, 244 P.3d 135 (Colo. 2010). Failure to give curative instruction not reversible error. Failure to give a curative instruction, in the absence of a request by defense counsel, did not constitute reversible error. People v. Rogers, 187 Colo. 128, 528 P.2d 1309 (1974). Curative jury instruction to disregard prior invalid conviction remedied any harm that may have resulted from reference to the invalid conviction. People v. McNeely, 68 P.3d 540 (Colo. App. 2002). Instructions as a whole held to have adequately advised jury on premeditation. Carroll v. People, 177 Colo. 288, 494 P.2d 80 (1972). Instruction reducing prosecutor's obligation prejudicial. Prejudice to the defendant is inevitable when the court instructs the jury in such a way as to reduce the prosecution's obligation to prove each element of its case beyond a reasonable doubt. People v. Kanan, 186 Colo. 255, 526 P.2d 1339 (1974); Lybarger v. People, 807 P.2d 570 (Colo. 1991). Cumulative instructions containing erroneous statements of law and which were at odds with the standard jury instructions on affirmative defenses had the effect of relieving the prosecution of its burden of proof in regard to affirmative defenses. Lybarger v. People, 807 P.2d 570 (Colo. 1991). Trial court's additional instruction in response to jury's inquiry not error because defendant acceded to instruction and the inquiry did not show any misunderstanding or confusion on a matter of law central to the defendant's guilt or innocence. People v. Phillips, 91 P.3d 476 (Colo. App. 2004). Giving of "Allen charge" prior to September 22, 1971, held not error. People v. Lovato, 181 Colo. 99, 507 P.2d 860 (1973). But error when no confusion in jurors' minds on the law. Ordinarily a trial judge is within his rightful province when he urges agreement upon a jury at loggerheads with itself; but this process has its limits, and it is a specifically delicate matter to importune unanimity when there is no indication of confusion or misapprehension in the minds of the jurors on the law of the case. Mogan v. People, 157 Colo. 395, 402 P.2d 928 (1965). "Time-fuse" instruction is plain error. The giving of a "time-fuse" instruction (which grants the jury a time limit to finish its deliberations, at the end of which the jury will be dismissed) constitutes plain error and requires reversal. Allen v. People, 660 P.2d 896 (Colo. 1983). Instruction that the jury could consider defendant's voluntary absence from the trial as evidence of guilt was not error. The court had made reasonable inquiry as to the defendant's whereabouts before continuing the trial. People v. Tafoya, 833 P.2d 841 (Colo. App. 1992). V. Motion for New Trial. Failure to comply with this rule will ordinarily result being precluded from raising an objection for the first time on motion for new trial. Arellano v. People, 177 Colo. 286, 493 P.2d 1362 (1972); Fresquez v. People, 178 Colo. 220, 497 P.2d 1246 (1972). Where grounds specified in motion are not the same as before court. Where the "grounds so specified" before the trial court are not the same as are thereafter urged in a motion for new trial, then the grounds may not be considered raised for the first time in the motion for a new trial. Zeiler v. People, 157 Colo. 332, 403 P.2d 439 (1965). VI. On Review. A. In General. Errors in instructions generally not basis for collateral attack. As a general rule, errors in jury instructions do not constitute fundamental error that would provide a basis for collateral attack. People v. Shearer, 181 Colo. 237, 508 P.2d 1249 (1973). Assumption that jury followed instructions. The reviewing court must assume, in the absence of evidence to the contrary, that the jury followed the court's instructions. People v. Palmer, 189 Colo. 354, 540 P.2d 341 (1975); People v. Montoya, 709 P.2d 58 (Colo. App. 1985), rev'd on other grounds, 736 P.2d 1208 (Colo. 1987). And that court properly instructed jury. On review, in the absence of all of the instructions, it will be assumed that the trial court properly instructed the jury on the law applicable to the facts and the issues. Luna v. People, 170 Colo. 1, 461 P.2d 724 (1969). Error benefiting party not prejudicial. Where one is benefited by an error in submitting or failing to submit an instruction, he cannot claim prejudicial error. Atwood v. People, 176 Colo. 183, 489 P.2d 1305 (1971). A party cannot complain when an instruction given is more favorable to him than the one refused. Lowdermilk v. People, 70 Colo. 459, 202 P. 118 (1921); Abshier v. People,

87 Colo. 507, 289 P. 1081 (1930). Where a court errs in giving an instruction that prejudices the state rather than the defendant in that it increases the state's burden beyond that required, no grounds for reversal are created. Early v. People, 178 Colo. 167, 496 P.2d 1021 (1972). No error where instructions support defendant's theory. Defendant cannot try the case on one theory and claim error on appeal where the trial court, in instructing the jury, acquiesced in that theory. People v. Lankford, 185 Colo. 445, 524 P.2d 1382 (1974). Or where approved by defense. Assignments of error based on instructions specifically approved by the defense will not be considered. Giacomozzi v. People, 72 Colo. 13, 209 P. 798 (1922). No error where defendant acquitted. Where the requested instructions went only to the question of a charge of which the defendant was acquitted, the refusal to give the instructions is not subject to review. Hughes v. People, 175 Colo. 351, 487 P.2d 810 (1971). Mere nondirection where no instruction is requested is not error. Brown v. People, 20 Colo. 161, 36 P. 1040 (1894); West v. People, 60 Colo. 488, 156 P. 137 (1915); Clarke v. People, 64 Colo. 164, 171 P. 69 (1918); Rowan v. People, 93 Colo. 473, 26 P.2d 1066 (1933). In reviewing claims based on clerical errors in instructions, the court must assume that the jury took a common sense view of the instruction. People v. Turner, 730 P.2d 333 (Colo. App. 1986). For court to determine the effect of particular instruction, it must be read in conjunction with the other instructions. People v. Zapata, 759 P.2d 754 (Colo. App. 1988), aff'd on other grounds, 779 P.2d 1307 (Colo. 1989). Under the doctrine of invited error, a party cannot complain where he has been the instrument for injecting error in the case, and any error caused by the failure of the trial court to give the jury an instruction due to the defendant's objections is error injected by the defendant and cannot be complained of on appeal. People v. Collins, 730 P.2d 293 (Colo. 1986). When a party injects or invites error in trial proceedings, he cannot later seek reversal on appeal because of that error. People v. Zapata, 759 P.2d 754 (Colo. App. 1988), aff'd on other grounds, 779 P.2d 1307 (Colo. 1989). A claim of plain error relative to a jury instruction must be tested by examining the sufficiency of the instructions as a whole. People v. Turner, 730 P. 2d 333 (Colo. App. 1986). The cumulative effect of improper jury instructions that contained erroneous statements of law which relegated to the jury the function of determining whether an affirmative defense was available in a case and which had the effect of relieving the prosecution of its burden of proof in regard to the affirmative defense was plain error even though a proper jury instruction was provided with the improper jury instruction. The proper jury instruction was insufficient to dispel the potential harm created by the erroneous jury instructions. Lybarger v. People, 807 P.2d 570 (Colo. 1991). Failure to instruct jury on element not necessarily structural, requiring reversal. If element uncontested, supported by overwhelming evidence, and jury verdict would have been same absent error, failure to instruct harmless. People v. Geisendorfer, 991 P.2d 308 (Colo. App. 1999). A trial court commits constitutional error when it correctly instructs the jury regarding the elements of the crime but instructs the jury that, as a matter of law, the prosecution has satisfied its burden of proving one of the elements, thereby withdrawing that element from the jury's consideration. People v. Gracey, 940 P.2d 1050 (Colo. App. 1996). B. Requirements. Failure to object at trial bars review. Where appellants argue that certain of the instructions given were erroneous, but they failed to raise any objection to these instructions at trial, offered no alternative instructions, and then failed to raise the issue in their motion for a new trial, an appellate court will not ordinarily review the assignment of error. People v. Buckner, 180 Colo. 65, 504 P.2d 669 (1972). See Morehead v. People, 167 Colo. 287, 447 P.2d 215 (1968); Tanksley v. People, 171 Colo. 77, 464 P.2d 862 (1970). Trial counsel must specify which instructions he is objecting to and tender correct instructions, and having failed to so object at trial, the issue cannot be raised on appeal. People v. Green, 183 Colo. 25, 514 P.2d 769 (1973). Where defendant did not object to the jury instruction, nor offer a substitute, or include the asserted ground in his motion for new trial, it will not be considered for the first time on appeal. Lamb v. People, 181 Colo. 446, 509 P.2d 1267 (1973). An appellate court ordinarily does not notice objections to instructions not raised at the trial court level. Keady v. People, 32 Colo. 57, 74 P. 892 (1903); Buschman v. People, 80 Colo. 173, 249 P. 652 (1926); Ruark v. People, 164 Colo. 257, 434 P.2d 124 (1967), cert. denied, 390 U.S. 1044, 88 S. Ct. 1644, 20 L. Ed. 2d 306 (1968). Ordinarily, the supreme court will not take note of erroneous instructions in the absence of a contemporaneous objection which gives the trial court an opportunity to correct error in its proceedings. People v. Meller, 185 Colo. 389, 524 P.2d 1366 (1974). Unless manifest prejudice amounting to plain error. Where the defendant does not object to an instruction given, or tender any alternate instruction which might more adequately set forth the law, his assignment of error is not valid unless there is manifest prejudice amounting to plain error. People v. Bercillio, 179 Colo. 383, 500 P.2d 975 (1972). Where defendant did not tender

118

his own instructions, nor did he object to the instructions given, nor did he raise objections to the instructions in his motion for a new trial, a reviewing court is not required to review the arguments raised for the first time, and would not do so unless fundamental error appears. People v. Manier, 184 Colo. 44, 518 P.2d 811 (1974). Where a defendant failed to object to the adequacy of the jury instructions in his motion for a new trial, a judgment will not be reversed unless plain error occurred. People v. Frysig, 628 P.2d 1004 (Colo. 1981). Where defendant only made a general objection to jury instructions, and failed to make a timely specific objection, supreme court will not consider argument by defendant that instructions were in error, absent plain error. People v. O'Donnell, 184 Colo. 104, 518 P.2d 945 (1974). Where the defendant failed to make any objection prior to submission of the instructions, absent plain error, the court would not consider the defendant's arguments on review. People v. Tilley, 184 Colo. 424, 520 P.2d 1046 (1974); People v. Casey, 185 Colo. 58, 521 P.2d 1250 (1974). Where defendant did not challenge the giving of the instruction at trial, only error so substantial as to constitute plain error requires reversal. People v. Turner, 730 P.2d 333 (Colo. App. 1986). Within the meaning of rule 52. Review as to an alleged error not previously specified to the trial court is precluded unless the alleged error be deemed "plain error" within the meaning of Crim. P. 52(b). People v. Brionez, 39 Colo. App. 396, 570 P.2d 1296 (1977). "Plain error" rule must be read in harmony with this rule. People v. Barker, 180 Colo. 28, 501 P.2d 1041 (1972). Review confined to whether plain error present. Where an instruction issue is raised for the first time on appeal, review is confined to a consideration of whether the error falls within the definition of plain error. People v. Barker, 180 Colo. 28, 501 P.2d 1041 (1972); People v. Zapata, 759 P.2d 754 (Colo. App. 1988), aff'd on other grounds, 779 P.2d 1307 (Colo. 1989); People v. Lybarger, 790 P.2d 855 (Colo. App. 1989), rev'd on other grounds, 807 P.2d 570 (Colo. 1991); People v. Knight, 167 P.3d 141 (Colo. App. 2006). Where instructions used by the trial court fail to define the statutory terms, failure to object to the tendered instructions or raise any constitutional objection to the statute at the trial court level raises the standard of review to one of "plain error". People v. Cardenas, 42 Colo. App. 61, 592 P.2d 1348 (1979). Appellate court reviews only for plain error where defendant fails to make all objections to the jury instructions before the instructions are submitted to the jury. People v. Sweeney, 78 P.3d 1133 (Colo. App. 2003). No plain error where a reasonable jury would not interpret the instructions to permit two aggravated robbery convictions where defendant took property from only one victim during a single episode. People v. Sweeney, 78 P.3d 1133 (Colo. App. 2003). "Plain error" not found. Where an instruction is not objected to by defendant when tendered by the court, the defendant does not tender a "proper" instruction, and he does not mention the asserted error in instruction in a motion for new trial, there is no plain error. People v. Green, 178 Colo. 77, 495 P.2d 549 (1972). Where from the court's review of all instructions it was satisfied that there was no "plain error" in the giving of the instruction which the defendant challenged for the first time on appeal, there was no need to discuss the several arguments advanced by the defendant. People v. Spinuzzi, 184 Colo. 412, 520 P.2d 1043 (1974). Broad objection insufficient for review. An objection in broad coverage, giving no basis whatever to point up with some reasonable particularity the nature of any shortcoming, is no objection at all and is not entitled to consideration on review. Cruz v. People, 165 Colo. 495, 441 P.2d 22 (1968). Where a great number of instructions are given, most of them dependent to some extent on each other, then, where they are full and fair to the defendant in a criminal case by stating the law correctly, an appellate court will not review them, or any part of them, upon a vague and general charge of error. Jones v. People, 6 Colo. 452, 45 Am. R. 526 (1882). Where instructions are given as a general charge and the exceptions are only general in their character, the party excepting is not in position to urge his objection on appeal. Liggett v. People, 26 Colo. 364, 58 P. 144 (1899). Refusal to give instruction not error if no prejudice. The court's refusal to give defendant's tendered instruction is not error where no prejudice to defendant is shown or apparent in record. Young v. People, 180 Colo. 62, 502 P.2d 81 (1972). Jury instruction that if defendant was found to be the initial aggressor he was not entitled to benefit of self-defense was harmless error. There was no real possibility the jury was misled and the instruction was at most cumulative of another instruction concerning self-defense. People v. Manzanares, 942 P.2d 1235 (Colo. App. 1996). Where record does not disclose any request during trial for the submission to the jury of a question, an appellate court declines to pass on the question of error in failure to submit. McClary v. People, 79 Colo. 205, 245 P. 491 (1926); McNulty v. People, 180 Colo. 246, 504 P.2d 335 (1972). No error in trial court's instruction on deadly weapon or in court's response to jury's question on deadly weapon where defense did not object to the instruction or tender an alternative instruction or object to the court's referral to the instruction in answering the question, and, in some circumstances, fists may be considered a deadly weapon. People v. Pennese, 830 P.2d 1085 (Colo. App. 1991). Jury instruction providing supplemental definition of "knowing" for the purposes of second degree murder was unnecessary, but was not reversible error. The trial court's instruction did not pose a barrier to the jury in considering fully the defendant's affirmative defense. People v. Baca, 852 P.2d 1302 (Colo. App. 1992). .

Rule 31 - Verdict

(a) Submission and Finding.

(1) Forms of Verdict. Before the jury retires the court shall submit to it written forms of verdict for its consideration.

(2) Retirement of Jury. When the jury retires to consider its verdict, the bailiff shall be sworn or affirmed to conduct the jury to some private and convenient place, and to the best of his ability to keep the jurors together until they have agreed upon a verdict. The bailiff shall not speak to any juror about the case except to ask if a verdict has been reached, nor shall he allow others to speak to the jurors. When they have agreed upon a verdict, the bailiff shall return the jury into court. However, in any case except where the punishment may be death or life imprisonment, the court, upon stipulation of counsel for all parties, may order that if the jury should agree upon a verdict during the recess or adjournment of court for the day, it shall seal its verdict, to be retained by the foreman and delivered by the jury to the judge at the opening of the court, and that thereupon the jury may separate, to meet in the jury box at the opening of court. Such a sealed verdict may be received by the court as the lawful verdict of the jury.

(3) Return. The verdict shall be unanimous and signed by the foreman. It shall be returned by the jury to the judge in open court.

(b) Several Defendants. If there are two or more defendants, the jury at any time during its deliberations may return a verdict or verdicts with respect to a defendant or defendants as to whom it has agreed; if the jury cannot agree with respect to all, the defendant or defendants as to whom it does not agree may be tried again.

(c) Conviction of Lesser Offense. The defendant may be found guilty of an offense necessarily included in the offense charged or of an attempt to commit either the offense charged or an offense necessarily included therein if the attempt is an offense.

(d) Poll of Jury. When a verdict is returned and before it is recorded, the jury shall be polled at the request of any party or upon the court's own motion. If upon the poll there is not unanimous concurrence, the jury may be directed to retire for further deliberations or may be discharged.

Colo. R. Crim. P. 31

Annotation I. General Consideration. Jury's verdict must be allowed to stand if supported by substantial evidence. People v. Chavez, 182 Colo. 216, 511 P.2d 883 (1973). Appellate courts cannot direct entry of directed verdicts of guilt. People v. Smith, 181 Colo. 203, 510 P.2d 315 (1973). Applied in People v. Morris, 190 Colo. 215, 545 P.2d 151 (1976); People v. Ledman, 622 P.2d 534 (Colo. 1981). II. Submission and Finding. A. Forms of Verdict. Where the crime charged can be committed in alternative ways, the written verdict form should not lump the ways together in the disjunctive or conjunctive, although the charge in the statute may be made in the disjunctive and the charge in the information may be made in the conjunctive. Hernandez v. People, 156 Colo. 23, 396 P.2d 952 (1964). Separate verdicts should be submitted or else there should be a general verdict given as a counterpart of the not guilty verdict, since evidence of any of the alternative ways a crime can be committed will support a general verdict. Hernandez v. People, 156 Colo. 23, 396 P.2d 952 (1964). B. Retirement of Jury. All communications should be made in open court with the parties afforded an opportunity to make timely objections to any action by the court or jury which might be deemed irregular. Barriner v. District Court, 174 Colo. 447, 484 P.2d 774 (1971). Informal communications improper. Informal communications between the court and jury via the bailiff are improper. Barriner v. District Court, 174 Colo. 447, 484 P.2d 774 (1971). Prejudice required to set aside verdict for improper jury communication. In order to constitute grounds for setting aside verdict because of unauthorized or improper communication with the jury, the defendant must show that he was prejudiced thereby. People v. Davis, 183 Colo. 228, 516 P.2d 120 (1973). Informal communication between court and jury must be examined in order to determine whether it is prejudicial. Ray v. People, 147 Colo. 587, 364 P.2d 578 (1961). Determination of prejudice within court's discretion. The determination of whether prejudice has occurred because of unauthorized or improper communication with the jury is within the sound discretion of the trial court, and only where that discretion has been abused will the verdict be set aside and a new trial ordered. People v. Davis, 183 Colo. 228, 516 P.2d 120 (1973). Communication without prejudice not reversible error.

Where the communication does not disclose that any prejudice whatever resulted to defendants, such communication between court and jury does not constitute reversible error. Ray v. People, 147 Colo. 587, 364 P.2d 578 (1961). This rule must receive a reasonable construction as prohibiting only communications of an improper or unnecessary character. McLean v. People, 66 Colo. 486, 180 P. 676 (1919). Ordinary physical necessities of jurors must be provided for. McLean v. People, 66 Colo. 486, 180 P. 676 (1919). Where trial testimony is read to the jury at its request during its deliberations, it is essential that the court observe caution that evidence is not so selected, nor used in such a manner, that there is a likelihood of it being given undue weight or emphasis by the jury, for this would be prejudicial abuse of discretion and constitute grounds for reversal. Settle v. People, 180 Colo. 262, 504 P.2d 680 (1972). Such reading is discretionary with trial court. The overwhelming weight of authority is that the reading of all or part of the testimony of one or more of the witnesses at trial, criminal or civil, at the specific request of the jury during its deliberations is discretionary with the trial court. Settle v. People, 180 Colo. 262, 504 P.2d 680 (1972). Court must determine whether jury is deadlocked. The trial court fails to exercise its power with that degree of caution which the circumstances demand where it fails to determine as a matter of fact that the jury is hopelessly deadlocked immediately before its discharge. Barriner v. District Court, 174 Colo. 447, 484 P.2d 774 (1971). When "consent" to discharge deemed invalid. Defendant's "consent" to the discharge of the jury has no force or validity where the conditions and assumptions upon which the consent is based are never legally met, such as where defendant agreed to a future situation where the jury was "hopelessly deadlocked" when he had a right to anticipate that the court would follow the usual procedures in discharging a jury, and not the declaration of a mistrial based upon hearsay and procedural violations of the bailiff done totally off the record and out of court where no objection to the procedure was possible. Barriner v. District Court, 174 Colo. 447, 484 P.2d 774 (1971). C. Return. Verdict in a criminal case should be certain and devoid of ambiguity, though it need not follow strict rules of pleading or be otherwise technical. Yeager v. People, 170 Colo. 405, 462 P.2d 487 (1969). Else conviction will not stand. When the language of the verdict permits reasonable uncertainty, defendant's conviction cannot be permitted to stand. Yeager v. People, 170 Colo. 405, 462 P.2d 487 (1969). Sealed verdict must be returned the next juridical day. Where the parties stipulated that the court direct the jury to the effect that should they agree upon a verdict during the recess or adjournment of court for the day, the jury should seal their verdict and thereafter, in the absence of defendant and his counsel, and without his knowledge, the court instructed the jury to return verdict one week later instead of the next juridical day, as this rule contemplates, such practice was improper. Denny v. People, 106 Colo. 328, 104 P.2d 610 (1940). Unanimity is required only with respect to the ultimate issue of defendant's guilt or innocence of the crime charged and not with respect to alternative means by which the crime was committed. People v. Taggart, 621 P.2d 1375 (Colo. 1981); People v. Vigil, 678 P.2d 554 (Colo. App. 1983). Unanimity in a verdict does not require the jurors to be in agreement as to specific elements of the crime. People v. Lewis, 710 P.2d 1110 (Colo. App. 1985). Where the intent of the jury can be ascertained from the verdict forms submitted, there is no reversible error as a result of the omission of a reference to conspiracy in the guilty verdict form. People v. Roberts, 705 P.2d 1030 (Colo. App. 1985). Jury verdicts will not be reversed for inconsistency when the crimes charged required different elements of proof, and the jury could find from the very same evidence that the element of one crime was present while at the same time finding that the element of another charged crime was absent. People v. Powell, 716 P.2d 1096 (Colo. 1986). No error in the trial court's decision to reassemble the jury for further deliberation and to enter judgment on the amended verdict where facts were insufficient to support a presumption that the jury was open to the influence of others after discharge and the defendant did not request that the jurors be questioned about their contact with others during the brief period after discharge. People v. Montanez, 944 P.2d 529 (Colo. App. 1996). Court properly instructed jury to resume deliberations where juror's statements were ambiguous and equivocal as to her concurrence in the verdict. People v. Barnard, 12 P.3d 290 (Colo. App. 2000). III. Conviction of Lesser Offense. Lesser included offense defined. If the greater of two offenses includes all the legal and factual elements of the lesser, the greater includes the lesser; but if the lesser offense requires the inclusion of some necessary element not so included in the greater offense, the lesser is not necessarily included in the greater. Sandoval v. People, 176 Colo. 414, 490 P.2d 1298 (1971). "The offense charged" as used in section (c), encompasses any lesser included offense of the one charged. Hunter v. District Court, 184 Colo. 238, 519 P.2d 941 (1974). Provisions of section (c) are embodiments of the rule at common law that the defendant was presumed to be on notice that he could be convicted of the crime charged or a lesser offense included therein. People v. Cooke,

186 Colo. 44, 525 P.2d 426 (1974). Section (c) and all prior Colorado case law provide that one may be convicted of a lesser included offense of the crime charged. Hunter v. District Court, 184 Colo. 238, 519 P.2d 941 (1974). If appellate court reverses a conviction as to a greater offense for insufficient evidence, it may direct entry of judgment on a lesser included offense supported by sufficient proof, even if jury was not instructed upon that lesser offense. People v. Valdez, 56 P.3d 1148 (Colo. App. 2002). A criminal defendant who maintains his or her innocence at trial is not automatically barred from seeking jury instructions for a voluntary intoxication defense. If an instruction is given in that case, there must be a rational basis for it in the evidence presented at trial. After a review of the record, there was no rational basis in the evidence for the voluntary intoxication instruction. Brown v. People, 239 P.3d 764 (Colo. 2010). Claim of innocence alone does not disentitle defendant to lesser included offense instruction. The instruction, however, must be supported by evidence at trial. There was no error in failing to instruct the jury on attempted first degree murder where victim's injuries were such that no rational jury could have found the shooter acted with anything but a premeditated intent to cause death. People v. Brown, 218 P.3d 733 (Colo. App. 2009), aff'd, 239 P.3d 764 (Colo. 2010). IV. Poll of Jury. A court may declare a mistrial without further questioning the jury if the record supports the determination that the jury is unlikely to reach a unanimous verdict. Section (d) specifically applies "when a verdict is returned" and contains no direction to poll jurors prior to a verdict. Although the rule contemplates that a juror may disagree with a verdict, thereby permitting the court to direct further deliberations or to discharge the jury, the rule contains no provision for the situation where the jury reports that it cannot, and likely will not, reach a verdict. People v. Rivers, 70 P.3d 531 (Colo. App. 2002). A jury poll ordinarily requires each juror to assent in the verdict. However, the right to a jury poll is not absolute, and matters relating to the manner of conducting a jury poll are generally committed to the discretion of the trial court. People v. Phillips, 91 P.3d 476 (Colo. App. 2004). Trial court properly refused defendant's request to poll the jury. If a single charge includes multiple degrees of offenses, the trial court may not conduct a partial verdict inquiry as to the offenses included within the charge. People v. Richardson, 184 P.3d 755 (Colo. 2008). Where no contemporaneous objection is made to an asserted defect occurring during the polling of the jury, review on appeal is limited to whether the defect rises to the level of ordinary plain error. Because the jurors in the case orally informed the court of their unanimous verdict and the record did not show a lack of unanimity, the court perceived no plain error where twelfth juror inexplicably not polled. People v. Phillips, 91 P.3d 476 (Colo. App. 2004).

Judgment

Rule 32 - Sentence and Judgment

(a)Presentence or Probation Investigation.

    (1)When Investigation and Report Required

        (i)In General. The probation officer must make a presentence investigation and written report to the court before the imposition of sentence or granting of probation:

            (a) In any case in which the defendant is to be sentenced for a felony and the court has discretion as to the punishment, or

            (b) When the court so orders in any case in which the defendant is to be sentenced for a misdemeanor.

        (ii) Waiver. The court, with the concurrence of the defendant and the prosecuting attorney, may dispense with the presentence investigation and report unless a presentence report is required by statute, including but not limited to the requirements of Section 16-11-102(1)(b), C.R.S.

    (2) Court May Order Examination. The court, upon its own motion or upon the petition of the probation officer, may order any defendant who is subject to presentence investigation or who has made application for probation to submit to a mental and physical examination.

    (3) Delivery of Report Copies. The probation officer must provide copies of the presentence report, including any recommendations as to probation, to the prosecuting attorney and to defense counsel or the defendant if unrepresented. The copies must be provided:

        (i) At least 72 hours before the sentencing hearing, or

        (ii) At least 7 days before the sentencing hearing if either the prosecuting attorney, defense counsel, or the defendant if unrepresented, so requests of the court within 7 days of the time the court sets the date for the sentencing hearing. If the probation department informs the court it cannot provide the report copies at least 7 days before the sentencing hearing, the court must grant the probation department additional time to complete the report and must reset the sentencing hearing so that it is held at least 7 days after the probation department provides the report copies.

(b)Sentence and judgment.

(1) Sentence shall be imposed without unreasonable delay. Before imposing sentence, the court shall afford the defendant an opportunity to make a statement in his or her own behalf, and to present any information in mitigation of punishment. The state also shall be given an opportunity to be heard on any matter material to the imposition of sentence. Alternatives in sentencing shall be as provided by law. When imposing sentence, the court shall consider restitution as required by Section 18-1.3-603(1), C.R.S.

(2) Upon conviction of guilt of a defendant of a class 1 felony, and after the sentencing hearing provided by law, the trial court shall impose such sentence as is authorized by law. At the time of imposition of a sentence of death, the trial court shall enter an order staying execution of the judgment and sentence until further order of the Supreme Court.

(3)Judgment.

(i) A judgment of conviction shall consist of a recital of the plea, the verdict or findings, the sentence, the finding of the amount of presentence confinement, and costs, if any are assessed against the defendant, the finding of the amount of earned time credit if the defendant had previously been placed in a community corrections program, an order or finding regarding restitution as required by Section 18-1.3-603 , C.R.S., and a statement that the defendant is required to register as a sex offender, if applicable.

(ii) If the defendant is found not guilty or for any other reason is entitled to be discharged, judgment shall be entered accordingly.

(iii) All judgments shall be signed by the trial judge and entered by the clerk in the register of actions.

(c) Advisement.

(1) Where judgment of conviction has been entered following a trial, the court shall, after passing sentence, inform the defendant of the right to seek review of the conviction and sentence, and the time limits for filing a notice of appeal. The court shall at that time make a determination whether the defendant is indigent, and if so, the court shall inform the defendant of the right to the assistance of appointed counsel upon review of the defendant's conviction and sentence, and of the defendant's right to obtain a record on appeal without payment of costs. In addition, the court shall, after passing sentence, inform the defendant of the right to seek postconviction reduction of sentence in the trial court under the provisions of Rule 35(b).

(2) Where judgment of conviction has been entered following a plea of guilty or nolo contendere, the court shall, after passing sentence, inform the defendant that the defendant may in certain circumstances have the right to appellate review of the sentence, of the time limits for filing a notice of appeal, and that the defendant may have a right to seek postconviction reduction of sentence in the trial court under the provisions of Rule 35(b).

(3) When the court imposes a sentence, enters a judgment, or issues an order that obligates a defendant to pay any monetary amount, the court shall instruct the defendant as follows:

(i) If at any time the defendant is unable to pay the monetary amount due, the defendant must contact the court's designated official or appear before the court to explain why he or she is unable to pay the monetary amount;

(ii) If the defendant lacks the present ability to pay the monetary amount due without undue hardship to the defendant or the defendant's dependents, the court shall not jail the defendant for failure to pay; and

(iii) If the defendant has the ability to pay the monetary amount as directed by the court or the court's designee but willfully fails to pay, the defendant may be imprisoned for failure to comply with the court's lawful order to pay pursuant to the terms of this section.

(d) Withdrawal of Plea of Guilty or Nolo Contendere. A motion to withdraw a plea of guilty or of nolo contendere may be made only before sentence is imposed or imposition of sentence is suspended. If the court decides that the final disposition should not include the charge or sentence concessions contemplated by a plea agreement, as provided in Rule 11(f) of these Rules, the court shall so advise the defendant and the district attorney and then call upon the defendant to either affirm or withdraw the plea of guilty or nolo contendere.

(e) Criteria for Granting Probation. The court in its discretion may grant probation to a defendant unless, having regard to the nature and circumstances of the offense and to the history and character of the defendant, it is satisfied that imprisonment is the more appropriate sentence for the protection of the public. The conditions of probation shall be as the court in its discretion deems reasonably necessary to ensure that the defendant will lead a law-abiding life and to assist the defendant to do so. The court shall provide as an explicit condition of every sentence to probation that the defendant not commit another offense during the period for which the sentence remains subject to revocation.

(f) Proceedings for Revocation of Probation.

(1) At the first appearance of the probationer in court, or at the commencement of the hearing, whichever is first in time, the court shall advise the probationer as provided in Rule 5(2)(I) through (VI) of these Rules insofar as such matters are applicable, except that there shall be no right to a trial by jury in proceedings for revocation of probation.

(2) At or prior to the commencement of the hearing, the court shall advise the probationer of the charges against the probationer and the possible penalty or penalties therefor, and shall require the probationer to admit or deny the charges.

(3) At the hearing, the prosecution shall have the burden of establishing by a preponderance of the evidence the violation of a condition or conditions of probation, except that the commission of a criminal offense must be established beyond a reasonable doubt unless the probationer has been convicted thereof in a criminal proceeding. The court may, when it appears that the alleged violation of conditions of probation consists of an offense with which the probationer is charged in a criminal proceeding then pending, continue the probation revocation hearing until the termination of such criminal proceeding. Any evidence having probative value shall be received regardless of its admissibility under the exclusionary rules of evidence if the defendant is accorded a fair opportunity to rebut the evidence.

(4) If the probationer is in custody, the hearing shall be held within 14 days after the filing of the complaint, unless delay or continuance is granted by the court at the instance or request of the probationer or for other good cause found by the court justifying further delay.

(5) If the court determines that a violation of a condition or conditions of probation has been committed, it shall within 7 days after the said hearing either revoke or continue the probation. In the event probation is revoked, the court may then impose any sentence, including probation which might originally have been imposed or granted.

(g) Proceedings in the Event of Failure to Pay. When a defendant fails to pay a monetary amount imposed by the court, the court shall follow the procedures set forth in Section 18-1.3-702(3), C.R.S.

Colo. R. Crim. P. 32

Source: a2, b to e, f2 amended and adopted September 7, 2006, effective 1/1/2007; a1 amended and effective 10/18/2007; f4 and f5 amended and adopted December 14, 2011, effective 7/1/2012. Amended and Adopted by the Court, En Banc, 5/22/2015, effective immediately; amended and adopted March 14, 2019, effective 3/14/2019.

Annotation I. General Consideration. Law reviews. For article, "Insanity and the Law", see 39 Dicta 325 (1962). For article, "Colorado Felony Sentencing", see 11 Colo. Law. 1478 (1982). For article, "Pronouncements of the U.S. Supreme Court Relating to the Criminal Law Field: 1985-1986", which discusses a recent case relating to increased sentences after retrial, see 15 Colo. Law. 1604 (1986). This rule is not unconstitutional because notice of a right to review is given to criminal defendants except in cases where judgment of conviction has been entered following a plea of guilty or nolo contendere. The reasonableness of the classification of defendants who have entered guilty pleas has been upheld in cases dealing with the federal counterpart. People v. Smith, 190 Colo. 449, 548 P.2d 603 (1976). A violation of this rule does not entitle defendant to a late appeal in the absence of prejudice. In order for the defendant to bring a claim alleging he or she was deprived of the right to appeal because the court failed to comply with this rule, the defendant must bring a timely postconviction action under Crim. P. 35(c) and request a remedy of a new appeal. People v. Boespflug, 107 P.3d 1118 (Colo. App. 2004). Applied in McClendon v. People, 175 Colo. 451, 488 P.2d 556 (1971); People v. Banks, 190 Colo. 295, 545 P.2d 1356 (1976); People v. District Court, 191 Colo. 558, 554 P.2d 1105 (1976); People v. Houpe, 41 Colo. App. 253, 586 P.2d 241 (1978); People v. Palmer, 42 Colo. App. 460, 595 P.2d 1060 (1979); People v. Baca, 44 Colo. App. 167, 610 P.2d 1083 (1980); People v. Horton, 628 P.2d 117 (Colo. App. 1980); People v. Quintana, 634 P.2d 413 (Colo. 1981); People v. Lawson, 634 P.2d 1019 (Colo. App. 1981); Hafelfinger v. District Court, 674 P.2d 375 (Colo. 1984); People v. Anderson, 703 P.2d 650 (Colo. App. 1985). II. Presentence or Probation Investigation. Even where evidence has been illegally seized, its use in a presentence hearing following a guilty plea is not error. Von Pickrell v. People, 163 Colo. 591, 431 P.2d 1003 (1967). III. Sentence. Equal protection requirements. In the context of sentencing for criminal offenses, equal protection requires only that those who have committed the same offense shall be subject to the same criminal sanctions in effect at the time the offense was committed. People v. Arellano, 185 Colo. 280, 524 P.2d 305 (1974). Imposition of sentence requires judicial discretion. The imposition of a criminal sentence in each individual case requires the exercise of judicial judgment, and it includes consideration of mitigating and aggravating circumstances, the power to impose an indeterminate sentence, and the right to suspend sentence, or the discretion to grant probation in appropriate cases. People v. Jenkins, 180 Colo. 35, 501 P.2d 742 (1972). Which does not deny equal protection. The exercise of the judge's discretionary power in sentencing does not deny an accused equal protection of the law. People v. Jenkins, 180 Colo. 35, 501 P.2d 742 (1972). Substance of American Bar Association standards deemed "authorized by law". The substance of the principles articulated in the American Bar Association Standards Relating to Sentencing Alternatives and Procedures § 3.5, insofar as they are consistent with the stated general purposes of the Colorado code of criminal procedure, may be deemed to be "authorized by law" within the meaning of section (b). People v. Lewis, 193 Colo. 203, 564 P.2d 111 (1977). Nothing requires court to assign reasons for imposing a sentence. People v. Pauldino, 187 Colo. 61, 528 P.2d 384 (1974). A sentencing court is required to state on the record the basic reasons for the imposition of sentence. The failure to do so creates a burdensome obstacle to effective and meaningful appellate review. People v. Luu, 983 P.2d 15 (Colo. App. 1998). A judgment of conviction is not final until sentence is imposed. Absent a specific finding that the victim did not suffer a pecuniary loss, restitution is a mandatory part of a sentence. Thus, absent such a finding, sentencing is not final until restitution is ordered. People v. Rosales, 134 P.3d 429 (Colo. App. 2005). Discretion to impose concurrent or consecutive sentence. A sentencing court has discretion to impose a sentence to be served concurrently with or consecutively to a sentence already imposed upon the defendant. People v. Garcia, 658 P.2d 1383 (Colo. App. 1983); People v. Cullen, 695 P.2d 750 (Colo. App. 1984). Delaying final sentencing on non-capital convictions until after sentencing on class 1 felony is appropriate where a court must sentence both for a class 1 felony and for other felonies. People v. Davis, 794 P.2d 159 (Colo. 1990). Six-year delay between defendant's conviction and legal sentencing did not divest court of jurisdiction or cause unreasonable delay, where the sentence was promptly imposed following defendant's conviction, but subsequent appeal and the defendant's election to invoke the discretionary procedure under the Sex Offender's Act of 1968 delayed the proceedings. People v. Wortham, 928 P.2d 771 (Colo. App. 1996). When court delays sentencing so that another case against defendant may be resolved that would allow the court to increase the sentence in case before the court, the court violates the requirement to impose sentence without "unreasonable delay". The delay in this case allowed the court to double the defendant's sentence which was substantial error that undermined the fundamental fairness of defendant's sentencing. People v. Sandoval-Candelaria, __ P.3d __ (Colo. App. 2011). Single sentence for more than one conviction does not constitute reversible error, although the preferable practice is to have a separate sentence for each conviction. People v. Pleasant, 182 Colo. 144, 511 P.2d 488 (1973). Reliance by court on probation report at time sentence imposed does not abuse the defendant's rights. People v. Canino, 181 Colo. 207, 508 P.2d 1273 (1973). Judge may consider truthfulness of voluntary statements. It is not a denial of due process for a judge, in connection with sentencing procedure, to consider the truthfulness of voluntary statements made by the defendant at a presentence hearing. People v. Quarles, 182 Colo. 321, 512 P.2d 1240 (1973). Deferred prosecution is relevant consideration in determining the sentence. People v. Lichtenwalter, 184 Colo. 340, 520 P.2d 583 (1974). There is no difference between plea of nolo contendere and plea of guilty for sentencing purposes. People v. Canino, 181 Colo. 207, 508 P.2d 1273 (1973). There is no requirement that codefendants be given equal sentences. People v. Martin, 670 P.2d 22 (Colo. App. 1983). Sentencing court should tailor sentence to defendant, keeping in mind past record, potential for rehabilitation, and protection of the public as well. People v. Alvarez, 187 Colo. 290, 530 P.2d 506 (1975). Sentencing court should attempt to tailor the sentence to the defendant. To achieve this goal, the court should be aware of defendant's entire record including his past encounters with the criminal justice system. People v. Lichtenwalter, 184 Colo. 340, 520 P.2d 583 (1974). Defendant must be notified when sentence will be pronounced. He has a right to be present in the court with legal counsel at that time, and he has a right of allocution before sentence is handed down which cannot be withheld from him. The failure of the court to properly insure these rights of a defendant renders invalid a sentence pronounced under those circumstances. People v. Emig, 177 Colo. 174, 493 P.2d 368 (1972). No right to evidentiary hearing. During a discretionary sentencing proceeding, rule does not require an evidentiary hearing on the validity of any prior conviction contained in a presentence report. People v. Padilla, 907 P.2d 601 (Colo. 1995). Prior to sentencing, the court must grant the defendant an opportunity to make a statement on his or her own behalf. The proper remedy for failing to allow the defendant to make a statement is resentencing. People v. Marquantte, 923 P.2d 180 (Colo. App. 1995). Effect of denial of allocution limited. Denial of the right of allocution under section (b) has no effect on the validity of the jury's determination of guilt. People v. Doyle, 193 Colo. 332, 565 P.2d 944 (1977). Relief from denial is resentencing. The defendant's relief from a denial of the right of allocution under section (b) is resentencing after being afforded his right to allocution. People v. Doyle, 193 Colo. 332, 565 P.2d 944 (1977). Where the presentence report is issued to counsel immediately prior to sentencing, and the trial court's refusal to continue the sentencing hearing to another day unduly abridges the defendant's rights to present evidence in rebuttal to the information and recommendations contained in the report, his sentence must be vacated and the case remanded for resentencing after a full sentencing hearing. People v. Wright, 672 P.2d 518 (Colo. 1983). However, the right of allocution is a statutory right, not a constitutional one, and reversal is not required if the failure to provide the defendant an opportunity to make a statement prior to sentencing is harmless. If a trial court imposes the minimum sentence permitted and does not have discretion to impose a lesser sentence, the lack of statement in allocution does not affect the sentence and is harmless. People v. Martinez, 83 P.3d 1174 (Colo. App. 2003). Sentencing must occur without unreasonable delay. Although the general assembly has prescribed no specific time within which sentence must be imposed, section (b) requires that sentencing occur without unreasonable delay. People ex rel. Gallagher v. District Court, 632 P.2d 1009 (Colo. 1981). Although sentencing was delayed for eight years, delay was excusable because the majority of it was attributable to defendant's own actions. Moody v. Corsentino, 843 P.2d 1355 (Colo. 1993). Although resentencing was delayed for 29 months, delay was excusable because of the timely imposition of defendant's original sentence, the substantial reduction of the original sentence upon resentencing, the consequent lack of prejudice resulting from the sentence imposed on remand, and the fact that all of the period of delay would be credited against the present sentence. People v. Luu, 983 P.2d 15 (Colo. App. 1998). Despite six-year delay, state had no duty to set defendant's probation revocation hearing until after termination of defendant's incarceration in another jurisdiction. People v. Smith, 183 P.3d 726 (Colo. App. 2008). One-year deferral of sentence imposition is unreasonable delay. Absent a legally justifiable reason, a one-year deferral of imposition of sentence constitutes an unreasonable delay in sentencing contrary to section (b). People ex rel. Gallagher v. District Court, 632 P.2d 1009 (Colo. 1981). Sentence imposed within statutory limits will not be disturbed. Ordinarily if a sentence imposed is within limits fixed by statute, it will not be disturbed on review. People v. Lutz, 183 Colo. 312, 516 P.2d 1132 (1973). Choice of place of confinement is within the sound discretion of the court. People v. Weihs, 187 Colo. 124, 529 P.2d 317 (1974). Length of term of imprisonment is within the discretion of the court. People v. Weihs, 187 Colo. 124, 529 P.2d 317 (1974). Sentencing judge is empowered to set the minimum sentence. Guerin v. Fullerton, 154 Colo. 142, 389 P.2d 84 (1964). Parole board has no authority to refuse to carry out the plain meaning of a sentence legally imposed by the sentencing judge. Guerin v. Fullerton, 154 Colo. 142, 389 P.2d 84 (1964). There is no constitutional right to credit of presentence jail time against sentence imposed. People v. Coy, 181 Colo. 393, 509 P.2d 1239 (1973); People v. Nelson, 182 Colo. 1, 510 P.2d 441 (1973). Presumption that court gave credit for presentence confinement. It will be conclusively presumed that the trial court gave credit for presentence time spent in confinement where the sentence imposed plus the prior time in confinement do not exceed the maximum possible sentence. Larkin v. People, 177 Colo. 156, 493 P.2d 1 (1972). Or otherwise acted properly. Where sentencing judge states only that he is taking time spent in jail prior to sentencing into consideration and thereafter gives the maximum, it must be presumed that he acted properly; that is, that he took the time spent into consideration and determined, as he had the right to do, not to grant the credit. People v. Nelson, 182 Colo. 1, 510 P.2d 441 (1973). But "giving credit" without applying it to sentence improper. Where the trial court in sentencing gives credit to the defendant for his presentence jail time but does not apply it to the maximum sentence, the court is, in fact, extending the sentence beyond the statutory limits. People v. Regan, 176 Colo. 59, 489 P.2d 194 (1971). Credit should be reflected in record. Trial judges would be well advised to follow the practice of causing the actual time spent by the defendant in jail prior to the imposition of sentence to be reflected in the record at the time sentence is imposed. People v. Jones, 176 Colo. 61, 489 P.2d 596 (1971). Cancellation of deferred sentence does not affect conviction. Where the trial court withdrew or cancelled the imposition of the deferred sentence, its order affected only the sentence, and did not touch the conviction. People v. Peretsky, 44 Colo. App. 270, 616 P.2d 170 (1980). Defendant's absence from the state was by

126

virtue of his own conduct and was justifiable reason for delay in sentencing. Defendant was incarcerated in another state for a probation violation. People v. Gould, 844 P.2d 1273 (Colo. App. 1992). Two and one-half month delay in sentencing following defendant's return to state was not unreasonable. People v. Gould, 844 P.2d 1273 (Colo. App. 1992). IV. Judgment. Intent of section (c). The intent behind section (c) is to establish some minimum guarantee that knowledge of the appellate process will be conveyed to defendants. People v. Boivin, 632 P.2d 1038 (Colo. App. 1981). Burden to show that defendant was advised of appellate rights. Once there is sufficient reason to believe that the trial court has not advised a defendant of his appellate rights, including the special rights of an indigent defendant, the burden falls upon the state to demonstrate that he was so advised. People v. Boivin, 632 P.2d 1038 (Colo. App. 1981). No "finality" standard for double jeopardy purposes. Section (c) does not provide a standard of "finality" for purposes of the constitutional prohibition against being twice placed in jeopardy for the same offense. People v. District Court, 663 P.2d 616 (Colo. 1983). For purposes of retroactive application of a new rule of law, a judgment of conviction in Colorado cannot be considered final so long as a defendant may directly appeal the conviction or sentence. People v. Sharp, 143 P.3d 1047 (Colo. App. 2005). Oral order does not become final judgment until order signed and entered in the judgment record. People v. Ganatta, 638 P.2d 268 (Colo. 1981). When judgment final for purposes of appeal. The final judgment was entered, for purposes of appeal, when trial court reversed its previous order imposing costs on the defendant, and therefore state's appeal, taken more than 30 days after sentencing was proper. People v. Fisher, 189 Colo. 297, 539 P.2d 1258 (1975). For purposes of § 16-5-402 and post-conviction review, a conviction occurs when the trial court enters judgment and sentence is imposed, if there is no appeal. The limitations of § 16-5-402 are applicable to a proportionality review of a sentence imposed pursuant to the habitual criminal statutes. People v. Talley, 934 P.2d 859 (Colo. App. 1996). Judgment in a criminal case is not final until after sentencing. Hellman v. Rhodes, 741 P.2d 1258 (Colo. 1987). An order of restitution becomes part of the sentence which, in accordance with section (c) of this rule, is part of the judgment of conviction. When a court orders a defendant, over his objection, to pay restitution to the victim or the victim's family as part of the judgment of conviction for a felony, the order of restitution is appealable pursuant to the statutory procedures applicable to the appellate review of a felony sentence. People v. Johnson, 780 P.2d 504 (Colo. 1989). Restitution component satisfied once ordered, even though specific amount not set until two years after sentence imposed. Once restitution ordered, although not set, judgment of conviction became final and appealable, even though district court retained jurisdiction to determine restitution amount. Sanoff v. People, 187 P.3d 576 (Colo. 2008). Post-final judgment orders void when court denied defendant's motion for new trial and imposed valid sentence. People v. Campbell, 738 P.2d 1179 (Colo. 1987). Constitutionality of imposing liability for costs. Statutes imposing liability for costs on a convicted defendant have been uniformly held to be constitutional. People v. Fisher, 189 Colo. 297, 539 P.2d 1258 (1975). For effect of rule on habitual criminal act, see Swift v. People, 174 Colo. 259, 488 P.2d 80 (1971). V. Withdrawal of Plea of Guilty or Nolo Contendere. A. In General. There is no ambiguity in this rule. Glaser v. People, 155 Colo. 504, 395 P.2d 461 (1964). No right to withdraw guilty plea. One may not, as a matter of right, have his plea of guilty withdrawn or changed. Maes v. People, 155 Colo. 570, 396 P.2d 457 (1964); McConnell v. People, 157 Colo. 235, 402 P.2d 75 (1965). Defendant does not have an absolute right to withdraw his guilty plea at any time before the court imposes sentence. People v. Riley, 187 Colo. 262, 529 P.2d 1312 (1975). Defendant not permitted to withdraw plea of nolo contendere. Defendant's assertion of innocence at the time his plea of nolo contendere was entered does not force the court to permit him to withdraw his plea of nolo contendere. People v. Canino, 181 Colo. 207, 508 P.2d 1273 (1973). Withdrawal of plea with court's discretion. An application for the withdrawal or change of such plea is addressed to the discretion of the trial court. Maes v. People, 155 Colo. 570, 396 P.2d 457 (1964); Bradley v. People, 175 Colo. 146, 485 P.2d 875 (1971). And court's ruling on such an application will not be reversed, except where there is a clear abuse of discretion. Maes v. People, 155 Colo. 570, 396 P.2d 457 (1964); Bradley v. People, 175 Colo. 146, 485 P.2d 875 (1971); People v. Miller, 685 P.2d 233 (Colo. App. 1984). Showing required to permit change of plea. To warrant the exercise of discretion favorable to a defendant concerning a change of plea, there must be some showing that justice will be subverted by a denial thereof, such as where a defendant may have been surprised or influenced into a plea of guilty when he had a defense, or where a plea of guilty was entered by mistake or under a misconception of the nature of the charge, or where such plea was entered through fear, fraud, or official misrepresentation, or where it was made involuntarily for some reason. Maes v. People, 155 Colo. 570, 396 P.2d 457 (1964); Crumb v.

127

People, 230 P.3d 726 (Colo. 2010). Defendant is entitled to withdraw plea of guilty where, at time plea was entered, neither court nor counsel was aware of defendant's parole status so defendant was improperly advised as to the minimum sentence, and where defendant promptly moved to withdraw guilty plea when parole status became known. People v. Chippewa, 751 P. 607 (Colo. 1988). Court should not consider sentence it intends to impose as a reason for denying motion to withdraw a guilty plea where plea was entered when neither court nor counsel was aware of defendant's parole status so that defendant was improperly advised as to minimum sentence. People v. Chippewa, 751 P.2d 607 (Colo. 1988). Defendant's motion to withdraw guilty plea must be granted where trial judge participated in plea negotiations. Because trial judge stepped out of his role as a neutral and impartial arbiter of justice by advising defendant and making other inappropriate remarks to influence defendant to agree to plea bargain, defendant has a fair and just reason to withdraw his plea. Crumb v. People, 230 P.3d 726 (Colo. 2010). Defendant was entitled to a hearing on motion to withdraw guilty plea where court understated minimum sentence that could be imposed and defendant's plea agreement was not in evidence. On remand, defendant must establish that his asserted belief that he would receive a sentence below the minimum sentence stated by the court was objectively reasonable. People v. Hodge, 205 P.3d 481 (Colo. App. 2008). Right to allocution not denied where extensive pretrial inquiry did not support defendant's last minute assertion of inability to speak in English at sentencing hearing. People v. Garcia, 752 P.2d 570 (Colo. 1988). When a defendant enters a plea agreement that includes a recommendation for a particular sentence, the fact that the sentence is rejected by the court removes the basis upon which the defendant entered his guilty plea and draws into question the voluntariness of the plea. Chae v. People, 780 P.2d 481 (Colo. 1989). Case must be remanded to allow defendant the opportunity to affirm or withdraw his guilty plea where the trial court's rejection of the sentence recommendation contained in the plea agreement calls into question the voluntariness of that plea and the defendant had no opportunity to affirm or withdraw that plea. People v. Walker, 46 P.3d 495 (Colo. App. 2002). When a defendant enters into a plea agreement that includes as a material element a recommendation for an illegal sentence and the illegal sentence is in fact imposed on the defendant, the guilty plea is invalid and must be vacated because the basis on which the defendant entered the plea included the impermissible inducement of an illegal sentence. Chae v. People, 780 P.2d 481 (Colo. 1989). Where there is a valid plea agreement but an illegal sentence imposed to enforce the valid and legal plea, the proper remedy is to modify the sentence to effect the intent of the plea agreement. People v. Antonio-Antimo, 29 P.3d 298 (Colo. 2000). It is not an abuse of the court's discretion to deny a motion pursuant to this rule even though the defendant is influenced by alcohol at the time of entry of a plea of guilty if the court finds that the defendant still has the mental capacity to understand the entry of a plea of guilty. People v. Lewis, 849 P.2d 855 (Colo. App. 1992). For a court to permit a defendant to withdraw his or her plea, there must be a fair and just reason. In this case, defendant's allegation of sentence misapprehension was contradicted by the record and the testimony of counsel, so there was no abuse of discretion in prohibiting defendant from withdrawing his plea. People v. Allen, ___ P.3d ___ (Colo. App. 2010). A claim of ineffective assistance of counsel that is conclusory or contradicted by the record is not a fair and just reason for withdrawing a guilty plea. People v. Lopez, 12 P.3d 869 (Colo. App. 2000). Fair and just reason for withdrawal of guilty plea is established where, immediately upon learning of the potential deportation consequences, the defendant filed a motion to withdraw his guilty plea before sentencing and where prosecution did not allege any prejudice arising from the withdrawal. People v. Luna, 852 P.2d 1326 (Colo. App. 1993). Defendant's motion to withdraw his guilty plea prior to sentencing without a hearing was duly denied, where defendant's expectation of a deferred sentence and judgment was merely a "wish and hope" that his counsel was unable to effectuate. People v. DiGuglielmo, 33 P.3d 1248 (Colo. App. 2001). Defendant's postconviction motion based on the voluntariness of his guilty plea as it related to the quality of his counsel was properly denied as successive under Crim. P. 35(c)(3)(VII), where lengthy evidentiary hearing was held on defendant's section 32(d) motion claiming that his plea was not knowing, voluntary, and intelligent due to ineffective assistance of counsel. People v. Vondra, 240 P.3d 493 (Colo. App. 2010). B. Sentence Concessions. Section (e) of this rule implements § 16-7-302(2) . People v. Wright, 38 Colo. App. 271, 559 P.2d 249 (1976), aff'd, 194 Colo. 448, 573 P.2d 551 (1978). Rule not limited to court-approved concessions. This rule, by its terms, is not limited to those situations where the court has first concurred in, or approved of, the sentence concessions. People v. Wright, 38 Colo. App. 271, 559 P.2d 249 (1976), aff'd, 194 Colo. 448, 573 P.2d 551 (1978). A sentence recommendation is a sentence concession whether or not the court approves or concurs. People v. Wright, 38 Colo. App. 271, 559 P.2d 249 (1976), aff'd,

194 Colo. 448, 573 P.2d 551 (1978). It is true that the district attorney has no authority to determine the sentence. However, sentence concessions must be equated with sentence recommendations; to hold otherwise would render the reference to sentence concessions in section (e) meaningless. People v. Wright, 38 Colo. App. 271, 559 P.2d 249 (1976), aff'd, 194 Colo. 448, 573 P.2d 551 (1978). The district attorney's agreement to recommend probation was a sentence concession contemplated by the plea agreement. People v. Wright, 38 Colo. App. 271, 559 P.2d 249 (1976), aff'd, 194 Colo. 448, 573 P.2d 551 (1978). But not all sentence concessions by the prosecution are sentence concessions. People v. Dawson, 89 P.3d 447 (Colo. App. 2003). "Sentence concessions" must refer only to the prosecution's making or not opposing favorable recommendations due to specific reference to Crim. P. 11(f). Prosecutor's agreement not to seek a sentence in the aggravated range does not constitute a sentence concession. People v. Dawson, 89 P.3d 447 (Colo. App. 2003). Court must comply with section (e). Merely informing the defendant, pursuant to Crim. P. 11(b)(5) that the court will not be bound by any recommendation or representation by anyone concerning sentencing or probation does not obviate the necessity of its complying with section (e). People v. Wright, 38 Colo. App. 271, 559 P.2d 249 (1976), aff'd, 194 Colo. 448, 573 P.2d 551 (1978). Court is not bound by a recommendation; in its discretion it may refuse to grant the district attorney's sentence concession. People v. Wright, 38 Colo. App. 271, 559 P.2d 249 (1976), aff'd, 194 Colo. 448, 573 P.2d 551 (1978). When plea bargain rejected, plea is not voluntary. When the trial judge rejects the plea bargain he removes it as the basis for the sentence. When this occurs, the plea can hardly be characterized as voluntary. People v. Wright, 38 Colo. App. 271, 559 P.2d 249 (1976), aff'd, 194 Colo. 448, 573 P.2d 551 (1978). And defendant may withdraw plea. A defendant is permitted to withdraw his guilty plea where the trial court chooses not to follow the prosecutor's sentence recommendation, regardless of whether the prosecution has promised that the court will follow the recommendation. People v. Wright, 194 Colo. 448, 573 P.2d 551 (1978). VI. Revocation of Probation. Power to alter sentence at time of revocation of probation is explicitly recognized in subsection (f)(5) of this rule, Crim. P. 35(a), and § 16-11-206(5). People v. Jenkins, 40 Colo. App. 140, 575 P.2d 13 (1977). Review of probation revocation order. Probation revocation orders are not reviewable only via Crim. P. 35, but may be reviewed by direct appeal. People v. Carr, 185 Colo. 293, 524 P.2d 301 (1974). Issue preclusion does not apply to bar the right of a defendant to a trial where defendant had been charged with the crime of driving with a revoked license, which constituted both a violation of his probation and a new criminal act. Defendant did not have a full and fair opportunity to litigate the issue in the probation revocation hearing. A determination of guilt or innocence in a probation revocation hearing would undermine the function of the criminal trial process. Byrd v. People, 58 P.3d 50 (Colo. 2002). Probation revocation hearings are held for different purposes, governed by different procedures, and do not protect a defendant's rights as does a criminal trial. Byrd v. People, 58 P.3d 50 (Colo. 2002).

Rule 32.1 - Death Penalty Sentencing Hearing

(a) **Purpose and Scope.** The purpose of this rule is to establish a uniform, expeditious procedure for conducting death penalty sentencing hearings in accordance with section 18-1.3-1201 , 6 C.R.S.

(b) **Statement of Intention to Seek Death Penalty.** In any class 1 felony case in which the prosecution intends to seek the death penalty, the prosecuting attorney shall file a written statement of that intention with the trial court no later than 63 days (9 weeks) after arraignment and shall serve a copy of the statement on the defendant's attorney of record or the defendant if appearing pro se.

(c) **Date of Sentencing Hearing.** After a verdict of guilt to a class 1 felony, the trial judge shall set a date for the sentencing hearing. The sentencing hearing shall be held as soon as practicable following the trial.

(d) **Discovery Procedures for Sentencing Hearing.** The following discovery provisions shall apply to the death penalty sentencing hearing:

(1) **Aggravating Factors.** Not later than 21 days after the filing of the written statement of intention required in subsection (b) of this rule, the prosecuting attorney shall provide to the defendant, and file with the court a list of the aggravating factors enumerated at section 18-1.3-1201(5), 6 C.R.S., and that the prosecuting attorney intends to prove at the hearing.

(2) **Prosecution Witnesses.** Not later than 21 days after the filing of the written statement of intention required in subsection (b) of this rule, the prosecuting attorney shall provide to the defendant a list of the witnesses whom the prosecuting attorney may call at the sentencing

129

hearing and shall promptly furnish the defendant with written notification of any such witnesses who subsequently become known or the materiality of whose testimony subsequently becomes known. Along with the name of the witness, the prosecuting attorney shall furnish the witness' address and date of birth, the subject matter of the witness' testimony, and any written or recorded statement of that witness, including notes.

(3) Prosecution Books, Papers, Documents. Not later than 21 days after the filing of the written statement of intention required in subsection (b) of this rule, the prosecuting attorney shall provide to the defendant a list of the books, papers, documents, photographs, or tangible objects, and access thereto, that the prosecuting attorney may introduce at the sentencing hearing and shall promptly furnish the defendant written notification of additional such items as they become known.

(4) Prosecution Experts. As soon as practicable but not later than 63 days (9 weeks) before trial, the prosecuting attorney shall provide to the defendant any reports, recorded statements, and notes, including results of physical or mental examinations and scientific tests, experiments, or comparisons, of any experts whom the prosecuting attorney intends to call as a witness at the sentencing hearing and shall promptly furnish the defendant additional such items as they become available.

(5) Material Favorable to the Accused. Not later than 21 days after the filing of the written statement of intention required in subsection (b) of this rule, the prosecuting attorney shall make available to the defendant any material or information within the prosecuting attorney's possession or control that would tend to mitigate or negate the finding of any of the aggravating factors the prosecuting attorney intends to prove at the sentencing hearing, and the prosecuting attorney shall promptly make available to the defendant any such material or information that subsequently comes into the prosecuting attorney's possession or control.

(6) Prosecution's Rebuttal Witnesses. Upon receipt of the information required by subsection (7), the prosecuting attorney shall notify the defendant as soon as practicable but not later than 14 days before trial of any additional witnesses whom the prosecuting attorney intends to call in response to the defendant's disclosures.

(7) Defendant's Disclosure.

(A) Subject to constitutional limitations, the defendant shall provide the prosecuting attorney with the following information and materials not later than 35 days before trial:

(I) A list of witnesses whom the defendant may call at the sentencing hearing. Along with the name of the witness, the defendant shall furnish the witness's address and date of birth, the subject matter of the witness's testimony, and any written or recorded statement of that witness, including notes, that comprise substantial recitations of witness statements and relate to the subject matter of the testimony;

(II) A list of the books, papers, documents, photographs, or tangible objects, and access thereto, that the defendant may introduce at the sentencing hearing;

(III) Any reports, recorded statements, and notes of any expert whom the defendant may call as a witness during the sentencing hearing, including results of physical or mental examinations and scientific tests, experiments, or comparisons.

(B) Any material subject to this subsection (7) that the defendant believes contains self-incriminating information that is privileged from disclosure to the prosecution prior to the sentencing hearing shall be submitted by the defendant to the trial judge under seal no later than 49 days before trial. The trial judge shall review any material submitted under seal pursuant to this paragraph (B) to determine whether it is in fact privileged.

(I) Any material submitted under seal pursuant to this paragraph (c) that the judge finds to be privileged from disclosure to the prosecution prior to the sentencing hearing shall be provided forthwith to the prosecution if the defendant is convicted of a class 1 felony.

(II) If the trial judge finds any of the material submitted under seal pursuant to this paragraph (B) to be not privileged from disclosure to the prosecution prior to the sentencing hearing, the trial judge shall notify the defense of its findings and allow the defense 7 days after such notification in which to seek a modification, review or stay of the court's order requiring disclosure.

(III) The trial judge may excise information it finds privileged from information it finds not privileged in order to disclose as provided in (II) above.

(8) Regulation of Discovery and Sanctions. No party shall be permitted to rely at the sentencing hearing upon any witness, material, or information that is subject to disclosure pursuant to this rule until it has been disclosed to the opposing party. The trial court, upon a showing of good cause, may grant an extension of time to comply with the requirements of this rule. If it is brought to the attention of the court that a party has failed to comply with this rule or with an order issued pursuant to this rule, the court may enter an order against such party that the court deems just under the circumstances, and which is consistent with constitutional limitations, including but not limited to an order to permit the discovery or inspection of materials not previously disclosed, to grant a continuance, to prohibit the offending party from introducing the information and materials, or impose sanctions against the offending party.

Colo. R. Crim. P. 32.1

Source: Entire rule adopted and effective 9/1/1995; f to h amended and effective 1/14/1999; f6III corrected, effective 3/2/1999; IPf6 corrected, effective 3/31/1999; entire rule amended and adopted March 11, 2004, effective 7/1/2004; b, d1 to d6, IPd7A, and d7B, amended and adopted December 14, 2011, effective 7/1/2012.

Rule 32.2 - Death Penalty Post-Trial Procedures

(a) Purpose and Scope. The purpose of this rule is to establish a fair, just and expeditious procedure for conducting trial court review of any post-trial motions and of any post-conviction motions, and for conducting appellate review of direct appeal and post-conviction review appeal in class one felony cases in which a sentence of death is imposed, as directed by section 16-12-201 , et seq.

(b) Trial Court Procedure.

(1) **Stay of Execution.** The trial judge, upon the imposition of a death sentence, shall set the time of execution pursuant to section 18-1.3-1205 and enter an order staying execution of the judgment and sentence until receipt of an order from the supreme court. The trial court shall immediately mail to the supreme court a copy of the judgment, sentence, and mittimus.

(2) **Motions for New Trial.** The defendant may file any post-trial motions, pursuant to Crim. P. 33, no later than 21 days after the imposition of sentence. The trial court, in its discretion, may rule on such motion before or after the sentencing hearing, but must rule no later than 91 days (13 weeks) after the imposition of sentence.

(3) **Advisement and Order.** Within 7 days after the imposition of a sentence of death, the court shall hold a hearing (advisement date) and shall advise the defendant pursuant to sections 16-12-204 and 205 . On the advisement date, the court shall:

(I) Appoint new counsel to represent the defendant concerning direct appeal and post-conviction review matters absent waiver by the defendant;

(II) Make specific findings as to whether any waiver by the defendant of the right to post-conviction review, direct appeal, or the appointment of new counsel is made knowingly, voluntarily and intelligently;

(III) Order the prosecuting attorney to deliver to counsel for the defendant within 7 days of the advisement date one copy of all material and information in the prosecuting attorney's possession or control that is discoverable under Crim. P. 16 or pertains to punishment, unless such material and information has been previously provided to that counsel. Costs of copying and delivery of such material and information shall be paid by the prosecuting attorney;

(IV) If new counsel is appointed for the defendant, order defendant's trial counsel, at his or her cost, to deliver a complete copy of trial counsel's file to new counsel within 7 days of the advisement date;

(V) Direct that any post-conviction review motions be filed within 154 days (22 weeks) of the advisement date; and

(VI) Order the production of three copies of a certified transcript of all proceedings in the case: one for the supreme court, one for the prosecution and one for the defense. Transcripts that are completed by the advisement date will be immediately provided to the prosecution and to defense counsel to the extent that counsel does not already possess those transcripts. All other transcripts shall be completed and delivered within 21 days of the advisement date or within 21 days of any subsequent hearing.

(4) **Resolution of Post-conviction Motions.** The court, upon receipt of any motion raising post-conviction review issues, as described in section 16-12-206 , shall promptly determine whether an evidentiary hearing is necessary, and if so, shall schedule the matter for hearing within 63 days (9 weeks) of the filing of such motions and enter its order on all motions within 35 days of the hearing. If no evidentiary hearing is required, the trial court shall rule within 35 days of the last day for filing the motions.

(5) **Record on Appeal.** In an appeal under this rule, the trial court shall designate the entire trial court record as the record on appeal. Within 21 days of the filing of the unitary notice of

appeal, the trial court shall deliver to the supreme court any portion of the record not previously delivered under subsection (b)(3)(VI) of this rule.

(6) Extension of Time. Upon a showing of extraordinary circumstances that could not have been foreseen and prevented, the court may grant an extension of time with regard to the time requirements of sections (b)(2), (3), (4) and (5) of this rule.

(c) Appellate Procedure.

(1) Unitary Notice of Appeal. The notice of appeal for the direct appeal and the notice of appeal for all post-conviction review shall be filed by unitary notice in the supreme court within 7 days after the trial court's order on post-conviction review motions, or within 7 days after the expiration of the deadline for filing post-conviction review motions if none have been filed. The unitary notice of appeal need conform only to the requirements of sections (1), (2), (6) and (8) of C.A.R. 3(g).

(2) Briefs. Counsel for defendant shall file an opening brief no later than 182 days (26 weeks) after the filing of the notice of appeal. The prosecution shall file an answer brief no later than 126 days (18 weeks) after filing of the opening brief. Counsel for defendant may file a reply brief no later than 63 days (9 weeks) after filing of the answer brief. Extensions of time will not be granted except on a showing of extraordinary circumstances that could not have been foreseen and prevented. The opening brief may not exceed 250 pages or, in the alternative, 79, 250 words; the answer brief may not exceed 250 pages or, in the alternative, 79, 250 words; and the reply brief may not exceed 100 pages or, in the alternative, 31,700 words. The Supreme Court may approve extensions not to exceed 75 pages or, in the alternative, 23,775 words for the opening and answer briefs, and 50 pages or 15, 850 words for the reply brief upon a showing of compelling need.

(3) Consolidation. Any direct appeal, any appeal of post-conviction review proceedings, and the review required by section 18-1.3-1201(6) (a), shall be consolidated and resolved in one proceeding before the supreme court.

(4) Further Proceedings.

(I) After the supreme court resolves the appeal, ineffective assistance of counsel on direct appeal may only be raised by a petition for rehearing filed in the supreme court, pursuant to section 16-12-204 ;

(II) Any notice of appeal concerning a trial court decision entered pursuant to section 16-12-209 or concerning any second or subsequent request for relief filed by the defendant, shall be filed in the supreme court within 35 days of the entry of the trial court's order. Such appeal shall be governed by the Colorado appellate rules as may be modified by the supreme court in case-specific orders designed to expedite the proceedings.

(d) Sanctions. The trial court and the supreme court may impose sanctions on counsel for willful failure to comply with this rule. This rule shall apply to class one felony offenses committed on or after January 1, 1998 for which a sentence of death is imposed.

Annotation

Section 16-12-208(3) does not impose an absolute two-year time limit on presenting a unitary appeal to the supreme court. Rather the statute directs the supreme court to create the limit in court rules. An absolute two-year time extension prohibition does not exist either in statute or rule. This rule implements the legislature's direction by imposing a series of highly specific time limits designed to meet the two-year goal when it can be accomplished without violating the defendant's constitutional rights or the legislature's expressly articulated goals. People v. Owens, 228 P.3d 969 (Colo. 2010).

Colo. R. Crim. P. 32.2

Source: Entire rule approved and adopted October 28, 1997, effective 1/1/1998; entire rule amended and adopted March 11, 2004, effective 7/1/2004; c2 amended and effective 4/3/2008; b2, IPb3, b3III, b3IV, b3V, b4, c1, c2, and c4II amended and adopted December 14, 2011, effective 7/1/2012; c1 amended and adopted June 21, 2012, effective 7/1/2012.

Rule 33 - New Trial

(a) Motions for New Trial or Other Relief Optional. The party claiming error in the trial of any case may move the trial court for a new trial or other relief. The party, however, need not raise all the issues it intends to raise on appeal in such motion to preserve them for appellate review. If such a motion is filed, the trial court may dispense with oral argument on the motion after it is filed.

(b) Motions for New Trial or Other Relief Directed by the Court. The court may direct a party to file a motion for a new trial or other relief on any issue. The failure of the party to file such a motion when so ordered shall preclude appellate review of the issues ordered to be raised in the motion. The party, however, need not raise all the issues it intends to raise on appeal in such motion to preserve them for appellate review.

(c) Motion; Contents; Time. The court may grant a defendant a new trial if required in the interests of justice. The motion for a new trial shall be in writing and shall point out with particularity the defects and errors complained of. A motion based upon newly discovered evidence or jury misconduct shall be supported by affidavits. A motion for a new trial based upon newly discovered evidence shall be filed as soon after entry of judgment as the facts supporting it become known to the defendant, but if a review is pending the court may grant the motion only on remand of the case. A motion for a new trial other than on the ground of newly discovered evidence shall be filed within 14 days after verdict or finding of guilt or within such additional time as the court may fix during the 14-day period.

(d) Appeal by Prosecution. The order of the trial court granting the motion is a final order reviewable on appeal.

Colo. R. Crim. P. 33

Source: Entire rule amended March 15, 1985, effective 7/1/1985; a amended October 29, 1987, effective 1/1/1989; d added4/20/2000, effective 7/1/2000; c amended and adopted December 14, 2011, effective 7/1/2012.

Annotation I. General Consideration. Law reviews. For note, "The Criminal Jury and Misconduct in Colorado", see 36 U. Colo. L. Rev. 245 (1964). For article, "Criminal Procedure", which discusses a recent Tenth Circuit decision dealing with a motion for a new trial based on recanted testimony, see 62 Den. U. L. Rev. 189 (1985). Prior to April, 1974, motion for new trial not required. Prior to April, 1974, there was no express language in any of the rules of criminal procedure or appellate rules that required a motion for new trial. People v. Martinez, 190 Colo. 507, 549 P.2d 758 (1976). Motion does not bar double jeopardy protection against retrial. A motion for a new trial does not relinquish the right to invoke double jeopardy guarantees against retrial of the charge upon which no verdict was returned. Ortiz v. District Court, 626 P.2d 642 (Colo. 1981). Federal court will deny "habeas corpus" where defendant fails to exhaust remedies under this rule. Tanksley v. Warden of State Penitentiary, 429 F.2d 1308 (10th Cir. 1970). Granting or denying motion for new trial does not constitute an appealable final judgment. People v. Jones, 690 P.2d 866 (Colo. App. 1984). Applied in People v. Pearson, 190 Colo. 313, 546 P.2d 1259 (1976); People v. Coca, 39 Colo. App. 264, 564 P.2d 431 (1977); People v. Vigil, 39 Colo. App. 371, 570 P.2d 13 (1977); People v. Davis, 194 Colo. 466, 573 P.2d 543 (1978); People v. Scott, 41 Colo. App. 66, 583 P.2d 939 (1978); People v. Reyes, 42 Colo. App. 73, 589 P.2d 1385 (1979); People v. Am. Health Care, Inc., 42 Colo. App. 209, 591 P.2d 1343 (1979); People v. Swain, 43 Colo. App. 343, 607 P.2d 396 (1979); People v. Rael, 199 Colo. 201, 612 P.2d 1095 (1980); People v. Glenn, 200 Colo. 416, 615 P.2d 700 (1980); People v. Smith, 620 P.2d 232 (Colo. 1980); People v. Trujillo, 624 P.2d 924 (Colo. 1980); People v. Dillon, 631 P.2d 1153 (Colo. App. 1981); People v. Holder, 632 P.2d 607 (Colo. App. 1981); People v. Dillon, 633 P.2d 504 (Colo. App. 1981); People v. Harris, 633 P.2d 1095 (Colo. App. 1981); People v. Allen, 636 P.2d 1329 (Colo. App. 1981); People v. Brassfield, 652 P.2d 588 (Colo. 1982); People v. Matthews, 662 P.2d 1108 (Colo. App. 1983); People v. Anderson, 703 P.2d 650 (Colo. App. 1985). II. No Review Unless Motion Made. Lack of contemporaneous objection is waiver. Lack of contemporaneous objection to testimony at time of trial constitutes waiver of new trial, and issue cannot be raised on appeal. People v. Routa, 180 Colo. 386, 505 P.2d 1298 (1973). Where defendant failed to object to an identification procedure at his preliminary hearing, and he made no objection to victim's testimony concerning the preliminary hearing identification at the trial or in his motion for new trial, defendant could not assert this objection for the first time on appeal. People v. Horne, 619 P.2d 53 (Colo. 1980). Appellate review is generally limited to errors presented to trial court for its consideration by a motion for new trial. Vigil v. People, 196 Colo. 522, 587 P.2d 1196 (1978). Only matters contained in the motion for new trial will be considered on appeal. Quintana v. People, 152 Colo. 127, 380 P.2d 667, cert. denied, 375 U.S. 863, 84 S. Ct. 132, 11 L. Ed. 2d 89 (1963); Cook v. People, 129 Colo. 14, 266 P.2d 776 (1954); Rueda v. People, 141 Colo. 502, 348 P.2d 957, cert. denied, 362 U.S. 923, 80 S.Ct. 673, 4 L. Ed. 2d 744 (1960); Wilson v. People, 143 Colo. 544, 354 P.2d 588 (1960); Dyer v. People, 148 Colo. 22, 364 P.2d 1062 (1961); Peterson v. People, 153 Colo. 23, 384 P.2d 460 (1963); Brown v. People, 158 Colo. 561, 408 P.2d 981 (1965); Lucero v. People, 158 Colo. 568, 409 P.2d 278 (1965). Failure to raise an issue in the motion for a new trial deprives the appellate court of jurisdiction to consider it unless the issue is one involving plain error affecting the substantial rights of the defendant. People v. Peterson,

656 P.2d 1301 (Colo. 1983). Failure to file a motion for new trial precludes consideration of issues raised on appeal. People v. Hallman, 44 Colo. App. 530, 624 P.2d 347 (1980); People v. Ullerich, 680 P.2d 1306 (Colo. App. 1983). Matters which counsel intends to raise on appeal must be preserved in a motion for a new trial. Diebold v. People, 175 Colo. 96, 485 P.2d 900 (1971). When errors alleged with regard to the admission of testimony were not raised during the trial or in the defendant's motion for a new trial, they need not be considered on appeal. Ortega v. People, 178 Colo. 419, 498 P.2d 1121 (1972). Absent a properly filed and acted on motion for new trial, appellate review is precluded. People v. Nisted, 653 P.2d 60 (Colo. App. 1980). Filing notice of appeal divests court of power to grant motion. Once the notice of appeal is filed, the trial court is left powerless to grant a motion for a new trial. People v. Dillon, 655 P.2d 841 (Colo. 1982). Motion prerequisite for review of probation revocation. A motion for new trial is a prerequisite for appellate review of a revocation of probation except when the propriety of a sentence is being appealed as provided in Rule 4(c), C.A.R. People v. Hallman, 44 Colo. App. 530, 624 P.2d 347 (1980). And motion required for review of revocation of deferred sentence. Compliance with the motion for a new trial requirement of section (a) is a prerequisite for appellate review of a trial court's judgment revoking a deferred sentence, and imposing a sentence. Hallman v. People, 652 P.2d 173 (Colo. 1982). Reasons need not be set forth in denial of motion. When a motion for a new trial is denied, reasons need not be set forth, because the motion is the basis and foundation for review of the judgment on appeal. Losavio v. District Court, 182 Colo. 186, 512 P.2d 264 (1973). But where there is a claim that the trial court committed plain error which was prejudicial to substantial rights of the defendant, appellate review may be had without the issue being raised in a new trial motion. People v. Ullerich, 680 P.2d 1306 (Colo. App. 1983). III. Motion, Contents, Time. A. In General. Purpose of a motion for a new trial is to accord the trial judge a fair opportunity to consider and correct, if necessary, any erroneous rulings, and to acquaint him with the specific objection to those rulings. Losavio v. District Court, 182 Colo. 186, 512 P.2d 264 (1973). The only purpose of requiring a motion for a new trial is to correct the trial court's own errors. Haas v. People, 155 Colo. 371, 394 P.2d 845 (1964). Timely motion for new trial is not jurisdictional in the sense that without it the court would lack authority to adjudicate the subject matter. People v. Moore, 193 Colo. 81, 562 P.2d 749 (1977). Unlike cases governed by the rules of civil procedure, in a criminal case the timely filing of a motion for new trial is not a jurisdictional prerequisite to the appeal of a judgment of conviction. People v. Masamba, 39 Colo. App. 197, 563 P.2d 382 (1977). An untimely filed motion for new trial does not divest an appellate court of jurisdiction to consider the issues raised on appeal which are also presented in the motion. People v. Hallman, 44 Colo. App. 530, 624 P.2d 347 (1980). Trial court may grant extension of filing time. In contrast to the provisions of the rules of civil procedure governing motions for new trial, upon a showing of excusable neglect the trial court is authorized under the criminal rules of procedure to grant an extension of time for filing the motion for new trial after the original 10 days had expired, or, after the expiration of any extended date granted by the trial court. People v. Masamba, 39 Colo. App. 197, 563 P.2d 382 (1977). Defendant may show excusable neglect for late filing. Where the prosecution objects to the late filing of a motion for new trial prior to the time of hearing on the motion, the defendant is afforded the opportunity to show, pursuant to Rule 45(b)(2), Crim. P., that the late filing was due to excusable neglect. People v. Masamba, 39 Colo. App. 197, 563 P.2d 382 (1977). Timeliness issue held waived. The prosecution, by failing to object to the trial court's hearing and deciding the new trial motion, waived their right to raise the timeliness issue on appeal. People v. Moore, 193 Colo. 81, 562 P.2d 749 (1977). Where there was no affirmative showing in the record on appeal that the prosecution objected to the late filing of defendant's motion for new trial prior to the time it was ruled upon by the trial court, that objection was deemed waived, and the prosecution was estopped to raise it for the first time on appeal. People v. Masamba, 39 Colo. App. 197, 563 P.2d 382 (1977). Granting of motion is in court's discretion. Where an error is called to the court's attention for the first time in a motion for new trial, the question of whether a new trial should be granted involves the exercise of the court's discretion. Abeyta v. People, 145 Colo. 173, 358 P.2d 12 (1960). Such as for misconduct of counsel. The question of whether a new trial should be granted for misconduct of counsel in his remarks to the jury rests in the sound judicial discretion of the trial court. Lee v. People, 170 Colo. 268, 460 P.2d 796 (1969). And this discretion will not be interfered with on appeal unless it manifestly appears that such discretion has been abused. Lee v. People, 170 Colo. 268, 460 P.2d 796 (1969). But this rule includes mandatory provision that motion based on newly discovered evidence be supported by affidavits, and this provision is impervious to judicial discretion. People ex rel. J.P.L., 214 P.3d 1072 (Colo. App. 2009). The standard by which to judge a court's grant of a new trial under this rule is whether the court abused its discretion. People v. Jones, 942 P.2d 1258 (Colo. App. 1996). Motion for new trial after trial on merits preserves errors alleged in sanity trial. A motion for a new trial after trial on the merits is sufficient to preserve for appeal errors alleged in the sanity trial, because the judgment declaring the defendant sane is not final for appeal purposes until defendant is found guilty of the crime charged. People v. Osborn, 42 Colo. App. 376, 599 P.2d 937 (1979). For differing considerations governing effect of time limitations in criminal cases and in civil cases, see People v. Moore, 193 Colo. 81, 562 P.2d 749 (1977). In order for a new trial to be granted on the basis of a prosecutor's remarks, in the absence of a contemporaneous objection, they must be particularly egregious. People v. Diefenderfer, 784 P.2d 741 (Colo. 1989). No basis in the record to conclude the jury's review of a silent videotape during deliberations was in any way prejudicial and the trial court therefore properly denied defendant's motion for a mistrial or new trial on this basis. People v. Blecha, 940 P.2d 1070 (Colo. App. 1996), aff'd, 962 P.2d 931 (Colo. 1998). B. Contents. Points of error must be raised with particularity. This rule requires the filing of a motion for new trial in which points of error must be raised with particularity. Feldstein v. People, 159 Colo. 107, 410 P.2d 188 (1966). See Jobe v. People, 158 Colo. 571, 408 P.2d 972 (1965); Cruz v. People, 165 Colo. 495, 441 P.2d 22 (1968). Attention should be drawn specifically to the alleged objectionable rulings in a motion for a new trial, and general objections and assignments of error fall far short of calling to the court's attention any specific error made in connection with its rulings. Losavio v. District Court, 182 Colo. 186, 512 P.2d 264 (1973). To give guidance to court. When the motion for a new trial does not set forth with particularity the reason that a new trial is required, a vacuum exists which leaves the trial judge without direction and without guidance as to how the new trial should be conducted. Losavio v. District Court, 182 Colo. 186, 512 P.2d 264 (1973). Testimony treated as substance of affidavit. A witness's testimony on direct examination may be treated as constituting the substance of the affidavit required for a new trial. Hernandez v. People, 175 Colo. 155, 486 P.2d 24 (1971). C. Based on Newly Discovered Evidence. Motion regarded with disfavor. A motion for new trial on grounds of newly discovered evidence is regarded with disfavor. People v. Gallegos, 187 Colo. 6, 528 P.2d 229 (1974); People v. Jones, 690 P.2d 866 (Colo. App. 1984); People v. Phillips, 732 P.2d 1226 (Colo. App. 1986); People v. Williams, 827 P.2d 612 (Colo. App. 1992); People v. Leonard, 872 P.2d 1325 (Colo. App. 1993); People v. Graham, 876 P.2d 68 (Colo. App. 1994). A motion for new trial based on newly discovered evidence is generally not looked upon with great favor because to do otherwise would encourage counsel to neglect to gather all available evidence for the first trial and, if unsuccessful, then to become diligent in securing other evidence to attempt to reverse the outcome on a second trial. People v. Mays, 186 Colo. 123, 525 P.2d 1165 (1974); People v. Scheidt, 187 Colo. 20, 528 P.2d 232 (1974). Motion addressed to court's discretion. A motion for new trial based upon newly discovered evidence is addressed to the sound discretion of the trial court. People v. Gallegos, 187 Colo. 6, 528 P.2d 229 (1974). And unless an abuse of discretion is affirmatively shown, the denial of a motion for a new trial based on newly discovered evidence will not be disturbed on appeal. People v. Gallegos, 187 Colo. 6, 528 P.2d 229 (1974); People v. Jones, 690 P.2d 866 (Colo. App. 1984); People v. Phillips, 732 P.2d 1226 (Colo. App. 1986); People v. Leonard, 872 P.2d 1325 (Colo. App. 1993). The denial of a motion for a new trial based upon newly discovered evidence will not be overturned unless there has been shown a clear abuse of the trial court's discretion. People v. Scheidt, 187 Colo. 20, 528 P.2d 232 (1974). Trial court did not abuse its discretion in denying motion for new trial due to newly discovered evidence because the evidence probably would not have resulted in an acquittal on retrial. People v. Leonard, 872 P.2d 1325 (Colo. App. 1993). To succeed on motion for new trial based upon newly discovered evidence, the defendant should show that the evidence was discovered after the trial; that defendant and his counsel exercised diligence to discover all possible evidence favorable to the defendant prior to and during the trial; that the newly discovered evidence is material to the issues involved, and not merely cumulative or impeaching; and that on retrial the newly discovered evidence would probably produce an acquittal. People v. Scheidt, 187 Colo. 20, 528 P.2d 232 (1974); People v. Jones, 690 P.2d 866 (Colo. App. 1984); People v. Williams, 827 P.2d 612 (Colo. App. 1992). Showing of diligent search and inquiry is a cardinal prerequisite of a new trial based upon newly discovered evidence. Isbell v. People, 158 Colo. 126, 405 P.2d 744 (1965); Pieramico v. People, 173 Colo. 276, 478 P.2d 304 (1970); People v. Jones, 690 P.2d 866 (Colo. App. 1984). When defense was aware of the possibility that someone else committed the crime but didn't pursue the theory and instead chose to rely on alibi witness, the motion for new trial was properly denied. People v. Stephens, 689 P.2d 666 (Colo. App. 1984). Else motion will be denied. Where the newly discovered evidence was cumulative in nature and could, with the exercise of due diligence, have been discovered before trial, motion for new trial was properly denied. People v. Mays, 186 Colo. 123, 525 P.2d 1165 (1974). When evidence could have been discovered with reasonable diligence and the result of the trial would probably not have been changed if the evidence had been presented, the trial court properly denied the motion for a new trial. People v. Phillips, 732 P.2d 1226 (Colo. App. 1986). Denial for motion for new trial based upon newly discovered evidence was proper where the asserted newly discovered evidence was either merely cumulative or impeaching and was neither material to the issues involved nor would it have probably produced a verdict of acquittal on retrial. People v. Williams, 827 P.2d 612 (Colo. App. 1992); People v. Graham, 876 P.2d 68 (Colo. App. 1994). Evidence must be of character to probably bring about acquittal. Newly discovered evidence must be of such a character as to probably bring about an acquittal verdict if presented at another trial. People v. Scheidt, 187 Colo. 20, 528 P.2d 232 (1974); People v. Jones, 690 P.2d 866 (Colo. App. 1984). As where codefendant is induced. Where the motion for new trial sets forth as newly discovered evidence the fact that following defendant's conviction the charge against a codefendant is dismissed, and that this casts grave doubt as to the truth of his testimony that no promise had been made to him, then the ends of justice require that the court conduct a hearing with the additional consideration of any probative evidence on the question of whether there was any inducement to procure the codefendant's testimony, the extent and nature thereof, if so, and then grant or deny the motion. Mitchell v. People, 170 Colo. 117, 459 P.2d 284 (1969). Evidence showing verdict influenced by false testimony sufficient. If newly discovered evidence is of such a character as to make it appear that the verdict was probably influenced by false or mistaken testimony and that upon another trial the result would probably, or might, be different, or even doubtful, then a new trial should be granted. Cheatwood v. People, 164 Colo. 334, 435 P.2d 402 (1967); Baker v. People, 176 Colo. 99, 489 P.2d 196 (1971); DeLuzio v. People, 177 Colo. 389, 494 P.2d 589 (1972). But cumulative evidence insufficient. Where the newly discovered evidence was cumulative in nature and could, with the exercise of due diligence, have been discovered before trial, and the outcome of the case on retrial would probably be the same, motion for new trial was properly denied. People v. Mays, 186 Colo. 123, 525 P.2d 1165 (1974). Evidence to discredit expert testimony insufficient. Newly discovered evidence that would merely tend to discredit or impeach expert testimony would not be grounds for a new trial. Roybal v. People, 177 Colo. 144, 493 P.2d 9 (1972). Evidence held not newly discovered as contemplated by this rule. See Steward v. People, 179 Colo. 31, 498 P.2d 933 (1972). Evidence within the defendant's knowledge before trial does not constitute newly discovered evidence as a basis for a new trial. People v. Gallegos, 187 Colo. 6, 528 P.2d 229 (1974). Where defendant filed a motion for a new trial based on newly discovered evidence, such evidence being that defendant was threatened with death if he testified in his own behalf and such threat was made without the knowledge of his attorney, the motion was properly denied since this was not a case of newly discovered evidence as the evidence presented consisted of facts which obviously were known to the defendant at the time of his trial. People v. Drumright, 189 Colo. 26, 536 P.2d 38 (1975). Magistrate did not abuse his discretion in denying motion for a new trial where movant failed to file mandatory supporting affidavits with the motion and magistrate denied motion based on this deficiency. People ex rel. J.P.L., 214 P.3d 1072 (Colo. App. 2009). A defendant who has pled guilty is not entitled to request a new trial under this rule because the defendant has been convicted not after trial but upon his or her own admissions. People v. Ambos, 51 P.3d 1070 (Colo. App. 2002). D. Based on Other Grounds. Trial court did not abuse discretion by denying motion for a new trial without a hearing where several hearings were set that had to be continued because of defendant's hostility and unwillingness to cooperate with counsel. People v. Eckert, 919 P.2d 962 (Colo. App. 1996). Trial court did not err in denying defendant a hearing on his motion for a new trial based on ineffective assistance of counsel where defendant failed to allege any acts or omissions of defense counsel that deprived him of a defense. In the absence of particularized facts supporting defendant's assertion of ineffective assistance of counsel, it was within the trial court's discretion to deny defendant a hearing on the motion. People v. Esquivel-Alaniz, 985 P.2d 22 (Colo. App. 1999). Motion denied where defendant received fair, although not perfect, trial. Although defendant did not receive a perfect trial, he did receive a fair trial, and because the law of Colorado entitles him to nothing more, his motion for a new trial was denied. People v. Scheidt, 182 Colo. 374, 513 P.2d 446 (1973). Fact that jury deliberates less than 45 minutes does not warrant the granting of a new trial. People v. Elliston, 181 Colo. 118, 508 P.2d 379 (1973). Evidence which is cumulative or corroborative will normally not support the granting of a motion for new trial. People v. Gallegos, 187 Colo. 6, 528 P.2d 229 (1974). Discovery of evidence unlikely to change verdict insufficient. A new trial is not required whenever a combing of the prosecutor's files after the trial has disclosed evidence possibly useful to the defense but not likely to have changed the verdict. Sandoval v. People, 180 Colo. 180, 503 P.2d 1020 (1972). New trial on basis of prosecution asking improper questions denied. See People v. Knapp, 180 Colo. 280, 505 P.2d 7 (1973). In order to justify a new trial based on a tainted jury, the defendant must show evidence of prejudice. People v. Barger, 732 P.2d 1225 (Colo. App. 1986). Prejudice occurring during jury sequestration. The determination of whether prejudice has occurred during jury sequestration is within the sound discretion of the trial court and only where that discretion has been abused will a new trial be ordered. People v. Mackey, 185 Colo. 24, 521 P.2d 910 (1974). Presence of armed uniformed officers in courtroom insufficient. The court did not abuse its discretion in overruling defendant's motion for a new trial where defendant asserted that the presence of two armed uniformed officers in the courtroom constituted prejudicial error. People v. Romero, 182 Colo. 50, 511 P.2d 466 (1973). Phone call by juror insufficient, absent showing of prejudice. It is not error to fail to grant a new trial because a juror allegedly makes a phone call out of the bailiff's presence, which is not shown to be prejudicial to the defendant. People v. Peery, 180 Colo. 161, 503 P.2d 350 (1972). Improper communications to jury are presumptively prejudicial, especially if the communications deal with the punishment or sentencing of a defendant. People v. Cornett, 685 P.2d 224 (Colo. App. 1984). Juror misconduct. Defendant must establish the truth of the allegations on which he bases his motion for a new trial and produce evidence of the alleged juror misconduct. People v. Stephens, 689 P.2d 666 (Colo. App. 1984). Allegations on which motion based must be supported by evidence. Mere hearsay allegations in an affidavit will warrant denial of motion. People v. Hernandez, 695 P.2d 308 (Colo. App. 1984). Failure to establish the truth of hearsay allegations contained in an affidavit will warrant denial of a motion for a new trial based on alleged juror misconduct. People v. Rogers, 706 P.2d 1288 (Colo. App. 1985). Misconduct of juror in sleeping through defense counsel's closing argument sufficiently prejudiced defendant to warrant a new trial. People v. Evans, 710 P.2d 1167 (Colo. App. 1985). Untruthful answers on voir dire concerning material matters do not entitle a party to a new trial per se. Under some circumstances, however, a juror's nondisclosure of information during jury selection may be grounds for a new trial. Allen v. Ramada Inn, Inc., 778 P.2d 291 (Colo. App. 1989). Only undisclosed information material to defendant's theory of the case and which might have affected the outcome of the trial will mandate reversal. People v. Rogers, 706 P.2d 1288 (Colo. App. 1985). Jurors learning of a co-defendant's guilty plea and capture of another co-defendant through the media insufficient absent a showing of prejudice. People v. Heller, 698 P.2d 1357 (Colo. App. 1984), rev'd on other grounds, 712 P.2d 1023 (Colo. 1986).

Rule 34 - Arrest of Judgment

The court shall arrest judgment if the indictment or information, complaint, or summons and complaint does not charge an offense, or if the court was without jurisdiction of the offense charged. The motion in arrest of judgment shall be made within 14 days after verdict or finding of guilt or within such further time as the court may fix during the 14-day period. A motion in arrest of judgment may be set forth alternatively as a part of a motion for a new trial.

Colo. R. Crim. P. 34

Source: Entire rule amended and adopted December 14, 2011, effective 7/1/2012.

Annotation Sufficiency of information may be raised after trial by motion. The sufficiency of an information is a matter of jurisdiction, which may be raised after trial by a motion in arrest of judgment. People v. Garner, 187 Colo. 294, 530 P.2d 496 (1975). Denial of motion held correct. People v. Ingersoll, 181 Colo. 1, 506 P.2d 364 (1973).

Rule 35 - Postconviction Remedies

(a) Correction of Illegal Sentence. The court may correct a sentence that was not authorized by law or that was imposed without jurisdiction at any time and may correct a sentence imposed in an illegal manner within the time provided herein for the reduction of sentence.

(b) Reduction of Sentence. The court may reduce the sentence provided that a motion for reduction of sentence is filed (1) within 126 days (18 weeks) after the sentence is imposed, or (2) within 126 days (18 weeks) after receipt by the court of a remittitur issued upon affirmance of the judgment or sentence or dismissal of the appeal, or (3) within 126 days (18 weeks) after entry of any order or judgment of the appellate court denying review or having the effect of upholding a judgment of conviction or sentence, or (4) at any time pursuant to a limited remand ordered by an appellate court in its discretion during the pendency of a direct appeal. The court may, after considering the motion and supporting documents, if any, deny the motion without a hearing. The court may reduce a sentence on its own initiative within any of the above periods of time.

(c) Other Remedies.

(1) If, prior to filing for relief pursuant to this paragraph (1), a person has sought appeal of a conviction within the time prescribed therefor and if judgment on that conviction has not then been affirmed upon appeal, that person may file an application for postconviction review upon the ground that there has been a significant change in the law, applied to the applicant's conviction or sentence, allowing in the interests of justice retroactive application of the changed legal standard.

(2) Notwithstanding the fact that no review of a conviction of crime was sought by appeal within the time prescribed therefor, or that a judgment of conviction was affirmed upon appeal, every person convicted of a crime is entitled as a matter of right to make application for postconviction review upon the grounds hereinafter set forth. Such an application for postconviction review must, in good faith, allege one or more of the following grounds to justify a hearing thereon:

(I) That the conviction was obtained or sentence imposed in violation of the Constitution or laws of the United States or the constitution or laws of this state;

(II) That the applicant was convicted under a statute that is in violation of the Constitution of the United States or the constitution of this state, or that the conduct for which the applicant was prosecuted is constitutionally protected;

(III) That the court rendering judgment was without jurisdiction over the person of the applicant or the subject matter;

(IV) Repealed.

(V) That there exists evidence of material facts, not theretofore presented and heard, which, by the exercise of reasonable diligence, could not have been known to or learned by the defendant or his attorney prior to the submission of the issues to the court or jury, and which requires vacation of the conviction or sentence in the interest of justice;

(VI) Any grounds otherwise properly the basis for collateral attack upon a criminal judgment; or

(VII) That the sentence imposed has been fully served or that there has been unlawful revocation of parole, probation, or conditional release.

(3) One who is aggrieved and claiming either a right to be released or to have a judgment of conviction set aside on one or more of the grounds enumerated in section (c)(2) of this Rule may file a motion in the court which imposed the sentence to vacate, set aside, or correct the sentence, or to make such order as necessary to correct a violation of his constitutional rights. The following procedures shall apply to the filing and hearing of such motions:

(I) Any motion filed outside of the time limits set forth in § 16-5-402 , 6 C.R.S., shall allege facts which, if true, would establish one of the exceptions listed in § 16-5-402(2), 6 C.R.S.

(II) Any motion filed shall substantially comply with the format of Form 4 and shall substantially contain the information identified in Form 4, Petition for Postconviction Relief Pursuant to Crim. P. 35(c)
. See Appendix to Chapter 29.

(III) If a motion fails to comply with Subsection (II) the court shall return to the defense a copy of the document filed along with a blank copy of Form 4 and direct that a motion in substantial compliance with the form be filed within 49 days.

(IV) The court shall promptly review all motions that substantially comply with Form 4, Petition for Postconviction Relief Pursuant to Crim. P. 35(c). In conducting this review, the court should consider, among other things, whether the motion is timely pursuant to § 16-5-402 , whether it fails to state adequate factual or legal grounds for relief, whether it states legal grounds for relief that are not meritorious, whether it states factual grounds that, even if true, do not entitle the party to relief, and whether it states factual grounds that, if true, entitle the party to relief, but the files and records of the case show to the satisfaction of the court that the factual allegations are untrue. If the motion and the files and record of the case show to the satisfaction of the court that the defendant is not entitled to relief, the court shall enter written findings of fact and conclusions of law in denying the motion. The court shall complete its review within 63 days (9 weeks) of filing or set a new date for completing its review and notify the parties of that date.

(V) If the court does not deny the motion under (IV) above, the court shall cause a complete copy of said motion to be served on the prosecuting attorney if one has not yet been served by counsel for the defendant. If the defendant has requested counsel be appointed in the motion, the court shall cause a complete copy of said motion to be served on the Public

Defender. Within 49 days, the Public Defender shall respond as to whether the Public Defender's Office intends to enter on behalf of the defendant pursuant to § 21-1-104(1)(b), 6 C.R.S. In such response, the Public Defender shall identify whether any conflict exists, request any additional time needed to investigate, and add any claims the Public Defender finds to have arguable merit. Upon receipt of the response of the Public Defender, or immediately if no counsel was requested by the defendant or if the defendant already has counsel, the court shall direct the prosecution to respond to the defendant's claims or request additional time to respond within 35 days and the defendant to reply to the prosecution's response within 21 days. The prosecution has no duty to respond until so directed by the court. Thereafter, the court shall grant a prompt hearing on the motion unless, based on the pleadings, the court finds that it is appropriate to enter a ruling containing written findings of fact and conclusions of law. At the hearing, the court shall take whatever evidence is necessary for the disposition of the motion. The court shall enter written or oral findings either granting or denying relief within 63 days (9 weeks) of the conclusion of the hearing or provide the parties a notice of the date by which the ruling will be issued. If the court finds that defendant is entitled to postconviction relief, the court shall make such orders as may appear appropriate to restore a right which was violated, such as vacating and setting aside the judgment, imposing a new sentence, granting a new trial, or discharging the defendant. The court may stay its order for discharge of the defendant pending appellate court review of the order. If the court orders a new trial, and there are witnesses who have died or otherwise become unavailable, the transcript of testimony of such witnesses at the trial which resulted in the vacated sentence may be used at the new trial.

(VI) The court shall deny any claim that was raised and resolved in a prior appeal or postconviction proceeding on behalf of the same defendant, except the following:

(a) Any claim based on evidence that could not have been discovered previously through the exercise of due diligence;

(b) Any claim based on a new rule of constitutional law that was previously unavailable, if that rule has been applied retroactively by the United States Supreme Court or Colorado appellate courts.

(VII) The court shall deny any claim that could have been presented in an appeal previously brought or postconviction proceeding previously brought except the following:

(a) Any claim based on events that occurred after initiation of the defendant's prior appeal or postconviction proceeding;

(b) Any claim based on evidence that could not have been discovered previously through the exercise of due diligence;

(c) Any claim based on a new rule of constitutional law that was previously unavailable, if that rule should be applied retroactively to cases on collateral review;

(d) Any claim that the sentencing court lacked subject matter jurisdiction;

(e) Any claim where an objective factor, external to the defense and not attributable to the defendant, made raising the claim impracticable.

(VIII) Notwithstanding (VII) above, the court shall not deny a postconviction claim of ineffective assistance of trial counsel on the ground that all or part of the claim could have been raised on direct appeal.

(IX) The order of the trial court granting or denying the motion is a final order reviewable on appeal.

Colo. R. Crim. P. 35

Source: c3 amended and adopted September 4, 1997, effective 1/1/1998; c3 amended and committee comment added January 7, 1999, effective 7/1/1999; entire section amended and adopted and committee comment repealed January 29, 2004, effective 7/1/2004; c3VIII corrected5/25/2004, nunc pro tunc1/29/2004, effective 7/1/2004; c3I, c3II, c3IV, and c3V corrected6/25/2004, nunc pro tunc1/29/2004, effective 7/1/2004; c3II and c3III amended and effective 12/11/2008; b, c3III, c3IV, 3cV 1supst/sup paragraph amended and adopted December 14, 2011, effective 7/1/2012; amended and adopted by the Court, En Banc, April 16, 2020, effective 4/16/2020, effective immediately.

Annotation I. General Consideration. Law reviews. For comment on Madrid v. People, 148 Colo. 149, 365 P.2d 39 (1961), appearing below, see Rocky Mtn. L. Rev. 400 (1962). For note, "Habeas Corpus Procedure", see 41 Den. L. Ctr. J. 111 (1964). For comment on Hackett v. People, 158 Colo. 304, 406 P.2d 331 (1965), appearing below, see 38 U. Colo. L. Rev. 417 (1966). For note, "Federal Habeas Corpus Confronts the Colorado Courts: Catalyst or Cataclysm?", see 39 U. Colo. L. Rev. 83 (1966). For note, "Colorado Appellate Procedure", see 40 U. Colo. L. Rev. 551 (1968). For note, "Defects in Ineffective Assistance Standards Used by

State Courts", see 50 U. Colo. L. Rev. 389 (1979). For article, "Attacking Prior Convictions in Habitual Criminal Cases: Avoiding the Third Strike", see 11 Colo. Law. 1225 (1982). For article, "Crim. P. 35(c): Colorado Law Regarding Postconviction Relief", see 22 Colo. Law. 729 (1993). Defendant not entitled to relief where sentence legal and constitutional. Where the sentence is within statutory limits and does not infringe upon the defendant's constitutional rights, he is not entitled to relief under this rule. People v. Mieyr, 176 Colo. 90, 489 P.2d 327 (1971). Previously, this rule provided in resentencing for credit for time already served. Stafford v. People, 165 Colo. 328, 438 P.2d 696 (1968). And made filing a motion under this rule a prerequisite to habeas corpus. Ralston v. People, 161 Colo. 523, 423 P.2d 326 (1967). This rule establishes postconviction remedies and is not an appropriate means to challenge rulings made in extradition proceedings. Hodges v. Barry, 701 P.2d 1240 (Colo. 1985). A habeas corpus petition seeking relief available under section (c) should be treated as a section (c) motion. Leske v. Golder, 124 P.3d 863 (Colo. App. 2005). Article II, § 16, of the Colorado Constitution does not create a constitutional right to counsel in a hearing under this rule. People v. Duran, 757 P.2d 1096 (Colo. App. 1988). The district court was not obliged to consider a subsequent motion that plainly treated the same issues as the original motion filed pursuant to section (c). People v. Adams, 905 P.2d 17 (Colo. App. 1995). A defendant may not use a proceeding under this rule to relitigate issues that were fully and finally resolved in an earlier appeal. People v. Johnson, 638 P.2d 61 (Colo. 1981); People v. Reali, 950 P.2d 645 (Colo. App. 1997). A hand-written letter that does not assert any claims for defendant's section (c) motion does not toll the time limit in § 16-5-402 . People v. Stovall, 2012 COA 7, ___ P.3d ___. Defendant needs only "assert", not necessarily "establish", a right to be released before being entitled to relief under section (c). People v. Gallegos, 975 P.2d 1135 (Colo. App. 1998). Defendant does not have a constitutional right to counsel in a Crim. P. 35 postconviction proceeding but does have a limited statutory right to counsel. An attorney appointed to assist defendant with a Crim. P. 35 proceeding who determines that defendant's claims are without merit may inform the court that he or she believes the claims are without merit and request permission to withdraw. If counsel is permitted to withdraw, defendant is not entitled to appointment of new counsel. People v. Starkweather, 159 P.3d 665 (Colo. App. 2006). A limited statutory right to counsel exists for a hearing pursuant to §§ 21-1-103 and 21-1-104 and the waiver of such right to counsel must be made voluntarily but need not be knowingly and intelligent. People v. Duran, 757 P.2d 1096 (Colo. App. 1988). No constitutional right to postconviction counsel exists; however, a limited statutory right exists. The statutory right to postconviction counsel is neither automatic nor unlimited. It is limited to cases where a defendant's section (c) petition is not wholly unfounded and has arguable merit, as determined by the court and the state public defender's office. Silva v. People, 156 P.3d 1164 (Colo. 2007). If postconviction counsel is required according to the limited statutory right, that counsel must provide effective assistance as measured by the two-pronged Strickland v. Washington test. Silva v. People, 156 P.3d 1164 (Colo. 2007). "Collateral attack" as used in § 16-5-402 includes relief sought pursuant to Crim. P. 35. People v. Robinson, 83 P.2d 832 (Colo. App. 1992). Collateral attack on an adjudication of habitual criminality includes relief sought under this rule. People v. Hampton, 876 P.2d 1236 (Colo. 1994). Defendant is not precluded from filing both a timely Crim. P. 35(b) motion and a Crim. P. 35(c) motion after conclusion of the direct appeal. People v. Metcalf, 979 P.2d 581 (Colo. App. 1999). The limitation period cannot commence until there is a right to pursue a collateral attack. People v. Manzanares, 85 P.3d 604 (Colo. App. 2003). Petitioner not entitled to appointed counsel when asserted claim for relief is wholly unfounded. Brinklow v. Riveland, 773 P.2d 517 (Colo. 1989); People v. Collier, 151 P.3d 668 (Colo. App. 2006). Plain error occurs if waiver of statutory right to counsel in postconviction proceeding is involuntary. People v. Duran, 757 P.2d 1096 (Colo. App. 1988). Without alleging specific facts for Crim. P. 35(c) motion that might appear in record to substantiate general allegations, defendant not entitled to have trial record provided to him at correctional facility. People v. Manners, 878 P.2d 71 (Colo. App. 1994). Trial court has no authority to retain jurisdiction over a defendant after sentencing for the reason that the law may be changed by a subsequent court decision even though the court, at the time of sentencing, is aware of a case appealed to the state supreme court which may change the interpretation of statute regarding credit against the sentence for presentence confinement. People v. Mortensen, 856 P.2d 45 (Colo. App. 1993). Motions under this rule are subject to statutory limitations in § 16-5-402 . People v. Robinson, 833 P.2d 832 (Colo. App. 1992); People v. Wiedemer, 852 P.2d 424 (Colo. 1993); People v. Wiedemer, 852 P.2d 449 (Colo. 1993); People v. Rodriguez, 914 P.2d 230 (Colo. 1996); People v. Ambos, 51 P.3d 1070 (Colo. App. 2002); People v. Collier, 151 P.3d 668 (Colo. App. 2006). The time limits in § 16-5-402(1) are specifically categorized by level of offense, so, in a case in which defendant is convicted of a class 1 felony and other felonies, the time limit for the class 1 felony does not control the time limit for all of the convictions that are not class 1 felonies. Defendant's challenges to the non-class 1 felonies in a section (c) motion were subject to the three-year statute of limitations. People v. Stovall, 2012 COA 7, __ P.3d __. Statutory limitations in § 16-5-402 do not usurp the supreme court's rulemaking authority. While the statute has an incidental effect on judicial procedure, it is primarily an expression of public policy, and therefore it prevails over terms of subsection (c)(3) of this rule stating that motion may be filed "at any time". People v. Robinson, 833 P.2d 832 (Colo. App. 1992). Justifiable excuse or excusable neglect would be established if the public defender's conflict of interest was the reason for not filing a motion for post-conviction relief on behalf of defendant. People v. Chang, 179 P.3d 240 (Colo. App. 2007). Justifiable excuse or excusable neglect would be established if the public defender's failure to file a motion for post-conviction relief on behalf of defendant was the result of ineffective counsel. People v. Chang, 179 P.3d 240 (Colo. App. 2007). In a hearing pursuant to this rule, the burden rests on the defendant to show that (1)counsel's performance was deficient, and (2)counsel's deficient performance prejudiced the defense of the defendant. People v. Duran, 757 P.2d 1096 (Colo. App. 1988); People v. Valdez, 789 P.2d 406 (Colo. 1990). Evidentiary hearing was required on defendant's claim of ineffective assistance of counsel, although not every such motion requires an evidentiary hearing. People v. Thomas, 867 P.2d 880 (Colo. 1994). Defendant could not be deprived of opportunity to prove counsel's choices lacked sound strategic motive unless the existing record clearly established otherwise or those choices could not have been prejudicial in any event. Ardolino v. People, 69 P.3d 73 (Colo. App. 2003). Defendant entitled to evidentiary hearing as long as the allegations of his motion, in light of the existing record, were not clearly insufficient to undermine confidence in the outcome of the trial by demonstrating a reasonable probability that but for counsel's challenged conduct, the defendant would not have been convicted. Ardolino v. People, 69 P.3d 73 (Colo. App. 2003). A second Crim. P. 35(c) motion cannot be used procedurally to raise mere ineffective assistance of counsel in a prior Crim. P. 35(c) proceeding. The ineffectiveness of appointed postconviction counsel does not constitute a statutory violation, because a defendant has no statutory right to such counsel. People v. Silva, 131 P.3d 1082 (Colo. App. 2005). Rule does not provide a method for reviewing the punishment assessed in a punitive contempt proceeding. In order to seek relief under this rule, a person must have been convicted of a crime. Conduct that results in punitive sanctions being imposed for contempt is not a common law or statutory crime. Benninghoven v. Dees, 849 P.2d 906 (Colo. App. 1992). Subsection (c)(3) requires a hearing and the entry of findings of fact and conclusions of law where defendant who was mistakenly released from custody before serving second sentence sought credit for time spent at liberty. People v. Stark, 902 P.2d 928 (Colo. App. 1995). Failure to review motion within 60 days as required by subsection (c)(3)(IV) does not entitle defendant to relief nor deprive the court of subject matter jurisdiction. The time limit is properly categorized as directory rather than jurisdictional. People v. Osorio, 170 P.3d 796 (Colo. App. 2007). Requirement that a copy of a motion be served on public defender is triggered when the court finds it necessary to consider matters outside of the motion, files, and record of the case. People v. Davis, 2012 COA 14, 272 P.3d 1167. The district court is required to make findings of fact and conclusions of law in every determination of a motion made pursuant to subsection (c)(3). People v. Breaman, 939 P.2d 1348 (Colo. 1997). A defendant cannot bring an illegal sentence claim under Crim. P. 35(a) if the sentence is consistent with the statutory scheme but imposed in an unconstitutional manner. Instead, the defendant must bring the claim under Crim. P. 35(c)(2)(I). People v. Wenzinger, 155 P.3d 415 (Colo. App. 2006). Prosecution may file a Crim. P. 35(a) motion to correct illegal sentence. People v. White, 179 P.3d 58 (Colo. App. 2007). The court simply stating, in denying a motion made pursuant to subsection (c)(3), that it "accepted appointed counsel's status report" was contrary to the requirement that the court make its own finding of facts and conclusions of law. People v. Breaman, 939 P.2d 1348 (Colo. 1997). Motion for post-conviction relief was timely when filed less than three years after the final decision on defendant's appeal. People v. Rivera, 964 P.2d 561 (Colo. App. 1998). For purposes of the time limit within which a section (c) motion must be filed, a defendant's conviction is final when his or her appeal rights have been exhausted. More specifically, it is final when the supreme court denies defendant's petition for a writ of certiorari and the mandate issues. People v. Stanley, 169 P.3d 258 (Colo. App. 2007). Trial court did not err in denying a section (c) motion as untimely where defendant did not raise a direct appeal or collateral attack of his Virginia conviction until almost 14 years after his conviction had entered. People v. Landis, 9 P.3d 1165 (Colo. App. 2000). A defendant cannot use this rule to relitigate matters fully and finally resolved in an

141

earlier appeal. Moreover an argument will be precluded if its review is nothing more than a second appeal on the same issues on some recently contrived constitutional theory. People v. Rodriguez, 914 P.2d 230 (Colo. 1996); People v. Martinez, 36 P.3d 201 (Colo. App. 2001); Leske v. Golder, 124 P.3d 863 (Colo. App. 2005). A properly filed section (b) motion tolls the one-year limitation period in § 2244(d)(1) of the federal Antiterrorism and Effective Death Penalty Act of 1996. Robinson v. Golder, 443 F.3d 718 (10th Cir.), cert. denied, 549 U.S. 867, 127 S. Ct. 166, 166 L. Ed. 2d 118 (2006). Pro se defendant's failure to file a Crim. P. 35(c) motion on form 4 does not deprive the trial court of subject matter jurisdiction. Section (c)(3)(II) requires only that pro se motions substantially comply with form 4. People v. Stanley, 169 P.3d 258 (Colo. App. 2007). Applied in Sides v. Tinsley, 333 F.2d 1002 (10th Cir. 1964); Sepulveda v. Colo., 335 F.2d 581 (10th Cir. 1964); Watson v. Patterson, 358 F.2d 297 (10th Cir.), cert. denied, 385 U.S. 876, 87 S. Ct. 153, 17 L. Ed. 2d 103 (1966); Terry v. Patterson, 372 F.2d 480 (10th Cir. 1967); Ralston v. People, 161 Colo. 523, 423 P.2d 326 (1967); Roberts v. People, 169 Colo. 115, 453 P.2d 793 (1969); Neighbors v. People, 171 Colo. 349, 467 P.2d 804 (1970); Ward v. People, 172 Colo. 244, 472 P.2d 673 (1970); Sawyer v. People, 173 Colo. 351, 478 P.2d 672 (1970); People ex rel. Wyse v. District Court, 180 Colo. 88, 503 P.2d 154 (1972); People v. Seymour, 182 Colo. 262, 512 P.2d 635 (1973); People v. Griswold, 190 Colo. 136, 543 P.2d 1251 (1975); People v. Taylor, 190 Colo. 144, 544 P.2d 392 (1975); People v. Martinez, 192 Colo. 388, 559 P.2d 228 (1977); People v. Lewis, 193 Colo. 203, 564 P.2d 111 (1977); People v. Mendoza, 195 Colo. 19, 575 P.2d 403 (1978); People v. Lipinski, 196 Colo. 50, 580 P.2d 1243 (1978); Carr v. Barnes, 196 Colo. 70, 580 P.2d 803 (1978); People v. Houpe, 41 Colo. App. 253, 586 P.2d 241 (1978); People v. McKnight, 41 Colo. App. 372, 588 P.2d 886 (1978); Mullins v. Evans, 473 F. Supp. 132 (D. Colo. 1979); Noe v. Dolan, 197 Colo. 32, 589 P.2d 483 (1979); People v. Blalock, 197 Colo. 320, 592 P.2d 406 (1979); People v. Calvaresi, 198 Colo. 321, 600 P.2d 57 (1979); People v. Jones, 198 Colo. 578, 604 P.2d 679 (1979); People v. Medina, 199 Colo. 1, 604 P.2d 682 (Colo. 1979); People v. Calloway, 42 Colo. App. 213, 591 P.2d 1346 (1979); People v. West, 42 Colo. App. 217, 592 P.2d 22 (1979); People v. Quintana, 42 Colo. App. 477, 601 P.2d 637 (1979); People v. Hardin, 199 Colo. 229, 607 P.2d 1291 (1980); Wiggins v. People, 199 Colo. 341, 608 P.2d 348 (1980); People v. McKenna, 199 Colo. 452, 611 P.2d 574 (1980); People v. Peretsky, 44 Colo. App. 270, 616 P.2d 170 (1980); People v. Horne, 619 P.2d 53 (Colo. 1980); People v. Aragon, 44 Colo. App. 550, 622 P.2d 579 (1980); Godbold v. Wilson, 518 F. Supp. 1265 (D. Colo. 1981); People v. Loggins, 628 P.2d 111 (Colo. 1981); People v. Francis, 630 P.2d 82 (Colo. 1981); People v. Trujillo, 631 P.2d 146 (Colo. 1981); People v. Small, 631 P.2d 148 (Colo. 1981); People v. Macias, 631 P.2d 584 (Colo. 1981); People v. District Court, 636 P.2d 689 (Colo. 1981); People v. Schultheis, 638 P.2d 8 (Colo. 1981); People v. Cushon, 631 P.2d 1164 (Colo. App. 1981); People v. Boivin, 632, P.2d 1038 (Colo. App. 1981); People v. Lawson, 634 P.2d 1019 (Colo. App. 1981); People v. Moore, 636 P.2d 1290 (Colo. App. 1981); People v. Martinez, 640 P.2d 255 (Colo. App. 1981); People v. Mascarenas, 643 P.2d 786 (Colo. App. 1981); People v. Lowery, 642 P.2d 515 (Colo. 1982); People v. Aragon, 643 P.2d 43 (Colo. 1982); People v. Gallegos, 644 P.2d 920 (Colo. 1982); People v. Montoya, 647 P.2d 1203 (Colo. 1982); People v. Cushon, 650 P.2d 527 (Colo. 1982); People v. Coyle, 654 P.2d 815 (Colo. 1982); People v. Peterson, 656 P.2d 1301 (Colo. 1983); People v. Turman, 659 P.2d 1368 (Colo. 1983); People v. Chavez, 659 P.2d 1381 (Colo. 1983); People v. Martinez, 660 P.2d 1292 (Colo. 1983); People v. McCall, 662 P.2d 178 (Colo. 1983); People v. Giles, 662 P.2d 1073 (Colo. 1983); People v. Brandt, 664 P.2d 712 (Colo. 1983); People v. Lesh, 668 P.2d 1362 (Colo. 1983); People v. Smith, 827 P.2d 577 (Colo. App. 1991); People v. Collier, 151 P.3d 668 (Colo. App. 2006). II. Correction of Illegal Sentence. When an original sentence is illegal, resentencing does not constitute double jeopardy even if the subsequent sentence is longer than the original, and even though the defendant has begun serving the original sentence. People v. District Court, 673 P.2d 991 (Colo. 1983). Court may correct an error in sentencing, and double jeopardy is not implicated when trial court corrects a sentencing error and imposes a longer sentence. People v. White, 179 P.3d 58 (Colo. App. 2007). Where sentence is illegal, sentencing court may correct it at any time. People v. Bradley, 169 Colo. 262, 455 P.2d 199 (1969); Mulkey v. Sullivan, 753 P.2d 1226 (Colo. 1988); Downing v. People, 895 P.2d 1046 (Colo. 1995). The imposition of an illegal sentence may be reviewed and corrected at any time. People v. Favors, 42 Colo. App. 263, 600 P.2d 78 (1979). When an illegal sentence is corrected pursuant to section (a), it renews the three-year deadline for collaterally attacking the original judgment of conviction pursuant to section (c). Leyva v. People, 184 P.3d 48 (Colo. 2008). When original judgment of conviction contains an illegal sentence on one count, the entire sentence is illegal. Leyva v. People, 184 P.3d 48 (Colo. 2008). The sentence is therefore subject to correction and the judgment of conviction is subject to amendment, making the judgment of conviction not final or fully valid. Leyva v. People, 184 P.3d 48 (Colo. 2008). Court has right and duty to set aside void sentence at any time. People v. Emig, 177 Colo. 174, 493 P.2d 368 (1972). So long as court retains jurisdiction. Where a trial court has jurisdiction of a person of the defendant and of the subject matter, and has imposed a sentence in error, the court retains jurisdiction to correct the sentence. Conversely, if the original sentence is a valid one, the trial court loses jurisdiction to change the sentence. Smith v. Johns, 187 Colo. 388, 532 P.2d 49 (1975). And where statutory provision changes erroneous sentence automatically, court loses jurisdiction. There is no irreconcilable inconsistency between § 16-11-303 which deals with a person wrongfully sentenced to a definite term in the state reformatory, and section (a) of this rule. Section 16-11-303 , changes the erroneous sentence automatically and a court, in altering the original sentence, acts in excess of jurisdiction. Smith v. Johns, 187 Colo. 388, 532 P.2d 49 (1975). The term "illegal sentence" no longer appears in section (a). That sentence was replaced with "a sentence that was not authorized by law". Under the current version of section (a), the only circumstance in which a sentence is "not authorized by law" is when it is inconsistent with the statutory scheme outlined by the legislature. People v. Wenzinger, 155 P.3d 415 (Colo. App. 2006); People v. Collier, 151 P.3d 668 (Colo. App. 2006). Illegal sentence is a sentence not in full compliance with sentencing statutes. Delgado v. People, 105 P.3d 634 (Colo. 2005); People v. White, 179 P.3d 58 (Colo. App. 2007). The sentence included an illegal parole term, therefore, it was an illegal sentence in its entirety. The imposition of an illegal sentence does not commence the 120-day deadline for filing a section (b) motion; only legal sentences trigger the rule's timeliness requirement. Delgado v. People, 105 P.3d 634 (Colo. 2005). Because an illegal sentence represents a type of jurisdictional defect, the trial court retains the authority to correct its own error. The 120-day time limit applies only if the court is asked to "correct a sentence imposed in an illegal manner". If the sentence itself is illegal, the court may act at any time. People v. White, 179 P.3d 58 (Colo. App. 2007). Defendant's claim that he was not given complete range of testing required by statute prior to sentencing is, in essence, a claim that the sentence was imposed in an illegal manner under section (a), and should have been asserted within 120 days of sentencing. People v. Collier, 151 P.3d 668 (Colo. App. 2006). Jurisdiction of appellate court. Where the district attorney claims that the trial court improperly considered the presumptive sentencing law and the defendant's conduct in prison as factors in evaluating a motion under section (b) for reduction of sentence, and that the trial court gave no consideration to the aggravated nature of the crimes for which the defendant was convicted, these claims are questions of law implicating the propriety of the proceeding itself and are sufficient to invoke appellate jurisdiction. People v. Bridges, 662 P.2d 161 (Colo. 1983). Matter of illegal sentence need not be raised on appeal. There is no requirement contained in this rule that the matter of an illegal sentence must be raised on appeal from the conviction or be thereafter waived. People v. Bradley, 169 Colo. 262, 455 P.2d 199 (1969). Successive postconviction motions under subsection (a) subject to law of the case doctrine. Under law of the case doctrine, where appropriate, a court may overlook the doctrine and grant relief where manifest injustice would result. People v. Tolbert, 216 P.3d 1 (Colo. App. 2007). Sentence to mandatory parole for attempted sexual assault committed between July 1, 1996 and July 1, 2002 is illegal. People v. Tolbert, 216 P.3d 1 (Colo. App. 2007). Action of judge in changing sentence without notice and hearing improper. The action of the sentencing judge in changing an original sentence without notice to the defendant and without opportunity for a hearing is improper, for while this rule permits a judge to correct a sentence of his own motion, where proper grounds exist, it does not permit him to do so without notice to the prisoner and an opportunity afforded for a hearing. Guerin v. Fullerton, 154 Colo. 142, 389 P.2d 84 (1964). Inmate had a protected liberty interest in a suspended sentence where his original sentence mandated a 10-year suspension when and if defendant could show successful completion of sex offender treatment. Defendant was entitled to due process protections before the trial court could modify the sentence. The court's order vacating the 10-year sentence reduction, sua sponte, denied defendant due process of law. The court erred in denying defendant's section (a) motion to correct the illegal sentence. People v. Sisson, 179 P.3d 193 (Colo. App. 2007). Upon defendant commencing sentence, judge cannot change sentence upon parole board's recommendation. The sentencing judge does not have the authority on the recommendation of the parole board to change a sentence he imposed upon a defendant after he commences serving his sentence, for such authority is present only when the sentence is erroneous or void under section (a), and not where the original sentence imposed is legal. Guerin v. Fullerton, 154 Colo. 142, 389 P.2d 84 (1964). And trial court cannot alter or amend commuted sentence imposed by the governor, because he has the exclusive power to grant reprieves, commutations, and pardons after conviction under § 7 of art. IV, Colo. Const. People ex rel. Dunbar v. District Court, 180 Colo. 107, 502 P.2d 420 (1972). Where several sentences concurrent, argument that some of sentences invalid falls. Where the defendant assumes that his sentences for several crimes are to run consecutively, but the governing judgments made the serving of all the sentences concurrent, the argument that some, but not all, sentences are invalid falls. Santistevan v. People, 177 Colo. 329, 494 P.2d 75 (1972). Sentence illegal where defendant not afforded benefit of amendatory legislation. A sentence imposed by the trial court which does not afford the defendant the benefit of amendatory legislation is not a valid and legal sentence. As such, it was subject to correction by the trial court at any time. People v. Jenkins, 40 Colo. App. 140, 575 P.2d 13 (1977). But defendant convicted of theft by receiving does not receive ameliorative benefit when retroactive application of amendatory legislation is clearly not intended by its own terms. Legislation that amended theft by receipt statute to provide that amendment shall apply to acts committed on or after July 1, 1985 makes it clear that amendment is to be applied prospectively only. People v. McCoy, 764 P.2d 1171 (Colo. 1988). Court may correct sentence to conform to "nolo contendere" plea. Error is harmless where after a court corrects a sentence it conforms to the advisement given a defendant pursuant to a plea of "nolo contendere". People v. Baca, 179 Colo. 156, 499 P.2d 317 (1972). Sentence in error because extraordinary aggravating circumstances not found. Judge erred in sentencing a 19-year old beyond the presumptive range because extraordinary aggravating circumstances justifying the sentence were not found even though the defendant was accused of committing five felonies in a nine-month period, including an arrest while on probation. People v. Jenkins, 674 P.2d 981 (Colo. App. 1983), rev'd on other grounds, 687 P.2d 455 (Colo. 1984). An unlawful sentence may be corrected by a sentencing court at any time. People v. Reynolds, 907 P.2d 670 (Colo. App. 1995). Court may correct the mittimus where the trial court neglected to specify that its sentence included a mandatory period of parole. People v. Mayes, 981 P.2d 1106 (Colo. App. 1999). Post-conviction motions that challenge the manner in which a plea is taken, such as whether the person was properly advised about the plea, are not challenges to the legality of the sentence and are properly brought pursuant to section (c), not section (a). People v. Green, 36 P.3d 125 (Colo. App. 2001); People v. Salinas, 55 P.3d 268 (Colo. App. 2002). Post-conviction motion challenging revocation of probation without a determination of ability to pay restitution should be brought under section (c), not section (a). People v. Shepard, 151 P.3d 580 (Colo. App. 2006). There is no constitutional right to credit of presentence jail time against sentence imposed. People v. Coy, 181 Colo. 393, 509 P.2d 1239 (1973). There is no constitutional right to credit for time spent in jail before sentence. People v. Nelson, 182 Colo. 1, 510 P.2d 441 (1973). But credit for presentence jail time presumed. Wherever it is possible, as a matter of mechanical calculation, that credit could have been given for presentence jail time, it will be conclusively presumed that it was given. This means that where the actual sentence imposed plus the time spent in jail prior to sentence do not exceed the maximum sentence which could be imposed, it will be conclusively presumed that the sentencing court gave the defendant credit for the presentence time spent in confinement. Maciel v. People, 172 Colo. 8, 469 P.2d 135 (1970). Where sentencing judge states only that he is taking time spent in jail prior to sentencing into consideration and thereafter gives the maximum, it must be presumed that he acted properly; that is, that he took the time spent into consideration and determined, as he had the right to do, not to grant the credit. People v. Nelson, 182 Colo. 1, 510 P.2d 441 (1973). And such rule outweighs any possible unfairness. The problems and expenditure of resources which would be caused by allowing each prisoner to attempt to demonstrate that in his particular case credit for presentencing confinement was not given outweighs any possible unfairness. Maciel v. People, 172 Colo. 8, 469 P.2d 135 (1970). Defendants found not entitled to credit for presentence jail time. People v. Puls, 176 Colo. 71, 489 P.2d 323 (1971). Use of polygraph results precluded at hearing to correct sentence. A jury determination of a defendant's guilt, which is upheld on appeal, precludes the use of the results of a polygraph examination on the issue of the defendant's guilt at a hearing to correct a sentence. People v. Reynolds, 638 P.2d 43 (Colo. 1981). Department of corrections may not intervene in a criminal case in order to file a motion to correct an illegal sentence. People v. Ham, 734 P.2d 623 (Colo. 1987). Appellate review precluded by the failure of the people to object at the sentencing hearing to the imposition of a sentence within the presumptive range when the defendant was convicted of possession of contraband while in a correctional institution, or to request the trial court, pursuant to this rule, to correct the sentence. People v. Gallegos, 764 P.2d 76 (Colo. 1988). If court determines sentence must be vacated, if original sentence was based at least in some important part upon the testimony of witnesses at original sentencing

144

hearing, and if original sentencing judge unavailable, there must be a new evidentiary hearing granted before a new sentence can be imposed. People v. Chetelat, 833 P.2d 771 (Colo. App. 1991). Rule does not provide a method for reviewing the punishment assessed in a punitive contempt proceeding. In order to seek relief under this rule, a person must have been convicted of a crime. Conduct that results in punitive sanctions being imposed for contempt is not a common law or statutory crime. Benninghoven v. Dees, 849 P.2d 906 (Colo. App. 1992). Claim that trial court's amended judgment and mittimus unlawfully increased defendant's sentence should have been brought as a motion to correct an illegal sentence. Graham v. Cooper, 874 P.2d 390 (Colo. 1994) (decided prior to 2004 amendment). A claim that the trial court aggravated a sentence in violation of Apprendi v. New Jersey, 530 U.S. 466 (2000), and Blakely v. Washington, 542 U.S. 296 (2004), is cognizable under section (c) and not section (a). People v. Collier, 151 P.3d 668 (Colo. App. 2006). Court order that changed sentence by eliminating suspended portion of it constituted an imposition of a sentence within the meaning of section (a) of this rule. Defendant was entitled, therefore, to proceed under section (a) to obtain relief. People v. Sisson, 179 P.3d 193 (Colo. App. 2007). Where defendant's challenge alleges that department of corrections (DOC) sentenced him under the wrong discretionary parole statute, section (a) does not give the trial court the authority to decide the issues raised in the defendant's motion because defendant's challenge was not to his sentence, but rather to an act of the DOC. People v. Huerta, 87 P.3d 266 (Colo. App. 2004). The court properly corrected illegal sentence, pursuant to a motion under section (c), but preserved provisions of valid and legal plea agreement. People v. Antonio-Antimo, 29 P.3d 298 (Colo. 2000). By entering into a plea agreement, defendant waives his or her Apprendi right to have any fact (the crime of violence charge) that increases the penalty beyond the prescribed maximum submitted to a jury and proved beyond a reasonable doubt. The plea agreement stated defendant waived his right to a jury trial and the right to have every element proven beyond a reasonable doubt. Thus, by pleading guilty the defendant waived the right to a factual basis for the charge and in effect admitted beyond a reasonable doubt the elements of the offense. People v. Munkus, 60 P.3d 767 (Colo. App. 2002); People v. Andracki, 68 P.3d 526 (Colo. App. 2002). In the case of the defendant's plea agreement, the term "illegal sentence" should be given its plain and ordinary meaning. Defendant's plea agreement did not use that term in the sense that it is used in this rule. In interpreting a plea agreement, the court focuses on the meaning a reasonable person would have attached to the agreement at the time the agreement was entered into. A reasonable person would understand the term "illegal sentence" as used in defendant's plea agreement to mean a sentence that is unlawful in some way. Defendant did not violate her plea agreement because the agreement did not waive her right to raise a challenge under Blakely v. Washington, 542 U.S. 296, 24 S. Ct. 2531, 159 L. Ed. 2d 403 (2004), to her aggravated sentence on appeal. Because defendant did not violate her plea agreement, the prosecution cannot withdraw from it. People v. Barton, 174 P.3d 786 (Colo. 2008). Failure to consider and fix amount of restitution at sentencing results in illegal sentence. People v. Dunlap, 222 P.3d 364 (Colo. App. 2009). Finality of judgment of conviction not affected by illegal sentence due to failure to consider and fix restitution at time of sentencing in circumstances where defendant has already directly appealed conviction and lost and, likewise, has failed to obtain postconviction relief from trial court and review by appellate court. Defendant may neither appeal anew from original conviction or the denial of a postconviction motion, nor may defendant seek application of cases announced after the conclusion of the direct appeal. People v. Dunlap, 222 P.3d 364 (Colo. App. 2009). Exclusion of DNA evidence not required. Where DNA evidence was obtained from defendant as a condition of probation as part of a plea bargain that resulted in an illegal sentence, the case does not implicate the judicially created exclusionary rule: (1) Constitutional error did not involve the police; and (2) the conduct failed the "assessment of flagrancy" test in that the conduct was not sufficiently deliberate that exclusion could meaningfully deter it. People v. Glasser, __ P.3d __ (Colo. App. 2011). Defendant's claim that the trial court erred in determining the amount of restitution is timed barred. Defendant is neither challenging the statutory basis for the award of restitution nor the court's subject matter jurisdiction to enter the order, but the manner in which the restitution hearing was conducted. A claim that the sentence was imposed in an illegal manner must be brought within 120 days. People v. Bowerman, 258 P.3d 314 (Colo. App. 2010). Guilty verdicts for both attempted after deliberation first degree murder and attempted extreme indifference first degree murder did not require inconsistent findings of fact; therefore, the sentences were not illegal. The information alleged different victims for the different charges, so it is not inconsistent to conclude that defendant had the specific intent to take the life of the specific targets and also showed an extreme indifference to *life in general to the other persons. People v. Stovall, 2012 COA 7, __ P.3d __. III. Reduction of Sentence. A. In General. Rule constitutional. Section (b) is a valid procedural rule promulgated pursuant to the rule-making power of the supreme court under § 21 of art. VI, Colo. Const., and it does not encroach upon the governor's exclusive power of commutation under § 7 of art. IV, Colo. Const. People v. Smith, 189 Colo. 50, 536 P.2d 820 (1975). As section (b), which suspends the finality of the conviction for a period of 120 days from the time sentence is imposed, or for 120 days after final disposition on appeal, to allow the filing of a motion for a reduction of sentence in the trial court, suspends the concept of finality of a criminal judgment of conviction, the rule does not offend the separation of powers doctrine under art. III, Colo. Const., nor the executive power of commutation. The court retains jurisdiction during the 120-day period for the filing of a motion for reduction of sentence. People v. Smith, 189 Colo. 50, 536 P.2d 820 (1975). Rule allows court to reconsider, in interests of justice, the sentence previously imposed, in the light of all relevant and material factors in the particular case which may or may not have been initially considered by the court and, in its sound discretion, to resentence the defendant to a lesser term within the statutory limits. People v. Smith, 189 Colo. 50, 536 P.2d 820 (1975); People v. Malacara, 199 Colo. 243, 606 P.2d 1300 (1980). This rule provides the trial court an opportunity to reconsider, in the interest of justice, a sentence previously imposed. Spann v. People, 193 Colo. 53, 561 P.2d 1268 (1977). The purpose of section (b) is to permit the trial court to reexamine the propriety of a sentence previously imposed. People v. Lyons, 44 Colo. App. 126, 618 P.2d 673 (1980). But section (b) cannot expand the trial court's authority in resentencing beyond that which it had initially. Death penalty statute, as it existed in 1993, mandated that a death sentence shall be binding unless the court, pursuant to the statute, determines the verdict was clearly erroneous. The trial court's determination that the sentence was not clearly erroneous, therefore, precludes granting postconviction relief under section (b) of this rule. People v. Dunlap, 36 P.3d 778 (Colo. 2001), cert. denied, 534 U.S. 1095, 122 S. Ct. 884, 151 L. Ed. 2d 722 (2002). But failure to appeal initial sentence forecloses later challenge. A defendant who fails to appeal an initial sentence is foreclosed from challenging that sentence later by means of motion under section (b). People v. Boykin, 631 P.2d 1149 (Colo. App. 1981) (but see Mikkleson v. People, 199 Colo. 319, 618 P.2d 1101 (1980)); Swainson v. People, 712 P.2d 479 (Colo. 1986). More than one sentence reduction is not permitted by former § 16-11-309 when read in conjunction with this rule. Although multiple sentence reductions are permitted under this rule if the sentence is reduced to a term within statutory limits, more than one sentence reduction under former § 16-11-309 would be outside the statutory limits. People v. Belgard, 58 P.3d 1077 (Colo. App. 2002). Jurisdiction to modify sentence retained only until conviction final. A trial court retains jurisdiction to take a "second look" at a sentence previously imposed only before the judgment of conviction underlying the sentence has become final. People v. Lyons, 44 Colo. App. 126, 618 P.2d 673 (1980); Swainson v. People, 712 P.2d 479 (Colo. 1986). If an illegal sentence is imposed, the time for filing a Crim. P. 35(b) motion does not start to run. The time period is triggered only by the imposition of a legal sentence. People v. Dean, 894 P.2d 13 (Colo. App. 1994). And conviction final 120 days after sentence imposed or appellate process concluded. For purposes of the rule's sentence reduction provisions, a conviction is final 120 days after the imposition of sentence when that conviction is not appealed, and 120 days after the conclusion of the appellate process if the conviction or sentence is directly appealed. People v. Lyons, 44 Colo. App. 126, 618 P.2d 673 (1980); Swainson v. People, 712 P.2d 479 (Colo. 1986). Where the defendant does not appeal his conviction but, some years later, challenges his conviction by a motion under section (c), which motion is denied by the trial court, the court of appeals' affirmance of the trial court's denial is not a "judgment" of that court "having the effect of upholding a judgment of conviction" and, thus, does not trigger a new 120-day period for filing a section (b) motion for reduction of sentence. People v. Akins, 662 P.2d 486 (Colo. 1983). Timely filing of a Crim. P. 35(b) motion suspends finality of sentence while the court reconsiders the original sentence. There is no support for the view that a sentence is final once a mandate is received. Ghrist v. People, 897 P.2d 809 (Colo. 1995). Framework for review of motions under section (b). First, the reviewing court must determine the timeliness of the motion, considering both when it is filed and when it is heard. The defendant's motivation for any delay attributable to the defendant is relevant to this determination, but delays that result from the court's inability to hear the matter should not be assessed against the defendant. Second, the court may consider all evidence presented at the hearing. Ghrist v. People, 897 P.2d 809 (Colo. 1995). Section (b) of this rule does not limit the evidence the trial court may consider. Ghrist v. People, 897 P.2d 809 (Colo. 1995). Decision to reduce a sentence is entrusted to the sound discretion of the trial court. Ghrist v. People, 897 P.2d 809 (Colo. 1995). Defendant required to file motion for reduction of sentence within 120 days after the date of successful completion of regimented inmate training program. This rule provides a 120-day time limitation for the filing of a motion for reduction of sentence, and § 17-27.7-104 requires that a motion to reduce sentence must be brought pursuant to Crim. P. 35(b). People v. Campbell, 75 P.3d 1151 (Colo. App. 2003). Jurisdiction retained after 120 days. If the defendant was unconstitutionally deprived of the opportunity to file his motion because of ineffective assistance of counsel, the trial court would have jurisdiction 120 days after the sentence is imposed and could extend the time limit for filing. Swainson v. People, 712 P.2d 479 (Colo. 1986). Therefore, it was error for the district court to dismiss defendant's motion without making any factual findings, on his claim of ineffective assistance of counsel. Swainson v. People, 712 P.2d 479 (Colo. 1986). One hundred twenty days to file a motion is not extended by Crim. P. 45 based upon family considerations or lack of knowledge of the law. The only excusable neglect recognized for extending the time to file a rule 35 motion is ineffective assistance of counsel. People v. Delgado, 83 P.3d 1144 (Colo. App. 2003), rev'd on other grounds, 105 P.3d 634 (Colo. 2005). Defendant should not be penalized for pursuing his right of appeal, or for any delay in deciding that matter. Ghrist v. People, 897 P.2d 809 (Colo. 1995). But, change in parole board policy not grounds for modification of defendant's sentence under subsection (c)(2)(v), and section (b) does not provide basis for review of a sentence if motion filed beyond 120-day time period required by rule. People v. Sorenson, 824 P.2d 38 (Colo. App. 1991). When defendant has filed a motion for reduction of sentence within 120 days after the imposition of sentence, this rule vests the court with jurisdiction to rule on the motion for a reasonable period of time after the expiration of the 120-day filing period. If the court fails to rule within a reasonable period of time, and the defendant fails to take reasonable efforts to secure an expeditious ruling on the motion, the motion may be deemed abandoned. People v. Fuqua, 764 P.2d 56 (Colo. 1988); People v. Cagle, 807 P.2d 1233 (Colo. App. 1991); Herr v. People, 198 P.3d 108 (Colo. 2008). Delay for the purpose of establishing a record of good behavior in the department of corrections is impermissible. A Crim. P. 35(b) motion is not a license to wait and reevaluate the sentencing decision in the light of subsequent developments. People v. Piotrowski, 855 P.2d 1 (Colo. App. 1992); Ghrist v. People, 897 P.2d 809 (Colo. 1995). Burden of going forward with motion pursuant to section (b) is on the defendant and a delay of 532 days is unreasonable and indicates that defendant abandoned the motion. Mamula v. People, 847 P.2d 1135 (Colo. 1993). Appeal of final judgment terminates trial court jurisdiction and does not restore it until the events described in subsections (2) and (3) of section (b) take place. People v. District Court, 638 P.2d 65 (Colo. 1981). Executive branch authorized to modify sentence after conviction final. The executive branch of government, not the judiciary, has the sole authority to modify a legally imposed criminal sentence after the conviction upon which it is based has become final. People v. Lyons, 44 Colo. App. 126, 618 P.2d 673 (1980). Power to alter sentence at time of revocation of probation is explicitly recognized in § 16-11-206(5), Crim. P. 32(f)(5), and section (b) of this rule. People v. Jenkins, 40 Colo. App. 140, 575 P.2d 13 (1977) (decided prior to 1979 amendment of this rule). Court obligated to exercise discretion in deciding whether to modify previously imposed sentence. The court has an affirmative obligation to exercise judicial discretion in deciding whether to modify the sentence previously imposed and to base the decision on relevant evidence, not personal whim. Spann v. People, 193 Colo. 53, 561 P.2d 1268 (1977); People v. Culbertson, 198 Colo. 153, 596 P.2d 1200 (1979); People v. Dunlap, 36 P.3d 778 (Colo. 2001), cert. denied, 534 U.S. 1095, 122 S. Ct. 884, 151 L. Ed. 2d 722 (2002). Implicit in a proceeding pursuant to section (b) is the duty of the trial court to use its discretion when considering the defendant's motion. Mikkleson v. People, 199 Colo. 319, 618 P.2d 1101 (1980); People v. Ellis, 873 P.2d 22 (Colo. App. 1993). Where evidence in support of defendant's section (b) motion was nearly identical to that presented at the sentencing hearing, trial court effectively considered all relevant evidence, and the findings it made at the sentencing hearing were sufficient to support its later exercise of discretion in denying defendant's motion. People v. Busch, 835 P.2d 582 (Colo. App. 1992); People v. Dunlap, 36 P.3d 778 (Colo. 2001), cert. denied, 534 U.S. 1095, 122 S. Ct. 884, 151 L. Ed. 2d 722 (2002). And is trial court's duty to consider all relevant and material factors, including new evidence, as well as facts known at the time the original sentence was pronounced. Spann v. People, 193 Colo. 53, 561 P.2d 1268 (1977); People v. Culbertson, 198 Colo. 153, 596 P.2d 1200 (1979); People v. Ellis, 873 P.2d 22 (Colo. App. 1993). The trial court in proceedings pursuant to section (b) must consider all relevant and material factors which may affect the decision on whether to reduce the original sentence. Mikkleson v. People, 199 Colo. 319, 618 P.2d 1101 (1980). But judicial discretion is not personal discretion. Judicial discretion cannot be distorted to camouflage or insulate from appellate review a decision based on the judge's personal caprice, hostility, or prejudice. Spann v. People, 193 Colo. 53, 561 P.2d 1268 (1977). Personal whim, hostility, or prejudice must not be basis for trial court's decision. People v. Culbertson, 198 Colo. 153, 596 P.2d 1200 (1979). Court considering a motion for reduction of sentence filed pursuant to § 17-27.7-104 must give complete consideration to all pertinent information provided by the offender, the offender's attorney, and the district attorney. People v. Smith, 971 P.2d 1056 (Colo. 1999). Trial court properly exercised judicial discretion under this section and complied with requirements of § 17-27.7-104 where, after careful review of case file, pre-sentence report, recommendation from regimented training program, and documents submitted by defendant, defendant's attorney, and prosecution, the court concluded that crime of vehicular assault was serious enough to warrant denial of motion for sentence reduction after completion of regimented inmate training program under § 17-27.7-103 . People v. Ellis, 873 P.2d 22 (Colo. App. 1993). Trial court gave complete consideration to defendant's Crim. P. 35(b) motion even though the record did not contain any information provided by defendant, his attorney, or the district attorney after defendant's acceptance into the regimented inmate training program. The court should not be precluded from ruling on defendant's motion simply because none of those entitled to provide additional information to the court chose to do so. People v. Morales-Uresti, 934 P.2d 856 (Colo. App. 1996). Defendant's argument that his denial for sentence reduction was based on race was without merit. Although defendant alleged that because he was African-American, he had been treated more harshly than a Caucasian inmate whose sentence had been modified, the two offenders were convicted of different offenses. People v. Ellis, 873 P.2d 22 (Colo. App. 1993). District attorney may withdraw from plea agreement when judge modifies sentence imposed. If a trial judge in the exercise of his discretion under this rule modifies or reduces a sentence imposed pursuant to a plea agreement, the district attorney must be permitted, in his discretion, to withdraw from the plea agreement, reinstate the charges which were dismissed, and proceed to trial as though no agreement had been made. People ex rel. VanMeveren v. District Court, 195 Colo. 34, 575 P.2d 4 (1978). But district attorney not permitted to withdraw from plea agreement when sentence reduced pursuant to the regimented inmate training program in § 17-27.7-104 . Because the plea agreement did not foreclose the future possibility of a reduction in sentence, the court-ordered sentence reduction could not amount to a substantial and material breach of the agreement between the parties. Keller v. People, 29 P.3d 290 (Colo. 2000). Generally, ruling on section (b) motion deemed final judgment, reviewable on appeal. When the trial court rules on a defendant's motion, filed pursuant to section (b), it is a final judgment as to the issue raised, and such ruling, except where the issue is propriety of sentence, is reviewable on appeal to the appropriate court. People v. Malacara, 199 Colo. 243, 606 P.2d 1300 (1980). There is no right of appeal as to a trial court's denial of a motion for reduction of sentence under this rule when the issue presented to and resolved by the court concerns the propriety of the sentence. People v. Busch, 835 P.2d 582 (Colo. App. 1992). Standard of review of sentencing by trial court is whether court abused discretion. People v. Mikkleson, 42 Colo. App. 77, 593 P.2d 975 (1979), rev'd on other grounds, 199 Colo. 314, 618 P.2d 1101 (1980); People v. Hudson, 709 P.2d 77 (Colo. App. 1985). And decision not reversed on appeal absent abuse. Absent an abuse of discretion, the decision of the reviewing court on a motion for the reduction of sentence under this rule will not be reversed. People v. Sundstrom, 638 P.2d 831 (Colo. App. 1981). American bar association standards relating to appellate review of sentences were used by court of appeals to review sentence imposed by trial court. People v. Hudson, 709 P.2d 77 (Colo. App. 1985). Disjunctive provisions of section (b) intended to recognize the different times at which a sentence might become final. People v. Cagle, 807 P.2d 1233 (Colo. App. 1991). Defendant cannot appeal motion's denial where issue one of propriety of sentence. A defendant has no right to appeal a denial of his motion filed pursuant to section (b) where the issue before the appellate court is the propriety of his sentence. People v. Malacara, 199 Colo. 243, 606 P.2d 1300 (1980); McKnight v. People, 199 Colo. 313, 607 P.2d 1007, cert. denied, 449 U.S. 873, 101 S. Ct. 214, 66 L. Ed. 2d 94 (1980); People v. Kerns, 629 P.2d 102 (Colo. 1981). Where the intrinsic fairness of defendants' sentence is reviewed by the trial court in proceedings pursuant to section (b), those determinations are not reviewed again on appeal. People v. Lopez, 624 P.2d 1301 (Colo. 1981). An argument challenging the intrinsic fairness of the sentence imposed and not the sentencing procedure utilized by the trial court will not be reconsidered on appeal to the supreme court. People v. Nemnich, 631 P.2d 1121 (Colo. 1981). There is no right of appeal to the denial by a trial court of a section (b) motion where the issue presented and resolved concerns the propriety of the sentence. People v. Dennis, 649 P.2d 321 (Colo. 1982). Or where issue treated as such. An appeal of the trial court's reduction of the defendant's sentence pursuant to this rule, seeking a further reduction of the sentence, is treated as an appeal of the "denial" of a section (b) motion raising the issue of the "propriety of the sentence", and is therefore dismissed. People v. Foster, 200 Colo. 283, 615 P.2d 652 (1980). Court may not sua sponte treat section (b) proceeding as section (c) proceeding. People v. Guitron, 191 Colo. 284, 552 P.2d 304 (1976). Failure of trial court to exercise any discretion renders proceeding defective. The failure of a trial court to exercise any discretion at all in reviewing a section (b) motion in effect renders the proceeding itself defective, and an appeal therefrom directly raises the issue of the propriety of that proceeding. Mikkleson v. People, 199 Colo. 319, 618 P.2d 1101 (1980). Such as where court refuses to consider mitigation information or make findings. It is only in such situations where the trial court has refused to consider any information in mitigation and does not make findings in support of its decision, that an error in denying a section (b) motion is sufficient to invoke appellate jurisdiction. Mikkleson v. People, 199 Colo. 319, 618 P.2d 1101 (1980). Where trial judge acts arbitrarily or capriciously, judgment vacated. Where the trial court exercises its discretion arbitrarily or capriciously, basing its decision to deny the petitioner's motion under section (b) on personal considerations rather than on the evidence, the trial court's judgment is vacated, and the motion is remanded for a prompt hearing before a different trial judge. Spann v. People, 193 Colo. 53, 561 P.2d 1268 (1977). Facts constituting abuse of discretion regarding court denial of work-release program. People v. Morrow, 197 Colo. 244, 591 P.2d 1026 (1979). Court may not increase an offender's original sentence unless it was erroneously imposed or is void. Downing v. People, 895 P.2d 1046 (Colo. 1995). Term of imprisonment that was longer than offender's original sentence constituted an increase in the sentence for purposes of section (b), regardless of whether the sentence was served in a community corrections facility under less severe conditions. Downing v. People, 895 P.2d 1046 (Colo. 1995). Since the granting of probation greatly reduces the level of restraint imposed on defendant, essentially allowing him to remain at liberty while complying with the terms of his probation, it does constitute a reduction under section (b), even when the length of the sentence increased. People v. Santana, 961 P.2d 498 (Colo. App. 1997). B. Proportionality Review. Proportionality determinations are reviewed de novo on appeal, because an appellate court is not bound by a trial court's conclusions of law. People v. Medina, 926 P.2d 149 (Colo. App. 1996). Three-part test adopted by U.S. supreme court in Solem v. Helm applies when reviewing proportionality of sentences under habitual-criminal statutes: (1) The gravity of the offense and the harshness of the penalty; (2) the sentences imposed on other criminals in the same jurisdiction; and (3) the sentences imposed for the commission of the same crime in other jurisdictions. People v. Cisneros, 855 P.2d 822 (Colo. 1993). Request for proportionality review alleging that sentence violates the eighth amendment to the U.S. constitution is subject to the limitation period set forth in § 16-5-402 . People v. Moore-El, 160 P.3d 393 (Colo. App. 2007). Concurrent life sentences held disproportionate where underlying crimes were relatively minor, none posed a major threat to society, and although defendant had a lengthy record, approval of a life sentence under the circumstances would drastically lower the "grave and serious" threshold. People v. Medina, 926 P.2d 149 (Colo. App. 1996). IV. Other Postconviction Remedies. A. General Purpose and Scope of Postconviction Review. Postconviction relief is founded upon constitutional principles. People v. Bucci, 184 Colo. 367, 520 P.2d 580 (1974). Rule is concerned with the validity of a sentence and judgment. Saiz v. People, 156 Colo. 43, 396 P.2d 963 (1964). A request for return of property is not within the scope of this rule, which is limited to challenges to a defendant's conviction or sentence. People v. Wiedemer, 692 P.2d 327 (Colo. App. 1984). Court may not sua sponte treat section (b) proceeding as section (c) proceeding. Where the proceeding is simply a proceeding under section (b) for the reduction of sentence, it is not within the province of the court, sua sponte, to treat it as a proceeding under section (c) and pass upon whether the defendant's guilty plea should be set aside, even though it is argued that the reduction was a part of a plea bargaining. People v. Guitron, 191 Colo. 284, 552 P.2d 304 (1976). Unless motion clearly raises section (c) issues. Where the defendant's motion seeks relief under section (b), but in substance it clearly raises issues and seeks relief available under section (c), the motion should be considered a motion for postconviction relief under section (c). People v. Ivery, 44 Colo. App. 511, 615 P.2d 80 (1980). Rule sets forth standards and procedure for postconviction relief. This rule sets the applicable standards and procedure required of a court when a motion to vacate, set aside, or correct a sentence is filed. Roberts v. People, 158 Colo. 76, 404 P.2d 848 (1965). And this rule similar to federal provision. Section (c) of this rule provides a method for postconviction relief to those sentenced by state courts in Colorado which is substantially the same as that of 28 U.S.C. § 2255. Henry v. Tinsley, 344 F.2d 109 (10th Cir. 1965); Ruark v. Tinsley, 350 F.2d 315 (10th Cir. 1965); Saxton v.*

149

Patterson, 370 F.2d 112 (10th Cir. 1966); Breckenridge v. Patterson, 374 F.2d 857 (10th Cir. 1967), cert. dismissed, 389 U.S. 801, 88 S. Ct. 9, 19 L. Ed. 2d 56 (1967). Section (c) of this rule authorizes postconviction relief without regard to time limitations for any sentence that "exceeded the maximum authorized by law, or is otherwise not in accordance with the sentence authorized by law". People v. Emig, 676 P.2d 1156 (Colo. 1984). Rule creates entirely new postconviction remedy. Section (c) of this rule is intended to fill the void created by the narrowness of the Colorado concept of "habeas corpus" by creating an entirely new postconviction remedy. Peters v. Dillon, 227 F. Supp. 487 (D. Colo. 1964), aff'd, 341 F.2d 337 (10th Cir. 1965). And attains same purpose as obsolete "habeas corpus" writ. The writ of "habeas corpus coram nobis" being obsolete, its purpose now is attained by the filing of a motion to set aside judgment. Grandbouche v. People, 104 Colo. 175, 89 P.2d 577 (1939); Hackett v. People, 158 Colo. 304, 406 P.2d 331 (1965). This rule affords all remedies which are available through writ of "habeas corpus". People ex rel. Wyse v. District Court, 180 Colo. 88, 503 P.2d 154 (1972); People v. Santisteven, 868 P.2d 415 (Colo. App. 1993). Section (c) affords a convicted person all the remedies which are available through a writ of habeas corpus. People v. Bucci, 184 Colo. 367, 520 P.2d 580 (1974). An improperly filed pro se habeas corpus petition should be treated as a Crim. P. 35(c) motion in order to provide review on the merits of the claims raised by a petitioner. Chatfield v. Colo. Court of Appeals, 775 P.2d 1168 (Colo. 1989). Pro se habeus corpus petition was improperly filed in case where an invalid judgment of conviction and sentence were rendered since relief was available under this rule and Crim. P. 36 and the district court should have treated petition as motion under subsection (c)(2) of this rule. Kailey v. Colo. Dept. of Corr., 807 P.2d 563 (Colo. 1991). Rather than dismissing an improper habeas corpus petition, the court should convert such petition into a motion under section (c) of this rule where the petitioner is acting pro se, the petitioner raises issues in the habeas corpus petition which should have been raised in a motion under section (c) of this rule, and the petitioner's claims are not barred by the statute of limitations. Graham v. Gunter, 855 P.2d 1384 (Colo. 1993). "Habeas corpus" is not proper remedy to gain review of purported constitutional violations. Breckenridge v. Patterson, 374 F.2d. 857 (10th Cir. 1967), cert. dismissed, 389 U.S. 801, 88 S. Ct. 9, 19, L. Ed. 2d 56 (1967). Rather, the proper procedure is motion under this rule, followed by an appeal. Breckenridge v. Patterson, 374, F.2d 857 (10th Cir.), cert. dismissed, 389 U.S. 801, 88 S. Ct. 9, 19 L. Ed. 2d 56 (1967). And "habeas corpus" petition raising constitutional questions treated as motion under this rule. Where the issues before a trial court in a "habeas corpus" proceeding raise substantive constitutional questions, the issues are within the purview of postconviction remedy, and the petition for "habeas corpus" will be treated as a motion under section (c). Dodge v. People, 178 Colo. 71, 495 P.2d 213 (1972). Under subsection (c)(3), the court must hold an evidentiary hearing unless the motion, the files, and the record of the case clearly establish that the allegations presented in the motion are without merit and do not warrant postconviction relief. White v. Denver District Court, 766 P.2d 632 (Colo. 1988). A habeas corpus petition that seeks relief available under this rule should be treated as a Crim. P. 35 motion based upon the substantive constitutional issues raised therein, rather than upon the label placed on the pleading. White v. Denver Dist. Ct., 766 P.2d 632 (Colo. 1988); DePineda v. Price, 915 P.2d 1278 (Colo. 1996). Defendant's challenges to procedures by which he was sentenced rather than the legality of his confinement may be raised by means of a motion under section (c) but not by means of a habeas corpus petition. Jones v. Zavaras, 926 P.2d 579 (Colo. 1996). Prisoner required to pursue remedies under rule before petitioning for "habeas corpus". The requirement that a prisoner must pursue his remedies under this rule before petitioning for "habeas corpus" does not constitute a suspension of the writ of "habeas corpus". People ex rel. Wyse v. District Court, 180 Colo. 88, 503 P.2d 154 (1972). So trial court judge abuses discretion when prematurely proceeds with "habeas corpus" hearing. When a motion for postconviction relief is heard and denied by one trial court judge and an appeal is pending, if the defense attorney files a "habeas corpus" petition on the same grounds, it is an abuse of discretion for a second trial court judge to proceed with a hearing on the "habeas corpus" petition. People ex rel. Wyse v. District Court, 180 Colo. 88, 503 P.2d 154 (1972). A motion under section (c) must be filed in the sentencing court because that court maintains the records relating to the conviction and sentence. Jones v. Zavaras, 926 P.2d 579 (Colo. 1996). Defendant may proceed pro se during postconviction proceedings pursuant to this rule. People v. Jones, 665 P.2d 127 (Colo. App. 1982). Contention that defendant has been wrongfully deprived of confinement credit is properly put forward in a motion under this rule at the time when defendant claims a right to be released. People v. Lepine, 744 P.2d 81 (Colo. 1987). An order of a trial court granting or denying a motion filed under section (c) of this rule is a final order reviewable on appeal. Such order becomes final after the period in which to perfect an appeal expires. People v. Janke, 852 P.2d 1271 (Colo. App. 1992). This rule governing postconviction remedies did not provide basis for granting habeas corpus relief where petition was not filed under postconviction rule, even though petition was assigned case number of petitioner's original criminal action. People v. Calyer, 736 P.2d 1204 (Colo. 1987). Defendant's motion does not seek relief from the judgment and sentence of the trial court but rather against the department of corrections. Therefore, it is not a claim cognizable under section (c). People v. Carrillo, 70 P.3d 529 (Colo. App. 2002). This rule does not address postconviction claim that defendant is being unconstitutionally denied the opportunity to be considered for parole. Naranjo v. Johnson, 770 P.2d 784 (Colo. 1989). Former clients are not required to obtain postconviction relief before bringing a malpractice action against their criminal defense attorneys. Rantz v. Kaufman, 109 P.3d 132 (Colo. 2005). The doctrine of issue preclusion can be used under appropriate circumstances to prevent a criminal defendant from relitigating issues that have been decided against him or her in a motion under section (c) in a subsequent malpractice suit. Rantz v. Kaufman, 109 P.3d 132 (Colo. 2005). Failure to seek or obtain postconviction relief is not a bar to bringing a malpractice suit. Smith v. Truman, 115 P.3d 1279 (Colo. 2005). When a postconviction claim is properly presented for evaluation on the merits, but is premised on trial error that was not preserved, the court must review the claim for plain error, employing the prejudice test articulated in Wilson v. People, 743 P.2d 415 (Colo. 1987). People v. Versteeg, 165 P.3d 760 (Colo. App. 2006). B. When Review Available. Previously, this rule was entitled "Post Conviction Remedy for Prisoner in Custody". Hudspeth v. People, 151 Colo. 5, 375 P.2d 518 (1962), cert. denied, 375 U.S. 838, 84 S. Ct. 82, 11 L. Ed. 2d 66 (1963). And previously limited to prisoner in custody. This rule was once expressly limited to where a prisoner was attacking a sentence under which he was "then" in custody. Hackett v. People, 158 Colo. 304, 406 P.2d 331 (1965). Such as person to whom probation granted. A person to whom probation has been granted is considered to be in "custody under sentence" and may raise a question as to whether his plea was voluntary. People v. Burger, 180 Colo. 415, 505 P.2d 1308 (1973). Presently, court cannot deny motion for sole reason petitioner not in custody. At the present time, on a sufficient section (c) motion, a trial court would not be justified in summarily denying the motion for the sole reason that a petitioner is not in custody under sentence pursuant to a conviction which he seeks to vacate. Hooker v. People, 173 Colo. 226, 477 P.2d 376 (1970). And this rule now applies to one who is aggrieved and claiming either a right to be released or to have a judgment of conviction set aside. Hooker v. People, 173 Colo. 226, 477 P.2d 376 (1970). A defendant who enters a guilty plea is entitled to file a Crim. P. 35(c) motion based on newly discovered evidence, and the rule does not limit postconviction review to those who have been convicted after trial or after entering an Alford plea. People v. Mason, 997 P.2d 1245 (Colo. App. 1999), aff'd on other grounds, 25 P.3d 764 (Colo. 2001). Postconviction relief is presently available where constitutional rights have been violated during trial. People v. Hubbard, 184 Colo. 243, 519 P.2d 945 (1974). Where defendant contended that the trial court imposed its sentence in an illegal manner, and not that it was an illegal sentence, defendant was required to file his motion within 120 days of the imposition of sentence. People v. Swainson, 674 P.2d 984 (Colo. App. 1983). Motion to dismiss may be treated as one filed pursuant to this rule. Where a motion to dismiss is filed after the defendant has pleaded guilty to and is sentenced for the charge involved, the trial court may elect to treat the motion as one filed pursuant to this rule. Wixson v. People, 175 Colo. 348, 487 P.2d 809 (1971). And review provided subsequent to appeal. The very purpose of a section (c) motion is to provide a postconviction remedy subsequent to an appeal to review constitutional errors made at trial. Lucero v. People, 173 Colo. 94, 476 P.2d 257 (1970). Or where time for appeal has passed. This rule provides for postconviction remedies to attack an unconstitutionally conducted trial although the time for appeal has passed. Baca v. Gobin, 165 Colo. 593, 441 P.2d 6 (1968). And in spite of fact appeal was dismissed for failure to file the requisite motion for new trial, and that the alleged error could have been raised had such an appeal been properly brought, nevertheless, where the error asserted would be a violation of a constitutionally protected right, it may be raised in a section (c) motion. Sackett v. People, 176 Colo. 18, 488 P.2d 885 (1971). Motion based upon change in law may be filed before conviction becomes "final". Motions pursuant to section (c) and § 18-1-410(1)(f) may be filed at any time before the conviction becomes "final", which does not take place until the date when a petition for rehearing, timely filed, has been denied. Litsey v. District Court, 193 Colo. 341, 565 P.2d 1343 (1977) (decided prior to 1979 amendment). Where an appellant files a motion for a postconviction review of his sentence based on a significant change in the law before his conviction becomes "final", the court has jurisdiction to entertain his motion for relief. People v. Thomas, 185 Colo. 395, 525

P.2d 1136 (1974). Relief from a validly imposed sentence because of amendatory legislation is only available if requested before a conviction becomes final. People v. Johnson, 638 P.2d 61 (Colo. 1981). Authority to modify sentence after conviction final. After a conviction has become final, relief from a validly imposed sentence cannot be obtained through the judiciary but must instead be sought through the executive department by way of commutation. People v. Akins, 662 P.2d 486 (Colo. 1983); People v. Piotrowski, 855 P.2d 1 (Colo. App. 1993). The limitations of § 16-5-402 are applicable to a proportionality review of a sentence imposed pursuant to the habitual criminal statutes. People v. Talley, 934 P.2d 859 (Colo. App. 1996). Because § 16-5-402 (1.5) is discretionary and because defendant's motion was premised on recent authority of constitutional magnitude, appellate court addressed the motion despite its untimeliness. People v. Gardner, 55 P.3d 231 (Colo. App. 2002). Defendant need not affirmatively assert that relief sought has not been previously denied, although an appeal duplicating an appeal previously denied may be dismissed. People v. Robinson, 833 P.2d 832 (Colo. App. 1992). Issue raised on appeal may be reviewed when Crim. P. 35(b) motion was inadvertently excluded from remainder of record transmitted to court and exclusion was not appellant's fault. People v. Olivas, 911 P.2d 675 (Colo. App. 1995). Review is appropriate when issues concern the sentencing proceeding and not the propriety of sentence itself. People v. Olivas, 911 P.2d 675 (Colo. App. 1995). Claims related to the department of corrections' sex offender classification are not reviewable under Crim. P. 35(c)(2). The proper claim is suit against the department of corrections. People v. McMurrey, 39 P.3d 1221 (Colo. App. 2001). Ripeness of claim for review. Subsections (c)(2) and (3) require an allegation that the applicant has a present right to be released because the sentence was imposed in violation of the constitution or laws of the United States or of Colorado and the sentence imposed was not in accordance with the sentence authorized by law. People v. Shackelford, 729 P.2d 1016 (Colo. App. 1986). Convict, who alleged that the department of corrections was incorrectly computing good-time credits for purposes of parole eligibility but who did not assert any defect in the sentence imposed upon him, and who presented his claim prior to the time when, even by his own calculations, he would be eligible for parole, did not present a dispute that was ripe for adjudication and did not state a cognizable claim. People v. Shackelford, 729 P.2d 1016 (Colo. App. 1986). State waived time bar to Crim. P. 35(c) motion by not raising it in trial court. People v. St. John, 934 P.2d 865 (Colo. App. 1996). When defendant entitled to review even though sentence served. When a defendant has completed service of a sentence and belatedly seeks postconviction relief, he may be charged with the burden of showing a present need for such relief. A sufficient showing is made when the defendant establishes that he is facing prosecution or has been convicted and the challenged conviction or sentence may be, or has been, a factor in sentencing for the current offense. People v. Montoya, 667 P.2d 1377 (Colo. 1983). A claim under this rule is not barred by a failure to challenge the conviction earlier as long as a postconviction motion states a claim cognizable under this rule, such as where the motion asserts facts which, if true, would invalidate a previously entered guilty plea, and the claim has not been fully and finally resolved in a prior judicial proceeding, the defendant is entitled to judicial review of the asserted error. People v. Montoya, 667 P.2d 1377 (Colo. 1983). A person seeking postconviction relief must allege with particularity in his motion that present need exists for relief sought and the present need must continue to exist until the time of the hearing on motion and, if a new present need arises prior to a hearing on motion for postconviction relief, defendant may amend his original pleading to reflect the change. Moland v. People, 757 P.2d 137 (Colo. 1988). Appellate court cannot review allegations not raised in a motion or hearing under section (c). People v. Goldman, 923 P.2d 374 (Colo. App. 1996). Constitutional error alleged need no longer be of sort not subject to appellate review. There is no longer any adherence to the rule that the constitutional error alleged must be of a sort not effectively subject to review on appeal from a conviction. People v. Bradley, 169 Colo. 262, 455 P.2d 199 (1969); Whitman v. People, 170 Colo. 189, 460 P.2d 767 (1969). The fact that defendant did not raise a constitutional claim on direct appeal does not preclude the defendant from raising the claim in a motion under section (c) or from seeking appellate review of the trial court's denial of such a motion. The defendant is entitled to review of a motion under this rule so long as the motion states a claim cognizable under this rule and the claim has not been fully and finally resolved in a prior judicial proceeding. People v. Corichi, 18 P.3d 807 (Colo. App. 2000). Defendant who has voluntarily and knowingly waived right to contest validity of prior convictions cannot apply for postconviction relief under section (c). People v. Gurule, 748 P.2d 1329 (Colo. App. 1987). But this rule is not a substitute for appeal or writ of error. People v. Shearer, 181 Colo. 237, 508 P.2d 1249 (1973). A motion under this rule is not a substitute for a writ of error. People v. Crawford, 183 Colo. 166, 515 P.2d 631 (1973).

152

And constitutional error previously disposed of on appeal cannot be raised again. An error consisting of a violation of constitutional rights of a defendant may be raised in a section (c) proceeding so long as it was not previously raised and disposed of on appeal. People v. Bradley, 169 Colo. 262, 455 P.2d 199 (1969); Whitman v. People, 170 Colo. 189, 460 P.2d 767 (1969). Where various matters raised in a motion under this rule have been considered on appeal and no constitutional issues are raised, the motion should be denied without hearing, as provided in this rule. McKenna v. People, 160 Colo. 369, 417 P.2d 505 (1966). Where a question is reviewed in depth in connection with the defendant's appeal, the matter is not subject to further review under section (c). Moore v. People, 174 Colo. 570, 485 P.2d 114 (1971). Once an issue has been reviewed on appeal it cannot be raised again by a petition to vacate judgment and sentence. Gallegos v. People, 175 Colo. 553, 488 P.2d 887 (1971). Unless otherwise required in the interests of justice, any grounds for postconviction relief which have been fully and finally litigated on a writ of error should not be relitigated. Morse v. People, 180 Colo. 49, 501 P.2d 1328 (1972). This rule is a vehicle for correcting errors of constitutional magnitude which were not previously raised and ruled upon. People v. Shearer, 181 Colo. 237, 508 P.2d 1249 (1973). An issue can be raised by a section (c) motion only when the alleged error involves a constitutional right and was not previously the subject of review on a writ of error. People v. Hill, 182 Colo. 253, 512 P.2d 257 (1973). Equitable principles permit a motion for postconviction relief to be denied without a hearing when the ground for postconviction relief relied upon has been fully and finally litigated in the proceedings leading to judgment of conviction, including an earlier appeal, and the interests of justice do not otherwise require another hearing. People v. Trujillo, 190 Colo. 497, 549 P.2d 1312 (1976). Once a claim has been raised and disposed of by the supreme court in an earlier appeal, it cannot be raised again in a later section (c) motion. People v. Johnson, 638 P.2d 61 (Colo. 1981); People v. Davis, 759 P.2d 742 (Colo. App. 1988). As there must be some finality in reviewing process. Although section (c) is primarily intended to provide procedure which will permit judicial review of alleged constitutional infirmities in criminal proceedings, it is couched in language which recognizes that there must be some finality in the reviewing process. People v. Hubbard, 184 Colo. 243, 519 P.2d 945 (1974). Rule not intended to establish perpetual review. This rule was not intended to establish a procedure which would allow continuing review of issues previously decided against the defendant. People v. Hubbard, 184 Colo. 243, 519 P.2d 945 (1974). Generally, this rule is not intended to provide a repetitive review of alleged errors. Buckles v. People, 162 Colo. 51, 424 P.2d 774 (1967). Postconviction proceedings are provided as a method of preventing injustices from occurring after a defendant has been convicted and sentenced, but not for the purpose of providing a perpetual right of review to every defendant in every case. People v. Hampton, 187 Colo. 131, 528 P.2d 1311 (1974). Second appellate review of the propriety of a sentence is prohibited. People v. Malacara, 199 Colo. 243, 606 P.2d 1300 (1980); People v. Jenkins, 687 P.2d 455 (Colo. 1984). A defendant is prohibited from using a proceeding under this rule to relitigate issues fully and finally resolved in an earlier appeal. People v. Johnson, 638 P.2d 61 (Colo. 1981); DePineda v. Price, 915 P.2d 1278 (Colo. 1996). A defendant is precluded from raising an issue under this rule if its review would be nothing more than a second appeal. DePineda v. Price, 915 P.2d 1278 (Colo. 1996). But if a significant change in the interpretation of the law, of constitutional magnitude, is determined after the defendant's direct appeal is affirmed, and if the change is binding precedent, then it is proper for the court of appeals to exercise its discretion to review the defendant's claims raised under this rule in a subsequent appeal. People v. Close, 22 P.3d 933 (Colo. App. 2000), rev'd on other grounds, 48 P.3d 528 (Colo. 2002). Rights of accused balanced against right to have final court determination. It is necessary to balance the rights of the accused to review a trial with postconviction proceedings against the right of society to have finality in court determinations. People v. Shearer, 181 Colo. 237, 508 P.2d 1249 (1973). Thus, American Bar Association Standards for Criminal Justice are to be followed. In balancing the rights of the accused in postconviction proceedings against the recurring problems which face the courts and society, the supreme court of Colorado has elected to follow the American Bar Association Standards for Criminal Justice relating to delayed applications for relief. People v. Hampton, 187 Colo. 131, 528 P.2d 1311 (1974). When appeal time expires, petitioner must show entitlement to relief. When the time for appeal has expired, there must be a showing by the petitioner that he would be entitled to relief under section (c). Valdez v. District Court, 171 Colo. 436, 467 P.2d 825 (1970). As must defendant who has completed challenged sentence. Where the defendant seeking postconviction relief has completed the sentences which were imposed on his challenged convictions, he has the burden of establishing a present need for relief under this rule. People v.

153

Hampton, 187 Colo. 131, 528 P.2d 1311 (1974). Where the defendant has long since served his sentence, time has dimmed memories, and court records are misplaced or unavailable, the defendant has the burden of demonstrating a present need for section (c) relief. People v. Bucci, 184 Colo. 367, 520 P.2d 580 (1974). A defendant who has fully discharged the sentence imposed against him and any parole obligation associated with the sentence, but who has made no further showing of the present need for relief, is not entitled to relief under section (c) of this rule. People v. Graham, 793 P.2d 600 (Colo. App. 1989). Motions under section (c) are subject to § 16-5-402(1), which prohibits a person convicted under a criminal statute from collaterally attacking the validity of the conviction unless the attack is commenced within three years of the conviction. People v. Green, 36 P.3d 125 (Colo. App. 2001); People v. Salinas, 55 P.3d 268 (Colo. App. 2002); People v. Collier, 151 P.3d 668 (Colo. App. 2006). However, an exception to the time limit in § 16-5-402(1), exists if a defendant demonstrates that the failure to seek timely relief was the result of justifiable excuse or excusable neglect. People v. Green, 36 P.3d 125 (Colo. App. 2001); People v. Salinas, 55 P.3d 268 (Colo. App. 2002). But the allegation that there was "justifiable excuse or excusable neglect" without specificity is insufficient and time barred. People v. Salinas, 55 P.3d 268 (Colo. App. 2002). Because there is no requirement that appellate counsel advise a defendant of time limitations for seeking postconviction relief, the absence of such advice is not a justifiable excuse for defendant's neglect. People v. Alexander, 129 P.3d 1051 (Colo. App. 2005). Postconviction motions that challenge the manner in which a plea is taken, such as whether the person was properly advised about the plea, are not challenges to the legality of the sentence and are properly brought pursuant to section (c), not section (a). People v. Green, 36 P.3d 125 (Colo. App. 2001); People v. Salinas, 55 P.3d 268 (Colo. App. 2002). When a deferred judgment and sentence agreement remains unrevoked, review under this rule is not available as it establishes postconviction remedies, and no conviction has entered. People ex rel. K.W.S., 192 P.3d 579 (Colo. App. 2008). Defendant who pleads guilty may not bring an as-applied equal protection postconviction challenge. People v. Ford, 232 P.3d 260 (Colo. App. 2009). C. Grounds Justifying Relief. 1. In General. Previously, this rule specifically limited the trial court's power to grant relief to situations where: (1) The sentence was imposed in violation of the constitution or laws of Colorado or of the United States; or (2) the court imposing the sentence was without jurisdiction to do so; or (3) the sentence was in excess of the maximum sentence authorized by law; or (4) the statute for the violation of which the sentence was imposed was unconstitutional or was repealed before the prisoner contravened its provisions. Saiz v. People, 156 Colo. 43, 396 P.2d 963 (1964); Hammons v. People, 156 Colo. 484, 400 P.2d 199 (1965). 2. Change of Law. Subsection (c)(1) appropriate where change intervenes before imposition of sentence. A defendant is given the right to make application for postconviction review when there has been a significant change in the law, applied to defendant's conviction or sentence, allowing in the interests of justice retroactive application of the changed legal standard. Hence, subsection (c)(1) is especially appropriate where a change in the law intervenes before conviction is had and sentence is imposed. People v. Thomas, 185 Colo. 395, 525 P.2d 1136 (1974). Where amendatory legislation mitigating the penalty for the offense became effective prior to imposition of the sentence, the defendant is entitled as a matter of law to be sentenced thereunder, although probation is imposed before the legislation and revocation with sentencing afterwards. People v. Jenkins, 40 Colo. App. 140, 575 P.2d 13 (1977). Standing to challenge conviction based upon change of law. Section (c) is proper motion for obtaining postconviction relief in circumstance in which one of the statutes under which the defendant was charged was later held unconstitutional, and therefore defendant had standing to bring such a motion. People v. Crespin, 682 P.2d 58 (Colo. App. 1984), rev'd on other grounds, 721 P.2d 688 (Colo. 1986). But where court overrules prior fourth amendment holding, suppression issues become moot upon entry of a guilty verdict and relief properly denied. People v. Waits, 695 P.2d 1176 (Colo. App. 1984), aff'd in part and rev'd in part on other grounds, 724 P.2d 1329 (Colo. 1986). Retroactive application of amendments to § 17-2-103(12), providing that a parole officer shall request that parole revocation proceedings be deferred pending a disposition of a criminal charge, denied under this rule because subsection (c)(1) provides a remedy to an offender whose conviction or sentence is affected by a change in the law during the pendency of a direct appeal of such conviction or sentence, but not to an offender claiming the benefit of changes in the law that occur during the pendency of other postconviction proceedings. People v. White, 804 P.2d 247 (Colo. App. 1990). 3. Constitutionally Infirm Judgment. Section (c) provides procedural mechanism to attack a conviction which is constitutionally infirm. People v. Ivery, 44 Colo. App. 511, 615 P.2d 80 (1980). Sufficiency of the evidence is a constitutional issue, cognizable under subsection (c)(2). People v. Nunez, 673 P.2d

154

53 (Colo. App. 1983). Postconviction questions pertaining to constitutionality of judgment of conviction are solely within rule. Shearer v. Patterson, 159 Colo. 319, 411 P.2d 247 (1966). A claim that the trial court aggravated a sentence in violation of Apprendi v. New Jersey, 530 U.S. 466 (2000), and Blakely v. Washington, 542 U.S. 296 (2004), is cognizable under section (c) and not section (a). People v. Collier, 151 P.3d 668 (Colo. App. 2006). Contention that sentence violates double jeopardy prohibition of the fifth amendment of the U.S. constitution is cognizable under section (c). People v. Collier, 151 P.3d 668 (Colo. App. 2006). Contention that sentencing scheme set forth in Colorado Sex Offender Lifetime Supervision Act violates equal protection is cognizable under section (c) of this rule. People v. Collier, 151 P.3d 668 (Colo. App. 2006). Contention that Colorado Sex Offender Lifetime Supervision Act violates due process because it does not provide for a continuing opportunity to be heard and does not give offenders a meaningful chance to demonstrate their rehabilitation is cognizable under section (c) of this rule. People v. Collier, 151 P.3d 668 (Colo. App. 2006). Contention that trial court used an unreliable test in sentencing defendant in violation of due process is cognizable under section (c) of this rule. People v. Collier, 151 P.3d 668 (Colo. App. 2006). If motion specifies violation of constitutional rights, hearing required. If a defendant's motion to vacate, or any attachments thereto, specify matters which are deemed to have violated his constitutional rights, then it would be incumbent upon the trial court to treat this motion in the nature of a section (c) motion and conduct a hearing to determine if there was a violation of any of the constitutional rights of the defendant. DeBaca v. People, 170 Colo. 415, 462 P.2d 496 (1969). Submission of the constitutionally infirm crime of extreme indifference murder under a general verdict to jury was not harmless error beyond a reasonable doubt. Crespin v. People, 721 P.2d 688 (Colo. 1986). 4. Unlawful Revocation of Sentence. Rule provides remedy for revocation of deferred sentence. A defendant may either appeal an order revoking a deferred sentence, pursuant to C.A.R. 1, or file a motion for postconviction review, pursuant to section (c) of this rule. People v. Boykin, 631 P.2d 1149 (Colo. App. 1981). As an order revoking deferred sentence is equivalent of revocation of conditional release for purposes of subsection (c)(2)(VII). People v. Boykin, 631 P.2d 1149 (Colo. App. 1981). Offender is not entitled to relief under section (c) of this rule when record demonstrates that offender was given statutorily required administrative review prior to termination from a community corrections program by the trial court in its role as the referring agency. People v. Rogers, 9 P.3d 371 (Colo. 2000). 5. Invalid Guilty Plea. State courts empowered to determine validity of pleas. Section (c) confers jurisdiction upon the state courts to hear and determine allegations which go to the validity of a petitioner's plea of guilty. Patterson v. Hampton, 355 F.2d 470 (10th Cir. 1966). As such allegations raise no question justiciable in "habeas corpus". Allegations of a petition which go to the validity of petitioner's plea of guilty are properly brought under this rule and raises no question properly justiciable in "habeas corpus". Stewart v. Tinsley, 157 Colo. 441, 403 P.2d 220 (1965); Martinez v. Tinsley, 158 Colo. 236, 405 P.2d 943 (1965). Defendant entitled to opportunity to prove allegations of coercion. No matter how improbable allegations of coercion may be, so long as they are not completely incredible, a defendant is entitled to the opportunity of trying to prove them at a hearing. Von Pickrell v. People, 163 Colo. 591, 431 P.2d 1003 (1967). And entitled to withdraw plea made under influence of drugs. If the defendant can show that he was under the influence of tranquilizing drugs at the time he changed his plea to guilty, to the extent that the guilty plea was not a free and voluntary act, he would be entitled to withdraw that plea and go to trial on a plea of not guilty, particularly where he alleges that he has a valid defense to the charges against him. Von Pickrell v. People, 163 Colo. 591, 431 P.2d 1003 (1967). Failure of court to advise or make inquiry precludes treating plea as voluntary. Failure of the trial court to advise or to make a proper inquiry precludes treating the defendant's plea of guilty as a voluntary and intelligent waiver of his constitutional rights, so defendant may withdraw his plea of guilty and be permitted to plea anew. People v. Harrington, 179 Colo. 312, 500 P.2d 360 (1972). And elements of crime charged must be explained in understandable terms. A guilty plea cannot stand as voluntarily and knowingly entered unless the defendant understands the nature of the crime charged, and this requirement is not met unless the critical elements of the crime charged are explained in terms which are understandable to the defendant. People v. Gorniak, 197 Colo. 289, 593 P.2d 349 (1979). But a defendant may plead guilty to a crime which does not exist and for which he could not be convicted at trial, and because the defendant receives a substantial benefit by pleading guilty to the lesser charges, postconviction relief will be denied. People v. Waits, 695 P.2d 1176 (Colo. App. 1984), aff'd in part and rev'd in part on other grounds, 724 P.2d 1329 (Colo. 1986). Defendant need not be advised on right to remain silent in competency evaluation for a postconviction motion under section (c) if the evaluation is not being used to establish guilt.

No self-incrimination issue exists, and procedural safeguards of § 16-8-117 do not apply because defendant already confessed, pleaded guilty, and was sentenced. People v. Karpierz, 165 P.3d 753 (Colo. App. 2006). The defendant must receive advisement of mandatory parole requirement when entering into a plea agreement so that the defendant has the requisite knowledge of the consequences of the plea agreement. Without sufficient advisement, the plea agreement can be withdrawn. People v. Seaney, 36 P.3d 81 (Colo. App. 2000). Hearing granted where no showing defendant aware of difference between felony and misdemeanor. Where the record fails to show defendant was aware of difference between felony and misdemeanor offenses when pleading guilty, he should be granted a hearing on his petition for postconviction relief. People v. Rivera, 185 Colo. 337, 524 P.2d 1082 (1974). Existence of prejudice resulting from ineffective assistance of counsel is not determined by underlying "truth" of a guilty plea, but rather by whether there is a reasonable probability that defendant would not have pleaded guilty but for counsel's failure to make him aware of the consequences of such plea. People v. Garcia, 799 P.2d 413 (Colo. App. 1990). Defendant who pleaded guilty to first degree sexual assault was resentenced to reflect terms of plea bargain as interpreted by court. Defendant's plea was based on court's interpretation of plea bargain that, if qualified under "good time law", he would serve no more than one-half of sentence agreed upon, but after defendant entered his plea, parole board determined that parole was discretionary, not mandatory, for sex offenders and that defendant may be required to serve the full sentence on his conviction. People v. Wilbur, 873 P.2d 1 (Colo. App. 1993). Trial court did not cause defendant's plea to be involuntarily made, where neither the People nor the trial court represented that defendant would be released on parole at any particular time, the court specifically stated to defendant that it would not be bound by any representations made to defendant concerning the penalty to be imposed or the granting or denial of probation, and neither the trial court nor the prosecutor referred to the parole board's early release policy. People v. Lustgarden, 914 P.2d 488 (Colo. App. 1995). Trial court's failure to advise defendant of the possibility of being sentenced pursuant to the Sex Offenders Act, former §§ 16-13-201 to 16-13-216 , was not grounds to set aside defendant's guilty plea entered a decade earlier; the failure to so advise was harmless since the defendant was not originally sentenced under the Act. People v. Lustgarden, 914 P.2d 488 (Colo. App. 1995). Defendant's postconviction motion based on the voluntariness of his guilty plea as it related to the quality of his counsel was properly denied as successive under subsection (c)(3)(VII) of this rule, where lengthy evidentiary hearing was held on defendant's Crim. P. 32(d) motion claiming that his plea was not knowing, voluntary, and intelligent due to ineffective assistance of counsel. People v. Vondra, 240 P.3d 493 (Colo. App. 2010). 6. Deprivation of Appellate Rights. Constitutional violation where deprivation of appellate rights by fraud or deception. A deprivation of constitutional rights has been held to exist where factors such as fraud or deception imposed upon a convicted person by his attorney deprive him of his appellate rights. Haines v. People, 169 Colo. 136, 454 P.2d 595 (1969). Otherwise, meritorious grounds for appellate review must be shown. Where a motion for postconviction relief is based on an alleged deprivation of the right to appeal, meritorious grounds for appellate review must be shown. Haines v. People, 169 Colo. 136, 454 P.2d 595 (1969). Indigent defendant is entitled to obtain a free transcript when necessary to exercise the right of appeal. People v. Shearer, 181 Colo. 237, 508 P.2d 1249 (1973). So long as furnishing of free transcript not "vain and useless" gesture. To warrant the furnishing of a free transcript, the petitioner must make some showing that the furnishing of such would not be just a "vain and useless" gesture, but that he is entitled to relief under this rule. Valdez v. District Court, 171 Colo. 436, 467 P.2d 825 (1970); Romero v. District Court, 178 Colo. 200, 496 P.2d 1049 (1972). Inasmuch as such would be the infliction of a needless expense. As to the right to have a free transcript on appeal, where petitioner does not come within the requirements of section (c) and no showing has been made why a very expensive transcript will be of any use to him, then the infliction of the needless expense to prepare such upon a small local unit of government under these circumstances would be an injustice. Peirce v. People, 158 Colo. 81, 404 P.2d 843 (1965). Allegations of ineffective assistance of counsel in appellate proceedings may be considered by the trial court in connection with motion for postconviction relief. People v. Williams, 736 P.2d 1229 (Colo. App. 1986). Attorney's performance found to be patently deficient in proceeding under this rule alleging ineffective assistance of counsel where such attorney failed to file a petition for writ of certiorari in a timely fashion after receiving three extensions of time from supreme court. People v. Valdez, 789 P.2d 406 (Colo. 1990). Motion for postconviction relief under this rule denied where defendant failed to establish that he had suffered prejudice due to patently deficient performance of attorney in handling criminal appeal. People v. Valdez, 789 P.2d 406 (Colo. 1990). A motion or petition for habeas corpus is a collateral attack that may be dismissed upon the defendant's death, since doing so does not deprive the defendant of the right to appeal the conviction. People v. Valdez, 911 P.2d 703 (Colo. App. 1996). 7. Other Grounds. Issue involving jurisdiction of court to impose certain sentence is subject to review under section (c). Johnson v. People, 174 Colo. 75, 482 P.2d 105 (1971). A defendant may not plead guilty to a crime after the general assembly has expressly repealed the statute defining that crime. Defendant's plea to first degree assault pursuant to § 18-3-202(1)(d), after such section was repealed, was illegal and, because it was material to his plea agreement, his plea agreement was vacated. People v. Wetter, 985 P.2d 79 (Colo. App. 1999). Due process failure where jury would not have convicted with later discovered evidence. If with later discovered evidence the jury would not have convicted the defendant, it can be said that the conviction can be laid at the door of inadequate preparation on the part of both sides, and this has the magnitude of a failure to due process, calling for a new trial. People v. Armstead, 179 Colo. 387, 501 P.2d 472 (1972). Where prior conviction is decreed a nullity by final judgment of court of appeals. The defendant cannot "reaffirm" the validity of a prior conviction at an habitual offender hearing when the court of appeals has decreed by final judgment that the prior conviction is a nullity. People v. Dugger, 673 P.2d 351 (Colo. 1983). Invited error doctrine not applicable as basis for denying postconviction relief. Defendant should not be estopped from challenging conviction on grounds that he invited the error by successfully objecting to submission of a special verdict form where court found that although the use of a general verdict form prevented a means of determining whether error raised in postconviction motion was harmless, the use of a general verdict form did not induce error by the trial court. People v. Crespin, 682 P.2d 58 (Colo. App. 1984), rev'd on other grounds, 721 P.2d 688 (Colo. 1986). Ineffective assistance of counsel. Defendant has burden to show inadequate representation, and a conviction will not be set aside unless, based on record as a whole, there was a denial of fundamental fairness. People v. Gies, 738 P.2d 398 (Colo. 1987); People v. Karpierz, 165 P.3d 753 (Colo. App. 2006). There is no need to inquire into trial errors or prejudice if trial counsel is found to be incompetent as a matter of law. In such case as trial counsel is found to be incompetent as a matter of law, defendant is entitled to new trial for this reason alone. People v. Kenny, 30 P.3d 734 (Colo. App. 2000). Trial counsel conflict of interest. If the trial court determines that a conflict of interest existed, such conflict adversely affected counsel's conduct, and that defendant did not voluntarily, knowingly, and intelligently waive the right to conflict-free representation, judgment of conviction must be vacated and a new trial should be conducted. People v. Kenny, 30 P.3d 734 (Colo. App. 2000). Strickland ineffective assistance standard requires that the court evaluate the evidence from the perspective of defense counsel as of the time of the representation in question and to indulge a strong presumption that defense counsel's efforts constituted effective assistance. People v. Naranjo, 840 P.2d 319 (Colo. 1992). If the court determines defense counsel's performance was not constitutionally deficient, it need not consider the prejudice prong of the ineffective assistance test. People v. Sparks, 914 P.2d 544 (Colo. App. 1996). Strickland test, while based on the constitutional right to counsel, is applicable to the determination of whether a defendant has received effective assistance of counsel in a postconviction proceeding. People v. Hickey, 914 P.2d 377 (Colo. App. 1995). In order to obtain relief based on a claim of ineffective assistance of counsel, a defendant must affirmatively prove both that his counsel's performance fell below the standard of professional reasonableness and that such performance prejudiced him, i.e., that there is reasonable probability that, but for such deficient performance, the outcome at trial would have been different. People v. Palmer, 888 P.2d 348 (Colo. App. 1994). Ineffective assistance of counsel may arise when an attorney's representation is intrinsically improper because of an actual conflict of interest. However, to make a showing of actual conflict of interest, the defendant must demonstrate a basis for the underlying ineffective assistance of counsel challenges. No basis was found where claim of ineffective assistance of counsel was based on bare allegations of failure to file an appeal with no showing of the existence of grounds for an appeal. People v. Rhorer, 946 P.2d 503 (Colo. App. 1997), rev'd on other grounds, 967 P.2d 147 (Colo. 1998). To succeed on a motion for new trial based on newly discovered evidence, the defendant must show that the evidence was discovered after the trial; that defendant and his counsel exercised diligence to discover all possible evidence favorable to the defendant prior to and during the trial; that the newly discovered evidence is material to the issues involved and not merely cumulative or impeaching; and lastly, that the newly discovered evidence is of such character as probably to bring about an acquittal verdict if presented at another trial. People v. Muniz, 928 P.2d 1352 (Colo. App. 1996); People v. Tomey, 969 P.2d 785 (Colo. App. 1998); People v. Mason, 997 P.2d 1245 (Colo. App. 1999), aff'd on other grounds, 25 P.3d 764 (Colo. 2001). Question in evaluating probability that new evidence would bring about an acquittal is not whether the court, in its experience, would consider a particular witness credible, but rather whether a reasonable jury would probably conclude that there existed a reasonable doubt of guilt based on all evidence, including the new evidence, as developed in the course of trial. People v. Estep, 799 P.2d 405 (Colo. 1990). Defendant entitled to a new trial upon the withdrawal of his guilty plea based upon newly discovered evidence. The defendant must present evidence from which the trial court may reasonably conclude that: (1) The newly discovered evidence was discovered after the entry of the plea, and in the exercise of reasonable diligence by the defendant and his or her counsel, could not have been discovered earlier; (2) the charges that the People filed against the defendant, or the charges to which the defendant pleaded guilty were actually false or unfounded; and (3) the newly discovered evidence would probably bring about a verdict of acquittal in a trial. People v. Schneider, 25 P.3d 755 (Colo. 2001); Mason v. People, 25 P.3d 764 (Colo. 2001). An Alford plea and a guilty plea are the same for purposes of analysis under Schneider. People v. Schneider, 25 P.3d 755 (Colo. 2001). A trial court may consider corroborating evidence in assessing a recanting witness's credibility. People v. Schneider, 25 P.3d 755 (Colo. 2001). Trial court record demonstrated defendant was aware that a crime of violence charge would increase his potential sentence and supported trial court's denial of motion to vacate upon finding that defendant's plea was knowingly and voluntarily entered. People v. Palmer, 888 P.2d 348 (Colo. App. 1994). It is extremely unlikely that a reasonable jury would acquit the defendant of drug charges in a new trial at which a witness now states, six years after the original trial, that she placed the drugs in the defendant's wallet. The trial court found it "rather incredible" that the witness would not mention that she had put the drugs in his wallet during the first trial and that the witness did not know that the defendant was in prison until six years later. The witness' testimony was further weakened by the fact that she was no longer subject to prosecution for her conduct and the fact that her testimony conflicted with her affidavit with respect to where she obtained the drugs. People v. Muniz, 928 P.2d 1352 (Colo. App. 1996). A defendant who enters a guilty plea is entitled to file a motion for post-conviction relief based on newly discovered evidence. People v. Tomey, 969 P.2d 785 (Colo. App. 1998). District court exceeded its statutory jurisdiction by ordering that defendant not have custody of her children as a condition of probation, since juvenile courts have exclusive jurisdiction to determine the legal custody of any child who is dependent and neglected under § 19-1-104 . People v. Forsythe, 43 P.3d 652 (Colo. App. 2001). D. Grounds Not Justifying Relief. 1. In General. Mere error, unless of constitutional dimension, is no grounds for postconviction relief. People v. Crawford, 183 Colo. 166, 515 P.2d 631 (1973). Such as failure to follow rule's formal requirements. For collateral relief such as habeas corpus to be available, more than a failure to follow the formal requirements of a rule of criminal procedure must be shown. Martinez v. Ricketts, 498 F. Supp. 893 (D. Colo. 1980). Trial court's failure to readvise defendant of elements of crime at providency hearing is not fatal to the conviction where record shows that defendant's plea was knowingly and understandingly made. People v. Reyes, 713 P.2d 1331 (Colo. App. 1985). Trial court's alleged error in refusing to permit defendant's wife to testify as to his nonviolent character and prior sexual conduct and allegation that prosecutor's remarks during cross-examination and closing argument were so prejudicial as to constitute reversible error were not proper grounds for postconviction relief. People v. Williams, 736 P.2d 1229 (Colo. App. 1986). Alleged defects in grand jury proceedings do not constitute grounds for relief from conviction, because once a defendant has been found guilty beyond a reasonable doubt, the issue of probable cause found at a grand jury proceeding becomes moot. People v. Tyler, 802 P.2d 1153 (Colo. App. 1990). Trial court's failure to advise defendant of the mandatory parole term did not constitute reversible error. Because the length of the defendant's sentence was less than the maximum that he was advised he could receive, the trial court properly determined that defendant had entered a valid guilty plea. Consequently, it committed no error in denying defendant's motion under this rule. People v. Tyus, 776 P.2d 1143 (Colo. App. 1989). Trial court's failure to advise defendant of mandatory parole term at the time he pleaded guilty to probation violation was not error because court had previously advised defendant when he pleaded guilty to the charge. People v. Wright, 53 P.3d 730 (Colo. App. 2002). Where mittimus does not reference a mandatory period of parole, remand is required for correction of the mittimus rather than granting defendant's Crim. P. 35(c) motion. People v. Barth, 981 P.2d 1102 (Colo. App. 1999). Allowing witness for defendant to appear in jail clothing is not reversible error where defendant cannot show he was prejudiced thereby. People v. Walters, 796 P.2d 13 (Colo. App. 1990); People v. Martinez, 32 P.3d 520 (Colo. App. 2001). Trial court's instruction that the jury could consider defendant's voluntary absence from the trial as evidence of guilt was not error. The court had made reasonable inquiry as to the defendant's whereabouts before continuing the trial. People v. Tafoya, 833 P.2d 841 (Colo. App. 1992). Where the only issue raised in a motion under this rule concerns the construction of statutes, failure of the trial court to make findings of fact and conclusions of law is harmless and does not require reversal. People v. Young, 908 P.2d 1147 (Colo. App. 1995). Defense counsel's failure to inform defendant of mandatory consecutive sentences did not result in ineffective assistance of counsel. The record supported the trial court's conclusion that defendant would not have accepted a plea bargain sentence in excess of 20 years, therefore defense counsel's failure to inform defendant of the mandatory consecutive sentence provision did not result in prejudice. People v. Williams, 908 P.2d 1157 (Colo. App. 1995). Defendant cannot claim ineffective assistance of counsel for failing to perfect appeal while defendant was a fugitive. Counsel's performance could not have prejudiced defendant by forcing forfeiture of an appeal because, by fleeing from justice while his appeal was pending, defendant himself forfeited his right to appellate review. People v. Brown, 250 P.3d 679 (Colo. App. 2010). Application of mandatory parole period did not violate equal protection where person is sentenced differently than others in same felony "class". Defendant is only "similarly situated" with defendants who commit the same or similar acts. People v. Friesen, 45 P.3d 784 (Colo. App. 2001); People v. Walker, 75 P.3d 722 (Colo. App. 2002). 2. Procedural Errors. Review on grounds of duplicity in charge is proper only by appeal to the conviction and not by means of this rule. Specht v. People, 156 Colo. 12, 396 P.2d 838 (1964). And mere surplusage in charge does not require court to hold a full-blown hearing into a motion to vacate, where it could be clearly seen from the motion itself that the particular matter was without merit, such being a matter of form not affecting the "real merits" of the offense charged. Carter v. People, 161 Colo. 10, 419 P.2d 654 (1966). Defendant cannot collaterally attack untrue record of arraignment and plea. Where the record as to arraignment and plea is not true, the defendant must reasonably call the defect to the court's attention by a motion for correction of error, but he cannot collaterally attack it. Madrid v. People, 148 Colo. 149, 365 P.2d 39 (1961). Hearing not required by delay where not oppressive or arbitrary. Where the record does not disclose any objection to a delay made by the defendant at the time of trial and the defendant's motion under this rule does not set forth any facts showing that the delay was in any manner oppressive or arbitrary, that he was in any way deprived of any defense, or that any witness was unavailable, then under such circumstances, the court is not required to hold an evidentiary hearing. Valdez v. People, 174 Colo. 268, 483 P.2d 1333 (1971). Attack on credibility of witnesses for the state is a matter not reviewable by motion under this rule, since it does not raise a constitutional question. Taylor v. People, 155 Colo. 15, 392 P.2d 294 (1964). Nor is admissibility of exhibit based on alleged lack of foundation. The issue as to the admissibility of an exhibit based on an alleged lack of foundation not based on any constitutional ground is not one which can form the basis for relief under section (c). Walters v. People, 166 Colo. 90, 441 P.2d 647 (1968). Tactical error regarding trial strategy insufficient basis for relief. Where counsel makes an informed decision regarding trial strategy and offers several theories of defense, only one of which is challenged as having been ineffectively presented at trial, this tactical error does not provide the necessary basis for postconviction relief. People v. Stroup, 624 P.2d 913 (Colo. App. 1980). As are, generally, errors in jury instructions. As a general rule, errors in jury instructions do not constitute fundamental error that would provide a basis for collateral attack. People v. Shearer, 181 Colo. 237, 508 P.2d 1249 (1973). And failure to appoint counsel on appeal. The failure to appoint counsel to carry an appeal does not authorize, or even permit, the setting aside of a judgment and sentence under this rule. Rather, the proper remedy is another request that he be appointed counsel to examine the trial record. Cruz v. People, 157 Colo. 479, 405 P.2d 213 (1965), cert. denied, 383 U.S. 915, 86 S. Ct. 905, 15 L. Ed. 2d 669 (1966). 3. Plea Bargaining and Disparate Sentences. Allegation of plea bargaining, standing alone, is not sufficient upon which to base a charge of coercion of a guilty plea. Smith v. People, 162 Colo. 558, 428 P.2d 69 (1967). Due process not denied where judge considers truthfulness of defendant's presentence statements. It is not a denial of due process for a judge, in connection with sentencing procedure, to consider the truthfulness of voluntary statements made by the defendant at a presentence hearing. People v. Quarles, 182 Colo. 321, 512 P.2d 1240 (1973). And relief cannot be given for disparity in sentences. A defendant is not entitled to relief under section (c) based on a lack of equal protection of the law due to the disparity of the sentences between himself and a codefendant. People v. Jenkins, 180 Colo. 35, 501 P.2d 742 (1972). Nor where defendant alleges that prison conditions constitute cruel and unusual punishment. The defendant's allegations that conditions at a prison constitute cruel and unusual punishment, making his sentence more onerous than that contemplated by the sentencing judge, do not present a claim for relief under this rule. People v. Sundstrom, 638 P.2d 831 (Colo. App. 1981). Defendant need not be advised on right to remain silent in competency evaluation for a postconviction motion under section (c) if the evaluation is not being used to establish guilt. No self-incrimination issue exists, and procedural safeguards of § 16-8-117 do not apply because defendant already confessed, pleaded guilty, and was sentenced. People v. Karpierz, 165 P.3d 753 (Colo. App. 2006). 4. Failure to Take Appeal. Mere failure to take appeal cannot support collateral attack. The mere failure, or even neglect, to take an appeal, "standing alone", whether excusable or not, raises no constitutional question, and, hence, does not support a collateral attack. Haines v. People, 169 Colo. 136, 454 P.2d 595 (1969); People v. Rhorer, 946 P.2d 503 (Colo. App. 1997), rev'd on other grounds, 967 P.2d 147 (Colo. 1998). Unless party precluded from appealing. Where a party has not availed himself of the normal appeal procedure, unless he has been effectively precluded from doing so, he cannot thereafter seize upon this remedy in order to seek relief from alleged grievances which are properly the subject of an appeal. Taylor v. People, 155 Colo. 15, 392 P.2d 294 (1964). Or where true prejudice to petitioner. Where a petitioner's time to sue out an appeal has long since passed and he has effectively and knowingly waived his right to file a motion for a new trial, he cannot, in the absence of any showing of true prejudice which could bring him under this rule, be heard to complain that his waiver had a legal effect he did not then contemplate. Peirce v. People, 158 Colo. 81, 404 P.2d 843 (1965). E. Motion and Hearing. 1. When Hearing Granted. If allegations set forth proper grounds for relief, court must grant prompt hearing. Patterson v. Hampton, 355 F.2d 470 (10th Cir. 1966). If a motion under section (c) sets forth facts constituting grounds for relief from a sentence, a prompt hearing by the trial court must be granted, unless the motions, files, and records satisfactorily show that the prisoner is not entitled to relief. Allen v. People, 157 Colo. 582, 404 P.2d 266 (1965); Roberts v. People, 158 Colo. 76, 404 P.2d 848 (1965); Coleman v. People, 174 Colo. 94, 482 P.2d 378 (1971). When defense counsel's ineffective assistance deprives defendant of a hearing on the merits of his or her postconviction claim, the remedy is to provide such a hearing. Thus, vindication of this statutory right trumps society's interest in the finality of convictions. People v. Valdez, 178 P.3d 1269 (Colo. App. 2007). Even when the record clearly demonstrates that postconviction counsel was ineffective in representing defendant through counsel's delay, proof of acquiescence could show defendant abandoned an ineffective assistance of counsel claim or waived the right to effective assistance of counsel. People v. Valdez, 178 P.3d 1269 (Colo. App. 2007). Whether a waiver of effective assistance of counsel was voluntary is a question of fact for the trial court. People v. Valdez, 178 P.3d 1269 (Colo. App. 2007). The allegation that defense counsel failed to inform defendant of his or her right to appeal plus the fact that the court did not advise the defendant of his or her right to appeal is sufficient to warrant an evidentiary hearing. People v. Boespflug, 107 P.3d 1118 (Colo. App. 2004). Evidentiary hearing not required where only legal issues to be decided by judge. An evidentiary hearing is not required under this rule where the motion, files, and record present only issues of law, or where the motion itself fails to specify the facts supporting the constitutional claim. People v. Trujillo, 190 Colo. 497, 549 P.2d 1312 (1976); People v. Johnson, 195 Colo. 350, 578 P.2d 226 (1978). Hearing unnecessary, and motion dismissed, where record shows no entitlement to relief. A motion under this rule may be dismissed without a hearing in the case where the motion, the files, and the record show to the satisfaction of the court that the prisoner is not entitled to relief. Whitman v. People, 170 Colo. 189, 460 P.2d 767 (1969). This rule permits a trial judge to deny the motion without granting a hearing, but only in those cases where the motion, the files, and the record in the case clearly establish that the allegations presented in the defendant's motion are without merit and do not warrant postconviction relief. People v. Hutton, 183 Colo. 388, 517 P.2d 392 (1973); People v. Breaman, 924 P.2d 1139 (Colo. App. 1996). Where the motion and the record of the case show, to the satisfaction of the court, that the prisoner is not entitled to relief, a hearing is not necessary. People v. Velarde, 200 Colo. 374, 616 P.2d 104 (1980). A motion under section (c) may be dismissed without a hearing if the motion, the files, and the record clearly establish that the defendant is not entitled to relief. People v. Hartkemeyer, 843 P.2d 92 (Colo. App. 1992); People v. Ruiz, 935 P.2d 68 (Colo. App. 1996); People v. Mayes, 981 P.2d 1106 (Colo. App. 1999); People v. Moriarity, 8 P.3d 566 (Colo. App. 2000); People v. Martinez, 36 P.3d 201 (Colo. App. 2001); People v. Salinas, 55 P.3d 268 (Colo. App. 2002); People v. Vieyra, 169 P.3d 205 (Colo. App. 2007). Trial court did not err in failing to grant defendant a hearing where the court referred only to information in the motion, record, and files in denying defendant's motion. People v. Fernandez, 53 P.3d 773 (Colo. App. 2002). Although the court may, after considering the motion and supporting documents, deny a motion pursuant to Crim. P. 35 without a hearing, the court may not grant the motion without a hearing. People v. Davis, 849 P.2d 857 (Colo. App. 1992), aff'd, 871 P.2d 769 (Colo. 1994). Court of appeals erred in vacating respondent's guilty plea based upon allegations contained in his or her section (c) motion. However, since the allegations, if true, may entitle respondent to relief, the district court must conduct an evidentiary hearing to ascertain the veracity of respondent's claims. People v. Simpson, 69 P.3d 79 (Colo. 2003). Before accepting a defendant's guilty plea, a trial court must adequately advise the defendant regarding a mandatory parole period. Appropriate remedy is to remand for a hearing to determine if defendant was aware of a mandatory parole term and, if not, whether he nevertheless would have pled guilty. People v. Calderon, 992 P.2d 1201 (Colo. App. 1999). 2. Sufficiency of Allegations. Bald allegation of constitutional error is sufficient for review when specific facts are not pleaded to support the claim. People v. Bruebaker, 189 Colo. 219, 539 P.2d 1277 (1975). Bare allegations of incompetence or coercion are not sufficient to entitle a defendant to an evidentiary hearing in section (c) proceeding. Von Pickrell v. People, 163 Colo. 591, 431 P.2d 1003 (1967); Bradley v. People, 175 Colo. 146, 485 P.2d 875 (1971). Bare allegations of incompetency of counsel are not sufficient to entitle a defendant to an evidentiary hearing in a proceeding under section (c). Moore v. People, 174 Colo. 570, 485 P.2d 114 (1971); People v. Osorio, 170 P.3d 796 (Colo. App. 2007). Bare assertions of mental exhaustion on the part of the defendant because of a series of continuances resulting in less than a month's delay is not equivalent to mental incompetence. Bradley v. People, 175 Colo. 146, 485 P.2d 875 (1971). And evidentiary hearings will not be granted on vague conclusional charges. DeBaca v. District Court, 163 Colo. 516, 431 P.2d 763 (1967). As where motion alleges sentence is "illegal" in violation of fourth and fifth amendments. It is impossible to glean from a motion any clear indication of how petitioner's constitutional rights may have been violated in connection with his conviction and sentence in the trial court where the motion does no more than allege that the sentence of the trial court was "illegal" and should be vacated because it was imposed in "violation of the fourth and fifth amendments", as such a motion contains no exposition of any facts from which a trial court could detect any basis for unconstitutional action or inaction. Hooker v. People, 173 Colo. 226, 477 P.2d 376 (1970). Specific facts to support the claim must appear in petition for postconviction relief. DeBaca v. District Court, 163 Colo. 516, 431 P.2d 763 (1967). A defendant need only assert facts that, if true, would provide a basis for relief to warrant a hearing. People v. Simpson, 69 P.3d 79 (Colo. 2003). Petitioner must allege ultimate facts with particularity. The petitioner has the burden to allege with particularity ultimate facts which support a conclusion that a judicial proceeding is illegal or irregular. Melton v. People, 157 Colo. 169, 401 P.2d 605 (1965), cert. denied, 382 U.S. 1014, 86 S. Ct. 624, 15 L. Ed. 2d 528 (1966). Motion for section (c) review is insufficient where it does not specify facts which constitute the basis for the unconstitutional charge. DeBaca v. People, 170 Colo. 415, 462 P.2d 496 (1969). Motion that fails to contain sufficient allegations to support the claim asserted as the basis for relief may be dismissed for failure to state a claim upon which relief may be granted. People v. Bossert, 772 P.2d 618 (Colo. 1989). And, failing specific facts, no hearing. Failing specific facts to support a claim, no issue is raised which demands an evidentiary hearing. DeBaca v. District Court, 163 Colo. 516, 431 P.2d 763 (1967). If the motion contains no allegations of facts upon which relief can be granted, there is no requirement that an evidentiary hearing be had or that an attorney be appointed to represent the defendant. Kostal v. People, 167 Colo. 317, 447 P.2d 536 (1968); People v. Lyons, 196 Colo. 384, 585 P.2d 916 (1978). And motion, and relief, denied. In a proceeding to compel the trial court to grant the defendant a free transcript of all proceedings had in connection with his criminal conviction, such may be refused where the defendant fails to allege sufficient facts which would warrant the granting of the transcript or which would warrant the granting of relief under section (c). Valdez v. District Court, 171 Colo. 436, 467 P.2d 825 (1970). A motion for review in the trial court as contemplated by the provisions of this rule is insufficient and may be summarily denied where it does not specify the facts which constitute the basis for the unconstitutional charge. Hooker v. People, 173 Colo. 226, 477 P.2d 376 (1970); People v. Rodriguez, 914 P.2d 230 (Colo. 1996). However, that prisoner's factual allegations seem unbelievable or improbable is not the test set forth in this rule for determining whether a hearing should or should not be afforded the prisoner; unless the motion itself, the files, or the record of the case show that the prisoner is not entitled to relief, he must be given an opportunity to support his allegations with evidence presented at a hearing. Roberts v. People, 158 Colo. 76, 404 P.2d 848 (1965). Court of appeals erred in vacating respondent's guilty plea based upon allegations contained in his or her section (c) motion. However, since the allegations, if true, may entitle respondent to relief, the district court must conduct an evidentiary hearing to ascertain the veracity of respondent's claims.

161

People v. Simpson, 69 P.3d 79 (Colo. 2003). Court may dismiss a motion without a hearing if the motion, the files, and the record clearly establish the right to relief. People v. Simons, 826 P.2d 382 (Colo. App. 1991). Defendant must allege with particularity in the motion that a present need exists for the relief sought such as the applicant may be disadvantaged in obtaining parole under a later sentence. People v. Santisteven, 868 P.2d 415 (Colo. App. 1993). Denial of free transcript not an abuse of discretion. Court did not abuse its discretion when it denied a request for free use of a transcript when an indigent defendant failed to demonstrate that he may be entitled to relief under section (c) and that the transcript might contain facts that substantiate his claim. Jurgevich v. District Ct., 907 P.2d 565 (Colo. 1995). 3. Contemporaneous Objection and Waiver. Like habeas corpus, proceeding under this rule governed by equitable principles. This rule affords a convicted person the remedies which are available through a writ of habeas corpus, and like the federal habeas corpus proceeding, a proceeding under this rule is governed by equitable principles. People v. Trujillo, 190 Colo. 497, 549 P.2d 1312 (1976); People v. Bravo, 692 P.2d 325 (Colo. App. 1984). Relief denied where right to counsel waived at trial. A trial court properly denies postconviction relief when the defendant knowingly waived his right to be represented by counsel at trial. Martinez v. People, 166 Colo. 132, 442 P.2d 422, cert. denied, 393 U.S. 990, 89 S. Ct. 474, 21 L. Ed. 2d 453 (1968). Rule is not designed to eliminate the requirement for contemporaneous objection and certain rights not raised at trial will be considered waived. Morse v. People, 180 Colo. 49, 501 P.2d 1328 (1972). Failure to raise search and seizure issue at trial tantamount to waiver. The contemporaneous objection rule applies to search and seizure issues, and the failure to raise the objection of an illegal search and seizure by proper objection at the trial level is tantamount to a waiver, in which case a trial court properly denies a motion for relief under section (c) based thereon. Brown v. People, 162 Colo. 406, 426 P.2d 764 (1967). As is failure to raise identification issue. Where there never was an issue raised in the trial as to the identification of defendant, this is a contrived issue, and a trial court is correct in refusing an evidentiary hearing based on petitioner's objection to lineup procedures. Whitman v. People, 170 Colo. 189, 460 P.2d 767 (1969). And failure to allege lack of speedy trial in motion to dismiss. Where the defendant claims that he pleaded guilty because he was promised that after he had entered his plea the trial court would consider a motion to dismiss for lack of a speedy trial, but makes no such allegation in his motion to dismiss, and there is nothing in the record which could even lead to the inference that such a promise might have been made, the court will not consider the argument. Wixson v. People, 175 Colo. 348, 487 P.2d 809 (1971). One who pleads guilty cannot claim search and seizure illegal. One who pleads guilty is not in a position to successfully move for vacation of judgment on claims of an alleged illegal search and seizure. Von Pickrell v. People, 163 Colo. 591, 431 P.2d 1003 (1967). No issue exists as to legality of plea bargain where sentence given vacated. Where the defendant first admitted his guilt upon being promised a minimum sentence prior to his first sentencing, but, upon being given more than that amount of time, his first sentence is vacated, the issue of the legality of his first plea bargain no longer exists in a subsequent motion. James v. People, 162 Colo. 577, 427 P.2d 878 (1967). 4. Burden of Proof. Legality of prior judgment and proceedings presumed. When attacking a conviction and sentence by a motion under this rule, the legality of the judgment and the regularity of the proceedings leading up to the judgment are presumed. Melton v. People, 157 Colo. 169, 401 P.2d 605 (1965), cert. denied, 382 U.S. 1014, 86 S. Ct. 624, 15 L. Ed. 2d 528 (1966); Lamb v. People, 174 Colo. 441, 484 P.2d 798 (1971). When a defendant attacks a conviction and sentence by a motion under section (c), the legality of the judgment and the regularity of the proceedings leading up to the judgment are presumed. People v. Brewer, 648 P.2d 167 (Colo. App. 1982). Burden of proof of allegations in a section (c) motion rests with petitioner. Bresnahan v. People, 175 Colo. 286, 487 P.2d 551 (1971); Bresnahan v. Patterson, 352 F. Supp. 1180 (D. Colo. 1973); People v. McClellan, 183 Colo. 176, 515 P.2d 1127 (1973); Kailey v. Colo. Dept. of Corr., 807 P.2d 563 (Colo. 1991); People v. Fleming, 867 P.2d 119 (Colo. App. 1993), rev'd on other grounds, 900 P.2d 19 (Colo. 1995); People v. Sickich, 935 P.2d 70 (Colo. App. 1996). Pleas of guilty induced by threats or promises are not valid, but upon postconviction procedures to set aside such a plea, it becomes the burden of the petitioner to establish that the plea was entered because of coercion. Normand v. People, 165 Colo. 509, 440 P.2d 282 (1968). The burden is on the defendant section (c) hearing to show that his plea was entered because of coercion. People v. Brewer, 648 P.2d 167 (Colo. App. 1982). And measure of proof on motion is ordinarily proof by preponderance of evidence. Bresnahan v. People, 175 Colo. 286, 487 P.2d 551 (1971); People v. Malouff, 721 P.2d 159 (Colo. App. 1986). The burden is upon the defendant to establish by at least the preponderance of the evidence the allegations of his section (c) motion. Lamb v. People, 174 Colo. 441, 484

P.2d 798 (1971); People v. McClellan, 183 Colo. 176, 515 P.2d 1127 (1973). In a Crim. P. 35(c) proceeding, the legality of the judgment and the regularity of the proceedings leading up to the judgment are presumed. The burden is upon the movant to establish by a preponderance of the evidence the allegations of the motion for post-conviction relief. If the evidence supports the district court's findings and order, the decision will not be disturbed on review. People v. Hendricks, 972 P.2d 1041 (Colo. App. 1998), rev'd on other grounds, 10 P.3d 1231 (Colo. 2000). District court properly required that petitioner who improperly filed habeus corpus petition establish entitlement to relief under this rule by a preponderance of evidence since the motion should have been treated by the court as a motion under subsection (c)(2) of this rule. Kailey v. Colo. Dept. of Corr., 807 P.2d 563 (Colo. 1991). State is under no duty to present any evidence if it believes that petitioner has failed to meet that burden. Bresnahan v. Patterson, 352 F. Supp. 1180 (D. Colo. 1973). Court need not grant defendant's motion because it denies state's motion for dismissal at the conclusion of the defendant's evidence. Bresnahan v. People, 175 Colo. 286, 487 P.2d 551 (1971). As denial afforded no effect on whether defendant meets burden. A state motion to dismiss and its denial can be afforded no effect as to whether the defendant meets his burden under this rule. Bresnahan v. People, 175 Colo, 286, 487 P.2d 551 (1971). 5. Evidence Examined. Section (c) hearing criminal, not civil. A section (c) hearing is but one phase of a criminal proceeding, and it is not a civil proceeding. Bresnahan v. District Court, 164 Colo. 263, 434 P.2d 419 (1967). Trial judge may utilize the complete trial record insofar as possible and pertinent when he rules on a section (c) motion. Bresnahan v. People, 175 Colo. 286, 487 P.2d 551 (1971). And judge should identify all documents before him at time of trial. The trial judge should identify for the purposes of the record in the section (c) hearing all documents, letters, and reports which were before him as of the time he permitted the defendant to plead at trial, such identification should be made without regard to the ultimate admissibility of the particular document at the section (c) hearing, and the documents thus identified should then be furnished to counsel for petitioners for the purpose of inspection, copying, and use by counsel in the section (c) hearing as applicable rules permit. Bresnahan v. District Court, 164 Colo. 263, 434 P.2d 419 (1967). However, rule's purpose cannot be disposed of by reference to trial record alone. The purpose of a section (c) hearing is to take evidence pertinent to the allegations, which cannot be disposed of by reference to the trial record alone. Bresnahan v. People, 175 Colo. 286, 487 P.2d 551 (1971). And absence of transcript of prior hearing not necessarily equivalent to silent record. The absence of a transcript of a prior providency hearing is not necessarily equivalent to a silent record at the postconviction review hearing, and whether a knowing and voluntary guilty plea was entered by the defendant may be determined by any evidence adduced at his section (c) hearing. People v. Brewer, 648 P.2d 167 (Colo. App. 1982). Taking of depositions governed by criminal rules and statutory provision. The taking of any deposition to be used in a section (c) hearing is governed by the rules on criminal procedure and the Uniform Act to Secure the Attendance of Witnesses from Without a State in Criminal Proceedings, contained in § 16-9-201 et seq. Bresnahan v. District Court, 164 Colo. 263, 434 P.2d 419 (1967). And so subpoenas may be served on out-of-state residents to compel attendance. That the Rules of Civil Procedure do not govern the taking of depositions in connection with a section (c) hearing is without prejudice to the right of a petitioner to serve subpoenas in accordance with the Rules of Criminal Procedure and § 16-9-201 et seq. on out-of-state residents and thereby compel their attendance at a section (c) hearing. Bresnahan v. District Court, 164 Colo. 263, 434 P.2d 419 (1967). Defendant's attorney for prior hearing and sentencing may testify in postconviction relief hearing. Regarding the voluntariness of a guilty plea, the defendant's knowledge of the elements of the crime may be developed in a postconviction relief hearing, and the defendant's attorney for the prior hearing and sentencing may testify in the postconviction relief hearing that the defendant knew and understood all the elements of the crime charged. People v. Keenan, 185 Colo. 317, 524 P.2d 604 (1974). 6. Role of Petitioner and Judge. Petitioner's presence generally necessary. If an evidentiary hearing under section (c) is required, then the petitioner's presence would be necessary under most circumstances. Hooker v. People, 173 Colo. 226, 477 P.2d 376 (1970). And assistance of counsel essential, unless claim wholly unfounded. An accused has a right to counsel at every stage of the proceeding, and, in the absence of a knowing and intelligent waiver, the assistance of counsel is essential in postconviction proceedings, unless the asserted claim for relief is wholly unfounded. People v. Hubbard, 184 Colo. 243, 519 P.2d 945 (1974). Where no hearing is necessary, no error is committed where petitioner is absent. Hooker v. People, 173 Colo. 226, 477 P.2d 376 (1970). Or where case is submitted on agreed statements of facts. Applications for postconviction relief can appropriately be decided on the merits without a plenary evidentiary hearing and without the

163

expense, risk, and inconvenience of transporting the applicants, if in custody, from the prison to the courthouse; such a summary disposition is proper in all cases where there is no factual issue and where the case is submitted on an agreed statement of facts. Dabbs v. People, 175 Colo. 273, 486 P.2d 1053 (1971). Rule contemplates hearing wherever possible before trial judge who presided over the case. A disqualification because he is familiar with what occurred at the trial renders the rule anomalous; familiarity with the circumstances surrounding the trial does not render the judge a material witness. Bresnahan v. Luby, 160 Colo. 455, 418 P.2d 171 (1966). Trial court erred in not holding a hearing on defendant's motions and instead directing defense counsel to conduct an investigation of pertinent allegations and accepting counsel's conclusion that they lacked merit. Such procedure was inappropriate first because defense counsel should not be placed in a position of warranting the validity of his client's assertions, and second because a court in passing upon the validity of a party's assertions must reach its own independent evaluation of such assertions. People v. Breaman, 924 P.2d 1139 (Colo. App. 1996). Weight and credibility given evidence within court's province. The weight and credibility to be given to the testimony of witnesses in a section (c) hearing is within the province of the trial court. Lamb v. People, 174 Colo. 441, 484 P.2d 798 (1971). Where the trial court found polygraph evidence to be of little weight, it was fully entitled to make such finding as the trier of facts on a motion for postconviction relief. People v. Armstead, 179 Colo. 387, 501 P.2d 472 (1972). Under this rule, the trial court determines all issues of fact and law. Swift v. People, 174 Colo. 259, 488 P.2d 80 (1971). And makes findings and conclusions. In a section (c) hearing the trial court is bound to determine the issues and make findings of fact and conclusions of law. Bresnahan v. People, 175 Colo. 286, 487 P.2d 551 (1971). Question of whether defendant's burden of proof is met is answered by findings made by the trial judge. Bresnahan v. People, 175 Colo. 286, 487 P.2d 551 (1971). Page-long comments, analysis, and conclusions by the trial judge are sufficient to establish that the requirement of this rule, that findings and conclusions must be made, was met. People v. Crater, 182 Colo. 248, 512 P.2d 623 (1973). Judge's findings are based upon trial record and evidence taken as postconviction hearing. Bresnahan v. People, 175 Colo. 286, 487 P.2d 551 (1971). Findings and conclusions required under rule must sufficiently set forth basis of ruling. People v. Crater, 182 Colo. 248, 512 P.2d 623 (1973); People v. Breaman, 924 P.2d 1139 (Colo. App. 1996). Unconstitutional to place undue emphasis on findings not supported by record. A denial of due process under this rule will exist when the trial court places undue emphasis on findings not supported by the record, and the denial is compounded when the trial court arbitrarily refuses to permit defense counsel to point out to the court the fact that matters not in evidence are being considered. Noland v. People, 175 Colo. 6, 485 P.2d 112 (1971). Trial court lacked jurisdiction to entertain motion to reconsider order denying motion under section (b) of this rule filed more than 120 days after the date of sentencing. People v. Gresl, 89 P.3d 499 (Colo. App. 2003). F. Determination. 1. Relief Granted. Resentencing where long-time intervals and defendant's status changes from juvenile to adult. Long-time intervals between the arrest and the making of the charge, between the arrest and the arraignment, and between the arrest and time of the appointment of an attorney to represent a defendant require a reversal and a remand of a case to the trial court for the purpose of vacating its prior sentence and resentencing a defendant when defendant's sentence was adversely affected by a change in status from juvenile to adult. England v. People, 175 Colo. 236, 486 P.2d 1055 (1971). New trial required where defendant's trial attorneys fail to present any favorable evidence. Where the defendant fails to receive a fair trial because of the failure of his trial attorneys to present any of the evidence favorable to the defendant which was clearly available and discoverable by even rudimentary investigation, and as a result the damaging prosecution's version of the incident is allowed to remain uncontradicted and unimpeached, even though there was evidence to challenge it, the defendant was denied his constitutional right to a fair trial, which requires that the defendant's conviction be vacated and that he be afforded a new trial. People v. Moya, 180 Colo. 228, 504 P.2d 352 (1972). Inquiry into question of effectiveness of counsel. Where guilty plea subjected defendant to deportation proceedings, inquiry must begin with initial determination that defense counsel in criminal case was aware that his client was an alien, and therefore was reasonably required to research relevant immigration law. People v. Pozo, 746 P.2d 523 (Colo. 1987). Guilty plea vacated where no explanation of elements of charge given defendant. Where the record of the hearing held under section (c) is devoid of any evidence that the defendant understood the nature of the charge, and the only explanation of the charge to the defendant was in the wording of the information, which the court did not even read to him, and the court admits on the record that no explanation was given defendant of the elements of the charge, and there is no other indication that he received the requisite knowledge

164

from other sources, his plea of guilty was improperly accepted and had to be vacated. People v. Brown, 187 Colo. 244, 529 P.2d 1338 (1974). And where plea results in sentence far in excess to that promised. Where a guilty plea results in a sentence far in excess of that which was promised by the district attorney, the prisoner is entitled to have the sentence vacated and to go to trial on a plea of not guilty when he alleges that he has a valid defense to the charge. Roberts v. People, 158 Colo. 76, 404 P.2d 848 (1965). And violation not remedied by resentencing defendant to same term for lesser offense. Resentencing a defendant years later to substantially the same term for a lesser offense does not remedy the violation of the defendant's right to withdraw his guilty plea or have a determination at the time of the trial whether or not he was guilty "as charged" for a greater offense. Burman v. People, 172 Colo. 247, 472 P.2d 121 (1970). Amended sentence invalid where defendant and attorney not notified and not present. An amended sentence handed down by the trial court is invalid where neither the defendant nor his attorney are notified of resentencing, neither is present, and the substantial rights of defendant are violated by these omissions. People v. Emig, 177 Colo. 174, 493 P.2d 368 (1972). Where jury not qualified to fix death penalty, entry of life-imprisonment sentence authorized. In a first-degree case, where the United States supreme court affirms the guilty verdict and invalidates the punishment portion of the verdict only because the jury was not constitutionally qualified to fix the death penalty, leaving the sole statutory alternative as to punishment available to the jury that of life imprisonment, the entry by the court of such a judgment is a mere ministerial act within the power and authority of the trial judge under the terms and within the contemplation of section (c). Segura v. District Court, 179 Colo. 20, 498 P.2d 926 (1972). Defendant cannot serve a county jail sentence while incarcerated in the penitentiary, and, conversely, he cannot serve a penitentiary sentence in the county jail. People v. Emig, 177 Colo. 174, 493 P.2d 368 (1972). Defendant cannot serve a misdemeanor sentence consecutively to a felony sentence while being held by corrections department. People v. Green, 734 P.2d 616 (Colo. 1987); People v. Battle, 742 P.2d 952 (Colo. App. 1987). 2. Relief Denied. Where confession's admission harmless error, defendant not prejudiced. Even assuming that a confession was involuntarily made, where its admission is harmless error, there is no prejudice to any substantive right of the petitioner. Melton v. People, 157 Colo. 169, 401 P.2d 605 (1965), cert. denied, 382 U.S. 1014, 86 S. Ct. 624, 15 L. Ed. 2d 528 (1966). Assistance of counsel effective where no evidence full consideration not given case. The effective assistance of counsel is not denied the defendant where there is no evidence to support the assertion that counsel did not keep defendant informed or that anything but full consideration was given to his case. People v. Crater, 182 Colo. 248, 512 P.2d 623 (1973). And constitutional for attorney not retained to give postconviction testimony. Postconviction testimony of an attorney contacted, but not retained, on behalf of the defendant discloses no violation of defendant's constitutional right to counsel. LaBlanc v. People, 177 Colo. 250, 493 P.2d 1089 (1972). Petitioner found not entitled to relief for denial of effective assistance of counsel. People v. Stephenson, 187 Colo. 120, 528 P.2d 1313 (1974). District court made detailed and extensive findings in determining that, while defense counsel's performance fell below the range of competency expected from him in certain areas, such deficiencies did not result in prejudice to defendant. Therefore, trial court did not err in denying defendant's Crim. P. 35(c) motion. People v. Hendricks, 972 P.2d 1041 (Colo. App. 1998), rev'd on other grounds, 10 P.3d 1231 (Colo. 2000). Even if counsel had presented certain witness's testimony and other evidence of the events surrounding the giving of defendant's statements in a successful effort to suppress them, in light of overwhelming independent evidence that defendant committed this offense, there was no reasonable probability that the outcome of the trial would have been different. Similarly, trial court did not err in determining that trial counsel's performance was not deficient in deciding not to raise the issue of defendant's competency. People v. Hendricks, 972 P.2d 1041 (Colo. App. 1998), rev'd on other grounds, 10 P.3d 1231 (Colo. 2000). Voluntary guilty plea not set aside. A plea of guilty should not be set aside if a factual basis exists for the plea and if the defendant has knowledge of the elements of the crime and enters the plea voluntarily. People v. Hutton, 183 Colo. 388, 517 P.2d 392 (1973). And plea voluntary where considered, deliberate, advised choice. Where the record indicates a considered, deliberate, advised choice on the part of the defendant to change his plea from not guilty to guilty, the trial court's finding that the guilty plea is voluntary and not coerced is amply supported by the record of the proceedings at the time of the entry of the plea, it not being shown to be otherwise by any evidence presented at the hearing on a section (c) motion. Workman v. People, 174 Colo. 194, 483 P.2d 213 (1971). And where defendant represented by able counsel and understands elements of charge. Where at all relevant times the defendant was represented by able counsel and neither in his motion to vacate the guilty plea, nor in the hearing thereon conducted under this rule, was there any indication that he did not understand the elements of the charge, the substance of the circumstances surrounding the plea indicates that it was voluntarily made with an understanding of the elements of the charge. People v. Edwards, 186 Colo. 129, 526 P.2d 144 (1974). Guilty plea upheld where trial judge makes careful and thorough inquiry of defendant. Where the trial court fully complied with the requirements of Crim. P. 11, before granting a defendant's request to withdraw his previous plea and to enter a guilty plea, but the defendant alleges in his Crim. P. 35(c) motion that his plea of guilty was entered because of fear and duress, the plea will be upheld when the record reflects that the trial judge did with care and thoroughness make inquiry of the defendant in order to assure himself that the defendant's act of pleading guilty was his free and voluntary act. Lamb v. People, 174 Colo. 441, 484 P.2d 798 (1971). Where the record on its face shows that the trial court in a providency hearing advised the petitioner of the possible sentence term, the sentence imposed was within that range, and the trial court did not treat the offense as a second offense, an evidentiary hearing on the petitioner's contention that the sentencing court failed to properly inform him of the possible penalties for crimes to which he entered a guilty plea is not required and the motion for relief will be denied. Hyde v. Hinton, 180 Colo. 324, 505 P.2d 376 (1973). The failure to advise a defendant of the provisions of mandatory parole after the defendant has entered into a plea agreement and the stipulated sentence and mandatory parole period is less than the maximum sentence the court could have imposed upon the defendant is harmless error, thus the court affirmed the trial court's order summarily denying the defendant's motion under this rule. People v. Munoz, 9 P.3d 1201 (Colo. App. 2000). Failure to convey a plea offer is deficient performance by defense counsel and a violation of the standard practice that a defense attorney should follow, but the failure did not constitute prejudice against defendant requiring reversal because the record did not show reasonable probability that the defendant would have accepted the offer if it had been timely communicated. People v. Perry, 68 P.3d 472 (Colo. App. 2002). No credit for presentence jail time where time taken into consideration in sentencing. Where the defendant is sentenced by the judge after the judge is advised of the time that the defendant has spent in jail before the sentence is imposed, where the defendant is advised by the judge at the time sentence is imposed that the time he spent in custody was taken into consideration in determining his sentence, and where the sentence imposed, plus the time spent in custody, is far less than the maximum penalty prescribed by law, the defendant is not entitled to credit for presentence jail time through a postconviction proceeding. People v. Puls, 176 Colo. 71, 489 P.2d 323 (1971). Failure to provide transcript on appeal found not to prejudice defendant. People v. Shearer, 181 Colo. 237, 508 P.2d 1249 (1973). The equitable doctrine of laches may be invoked to bar postconviction relief. People v. Bravo, 692 P.2d 325 (Colo. App. 1984). Defendant pleading guilty was sufficiently informed of mens rea element of the offense of rape by information read to him that contained the term "feloniously" and, therefore, postconviction relief was properly denied. Wilson v. People, 708 P.2d 792 (Colo. 1985). Present need standard for postconviction relief not established under collateral attack statute for 30-year-old conviction for violations of municipal ordinances. City and County of Denver v. Rhinehart, 742 P.2d 948 (Colo. App. 1987). The trial court was correct in denying defendant's motion under this rule since defendant, who was extradited to Colorado for trial on two charges, was not entitled to credit in second sentence for time spent in confinement prior to imposition of first sentence, if the first sentence had allowed presentence confinement credit for that period of time. People v. Garcia, 757 P.2d 1110 (Colo. App. 1988). Court correctly denied Crim. P. 35(c) motion and held that no conflict of interest existed to defeat defendant's right to counsel. Public defender represented both the defendant and another person against whom the authorities had no evidence, but whom the defendant had admitted to be a co-participant in the burglary. The court stated that the defendant could not seek to profit from the collapse of a self-created situation. People v. Wood, 844 P.2d 1299 (Colo. App. 1992). Defendant may not seek review of felony conviction under section (c) because, under the plea agreement, judgment and sentencing did not enter but were deferred. People v. Kazadi, __ P.3d __ (Colo. App. 2011). When a criminal defendant, who pled guilty to charge, dies while his appeal for relief from his sentence is pending, an abatement of the underlying conviction is not warranted. People v. Rickstrew, 961 P.2d 1139 (Colo. App. 1998). A witness's exercise of the privilege against self-incrimination does not give rise to a violation of the defendant's right to a fair trial or to present a defense. People v. Coit, 50 P.3d 936 (Colo. App. 2002). Because the United States supreme court's decision in Crawford v. Washington, 541 U.S. 36 (2004), established a procedural, not a substantive, rule and it was not a "watershed" rule, Crawford does not apply retroactively to cases on collateral review where the defendant's conviction became final prior to Crawford. Under prior case law, out-of-court statements properly admitted. People v. Edwards, 101 P.3d 1118 (Colo. App. 2004), aff'd, 129 P.3d 977 (Colo. 2006). G. Successive Motions. Repetitive postconviction proceedings with some legal and factual claims not afforded by constitution. Although postconviction relief is grounded upon constitutional principles, it does not afford any person the right to clog the judicial machinery with repetitive postconviction proceedings seeking relief on the same principles of law and the same factual claims. People ex rel. Wyse v. District Court, 180 Colo. 88, 503 P.2d 154 (1972). Defendant is unauthorized to file successive motions based upon same or similar allegations in the hope that a sympathetic judicial ear may eventually be found. People v. Hubbard, 184 Colo. 243, 519 P.2d 945 (1974). Especially where defendant fails to seek review of denial of first similar claim. Where the defendant fails to avail himself of the right to have review of the propriety of the trial court's denial of his motion and thereafter files a second motion to vacate in which he reurges the same grounds raised in the first motion, the trial court under section (c), need not entertain such second and successive motion. Henson v. People, 163 Colo. 302, 430 P.2d 475 (1967). The court is not required to entertain successive motions for similar postconviction relief on behalf of the same prisoner. Graham v. Zavaras, 877 P.2d 363 (Colo. 1994); People v. Harmon, 3 P.3d 480 (Colo. App. 2000). Standards on successive motions for review. In the case of a successive motion for postconviction review, the appropriate consideration is whether the defendant's constitutional claim has been fully and finally litigated in the prior postconviction proceeding. People v. Billips, 652 P.2d 1060 (Colo. 1982). The doctrine of res judicata is not an appropriate standard for the resolution of postconviction claims. People v. Billips, 652 P.2d 1060 (Colo. 1982). Collateral estoppel inapplicable. Although the doctrine of estoppel is as applicable to criminal proceedings as it is to civil proceedings, it is inapplicable in a section (c) proceeding. People v. Wright, 662 P.2d 489 (Colo. App. 1982). All allegations relating to constitutional violations should be included in single motion. In light of the right to counsel in postconviction proceedings, all allegations relating to the violation of a defendant's constitutional rights should be included in a single section (c) motion. People v. Hubbard, 184 Colo. 243, 519 P.2d 945 (1974). All allegations relating to the violation of defendant's constitutional rights should be included in a single section (c) motion. People v. Bucci, 184 Colo. 367, 520 P.2d 580 (1974). And failure to do so results in summary denial of second similar application. The failure of an application to contain all factual and legal contentions will, unless special circumstances exist, ordinarily result in a second application containing such grounds being summarily denied. People v. Scheer, 184 Colo. 15, 518 P.2d 833 (1974). And prisoner deliberately withholding ground for postconviction relief waives right to second hearing. If a prisoner deliberately withholds one of two grounds for postconviction relief at the time of filing his first application, he may be deemed to have waived his right to a hearing on the second ground in subsequent application. This interpretation is not intended to eliminate any judicial determination on the merits of a prisoner's claims, but rather is to ensure that all claims are considered in one proceeding. People v. Hubbard, 184 Colo. 243, 519 P.2d 945 (1974). Second motion dismissed unless failure to include newly-asserted grounds in first motion excusable. If a second or successive motion is filed, it may be summarily dismissed without a hearing unless the trial judge finds that the failure to include newly-asserted grounds for relief in the first motion is excusable. People v. Hubbard, 184 Colo. 243, 519 P.2d 945 (1974). Such as where defendant urges incompetency of counsel representing him in first hearing. Ordinarily, a defendant would be expected to raise the matter of competency of counsel in a section (c) proceeding, but where his trial counsel is still representing him, and this same counsel prepares the motion of a new trial which does not mention the subject and a new counsel then comes into the case, then under these particular circumstances, if the defendant wishes to urge the point of incompetency of his initial counsel, he may attempt to raise the point in a further section (c) proceeding in the trial court. Stone v. People, 174 Colo. 504, 485 P.2d 495 (1971). Such as where the factual and legal allegations raised in the second motion have not previously been fully and finally decided. People v. Wimer, 681 P.2d 967 (Colo. App. 1983). In the absence of special circumstances, courts need not consider successive requests for the same relief based on the same or similar allegations on behalf of the same prisoner. People v. Holmes, 819 P.2d 541 (Colo. App. 1991). Because defendant did not know of the changed double jeopardy standard when the defendant filed his first motion under section (c), the provisions of subsection (c)(1) mandate that the defendant's application for relief is not barred under the provisions of subsection (c)(3). People v. Allen, 843 P.2d 97 (Colo. App. 1992). Defendant's actions in specifically withdrawing those claims from the trial court's consideration at an earlier proceeding which he argues should have been addressed in the second proceeding, constitute an abandonment of those claims. People v. Abeyta, 923 P.2d 318 (Colo. App. 1996). Defendant's section (c) motion raising cognizable constitutional claims is not successive merely because he had unsuccessfully attempted to raise those claims in his prior appeal. People v. Diaz, 985 P.2d 83 (Colo. App. 1999). Defendant's postconviction motion based on the voluntariness of his guilty plea as it related to the quality of his counsel was properly denied as successive under subsection (c)(3)(VII) of this rule, where lengthy evidentiary hearing was held on defendant's Crim. P. 32(d) motion claiming that his plea was not knowing, voluntary, and intelligent due to ineffective assistance of counsel. People v. Vondra, 240 P.3d 493 (Colo. App. 2010). Missouri v. Seibert, 542 U.S. 600 (2004), not a "watershed rule of criminal procedure". Therefore it is not applied retroactively to defendant's conviction that was final prior to its announcement. Court properly denied hearing on defendant's section (c) motion because it did not meet the exception in subsection (c)(3)(VI)(b). People v. McDowell, 219 P.3d 332 (Colo. App. 2009). H. Review on Appeal. Appellate review of decisions made under this rule may be made. Henry v. Tinsley, 344 F.2d 109 (10th Cir. 1965); Ruark v. Tinsley, 350 F.2d 315 (10th Cir. 1965). Including review of order denying relief. Previously, it was not clear whether an order denying relief sought under this rule was appealable. Nevertheless, denial of such relief can now be appealed. Smith v. Tinsley, 223 F. Supp. 68 (D. Colo. 1963). An order of a trial court denying a motion to vacate is a final order reviewable on appeal. Henson v. People, 163 Colo. 302, 430 P.2d 475 (1967). Question raised for first time in postconviction motion properly before appellate court. A question presented on appeal which was raised for the first time in a postconviction motion and has not been previously considered or disposed of on appeal is properly before an appellate court. Trujillo v. People, 178 Colo. 136, 496 P.2d 1026 (1972). Including matters not raised in new trial motion. While it is true that on appeal an appellate court will not consider a matter not raised in a new trial motion, this constraint does not apply to a section (c) motion. Lucero v. People, 173 Colo. 94, 476 P.2d 257 (1970). But matters not contained in motion cannot be considered on appeal. The ground that certain exhibits were erroneously received upon trial because of an alleged lack of foundation, not having been contained in the section (c) motion filed in the trial court, cannot be raised for the first time on appeal. Walters v. People, 166 Colo. 90, 441 P.2d 647 (1968). Issue not raised in motion or hearing not reviewable. An issue not raised in either section (c) motion or at the trial court hearing is not properly before the appellate court for review. People v. McClellan, 183 Colo. 176, 515 P.2d 1127 (1973); People v. Simms, 185 Colo. 214, 523 P.2d 463 (1974). Relief pursuant to section (b) of this rule is discretionary and the exercise of the sentencing court's discretion is generally not subject to appeal. However, defendant's appeal was not barred where the sentencing court declined to entertain the defendant's motion and exercise its discretion for the reason that it erroneously considered itself bound to impose a sentence to the department of corrections by statute. Shipley v. People, 45 P.3d 1277 (Colo. 2002). Defendant's claim of statutory violation in imposition of consecutive sentences is barred in postconviction proceeding because it was available to defendant to be raised on his direct appeal and was not raised at that time. People v. Banks, 924 P.2d 1161 (Colo. App. 1996). To merely charge that a trial proceeding was "unconstitutional" is wholly insufficient as a basis for relief or review in an appellate court. Peirce v. People, 158 Colo, 81, 404 P.2d 843 (1965). Where motion specifies grounds for relief, trial court conducts hearing before appeal determined. Before the merits of an appeal can be determined, it might be necessary first that the trial court conduct a hearing into the merits of the allegations made in the petition for section (c) relief where the motion sets forth facts constituting proper grounds for relief. Roberts v. People, 158 Colo. 76, 404 P.2d 848 (1965); Black v. People, 166 Colo. 358, 443 P.2d 732 (1968). And hearing should be granted where facts supporting claim appear outside record. Where the very basis of defendant's claim of error is that the trial court should have granted an evidentiary hearing because the facts he alleges in his motion do not appear in the record, then, however regular the proceedings might appear from the trial transcript, it still might be the case that the petitioner did not make an intelligent and understanding waiver of his constitutional rights at trial if the facts on which petitioner's claim is predicated are outside the record, and the court should have granted evidentiary hearing. Von Pickrell v. People, 163 Colo. 591, 431 P.2d 1003 (1967). Otherwise, state to furnish transcript on appeal to justify trial court's determination. Where the defendant asserts that his plea was involuntary for reasons not appearing on the record, it is incumbent on the state to provide the appellate court with a transcript which shows that the trial court at the time of a guilty plea made such inquiry as to justify its determination without a hearing on a section (c) petition that defendant's plea was voluntarily made. Von Pickrell v. People, 163 Colo. 591, 431 P.2d 1003 (1967). Trial court's judgment not disturbed where evidence amply supports findings. Where the evidence before the trial court amply supports the findings and holding of the trial court, the judgment of the trial

168

court on a section (c) motion will not be disturbed on review. Lamb v. People, 174 Colo. 441, 484 P.2d 798 (1971). Vacation of guilty plea not upset absent extreme circumstances. When a trial judge holds a hearing on a section (c) motion and determines after hearing the testimony that the interests of justice require the vacation of a guilty plea and that a trial be held on the question of guilt or innocence, this determination will not be upset by an appellate court, except in extreme circumstances. People v. Gantner, 173 Colo. 92, 476 P.2d 998 (1970). Denial of motion upheld where sufficient evidence to convict the defendant is found. People v. Grass, 180 Colo. 346, 505 P.2d 1301 (1973). Including testimony of defendant at postconviction hearing concerning truth of probation report. Where a motion under this rule asserts that the defendant was denied the opportunity to confront the witnesses furnishing the information contained in a probation report which he contends was incorrect and prejudicial to him, but at the hearing on this motion defendant was permitted to testify concerning the truth of the matters contained in the probation report and to give his explanation of them, the record supports the trial court's denial of the motion. Wolford v. People, 178 Colo. 203, 496 P.2d 1011 (1972). Trial court errs in not setting aside conviction where massive, prejudicial publicity. A trial court errs in determining that it cannot compare present day standards of newspaper conduct to past happenings in denying a motion under section (c) to set aside the conviction of a defendant, since the line of cases culminating in Sheppard v. Maxwell, 384 U.S. 333, 86 S. Ct. 1507, 16 L. Ed. 2d 600 (1966), hold that the publicity can be so "massive, pervasive, and prejudicial" that the denial of a fair trial may be presumed, and the court therefore also erred in holding that a showing must be made that the jurors were actually and directly affected by the publicity. Walker v. People, 169 Colo. 467, 458 P.2d 238 (1969). And order denying motion reversed where rule on judicial plea-bargain inquiry not followed. The failure of a trial court to follow the requirements of Crim. P. 11, as to the inquiry to be conducted before the acceptance of a plea necessitates a reversal of the order of the trial court denying defendant's section (c) motion. Westendorf v. People, 171 Colo. 123, 464 P.2d 866 (1970). Denial of motion reversed with directions to conduct new hearing. People v. Burger, 180 Colo. 415, 505 P.2d 1308 (1973). Trial court erred in denying defendant's motion where defendant was not advised that, in addition to any term of incarceration, a separate and additional term of parole was a required consequence of his plea. People v. Espinoza, 985 P.2d 68 (Colo. App. 1999). Setting definite execution date in order granting stay of execution not unconstitutional. The fact that an appellate court sets definite execution date in order granting a stay of execution pending the determination of postconviction relief is not "suggestion of predetermination" in violation of due process and does not constitute an implied direction to deny petitioner relief. Bell v. Patterson, 279 F. Supp. 760 (D. Colo. 1968), aff'd, 402 F.2d 394 (10th Cir. 1968), cert. denied, 403 U.S. 955, 91 S. Ct. 2279, 29 L. Ed. 2d 865 (1971). Court of appeals has jurisdiction to decide if trial court erred in granting a new trial under postconviction relief motion when issues in motion were brought pursuant to the "other remedies" portion of this rule. People v. Naranjo, 821 P.2d 836 (Colo. App. 1991). An order of a trial court granting or denying a motion filed under section (c) of this rule is a final order reviewable on appeal. Such order becomes final after the period in which to perfect an appeal expires. People v. Janke, 852 P.2d 1271 (Colo. App. 1992); People v. Ovalle, 51 P.3d 1073 (Colo. App. 2002). Since an appellate court is not in as good a position as the trial court to make factual findings, the court of appeals erred in vacating respondent's conviction where the trial court denied the section (c) motion without a hearing. People v. Simpson, 69 P.3d 79 (Colo. 2003). Trial court did not abuse its discretion in denying defendant's Crim. P. 35(c) motion without an evidentiary hearing on ineffective assistance of counsel claim. The defendant received sufficient notice from the Crim. P. 11 advisement form and had an affirmative obligation to request clarification at the providency hearing. People v. DiGuglielmo, 33 P.3d 1248 (Colo. App. 2001). Once a final order under this rule is entered, the only means by which a trial court may alter, amend, or vacate such order is by an appropriate motion under C.R.C.P. 59 or 60. Accordingly, people's argument that the doctrine of law of the case authorizes trial court to reconsider final order is rejected. People v. Janke, 852 P.2d 1271 (Colo. App. 1992). I. Federal Habeas Corpus. In Colorado, habeas corpus is not a substitute for review by an appeal. Martinez v. Patterson, 382 F.2d 1002 (10th Cir. 1967). Federal relief denied where state remedies under this rule not exhausted. A federal court will deny "habeas corpus" where one fails to exhaust state remedies by failing to seek state review of a trial court's denial of a motion under this rule. Breckenridge v. Patterson, 374 F.2d 857 (10th Cir.), cert. dismissed, 389 U.S. 801, 88 S. Ct. 9, 19 L. Ed. 2d 56 (1967); Kanan v. Denver Dist. Court, 438 F.2d 521 (10th Cir. 1971). Where the petitioner fails to raise any of his allegations of error in state courts either by direct appeal or by means of this rule, he has not exhausted his state remedies on these issues

and cannot obtain habeas corpus relief from the federal courts. Thompson v. Ricketts, 500 F.
Supp. 688 (D. Colo. 1980). But mere availability of possible remedy under this rule cannot
preclude federal writ of "habeas corpus". Smith v. Tinsley, 223 F. Supp. 68 (D. Colo. 1963). But
see Breckenridge v. Patterson, 374 F.2d 857 (10th Cir.), cert. dismissed, 389 U.S. 801, 88 S. Ct.
9, 19 L. Ed. 2d 56 (1967); Kanan v. Denver Dist. Court, 438 F.2d 521 (10th Cir. 1971).
Postconviction hearing unnecessary where state supreme court decision already controls
question. Where the Colorado supreme court reaches a conclusion on the substantive issue
stating it in such a way that under ordinary circumstances a trial court would feel bound by the
decision, even though it is only dictum, and would therefore deny a motion made pursuant to
section (c), on the grounds that the Colorado supreme court has already decided the question,
then, for all practical purposes, the petitioner has exhausted his state remedies, and a petition for
federal "habeas corpus" is proper. Peters v. Dillon, 227 F. Supp. 487 (D. Colo. 1964), aff'd, 341
F.2d 337 (10th Cir. 1965). State remedies exhausted by prior prosecution of state "habeas"
action. Where the federal "habeas corpus" act requires that a defendant exhaust one of his
available alternative state remedies, the maintenance of a motion under this rule is not necessary
where there has been prior prosecution of a "habeas corpus" action. Martinez v. Tinsley, 241 F.
Supp. 730 (D. Colo. 1965).

Rule 36 - Clerical Mistakes

Clerical mistakes in judgments, orders, or other parts of the record and errors in the record
arising from oversight or omission may be corrected by the court at any time and after such
notice, if any, as the court orders.

Colo. R. Crim. P. 36

Annotation Correction of error discretionary. The language of this rule indicates that the
decision to correct an error is discretionary rather than mandatory. Quintana v. People, 200
Colo. 258, 613 P.2d 1308 (1980). Judge may correct grammar and strike meaningless
repetitions. A judge may correct or amend a record, to make certain perfunctory changes to
correct grammar, and to strike meaningless repetitions. People v. Emeson, 179 Colo. 308, 500
P.2d 368 (1972). And may correct mittimus to reflect sentence actually imposed. Where a
mittimus recites what purports to be the sentence imposed, but a clerical error in the mittimus
quite obviously does not reflect the actual sentence intended to be imposed by the sentencing
judge, the order of the trial judge correcting the mittimus to reflect the sentences actually
imposed by the sentencing judge is the proper procedure. People v. Mason, 188 Colo. 410, 535
P.2d 506 (1975). But cannot correct mistakes after commutation of sentence. Since the courts
lack jurisdiction to alter or amend a commuted sentence imposed by the executive, a motion
under this rule to correct clerical oversights in sentencing may not be granted after
commutation. People v. Quintana, 42 Colo. App. 477, 601 P.2d 637 (1979), aff'd, 200 Colo. 258,
613 P.2d 1308 (1980). Clerical error in judgment of conviction, sentence, and mittimus
concerning the sentences imposed for sexual assault and kidnapping is proper grounds for
remand to correct the error. People v. Turner, 730 P.2d 333 (Colo. App. 1986).

Rule 37 - Appeals from County Court

(a) Filing Notice of Appeal and Docketing Appeal. The district attorney may appeal a question
of law, and the defendant may appeal a judgment of the county court in a criminal action under
simplified procedure to the district court of the county. To appeal the appellant shall, within 35
days after the date of entry of the judgment or the denial of posttrial motions, whichever is later,
file notice of appeal in the county court, post such advance costs as may be required for the
preparation of the record and serve a copy of the notice of appeal upon the appellee. He shall
also, within such 35 days, docket the appeal in the district court and pay the docket fee. No
motion for new trial or in arrest of judgment shall be required as a prerequisite to an appeal, but
such motions if filed shall be pursuant to Rule 33(b) of these Rules.

(b) Contents of Notice of Appeal and Designation of Record. The notice of appeal shall state
with particularity the alleged errors of the county court or other grounds relied upon for the
appeal, and shall include a stipulation or designation of the evidence and other proceedings
which the appellant desires to have included in the record certified to the district court. If the
appellant intends to urge upon appeal that the judgment or a finding or conclusion is unsupported
by the evidence or is contrary to the evidence, the appellant shall include in the record a
transcript of all evidence relevant to such finding or conclusion. The appellee shall have 14 days
after service upon him of the notice of appeal to file with the clerk of the county court and serve
upon the appellant a designation of any additional parts of the transcript or record which he
deems necessary. The advance cost of preparing the additional record shall be posted by the

appellant with the clerk of the county court within 7 days after service upon him of the appellee's designation, or the appeal will be dismissed. If the district court finds that any part of the additional record designated by the appellee was unessential to a complete understanding of the questions raised by the appeal, it shall order the appellee to reimburse the appellant for the cost advanced for the preparation of such part without regard to the outcome of the appeal.

(c) Contents of Record on Appeal. Upon the filing of a notice of appeal and upon the posting of any advance costs by the appellant, as are required for the preparation of a record, unless the appellant is granted leave to proceed as an indigent, the clerk of the county court shall prepare and issue as soon as possible a record of the proceedings in the county court, including the summons and complaint or warrant, the separate complaint if any has been issued, and the judgment. The record shall also include a transcription or a joint stipulation of such part of the actual evidence and other proceedings as the parties designate. If the proceedings have been recorded electrically, the transcription of designated evidence and proceedings shall be prepared in the office of the clerk of the court, either by him or her or under his or her supervision, within 42 days after the filing of the notice of appeal or within such additional time as may be granted by the county court. The clerk shall notify in writing the opposing parties of the completion of the record, and such parties shall have 14 days within which to file objections. If none are received, the record shall be certified forthwith by the CLERK. If objections are made, the parties shall be called for hearing and the objections settled by the county judge and the record then certified.

(d) Filing of Record. When the record has been duly certified and any additional fees therefor paid, it shall be filed with the clerk of the district court by the clerk of the county court, and the opposing parties shall be notified by the clerk of the county court of such filing.

(e) Briefs. A written brief setting out matters relied upon as constituting error and outlining any arguments to be made shall be filed in the district court by the appellant within 21 days after certification of the record. A copy of the appellant's brief shall be served upon the appellee. The appellee may file an answering brief within 21 days after such service. A reply brief may be filed within 14 days after service of the answering brief. In the discretion of the district court, the time for filing briefs and answers may be extended.

(f) Stay of Execution. Pending the docketing of the appeal, a stay of execution shall be granted by the county court upon request. If a sentence of imprisonment has been imposed, the defendant may be required to post bail, and if a fine and costs have been imposed, a deposit of the amount thereof may be required by the county court. Upon a request for stay of execution made any time after the docketing of the appeal, such action may be taken by the district court. Stays of execution granted by the county court or district court and, with the written consent of the sureties if any, bonds posted with such courts shall remain in effect until after final disposition of the appeal, unless modified by the district court.

(g) Trials de Novo; Penalty Not Increased. If for any reason an adequate record cannot be certified to the district court the case shall be tried de novo in that court. No action on appeal shall result in an increase in penalty.

(h) Judgment; How Enforced. Unless there is further review by the Supreme Court upon writ of certiorari pursuant to the rules of such court, after final disposition of the appeal the judgment on appeal entered by the district court shall be certified to the county court for action as directed by the district court, except in cases tried de novo by the district court or in cases in which the district court modifies the county court judgment, and in such cases, the judgment on appeal shall be that of the district court and so enforceable.

(i) Appeals to Superior Court. In counties in which a superior court has been established, appeals from the county court shall be taken to the superior court rather than the district court. All of the provisions of this section governing appeals from the county court to the district court are applicable when the appeal is taken to the superior court, and the term "district court" as used in this section shall be understood to include the superior court.

Colo. R. Crim. P. 37

Source: a, b, c, and e amended and adopted December 14, 2011, effective 7/1/2012; c amended and effective 1/16/2014.

Annotation Law reviews. For article, "Pronouncements of the U.S. Supreme Court Relating to the Criminal Law Field: 1985-1986", which discusses a recent case relating to the right of appeal, see 15 Colo. Law. 1613 (1986). Appeals between county and superior courts. The district court has no jurisdiction to interfere with the appeal process between the county and superior courts. Petry v. County Court, 666 P.2d 1125 (Colo. App. 1983). This rule does not give authority to the court of appeals to hear an appeal of a district court judgment modifying a county court decision. The modified county judgment becomes a district court judgment only for purposes of enforcement. People v. Smith, 874 P.2d 452 (Colo. App. 1993). Because appellant's conviction originated in a municipal court of record, appellant had 30 days following the judgment of conviction to file the notice of appeal pursuant to § 13-10-116 , this rule, and C.M.C.R. 237. Normandin v. Town of Parachute, 91 P.3d 383 (Colo. 2004). Finality attaches upon expiration of 30 days from judgment. Where judgment and sentence had been entered in the county court, at the expiration of 30 days-no notice of appeal having been filed-it became final. Mills v. People, 181 Colo. 168, 509 P.2d 594 (1973). And time to file appeal not automatically extended by new trial motion. The filing of a motion for a new trial does not have the effect of automatically extending the time to file a notice of appeal as prescribed by this rule. Mills v. People, 181 Colo. 168, 509 P.2d 594 (1973). Appeals filing period begins to run when the judgment becomes final-that is when sentence has been passed-even though sentencing has been delayed for over a year due to defendant's voluntary unavailability. Hellman v. Rhodes, 741 P.2d 1258 (Colo. 1987). For purposes of appeal, a final judgment must include the sentence. Therefore, after the sentence was vacated on appeal, an order withdrawing plea of guilty was not a final judgment. Ellsworth v. People, 987 P.2d 264 (Colo. 1999). A trial de novo conducted by the district court is not a review of the county court judgment; it is an entirely new proceeding. Bovard v. People, 99 P.3d 585 (Colo. 2004). Only in cases tried de novo by the district court will the district court judgment be subject to direct appeal. Justifiably, then, the defendant may seek direct appeal when the district court enters its judgment from a de novo trial. Bovard v. People, 99 P.3d 585 (Colo. 2004). Certiorari review does not suffice as an appellate review from a final judgment of the district court. Bovard v. People, 99 P.3d 585 (Colo. 2004). Transcript of all evidence presented to lower court relevant to challenged ruling required. Where an appellant challenges a ruling that was based, either in whole or in part, on evidence presented to the lower court, a transcript of all evidence pertaining to the decision must be included in the record; however, the appellant is not required by Crim. P. 37(b), to include in the record a transcript of evidence that is not relevant to the issues raised on appeal. Holcomb v. City & County of Denver, 199 Colo. 251, 606 P.2d 858 (1980); People v. Campbell, 174 P.3d 860 (Colo. App. 2007). Filing a notice of appeal in the county court is not a jurisdictional requirement of subsection (a) of this rule, but timely docketing an appeal in the district court is sufficient to invoke the appellate jurisdiction of that court. Peterson v. People, 113 P.3d 706 (Colo. 2005). Timely filing of a brief is not jurisdictional under this rule, and a trial court's discretion to extend the time to file a brief under section (e) is not restricted to extensions requested within the normal filing time. People v. Chapman, 192 Colo. 322, 557 P.2d 1211 (1977). Excusable or inexcusable neglect considered in deciding whether to reinstate after late brief. Although no "excusable neglect" prerequisite appears in section (e), the court may consider excusable or inexcusable neglect among other factors in deciding whether to grant a motion to reinstate after late filing of a brief. People v. Chapman, 192 Colo. 322, 557 P.2d 1211 (1977). Unavailability or inadequacy of record mandates trial de novo. If the record is unavailable, a defendant should not suffer for the lack thereof, but should be afforded an entirely new trial; if a record is inadequate, the district court must grant a trial de novo under section (g). It has no discretion in the matter. Hawkins v. Superior Court, 196 Colo. 86, 580 P.2d 811 (1978). Applied in People v. Lessar, 629 P.2d 577 (Colo. 1981); People v. Luna, 648 P.2d 624 (Colo. App. 1982); Waltemeyer v. People ex rel. City of Arvada, 658 P.2d 264 (Colo. 1983); Dike v. People, 30 P.3d 197 (Colo. 2001).

Rule 37.1 - Interlocutory Appeal from County Court

(a) Grounds. The prosecuting attorney may file an interlocutory appeal in the district court from a ruling of a county court granting a motion made in advance of trial by the defendant for return of property and to suppress evidence or granting a motion to suppress evidence or granting a motion to suppress an extra-judicial confession or admission; provided that the prosecuting attorney certifies to the judge who granted such motion and to the district court that the appeal is not taken for purposes of delay and that the evidence is a substantial part of the proof of the charge pending against the defendant.

(b) Filing Notice of Appeal. The prosecuting attorney shall file the notice of appeal with the clerk of the district court and shall serve the defendant and the clerk of the trial court with a copy thereof. Such notice of appeal shall be filed within 14 days of the entry of the order being appealed and any docket fee shall be paid at the time of the filing.

(c) Contents of Record on Appeal. The record for an interlocutory appeal shall consist of the information or charging document, the motions filed by the defendant or defendants and the grounds stated in section (a) above, a transcript of all testimony taken at the hearing on said motions and such exhibits or reasonable copies, facsimiles, or photographs thereof as the parties may designate (subject to the provisions in C.A.R. 11(b) pertaining to exhibits of bulk), the order of court ruling on said motions and the date, if one has been fixed, that the case is set for trial or a certificate by the clerk that the case has not been set for trial. The record shall be filed within 14 days of the date of filing the notice of appeal, and may be supplemented by order of the district court.

(d) Briefs. Within 14 days after the record has been filed in the district court, the prosecuting attorney shall file an opening brief. Within 14 days after service of said opening brief, the defendant shall file an answer brief, and the prosecuting attorney shall have 7 days after service of said answer brief to file a reply brief.

(e) Disposition of Cause. Unless oral argument is ordered by the court and it rules on the record and in the presence of the parties, the decision of the court shall be by written opinion, copies of which shall be transmitted by the clerk of the court by mail to the trial judge and to all parties. No petition for rehearing shall be permitted. A certified copy of the judgment and directions to the county court, and a copy of the written opinion, if any, shall constitute the mandate of the district court, concluding the appeal and restoring jurisdiction to the county court. Such mandate shall issue and be transmitted by the clerk of the court by mail to the trial judge and all parties on the 44SUPth/SUP day after the district court's oral or written order, unless the district court is given notice by one of the parties that it has sought further review by the supreme court upon a writ of certiorari pursuant to the rules of that court, in which case the mandate shall issue upon notification that certiorari has been denied or upon receiving the remittitur of the supreme court.

(f) Time. The time limits herein may only be enlarged by order of the appropriate court before the existing time limit has expired.

(g) If no procedure is specifically prescribed by this rule, the court shall look to the Rules of Appellate Procedure for guidance.

(h) Nothing in this Rule 37.1 shall be construed to deprive the county court of jurisdiction to consider bail issues during the pendency of the interlocutory appeal.

Annotation

The 10-day time frame under subsection (b) for filing an interlocutory appeal is to be calculated according to C.A.R. 26(a), with intervening Saturdays, Sundays, and legal holidays excluded in the computation. People v. Zhuk, 239 P.3d 437 (Colo. 2010).

Colo. R. Crim. P. 37.1

Source: Added July 16, 1992, effective 11/1/1992; b to e amended and adopted December 14, 2011, effective 7/1/2012.

Rule 38 - Appeals from the District Court

Appeals from the district court shall be conducted pursuant to the Colorado Appellate Rules.

Colo. R. Crim. P. 38

Source: Entire rule amended and adopted June 27, 2002, effective 7/1/2002.

Rule 39 - Stays

The filing of an interlocutory appeal or an appeal from an order that dismisses one or more counts of a charging document prior to trial automatically stays all proceedings until final determination of the appeal, unless the appellate court lifts such stay in whole or in part.

Colo. R. Crim. P. 39

Source: Entire rule added and adopted June 27, 2002, effective 7/1/2002.

Supplementary and Special Proceedings

Rule 41 - Search, Seizure, and Confession

(a)Authority to Issue Warrant. A search warrant authorized by this Rule may be issued by any judge of a court of record.

(b)Grounds for Issuance. A search warrant may be issued under this Rule to search for and seize any property:

(1) Which is stolen or embezzled; or

(2) Which is designed or intended for use as a means of committing a criminal offense; or

(3) Which is or has been used as a means of committing a criminal offense; or

(4) The possession of which is illegal; or

(5) Which would be material evidence in a subsequent criminal prosecution in this state or in another state; or

(6) The seizure of which is expressly required, authorized, or permitted by any statute of this state; or

(7) Which is kept, stored, maintained, transported, sold, dispensed, or possessed in violation of a statute of this state, under circumstances involving a serious threat to public safety or order, or to public health.

(c) Application for Search Warrant.

(1) A search warrant shall issue only on affidavit sworn or affirmed to before the judge, except as provided in (c)(3). Such affidavit shall relate facts sufficient to:

(I) Identify or describe, as nearly as may be, the premises, person, place, or thing to be searched;

(II) Identify or describe, as nearly as may be, the property to be searched for, seized, or inspected;

(III) Establish the grounds for issuance of the warrant, or probable cause to believe that such grounds exist; and

(IV) Establish probable cause to believe that the property to be searched for, seized, or inspected is located at, in, or upon the premises, person, place, or thing to be searched.

(2) The affidavit required by this section may include sworn testimony reduced to writing and signed under oath by the witness giving the testimony before issuance of the warrant. A copy of the affidavit and a copy of the transcript of testimony taken in support of the request for a search warrant shall be attached to the search warrant filed with the court.

(2.5) A no-knock search warrant, which means, for purposes of this section, a search warrant authorized by the court to be executed by law enforcement officers through a forcible entry without first announcing their identity, purpose, and authority, shall be issued only if the affidavit for such warrant:

(I) Complies with the provisions of subsections (1) and (2) of this section (c) and section 16-3-303(4), C.R.S.;

(II) Specifically requests the issuance of a no-knock search warrant;

(III) Relates sufficient circumstances to support the issuance of a no-knock search warrant;

(IV) Has been reviewed and approved for legal sufficiency and signed by a district attorney with the date and his or her attorney registration number on the affidavit, pursuant to section 20-1-106.1(2), C.R.S.; and

(V) If the grounds for the issuance of a no-knock warrant are established by a confidential informant, the affidavit for such warrant shall contain a statement by the affiant concerning when such grounds became known or were verified by the affiant, but such statement shall not identify the confidential informant.

(3) Application and Issuance of a Warrant by Facsimile or Electronic Transmission. A warrant, signed affidavit, and accompanying documents may be transmitted by electronic facsimile transmission (fax) or by electronic transfer with electronic signatures to the judge, who may act upon the transmitted documents as if they were originals. A warrant affidavit may be sworn to or affirmed by administration of the oath over the telephone by the judge. The affidavit with electronic signature received by the judge or magistrate and the warrant approved by the judge or magistrate, signed with electronic signature, shall be deemed originals. The judge or magistrate shall facilitate the filing of the original affidavit and original warrant with the clerk of the court and shall take reasonable steps to prevent the tampering with the affidavit and warrant. The issuing judge or magistrate shall also forward a copy of the warrant and affidavit, with electronic signatures, to the affiant. This subsection (c)(3) does not authorize the court to issue warrants without having in its possession either a faxed copy of the signed affidavit and warrant or an electronic copy of the affidavit and warrant with electronic signatures.

(d) Issuance, Contents, Execution, and Return of Warrant.

(1) If the judge is satisfied that grounds for the application exist, or that there is probable cause to believe that such grounds exist, he shall issue a search warrant, which shall:

(I) Identify or describe, as nearly as may be, the premises, person, place, or thing to be searched;

(II) Identify or describe, as nearly as may be, the property to be searched for, seized, or inspected;

(III) State the grounds or probable cause for its issuance; and

(IV) State the names of the persons whose affidavits of testimony have been taken in support thereof.

(2) The search warrant may also contain such other and further orders as the judge may deem necessary to comply with the provisions of a statute, charter, or ordinance, or to provide for the

174

custody or delivery to the proper officer of any property seized under the warrant, or otherwise to accomplish the purposes of the warrant.

(3) Unless the court otherwise directs, every search warrant authorizes the officer executing the same:

(I) To execute and serve the warrant at any time; and

(II) To use and employ such force as may reasonably be necessary in the performance of the duties commanded by the warrant.

(4) Joinder. The search of one or more persons, premises, places, or things, may be commanded in a single warrant or in separate warrants, if compliance is made with Rule 41(c)(1)(IV) of these Rules.

(5) Execution and Return.

(I) Except as otherwise provided in this Rule, a search warrant shall be directed to any officer authorized by law to execute it in the county wherein the property is located.

(II) Any judge issuing a search warrant, for the search of a person or for the search of any motor vehicle, aircraft, or other object which is mobile or capable of being transported may make an order authorizing a peace officer to be named in such warrant to execute the same, and the person named in such order may execute such warrant anywhere in the state. All sheriffs, coroners, police officers, and officers of the Colorado State Patrol, when required, in their respective counties, shall aid and assist in the execution of such warrant. The order authorized by this subsection (5) may also authorize execution of the warrant by any officer authorized by law to execute it in the county wherein the property is located.

(III) When any officer, having a warrant for the search of a person or for the search of any motor vehicle, aircraft, or other object which is mobile or capable of being transported, shall be in pursuit thereof and such person, motor vehicle, aircraft, or other object shall cross or enter into another county, such officer is authorized to execute the warrant in such other county.

(IV) It shall be the duty of all peace officers into whose hands any search warrant shall come, to execute the same, in their respective counties or municipalities, and make due return thereof.

(V) The officers executing a search warrant shall first announce their identity, purpose, and authority, and if they are not admitted, may make a forcible entry into the place to be searched; however, the officers may make forcible entry without such prior announcement if the warrant expressly authorizes them to do so or if the particular facts and circumstances known to them at the time the warrant is to be executed adequately justify dispensing with this requirement.

(VI) A search warrant shall be executed within 14 days after its date. The officer taking property under the warrant shall give to the person from whom or from whose premises the property was taken a copy of the warrant and a receipt for the property or shall leave the copy and receipt at the place from which the property was taken. The return shall be made promptly and shall be accompanied by a written inventory of any property taken. The inventory shall be made in the presence of the applicant for the warrant and the person from whose possession or premises the property was taken, if they are present, or in the presence of at least one credible person other than the applicant for the warrant or the person from whose possession or premises the property was taken, and shall be verified by the officer. In a case involving the seizure of electronic storage media or the seizure or copying of electronically stored information, the inventory may be limited to describing the physical storage media that were seized or copied. The officer may retain a copy of the electronically stored information that was seized or copied. The judge upon request shall deliver a copy of the inventory to the person from whom or from whose premises the property was taken and to the applicant for the warrant.

(VII) A warrant under Rule 41(b) may authorize the seizure of electronic storage media or the seizure or copying of electronically stored information. Unless otherwise specified, the warrant authorizes a later review of the media or information consistent with the warrant. The time for executing the warrant in Rule 41(d)(5)(VI) refers to the seizure or on-site copying of the media or information, and not to any later off-site copying or review.

(e) Motion for Return of Property and to Suppress Evidence. A person aggrieved by an unlawful search and seizure may move the district court for the county where the property was seized for the return of the property and to suppress for use as evidence anything so obtained on the ground that:

(1) The property was illegally seized without warrant; or

(2) The warrant is insufficient on its face; or

(3) The property seized is not that described in the warrant; or

175

(4) There was not probable cause for believing the existence of the grounds on which the warrant was issued; or

(5) The warrant was illegally executed. The judge shall receive evidence on any issue of fact necessary to the decision of the motion. If the motion is granted the property shall be restored unless otherwise subject to lawful detention and it shall not be admissible in evidence at any hearing or trial. The motion to suppress evidence may also be made in the court where the trial is to be had. The motion shall be made and heard before trial unless opportunity therefor did not exist or the defendant was not aware of the grounds for the motion, but the court, in its discretion, may entertain the motion at the trial.

(f) Return of Papers to Clerk. The judge who has issued a warrant shall attach to the warrant a copy of the return, inventory, and all other documents in connection therewith, including any affidavit in application for the warrant, and shall file them with the clerk of the district court for the county of origin. If a case has been filed in the district court after issuance of the warrant, the clerk of the district court shall notify the clerk of the county court which issued it that the warrant has been filed in the district court. When the warrant has been issued by the county judge and there is no subsequent filing in the district court, after the issuance of the warrant, the documents shall remain in the county court. Any documents transmitted by fax or electronic transmission to the judge to obtain the warrant and the documents transmitted by the judge to the applicant shall be filed with the clerk of the court.

(g) Suppression of Confession or Admission. A defendant aggrieved by an alleged involuntary confession or admission made by him, may make a motion under this Rule to suppress said confession or admission. The motion shall be made and heard before trial unless opportunity therefor did not exist or defendant was not aware of the grounds for the motion, but the court, in its discretion, may entertain the motion at the trial. The judge shall receive evidence on any issue of fact necessary to the decision of the motion.

(h) Scope and Definition. This Rule does not modify any statute, inconsistent with it, regulating search, seizure, and the issuance and execution of search warrants in circumstances for which special provision is made. Editor's note: The 2001 amendments to this section added a new (d)(5)(V) and renumbered the existing (d)(5)(V) as (d)(5)(VI).

Colo. R. Crim. P. 41

Source: The introductory portion to c, c3, and f amended July 16, 1993, effective 11/1/1992; entire rule amended and effective 10/4/2001; entire rule corrected and effective 10/22/2001; entire rule corrected and effective 10/25/2001; d5VI amended May 7, 2009, effective 7/1/2009; c3 and f amended and effective 2/10/2011; c3 amended and effective 6/16/2011; d5VI amended and adopted December 14, 2011, effective 7/1/2012; amended January 11, 2018, effective 1/11/2018.

Committee Comment to (c)For purposes of this rule, the term "electronic signature" has the same meaning as used in C.R.S. § 16-1-106(4)(c). Committee Comment to (h)This rule is intended to facilitate the issuance of warrants by eliminating the need to physically carry the supporting affidavit to the judge.

Annotation I. General Consideration. Law reviews. For note, "Search and Seizure Since Mapp", see 36 U. Colo. L. Rev. 391 (1964). For comment on Hernandez v. People, 153 Colo. 316, 385 P.2d 996 (1963), appearing below, see 36 U. Colo. L. Rev. 435 (1964). For article, "Attacking the Seizure-Overcoming Good Faith", see 11 Colo. Law. 2395 (1982). For comment, "Colorado's Approach to Searches and Seizures in Law Offices", see 54 U. Colo. L. Rev. 571 (1983). For article, "Criminal Procedure", which discusses a recent Tenth Circuit decision dealing with post-arrest silence and searches, see 61 Den. L.J. 281 (1984). For article, "The Demise of the Aquilar-Spinelli Rule: A Case of Faulty Reception", see 61 Den. L.J. 431 (1984). For comment, "The Good Faith Exception: The Seventh Circuit Limits the Exclusionary Rule in the Administrative Context", see 61 Den. L.J. 597 (1984). For article, "Veracity Challenges in Colorado: A Primer", see 14 Colo. Law. 227 (1985). For article, "Consent Searches: A Brief Review", see 14 Colo. Law. 795 (1985). For article, "Criminal Procedure", which discusses recent Tenth Circuit decisions dealing with searches, see 62 Den. U. L. Rev. 159 (1985). For article, "Civil Action for Return of Property: 'Anomalous' Federal Jurisdiction in Search of Justification", see 62 Den. U. L. Rev. 741 (1985). For article, "People v. Mitchell: The Good Faith Exception in Colorado", see 62 Den. U. L. Rev. 841 (1985). For article, "Pronouncements of the U.S. Supreme Court Relating to the Criminal Law Field: 1985-1986", which discusses recent cases relating to protection from searches and warrant requirements, see 15 Colo. Law. 1564 and 1566 (1986). For article, "Criminal Procedure", which discusses recent Tenth Circuit decisions dealing with unreasonable searches and seizures, see 65 Den. U. L. Rev. 535 (1988).

Applied in Seccombe v. District Court, 180 Colo. 420, 506 P.2d 153 (1973); People v. Hoinville, 191 Colo. 357, 553 P.2d 777 (1976); People v. Fletcher, 193 Colo. 314, 566 P.2d 345 (1977); People v. Valdez, 621 P.2d 332 (Colo. 1981); People v. Conwell, 649 P.2d 1099 (Colo. 1982); People v. Lindsey, 660 P.2d 502 (Colo. 1983); People v. Roybal, 672 P.2d 1003 (Colo. 1983). II. Constitutional Protections. State courts to resolve search and seizure problems in light of constitutional guarantees. Mapp v. Ohio, 367 U.S. 643, 81 S. Ct. 1684, 6 L. Ed. 2d 1081 (1961), does not by its terms nationalize the law of search and seizure, but it does compel state courts to examine and resolve the problems arising from the search for and the seizure of evidence in the light of state and federal constitutional guarantees against unlawful searches and seizures. Hernandez v. People, 153 Colo. 316, 385 P.2d 996 (1963). And state rules proper, provided they do not violate federal constitution. Rules establishing workable state procedures governing searches and seizures, even though they may not be strictly in accord with federal procedures, are proper provided that such rules do not violate the fourth amendment proscription against unreasonable searches and seizures. Hernandez v. People, 153 Colo. 316, 385 P.2d 996 (1963). Thus, this rule issued to implement constitutional guarantees. As a result of Mapp v. Ohio, 367 U.S. 643, 81 S. Ct. 1684, 6 L. Ed. 2d 1081 (1961), and to implement the constitutional guarantees against unlawful searches and seizures, the supreme court of Colorado on November 1, 1961, initially issued this rule providing for the manner in which search warrants should be issued and making property obtained by an unlawful search and seizure inadmissible in evidence in the courts of this state, provided timely motions to suppress are made. Hernandez v. People, 153 Colo. 316, 385 P.2d 996 (1963). Though use of search warrant has long been encouraged in Colorado. It has long been the policy of the supreme court of Colorado and other courts to encourage the use of the search warrant as a most desirable method of protecting and preserving the constitutional rights of the accused. People v. Whisenhunt, 173 Colo. 109, 476 P.2d 997 (1970). But previous statute on issuance of search warrants held unconstitutional. People v. Leahy, 173 Colo. 339, 484 P.2d 778 (1970); People v. Singleton, 174 Colo. 138, 482 P.2d 978 (1971) (decided under § 48-5-11(3), C.R.S. 1963). Federal constitution guarantees security of persons against unreasonable searches. The fourth amendment to the United States Constitution does not guarantee the security of persons against all searches but only those which are unreasonable. Moore v. People, 171 Colo. 338, 467 P.2d 50 (1970). And practical accuracy determines whether warrant complies with constitutional requirements. The standard for determining whether search warrant complies with constitutional requirements is one of practical accuracy rather than technical nicety. People v. Ragulsky, 184 Colo. 86, 518 P.2d 286 (1974). No constitutional violation when prison cells "shaken down". Considering normal and necessary prison practices and the charge placed upon prison officials to supervise the operation of state prisons, to preserve order and discipline therein, and to maintain prison security, there is no violation of the fourth amendment prohibition against unreasonable search and seizure when prison cells are searched or "shaken down" in carrying out this charge. Moore v. People, 171 Colo. 338, 467 P.2d 50 (1970). So long as searches not cruel, or conducted for harassing or humiliating purposes. Searches conducted by prison officials entrusted with the orderly operation of the prisons are not unreasonable so long as they are not conducted for the purpose of harassing or humiliating the inmate or in a cruel or unusual manner. Moore v. People, 171 Colo. 338, 467 P.2d 50 (1970). And seizure of business records not unconstitutional where records instrumentalities of crime. Seizure of records does not violate defendant's privilege against self-incrimination where defendant is not "compelled" to produce the papers, the papers are not communicative in nature, they are business records of which others must have knowledge rather than personal and private writings, and they are instrumentalities of the crime with which defendant is charged. People v. Tucci, 179 Colo. 373, 500 P.2d 815 (1972). Voluntary surrender of nontestimonial evidence waives any constitutional protections. People v. Mattas, 645 P.2d 254 (Colo. 1982). III. Applicability of Rule. Validity of a search warrant is to be judged under this rule. People v. Leahy, 173 Colo. 339, 484 P.2d 778 (1970); People v. Ferris, 173 Colo. 494, 480 P.2d 552 (1971). Consequently, it is necessary for search warrant to comply with provisions of this rule. People v. Henry, 173 Colo. 523, 482 P.2d 357 (1971). But only unlawfully seized or obtained evidence or confession suppressed. This rule provides only for motions to suppress physical evidence unlawfully seized, as well as confessions and statements unlawfully obtained, from accused defendants. People v. McNulty, 173 Colo. 491, 480 P.2d 560 (1971). Mandatory pretrial suppression of evidence hearing only for matters listed in rule. There is nothing in the Colorado Rules of Criminal Procedure which contemplates a mandatory pretrial suppression of evidence hearing other than for the matters listed in sections (e) and (g) of this rule, viz., evidence obtained because of an illegal search and seizure or an extrajudicial confession or

177

admission. People v. Thornburg, 173 Colo. 230, 477 P.2d 372 (1970). Therefore, this rule does not encompass motions for suppression of testimonial evidence. People v. McNulty, 173 Colo. 491, 480 P.2d 560 (1971). Nor motions for suppression of identification testimony. Where the defendant contends that he was not afforded counsel during a lineup and that the lineup was overly suggestive, so that identification testimony should not be allowed into evidence, such a matter is to be resolved at trial rather than pursuant to this rule. People v. Thornburg, 173 Colo. 230, 477 P.2d 372 (1970). Likewise, whether an arrest is without probable cause is a subject which may not properly be considered under a motion to suppress. People v. Henry, 173 Colo. 523, 482 P.2d 357 (1971). Interlocutory appeals by state made only from adverse suppression rulings governed by rules. C.A.R. 4.1, which provides for interlocutory appeals by the state, is designed to review rulings of the trial court made upon suppression hearings under sections (e) and (g) of this rule; where objections to proposed evidence do not come within these sections, rulings on the same are not subject to review under C.A.R. 4.1. People v. Thornburg, 173 Colo. 230, 477 P.2d 372 (1970); People v. McNulty, 173 Colo. 491, 480 P.2d 560 (1971); People v. Henry, 173 Colo. 523, 482 P.2d 357 (1971); People v. Patterson, 175 Colo. 19, 485 P.2d 494 (1971); People v. Fidler, 175 Colo. 90, 485 P.2d 725 (1971) (all cases decided prior to 1979 amendment of C.A.R. 4.1). Under C.A.R. 4.1, interlocutory appeals may only be made by the state from adverse rulings by a district court to motions made pursuant to sections (e) and (g) of this rule and Crim. P. 41.1(i). People v. Morgan, 619 P.2d 64 (Colo. 1980). IV. Authority to Issue Warrant. Only judicial officer may issue search warrant. Hernandez v. People, 153 Colo. 316, 385 P.2d 996 (1963); Mayorga v. People, 178 Colo. 106, 496 P.2d 304 (1972). And only such authority may modify warrant. It is axiomatic that the right to alter, modify, or correct a warrant is necessarily vested only in a judicial authority. Hernandez v. People, 153 Colo. 316, 385 P.2d 996 (1963); Mayorga v. People, 178 Colo. 106, 496 P.2d 304 (1972). So, alteration of search warrant by police officer is usurpation of judicial function and is therefore improper. Hernandez v. People, 153 Colo. 316, 385 P.2d 996 (1963). But warrant modified before issued by judge not subject to challenge. Where changes and modifications on a search warrant take place before it is signed and issued by a judge, the validity of the search warrant is not subject to challenge. People v. Ferris, 173 Colo. 494, 480 P.2d 552 (1971). V. Application for Warrant. A. General Procedural Requirements. Rule requires affidavit to support search warrant, which establishes the grounds for the issuance of the warrant, and demands that the affidavit be sworn to before a judge. People v. Brethauer, 174 Colo. 29, 482 P.2d 369 (1971). Which must comply with United States supreme court standards. If a search warrant is to be sustained, the affidavit must comply with the standards set forth in Aguilar v. Texas, 378 U.S. 108, 84 S. Ct. 1509, 12 L. Ed. 2d 723, 10 A.L.R.3d 359 (1966), and in Spinelli v. United States, 393 U.S. 410, 89 S. Ct. 584, 21 L. Ed. 2d 637 (1969). People v. Brethauer, 174 Colo. 29, 482 P.2d 369 (1971). But technical requirements and elaborate specificity are not required in the drafting of affidavits for search warrants. People v. Padilla, 182 Colo. 101, 511 P.2d 480 (1973). Probable cause must be supported by oath or affirmation reduced to writing. The fourth amendment to the United States constitution requires probable cause supported by oath or affirmation as a condition precedent to the valid issuance of a search warrant; § 7 of art. II, Colo. Const., is even more restrictive and provides that probable cause must be supported by oath or affirmation reduced to writing. Hernandez v. People, 153 Colo. 316, 385 P.2d 996 (1963); People v. Brethauer, 174 Colo. 29, 482 P.2d 369 (1971). Under the Colorado Constitution, the warrant can only be issued upon probable cause supported by oath or affirmation which is "reduced to writing". People v. Brethauer, 174 Colo. 29, 482 P.2d 369 (1971). And verbal communication insufficient. Verbal communication of facts, as contrasted with written communication, will not suffice to establish probable cause. People v. Padilla, 182 Colo. 101, 511 P.2d 480 (1973). Previously, this rule did not require affidavit to be attached to search warrant. People v. Ferris, 173 Colo. 494, 480 P.2d 552 (1971); People v. Singleton, 174 Colo. 138, 482 P.2d 978 (1971). Admission of evidence seized from a defendant's residence pursuant to a defective warrant did not constitute reversible error, even though warrant was issued based on an affidavit inadvertently failing to allege facts linking defendant to the residence to be searched. People v. Deitchman, 695 P.2d 1146 (Colo. 1985). Failure for good cause to comply with subsection (c)(1) of this rule, which requires affidavits for search warrants to be sworn to or affirmed before the issuing judge, does not constitute a constitutional violation that automatically triggers the exclusionary rule. People v. Fournier, 793 P.2d 1176 (Colo. 1990). B. Role of Courts and Police. Probable cause determined by detached magistrate, not police officer. Search warrants must be supported by evidentiary affidavits containing sufficient facts to allow "probable cause" to be determined by a detached magistrate instead of the accusing police officer. Brown v. Patterson, 275 F. Supp. 629 (D. Colo.

178

1967), aff'd, 393 F. 2d 733 (10th Cir. 1968). Existence of probable cause must be determined by a member of the judiciary rather than by a law enforcement officer who is employed to apprehend criminals and to bring before the courts for trial those who would violate the law. People v. Brethauer, 174 Colo. 29, 482 P.2d 369 (1971). Be it a judge of the supreme, district, county, or superior court. The determination of whether probable cause exists is a judicial function to be performed by the issuing magistrate, which in Colorado may be any judge of the supreme, district, county, or superior court under this rule, and is not a matter to be left to the discretion of a police officer. Hernandez v. People, 153 Colo. 316, 385 P.2d 996 (1963); People v. Brethauer, 174 Colo. 29, 482 P.2d 369 (1971). And to dispense with this requirement would render search warrant itself meaningless, since it would allow a police officer to subjectively determine probable cause. Brown v. Patterson, 275 F. Supp. 629 (D. Colo. 1967), aff'd, 393 F.2d 733 (10th Cir. 1968). Police officer's role limited to providing judge with facts to make proper determination. The role of the police officer in search warrant practice is limited solely to providing the judge with facts and trustworthy information upon which he, as a neutral and detached judicial officer, may make a proper determination. People v. Brethauer, 174 Colo. 29, 482 P.2d 369 (1971). Affidavits for warrants interpreted by magistrates in common-sense fashion. Affidavits for search warrants must be tested and interpreted by magistrates and courts in a common-sense and realistic fashion. People v. Whisenhunt, 173 Colo. 109, 476 P.2d 997 (1970). And judge, in determining sufficiency, looks to four corners of affidavit. In determining whether the affidavit is sufficient, the judge must look within the four corners of the affidavit to determine whether there are grounds for the issuance of a search warrant. People v. Brethauer, 174 Colo. 29, 482 P.2d 369 (1971); People v. Woods, 175 Colo. 34, 485 P.2d 491 (1971); People v. Padilla, 182 Colo. 101, 511 P.2d 480 (1973). Issuing magistrate need only state result that probable cause exists. This rule was not intended to require the issuing magistrate to reiterate his mental process for reaching the result that probable cause exists, but rather to require only that he state that the result has been reached. People v. Singleton, 174 Colo. 138, 482 P.2d 978 (1971); People v. Noble, 635 P.2d 203 (Colo. 1981). Reasons given for search judicially reviewed by standards appropriate for reasonable police officer. Where an officer believes he has probable cause to search and states his reasons, an appellate court will not examine such reasons grudgingly, but will measure them by standards appropriate for a reasonable, cautious, and prudent police officer trained in the type of investigation which he is making. People v. Singleton, 174 Colo. 138, 482 P.2d 978 (1971). For negative attitude by reviewing courts discourages police from submitting evidence before acting. A grudging or negative attitude by reviewing courts toward warrants will tend to discourage police officers from submitting their evidence to a judicial officer before acting. People v. Whisenhunt, 173 Colo. 109, 476 P.2d 997 (1970). C. Underlying Facts and Circumstances. Issuing magistrate to be apprised of underlying facts and circumstances showing probable cause. Before the issuing magistrate can properly perform his official function he must be apprised of the underlying facts and circumstances which show that there is probable cause to believe that proper grounds for the issuance of the warrant exist. Hernandez v. People, 153 Colo. 316, 385 P.2d 996 (1963); Brown v. Patterson, 275 F. Supp. 629 (D. Colo. 1967), aff'd, 393 F.2d 733 (10th Cir. 1968); People v. Brethauer, 174 Colo. 29, 482 P.2d 369 (1971); People v. Padilla, 182 Colo. 101, 511 P.2d 480 (1973); People v. Clavey, 187 Colo. 305, 530 P.2d 491 (1975). The police must show to the issuing magistrate the underlying facts and circumstances upon which the magistrate can determine that probable cause exists for the issuance of a warrant. People v. Massey, 178 Colo. 141, 495 P.2d 1141 (1972). And it is elementary and of no consequence that police have additional information which could provide a basis for the issuance of the warrant. People v. Brethauer, 174 Colo. 29, 482 P.2d 369 (1971). Mere affirmance of the belief or suspicion on the officer's part is not enough, for to hold otherwise would attach controlling significance to the officer's belief rather than to the magistrate's judicial determination. Hernandez v. People, 153 Colo. 316, 385 P.2d 996 (1963); People v. Brethauer, 174 Colo. 29, 482 P.2d 369 (1971). Mere conclusory belief or suspicion by an affiant officer is not enough upon which to base the issuance of a search warrant. People v. Clavey, 187 Colo. 305, 530 P.2d 491 (1975). Nor will affiant's conclusory declaration that he has probable cause add strength to the showing made. People v. Padilla, 182 Colo. 101, 511 P.2d 480 (1973). For without facts, affidavits fatally defective. Affidavits containing only the conclusion of the police officer that he believes that certain property is on the premises or person and that such property is designed, or intended, or is, or has been, used as a means of committing a criminal offense, or the possession of which is illegal, without setting forth facts and circumstances from which the judicial officer can determine whether probable cause exists are fatally defective. Hernandez v. People, 153 Colo. 316, 385

P.2d 996 (1963). And warrant issued on basis of mere conclusion deemed nullity. Where the mere conclusions by an officer provide nothing from which the judge can make an independent determination of probable cause, a warrant issued on the basis of such an affidavit is a nullity. People v. Baird, 172 Colo. 112, 470 P.2d 20 (1970). But a search warrant may be based on hearsay, as long as a substantial basis for crediting the hearsay exists. People v. Woods, 175 Colo. 34, 485 P.2d 491 (1971). Police officer's statements in affidavit that are erroneous and false must be stricken and may not be considered in determining whether the affidavit will support the issuance of a search warrant. People v. Malone, 175 Colo. 31, 485 P.2d 499 (1971). Where the information supplied by an affiant which supports the issuance of a search warrant is false, the trial court has no alternative but to strike the admittedly erroneous information which the affiant supplied. People v. Hampton, 196 Colo. 466, 587 P.2d 275 (1978). But other information supplied by affidavit not ignored. Fact that some portions of affidavit are erroneous does not require the issuing magistrate to ignore the other information supplied by the affidavit. People v. Hampton, 196 Colo. 466, 587 P.2d 275 (1978). And where affidavit still sufficient, court will not strike down warrant. Where the affidavit still contains material facts sufficient as a matter of law to support the issuance of a warrant after the deletion of erroneous statements, the court will not strike down the warrant because the affidavit is not completely accurate. People v. Malone, 175 Colo. 31, 485 P.2d 499 (1971). Verbal communications cannot correct deficient affidavit. Verbal communications, to the magistrate, of additional supporting information cannot correct an affidavit which is basically deficient in its statement of the underlying facts and the circumstances relied upon. People v. Padilla, 182 Colo. 101, 511 P.2d 480 (1973). But sworn testimony to supplement warrant, or amendment of affidavit, may be required. Should the judge to whom application has been made for the issuance of a search warrant determine that the affidavit is insufficient, he can require that sworn testimony be offered to supplement the warrant or can demand that the affidavit be amended to disclose additional facts, if a search warrant is to be issued. People v. Brethauer, 174 Colo. 29, 482 P.2d 369 (1971). Affidavit containing stale information. Although crimes were perpetrated eight months prior to application for search warrant, because officers proceeded with all due diligence upon discovery of information upon which to base request for a search warrant, the affidavit was sufficient to establish probable cause. People v. Cullen, 695 P.2d 750 (Colo. App. 1984). Anticipatory warrants are barred by language of rule and identical language in § 16-3-303 requiring that property to be searched for, seized, or inspected "is located at, in, or upon" premise, person, place, or thing to be searched. People v. Poirez, 904 P.2d 880 (Colo. 1995). D. Finding of Probable Cause. Police entry into individual's private domain made only upon showing of probable cause. It is only upon a showing of probable cause that the legal doors are opened to allow the police to gain official entry into an individual's domain of privacy for the purpose of conducting a search or to make an official seizure under the constitution. People v. Brethauer, 174 Colo. 29, 482 P.2d 369 (1971). Not necessary to specifically allege that possession of articles illegal. To establish the grounds in an affidavit it is not necessary that the person seeking the search warrant specifically allege therein the conclusion that the possession of the articles is illegal. People v. Whisenhunt, 173 Colo. 109, 476 P.2d 997 (1970); People v. Martin, 176 Colo. 322, 490 P.2d 924 (1971). Or that the use thereof is illegal. Where an affidavit identifies the articles in question and alleges where they are located, but does not state that the possession or use thereof is illegal, the fact that the illegality is not set forth in the affidavit does not prevent the issuance of a search warrant. People v. Martin, 176 Colo. 322, 490 P.2d 924 (1971). But warrant issues upon judge finding grounds established, or probable cause therefor. This rule provides that if the judge is satisfied from the facts alleged in the affidavit that the existence of one or more of the grounds for the issuance of a warrant has been established or that there is probable cause to believe that one or more grounds for issuing the warrant exist, then it should issue. People v. Whisenhunt, 173 Colo. 109, 476 P.2d 997 (1970); People v. Martin, 176 Colo. 322, 490 P.2d 924 (1971). Warrant authorized upon connection being provided between evidence and criminal activity. One test for authorizing a search warrant for the seizure of certain articles is: Does the evidence in itself or with facts known to the officer prior to the search, excluding any facts subsequently developed, provide a connection between the evidence and criminal activity? People v. Henry, 173 Colo. 523, 482 P.2d 357 (1971). Probable cause exists where facts warrant reasonable belief offense committed. Probable cause exists where the facts and circumstances within the officers' knowledge, and of which they had reasonably trustworthy information, are sufficient in themselves to warrant a man of reasonable caution in the belief that an offense has been, or is being, committed. People v. Brethauer, 174 Colo. 29, 482 P.2d 369 (1971); Finley v. People, 176 Colo. 1, 488 P.2d 883 (1971). Moreover, in dealing with probable cause, one deals with probabilities; these are not technical; they are the factual and practical considerations of everyday life on which reasonable and prudent men, not legal technicians, act. People v. Brethauer, 174 Colo. 29, 482 P.2d 369 (1971); Finley v. People, 176 Colo. 11, 488 P.2d 883 (1971). Hence, the odor of a decomposing body is certainly probable cause for obtaining a search warrant. Condon v. People, 176 Colo. 212, 489 P.2d 1297 (1971). Affidavit must support probable cause finding as to each place searched. The fact that places to be searched were apartments rather than single-family residences does not alter the rule that an affidavit must support a finding of probable cause as to each separate place to be searched. People v. Arnold, 181 Colo. 432, 509 P.2d 1248 (1973). Affidavit detailing various items at named address presents sufficient facts showing probable cause. Where the affidavit of a police officer in support of a search warrant sets forth at length the various items of information regarding the presence of certain articles at a named address, elaborating in detail on the items of police surveillance and discovery of such, such an affidavit presents ample and sufficient facts showing probable cause for the issuance of the search warrant. People v. Ferris, 173 Colo. 494, 480 P.2d 552 (1971). Officers rightly in defendant's residence entitled to seize stolen items in plain view. If the supporting affidavit was sufficient to provide probable cause for issuance of a warrant, are the searching officers rightfully in the defendant's residence, then the officers are entitled to seize items in plain view which they recognize as stolen. People v. Espinoza, 195 Colo. 127, 575 P.2d 851 (1978). Even if not false, statements of officer-affiants may be so misleading that a finding of probable cause may be deemed erroneous. People v. Winden, 689 P.2d 578 (Colo. 1984). Probable cause to issue a search warrant for a residence was sufficiently established by affidavit that was based primarily on information provided by confidential police informant and only thinly corroborated by independent police investigation. The "totality of circumstances" test for determining whether probable cause existed for issuing warrant was met. People v. Paquin, 811 P.2d 394 (Colo. 1991). Where only non-criminal activity is corroborated by independent police investigation, the question of whether probable cause exists focuses on the degree of suspicion that attaches to the types of corroborated non-criminal acts and whether the informant provides details that are not easily obtained. People v. Pacheco, 175 P.3d 91 (Colo. 2006). E. Informers. Affidavit for search warrant based on an informant's information must meet a two-pronged test requiring that the officer establish: (1) The underlying circumstances from which the informant concluded what he claims, and (2) some of the underlying circumstances from which the officer concludes that the informant is credible or his information reliable. People v. Peppers, 172 Colo. 556, 475 P.2d 337 (1970); People v. Glaubman, 175 Colo. 41, 485 P.2d 711 (1971); Stork v. People, 175 Colo. 324, 488 P.2d 76 (1971). The standards of probable cause for issuance of search warrant based on information given to affiant police officer by unidentified informant are that the affidavit must: (1) Allege facts from which the issuing magistrate can independently determine whether there are reasonable grounds to believe that an illegal activity is being carried on in the place to be searched; and (2) set forth sufficient facts to allow the magistrate to determine independently if the informer is credible or his information reliable. People v. Peschong, 181 Colo. 29, 506 P.2d 1232 (1973); People v. Harris, 182 Colo. 75, 510 P.2d 1374 (1973); People v. Baird, 182 Colo. 284, 512 P.2d 629 (1973); People v. Masson, 185 Colo. 65, 521 P.2d 1246 (1974). The two-pronged test which emphasizes the basis upon which an informer's tip will provide a foundation for the issuance of a search warrant requires that the affidavit set forth: (1) The underlying circumstances necessary to enable the magistrate independently to judge the validity of the informant's conclusion; and (2) support of the affiant's claim that the informant was credible or his information reliable. People v. McGill, 187 Colo. 65, 528 P.2d 386 (1974); People v. Dailey, 639 P.2d 1068 (Colo. 1982). And informant's personal knowledge satisfies first prong of test. Personal observation by informant of the objects of the search within the place to be searched satisfied the first prong of establishing probable cause. People v. Ward, 181 Colo. 246, 508 P.2d 1257 (1973); People v. Harris, 182 Colo. 75, 510 P.2d 1374 (1973). The requirement that the affidavit for a search warrant set forth underlying circumstances so as to enable a magistrate to independently judge the validity of the informant's conclusion that criminal activity exists can be satisfied by the assertion of personal knowledge of the informant. People v. Montoya, 189 Colo. 106, 538 P.2d 1332 (1975). Where the affiant states that the informant personally observed illegal property in the premises to be searched, this statement is sufficient to permit the issuing magistrate to determine independently that there were reasonable grounds to believe that illegal activity was being carried on in the place to be searched. People v. Harris, 182 Colo. 75, 510 P.2d 1374 (1973). Where it appears that the informant personally saw an illegal narcotic on the premises, that he was given an illegal narcotic by someone on the premises and that he observed other illegal narcotics at the

181

time he left the premises, these facts are sufficient to allow a magistrate to determine whether there was probable cause to determine presence of illegal activity. People v. Baird, 182 Colo. 284, 512 P.2d 629 (1973). But informant's information insufficient where place searched not connected with illegal substance. An affidavit, while stating that an informant was present when defendants sold contraband, but does not state that he was ever in the defendants' place, that he had seen such contraband in the defendants' place, or that he had witnessed the sale of such in the defendants' place is not sufficient information upon which to base a search warrant of defendants' place. People v. Massey, 178 Colo. 141, 495 P.2d 1141 (1972). Also, affidavit insufficient if no explanation of how information received. An affidavit is insufficient to support a finding of probable cause where the officer does not more than state that he received information from an investigator who received the information from a reliable source and there is nothing in the affidavit concerning personal knowledge of the facts on the part of either officer, the facts upon which the informant based his information, or the circumstances from which the officers could conclude that the informant is credible or his information reliable. People v. Baird, 172 Colo. 112, 470 P.2d 20 (1970). An affidavit does not meet the test if there is no explanation as to how the police obtained the information, nor does the affidavit set forth who made the observation or whether the information was obtained from an eyewitness or from a person who received the information indirectly. People v. Myers, 175 Colo. 109, 485 P.2d 877 (1971). Magistrate must be shown facts to form basis for believing informant's information reliable. Some facts must also be shown to a magistrate upon which he can form a basis for believing information supplied by an informer is credible or the informer reliable. People v. Massey, 178 Colo. 141, 495 P.2d 1141 (1972). There must be a comprehensive statement of underlying facts upon which the magistrate can make an independent determination that the informant is credible or his information reliable. People v. Aragon, 187 Colo. 206, 529 P.2d 644 (1974). And merely stating informant known to be reliable does not establish his credibility. An affidavit does not establish the credibility of an informant by merely stating that the informant is known to be reliable, nor does an affidavit establish the credibility of an informant by merely stating that the informant is known to be reliable based on "past information" supplied by the informer which has proved to be accurate. Although the words "past information" might conjure up in the mind of the officer some knowledge of the underlying circumstances from which the officer might conclude that the informant is reliable, the judge has not been apprised of such facts, and consequently, he cannot make a disinterested determination based upon such facts. People v. Brethauer, 174 Colo. 29, 482 P.2d 369 (1971). As a basis for issuing a search warrant, the mere assertion of reliability is not sufficient to establish an informant's credibility. People v. Aragon, 187 Colo. 206, 529 P.2d 644 (1974). An affidavit for a search warrant seeking to show an informant's credibility is not satisfactory by merely stating that the informant is reliable, or that he has supplied information in the past which proved to be accurate. Nor are irrelevant, albeit correct, details sufficient. People v. Montoya, 189 Colo. 106, 538 P.2d 1332 (1975). Where the only recital in the affidavit for a search warrant bearing upon the informant's credibility or the reliability of the information supplied was as follows: "That the confidential informant has related information to the affiant regarding several previous narcotics and dangerous drugs sellers and users which has been confirmed and proven reliable by the affiant", this was totally conclusory and devoid of details sufficient to support an independent finding of credibility or reliability. People v. Bowen, 189 Colo. 126, 538 P.2d 1336 (1975). Neither does allegation of suspect's criminal reputation. An allegation of suspect's criminal reputation standing alone does not set forth sufficient facts to allow a magistrate to determine independently reliability of information supplied by an informant. People v. Peschong, 181 Colo. 29, 506 P.2d 1232 (1973). But three ways to allow magistrate to determine reliability of informant's information. There are at least three ways in which an affidavit might allow a magistrate to determine the reliability of an informant's information so as to issue a search warrant: (1) By stating that the informant had previously given reliable information; (2) by presenting the information in detail which clearly manifests its reliability; and (3) by presenting facts which corroborate the informant's information. People v. Masson, 185 Colo. 65, 521 P.2d 1246 (1974). Reliability of informant. Where an affidavit is based upon an informer's tip, the totality of the circumstances inquiry looks to all indicia of reliability, including the informer's veracity, the basis of his knowledge, the amount of detail provided by the informer, and whether the information provided was current. People v. Leftwich, 869 P.2d 1260 (Colo. 1994); People v. Randolph, 4 P.3d 477 (Colo. 2000); People v. Pacheco, 175 P.3d 91 (Colo. 2006). Assertion that informant previously furnished solid information of criminal activity shows his credibility. The requirement that the affiant-police officer support his request for a search warrant with information showing that the informant was credible, or his information was reliable, may be satisfied by an assertion that the informant has previously furnished solid material information of specified criminal activity. People v. Montoya, 189 Colo. 106, 538 P.2d 1332 (1975). Previously furnished information leading to arrests sufficient to find informant reliable. Where the affidavit related that the informant had, within the past 14 months, supplied information which led to the arrest and conviction of an individual for possession of a narcotic drug, and that the informant had, within the past 24 hours, supplied information which resulted in arrests and the seizure of a quantity of marijuana, this information was sufficient to permit the issuing magistrate to find that the informant was reliable. People v. Harris, 182 Colo. 75, 510 P.2d 1374 (1973). Where the affidavit states that the informant has "given information in the past that has resulted in seizures and arrests" and that the informant "reported that he has just left this location and observed the described articles", then a fair reading of these statements compels one to conclude that the informant is personally aware of the location and the identity of the articles and additional details, such as the name of the person who led the informant to the location of the articles; these constitute examples of that type of essential information that allows the judge who issues the warrant to determine the underlying circumstances from which the officer who signs the affidavit concluded that these articles are on the premises. People v. Peppers, 172 Colo. 556, 475 P.2d 337 (1970). Where informant had furnished information which "has been the cause of approximately 20 narcotic and dangerous drug arrests in the past year", the magistrate could independently conclude that the police would not repeatedly accept information from one who has not proven by experience to be reliable, and hence, the magistrate could determine that the informant was credible. People v. Baird, 182 Colo. 284, 512 P.2d 629 (1973). Additionally, reliability of informant can be corroborated by descriptions in police reports. Where defendant contends that an affidavit does not contain sufficient corroborative information as to reliability of informant, such is without merit when the similarity of descriptions given by the informant, as well as by police employee, of articles matches descriptions contained in police (e.g., theft) reports; this is sufficient independent proof of reliability of informant, and employee, and constitutes sufficient probable cause for issuance of a warrant. People v. Greathouse, 173 Colo. 103, 476 P.2d 259 (1970). Citizen-informer not considered on same basis as ordinary informant. Colorado follows the citizen-informer rule and will recognize that a citizen who is identified by name and address and was a witness to criminal activity cannot be considered on the same basis as the ordinary informant. People v. Glaubman, 175 Colo. 41, 485 P.2d 711 (1971). And not necessary that affidavit contains facts showing reliability of citizen-informer. Where the citizen-informant rule applies to information contained in an affidavit for issuance of a search warrant, it is not necessary that the affidavit contain a statement of facts showing the reliability of the citizen-informant, as is the case when the informant is confidential and unidentified. People v. Schamber, 182 Colo. 355, 513 P.2d 205 (1973). Totality of circumstances test adopted. People v. Pannebaker, 714 P.2d 904 (Colo. 1986). VI. Issuance, Contents, Execution, and Return. A. Issuance and Contents. Affidavit must support finding of probable cause as to each warrant issued. While more than one search warrant may be issued on the basis of a single affidavit, the affidavit must support a finding of probable cause as to each separate warrant or each separate place to be searched. People v. Arnold, 181 Colo. 432, 509 P.2d 1248 (1973). Search warrant should not be broader than the justifying basis of facts. People v. Clavey, 187 Colo. 305, 530 P.2d 491 (1975). Description sufficient where person presented with warrant knows place authorized to be searched. The description in a warrant is sufficient where any person, upon being presented with the warrant, would know immediately in which place the search is authorized. People v. Peppers, 172 Colo. 556, 475 P.2d 337 (1970). And number of place searched not required where location specifically indicated. It is unrealistic to require the technicality of indicating the number of the place to be searched when the location is otherwise indicated with reasonable specificity. People v. Peppers, 172 Colo. 556, 475 P.2d 337 (1970). Warrant describing house as within Denver when in fact the house lay one-half block outside Denver was not for that reason invalid. People v. Martinez, 898 P.2d 28 (Colo. 1995). Illicit property may be described generally. If the purpose of search is to seize not a specific property but any property of a specified character which by reason of its character is illicit or contraband, a specific particular description of the property is unnecessary, and it may be described generally as to its nature or character. People v. Benson, 176 Colo. 421, 490 P.2d 1287 (1971). Such as "a quantity of narcotic drugs". Where the affidavit contains information which justifies the magistrate in believing that upon a search of the particular premises not only marijuana but other narcotics might be found, a warrant describing "a quantity of narcotic drugs" is in order. People v. Benson, 176 Colo. 421, 490 P.2d 1287 (1971). Historically, problem has arisen in execution of warrant at night. Historically, there has not been a question about executing a search warrant during the daytime; the problem has arisen in the execution of a warrant at night when the warrant did not specifically so authorize such execution. People v. Henry, 173 Colo. 523, 482 P.2d 357 (1971). Thus, under rule, warrant without specified time may be executed in daytime. Under this rule, when a search warrant does not specify the time at which it is to be served, or that it may be served at any time, its validity is not affected, and it may be executed in the daytime. People v. Henry, 173 Colo. 523, 482 P.2d 357 (1971). Or at any time. Unless and until a warrant specifically indicates that it must be served in the daytime, it may be served at any time. People v. Singleton, 174 Colo. 138, 482 P.2d 978 (1971). Language sufficient to identify affiant. People v. Singleton, 174 Colo. 138, 482 P.2d 978 (1971). B. Execution and Return. The fourth amendment generally requires officers to knock before executing a search warrant except when the warrant specifically authorizes a "no-knock" or the particular facts and circumstances known to them at the time the warrant is executed adequately justify dispensing with the requirement to knock. In this case the officers had reasonable suspicion that knocking would result in destruction of the drugs subject to seizure. People v. King, __ P.3d __ (Colo. App. 2011). Execution means searching premises authorized to be searched in warrant. The execution of a search warrant means carrying out the judicial command of the warrant to conduct a search of the premises authorized to be searched. Mayorga v. People, 178 Colo. 106, 496 P.2d 304 (1972). Warrant directed to "authorized" officers sufficient, as name of specific officer not required. The contention that a search warrant which directs "all sheriffs and peace officers" is improperly directed and should be specifically directed to officers in a certain county is without merit where it is implicit after considering all the language of the warrant that its direction or command is to officers in a certain county and that in this respect it complies with section (d). People v. Ferris, 173 Colo. 494, 480 P.2d 552 (1971). A search warrant addressed to "any person authorized by law to execute warrants within the state of Colorado" complies with the provisions of this rule and is not deemed insufficient merely because it does not contain the name of the officer who would execute it. People v. Henry, 173 Colo. 523, 482 P.2d 357 (1971). Rule's requirements relating to making of return and inventory are ministerial in nature. People v. Schmidt, 172 Colo. 285, 473 P.2d 698 (1970). And the failure to make a proper return can always be corrected at a later time in the proceedings. Deficiencies, if any exist in the return, can always be corrected by order of court. People v. Schmidt, 172 Colo. 285, 473 P.2d 698 (1970). Technical perfection not required. Where warrant specified a street address that was adjacent to defendant's residence and owned by the same owner, and defendant's residence was not itself searched, both the warrant and the search were valid. People v. Schrader, 898 P.2d 33 (Colo. 1995). Not every violation of subsection (c)(1) of this rule requires suppression of evidence under the exclusionary rule. Where search warrant was executed one-half block outside officers' jurisdiction, but city boundaries were not clear and officers promptly notified the proper authorities when the error was discovered, no violation of defendant's constitutional rights occurred. People v. Martinez, 898 P.2d 28 (Colo. 1995). VII. Motion to Suppress Evidence. A. In General. Annotator's note. For further annotations concerning search and seizure, see § 7 of art. II, Colo. Const., part 3 of article 3 of title 16, and Crim. P. 26. Previously, evidence obtained in unlawful search was admissible in criminal prosecution. Until June 19, 1961, when the supreme court of the United States decided Mapp v. Ohio, 367 U.S. 643, 81 S. Ct. 1684, 6 L. Ed. 2d 1081 (1961), the rule in Colorado was that evidence, even though obtained as a result of an unlawful search and seizure, was admissible in a prosecution for a criminal offense. Hernandez v. People, 153 Colo. 316, 385 P.2d 996 (1963). But now is inadmissible. The fruits of an unlawful search are, by Mapp v. Ohio, 367 U.S. 643, 81 S. Ct. 1684, 6 L. Ed. 2d 1081 (1961), and by this rule, inadmissible in evidence. Hernandez v. People, 153 Colo. 316, 385 P.2d 996 (1963). This rule specifically provides for motion to suppress. A motion to suppress is excluded by definition from Crim. P. 12(b), but section (e) of this rule specifically provides for such a motion. Adargo v. People, 173 Colo. 323, 478 P.2d 308 (1970). Only purpose served by suppressing evidence is preventing use by prosecution. The only purpose that can be served by suppressing the evidence which is seized by the police is to prevent its use by the prosecution at the trial. Lucero v. People, 164 Colo. 247, 434 P.2d 128 (1967). Habeas corpus is not correct vehicle to raise the issue of illegal evidence having been secured through wiretapping. Ferrell v. Vogt, 161 Colo. 549, 423 P.2d 844 (1967). Not every violation of subsection (c)(1) of this rule requires suppression of evidence under the exclusionary rule. Where search warrant was executed one-half block outside officers' jurisdiction, but city boundaries were not clear and officers promptly notified the proper authorities when the error was discovered, no violation of defendant's constitutional rights occurred. People v. Martinez, 898 P.2d 28 (Colo. 1995). Trial court erred in holding that defendant abandoned the motions to *suppress when he failed to appear at the suppression hearings. The court could have heard and decided the motions on the merits though defendant was absent. People v. Dashner, 77 P.3d 787 (Colo. App. 2003). Defendant's incriminating statements were obtained in violation of his Miranda rights, and trial court's order to suppress the statements was appropriate. A reasonable person in defendant's circumstances would have felt deprived of his or her freedom of action in a manner similar to a formal arrest. Therefore, defendant was in custody and subject to interrogation without being advised of his Miranda rights. People v. Holt, 233 P.3d 1194 (Colo. 2010). B. Aggrieved Party. Defendant has the burden of showing that he is an aggrieved person under the provisions of this rule. People v. Towers, 176 Colo. 295, 490 P.2d 302 (1971). And where burden not established, motion denied. Where the defendant does not meet his burden and does not establish that he has standing to object to the search and seizure, his motion to suppress is properly denied. People v. Towers, 176 Colo. 295, 490 P.2d 302 (1971). Prosecutor bears no burden at suppression hearing to prove that defendant was the victim of the claimed illegal police conduct because, when a defendant files a motion to suppress claiming his or her fourth amendment rights were violated, this initial allegation suffices to establish that he or she was the victim or aggrieved party of the alleged invasion of privacy. People v. Jorlantin, 196 P.3d 258 (Colo. 2008). Defendant legitimately on premises when search occurs possesses standing to object. A defendant has standing to object to a search or to a seizure if he is legitimately on the premises when the search occurs. People v. Towers, 176 Colo. 295, 490 P.2d 302 (1971). When fruits of search to be used against him. Anyone legitimately on the premises where a search occurs may challenge its legality by way of a motion to suppress, when its fruits are proposed to be used against him. Lanford v. People, 176 Colo. 109, 489 P.2d 210 (1971). Including a child subject to delinquency adjudication. Since a child subject to a delinquency adjudication is entitled to same constitutional safeguards as adult accused of crime, evidence obtained as result of unlawful search should be suppressed. In re People in Interest of B.M.C., 32 Colo. App. 79, 506 P.2d 409 (1973). Hence, defendant "aggrieved" where search occurs in sister's home while defendant there. Where the search and seizure which a defendant challenges occurred in the home of his sister and the defendant was there with the permission of his sister, the defendant qualifies under this rule as a person "aggrieved", where the search, if valid, produces evidence which is relevant to the issue of his guilt, for under the circumstances, he has standing to have the question of the validity of the search determined upon its merits. Adargo v. People, 173 Colo. 323, 478 P.2d 308 (1970). One not legitimately on the premises has no standing to move to suppress the fruits of a search and seizure of those premises. People v. Trusty, 183 Colo. 291, 516 P.2d 423 (1973). And defendant cannot urge standing on basis of fleeting presence before search. Where a defendant neither claims nor has a possessory interest in premises and has no personal expectation of privacy, he cannot successfully urge standing on the basis of his fleeting presence in the premises before the search. People v. Towers, 176 Colo. 295, 490 P.2d 302 (1971). State precluded from denying defendant's possessory interest when possession essential element of offense. When possession of the seized evidence is itself an essential element of the offense charged, the state is precluded from denying that the defendant has the requisite possessory interest to challenge the admission of the evidence. People v. Towers, 176 Colo. 295, 490 P.2d 302 (1971). Defendant did not have automatic standing to challenge automobile search. Where the defendant was found unconscious inside an automobile which upon a search was found to contain the deceased's body, and it was not an instance where the basis for defendant's prosecution was possession of the vehicle, the defendant did not have automatic standing to challenge the vehicle's search and seizure. People v. Trusty, 183 Colo. 291, 516 P.2d 423 (1973). Likewise, where defendant has abandoned a car, he has no standing to suppress the evidence seized in a warrantless search of the car as "a person aggrieved". Kurtz v. People, 177 Colo. 306, 494 P.2d 97 (1972). A person who has abandoned a vehicle is not an "aggrieved" person under section (e) and has no standing to suppress evidence seized in a search of that vehicle. People v. Parker, 189 Colo. 370, 541 P.2d 74 (1975). Jail not place where defendant can claim constitutional immunity from search. A public jail is not the equivalent of a man's "house" or a place where he can claim constitutional immunity from search or seizure of his person, his papers, or his effects. A jail shares none of the attributes of privacy of a home, an automobile, an office, or a hotel room. In prison, official surveillance has traditionally been the order of the day. Moore v. People, 171 Colo. 338, 467 P.2d 50 (1970). C. Grounds. 1. In General. Motion has limited reach. A brief examination of the five grounds that support a motion to suppress discloses the limited reach of the motion. People v. Fidler, 175 Colo. 90, 485 P.2d 725 (1971). A court cannot exclude all of a witness's testimony based on a violation of the constitution. The court has the authority to suppress only the tainted evidence, not the untainted evidence. People v. Cowart, 244 P.3d 1199 (Colo. 2010). Entrapment does not present a question of admissibility of evidence, but presents rather the proposition that a conviction may not be obtained, no matter what the evidence, where the authorities instigated the acts complained of, and this is generally a question of fact for a jury; therefore, entrapment is not within the scope of section (e) of this rule, which deals solely with the question of admissibility. People v. Patterson, 175 Colo. 19, 485 P.2d 494 (1971). Absence of "chain of evidence" not within rule's perimeters. When the defendant argues that there is no "chain of evidence" to establish that a specimen analyzed is one obtained from the defendant, then, in the absence of any averment of constitutional overtones for this claim, this ground does not fall within the perimeters set forth in section (e) of this rule, and to which interlocutory appeals are limited. People v. Kokesh, 175 Colo. 206, 486 P.2d 429 (1971). Where no constitutional rights invaded under official authority, motion denied. Where no constitutional rights are invaded by or under color of official authority, a motion to suppress will be denied. People v. Benson, 176 Colo. 421, 490 P.2d 1287 (1971). Rule not expanded to exclude evidence obtained by private persons. Even though the rule as to the exclusion of evidence obtained by an unreasonable search and seizure has been broadened and expanded, it has not been expanded to the extent that evidence obtained by persons not acting in concert with either state or federal officials must be excluded. People v. Benson, 176 Colo. 421, 490 P.2d 1287 (1971). But question whether items seized inadmissible on other grounds determined at trial. The question of whether the items seized are inadmissible in evidence on grounds other than those specified in this rule must be determined at the time of trial. People v. Towers, 176 Colo. 295, 490 P.2d 302 (1971). Rule applicable to evaluate validity of arrest prior to search. This rule does apply when the validity of an arrest must be evaluated before the court can rule upon a motion to suppress items seized in a search incident to the arrest. People v. Lott, 197 Colo. 78, 589 P.2d 945 (1979). Evidence need not be suppressed if it is obtained in violation of a statutory provision unless it also amounts to a constitutional violation. People v. Mandez, 997 P.2d 1254 (Colo. App. 1999). Police search of cloth glove not unconstitutional. Like the plain view doctrine, the plain feel doctrine allows police to seize contraband discovered through the sense of touch during an otherwise lawful search; therefore, trial court erred in suppressing evidence. People v. Brant, 252 P.3d 459 (Colo. 2011). Where search warrant validly is obtained, motion to suppress evidence is not valid. People v. Buttorff, 179 Colo. 406, 500 P.2d 979 (1972). Preservation of hazardous substances not required. The destruction of evidence rule cannot be applied mechanically in a way that endangers the lives of public safety officers or forces the police to preserve hazardous substances which cannot be stored safely. People v. Clements, 661 P.2d 267 (Colo. 1983). Such as high explosives. The prosecution does not have the duty to preserve high explosives, homemade bombs or dangerous materials if that requirement would endanger lives and the public safety. People v. Clements, 661 P.2d 267 (Colo. 1983). Failure for good cause to comply with subsection (c)(1) of this rule, which requires affidavits for search warrants to be sworn to or affirmed before the issuing judge, does not constitute a constitutional violation that automatically triggers the exclusionary rule. People v. Fournier, 793 P.2d 1176 (Colo. 1990). 2. Illegal Seizure Without Warrant. Not every search that is conducted without search warrant is "unreasonable" or "illegal" as those words are used in the United States Constitution and in this rule. More v. People, 171 Colo. 338, 467 P.2d 50 (1970). Nor does Mapp decision exclude all evidence incident to arrest without warrant. The decision of the supreme court of the United States in Mapp v. Ohio, 367 U.S. 643, 81 S. Ct. 1684, 6 L. Ed. 2d 1081 (1961), went no further than to exclude in state courts the use of evidence obtained by unreasonable search and seizure prohibited by the fourth amendment; it does not exclude all evidence which might be obtained as an incident to a lawful arrest, nor does it preclude admission of all evidence which may have been obtained without the sanction of a search warrant. Peters v. People, 151 Colo. 35, 376 P.2d 170 (1962). But probable cause requirements are at least as strict in warrantless searches as in those pursuant to a warrant. People v. Thompson, 185 Colo. 208, 523 P.2d 128 (1974). Where search illegal at inception, nothing intervening can render search legal. Where a search is illegal at its inception, nothing intervening, including the last minute obtaining of a search warrant, can render any part of the search legal. Condon v. People, 176 Colo. 212, 489 P.2d 1297 (1971). But where warrantless entry and arrest legal, evidence seized not inadmissible. Where warrantless entry and arrest are based on probable cause and a search warrant is issued subsequent to the entry and arrest, the evidence seized is not inadmissible because the entry and arrest were without warrant. People v. Vaughns, 175 Colo. 369, 489 P.2d 591 (1971). Except where supposed legitimate entry utterly vitiated by method of entry. Where any supposed legitimate entry is utterly vitiated by the method of entry, the evidence observed by the officers is tainted, cannot be used as the basis for probable cause to arrest or seized as incident to a lawful arrest, and is therefore properly suppressed. People v. Godinas, 176 Colo. 391, 490 P.2d 945 (1971). Warrant needed where article believed concealed. A belief, no matter how well-founded, that an article sought is concealed in a dwelling furnishes no justification for the search of the dwelling without a lawful warrant. People v. McGahey, 179 Colo. 401, 500 P.2d 977 (1972). Defendant's allegedly criminal acts were sufficiently attenuated from any illegal conduct of sheriff's deputies so that exclusion of evidence was not appropriate. Evidence of a new crime committed in response to an unlawful trespass is admissible. People v. Doke, 171 P.3d 237 (Colo. 2007). "Emergency doctrine" tested on particular facts of each case. In applying the "emergency doctrine" to warrantless searches each case must be tested on its own particular facts. Condon v. People, 176 Colo. 212, 489 P.2d 1297 (1971). And the test is reasonableness under the circumstances. Condon v. People, 176 Colo. 212, 489 P.2d 1297 (1971). But odor of decomposing body not emergency. The detection of an odor which might be that of a decomposing body does not create, in and of itself, an emergency sufficient to justify a warrantless search. Condon v. People, 176 Colo. 212, 489 P.2d 1297 (1971). Burden of proving probable cause for arrest without warrant is on the prosecution. People v. Chacon, 177 Colo. 368, 494 P.2d 79 (1972). As is burden to establish probable cause for warrantless search. The burden is upon the state at a suppression hearing to establish that probable cause existed which would justify a warrantless search of the defendant's person. People v. Ware, 174 Colo. 419, 484 P.2d 103 (1971). Burden of proof for warrantless arrest and search. Where defendant is arrested without a warrant and moves to suppress evidence seized in course of his arrest, burden of proof is upon prosecution to prove constitutional validity of arrest and search. People v. Crow, 789 P.2d 1104 (Colo. 1990). "Reasonable" search may be made in the place where a lawful arrest occurs in order to find and seize articles connected with the crime as its fruits or as the means by which it was committed. Hernandez v. People, 153 Colo. 316, 385 P.2d 996 (1963). And police entitled to made contemporaneous search of person. When a person is lawfully arrested, the police have the right, without a search warrant, to made a contemporaneous search of the person of the accused for weapons or for the fruits of or implements used to commit a crime. People v. Vigil, 175 Colo. 421, 489 P.2d 593 (1971). And such searches not violative of constitutions. Even if there is a search, where the arrest is legal the search is not violative of the state and federal constitutions regarding unreasonable search and seizure. People v. Clark, 173 Colo. 129, 476 P.2d 564 (1970). So long as not too much time between search and arrest. The lapse of too much time between the inception of the search and the arrest falls short of the requirement that the two acts (search and arrest) be nearly simultaneous and constitute for all practical purposes one transaction. People v. Drumright, 172 Colo. 577, 475 P.2d 329 (1970). Search incident to arrest limited to evidence related to offense. The scope of a warrantless evidentiary search incident to arrest is limited to evidence related to offense for which arrest is made. In re People in Interest of B. M. C., 32 Colo. App. 79, 506 P.2d 409 (1973). And extends to things under accused's immediate control and place of arrest. The right to search and seize without a search warrant incident to a lawful arrest extends to things under the accused's immediate control and to an extent, depending on the circumstances of the case, to the place where he is arrested. People v. Vigil, 175 Colo. 421, 489 P.2d 593 (1971). Including police station. A police station, immediately following an arrest, cannot be held to be too remote from the place of arrest in a search and seizure case. Glass v. People, 177 Colo. 267, 493 P.2d 1347 (1972). Search following arrest may also be conducted as inventory procedure. A warrantless search of defendant's purse that followed her arrest for drug use and the seizure of the contraband found therein may be upheld either as a search incident to an arrest or as an inventory procedure conducted prior to incarceration. Avalos v. People, 179 Colo. 88, 498 P.2d 1141 (1972). Where probable cause for a warrantless arrest is lacking, subsequent search is invalid. People v. Trujillo, 179 Colo. 428, 500 P.2d 1176 (1972). And fact contraband found in search does not make arrest valid. Where police officers when they arrest a defendant have no idea of what the charge is for which they are arresting him, the fact that contraband is found in an illegal search does not make such an arrest valid. Gallegos v. People, 157 Colo. 173, 401 P.2d 613 (1965). Fruits of unlawful arrest inadmissible. The prosecution's failure to present evidence to support a determination that the arrest of the defendant was supported by probable cause leaves the court with no alternative but to hold that the arrest was unlawful and its fruits inadmissible. People v. Chacon, 177 Colo. 368, 494 P.2d 79 (1972). And the defendant's motion to suppress should be granted where the police conducted a warrantless search and arrest without probable cause. People v. Henderson, 175 Colo. 400, 487 P.2d 1108 (1971). Test of admissibility of evidence seized in lawful search following unlawful search is whether, granting establishment of the primary illegality, the evidence to which instant objection is made has been arrived at by exploitation of that illegality, or instead by means sufficiently distinguishable to be purged of the primary taint. People v. Hannah, 183 Colo. 9, 514 P.2d 320 (1973). "Pat down" or "stop and frisk" search justified for potentially armed individual. It is well established that an officer may conduct a limited search for weapons (a so-called "pat down" or "stop and frisk") for his own safety when he is justified in believing that he is dealing with a potentially armed and dangerous individual. Finley v. People, 176 Colo. 1, 488 P.2d 883 (1971). Limited searches of person for weapons during investigative detention, where probable cause for arrest is lacking, is permissible, but there must be: (a) Some reason for the officer to confront the citizen in the first place; (b) something in the circumstances, including the citizen's reaction to the confrontation, must give the officer reason to suspect that the citizen may be armed and, thus, dangerous to the officer or others; and (c) the search must be limited to a frisk directed at discovery and appropriation of weapons and not at evidence in general. People v. Martineau, 185 Colo. 194, 523 P.2d 126 (1974). And evidence of crime uncovered is competent and admissible. Where the search was limited to a frisk directed at the discovery and appropriation of weapons, and not to uncover evidence as such, evidence of a crime having thus been lawfully uncovered, it is competent and admissible in evidence as relevant proof of the charges of which defendant is accused. People v. Martineau, 185 Colo. 194, 523 P.2d 126 (1974). Objects in plain view of officer subject to seizure. Objects falling in the plain view of an officer who has a right to be in the position to have that view are subject to seizure and may be introduced in evidence. People v. McGahey, 179 Colo. 401, 500 P.2d 977 (1972). Where the record fails to support defendant's contention that the officers were engaged in a search when they observed the evidence in plain view, suppression is not required. Blincoe v. People, 178 Colo. 34, 494 P.2d 1285 (1972). As such does not constitute a search. The discovery of the fruits of a crime or of contraband lying free in the open does not constitute any kind of search. Alire v. People, 157 Colo. 103, 402 P.2d 610 (1965). Police protective search of passenger compartment of vehicle justified. People v. Brant, 252 P.3d 459 (Colo. 2011). Applying the "plain feel" doctrine, police properly seized evidence discovered in cloth glove. People v. Brant, 252 P.3d 459 (Colo. 2011). Validity of automobile searches turn upon their own peculiar circumstances. Kurtz v. People, 177 Colo. 306, 494 P.2d 97 (1972). Police officer entitled to approach suspicious parked automobile and look inside. Where a police officer approaches a parked automobile, in which the defendant is seated, he has a right to flash his light inside, and any contraband which he sees in the automobile and seizes is admissible against the defendant. People v. Shriver, 186 Colo. 405, 528 P.2d 242 (1974). Plain view exception applies to contraband in defendant's home observed by officers using a flashlight to view inside defendant's residence. Officers who were lawfully on defendant's porch when defendant left front door open could use flashlights to peer into the home. The fact that the officers used their flashlights to see inside defendant's home did not transform their plain view observations into an illegal search because, had it been daylight, the contraband on the table inside the home would have been plainly visible to the officers. People v. Glick, 250 P.3d 578 (Colo. 2011). Lawful to stop vehicle for investigatory purposes, and search where probable cause. Where police officer obtained probable cause to search a vehicle and seize evidence in the process of making a lawful stop for threshold investigatory purposes, the defendant's motion to suppress this evidence was properly denied. People v. Lucero, 182 Colo. 39, 511 P.2d 468 (1973). Stopping automobile not "unreasonable" where probable cause offense committed. Stopping an automobile and conducting a search and seizure is not "unreasonable" where the officer conducting it has a probable and reasonable belief that an offense has been committed. Hopper v. People, 152 Colo. 405, 382 P.2d 540 (1963). If probable cause to search car, right to search without warrant. If there is probable cause to obtain a warrant to search a car, police officers have the right to stop and search it without a warrant. People v. Chavez, 175 Colo. 25, 485 P.2d 708 (1971). And items found admissible into evidence. Where police officers have probable cause to search defendants' automobile, the search of defendants' automobile without a warrant is proper, and it is not error to admit the items found into evidence. Atwood v. People, 176 Colo. 183, 489 P.2d 1305 (1971). Search of vehicle which is made substantially contemporaneously with an arrest is permissible as an incident to the arrest. People v. Olson, 175 Colo. 140, 485 P.2d 891 (1971). And evidence seized during arrest not suppressed. The denial of a motion to suppress evidence seized during a warrantless arrest of fleeing felons in an automobile should be affirmed. People v. Duncan, 179 Colo. 253, 500 P.2d 137 (1972). Where defendant stopped for careless driving, exposed contraband seized. The fact that a defendant is stopped by police officers because of his careless driving will not prevent them from seizing contraband found lying exposed on the seat of the automobile. Alire v. People, 157 Colo. 103, 402 P.2d 610 (1965). As inspection protected by "plain view rule". Where a police officer*

188

properly stops a car for careless driving, that officer has every right to look into the car and seize anything that is contraband, for such an inspection is held to be protected by the "plain view rule". People v. Teague, 173 Colo. 120, 476 P.2d 751 (1970). And items in "plain view" admissible in evidence. Where an arrest is made with probable cause, any items in "plain view" after the defendant exits from a vehicle can properly be used in evidence against him. People v. Clark, 173 Colo. 129, 476 P.2d 564 (1970). Probable cause must exist at moment arrest or automobile search made. In order for a warrantless search of an automobile to be excused under exigent circumstances, probable cause must exist at the moment the arrest or the search is made. People v. Thompson, 185 Colo. 208, 523 P.2d 128 (1974). Factors which lead to the conclusion that a warrantless search of a car was reasonable include the commission of a felony, abandonment of the car by the suspects at the scene of the crime, and their flight from the scene on foot into the night and their remaining at large. Kurtz v. People, 177 Colo. 306, 494 P.2d 97 (1972). Suspicious demeanor and odor supports probable cause for possession of marijuana in car. The combination of the suspicious demeanor of the occupants of a vehicle and the subsequent odor of marijuana emanating from within the car moments after the occupants had exited was a sufficient basis upon which to predicate probable cause for the belief that the offense of possession of marijuana had been recently committed. People v. Olson, 175 Colo. 140, 485 P.2d 891 (1971). Moreover, it is unnecessary for officer to have a chemical analysis of a suspected narcotic prior to making a valid seizure; it is only necessary that he have reason to believe that the article seized is a narcotic. Alire v. People, 157 Colo. 103, 402 P.2d 610 (1965). But mere exploratory search not sustained. Where a police officer has no cause to believe that a car contains any contraband, a search is exploratory only and cannot be sustained. People v. Singleton, 174 Colo. 138, 482 P.2d 978 (1971). Search not incident to arrest where defendant in custody, car outside search area. The defendant was in custody so there was no danger of his destroying any evidence in his car, and the car was without the area authorized to be searched by a warrant, the search was not incident to the arrest. People v. Singleton, 174 Colo. 138, 482 P.2d 978 (1971). Suppression of evidence proper where it was undisputed that defendant had already been arrested, handcuffed, and placed in patrol car at the time of the search of defendant's vehicle and because it would not have been reasonable for officers to believe that defendant's vehicle might contain evidence relevant to the false reporting crime. People v. Chamberlain, 229 P.3d 1054 (Colo. 2010). Permissive search is not unreasonable search and seizure within the coverage of Mapp v. Ohio (367 U.S. 643, 81 S. Ct. 1684, 6 L. Ed. 2d 1081 (1961)). Peters v. People, 151 Colo. 35, 376 P.2d 170 (1962). Hence, a search loses its illegal effect when defendant gives permission for such a search of the premises, as this consent removes the applicability of the constitutional guaranty. Williams v. People, 136 Colo. 164, 315 P.2d 189 (1957); Hopper v. People, 152 Colo. 405, 382 P.2d 540 (1963). But search must be voluntary. A search conducted without a warrant but with the voluntary consent of the person whose place is searched is reasonable and not in violation of the state or federal constitutions. Phillips v. People, 170 Colo. 520, 462 P.2d 594 (1969). And voluntary means that the consent is intelligently and freely given. Phillips v. People, 170 Colo. 520, 462 P.2d 594 (1969). Burden of proof as to consent to warrantless search on people. The burden of proof in the determination of whether a consent to a warrantless search is intelligently and freely given rests firmly on the people. People v. Neyra, 189 Colo. 367, 540 P.2d 1077 (1975). Whether consent voluntary determined from each case's total circumstances. Whether or not the consent which is given to a search in a particular case is voluntary is a question to be determined from the totality of the circumstances in each case. The circumstances of a case may indicate that a defendant was fully aware that the police were his adversaries and that evidence seized by them could be used against him at trial. Phillips v. People, 170 Colo. 520, 462 P.2d 594 (1969). Miranda decision not applicable to fourth amendment searches and seizures. Miranda v. Arizona, 384 U.S. 436, 86 S. Ct. 1602, 16 L. Ed. 2d 694, 10 A.L.R.3d 974 (1966), has no application to the area of fourth amendment searches and seizures, since the ruling therein was designed as a prophylactic rule to correct and prevent abusive police practices in the area of confessions, and the United States Supreme Court has not acted to extend the rule in Miranda to the fourth amendment. Phillips v. People, 170 Colo. 520, 462 P.2d 594 (1969). But warning that defendant does not have to consent to search constitutionally sufficient. Where a defendant is informed that he does not have to consent to a warrantless search of his premises, such a warning is sufficient to apprise the defendant of his rights under the fourth amendment of the U. S. Constitution and § 7 of art. II, Colo. Const. Phillips v. People, 170 Colo. 520, 462 P.2d 594 (1969). Resident of a place has the ability to consent to a search of the premises, and a search based on such consent is not illegal. Lanford v. People, 176 Colo. 109, 489 P.2d 210 (1971). Likewise, one of two or more persons occupying premises may authorize search. When two or more persons have an equal right of ownership, occupancy, or other possessory interest in the premises searched or the property seized, any one of such persons may authorize a search and seizure thereof thereby binding the others, waiving their rights to object. Lanford v. People, 176 Colo. 109, 489 P.2d 210 (1971). But a landlord is not a proper person to give consent to the search of his tenant's residence. Condon v. People, 176 Colo. 212, 489 P.2d 1297 (1971). After consent has been granted to conduct search, that consent cannot be withdrawn. People v. Kennard, 175 Colo. 479, 488 P.2d 563 (1971). Prisoner cannot expect to be free from warrantless searches. A prison cell is not a place in which the occupant can expect to be free from all searches unless accompanied by a warrant. Moore v. People, 171 Colo. 338, 467 P.2d 50 (1970). 3. Warrant Insufficient on Face. Affidavits have not been required to be attached to warrants. People v. Leahy, 173 Colo. 339, 484 P.2d 778 (1970). Warrant not insufficient because affidavit does not allege possession of articles is crime. Where an affidavit upon which a search warrant is issued does not allege that possession of the articles in question is a crime, this does not render the warrant insufficient. People v. Whisenhunt, 173 Colo. 109, 476 P.2d 997 (1970). The fact that the affidavit details activities that are lawful does not cause it to be a bare bones affidavit; a combination of otherwise lawful circumstances may well lead to a legitimate inference of criminal activity. People v. Altman, 960 P.2d 1164 (Colo. 1998). But, constitutionally, probable cause must appear on face of affidavit. The express Colorado constitutional requirement of a written oath or affirmation makes it clear beyond a doubt that sufficient facts to support a magistrate's determination of probable cause must appear on the face of a written affidavit. People v. Baird, 172 Colo. 112, 470 P.2d 20 (1970). Otherwise, warrants issued on such fatally defective affidavits are nullities, any search conducted under them was unlawful, and the fruits of such a search are inadmissible in evidence. Hernandez v. People, 153 Colo. 316, 385 P.2d 996 (1963); People v. Baird, 173 Colo. 112, 470 P.2d 20 (1970); People v. Brethauer, 174 Colo. 29, 482 P.2d 369 (1971). Affidavit in support of warrant held fatally defective. People v. Peschong, 181 Colo. 29, 506 P.2d 1232 (1973). On review, search warrants are tested and interpreted in common sense and realistic fashion. People v. Lamirato, 180 Colo. 250, 504 P.2d 661 (1972). Where statements concerning reliability of informer are not true, warrant cannot stand. Where information attributed to an informer is sufficient upon which to base a warrant, but statements made to the issuing magistrate by a policeman concerning the reliability of the informer are not true, a search warrant issued by the magistrate based on the false allegations of the police officer cannot stand. People v. Massey, 178 Colo. 141, 495 P.2d 1141 (1972). Warrant's validity cannot be challenged where modified before issuance. Where changes and modifications on a search warrant take place before it is signed and issued by a judge, the validity of the search warrant is not subject to challenge. People v. Ferris, 173 Colo. 494, 480 P.2d 552 (1971). Warrant not invalidated because descriptions therein vary from affidavit's. That there exists a variation between the descriptions in the warrant and in the affidavit does not in itself render the warrant invalid, unless the variance is material. People v. Peppers, 172 Colo. 556, 475 P.2d 337 (1970). So long as description adequately identifies premises. A slight variation from the description in the affidavit will not affect the validity of a search warrant as long as the remainder of the descriptive language adequately identifies the premises to be searched. People v. Peppers, 172 Colo. 556, 475 P.2d 337 (1970). And warrant specifically describing premises not rendered insufficient by command portion of warrant. A command portion of search warrant which reads: "You are therefore commanded to search forthwith the above described property for the property described" did not render the warrant insufficient on its face where the property to be searched had been specifically described "above" in the warrant. People v. Ragulsky, 184 Colo. 86, 518 P.2d 286 (1974). Test for determining whether the sufficiency of a description in a search warrant is adequate is if the officer executing the warrant can with reasonable effort ascertain and identify the place intended to be searched. People v. Ragulsky, 184 Colo. 86, 518 P.2d 286 (1974). Where city not specified in warrant, absence not fatal where location clear. Where a warrant specified the place to be searched as to street, county, and state, although not as to city, but the district attorney made a showing to the trial court that the place searched was the only one in the indicated county having such a street address, and the trial court found that there was sufficient clarity as to the location in the minds of all parties involved, then the absence of the name of the city was not fatal or prejudicial. People v. Leahy, 173 Colo. 339, 484 P.2d 778 (1970). But omission of description of property to be seized not excused. Where in the space provided in a warrant for the description of the property to be seized there appears a description of the location of the place to be searched, then, although it may be presumed that this incorrect language doubtless was inserted by mistake and that the person who completed the

190

warrant intended to insert the required description of the property to be seized, this is, however, not the type of mere "technical omission" that is excused, since it goes rather to the very essence of the constitutional requirement that a warrant describe "the person or thing to be seized, as near as may be" contained in § 7 of art. II, Colo. Const. People v. Drumright, 172 Colo. 577, 475 P.2d 329 (1970). Warrant commanding officers to enter designated place for certain property valid. A search warrant directed to all peace officers which in essence states that certain articles are concealed at a designated address, that complaint made by a named person set forth reasons which show that probable cause exists, and commands such persons to enter the place and search for certain property fully sets forth the information required by this rule, and is therefore valid. People v. Ferris, 173 Colo. 494, 480 P.2d 552 (1971). Failure to insert names indicating to whom return to be made is ministerial deficiency. The failure to insert names in blank spaces provided in a search warrant for purpose of indicating to whom return is to be made and to whom written inventory of seized property is to be made is ministerial deficiency and not such as to render a warrant invalid. Brown v. People, 158 Colo. 561, 408 P.2d 981 (1965). Substantial compliance with contemporary objection rule exists where continuous general objection is made on ground that evidence is product of search under invalid warrant. Brown v. Patterson, 275 F. Supp. 629 (D. Colo. 1967), aff'd, 393 F.2d 733 (10th Cir. 1968). But even if objection insufficient, federal habeas relief not precluded. Even if failure to specifically attack insufficiency of affidavit supporting warrant renders objection insufficient under this rule, a state court conviction based thereon will not preclude procuring federal habeas corpus relief. Brown v. Patterson, 275 F. Supp. 629 (D. Colo. 1967), aff'd, 393 F.2d 733 (10th Cir. 1968). 4. Property Not Described in Warrant. Description of items to be seized in search warrant must be specific. People v. Clavey, 187 Colo. 305, 530 P.2d 491 (1975). And items seized under warrant with insufficient description suppressed. All items seized under a search warrant that failed to describe the things to be seized with sufficient particularity should be suppressed. People ex rel. McKevitt v. Harvey, 176 Colo. 447, 491 P.2d 563 (1971). But the seizure of property not specified does not render specified items inadmissible. People v. Greathouse, 173 Colo. 103, 476 P.2d 259 (1970). Warrant not too broad where authorizes seizure of "narcotics" and "paraphernalia". The language in a warrant which specifies the items to be seized is not so broad and ambiguous as to make it a general warrant where the warrant authorizes seizure of: (1) Any and all narcotics and dangerous drugs as defined by the applicable Colorado statutes, the possession of which is illegal; and (2) all implements, paraphernalia, articles, papers, and records pertaining to, or which would be evidence of, the illegal use, possession, or sale of narcotics and/or dangerous drugs. People v. Leahy, 173 Colo. 339, 484 P.2d 778 (1970). And "narcotics" includes marijuana. Where a search warrant authorizes a search for "narcotics, dangerous drugs, and narcotics paraphernalia", then, since the word "narcotics" includes marijuana, the seizure of marijuana is properly authorized under the warrant. People v. Henry, 173 Colo. 523, 482 P.2d 357 (1971). Term "narcotics paraphernalia" is not so vague as to make document general warrant. People v. Henry, 173 Colo. 523, 482 P.2d 357 (1971). Seized items held sufficiently within warrant description. People v. Lamirato, 180 Colo. 250, 504 P.2d 661 (1972). Search must be conducted for specific articles. The search, whether under a valid search warrant or whether as incident to a lawful arrest, must be one in which the officers are looking for specific articles and must be conducted in a manner reasonably calculated to uncover such articles. Hernandez v. People, 153 Colo. 316, 385 P.2d 996 (1963); People v. Drumright, 172 Colo. 577, 475 P.2d 329 (1970). And any search more extensive than this constitutes a general exploratory search and is squarely within the interdiction of the constitutional guarantee against unreasonable search and seizure. Hernandez v. People, 153 Colo. 316, 385 P.2d 996 (1963); People v. Drumright, 172 Colo. 577, 475 P.2d 329 (1970); In re People in Interest of B.M.C., 32 Colo. App. 79, 506 P.2d 409 (1972). Entire search only becomes invalid if general tenor is that of exploratory search for evidence not specifically related to the search warrant. People v. Tucci, 179 Colo. 373, 500 P.2d 815 (1972). And where execution of warrant in good faith, not all evidence obtained suppressed. Where evidence is without conflict that the persons executing the search warrant were trying in good faith to obtain items relating to that prescribed in the warrant, a ruling requiring suppression of all evidence obtained during the search of defendant's premises is disapproved. People v. Tucci, 179 Colo. 373, 500 P.2d 815 (1972). Evidence seized during general exploratory search will be suppressed. Where evidence was seized during a general exploratory search for which no probable cause existed, defendant's motion to suppress the evidence will be granted. People v. Valdez, 182 Colo. 80, 511 P.2d 472 (1973). "Other" articles found in course of "proper" search are admissible. If an officer is conducting a search, either under a valid search warrant or incident to a valid arrest, where the search is such as is reasonably designed to uncover the articles for which he is looking and in the course of such search discovers contraband or articles the possession of which is a crime, other than those for which he was originally searching, he is not required to shut his eyes and refrain from seizing that material under the penalty that if he does seize it, it cannot be admitted in evidence. Hernandez v. People, 153 Colo. 316, 385 P.2d 996 (1963). And no suppression of fruits or instruments of crime, and contraband. Harris v. United States, 331 U.S. 145, 67 S. Ct. 1098, 91 L. Ed. 1399 (1947), upheld the validity of seizure of fruits of a crime, instrumentalities of a crime, and contraband articles; such items may be referred to as "Harris articles", and where items are "Harris articles", a trial court is correct in denying a suppression motion with respect to them. People v. Henry, 173 Colo. 523, 482 P.2d 357 (1971). But burden on state where such articles not connected with crime "per se". When a defendant demonstrates that an article is not specifically described in the search warrant and it is not "per se" connected with criminal activity, the burden of showing that it is so connected falls upon the state. People v. Henry, 173 Colo. 523, 482 P.2d 357 (1971); People v. Wilson, 173 Colo. 536, 482 P.2d 355 (1971). And if state sustains burden, the articles should not be suppressed. People v. Wilson, 173 Colo. 536, 482 P.2d 355 (1971). However, where showing not made, nonspecified articles suppressed. When the district attorney fails to make the requisite showing, the trial court should sustain the motion as it relates to nonspecified articles not "per se" connected with criminal activity. People v. Wilson, 173 Colo. 536, 482 P.2d 355 (1971). "Mere evidence" seized must be shown to have a "nexus" with case and defendant. "Mere evidence" consists of articles which are not fruits, instrumentalities, or contraband, and which are not "per se" associated with criminal activity, but which an officer executing a warrant has probable cause to believe are associated with criminal activity, and "mere evidence" which is seized within the scope of the search authorized by a warrant must be shown to have a "nexus" with the case in which a motion to suppress is filed and with at least one of the defendants in the case. People v. Henry, 173 Colo. 523, 482 P.2d 357 (1971); People v. LaRocco, 178 Colo. 196, 496 P.2d 314 (1972). 5. No Probable Cause. Matter of probable cause not "res judicata". The trial court is not bound to conclude that because a search warrant had been issued the matter of the existence of probable cause for the issuance thereof was "res judicata", inasmuch as it is for the judge who determines the adversary proceeding to decide all questions relating to the admissibility of the evidence offered by the litigants. Gonzales v. District Court, 164 Colo. 433, 435 P.2d 384 (1967). Warrant routinely issued at request of accusing officer clearly unconstitutional. Where a search warrant was routinely issued at the request of the accusing officer, without the slightest showing of probable cause, it therefore clearly violates the fundamental principle that the basis for the issuance of a search warrant must be determined by a judicial officer based on facts and not on the conclusion of the applicant. Consequently, such a search warrant is issued in violation of long-established fundamental constitutional standards, and any evidence seized under its authority should be excluded from evidence in the trial court, unless there is other legal basis for its admission. Brown v. Patterson, 275 F. Supp. 629 (D. Colo. 1967), aff'd, 393 F.2d 733 (10th Cir. 1968). Independent determination of probable cause to search specified place. The fact that the police did not request a warrant to search additional places likely to contain incriminating evidence is irrelevant to the independent determination of probable cause to search the place specified in the warrant. People v. Chase, 675 P.2d 315 (Colo, 1984). Affidavit introduced where warrant challenged for lack of probable cause. When a search warrant is challenged for lack of probable cause, the supporting affidavit is an essential element to be introduced in evidence. People v. Espinoza, 195 Colo. 127, 575 P.2d 851 (1978). Where supporting affidavit lacks probable cause, warrant invalid. Where the affidavit upon which a search warrant was issued was not sufficient to establish probable cause, the search and resultant arrest of defendant are part of the illegal fruits of an invalid warrant. Zamora v. People, 175 Colo. 340, 487 P.2d 1116 (1971). Warrant based on observations of police employee in response to invitation not invalid. Where a visit by a police employee is legitimately in response to an invitation by the defendant, a later search is not invalidated by the fact that the employee made observations which became part of the basis for the warrant. People v. Greathouse, 173 Colo. 103, 476 P.2d 259 (1970). Affidavit in support of search warrant was not insufficient because it was predicated upon "double hearsay". People v. Quintana, 183 Colo. 81, 514 P.2d 1325 (1973). But where the affidavit upon which a search warrant was predicated was based on "double hearsay", such does not render the warrant invalid. People v. Leahy, 173 Colo. 339, 484 P.2d 778 (1970). Such as where the information is conveyed by one police officer to another police officer. People v. Quintana, 183 Colo. 81, 514 P.2d 1325 (1973). Even if hearsay turns out to be incorrect. If the material in the affidavit is stated to be or appears to be hearsay information obtained from an informant or other person

192

and the information turns out to be incorrect, a court will not use hindsight as a test to determine whether the search warrant should or should not have been issued. People v. Woods, 175 Colo. 34, 485 P.2d 491 (1971). Reliability of detective need not be shown. The fact that the affidavit did nothing to disclose the reliability of a detective-except the fact that he was a detective-does not affect its validity, since there is nothing requiring a showing of reliability of a detective. People v. Leahy, 173 Colo. 339, 484 P.2d 778 (1970). Facts held sufficient to establish probable cause. People v. Henry, 173 Colo. 523, 482 P.2d 357 (1971); People v. Vigil, 175 Colo. 421, 489 P.2d 593 (1971); Atwood v. People, 176 Colo. 183, 489 P.2d 1305 (1971). Facts held not sufficient to establish probable cause. People v. Brethauer, 174 Colo. 29, 482 P.2d 369 (1971).
6. Illegal Execution. Officers must identify themselves before forced entry. Even with a valid warrant, before police officers attempt a forced entry into a place, they must first identify themselves and make their purpose known. People v. Godinas, 176 Colo. 391, 490 P.2d 945 (1971). And forceful entries include entries without permission. Forceful entries need not involve the actual breaking of doors and windows, but may include merely entries made without permission. Thus, where officers enter through a door which is ajar without right and they do not announce their purpose, a subsequent knock on an interior door is made after an illegal entry and without announcing identity and purpose. People v. Godinas, 176 Colo. 391, 490 P.2d 945 (1971). Copy of warrant need not be left personally with one confined in jail. The argument that the execution of a search warrant did not comply with this rule in that a copy of the warrant was not left with defendant personally is without merit where at the time of the search defendant was confined in jail, the officer upon whose affidavit the warrant was issued exhibited the warrant, receipt, and inventory of what was seized to defendant after seizure, and the copy of the warrant, receipt, and inventory was then placed in defendant's locker in the jail which contained his other personal belongings; in the absence of a showing of any prejudice resulting from this particular procedure, there is no reversible error. People v. Aguilar, 173 Colo. 260, 477 P.2d 462 (1970). Warrant need not have copy of affidavit attached. There is nothing which requires that a person given a warrant must receive a copy of the underlying affidavit or that a copy thereof must be attached to the copy of the warrant which is served at the time of the search. People v. Papez, 652 P.2d 619 (Colo. App. 1982). Where one recites he has "duly executed" warrant, authority to execute inferred. Where in the return and inventory made following the execution of a warrant, one recites that he has "duly executed the within search warrant", this alone justifies an inference and finding that the individual was authorized by law to execute such, and it thereupon becomes incumbent upon the defendant to show that he was not. People v. Henry, 173 Colo. 523, 482 P.2d 357 (1971). Warrant not invalidated by failure to follow requirements as to return and inventory. Since the requirements of this rule relating to the making of the return and inventory are ministerial in nature, a failure to comply does not render the search warrant or the seizure of the property pursuant thereto invalid. People v. Schmidt, 172 Colo. 285, 473 P.2d 698 (1970). Hence, failure to file the return within 10 days does not invalidate a search. People v. Wilson, 173 Colo. 536, 482 P.2d 355 (1971). D. Hearing. 1. When Motion Made. Suppression remedy not extended to grand jury proceedings. The remedy of suppression of evidence applies to a trial once an indictment has been returned, but has not been extended to grand jury proceedings considering an indictment. People ex rel. Dunbar v. District Court, 179 Colo. 321, 500 P.2d 819 (1972). Purpose of rule to prevent introduction of issue of police misconduct into trial. The purpose of this rule is to prevent, whenever possible, the introduction of a collateral issue, that of whether the police acted improperly, into the trial on the issue of guilt. Morgan v. People, 166 Colo. 451, 444 P.2d 386 (1968). Rule on time to serve motions preserves right to raise fourth amendment issues. Crim. P. 45(d), which must be read in conjunction with this rule, can adequately preserve the defendant's right to raise fourth amendment issues, while carrying out the salutary purpose of not commingling the fourth amendment issues with the guilt issue. Morgan v. People, 166 Colo. 451, 444 P.2d 386 (1968). Motion to suppress filed on the morning of the trial is not timely. Morgan v. People, 166 Colo. 451, 444 P.2d 386 (1968). Trial court's consideration of merits of a suppression motion does not render moot ruling by trial court that the motion was untimely. People v. Tyler, 874 P.2d 1037 (Colo. 1994). Nor is motion filed day before trial, where grounds raised therein previously apparent. Where defendant files his motion to suppress on the afternoon before the day on which the trial is to begin, but all the grounds raised therein were clearly apparent in the record from the very first time counsel appeared, then under such circumstances the motion is not timely filed. Morgan v. People, 166 Colo. 451, 444 P.2d 386 (1968). Motion untimely where defendant possesses all pertinent information prior to trial. Where defendant possessed prior to trial all pertinent information relative to the seizure of evidence and its possible suppression, the trial court did not abuse its discretion in declaring the

193

motion to suppress untimely. People v. Hinchman, 40 Colo. App. 9, 574 P.2d 866 (1977), rev'd on other grounds, 196 Colo. 526, 589 P.2d 917, cert. denied, 442 U.S. 941, 99 S. Ct. 2883, 61 L. Ed. 2d 311 (1979). But trial court has discretionary power to entertain a suppression motion at trial. People v. Stevens, 183 Colo. 399, 517 P.2d 1336 (1973). And if court rules on untimely motion, matter not waived unless discretion abused. If the trial court elects to rule on a untimely suppression motion raised at trial, an appellate court should not consider the matter waived unless it can be shown that the trial court abused its discretion in ruling on the merits of the motion. People v. Stevens, 183 Colo. 399, 517 P.2d 1336 (1973). Defendant not to be penalized because belated motion to suppress heard. There cannot be read into this rule any intendment that the defendant is to be penalized because the court chose to hear and consider his belated motion to suppress. People v. Voss, 191 Colo. 338, 552 P.2d 1012 (1976). Where proper pretrial request denied, court errs in not holding hearing at trial. Where the defendant is entitled to such a pretrial hearing which he requests, then a court which fails to grant a pretrial hearing again errs in not holding a hearing at the time the property objected to is offered in evidence by the prosecution; the defendant having made a proper request, the trial court errs in not holding a hearing. Adargo v. People, 173 Colo. 323, 478 P.2d 308 (1970). Pretrial ruling on a motion to suppress does not necessarily bind the trial judge, and under certain circumstances, the trial court has a duty to consider "de novo" the issue of suppression. Gibbons v. People, 167 Colo. 83, 445 P.2d 408 (1968). And within judge's discretion to hold additional evidentiary hearing. If it is necessary for the trial judge to hold an additional evidentiary hearing in order to arrive at the truth concerning a suppression of evidence motion, it is within his discretion to do so. People v. Duncan, 179 Colo. 253, 500 P.2d 137 (1972). 2. Procedure. Rule provides for procedure to be followed when motion to suppress is filed. Adargo v. People, 173 Colo. 323, 478 P.2d 308 (1970). Motion to suppress is interlocutory in character, and neither res judicata nor collateral estoppel applies to a ruling which is less than a final judgment. People v. Lewis, 659 P.2d 676 (Colo. 1983). Court makes inquiry and bases determination solely on evidence presented. The trial court shall make an inquiry concerning the validity of the search and base its determination solely upon the evidence presented upon a hearing conducted by it on the motion of the petitioners. Gonzales v. District Court, 164 Colo. 433, 435 P.2d 384 (1967). Burden is upon the state at a suppression hearing to show a connection between the evidence seized and the criminal activity for which the search was initiated in order that the evidence not be suppressed. People v. LaRocco, 178 Colo. 196, 496 P.2d 314 (1972). When granting or denying a motion, the court should state appropriate findings of fact. People v. Vigil, 175 Colo. 373, 489 P.2d 588 (1971). It is the function of the court to determine the factual issues presented by a motion to suppress, and this fact in turn requires the judge to make findings of fact whenever he rules on a motion to suppress. People v. Duncan, 176 Colo. 427, 498 P.2d 941 (1971); People v. Brazzel, 18 P.3d 1285 (Colo. 2001). And making conclusion of law instead is error. In a suppression hearing, when the court makes a conclusion of law rather than a required finding of fact, there is error. People v. Duncan, 176 Colo. 427, 498 P.2d 941 (1972). But findings in second case may suffice for findings in identical first case. Where in one case the judge, in denying the motion to suppress, does not make sufficient findings, but in another case the findings upon denial of the motion to suppress are amply sufficient, then where the findings in the second case are by the same court although by a different judge, the rulings by both judges are the same, and the parties and the search - and in substantial effect the testimony - are identical, an appellate court is justified in considering the findings in the second case as governing the first case, for it would be useless to remand the first case for findings. People v. Ramey, 174 Colo. 250, 483 P.2d 374 (1971). Finding that lesser crimes not included in wiretap statute, grounds for suppression. A finding that lesser crimes are not intended by congress to be included in the class of crimes for which a wiretap can be authorized does not render an entire state statute invalid, but is merely grounds for suppression. People v. Martin, 176 Colo. 322, 490 P.2d 924 (1971). District judge may reconsider a motion to suppress previously denied by another district judge. People v. Lewis, 659 P.2d 676 (Colo. 1983). Fourth amendment exclusionary rule is designed to deter police misconduct. Illegal police searches and district attorney preparedness are unrelated. The court ruling granting suppression of all evidence was tantamount to dismissal of the case, which was outside the court's authority to dismiss. People v. Bakari, 780 P.2d 1089 (Colo. 1989). Suppression for a procedural flaw in argument does not serve the purpose of the exclusionary rule, which is solely to deter police misconduct, not prosecutorial error. People v. Kirk, 103 P.3d 918 (Colo. 2005). 3. Return of Property. No right to return of illegal property. If property is legally seized and it is designed or intended for use as a means of committing a criminal offense or the possession of which is illegal, there is no right to have it returned. People v. Angerstein,

194 Colo. 376, 572 P.2d 479 (1977). Return can be made only upon determination by judge. If certain property is seized under and by virtue of a search warrant, it was incumbent upon the officers seizing same to deal with it only in accordance with the provisions and terms of this rule; consequently, they cannot rightfully restore it to the party from whom taken until a judge has examined witnesses and made a determination. Guyton v. Neal, 48 Colo. 549, 111 P. 84 (1910). Mandamus lies to compel officer to obey order to return goods. Where goods seized under a search warrant are ordered by the magistrate, on a hearing pursuant to this rule, to be returned by the officer to the person from whose premises they were taken, mandamus lies to compel the discharge of this ministerial duty. Bell v. Thomas, 49 Colo. 76, 111 P. 76, 31 L.R.A. (n.s.) 664 (1910). But mandamus cannot lie to return goods while proceedings still pending. Mandamus will not lie to compel an officer to surrender goods seized upon a search warrant, in excess of what is described therein, while the proceedings under the search warrant are still pending. Guyton v. Neal, 48 Colo. 549, 111 P. 84 (1910). A decision on a motion for return of property is ordinarily interlocutory and therefore unappealable, but actions for return of property prior to the initiation of any civil or criminal proceedings may be reviewed. In re Search Warrant for 2045 Franklin, Denver, 709 P.2d 597 (Colo. App. 1985). 4. Judicial Review. Appellate procedures cannot be invoked to test propriety of suppression order. The order of a trial court by which a motion to suppress evidence is sustained is not a final judgment and, accordingly, does not come within any exceptions provided by rule or statute under which appellate procedures can be invoked to test the propriety of the order. People v. Hernandez, 155 Colo. 519, 395 P.2d 733 (1964). But interlocutory appeals may be taken pursuant to C.A.R. 4.1. People v. Thornburg, 173 Colo. 230, 477 P.2d 372 (1970); People v. McNulty, 173 Colo. 491, 480 P.2d 560 (1971); People v. Henry, 173 Colo. 523, 482 P.2d 357 (1971); People v. Patterson, 175 Colo. 19, 485 P.2d 494 (1971); People v. Fidler, 175 Colo. 90, 485 P.2d 725 (1971). Contemporaneous objection rule applies to search and seizure issues. Brown v. People, 162 Colo. 406, 426 P.2d 764 (1967). Issue of illegal evidence should be brought to attention of the trial court either by a pretrial motion to suppress or at the trial when the prosecution offers evidence which the defendant claims is "tainted" because of the manner in which it was obtained by the prosecution. Ferrell v. Vogt, 161 Colo. 549, 423 P.2d 844 (1967). And failure to raise objection tantamount to waiver. The failure to raise the objection of an illegal search and seizure by proper objection at the trial level is tantamount to a waiver. Brown v. People, 162 Colo. 406, 426 P.2d 764 (1967). To preserve an issue for appeal, defendant must alert trial court to the particular issue. In case where defendant argued on appeal that search of his vehicle violated the fourth amendment and that trial court erred in admitting evidence found in the vehicle, defendant had waived the issue by failing to contest it at trial. Trial court's ruling that the search and seizure of the evidence was proper did not negate the waiver or preserve the issue for appeal. People v. Cordova, ___ P.3d ___ (Colo. App. 2011). In absence of motion, ground of error disregarded. In the absence of a motion for return of items or to suppress them as evidence on the ground of illegal search and seizure, an alleged ground of error based thereon will be disregarded. Salazar v. People, 153 Colo. 93, 384 P.2d 725 (1963). Where defendant denies possessory interest at hearing, cannot later claim possessory interest. At a suppression hearing where a defendant denies that he has a possessory interest in any of the items found, he cannot be allowed to later claim a possessory interest unsupported by the record and in direct contradiction of his own testimony in order to challenge the admission of the seized evidence. People v. Towers, 176 Colo. 295, 490 P.2d 302 (1971). And guilty plea makes question of search's validity moot. The question of the validity of the search for and seizure of contraband goods becomes moot upon the entry of the plea of guilty. Lucero v. People, 164 Colo. 247, 434 P.2d 128 (1967). Suppression order sustained where facts not shown on record on appeal. Order sustaining motion to suppress admission in evidence of items seized in execution of search warrant will be affirmed where record on appeal does not show essential facts on which trial court predicated its ruling. People v. Cram, 180 Colo. 418, 505 P.2d 1299 (1973). Granting of motion to suppress held invalid. People v. McGahey, 179 Colo. 401, 500 P.2d 977 (1972). Denial of motion to suppress upheld. People v. Hankin, 179 Colo. 70, 498 P.2d 1116 (1972); People v. Tucci, 179 Colo. 373, 500 P.2d 815 (1972); People v. Cram, 180 Colo. 418, 505 P.2d 1299 (1973). VIII. Return of Papers to Clerk. Warrant not invalidated by failure to indicate to whom papers to be returned. The failure to insert the names in the blank spaces provided in a search warrant for the purpose of indicating to whom the return is to be made and to whom a written inventory of the seized property is to be made is a deficiency of a ministerial nature and not such as to render a warrant invalid. Brown v. People, 158 Colo. 561, 408 P.2d 981 (1965). And where return made to issuing court, no prejudice to defendant. Where the record supports the conclusion that the return was made to the court which issued the warrant, then, such being the state of the record and the obvious intent of the issuing magistrate, there can be no finding of prejudice to the defendant in regard to such an alleged deficiency of the warrant. Brown v. People, 158 Colo. 561, 408 P.2d 981 (1965). IX. Suppression of Confession or Admission. A. Grounds. Confession deemed acknowledgment of truth of guilty fact. A confession is an acknowledgment in express words, by the accused in a criminal case, of the truth of the guilty fact charged or of some essential part of it. Jones v. People, 146 Colo. 40, 360 P.2d 686 (1961). Statement taken as result of and following an unlawful arrest must be suppressed. People v. Moreno, 176 Colo. 488, 491 P.2d 575 (1971). And no distrinction between "inculpatory" or "exculpatory" statements. No distinction may be drawn between "inculpatory" statements made by defendant and statements alleged to be merely "exculpatory", following an unlawful arrest. People v. Moreno, 176 Colo. 488, 491 P.2d 575 (1971). Not between formal arrest and police custody. The fact that the defendant is not under formal arrest at the time he made such statements is unimportant where he is in police custody, he is the main suspect, and the accusing finger is surely directed at defendant, in which case the questions of a police officer in this posture are obviously for the main purpose of eliciting incriminating statements from the defendant, and therefore, the trial court should exclude any oral incriminating statements. Nez v. People, 167 Colo. 23, 445 P.2d 68 (1968). Prosecution has burden at suppression hearing to show that defendant was lawfully arrested. People v. Moreno, 176 Colo. 488, 491 P.2d 575 (1971). Judge may suppress statements made by defendant before he was given "Miranda warning", but deny the suppression of statements made after the warning has been given. People v. Garrison, 176 Colo. 516, 491 P.2d 917 (1971). Confession obtained after inadequate warning should be suppressed. Where defendant's confession is obtained after a warning of his rights, which does not meet the requirements of Miranda, a motion to suppress the confession should be granted. People v. Vigil, 175 Colo. 373, 489 P.2d 588 (1971). Suppression of incriminating statements warranted when defendant was subject to interrogation by police officers before being advised of Miranda rights. A routine encounter turned into a custodial situation, as defendant was physically surrounded by officers, was not free to go during questioning, and had "objective reasons to believe that he was under arrest"; such circumstances constituted custody. People v. Null, 233 P.3d 670 (Colo. 2010). Stereotype warning cannot be the sole basis of the court's determination that a statement was voluntary and that the defendant was aware of his rights and waived and relinquished those rights. People v. Moreno, 176 Colo. 488, 491 P.2d 575 (1971). If written confession is direct exploitation of prior illegality, it is inadmissible as the "fruit of the poisonous tree". People v. Algien, 180 Colo. 1, 501 P.2d 468 (1972). Similarly, search conducted pursuant to illegal confession must be suppressed. Where the sole basis of a probable cause for the search of the defendant's home presented in the affidavit is his confession and that confession was illegally obtained, then, under the "fruit of the poison tree" doctrine, any articles obtained must be suppressed. People v. Vigil, 175 Colo. 373, 489 P.2d 588 (1971). Good faith basis required to challenge warrant affidavits. As conditions to a veracity hearing testing the truth of averments contained in a warrant affidavit, a motion to suppress must be supported by one or more affidavits reflecting a good faith basis for the challenge and contain a specification of the precise statements challenged. People v. Dailey, 639 P.2d 1068 (Colo. 1982). Voluntariness should be determined based on the totality of the circumstances, including the occurrences and events surrounding the confession and the presence or absence of official misconduct. People v. Sparks, 748 P.2d 795 (Colo. 1988); People v. Mounts, 801 P.2d 1199 (Colo. 1990). Confession given after proper warnings not defective just because prior statements illegal. A confession obtained after proper constitutional warnings are given is not defective just because prior statements might be tainted with illegality. People v. Potter, 176 Colo. 510, 491 P.2d 974 (1971). But time lapse between interrogations found insufficient to remove original taint from confession. People v. Algien, 180 Colo. 1, 501 P.2d 468 (1972). "Totality of circumstances" standard. Courts must determine whether a confession given in a noncustodial setting is voluntary under the "totality of circumstances" standard. People v. Johnson, 671 P.2d 958 (Colo. 1983). Confession properly suppressed where defendant's will was overborne by coercive conduct of police. Defendant's statements concerning drugs in his pockets were made after sustaining serious facial fractures and other injuries from the police and while he feared the police would use further force. People v. Vigil, 242 P.3d 1092 (Colo. 2010). Trial court must consider all attendant circumstances to determine whether coercion of first confession infected second confession. Officers receiving subsequent confessions cannot merely be the beneficiaries of earlier pressure improperly applied to defendant. Defendant declined further medical treatment for his serious injuries, was released to the same officers who had inflicted the injuries, and was interrogated by those officers at 2:00 a.m. The evidence supports the trial court's ruling that defendant's subsequent statements were made under the lingering coercion of the physical force used against him and were thus properly suppressed. People v. Vigil, 242 P.3d 1092 (Colo. 2010). **B. When Motion Made.** *Defendant entitled to object to confession's use at some stage in proceedings. A defendant has a constitutional right at some stage in the proceedings to object to the use of a confession and to have a "fair and reliable determination" on the issue of voluntariness. Compton v. People, 166 Colo. 419, 444 P.2d 263 (1968); Whitman v. People, 170 Colo. 189, 460 P.2d 767 (1969). But pretrial hearing not constitutional requirement. While the better practice, at least with questions involving the admissibility of confessions and admissions, is to conduct a hearing before the jury becomes aware that the evidence exists, such has never been made a pretrial hearing a constitutional requirement. Whether or not a reference to such evidence before the jury might result in a denial of the defendant's constitutional rights is a matter to be considered on a case-by-case basis. People v. Renfrow, 172 Colo. 399, 473 P.2d 957 (1970). Issue of timeliness of motion moot when court entertains motion. When the court determines to entertain a motion to suppress and conduct a hearing thereon, the issue of the timeliness of the motion becomes moot and can no longer be a proper ground for denial thereof. People v. Robertson, 40 Colo. App. 386, 577 P.2d 314 (1978).* **C. Procedure.** *Procedural guidelines same for determining admissibility of confession and "voluntariness" of blood test. It is proper for a trial judge to resolve the matter as to the "voluntariness" of the blood alcohol test along the same procedural lines as would be followed in determining the admissibility, or nonadmissibility, of a confession. Compton v. People, 166 Colo. 419, 444 P.2d 263 (1968). Express or contemporaneous objection to admission of confession unnecessary where voluntariness issue evident. It is not necessary that there be an express objection by the defendant to the admission of the confession by a motion to suppress or by contemporaneous objection, for the trial judge is required to conduct a hearing when it becomes evident to him that voluntariness is in issue, and an awareness on the part of the trial judge that the defendant is questioning the circumstances under which the statements were obtained is sufficient. Whitman v. People, 170 Colo. 189, 460 P.2d 767 (1969). Denial of hearing on voluntariness is error. The denial of defense counsel's request for a hearing to determine whether defendant's statements following his arrest were voluntarily made is error. Hervey v. People, 178 Colo. 38, 495 P.2d 204 (1972). Trial judge, and not the jury, determines the admissibility of a confession where objection is made on the ground that the confession was involuntarily made. Compton v. People, 166 Colo. 419, 444 P.2d 263 (1968). And court must make findings of fact and law. Before incriminating statements or confessions, to which objections have been made, can be admitted in evidence, the court must make findings of fact and law that the statements and confessions under consideration were voluntarily given with full understanding of the accused's rights. Compton v. People, 166 Colo. 419, 444 P.2d 263 (1968); Espinoza v. People, 178 Colo. 391, 497 P.2d 994 (1972). Before a trial court may rule that a confession is voluntary and admissible, or that it is involuntary and must be suppressed, the court must make sufficiently clear and detailed findings of fact and conclusions of law on the record to permit meaningful appellate review. People v. McIntyre, 789 P.2d 1108 (Colo. 1990). And the mere denial of defendant's motion to suppress, without more, does not satisfy these requirements. Espinoza v. People, 178 Colo. 391, 497 P.2d 994 (1972). Showings required for admission of confession. On a motion to suppress a confession made to police officers without assistance of an attorney, the prosecution must prove, by clear and convincing evidence, that the defendant knowingly, voluntarily and intelligently waived his right to counsel and his right against self-incrimination and must prove, by a preponderance of the evidence, that the confession was made voluntarily. People v. Fish, 660 P.2d 505 (Colo. 1983). Court finds whether statement voluntary, and whether defendant voluntarily waived constitutional privileges. Where the defendant makes a motion under this rule, it is incumbent upon the trial court to find whether the statement was given freely and voluntarily without any improper compelling influences and whether the defendant voluntarily, knowingly, and intelligently waived his privilege against self-incrimination and his right to retained or appointed counsel. Espinoza v. People, 178 Colo. 391, 497 P.2d 994 (1972). And trial judge must find that the statement was voluntary beyond a reasonable doubt. People v. Moreno, 176 Colo. 488, 491 P.2d 575 (1971). Jury precluded from fully resolving issue of voluntariness. Under the federal constitution, a fair and reliable determination of the voluntariness of a confession precludes the conflicting jury from fully resolving the issue. Compton v. People, 166 Colo. 419, 444 P.2d 263 (1968). Including the taking of a blood alcohol test. The defendant has the right to a "fair and reliable determination" on the issue as to whether he gave his consent to the taking of a blood alcohol test, and therefore, it is improper for the trial court to permit the jury to "fully resolve" this matter. Compton v.*

197

People, 166 Colo. 419, 444 P.2d 263 (1968). But where issues resolved against defendant, weight given to confession left to jury. Where the trial court conducts a full "in camera" hearing to determine whether defendant's confession was voluntary and to ascertain whether defendant was advised of rights afforded him by Miranda v. Arizona, then, where these issues are resolved against defendant, the weight to be given to defendant's confession is properly left to jury. People v. Lovato, 180 Colo. 445, 506 P.2d 361 (1973). And where evidence not sufficient to require exclusion, confession's voluntariness question for jury. Whenever there is evidence, not sufficient to require exclusion of the alleged confession, but sufficient to raise a question as to the weight to which it is entitled at the hands of the jury, the court must refer the question of the voluntariness of the confession to the jury under proper instructions. Baker v. People, 168 Colo. 11, 449 P.2d 815 (1969) (but see Compton v. People, 166 Colo. 419, 444 P.2d 263 (1968); People v. Lovato, 180 Colo. 445, 506 P.2d 361 (1973). However, judge must first affirmatively find confession voluntarily given before submitted to jury. The fact that the jury determines the weight to be given a confession, or, as is sometimes the practice, the fact that the issue of the voluntariness of a confession, though already determined by the trial court, is also submitted to the jury under proper instructions, in nowise alters the fundamental rule that before a confession is admitted into evidence the trial judge must first affirmatively find that the confession was voluntarily given. Compton v. People, 166 Colo. 419, 444 P.2d 263 (1968). Or that blood alcohol test was taken with consent. Where an objection is made by a defendant to the introduction into evidence of the results of a blood alcohol test on the ground that the test was taken without his consent, the trial court, after hearing, must make a specific and affirmative finding that such consent was given before this line of testimony may with propriety be submitted to the jury for its consideration. Compton v. People, 166 Colo. 419, 444 P.2d 263 (1968). When no evidence on voluntariness, matter not submitted to jury. When there is no evidence which raises a question as to the voluntariness of a confession, the matter need not be submitted to the jury. Baker v. People, 168 Colo. 11, 449 P.2d 815 (1969). Evidence held sufficient to support finding of voluntary confession. People v. Valencia, 181 Colo. 36, 506 P.2d 743 (1973).

Rule 41.1 - Court Order for Nontestimonial Identification

(a) Authority to Issue Order. A nontestimonial identification order authorized by this Rule may be issued by any judge of the Supreme, District, Superior, County Court, or Court of Appeals.

(b) Time of Application. A request for a nontestimonial identification order may be made prior to the arrest of a suspect, after arrest and prior to trial or, when special circumstances of the case make it appropriate, during trial.

(c) Basis for Order. An order shall issue only on an affidavit or affidavits sworn to or affirmed before the judge, or by the procedures set forth in Crim. P. 41(c)(3), and establishing the following grounds for the order:

(1) That there is probable cause to believe that an offense has been committed;

(2) That there are reasonable grounds, not amounting to probable cause to arrest, to suspect that the person named or described in the affidavit committed the offense; and

(3) That the results of specific nontestimonial identification procedures will be of material aid in determining whether the person named in the affidavit committed the offense.

(d) Issuance. Upon a showing that the grounds specified in section (c) exist, the judge shall issue an order directed to any peace officer to take the person named in the affidavit into custody to obtain nontestimonial identification. The judge shall direct that the designated nontestimonial identification procedures be conducted expeditiously. After such identification procedures have been completed, the person shall be released or charged with an offense.

(e) Contents of Order. An order to take into custody for nontestimonial identification shall contain:

(1) The name or description of the individual who is to give the nontestimonial identification;

(2) The names of any persons making affidavits for issuance of the order;

(3) The criminal offense concerning which the order has been issued and the nontestimonial identification procedures to be conducted specified therein;

(4) A mandate to the officer to whom the order is directed to detain the person for only such time as is necessary to obtain the nontestimonial identification;

(5) The typewritten or printed name of the judge issuing the order and his signature.

(f) Execution and Return.

(1) Nontestimonial identification procedures may be conducted by any peace officer or other person designated by the judge. Blood tests shall be conducted under medical supervision, and the judge may require medical supervision for any other test ordered pursuant to this section

when he deems such supervision necessary. No person who appears under an order of appearance issued pursuant to this section (f) shall be detained longer than is reasonably necessary to conduct the specified nontestimonial identification procedures unless he is arrested for an offense.

(2) The order may be executed and returned only within 14 days after its date.

(3) The order shall be executed in the daytime unless the issuing judge shall endorse thereupon that it may be served at any time, because it appears that the suspect may flee the jurisdiction if the order is not served forthwith.

(4) The officer executing the order shall give a copy of the order to the person upon which it is served.

(5) No search of the person who is to give nontestimonial identification may be made, except a protective search for weapons, unless a separate search warrant has been issued.

(6) A return shall be made to the issuing judge showing whether the person named has been:

(I) Detained for such nontestimonial identification;

(II) Released or arrested.

(7) If, at the time of such return, probable cause does not exist to believe that such person has committed the offense named in the affidavit or any other offense, the person named in the affidavit shall be entitled to move that the judge issue an order directing that the products of the nontestimonial identification procedures, and all copies thereof, be destroyed. Such motion shall, except for good cause shown, be granted.

(g) Nontestimonial Identification Order at Request of Defendant. A person arrested for or charged with an offense may request a judge to order a nontestimonial identification procedure. If it appears that the results of specific nontestimonial identification procedures will be of material aid in determining whether the defendant committed the offense, the judge shall order the state to conduct such identification procedure involving the defendant under such terms and conditions as the judge shall prescribe.

(h) Definition of Terms. As used in this Rule, the following terms have the designated meanings:

(1) "Offense" means any felony, class 1 misdemeanor, or other crime which is punishable by imprisonment for more than one year.

(2) "Nontestimonial identification" includes, but is not limited to, identification by fingerprints, palm prints, footprints, measurements, blood specimens, urine specimens, saliva samples, hair samples, specimens of material under fingernails, or other reasonable physical or medical examination, handwriting exemplars, voice samples, photographs, appearing in lineups, and trying on articles of clothing.

(i) Motion to Suppress. A person aggrieved by an order issued under this Rule may file a motion to suppress nontestimonial identification seized pursuant to such order and the said motion shall be granted if there were insufficient grounds for the issuance or the order was improperly issued. The motion to suppress the use of such nontestimonial identification as evidence shall be made before trial unless opportunity therefor did not exist or the defendant was not aware of the grounds for the motion, but the court, in its discretion, may entertain the motion at the trial.

Colo. R. Crim. P. 41.1

Source: f2 amended May 7, 2009, effective 7/1/2009; IPc amended and effective 2/10/2011; f2 amended and adopted December 14, 2011, effective 7/1/2012.

Annotation Law reviews. For comment, "Beyond the Davis Dictum: Reforming Nontestimonial Identification Evidence Rules and Statutes", see 79 U. Colo. L. Rev. 189 (2008). Limited intrusions into privacy on less than probable cause are constitutional when: (1) There must be an articulable and specific basis in fact for suspecting criminal activity at the outset; (2) the intrusion must be limited in scope, purpose, and duration; (3) the intrusion must be justified by substantial law-enforcement interests; and (4) there must be an opportunity at some point to subject the intrusion to the neutral and detached scrutiny of a judicial officer before the evidence obtained therefrom may be admitted in a criminal proceeding against the accused. People v. Madson, 638 P.2d 18 (Colo. 1981); People v. Harris, 762 P.2d 651 (Colo. 1988), cert. denied, 488 U.S. 985, 109 S. Ct. 541, 102 L. Ed. 2d 572 (1988). This rule is limited to nontestimonial identification evidence only and does not authorize the acquisition of testimony of communications protected by the privilege against self-incrimination. People v. Harris, 729 P.2d 1000 (Colo. App. 1986), aff'd, 762 P.2d 651 (Colo. 1988), cert. denied, 488 U.S. 985, 109 S. Ct. 541, 102 L. Ed. 2d 572 (1988). And this rule constitutional. This rule does not violate either the fourth amendment to the federal constitution or § 7 of art. II, Colo. Const. People v. Madson,

638 P.2d 18 (Colo. 1981); People v. Harris, 729 P.2d 1000 (Colo. 1986), aff'd, 762 P.2d 651 (Colo. 1988), cert. denied, 485 U.S. 985, 109 S. Ct. 541, 102 L. Ed. 2d 572 (1988). Voluntary surrender of nontestimonial evidence waives constitutional protections. People v. Mattas, 645 P.2d 254 (Colo. 1982). Propriety of examination determined by totality of circumstances. When the propriety of an identification is at issue, such as a lineup identification, the question of whether there is a substantial likelihood of irreparable misidentification is determined by examining the totality of the circumstances. People v. Johnson, 653 P.2d 737 (Colo. 1982). Judicial order necessary only when authorities take someone into custody. Authorities must obtain a judicial order pursuant to this rule only when they take someone presently at liberty into custody for purposes of the nontestimonial identification. People v. Peoples, 200 Colo. 509, 616 P.2d 131 (1980). And rule not applicable to suspect under arrest. The authority of law-enforcement officers to photograph, fingerprint, and measure a suspect while he is under arrest, confined, or awaiting trial has long been recognized, as well as the propriety of using photographs obtained thereby for identification purposes, and this rule is not applicable under those circumstances. People v. Reynolds, 38 Colo. App. 258, 559 P.2d 714 (1976). This rule is not applicable to nontestimonial identifications of persons already in police custody pursuant to a lawful arrest. People v. Peoples, 200 Colo. 509, 616 P.2d 131 (1980). Once probable cause exists to arrest, this rule is inapplicable. People v. Harris, 729 P.2d 1000 (Colo. App. 1986), aff'd, 762 P.2d 651 (Colo. 1988), cert. denied, 488 U.S. 985, 109 S. Ct. 541, 102 L. Ed. 2d 572 (1988). Nor where defendant voluntarily submits to investigatory procedures. The court need not concern itself with the investigatory procedures of this rule where defendants voluntarily submit to fingerprinting, thereby waiving their constitutional protections. People v. Hannaman, 181 Colo. 82, 507 P.2d 466 (1973). Rule applies only to obtaining nontestimonial identification from the defendant himself and not to procedures on a third party. People v. Braxton, 807 P.2d 1214 (Colo. App. 1990). Prosecution could not be sanctioned for police conduct in which it did not participate. Trial court may not preclude prosecution from applying for and obtaining order for nontestimonial identification evidence though blood and hair samples obtained by police through a warrantless search were suppressed. People v. Diaz, 55 P.3d 1171 (Colo. 2002). Judge may order fingerprints of individual to be obtained when it is shown by an affidavit that: (1) A known criminal offense has been committed; (2) there is reason to suspect that the individual is connected with the perpetration of a crime; and (3) the individual's fingerprints are not in the files of the applying agency. Stone v. People, 174 Colo. 504, 485 P.2d 495 (1971). Information obtained from anonymous tip may form basis for affidavit used to obtain an order for nontestimonial identification pursuant to this rule. People v. Davis, 669 P.2d 130 (Colo. 1983). Nontestimonial evidence suppressed where prosecution fails to establish that affidavits sworn to. Where the prosecution fails to establish at trial that the affidavits required by section (c) of this rule were sworn to or affirmed before the court which issued the nontestimonial identification order, the nontestimonial evidence is properly suppressed. People v. Hampton, 198 Colo. 566, 603 P.2d 133 (1979). No deprivation of procedural safeguards when county court issued a nontestimonial identification order even though the offenses involved were committed in another jurisdiction. Ginn v. County Court, 677 P.2d 1387 (Colo. App. 1984). Admissibility of statements of defendant while in custody for nontestimonial identification procedures. A statement of a suspect who is detained pursuant to an order to obtain nontestimonial evidence may be admissible under circumstances in which the suspect initiates a conversation with police and, despite a lack of coercion or interrogation, voluntarily offers information. People v. Wilson, 841 P.2d 337 (Colo. App. 1992). This rule not for exclusive use of Colorado officials investigating offenses occurring in Colorado. Where the requirements of this rule are met, it is not an abuse of discretion for a county court to issue a nontestimonial identification order even though the offenses involved were committed in another jurisdiction. Ginn v. County Court, 677 P.2d 1387 (Colo. App. 1984). Statement in affidavit not a judicial admission. Statement that probable cause for arrest did not yet exist in an affidavit in support of an order for nontestimonial identification is not a judicial admission. People v. Page, 907 P.2d 624 (Colo. App. 1995). Applied in People v. Morgan, 619 P.2d 64 (Colo. 1980); Richardson v. District Court, 632 P.2d 595 (Colo. 1981); People v. District Court, 664 P.2d 247 (Colo. 1983).

Rule 41.2 - Interlocutory Appeal from the County Court

Colo. R. Crim. P. 41.2

Repealed July 16, 1992, effective 11/1/1992.

Rule 41.3 - Interlocutory Appeal from District Court

See Colorado Appellate Rules.

Rule 42 - No Colorado Rule
Colo. R. Crim. P. 42

Rule 43 - Presence of the Defendant

(a) Presence Required. The defendant shall be present at the preliminary hearing, at the arraignment, at the time of the plea, at every stage of the trial including the impaneling of the jury and the return of the verdict, and at the imposition of sentence, except as otherwise provided by this rule.

(b) Continued Presence Not Required. The trial court in its discretion may complete the trial, and the defendant shall be considered to have waived his right to be present, whenever a defendant, initially present:

(1) Voluntarily absents himself after the trial has commenced, whether or not he has been informed by the court of his obligation to remain during the trial, or

(2) After being warned by the court that disruptive conduct will cause him to be removed from the courtroom, persists in conduct which is such as to justify his being excluded from the courtroom.

(c) Presence Not Required. A defendant need not be present in the following situations:

(1) A corporation may appear by counsel for all purposes.

(2) At a conference or argument upon a question of law.

(3) At a reduction of sentence under Rule 35.

(d) Waiver. The voluntary failure of the defendant to appear at the preliminary hearing may be construed by the court as an implied waiver of his right to a preliminary hearing.

(e) Presence of the Defendant by Interactive Audiovisual Device or Interactive Audio Device.

(1) As used in this Rule 43:

(I) "Interactive audiovisual device" means a television- or computer-based audiovisual system capable of two-way transmission and of sufficient audio and visual quality that persons using the system can view and converse with each other.

(II) "Interactive audio device" means a telephone- or computer-based audio system capable of two-way transmission and of sufficient audio quality that persons using the system can converse with each other.

(2) With the court's approval, the defendant may be present within the meaning of this Rule 43 by the use of an interactive audiovisual device or an interactive audio device for any proceeding that does not involve a jury.

(3) The consent of the defendant shall be required prior to conducting any of the following types of proceedings by the use of an interactive audiovisual device or an interactive audio device pursuant to this subsection (e):

(I) Entry of guilty plea;

(II) Trial to the court;

(III) Sentencing hearings;

(IV) Probation and deferred sentence revocation hearings;

(V) Preliminary hearings;

(VI) Pre-trial motions hearings;

(VII) Hearings to modify bail;

(VIII) Restitution hearings; and

(IX) Crim. P. 35(b) and (c) hearings.

(4) The court shall advise the defendant of the following prior to any proceeding conducted pursuant to subsection (e)(3) of this rule:

(I) The defendant has the right to appear in person;

(II) The defendant has the right to have his or her counsel appear with him or her at the same physical location;

(III) The defendant's decision to appear by use of an interactive audiovisual device or an interactive audio device must be voluntary and must not be the result of undue influence or coercion on the part of anyone; and

(IV) If the defendant is pro se, he or she has the right to request that the identity and role of all individuals with whom he or she may have contact during the proceeding be disclosed.

(5) Every use of an interactive audiovisual device or an interactive audio device must comply with the following minimum standards:

(I) If defense counsel appears, such appearance shall be at the same physical location as the defendant if so requested by the defendant. If defense counsel does not appear in the same location as the defendant, a separate confidential communication line, such as a phone line, shall be provided to allow for private and confidential communication between the defendant and counsel.

(II) Installation of an interactive audiovisual device or an interactive audio device in the courtroom shall be done in such a manner that members of the public are reasonably able to observe or listen to, and (where appropriate) participate in, the hearing.

(III) Unless the court determines otherwise, parties must have the ability to electronically transfer exhibits to the court, a witness, and each other during any proceeding conducted by an interactive audiovisual device or an interactive audio device pursuant to this subsection (e). Any exhibits electronically transferred to the court shall be treated as if they had been submitted in person.

Colo. R. Crim. P. 43

Source: e added and adopted December 19, 1996, effective 3/1/1997; e amended and adopted and comment added and adopted May 11, 2006, effective 7/1/2006; e amended and effective 6/17/2010; amended and adopted March 19, 2020, effective 3/19/2020; amended and adopted March 23, 2020, effective 3/23/2020; amended and adopted March 30, 2020, effective 3/30/2020; amended and adopted April 7, 2020, effective 4/7/2020; amended and adopted November 16, 2020, effective 11/16/2020; amended and adopted by the court, en banc, July 15, 2021, effective 7/15/2021; amended and adopted by the court, en banc, June 28, 2022, effective 7/1/2022.

CommentThe court recommends that defendants be informed of their rights pursuant to this rule by showing such defendants a pre-recorded video containing the judicial advisement contained in this rule. The video should be shown prior to any jail authorities asking whether a defendant planned to elect to participate by audiovisual device. The court recognized that such audiovisual devices will be used to conduct plea discussions. Accordingly, the pre-recorded video should also explain the plea discussion process.

Annotation Waiver required for absence from trial. The trial court must establish a voluntary and intelligent waiver by a defendant concerning an absence from trial. People v. Campbell, 785 P.2d 153 (Colo. App. 1989), rev'd on other grounds, 814 P.2d 1 (Colo. 1991). Waiver must be knowing, intelligent, and voluntary. Waiver is knowing and intelligent when a defendant has had notice of the consequences of not appearing. People v. Stephenson, 165 P.3d 860 (Colo. App. 2007). Absence from trial compelled by medical necessity may generally be deemed voluntary, and the determination of whether defendant is "voluntarily absent" requires a fact-specific inquiry into the type of medical condition, the circumstances surrounding the absence, and defendant's conduct and statements. People v. Stephenson, 165 P.3d 860 (Colo. App. 2007). A defendant's absence may be deemed voluntary when the record establishes that defendant created the medical necessity by attempting suicide in order to effect his or her absence from trial. People v. Price, 240 P.3d 557 (Colo. App. 2010). Removal of defendant from court during trial did not abridge defendant's constitutional rights. Where defendant had been warned numerous times about his courtroom behavior including getting up from his seat and moving towards judge on one occasion and physically attacking a witness on the witness stand on another so that court would either have to shackle, bind, and gag defendant in court or remove him to another room where he could watch the trial via closed-circuit television and freely talk to his attorney by telephone, trial court used constitutionally permissible method pursuant to (b)(2) to deal with disruptive defendant. People v. Davis, 851 P.2d 239 (Colo. App. 1993). Although the trial court failed to include the mandatory parole period during the sentencing period and mittimus, it is not a violation of the defendant's right to be present at sentencing to subsequently correct the mittimus to include the mandatory parole period. People v. Nelson, 9 P.3d 1177 (Colo. App. 2000). Trial court's action in making its resentencing decision the subject of a written order, rather than reconvening a hearing to announce that decision, was harmless. Defendant was present at both his sentencing and resentencing hearings when the information relied upon by the court for its sentencing decision was presented, and defendant raised no objection when, at the completion of the resentencing hearing, the court reserved its decision on resentencing and stated its intention to announce that decision at a later date. People v. Luu, 983 P.2d 15 (Colo. App. 1998). Due process does not require the defendant's presence when his presence would be useless, or the benefit nebulous. People v. Luu, 983 P.2d 15 (Colo. App. 1998). Applied in People v. Trefethen, 751 P.2d 657 (Colo. App. 1987).

Rule 44 - Appearance of Counsel

(a) Appointment of Counsel. If the defendant appears in court without counsel, the court shall advise the defendant of the right to counsel. In an appropriate case, if, upon the defendant's affidavit or sworn testimony and other investigation, the court finds that the defendant is financially unable to obtain counsel, an attorney shall be assigned to represent the defendant at every stage of the trial court proceedings. In any misdemeanor case the court may appoint as counsel law students who shall act under the provisions of C.R.C.P. 226. No lawyer need be appointed for a defendant who, after being advised, with full knowledge of his rights thereto, elects to proceed without counsel. Except in a case in which a law student has been appointed, unless good cause exists otherwise, the court shall appoint the state public defender.

(b) Multiple Representation by Counsel. Whenever two or more defendants have been jointly charged pursuant to Rule 8(b) or have been joined for trial pursuant to Rule 13, and are represented by the same retained or assigned counsel or by retained or assigned counsel who are associated in the practice of law, the court shall promptly inquire with respect to such joint representation and shall personally advise each defendant of the right to the effective assistance of counsel, including separate representation. Unless it appears that there is good cause to believe no conflict of interest is likely to arise, the court shall take such measures as may be appropriate to protect each defendant's right to counsel.

(c) Request for Withdrawal of a Lawyer During Proceedings. Except as provided in section (e), withdrawal of a lawyer in a criminal case is a matter within the sound discretion of the court. In exercising such discretion, the court shall balance the need for orderly administration of justice with the facts underlying the request.

(d) Procedure for Withdrawal During Proceedings.

(1) A lawyer may withdraw from a case only upon order of the court. In the discretion of the court, a hearing on a motion to withdraw may be waived with the consent of the prosecution and if a written substitution of counsel is filed which is signed by current counsel, future counsel and the defendant. A request to withdraw shall be in writing or may be made orally in the discretion of the court and shall state the grounds for the request. A request to withdraw shall be made as soon as practicable upon the lawyer becoming aware of the grounds for withdrawal. Advance notice of a request to withdraw shall be given to the defendant before any hearing, if practicable. Such notice to withdraw shall include:

(I) That the attorney wishes to withdraw;

(II) The grounds for withdrawal;

(III) That the defendant has the right to object to withdrawal;

(IV) That a hearing will be held and withdrawal will only be allowed if the court approves;

(V) That the defendant has the obligation to appear at all previously scheduled court dates;

(VI) That if the request to withdraw is granted, then the defendant will have the obligation to hire other counsel, request the appointment of counsel by the court or elect to represent himself or herself.

(2) Upon setting of a hearing on a motion to withdraw, the lawyer shall make reasonable efforts to give the defendant actual notice of the date, time and place of the hearing. No hearing shall be conducted without the presence of the defendant unless the motion is made subsequent to the failure of the defendant to appear in court as scheduled. A hearing need not be held and notice need not be given to a defendant when a motion to withdraw is filed after a defendant has failed to appear for a scheduled court appearance and has not reappeared within six months.

(e) Termination of Representation.

(1) Unless otherwise directed by the trial court or extended by an agreement between counsel and a defendant, counsel's representation of a defendant, whether retained or appointed, shall terminate when trial court proceedings have concluded. Trial court proceedings "have concluded" when restitution, if applicable, is finally determined and at the point in time:

(I) When dismissal is granted by the court and no timely appeal has been filed;

(II) When the parties have entered into an agreement for pretrial diversion or when an order enters granting a deferred sentence or probation if no sentence to incarceration is imposed;

(III) After a sentence to incarceration is imposed upon conviction when no motion has been timely filed pursuant to Crim. P. 35(b) or such motion so filed is ruled on; or

(IV) When a timely notice of appeal is filed by the defendant.

(2) At the time a pretrial diversion order is entered or deferred sentence is granted or at the time sentence is imposed upon conviction, the court shall inform the defendant when representation shall terminate.

Colo. R. Crim. P. 44

Source: Entire rule amended June 19, 1986, effective 1/1/1987; entire rule amended and adopted December 19, 1996, effective 3/1/1997; e amended and adopted September 10, 2009, effective 1/1/2010; amended and adopted October 24, 2019, effective 10/24/2019.

Annotation Law reviews. For note, "Right to Counsel in Colorado", see 34 Rocky Mtn. L. Rev. 343 (1962). For article, "Hearsay in Criminal Cases Under the Colorado Rules of Evidence: An Overview", see 50 U. Colo. L. Rev. 277 (1979). For article, "Pronouncements of the U.S. Supreme Court Relating to the Criminal Law Field: 1985-1986", which discusses recent cases relating to the right to counsel, see 15 Colo. Law. 1578 (1986). Annotator's note. For other annotations concerning legal counsel for the indigent, see § 16 of art. II, Colo. Const., and § 18-1-403 . Court to advise defendant of right to counsel and to make financial inquiry. The rule imposes upon the trial court an affirmative duty to advise all criminal defendants, whether affluent or indigent, who appear without counsel of the right to counsel, and to inquire into the defendant's financial ability to employ counsel if pertinent. Allen v. People, 157 Colo. 582, 404 P.2d 266 (1965). However, a defendant is not entitled to a presumption of poverty. Allen v. People, 157 Colo. 582, 404 P.2d 266 (1965). Defendant with sufficient means accorded reasonable opportunity to employ attorney. If it appears that a defendant has sufficient means to employ an attorney of his own choosing, then he must be accorded a reasonable opportunity to do so. Allen v. People, 157 Colo. 582, 404 P.2d 266 (1965). Attorney assigned to represent indigent defendant at every stage of trial court proceedings. If upon the defendant's affidavit or sworn testimony and other investigation the court finds that the defendant is financially unable to obtain counsel, an attorney shall be assigned to represent him at every stage of the trial court proceedings. Allen v. People, 157 Colo. 582, 404 P.2d 266 (1965). Including imposition of sentence. This rule provides that in the case of an indigent defendant in a criminal proceeding, an attorney shall be assigned to represent him at every stage of the trial court proceedings, which includes imposition of sentence. The imposition of sentence is certainly one stage of the proceedings before the trial court; indeed, it is perhaps the most critical stage of the proceeding. John Doe v. People, 160 Colo. 215, 416 P.2d 376 (1966); Gehl v. People, 161 Colo. 535, 423 P.2d 332 (1967). So, if a defendant later insists on this right, he is entitled to have the sentence vacated and a new one imposed, at which time he should be represented by an attorney and provided counsel if he is unable to employ his own lawyer. Gehl v. People, 161 Colo. 535, 423 P.2d 332 (1967). Right to counsel extended to contempt proceedings resulting in imprisonment. The right to counsel must be extended to all contempt proceedings, whether labeled civil or criminal, which result in the imprisonment of the witness. Padilla v. Padilla, 645 P.2d 1327 (Colo. App. 1982). Previously, appointment of counsel on appeal was generally denied to indigents in all cases except capital. In re Petition of Griffin, 152 Colo. 347, 382 P.2d 202 (1963). Court must establish that waiver of right made knowingly and intelligently. Once it is established that a defendant has a right to counsel, the court must establish that any waiver of that constitutional right is made knowingly and intelligently. Padilla v. Padilla, 645 P.2d 1327 (Colo. App. 1982). Court obligated to see that appointed counsel of sufficient ability and experience. When a court is called upon to appoint counsel for a defendant in a criminal case, it is its duty to see that counsel of sufficient ability and experience is assigned to fairly represent the defendant. Carlson v. People, 91 Colo. 418, 15 P.2d 625 (1932). One consenting to representation by counsel employed by another cannot complain counsel ineffective. One who has knowledge that he could have court appoint counsel if desired but consents to representation by counsel employed by another for him, cannot complain that counsel was ineffective without a showing of substantial prejudice to the defendant because of counsel's representation. Bresnahan v. People, 175 Colo. 286, 487 P.2d 551 (1971). Joint representation does not result in a per se violation of the right to effective counsel. Neither defendant testified, so defense counsel was not faced with the possibility of commenting on the credibility of one to the detriment of the other. People v. Tafoya, 833 P.2d 841 (Colo. App. 1992). Trial counsel was counsel of record at the time the 45-day period for filing a notice of appeal under C.A.R. 4(b) expired where trial counsel filed a Crim. P. 35(b) motion before appellate counsel was appointed and trial counsel had not moved to withdraw. People v. Baker, 104 P.3d 893 (Colo. 2005). Applied in Buckles v. People, 162 Colo. 51, 424 P.2d 774 (1967).

Rule 45 - Time

(a) Computation. In computing any period of time prescribed or allowed by these rules, the day of the event from which the designated period of time begins to run is not to be included. Thereafter, every day shall be counted including holidays, Saturdays, and Sundays. The last day of the period so computed is to be included, unless it is a Saturday, a Sunday, or a legal holiday, in which event the period runs until the end of the next day which is not a Saturday, a Sunday, or a legal holiday. The "next day" is determined by continuing to count forward when the period is measured after an event and backward when measured before an event. As used in these Rules, "legal holiday" includes the first day of January, observed as New Year's Day; the third Monday in January, observed as Martin Luther King Day; the third Monday in February, observed as Washington-Lincoln Day; the last Monday in May, observed as Memorial Day; the fourth day of July, observed as Independence Day; the first Monday in September, observed as Labor Day; the second Monday in October, observed as Columbus Day; the 11th day of November, observed as Veteran's Day; the fourth Thursday in November, observed as Thanksgiving Day; the twenty-fifth day of December, observed as Christmas Day, and any other day except Saturday or Sunday when the court is closed.

(b) Enlargement. When an act is required or allowed to be performed at or within a specified time, the court for cause shown may at any time in its discretion:

(1) With or without motion or notice, order the period enlarged if application therefor is made before expiration of the period originally prescribed or of that period as extended by a previous order; or,

(2) Upon motion, permit the act to be done after expiration of the specified period if the failure to act on time was the result of excusable neglect.

(c) to (e) Repealed.

(f) Inmate Filings. A document filed by an inmate confined in an institution is timely filed with the court if deposited in the institution's internal mailing system on or before the last day for fling. If an institution has a system designed for legal mail, the inmate must use that system to receive the benefit of this rule.

Colo. R. Crim. P. 45

Source: Entire rule amended and adopted May 17, 2001, effective 7/1/2001; a and e amended and Comment added May 7, 2009, effective 7/1/2009; a amended, c, d, and e repealed, and comment deleted and adopted December 14, 2011, effective 7/1/2012; comment added and adopted June 21, 2012, effective 7/1/2012.

CommentAfter the particular effective date, time computation in most situations is intended to incorporate the Rule of Seven. Under the Rule of Seven, a day is a day, and because calendars are divided into 7-day week intervals, groupings of days are in 7-day or multiples of 7-day intervals. Groupings of less than 7 days have been left as they were because such small numbers do not interfere with the underlying concept. Details of the Rule of Seven reform are set forth in an article by Richard P. Holme, 41 Colo. Lawyer, Vol. 1, P 33 (January 2012). Time computation is sometimes "forward," meaning starting the count at a particular stated event such as date of filing and counting forward to the deadline date. Counting "backward" means counting backward from the event to reach the deadline date such as a stated number of days being allowed before the commencement of trial . In determining the effective date of the Rule of Seven time computation/time interval amendments having a statutory basis, said amendments take effect on July 1, 2012 and regardless of whether time intervals are counted forward or backward, both the time computation start date and deadline date must be after June 30, 2012. Further, the time computation/time interval amendments do not apply to modify the settings of any dates or time intervals set by an order of a court entered before July 1, 2012.

Annotation Law reviews. For article, "'Rule of Seven' for Trial Lawyers: Calculating Litigation Deadlines", see 41 Colo. Law. 33 (January 2012). Rule preserves defendant's right to raise fourth amendment issue. Section (d) of this rule which must be read in conjunction with Rule 41(e), Crim. P., adequately preserves a defendant's right to raise a fourth amendment issue, while carrying out the salutary purpose of not commingling the fourth amendment issue with the guilt issue. Morgan v. People, 166 Colo. 451, 444 P.2d 386 (1968). Purpose of section (d) is to allow time for adequate preparation. People v. District Court, 189 Colo. 159, 538 P.2d 887 (1975). And notice served same day as pretrial hearing clear violation of rule. Where notice of motion to disqualify the district attorney from further participation in a criminal case is given to the district attorney's office the same morning that the hearing on the motion was held, the consideration of this motion by the trial court when the district attorney did not have fair notice and an opportunity to defend himself is a clear violation of the provisions of this rule. People v. District Court, 189 Colo. 159, 538 P.2d 887 (1975). But failure to object to lack of notice constitutes waiver. If defendant fails to object to the lack of notice at the hearing prior to trial or fails to request a continuance, his silence constitutes a waiver of the five-day notice. Maraggos v. People, 175 Colo. 130, 486 P.2d 1 (1971). Timely motion for new trial is not jurisdictional in the sense that without it the court would lack authority to adjudicate the subject matter. People v. Moore, 193 Colo. 81, 562 P.2d 749 (1977). Rather, it is a procedural prerequisite intended to assure that the matters appealed have been considered by the trial court. People v. Moore, 193 Colo. 81, 562 P.2d 749 (1977). And prosecution's failure to object waives timeliness issue on appeal. The people, by failing to object to the trial court's hearing and deciding the new trial motion, waived their right to raise the timeliness issue on appeal. People v. Moore, 193 Colo. 81, 562 P.2d 749 (1977). Excusable neglect. A trial court may extend the time for filing a motion on the basis that failure to act on time was the result of excusable neglect if there was a factual finding to support a claim of ineffective assistance of counsel. Swainson v. People, 712 P.2d 479 (Colo. 1986). Excusable neglect does not include family considerations or lack of knowledge of the law for purposes of extending the time to file a Crim. P. 35 motion. People v. Delgado, 83 P.3d 1144 (Colo. App. 2003), rev'd on other grounds, 105 P.3d 634 (Colo. 2005). Burden of showing excusable neglect under section (b) is upon the defendant. People v. Dillon, 655 P.2d 841 (Colo. 1982). Defendant wrongfully believing appeal being processed by attorney allowed to file untimely motion. In light of the defendant's uncontroverted belief that his attorney is processing his appeal, the trial court abuses its discretion when it later denies defendant's motion to file an untimely motion and thereby perfect his appeal. People v. Dillon, 631 P.2d 1153 (Colo. App. 1981). Considerations governing determination of effect of time limitations in criminal cases and in civil cases. People v. Moore, 193 Colo. 81, 562 P.2d 749 (1977). Mere speculation regarding the court's disposition of a motion for a continuance or to recall a witness does not obviate the defendant's duty to seek such procedures if the defendant is to base his claim of prejudice on the inability to prepare new theories of defense or to cross-examine past witnesses in light of previously undisclosed evidence. Salazar v. People, 870 P.2d 1215 (Colo. 1994). Applied in People v. Masamba, 39 Colo. App. 187, 563 P.2d 382 (1977); People v. Houpe, 41 Colo. App. 253, 586 P.2d 241 (1978); People v. Peterson, 656 P.2d 1301 (Colo. 1983).

Rule 46 - Bail

In considering the question of bail, the Court shall be governed by the statutes and the Constitution of the State of Colorado and the United States Constitution.

Colo. R. Crim. P. 46

Source: Entire rule repealed and readopted April 2, 1987, effective 9/1/1987.

Annotation Rule does not authorize setting aside a judgment on a forfeiture of a bond. People v. Caro, 753 P.2d 196 (Colo. 1988) (decided under rule before 1987 repeal and readoption).

For right to bail and exceptions thereto, see § 19 of article II of the state constitution; for prohibition on excessive bail, see § 20 of article II of the state constitution; for bailable offenses, see article 4 of title 16, C.R.S.

Rule 46.1 - Bail-County Courts

Colo. R. Crim. P. 46.1

Repealed April 2, 1987, effective 9/1/1987.

Rule 47 - Motions

(a) An application to the court for an order shall be by motion. A motion other than one made during a trial or hearing shall be in writing unless the court permits it to be made orally. It shall state the grounds upon which it is made and shall set forth the relief or order sought. It may be supported by affidavit.

(b) A written motion, other than one which may be heard ex parte, and notice of the hearing thereof, shall be served not later than 7 days before the time specified for the hearing unless a different period is fixed by rule or order of the court. For cause shown such an order may be made on ex parte application. When a motion is supported by affidavit, the affidavit shall be served with the motion, and opposing affidavits may be served not less than one day before the hearing unless the court permits them to be served at a later time.

Colo. R. Crim. P. 47

Source: Entire rule amended and adopted December 14, 2011, effective 7/1/2012.

Annotation Court is justified in considering statements in affidavits in support of motion to dismiss indictments as evidence of the facts asserted. People v. Lewis, 183 Colo. 236, 516 P.2d 416 (1973). If party disagrees with allegations in affidavits attached to motion to dismiss indictments, he should file counter affidavits or call witnesses to dispute the allegations. People v. Lewis, 183 Colo. 236, 516 P.2d 416 (1973). Applied in People v. Martinez, 43 Colo. App. 419, 608 P.2d 359 (1979); People v. Buggs, 631 P.2d 1200 (Colo. App. 1981).

Rule 48 - Dismissal

(a) By the State. No criminal case pending in any court shall be dismissed or a nolle prosequi therein entered by any prosecuting attorney or his deputy, unless upon a motion in open court, and with the court's consent and approval. Such a motion shall be supported or accompanied by a written statement concisely stating the reasons for the action. The statement shall be filed with the record of the particular case and be open to public inspection. Such a dismissal may not be filed during the trial without the defendant's consent.

(b) By the Court.

(1) If, after the filing of a complaint, there is unnecessary delay in finding an indictment or filing an information against a defendant who has been held to answer in a district court, the court may dismiss the prosecution. Except as otherwise provided in this Rule, if a defendant is not brought to trial on the issues raised by the complaint, information, or indictment within six months from the entry of a plea of not guilty, he shall be discharged from custody if he has not been admitted to bail, the pending charges shall be dismissed, whether he is in custody or on bail, and the defendant shall not again be indicted, informed against, or committed for the same offense, or for another offense based upon the same act or series of acts arising out of the same criminal episode.

(2) If trial results in conviction which is reversed on appeal, any new trial must be commenced within six months after the date of the receipt by the trial court of the mandate from the appellate court.

(3) If a trial date has been fixed by the court, and thereafter the defendant requests and is granted a continuance for trial, the period within which the trial shall be had is extended for an additional six months period from the date upon which the continuance was granted.

(3.5) If a trial date has been fixed by the court and the defendant fails to make an appearance in person on the trial date, the period in which the trial shall be had is extended for an additional six months' period from the date of the defendant's next appearance.

(4) If a trial date has been fixed by the court, and thereafter the prosecuting attorney requests and is granted a continuance, the time is not thereby extended within which the trial shall be had, as is provided in subsection (b)(1) of this Rule, unless the defendant in person or by his counsel in open court of record expressly agrees to the continuance. The time for trial, in the event of such agreement, is then extended by the number of days intervening between the granting of such continuance and the date to which trial is continued.

(5) To be entitled to a dismissal under subsection (b)(1) of this Rule, the defendant must move for dismissal prior to the commencement of his trial or the entry of a plea of guilty to the charge or an included offense. Failure so to move is a waiver of the defendant's rights under this section.

(5.1) If a trial date is offered by the court to a defendant who is represented by counsel and neither the defendant nor his counsel expressly objects to the offered date as beyond the time within which the trial shall be had pursuant to this rule, then the period within which the trial shall be had is extended until such trial date and may be extended further pursuant to any other applicable provision of this rule.

(6) In computing the time within which a defendant shall be brought to trial as provided in subsection (b)(1) of this Rule, the following periods of time shall be excluded:

(I) Any period during which the defendant is incompetent to stand trial or is unable to appear by reason of illness or physical disability or is under observation or examination at any time the issue of insanity, incompetency or impaired mental condition is raised;

(II) The period of delay caused by an interlocutory appeal, an appeal from an order that dismisses one or more counts of a charging document prior to trial, or after issuance of a rule to show cause in an original action brought under Colorado Appellate Rule 21, whether commenced by the defendant or by the prosecution;

(III) A reasonable period of delay when the defendant is joined for trial with a codefendant as to whom the time for trial has not run and there is good cause for not granting a severance;

(IV) The period or delay resulting from the voluntary absence or unavailability of the defendant; however, a defendant shall be considered unavailable whenever his whereabouts are known but his presence for trial cannot be obtained, or he resists being returned to the state for trial;

(V) The period of delay caused by any mistrial, not to exceed three months for each mistrial;

(VI) The period of delay caused at the instance of the defendant;

(VII) The period of delay not exceeding six months resulting from a continuance granted at the request of the prosecuting attorney, without the consent of the defendant, if:

(A) The continuance is granted because of the unavailability of evidence material to the state's case, when the prosecuting attorney has exercised due diligence to obtain such evidence and there are reasonable grounds to believe that such evidence will be available at the later date; or

(B) The continuance is granted to allow the prosecuting attorney additional time in felony cases to prepare the state's case and additional time is justified because of exceptional circumstances of the case and the court entered specific findings with respect to the justification.

(VIII) The period of delay between the new date set for trial following the expiration of the time periods excluded by paragraphs (I), (II), (III), (IV), and (V) of this subsection (6), not to exceed three months.

(IX) The period of delay between the filing of a motion pursuant to section 18-1-202(11) and any decision by the court regarding such motion, and if such decision by the court transfers the case to another county, the period of delay until the first appearance of all the parties in a court of appropriate jurisdiction in the county to which the case has been transferred, and in such event the provisions of subsection (7) of this section shall apply.

(7) If a trial date has been fixed by the court and the case is subsequently transferred to a court in another county, the period within which trial must be had is extended for an additional three months from the date of the first appearance of all the parties in a court of appropriate jurisdiction in the county to which the case has been transferred.

Colo. R. Crim. P. 48

Source: b3.5, b5.1, b6VIII, b6IX, and b7 added February 4, 1993, effective 4/1/1993; b6I amended and committee comment added, effective 1/26/1995; entire rule amended and adopted June 27, 2002, effective 7/1/2002.

Committee CommentThis amendment to Crim. P. 48(b)(6)(I) is designed to bring this Rule into conformity with its corresponding statute, Section 18-1-405(6)(A), 8 B C.R.S. (1994 Supp.).

Annotation I. General Consideration. Law reviews. For article, "Criminal Procedure", which discusses a recent Tenth Circuit decision dealing with dismissal of indictments without prejudice, see 62 Den. U. L. Rev. 185 (1985). For article, "Pronouncements of the U.S. Supreme Court Relating to the Criminal Law Field: 1985-1986", which discusses recent cases relating to speedy trials, see 15 Colo. Law. 1595 and 1617 (1986). For article, "The Ins and Outs, Stops and Starts of Speedy Trial Rights in Colorado-Part I", see 31 Colo. Law. 115 (July 2002). For article, "The Ins and Outs, Stops and Starts of Speedy Trial Rights in Colorado-Part II", see 31 Colo. Law. 59 (August 2002). Annotator's note. For other annotations concerning speedy trials, see § 16 of art. II, Colo. Const., and § 18-1-405 . Intent of rule. This rule was designed to render the federal and state constitutional rights to a speedy trial more effective. Sweet v. Myers, 200 Colo. 50, 612 P.2d 75 (1980); People v. Sanchez, 649 P.2d 1049 (Colo. 1982). An accused person's right to a speedy trial is ultimately grounded on the federal and state constitutions, and statutes relating to speedy trial are intended to render these constitutional guarantees more effective. Simakis v. District Court, 194 Colo. 436, 577 P.2d 3 (1978). This rule was designed to substantially conform to § 18-1-405 . Carr v. District Court, 190 Colo. 125, 543 P.2d 1253 (1975). Both simplify constitutional parameters. This rule and § 18-1-405 clarify and simplify the parameters of the constitutional right to a speedy trial. Carr v. District Court, 190 Colo. 125, 543 P.2d 1253 (1975); People v. Cisneros, 193 Colo. 141, 563 P.2d 355 (1977); People v. Chavez, 779 P.2d 375 (Colo. 1989). Policies underlying this rule and § 18-1-405 , are the same as those relative to the uniform mandatory disposition of detainers act, §§ 16-14-101 to 16-14-108 . People v. Lopez, 41 Colo. App. 206, 587 P.2d 792 (1978). Applied in People v. Flowers, 190 Colo. 453, 548 P.2d 918 (1976); Murphy v. District Court, 195 Colo. 149, 576 P.2d 163 (1978); Reliford v. People, 195 Colo. 549, 579 P.2d 1145 (1978); People v. District Court, 196 Colo. 420, 586 P.2d 1329 (1978); People v. Gonzales, 198 Colo. 546, 603 P.2d 139 (1979); People v. Wimer, 43 Colo. App. 237, 604 P.2d 1183 (1979); Jeffrey v. District Court, 626 P.2d 631 (Colo. 1981); People v. Small, 631 P.2d 148 (Colo. 1981); People v. Jones, 631 P.2d 1132

(Colo. 1981); People v. District Court, 632 P.2d 1022 (Colo. 1981); People v. Marquez, 644 P.2d 59 (Colo. App. 1981); People v. Velasquez, 641 P.2d 943 (Colo. 1982); People v. Ashton, 661 P.2d 291 (Colo. App. 1982); People v. Olds, 656 P.2d 705 (Colo. 1983); People v. Watson, 666 P.2d 1114 (Colo. App. 1983); People v. Harding, 671 P.2d 975 (Colo. App. 1983); People v. Castango, 674 P.2d 978 (Colo. App. 1983). II. By the State. District attorney's common-law power to enter nolle prosequi. Prior to the enactment of this rule, the common-law rule was that the district attorney had the power to enter a nolle prosequi in a criminal case without the consent of the court. People v. Lichtenstein, 630 P.2d 70 (Colo. 1981). Dismissal is function of district attorney. Neither the complaining witness nor the trial judge may dismiss a prosecution on behalf of the state; that is the function of the district attorney. People v. Dennis, 164 Colo. 163, 433 P.2d 339 (1967). Trial court's discretion in reviewing motion to dismiss. In exercising its discretion in reviewing a motion to dismiss charges, the trial court should not serve merely as a rubber stamp for the prosecutor's decision. People v. Lichtenstein, 630 P.2d 70 (Colo. 1981). The trial court's refusal to consent to a dismissal of charges is appropriate only where the evidence is clear and convincing that the interests of the defendant or the public are jeopardized by the district attorney's refusal to prosecute. People v. Lichtenstein, 630 P.2d 70 (Colo. 1981). III. By the Court. A. In General. Rule is independent of constitutional provisions. This rule is tied to the historical right and the inherent power of the court to dismiss a case for want of prosecution and is separate and independent of the constitutional right to a speedy trial. People ex rel. Coca v. District Court, 187 Colo. 280, 530 P.2d 958 (1975). The right to a speedy trial is guaranteed by § 16 of art. II, Colo. Const., and this constitutional protection is independent of any right established by statute or rule. People v. Slender Wrap, Inc., 36 Colo. App. 11, 536 P.2d 850 (1975). Provisions of this rule and the constitutional issue as to denial of speedy trial are mutually exclusive, and the resolution of one does not necessarily determine the resolution of the other. Potter v. District Court, 186 Colo. 1, 525 P.2d 429 (1974). The obvious purpose of this rule is to prevent "dillydallying" on the part of the district attorney or the court in a criminal proceeding. People v. Bates, 155 Colo. 277, 394 P.2d 134 (1964); Jaramillo v. District Court, 174 Colo. 561, 484 P.2d 1219 (1971). Dismissal of charges sufficient to protect defendant's rights. Where defendant's trial took place within six months of defendant's plea of not guilty to the charges in the second indictment, and while the trial was not held until more than six months after defendant's plea to the charges of the original indictment, those charges were dismissed by the trial court, such dismissal was sufficient to protect defendant's rights under § 18-1-405 and section (b)(1) of this rule. People v. Wilkinson, 37 Colo. App. 531, 555 P.2d 1167 (1976). Speedy trial is calculated separately for each criminal complaint. When charges in a complaint are properly dismissed within the speedy trial period without prejudice, they are a nullity. If defendant is arraigned under new charges, even if they are identical to the dismissed charges, the speedy trial period begins anew. Huang v. County Court of Douglas County, 98 P.3d 924 (Colo. App. 2003). No dismissal where not authorized by rule or due process. The trial court may not, on its own motion, dismiss an action on behalf of the defendant prior to trial over the objection of the district attorney where such dismissal is not authorized under the rules and is not required by due process. People v. Butz, 37 Colo. App. 212, 547 P.2d 262 (1975). Outrageous governmental conduct need not be prejudicial to defendant to constitute a violation of due process. People v. Auld, 815 P.2d 956 (Colo. App. 1991). Trial court had no authority to dismiss case based on the theory that it was an abuse of prosecutorial discretion to retry the case. A district attorney has broad discretion in determining who shall be prosecuted and what crimes shall be charged, and such discretion may not be controlled or limited by judicial intervention, except in unusual circumstances which result in a denial of a particular defendant's due process right to fundamental fairness. People v. Schwartz, 678 P.2d 1000 (Colo. 1984). Court's practice of postponing arraignment until all pretrial matters are concluded thwarts purpose of this rule and § 18-1-405 . People v. Chavez, 779 P.2d 375 (Colo. 1989). It is the joint responsibility of the district attorney and the trial court to assiduously avoid any occasion for a useless and unnecessary delay in the trial of a criminal case. People v. Murphy, 183 Colo. 106, 515 P.2d 107 (1973). Relief in nature of prohibition appropriate remedy. Relief in the nature of prohibition under C.A.R. 21, is an appropriate remedy when a district court is proceeding without jurisdiction to try a defendant in violation of his right to a speedy trial. Marquez v. District Court, 200 Colo. 55, 613 P.2d 1302 (1980). Relation of section (b) to Rule 248(b), C.M.C.R. Section (b) is the parallel rule to Rule 248(b), C.M.C.R. Bachicha v. Municipal Court, 41 Colo. App. 198, 581 P.2d 746 (1978). Uniform Mandatory Disposition of Detainers Act controls in conflict with rule. When there is a conflict with the general speedy trial provisions of the Uniform Mandatory Disposition of Detainers Act and this rule, the provisions of the uniform

act control. People v. Swazo, 199 Colo. 486, 610 P.2d 1072 (1980). B. Right to Speedy Trial.
Right to a speedy trial is not only for the benefit of the accused, but also for the protection of the
public. It is essential that an early determination of guilt be made so that the innocent may be
exonerated and the guilty punished. Jaramillo v. District Court, 174 Colo. 561, 484 P.2d 1219
(1971); People v. Martin, 732 P.2d 1210 (Colo. 1987). Speedy trial provisions are designed to
foster more effective prisoner treatment and rehabilitation by eliminating, as expeditiously as
possible, the uncertainties surrounding outstanding criminal charges. Simakis v. District Court,
194 Colo. 436, 577 P.2d 3 (1978). Court lacks jurisdiction to try defendant in violation of speedy
trial right. A court would be proceeding without jurisdiction if it were to try criminal defendant
in violation of his rights under the Colorado speedy trial statute and the rules of the Colorado
supreme court. Hampton v. District Court, 199 Colo. 104, 605 P.2d 54 (1980). Determination of
denial of speedy trial is judicial question. The question of determining when an accused has been
denied a speedy trial under this rule, or under the constitution, is necessarily a judicial question.
Jaramillo v. District Court, 174 Colo. 561, 484 P.2d 1219 (1971). Appealability. Where
determination that delays in bringing defendant to trial involved resolutions of fact questions, the
district attorney could not appeal such determinations. People v. Murphy, 183 Colo. 106, 515
P.2d 107 (1973). Speedy public trial is a relative concept requiring judicial determination on a
case-by-case basis. Lucero v. People, 171 Colo. 167, 465 P.2d 504 (1970). Determined by
circumstances of each case. A speedy public trial is a relative concept, because the
circumstances of each case determine whether it has been afforded. Maes v. People, 169 Colo.
200, 454 P.2d 792 (1969). The circumstances of each case must be examined to determine
whether a speedy trial has been afforded, and in making this determination the court must
consider the length of the pretrial delay, the reasons for it, whether the defendant has demanded
a speedy trial, and whether any prejudice actually resulted to the defendant. All of these factors
are interrelated and must be considered together with any other relevant circumstances. Gelfand
v. People, 196 Colo. 487, 586 P.2d 1331 (1978). Such as defendant's understanding of when six-
month period begins to run. Where defendant's expressed understanding was that the six-month
period of the speedy trial statute would commence to run at the end of his continuance, the
failure to try defendant within six months of the granting of the continuance does not entitle him
to dismissal of charges. Baca v. District Court, 198 Colo. 486, 603 P.2d 940 (1979). The speedy
trial statute (§ 18-1-405) is intended to implement the constitutional right to a speedy trial by
requiring dismissal of the case whenever the defendant is not tried within the six-month period
and the delay does not qualify for one of the express exclusionary categories set out in the
statute. People v. Deason, 670 P.2d 792 (Colo. 1983). Section (b) and § 18-1-405 are virtually
identical. Since section (b) of this rule is the procedural counterpart to the speedy trial statute
and is virtually identical to § 18-1-405 , the resolution of a speed trial issue if the same whether
the analysis proceeds from the statute or the rule. People v. Deason, 670 P.2d 792 (Colo. 1983).
Section 18-1-405 refers to trial resolving ultimate guilt or innocence. The phrase "brought to
trial on the issues raised by the ... information", as used in § 18-1-405 , refers to a trial which
resolves the ultimate guilt or innocence of the accused as to the charges filed against him and
not a sanity trial, even when the defendant pleads not guilty by reason of insanity. People v.
Deason, 670 P.2d 792 (Colo. 1983). And commencement of a sanity trial is not the functional
equivalent of a trial on the merits for purposes of satisfying the state's speedy trial obligation.
People v. Deason, 670 P.2d 792 (Colo. 1983). Constitutional right to speedy trial not controlled
by six-month statutory period. A defendant is not precluded from asserting her constitutional
right to a speedy trial simply because the trial was held within the required statutory period; the
defendant, however, has the burden of proving that her constitutional speedy trial right has been
denied. Gelfand v. People, 196 Colo. 487, 586 P.2d 1331 (1978). Simply because a trial is held
within six months, the defendant is not precluded from raising his right to a speedy public trial as
embodied in § 16 of art. II, Colo. Const. Casias v. People, 160 Colo. 152, 415 P.2d 344, cert.
denied, 385 U.S. 979, 87 S. Ct. 523, 17 L. Ed. 2d 441 (1966). For the six-month proscription of
this rule defines the outside limits for prosecution. People v. Small, 177 Colo. 118, 493 P.2d 15
(1972). This rule is not a statement of the minimum time that must expire before a defendant can
look for relief for denial of a speedy trial. People v. Mayes, 178 Colo. 429, 498 P.2d 1123
(1972). The six-month provision sets up a maximum limitation beyond which a defendant shall
not be tried for the offense charged, provided the delay was not occasioned by his action or
request. Casias v. People, 160 Colo. 152, 415 P.2d 344, cert. denied, 385 U.S. 979, 87 S. Ct.
523, 17 L. Ed. 2d 441 (1966). Prejudice to the defendant could dictate that a case be dismissed
for failure to grant a speedy trial, even though the six-month period set forth in the rule has not
expired. People v. Small, 177 Colo. 118, 493 P.2d 15 (1972). Six-month limitation begins to run.

210

The six-month limitation of both § 18-1-405 and section (b)(1) of this rule runs from the date that defendant's plea is entered. People v. Wilkinson, 37 Colo. App. 531, 555 P.2d 1167 (1976). Subsection (b)(1) plainly requires that the defendant be brought to trial within six months of the date upon which he enters a plea of not guilty to the charges set forth in the information. People v. Romero, 196 Colo. 520, 587 P.2d 789 (1978). The six-month period commences upon the arraignment for the last information. People v. Dunhill, 40 Colo. App. 137, 570 P.2d 1097 (1977). The six-month period, provided for in section (b), commences to run upon the defendant's arraignment on the last of three informations where two prior informations have been dismissed. People v. Lopez, 41 Colo. App. 206, 587 P.2d 792 (1978). Record to show compliance. The burden of establishing compliance with the speedy trial statute includes making a record sufficient for an appellate court to determine such statutory compliance. Marquez v. District Court, 200 Colo. 55, 613 P.2d 1302 (1980). Court cannot dismiss on own motion. Where defendant and counsel failed to appear at trial date, this rule does not authorize a district court, on its own motion, to dismiss a criminal case over the district attorney's objection, even though it appears that further prosecution will be useless and unnecessarily costly. People v. Hale, 194 Colo. 503, 573 P.2d 935 (1978). Speedy trial requirements apply in juvenile proceedings. Trial courts are bound by the statutory and constitutional speedy trial requirements in juvenile as well as adult proceedings; fundamental fairness requires no less. P.V. v. District Court, 199 Colo. 357, 609 P.2d 110 (1980). A trial court conducting a juvenile proceeding is bound by the same statutory and constitutional speedy trial requirements that are applicable in adult proceedings. People in Interest of T.F.B., 199 Colo. 474, 610 P.2d 501 (1980). But not in trial de novo for violation of ordinance. Six-month speedy trial rule does not apply in a trial de novo in the county court for violation of a municipal ordinance. Rainwater v. County Court, 43 Colo. App. 477, 604 P.2d 1195 (1979). Special time limitations of § 24-60-501 prevail, when conflicts arise, over the more general criminal procedure provisions of § 18-1-405 and this rule. Simakis v. District Court, 194 Colo. 436, 577 P.2d 3 (1978). Defendant must enter plea before he may take advantage of the restriction of § 18-1-405 and subsection (b) (1) of this rule. People v. Wilkinson, 37 Colo. App. 531, 555 P.2d 1167 (1976). Where no plea has been entered, there has been no violation of the rule. Potter v. District Court, 186 Colo. 1, 525 P.2d 429 (1974). Defendant only required to move for dismissal. The burden of insuring compliance with the time requirements of section (b) is on the prosecution and the trial court, to the point that the only affirmative action required on the part of the defendant is that he move for a dismissal prior to trial. People v. Abeyta, 195 Colo. 338, 578 P.2d 645 (1978). To properly raise the question, the accused may apply for his discharge or for dismissal for lack of a speedy trial. Jaramillo v. District Court, 174 Colo. 561, 484 P.2d 1219 (1971). And must show he was not afforded speedy trial. A motion for discharge or for dismissal for want of due prosecution of a charge of crime must be sustained by the accused, as he has the burden of showing that he was not afforded a speedy trial. Jaramillo v. District Court, 174 Colo. 561, 484 P.2d 1219 (1971). The burden is upon the defendant to show that an expeditious trial was denied him. Maes v. People, 169 Colo. 200, 454 P.2d 792 (1969); Ziatz v. People, 171 Colo. 58, 465 P.2d 406 (1970). The burden is upon the defendant to establish that he has been denied a speedy trial in violation of the statute or rule or that his constitutional right to a speedy trial requires dismissal. Saiz v. District Court, 189 Colo. 555, 542 P.2d 1293 (1975); People v. Chavez, 779 P.2d 375 (Colo. 1989). Although there is considerable delay in bringing the defendants to trial, such is immaterial where it is still accomplished within the six-month requirement, and defendants fail to meet the burden of showing they were denied an expeditious trial, and that they were prejudiced thereby. Casias v. Patterson, 398 F.2d 486 (10th Cir. 1968), cert. denied, 393 U.S. 1108, 89 S. Ct. 918, 21 L. Ed. 2d 804 (1969). Although not because bail is granted. The right to a speedy trial is not dissipated by the fact that the defendant is granted bail. Jaramillo v. District Court, 174 Colo. 561, 484 P.2d 1219 (1971). Consistent with court's trial docket. The burden is upon defendant who asserts denial of speedy trial to show facts establishing that, consistent with court's trial docket conditions, he could have been afforded trial. Rowse v. District Court, 180 Colo. 44, 502 P.2d 422 (1972). As a speedy trial envisions a public trial consistent with the court's business. Lucero v. People, 171 Colo. 167, 465 P.2d 504 (1970). The constitutional right to a speedy trial means a trial consistent with the court's business. People v. Mayes, 178 Colo. 429, 498 P.2d 1123 (1972). And not immediately after apprehension and indictment. Speedy public trial does not mean trial immediately after the accused is apprehended and indicted, but public trial consistent with the court's business. Maes v. People, 169 Colo. 200, 454 P.2d 792 (1969). Congestion of docket must be considered. One circumstance to be considered in determining whether the defendant received a speedy trial is the extent of congestion of the docket of the trial court. Lucero v.

People, 171 Colo. 167, 465 P.2d 504 (1970). Although it is clear that docket congestion would not warrant a retrial later than the three-month maximum period for delay caused by a mistrial, it is a factor in determining the reasonableness of the delay within the statutory and procedural time periods of § 18-1-405(6)(e) and section (b)(6)(V) of this rule. Pinelli v. District Court, 197 Colo. 555, 595 P.2d 225 (1979). When a trial court continues a case due to docket congestion, but makes a reasonable effort to reschedule within the speedy trial period, and defense counsel's scheduling conflict does not permit a new date within the speedy trial deadline, the resulting delay is attributable to defendant. The period of delay is excludable from time calculations for purposes of the applicable speedy trial provision. Hills v. Westminster Mun. Court, 245 P.3d 947 (Colo. 2011). Delays which are occasioned by a district attorney are to be considered by a trial court in determining whether defendant had been denied his constitutional right to a speedy trial. People v. Mayes, 178 Colo. 429, 498 P.2d 1123 (1972). Deliberate election of district attorney to postpone trial is denial. Where the facts clearly establish that a defendant was denied a speedy trial through no fault of his own and as a result of the deliberate election of the district attorney to postpone the trial, the defendant has been denied a speedy trial under the provisions of section (b) of this rule. Jaramillo v. District Court, 174 Colo. 561, 484 P.2d 1219 (1971). Delay caused by change of venue. When a change of venue is granted after arraignment, it is incumbent upon the prosecuting attorney to make a motion to obtain additional time to bring the defendant to trial because of the exceptional circumstances of the case, and the trial court must then make specific findings with respect to the justification. People v. Colantonio, 196 Colo. 242, 583 P.2d 919 (1978). State cannot dismiss and refile charges indiscriminately and avoid the mandate of this rule. Schiffner v. People, 173 Colo. 123, 476 P.2d 756 (1970). The prosecution cannot indiscriminately dismiss and refile charges in order to avoid the mandate of § 18-1-405 and section (b)(1) of this rule. People v. Wilkinson, 37 Colo. App. 531, 555 P.2d 1167 (1976). And subsequent indictment charging same offense must be dismissed. Where defendant was charged with an offense in one indictment and was subject to jurisdiction of court for more than one year, a subsequent indictment charging the defendant with same offense had to be dismissed for lack of speedy trial. Rowse v. District Court, 180 Colo. 44, 502 P.2d 422 (1972). Provided defendant proves presecution's course of action. To be entitled to dismissal on these grounds, the defendant must affirmatively establish the existence of such a course of action on the part of the prosecution. People v. Wilkinson, 37 Colo. App. 531, 555 P.2d 1167 (1976). The burden of establishing that the prosecution indiscriminately dismissed and refiled charges in order to avoid the mandate of § 18-1-405 and section (b)(1) of this rule is not satisfied by proof only that the district attorney sought and obtained a subsequent indictment for different offenses arising from the same transaction. People v. Wilkinson, 37 Colo. App. 531, 555 P.2d 1167 (1976). But where actions of district attorney in refiling are result of change in circumstances which justify that action, no violation of this rule occurs. Schiffner v. People, 173 Colo. 123, 476 P.2d 756 (1970). As where federal sanctions are nullified after state action is dismissed. Where the district attorney was acting for the benefit of the defendant when he dismissed the original information based on the assumption that the defendant should not be punished twice for the same transaction, then when it becomes apparent that the defendant is to escape federal sanctions by reason of a technical objection, it is certainly proper for the district attorney to refile the state charges, and the actions of the district attorney are within the spirit of this rule. Schiffner v. People, 173 Colo. 123, 476 P.2d 756 (1970). Effect of prosecution's filing amended complaint. When the prosecution files an amended complaint charging new material after the defendant's initial guilty plea, the period of time for dismissal under the speedy trial provisions is measured from the second guilty plea unless the prosecution has shown bad faith in amending the complaint. If the amended complaint does not charge new material, the time period is measured from the original guilty plea. Amon v. People, 198 Colo. 172, 597 P.2d 569 (1979). Mistrials due to prosecutor's actions not treated differently. Neither subparagraph (b)(6)(V) of this rule nor § 18-1-405(6)(e), treats mistrials due to the prosecutor's actions differently from mistrials due to other reasons. People v. Erickson, 194 Colo. 557, 574 P.2d 504 (1978). For purposes of six-month period, new trial order similar to reversal. A new trial order pursuant to a new trial motion is similar to a reversal on appeal for purposes of the speedy trial provisions and results in a six-month speedy trial period. People v. Jamerson, 196 Colo. 63, 580 P.2d 805 (1978). Failure to demand dismissal waives speedy trial objection. Failure to bring defendant to trial within the allotted time does not automatically deprive the trial court of jurisdiction, because defendant's failure to demand dismissal prior to trial waives any speedy trial objection. People v. Anderson, 649 P.2d 720 (Colo. App. 1982). In accordance with the express language of § 18-1-405(5), defendant waived his right to a speedy trial by failing to move for dismissal of charges

212

prior to entering a guilty plea. This did not, however, automatically waive the defendant's constitutional right to a speedy trial. Moody v. Corsentino, 843 P.2d 1355 (Colo. 1993). Delay caused by briefing and determining defendant's motion to dismiss properly charged to defendant. Williamsen v. People, 735 P.2d 176 (Colo. 1987). Determination that delay was caused by substitution of counsel not supported by record and not properly chargeable to defendant. Defendant's actions did not require a substitution of counsel, he was not counseled by the court on a need for a continuance, and court did not attempt to find other counsel who could meet the deadline. People ex rel. Gallagher v. District Court, 933 P.2d 583 (Colo. 1997). Express waiver or other affirmative conduct evidencing a waiver of the right to a speedy trial must be shown before a trial court may deny a dismissal motion. People v. Gallegos, 192 Colo. 450, 560 P.2d 93 (1977); Rance v. County Court, 193 Colo. 220, 564 P.2d 422 (1977); People v. Abeyta, 195 Colo. 338, 578 P.2d 645 (1978). Mere silence by a defense counsel to a trial setting beyond the speedy trial period shall not be construed as a waiver of a defendant's right to a speedy trial. Rance v. County Court, 193 Colo. 220, 564 P.2d 422 (1977); People v. Abeyta, 195 Colo. 338, 578 P.2d 645 (1978); People v. Lopez, 41 Colo. App. 206, 587 P.2d 792 (1978). Defendant's waiver limited. Where petitioner moved to continue his arraignment date, his written motion contained a statement to the effect that "the defendant waives his right to a speedy trial", this statement was intended only as a waiver of the right to challenge any speedy trial violation caused by the request for a continuance of the arraignment date and was not effective with respect to any subsequently occurring statutory speedy trial violation. Sweet v. Myers, 200 Colo. 50, 612 P.2d 75 (1980). Failure of each defendant to interpose any objection to a trial setting in county court beyond the six-month speedy trial period did not waive his right to a speedy trial. Rance v. County Court, 193 Colo. 220, 564 P.2d 422 (1977). Waiver after six-month period questionable. It is questionable whether a waiver of the right to a dismissal for failure to be granted a speedy trial could ever occur after the right to dismissal has already accrued. People v. Abeyta, 195 Colo. 338, 578 P.2d 645 (1978). Presence of defendant or counsel for subdivision (b)(6)(VII)(A) continuance. It is not clear under subdivision (b)(6)(VII)(A) of this rule whether the presence of the defendant or his counsel in open court is required. People v. Baker, 38 Colo. 101, 556 P.2d 90 (1976). Showing required by subdivision (b)(6)(VII)(A). Subdivision (b)(6)(VII)(A) requires a showing not only that the evidence is material and unavailable but also that the prosecuting attorney has exercised due diligence to obtain it. People v. Baker, 38 Colo. 101, 556 P.2d 90 (1976). C. Exclusion of Periods of Delay. Exclusion of delay caused by defendant. This rule excludes delay which is caused by, agreed to, or created at the instance of the defendant. Saiz v. District Court, 189 Colo. 555, 542 P.2d 1293 (1975). Where the delay has been initially caused by the defendant, he cannot invoke this rule. Lucero v. People, 171 Colo. 167, 465 P.2d 504 (1970). A defendant is not entitled to be discharged if he requests a postponement of his trial or otherwise causes the delay. People v. Bates, 155 Colo. 277, 394 P.2d 134 (1964). Where attributable to affirmative action by defendant. In computing the time within which a defendant must be brought to trial, in order for the delay to be charged to the defendant, it must be attributable to affirmative action on defendant's part, or to defendant's express consent to the delay, or to other affirmative conduct evidencing such consent. Tassett v. Yeager, 195 Colo. 190, 576 P.2d 558 (1978). An express consent to the delay or other affirmative evidencing such consent must be shown before the delay is chargeable to the defendant. People v. Lopez, 41 Colo. App. 206, 587 P.2d 792 (1978). Since the six-month provision of this rule is conditioned upon the proposition that the delay is not caused by the action or request of the defendant. Lucero v. People, 171 Colo. 167, 465 P.2d 504 (1970). Factors authorized a continuance and thereby extended the speedy trial time where a period of delay was attributable to the inability of the prosecution, despite its exercise of due diligence, to obtain the victim's presence for trial and prosecution demonstrated the victim would be available to testify at a later date. People v. Grenemyer, 827 P.2d 603 (Colo. App. 1992). Period of delay was excluded from the speedy trial period under the provisions of subsection (b)(6)(III). The trial court did not abuse its discretion in refusing to grant a severance, therefore the continuance granted to the codefendant was chargeable to the defendant, and the defendant was not denied his right to a speedy trial. People v. Backus, 952 P.2d 846 (Colo. App. 1998). Exclusion applies to entire period fairly attributed to absence. The exclusion provision applicable to the defendant's voluntary absence or unavailability applies to the entire period of delay that may be fairly attributed to such absence. People v. Sanchez, 649 P.2d 1049 (Colo. 1982); People v. Gray, 710 P.2d 1149 (Colo. App. 1985). Defendant confined to mental institution. When a defendant is confined to a mental institution or hospital for observation or examination prior to a determination of mental competency, he cannot complain of a denial of his constitutional right to

213

a speedy trial because of the delay occasioned by that confinement, People v. Jones, 677 P.2d 383 (Colo. App. 1983), aff'd in part, rev'd in part on other grounds, 711 P.2d 1270 (Colo. 1986). Excludable period may be longer than period of absence. The excludable period of delay resulting from defendant's absence, may, in some cases, be longer than merely the period of defendant's absence. People v. Alward, 654 P.2d 327 (Colo. App. 1982), cert. dismissed, 677 P.2d 948 (Colo. 1984). The period between a mistrial and commencement of a completed trial is properly excludable from the statutory speedy trial period requirement. People v. Martinez, 712 P.2d 1070 (Colo. App. 1985). Short delay is of no consequence where there have been numerous appearances already. The record is devoid of any showing that the trial was not held as soon as consistent with the court's business or that defendant suffered any prejudice by reason of the short delay when, between the date of charge and the date of trial, defendant, with his counsel, made numerous appearances in court to dispose of various pretrial matters. Maes v. People, 169 Colo. 200, 454 P.2d 792 (1969). Prearrest delay excluded from computation. Subsection (b)(1) supports a motion to dismiss only when the delay occurs after charges are made or an arrest has been effected and is not directed to delay which transpires prior to arrest. People ex rel. Coca v. District Court, 187 Colo. 280, 530 P.2d 958 (1975). Where a complaint was filed against defendant and a warrant for his arrest was issued, but there was no evidence that defendant was in the county during the period between the complaint and his arrest, the defendant was not entitled to a dismissal under this rule. People v. Tull, 178 Colo. 151, 497 P.2d 3 (1972). Period tolled by defendant's failure to make court appearance. When a defendant fails to make a scheduled bond appearance before the trial court, the six-month speedy trial period is tolled until he makes himself available to the court, even where some of time that he is unavailable he is incarcerated in another jurisdiction. People v. Moye, 635 P.2d 194 (Colo. 1981). Where defendant's criminal behavior causes him to be in the penitentiary when his case is set for trial, the delay that occurs cannot be interpreted to be a violation of his constitutional rights. Scott v. People, 176 Colo. 289, 490 P.2d 1295 (1971). Period of delay caused by mistrial not included. The computation of the six-month period allowed for in section (b)(1) shall not include any period of delay caused by a mistrial, nor the extension provided following a mistrial, being part of the delay caused thereby. Pinelli v. District Court, 197 Colo. 555, 595 P.2d 225 (1979). The length of delay "caused by any mistrial" must be calculated to include the days on which the aborted trial or trials were in progress. People v. Erickson, 194 Colo. 557, 574 P.2d 504 (1978). Three-month exclusion following mistrial. Section 18-1 -405(6)(e) and subdivision (b)(6)(V) of this rule grant the prosecution a three-month exclusion in which to retry a case after a mistrial, provided that the delays are reasonable. People v. Pipkin, 655 P.2d 1360 (Colo. 1982); Mason v. People, 932 P.2d 1377 (Colo. 1997). The general assembly intended to grant no more than three months as an exclusion from the speedy trial period, which is one-half of the statutory speedy trial period, following a mistrial. People v. Pitkin, 655 P.2d 1360 (Colo. 1982). Whether jeopardy has attached is irrelevant. If the court is forced to dismiss the jurors, or prospective jurors, and reschedule the trial, whether jeopardy has yet attached is irrelevant in computing the length of delay excluded due to mistrial. People v. Erickson, 194 Colo. 557, 574 P.2d 504 (1978). Where continuances requested to effect plea bargain. A defendant was not denied a speedy trial when the trial was held more than one year after he was charged where the delay was occasioned, to a large extent, by the defendant who requested and obtained numerous continuances in an attempt to effectuate a plea bargain. Maynes v. People, 178 Colo. 88, 495 P.2d 551 (1972). Speedy trial period tolled by appeal. The period of time necessary to go through the appellate process, where the appeal stems from a dismissal upon the defendant's motion, tolls the statutory speedy trial period. People v. Jamerson, 198 Colo. 92, 596 P.2d 764 (1979). This rule excludes from the computation of the time for speedy trial purposes the period of delay caused by an interlocutory appeal, but an original proceeding under C.A.R. 21 is, technically speaking, not an interlocutory appeal. People v. Medina, 40 Colo. App. 490, 583 P.2d 293 (1978). And for filing of psychiatric reports. When a defendant pleads not guilty by reason of insanity, the period from the time of commitment until the filing of the final psychiatric report, if filed within a reasonable time, is excludable for purposes of the six-month period. People v. Renfrow, 193 Colo. 131, 564 P.2d 411 (1977). The defendant need not be committed to an institution for examination before a reasonable time can be excluded from the speedy trial computation for the filing of psychiatric reports. People v. Brown, 44 Colo. App. 397, 622 P.2d 573 (1980). Tactical decision to seek continuance chargeable to defendant, absent prosecutor's bad faith. For purposes of section (b), a tactical decision to seek a continuance is chargeable to the defendant in the absence of a showing of bad faith on the part of the prosecutor. People v. Medina, 40 Colo. App. 490, 583 P.2d 293 (1978). In the absence of a showing of bad faith on the

214

part of the prosecutor in endorsing a witness on the day of the trial, the delay resulting from the defendant's tactical decision to seek a continuance as a result of the late endorsement is chargeable to her. *People v. Steele, 193 Colo. 87, 563 P.2d 6 (1977)*. Defense counsel's action held tantamount to request for continuance. When defense counsel insists he could not try the case prior to expiration of the six-month speedy trial period, this is tantamount to a request for a continuance. *People v. Chavez, 650 P.2d 1310 (Colo. App. 1982)*. Counsel may obtain continuance without defendant's consent. Defendant's attorney, without defendant's personal consent, may obtain a continuance of a trial setting subject to the discretion of the trial court,and the continuance will extend the speedy trial deadline an additional six months from the granting of the continuance. *People v. Anderson, 649 P.2d 720 (Colo. App. 1982)*. Defendant's speedy trial rights were not violated when, in response to the testimony of defendant's mental health expert during a suppression hearing that defendant's statements were involuntary because of a mental disorder, prosecution requested, and was granted, three month continuance in order to arrange for expert testimony and analyze the alleged mental disorder. *People v. Whalin, 885 P.2d 293 (Colo. App. 1994)*.

Rule 49 - Service and Filing of Papers

(a) Service-When Required. Written motions other than those which are heard ex parte, written notices, and similar papers shall be served upon the adverse parties. A motion or other pleading that includes a claim alleging a state statute or municipal ordinance is unconstitutional shall also be served upon the Attorney General.

(b) Service-How Made. Whenever under these Rules or by court order service is required or permitted to be made upon a party represented by an attorney, the service shall be made upon the attorney unless service upon the party himself is ordered by the court. Service upon the attorney or upon a party shall be made in the manner provided for civil actions unless otherwise ordered by the court.

(c) Notice of Orders. Immediately upon entry of any order made out of the presence of the parties after the information or indictment is filed, the clerk shall mail to each party affected a notice of the order and shall note the mailing in the docket.

Colo. R. Crim. P. 49

Source: a amended and effective 10/18/2007.

Annotation Reversal of verdict on the basis of failure to disclose certain information to the defendant is mandated only where the information might have affected the outcome of the trial. However, failure of prosecution to give notice to defendant of grants of immunity to two witnesses was not reversible error in that the ex parte order was available to the defense counsel in court records and there was nothing to indicate that the defense counsel's lack of knowledge regarding the grants of immunity might have in any way prejudiced the defendant so as to have affected the outcome of the trial. People v. Hickam, 684 P.2d 228 (Colo. 1984).

For the manner of service in civil actions, see C.R.C.P. 5.

Rule 49.5 - Electronic Filing and Service System

(a) Types of Cases Applicable. E-Filing and E-Service may be used for certain cases filed in the courts of Colorado as the service becomes available.

(b) E-Filing May be Mandated. With the permission of the Chief Justice, a chief judge may mandate E-Filing within a county or judicial district for specific case classes or types of cases. A judicial officer may mandate E-Filing and E-Service in that judicial officer's division for specific cases, for submitting documents to the court, and for serving documents on case parties. Where E-Filing is mandatory, the court may thereafter accept a document in paper form and the court shall scan the document and upload it to the E-System Provider. After notice to an attorney that all future documents are to be E-Filed, the court may charge a fee of $50 per document for the service of scanning and uploading a document filed in paper form. Where E-Filing and E-Service are mandatory, the chief judge or appropriate judicial officer may exclude pro se parties from mandatory E-Filing requirements.

(c) Definitions.

(1) Document. A pleading, motion, writing, or other paper filed or served under the E-System.

(2) E-Filing/Service System. The E-Filing/Service System (**"E-System"**) approved by the Colorado Supreme Court for filing and service of documents via the Internet through the Court-authorized E-System provider.

(3) Electronic Filing. Electronic filing (**"E-Filing"**) is the transmission of documents to the clerk of the court, and from the court, via the E-System.

(4) Electronic Service. Electronic service ("**E-Service**") is the transmission of documents to any party in a case via the E-System. Parties who have subscribed to the E-System have agreed to receive service of filings via the E-System, except when personal service is required.

(5) E-System Provider. The E-Filing/E-Service System Provider authorized by the Colorado Supreme Court.

(6) Signatures.

(I) Electronic Signature. An electronic sound, symbol, or process attached to or logically associated with an electronic record and executed or adopted by the person with the intent to sign the E-Filed or E-Served document.

(II) Scanned Signature. A graphic image of a handwritten signature.

(d) To Whom Applicable.

(1) Attorneys licensed or certified to practice law in Colorado, or admitted pro hac vice under C.R.C.P. 205.3 or 205.5 may register to use the E-System. The E-System Provider will provide an attorney permitted to appear pursuant to C.R.C.P 205.3 or 205.5 with a special user account for purposes of E-Filing and E-Service only in the case identified by a court order approving pro hac vice admission. In districts where E-Filing is mandated pursuant to Subsection (b) of this Rule 49.5, attorneys must register and use the E-System.

(2) Where the system and necessary equipment are in place to permit it, pro se parties and government entities and agencies may register to use the E-System.

(e) E-Filing-Date and Time of Filing. Documents filed in cases on the E-System may be filed underCrim. P. 49 through E-Filing. A document transmitted to the E-System Provider by 11:59 p.m. Colorado time shall be deemed to have been filed with the clerk of the court on that date.

(f) E-Service When Required Date and Time of Service. Documents submitted to the court through E-Filing shall be served in accordance with Crim. P. 49 by E-Service to parties who have subscribed to the E-System. A document transmitted to the E-System Provider for service by 11:59 p.m. Colorado time shall be deemed to have been served on that date.

(g) Filing Party to Maintain the Signed Copy Paper Document Not to be Filed Duration of Maintaining of Document. A printed or printable copy of an E-Filed or E-Served document with original, electronic, or scanned signatures shall be maintained by the filing party and made available for inspection by other parties or the court upon request, but shall not be filed with the court. Documents shall be maintained in accordance with the Rules of Professional Conduct.

(h) Documents Requiring E-Filed Signatures. For E-Filed and E-Served documents, signatures of attorneys, parties, witnesses, notaries and notary stamps may be affixed electronically or handwritten and scanned.

(i) Documents Under Seal. A motion for leave to file documents under seal may be E-Filed. Documents to be filed under seal pursuant to an order of the court, if filed electronically, must be submitted separately from the Motion to Seal.

(j) Transmitting of Orders, Notices, and Other Court Entries. Courts shall distribute orders, notices, and other court entries using the E-System in cases where E-Filings were received from any party.

(k) Form of E-Filed Documents.C.R.C.P. 10 shall apply to E-Filed documents.

(l) Relief in the Event of Technical Difficulties.

(1) The court may enter an order permitting a document to be filed nunc pro tunc to the date it was first attempted to be sent electronically upon satisfactory proof that E-Filing or E-Service of the document was not completed because of: (I) an error in the transmission of the document to the E-System Provider which was unknown to the sending party; (II) a failure of the E-System Provider to process the E-Filed document(s) when received; or (III) other technical problems experienced by the filer or E-System Provider.

(2) Upon satisfactory proof that an E-Served document was not received by or unavailable to a party served, the court may enter an order extending the time for responding to that document.

(m) Form of Electronic Documents.

(1) Electronic Document Format, Size, and Density. Electronic document format, size, and density shall be as specified by Chief Justice Directive # 11-01.

(2) Multiple Documents. Multiple documents (including proposed orders) may be filed in a single electronic filing transaction. Each document (including proposed orders) in that filing must bear a separate document title.

(3) Proposed Orders. Proposed orders shall be E-Filed in editable format. Proposed orders that are E-Filed in a non-editable format shall be rejected by the clerk's office and must be resubmitted. In courts where proposed orders are not required, a proposed order need not be filed with the court.

(n) Document Security Level. Documents filed in a criminal case will not be electronically available to persons other than the parties until reviewed and provided by the clerk of court or his or her designee.

(o) Protective Orders. Nothing in these rules shall prohibit a court from ordering the limitation or prohibition of a nonparty's remote electronic access to a document filed with the court.

Colo. R. Crim. P. 49.5

Subdivision (a) and Comments amended and adopted by the Court, En Banc, 3/2/2017, effective immediately; amended September 6, 2018, effective 9/6/2018.

COMMENTS2014 [1] The Court authorized service provider for the program is the Integrated Colorado Courts E-Filing System (http://www.jbits.courts.state.co.us/icces). [2] "Editable Format" is one which is subject to modification by the court using standard means, such as Word or WordPerfect format. [3] C.R.C.P. 77 provides that courts are always open for business. This rule is intended to comport with that rule. 2017 [4] Effective November 1, 2016, the name of the court authorized service provider changed from the "Integrated Colorado Courts E-Filing System" to "Colorado Courts E-Filing" (www.jbits.courts.state.co.us/efiling/).2018[5] The website for the Colorado Courts E-filing system is now www.courts.state.co.us/efiling.

Rule 50 - Calendars

The courts of record may provide for placing criminal proceedings upon appropriate calendars. Preference shall be given to criminal proceedings.

Colo. R. Crim. P. 50

Annotation Am. Jur.2d. See 20 Am. Jur.2d, Courts, § 22.

Rule 51 - Exceptions Unnecessary

Exceptions to ruling or orders of the court are unnecessary. For all purposes for which an exception has heretofore been necessary it is sufficient that a party, at the time the court ruling or order is made or sought, makes known to the court the action which he desires the court to take or his objection to the court's action and the grounds therefor. But if a party has no opportunity to object to a ruling or order, the absence of an objection does not thereafter prejudice him.

Colo. R. Crim. P. 51

Annotation Allegation of prejudice gives standing for review, regardless of lack of objection. A defendant's claim that the trial court's ruling adversely affected the exercise of his right to testify in his own defense alleges sufficient prejudice to give him standing to seek review of that ruling, whether or not he objected when the ruling was made. People v. Evans, 630 P.2d 94 (Colo. App. 1981). Court must allow contemporaneous objections to evidence and the court's rulings. Without a contemporaneous record of the grounds that a party stated at the time of a objection, disputes as to the grounds asserted for error may arise. Jones v. District Court, 780 P.2d 526 (Colo. 1989). Applied in People v. Peterson, 656 P.2d 1301 (Colo. 1983).

Rule 52 - Harmless Error and Plain Error

(a) Harmless Error. Any error, defect, irregularity, or variance which does not affect substantial rights shall be disregarded.

(b) Plain Error. Plain errors or defects affecting substantial rights may be noticed although they were not brought to the attention of the court.

Colo. R. Crim. P. 52

Annotation I. General Consideration. Law reviews. For article, "United States Supreme Court Review of Tenth Circuit Decisions", which discusses attorney misconduct as harmless error, see 63 Den. U. L. Rev. 473 (1986). For article, "Pronouncements of the U.S. Supreme Court Relating to the Criminal Law Field: 1985-1986", which discusses a recent case relating to harmless error, see 15 Colo. Law. 1616 (1986). For article, "Standards of Appellate Review in State Versus Federal Courts", see 35 Colo. Law. 43 (April 2006). Applied in Ruark v. People, 164 Colo. 257, 434 P.2d 124 (1967), cert. denied, 390 U.S. 1044, 88 S. Ct. 1644, 20 L. Ed. 2d 306 (1968); Morehead v. People, 167 Colo. 287, 447 P.2d 215 (1968); Wiseman v. People, 179 Colo. 101, 498 P.2d 930 (1972); Scott v. People, 179 Colo. 126, 498 P.2d 940 (1972); People v. Baca, 179 Colo. 156, 499 P.2d 317 (1972); People v. Vigil, 180 Colo. 104, 502 P.2d 418 (1972); People v. Spinuzzi, 184 Colo. 412, 520 P.2d 1043 (1974); People v. Mullins, 188 Colo. 23, 532 P.2d 733 (1975); People v. McClure, 190 Colo. 250, 545 P.2d 1038 (1976); People v. LeFebre, 190 Colo. 307, 546 P.2d 952 (1976); People v. Bastardo, 191 Colo. 521, 554 P.2d 297 (1976); Chandler Trailer Convoy, Inc. v. Rocky Mt. Mobile Home Towing Servs., Inc., 37 Colo. App. 520, 552 P.2d 522 (1976); People v. Brionez, 39 Colo. App. 396, 570 P.2d 1296 (1977); People v. Thorpe, 40 Colo. App. 159, 570 P.2d 1311 (1977); People v. Stitt, 40 Colo. App. 355, 575 P.2d

446 (1978); People v. Taylor, 191 Colo. 161, 591 P.2d 1017 (1979); People v. Reyes, 42 Colo. App. 73, 589 P.2d 1385 (1979); People v. Am. Health Care, Inc., 42 Colo. App. 209, 591 P.2d 1343 (1979); People v. Davenport, 43 Colo. App. 41, 602 P.2d 871 (1979); People v. Glenn, 200 Colo. 416, 615 P.2d 700 (1980); People v. Smith, 620 P.2d 232 (Colo. 1980); People v. Hallman, 44 Colo. App. 530, 624 P.2d 347 (1980); People v. Massey, 649 P.2d 1112 (Colo. App. 1980), aff'd, 649 P.2d 1070 (Colo. 1982); People v. Nisted, 653 P.2d 60 (Colo. App. 1980); People v. Small, 631 P.2d 148 (Colo. 1981); People v. Christian, 632 P.2d 1031 (Colo. 1981); People v. Padilla, 638 P.2d 15 (Colo. 1981); People v. Swanson, 638 P.2d 45 (Colo. 1981); People v. Founds, 631 P.2d 1166 (Colo. App. 1981); People v. Dillon, 633 P.2d 504 (Colo. App. 1981); People v. Roark, 643 P.2d 756 (Colo. 1982); People v. Gallegos, 644 P.2d 920 (Colo. 1982); People v. Handy, 657 P.2d 963 (Colo. App. 1982); People v. Jones, 665 P.2d 127 (Colo. App. 1982); People v. Hart, 658 P.2d 857 (Colo. 1983); People v. Cisneros, 665 P.2d 145 (Colo. App. 1983); People v. Priest, 672 P.2d 539 (Colo. App. 1983); People v. Beasley, 683 P.2d 1210 (Colo. App. 1984); Callis v. People, 692 P.2d 1045 (Colo. 1984); People v. Armstrong, 704 P.2d 877 (Colo. App. 1985); Williams v. People, 724 P.2d 1279 (Colo. 1986); People v. Wieghard, 727 P.2d 383 (Colo. App. 1986); People v. Rivers, 727 P.2d 394 (Colo. App. 1986); People v. Galimanis, 765 P.2d 644 (Colo. App. 1988), cert. granted, 783 P.2d 838 (Colo. 1989), cert. denied, 805 P.2d 1116 (Colo. 1991); People v. Schuett, 833 P.2d 44 (Colo. 1992); People v. Corpening, 837 P.2d 249 (Colo. App. 1992); People v. Ornelas, 937 P.2d 867 (Colo. App. 1996); People v. Thompson, 950 P.2d 608 (Colo. App. 1997); People v. Gallegos, 950 P.2d 629 (Colo. App. 1997). II. Harmless Error. No reversal where insufficient error. Where there is no error of sufficient magnitude, reversal of judgment of conviction is not required. Early v. People, 178 Colo. 167, 496 P.2d 1021 (1972). Harmless, constitutional error. The admission of an in-court identification without first determining that it is not tainted by an illegal lineup but is of independent origin may be constitutional error; but such error may be considered harmless even if there has been an illegal lineup confrontation, if the identification witness makes an in-court identification based on sufficient independent observations of the defendant, disassociated from the pretrial lineup. Espinoza v. People, 178 Colo. 391, 497 P.2d 994 (1972). Constitutional errors may be characterized as harmless only when the case against a defendant is so overwhelming that the constitutional violation is harmless beyond a reasonable doubt. People v. Matthews, 662 P.2d 1108 (Colo. App. 1983); People v. Jensen, 747 P.2d 1247 (Colo. 1987); Topping v. People, 793 P.2d 1168 (Colo. 1990); People v. Denton, 91 P.3d 388 (Colo. App. 2003); People v. Delgado-Elizarras, 131 P.3d 1110 (Colo. App. 2005). Before an error affecting a defendant's constitutional right to testify in his own behalf can be deemed harmless, an appellate court must determine beyond a reasonable doubt that the error did not contribute to the verdict. People v. Evans, 630 P.2d 94 (Colo. App. 1981); Crespin v. People, 721 P.2d 688 (Colo. 1986); Topping v. People, 793 P.2d 1168 (Colo. 1990). Absence of defense counsel at critical stage of proceedings, which is a constitutional error, can be harmless if the error is a "trial error" that can be quantitatively assessed on appellate review as opposed to "structural defect" that affects the framework within which the trial proceeds. Key v. People, 865 P.2d 822 (Colo. 1994). The standard for harmless error is the prosecution must show that the error did not contribute to a defendant's conviction. If there is reasonable probability from review of the entire record that a defendant could be prejudiced the error is not harmless. Key v. People, 865 P.2d 822 (Colo. 1994). An ex parte scheduling conference with jurors during deliberations occurred at a critical stage of the criminal proceedings and was not harmless error. Key v. People, 865 P.2d 822 (Colo. 1994). Markings from codefendant's trial on exhibits harmless. Fact that certain exhibits used in defendant's trial had court reporter's identification marks on them remaining from their use in the codefendant's trial, did not result in any prejudice and, at most, the marks constituted harmless error which is not ground for reversal. People v. Gallegos, 181 Colo. 264, 509 P.2d 596 (1973). As may be use of void prior convictions for impeachment. The error implicit in the use of void prior convictions for impeachment purposes need not necessarily require reversal, particularly where the error is found to be harmless beyond a reasonable doubt. People v. Neal, 187 Colo. 12, 528 P.2d 220 (1974). Or failure to properly instruct jury. Where jury instruction failed to include an essential part of the two-witness rule in prosecution for perjury, i.e., that the corroborating evidence must be deemed of equal weight to the testimony of another witness, this omission was harmless error inasmuch as there was direct testimony by three witnesses contradicting the defendant's grand jury testimony. People v. Mazza, 182 Colo. 166, 511 P.2d 885 (1973). Where the admissions of a defendant as either extrajudicial statements or a confession is not an issue of significance, the giving of an instruction on them is not grounds for relief. Yerby v. People, 176 Colo. 115, 489 P.2d 1308 (1971). Where one is benefited by an error in submitting or failing to submit an instruction, he cannot claim prejudicial error. *Atwood v. People, 176 Colo. 183, 489 P.2d 1305 (1971).* Where evidence of a petty offense by defendants is introduced during a felony trial, the trial judge should instruct the jury as to its limited purpose, but his failure to do so is harmless error, considering the nature of the petty offense as compared with the gravity of the charge against the defendants. *Kurtz v. People, 177 Colo. 306, 494 P.2d 97 (1972).* Where a court errs in giving an instruction that prejudices the state rather than the defendant in that it increases the state's burden beyond that required, no grounds for reversal are created. *Early v. People, 178 Colo. 167, 496 P.2d 1021 (1972).* While it is unnecessary and poor practice to give the jury a separate instruction on the credibility of a defendant as a witness, the giving of such an instruction does not constitute reversible error. *People v. Hankin, 179 Colo. 70, 498 P.2d 1116 (1972).* Where there is overwhelming evidence of the defendant's deliberation in a first degree murder case, the use of an outmoded jury instruction on the law of deliberation is harmless error. *People v. Key, 680 P.2d 1313 (Colo. App. 1984).* Inclusion of allegation of aggravation in jury instruction for simple robbery charge which was basis of felony murder charge constituted harmless error as instruction inured to benefit of defendant. *People v. Driggers, 812 P.2d 702 (Colo. App. 1991).* **Or admission of challenged statement.** Where the defendant's substantial rights were not affected by the admission into evidence of a challenged statement, no reversible error occurs. *People v. McKnight, 626 P.2d 678 (Colo. 1981).* **Or improper questioning concerning coconspirator's guilty plea.** While a prosecutor should not elicit testimony concerning a coconspirator's guilty plea, when the evidence of a defendant's guilt is overwhelming, reference to the guilty plea is harmless error, especially when defense counsel questions the witness about this guilty plea in an effort to impeach his credibility. *People v. Craig, 179 Colo. 115, 498 P.2d 942, cert. denied, 409 U.S. 1077, 93 S. Ct. 690, 34 L. Ed. 2d 666 (1972).* **Or error in admitting testimony of codefendant.** Error, if any, in admitting testimony as to admissions which were made by codefendant who under prosecution theory was principal perpetrator of robbery and murder that constituted basis for first-degree murder charge of defendant as an accessory, which indicated that another person was present and the admission of which allegedly violated defendant's sixth amendment right of confrontation was harmless, where additional evidence consisting of testimony of three eyewitnesses also established that the robbery was committed by two men. *People v. Knapp, 180 Colo. 280, 505 P.2d 7 (1973).* It is not reversible error to admit evidence concerning a description of defendants just because it is testimony of a codefendant as to whom the severance has been granted, thereby operating so as either to deprive defendants of an opportunity to cross-examine or to require a waiver of the benefits of a severance to which they are entitled, where in view of the inconclusive nature of the identification, it cannot be said that there is any prejudice to the defendants from the admission of this evidence, although it would clearly be a better procedure to conceal the source of the extrajudicial identifications. *Kurtz v. People, 177 Colo. 306, 494 P.2d 97 (1972).* **Failure to grant continuance or mistrial where witness fails to appear held harmless error.** *People v. Lee, 180 Colo. 376, 506 P.2d 136 (1973).* **Failure to provide definition of "custody" and "confinement" to the jury was harmless error** under the circumstances portrayed by the record. A trial court is under an obligation to instruct the jury properly, and a failure to do so as to every element of a crime charged is error. However, the lack of instruction by the court as to the meanings of "custody" and "confinement" inured to the defendant's benefit and thus the instructional failure here constituted harmless error. *People v. Atkins, 885 P.2d 243 (Colo. App. 1994).* **Failure to grant motion for mistrial not an abuse of discretion** where trial court sustained defendant's objection to question suggesting prior criminal conduct, defendant did not request that a curative instruction be given to the jury and none was given, and no substantial prejudice to defendant was demonstrated. *People v. Talley, 677 P.2d 394 (Colo. App. 1983).* **Improper admission of defendant's refusal to sign a written Miranda advisement held harmless error.** *People v. Mack, 638 P.2d 257 (Colo. 1981).* **Improper admission of evidence to which hearsay exceptions did not apply held harmless error** since the admission did not contribute to defendant's conviction, nor did it prejudice the proceedings. *People v. Blecha, 940 P.2d 1070 (Colo. App. 1996), aff'd, 962 P.2d 931 (Colo. 1998).* **When misstatements at trial do not require reversal.** Where misstatements do not so inflict the trial as to require more than an admonition given to the jury by the trial judge in the exercise of his discretion and no motion for mistrial on these grounds is made at the time of the statements, there are not substantial grounds for reversal. *Fernandez v. People, 176 Colo. 346, 490 P.2d 690 (1971).* **Nor improper argument by prosecutor.** A prosecutor's argument is not prejudicial and does not require reversal when the trial judge tells the prosecution to terminate the line of argument and instructs the jury that argument is not evidence. *People v. Motley, 179*

Colo. 77, 498 P.2d 339 (1972). Attorney prohibited from characterizing a witness's testimony or his character for truthfulness with any form of the word "lie". A violation of this prohibition, although sanctionable in other ways, does not warrant reversal if it was harmless. Domingo-Gomez v. People, 125 P.3d 1043 (Colo. 2005); Crider v. People, 186 P.3d 39 (Colo. 2008). Prosecutor prohibited from making generic tailoring arguments, which are improper because they are not based on reasonable inferences from evidence in the record. Martinez v. People, 244 P.3d 135 (Colo. 2010). Prosecutor's closing argument that defendant who testified at trial had an opportunity to listen to all of the testimony and tailor his testimony to fit that of other witnesses improper. Martinez v. People, 244 P.3d 135 (Colo. 2010). Prosecutor's generic tailoring comments harmless, however, because defendant commented on and expressly incorporated testimony of prior witnesses and because of substantial evidence calling into question defendant's credibility. No reasonable probability existed that prosecutor's generic tailoring argument, even though improper, influenced jury's determination of defendant's credibility or guilt. Martinez v. People, 244 P.3d 135 (Colo. 2010). Nor giving of stock instruction. The giving of a stock instruction on the presumption of innocence does not constitute reversible error just because of its historical use. Jorgensen v. People, 178 Colo. 8, 495 P.2d 1130 (1972). Nor failure to allow examination of grand jury testimony. The failure of a trial judge to grant a defendant and his counsel the right to examine grand jury testimony is not reversible error. Robles v. People, 178 Colo. 181, 496 P.2d 1003 (1972). Nor inclusion of hearsay. The admission of a death certificate containing the statement that the victim was "helping neighbor investigate burglary of neighbor's store and was shot by one of the burglars during this investigation" is not reversible error, particularly when the court later instructs the jury to ignore that portion of the certificate, although it would be much better practice to delete such included hearsay. Kurtz v. People, 177 Colo. 306, 494 P.2d 97 (1972). Even if extrajudicial identifications are inadmissible hearsay, when in light of the other material evidence relating defendants to the crime, such identification is clearly cumulative, and any error is harmless. Kurtz v. People, 177 Colo. 306, 494 P.2d 97 (1972). Nor verbal slip by judge. A defendant is not prejudiced by the trial judge's use of the word "offense" when the judge gives the jury a cautionary oral instruction at the time evidence of another transaction is introduced, and it is not reversible error. Howe v. People, 178 Colo. 248, 496 P.2d 1040 (1972). Nor failure to administer an oath or affirmation of true translation to interpreter. People v. Avila, 797 P.2d 804 (Colo. App. 1990). Nor failure to conduct a hearing on the admissibility of scientific evidence. Where DNA evidence relates solely to similar transaction evidence, the admission of such evidence, absent a preliminary hearing on its admissibility, is harmless error. People v. Groves, 854 P.2d 1310 (Colo. App. 1992). Nor failure to swear jury prior to beginning of testimony where jury sworn before deliberations. People v. Clouse, 859 P.2d 228 (Colo. App. 1992). Nor where comment on defendant's failure to testify. A comment by the district attorney on defendant's failure to testify was not prejudicial enough to warrant reversal because the trial court properly instructed the jury that the defendant's failure to testify cannot be considered as evidence of guilt or innocence and it is generally accepted that defense counsel may by improper argumentative comment open the door to a response by the prosecuting attorney. Kurtz v. People, 177 Colo. 306, 494 P.2d 97 (1972). When the prosecution calls oblique attention to the possible silence of the defendant, but does not make direct reference to the defendant's silence, there is error, but not reversible error. People v. Calise, 179 Colo. 162, 498 P.2d 1154 (1972). Nor admission of defendant's mug shot. Where the evidence of guilt is substantial, the sole error of admitting the defendant's mug shot does not, in and of itself, constitute reversible error. People v. Bugarin, 181 Colo. 57, 507 P.2d 879 (1973). If testimony accompanying introduction of a mug shot does not imply that defendant has a past criminal history, the introduction of the mug shot does not necessitate the granting of a mistrial. People v. Borghesi, 40 P.3d 15 (Colo. App. 2001), aff'd in part and rev'd in part on other grounds, 66 P.3d 93 (Colo. 2003). Nor where material witness functions as officer of court. Where the court, over defendants' objection, allowed the sheriff, who was a material witness for the state, to take part in the conduct of the trial by daily calling the court to order as well as select a few prospective jurors on open venire and the court also refused to give an instruction to the effect that no particular weight was to be attached to the sheriff's testimony by reason of his court functions, but he was not placed in charge of the jury at any time, then reversible error was not committed, although it is a better practice not to permit a material witness to function as an officer of the court. Kurtz v. People, 177 Colo. 306, 494 P.2d 97 (1972). Nor limitation of cross-examination of defendant's coconspirator by refusing to allow inquiry into coconspirator's subjective understanding of his plea arrangement is not reversible error. People v. McCall, 43 Colo. App. 117, 603 P.2d 950

(1979), rev'd on other grounds, 623 P.2d 397 (Colo. 1981). Variance between charge and proof held not fatal. People v. Incerto, 180 Colo. 366, 505 P.2d 1309 (1973). Where transaction charged and the one proved are substantially the same, although not all those allegedly involved in conspiracy are found to have participated, and the object of conspiracy is proved as laid, variance is not reversible error as substantial rights of defendant are not affected. People v. Incerto, 180 Colo. 366, 505 P.2d 1309 (1973). Witness' statement that defendant had been in jail several times held not prejudicial. People v. Gallegos, 179 Colo. 211, 499 P.2d 315 (1972). Failure to record final arguments in a trial to the court is not prejudicial error. People in Interest of B.L.M. v. B.L.M., 31 Colo. App. 106, 500 P.2d 146 (1972). Despite defendant's contention that unauthorized persons were allowed in grand jury room and proceedings were not kept secret, the alleged violations did not affect defendant's substantial rights. Petit jury's subsequent guilty verdict made alleged error in grand jury proceeding harmless beyond a reasonable doubt. People v. Cerrone, 867 P.2d 143 (Colo. App. 1993); aff'd on other grounds, 900 P.2d 45 (Colo. 1995). Prejudicial opening statement made in bad faith reversible. Error cannot be predicated upon opening statement of attorney as to what he expects to prove, although his statement is not completely supported by evidence adduced at trial, unless unsupported portion of statement was made in bad faith and was manifestly prejudicial. People v. Jacobs, 179 Colo. 182, 499 P.2d 615 (1972). Trial judge to determine effect of potentially prejudicial evidence on jury. The trial judge is in preeminent position to determine potential effects of allegedly prejudicial statements on jurors, and his judgment will only be overturned upon an abuse of discretion. People v. Jacobs, 179 Colo. 182, 499 P.2d 615 (1972). Where the judge examines the jury as to the effect certain knowledge would have upon their ability to render a fair and impartial verdict in a criminal proceeding and is satisfied that their ability would not be impaired, his denial of motion for mistrial is not an abuse of discretion and will not be disturbed on review. Atwood v. People, 176 Colo. 183, 489 P.2d 1305 (1971). Error may be rendered harmless and therefore become not reversible by subsequent proceedings in the case or by the result thereof. Walker v. People, 175 Colo. 173, 489 P.2d 584 (1971). A harmless error argument does not apply when the trial court erroneously disqualifies a defendant's retained counsel of choice. Anaya v. People, 764 P.2d 779 (Colo. 1988). Since testimony implicated another person and not defendant, the testimony was not prejudicial to defendant. Any error in the admission of such testimony is harmless. People v. Mapps, 231 P.3d 5 (Colo. App. 2009). Admission of testimony was harmless since it did not substantially influence the verdict or impair the fairness of defendant's trial. People v. Mapps, 231 P.3d 5 (Colo. App. 2009). III. Plain Error. Authority of appellate court to consider plain error. Section (b) permits an appellate court to consider an alleged error which was not brought to the attention of the trial court, if the error affects the substantial rights of the defendant and it is "plain error". Vigil v. People, 196 Colo. 522, 587 P.2d 1196 (1978). A trial error to which no objection is made is forfeited and, therefore, not reviewable. However, such errors can be reviewed for plain error, which means an error must be plain and must affect a substantial right of a party. People v. O'Connell, 134 P.3d 460 (Colo. App. 2005). If no contemporaneous objection to alleged prosecutorial misconduct is made at trial, subsection (b) limits appellate review to a determination of plain error. People v. Fell, 832 P.2d 1015 (Colo. App. 1991). Appellate court cannot correct an error pursuant to section (b) unless the error is clear under current law. People v. O'Connell, 134 P.3d 460 (Colo. App. 2005). If the law is unsettled at the time of trial, the plain error analysis will be conducted using the status of the law at the time of trial. People v. O'Connell, 134 P.3d 460 (Colo. App. 2005). "Plain error" means error both obvious and substantial and those grave errors which seriously affect substantial rights of the accused. People v. Barker, 180 Colo. 28, 501 P.2d 1041 (1972); People v. Koon, 724 P.2d 1367 (Colo. App. 1986); People v. Roberts, 738 P.2d 380 (Colo. App. 1986). "Plain" is synonymous with "clear" or, equivalently, "obvious". People v. O'Connell, 134 P.3d 460 (Colo. App. 2005). A plain error is an error seriously affecting substantial rights of the accused. People v. Miller, 37 Colo. App. 294, 549 P.2d 1092 (1976), aff'd, 193 Colo. 415, 566 P.2d 1059 (1977); People v. Constant, 44 Colo. App. 544, 623 P.2d 63 (1980), rev'd on other grounds, 645 P.2d 843 (Colo. 1982); People v. Green, 759 P.2d 814 (Colo. App. 1988); Harris v. People, 888 P.2d 259 (Colo. 1995). Only error which is obvious and grave can rise to the status of plain error. People v. Mills, 192 Colo. 260, 557 P.2d 1192 (1976); People v. Vialpando, 804 P.2d 219 (Colo. App. 1990). Plain error is error which is "obvious and grave". People v. Peterson, 656 P.2d 1301 (Colo. 1983); People v. Vialpando, 804 P.2d 219 (Colo. App. 1990). The proper inquiry in determining a harmless error question is whether the error substantially influenced the verdict or affected the fairness of the trial proceedings. People v. Quintana, 665 P.2d 605 (Colo. 1983). Plain error occurs when, after

review of entire record, the error so undermined trial's fundamental fairness as to cast serious doubt on reliability of conviction. People v. Kruse, 839 P.2d 1 (Colo. 1992); People v. Hampton, 857 P.2d 441 (Colo. App. 1992), aff'd, 876 P.2d 1236 (Colo. 1994); People v. Herr, 868 P.2d 1121 (Colo. App. 1993); Harris v. People, 888 P.2d 259 (Colo. 1995); People v. Kerber, 64 P.3d 930 (Colo. App. 2002); People v. Mullins, 104 P.3d 299 (Colo. App. 2004). A plain error analysis requires a consideration of various factors including the strength of the evidence against the defendant, the posture of the defense, and any persistent, improper remarks by the defendant. People v. Mullins, 104 P.3d 299 (Colo. App. 2004). To meet the burden of plain error, there must be a reasonable possibility that the alleged error contributed to the defendant's conviction. People v. Valdez, 725 P.2d 29 (Colo. App. 1986), aff'd, 789 P.2d 406 (Colo. 1990). No definition of plain error will fit every case, and each case must be resolved on the particular facts or laws which are in issue. People v. Barker, 180 Colo. 28, 501 P.2d 1041 (1972). Each case must be resolved on the particular facts and law at issue. People v. Miller, 37 Colo. App. 294, 549 P.2d 1092 (1976), aff'd, 193 Colo. 415, 566 P.2d 1059 (1977). Each case in which it is argued that plain error has been committed must be resolved in light of its particular facts and the law that applies to those facts. People v. Mills, 192 Colo. 260, 557 P.2d 1192 (1976); People v. Peterson, 656 P.2d 1301 (Colo. 1983). And reviewing court to determine existence of plain error. It is incumbent upon a reviewing court, from its own reading of the record, to determine whether "plain error" occurred. People v. Barker, 180 Colo. 28, 501 P.2d 1041 (1972). Even though raised for first time on appeal. Where plain error affecting substantial rights appears, an appellate court, in the interest of justice, may, and should, deal with it, even though it is raised for the first time on appeal. People v. Archuleta, 180 Colo. 156, 503 P.2d 346 (1972); People v. Meller, 185 Colo. 389, 524 P.2d 1366 (1974); People v. Bridges, 620 P.2d 1 (Colo. 1980). Issues not properly preserved at trial can serve as a basis for reversal only if they involve plain error. People v. Mattas, 44 Colo. App. 139, 618 P.2d 675 (1980), aff'd, 645 P.2d 254 (Colo. 1982). An error in trial proceedings to which the accused fails to make a contemporaneous objection will not support reversal unless it casts serious doubt upon the basic fairness of the trial. Wilson v. People, 743 P.2d 415 (Colo. 1987); People v. Winters, 765 P.2d 1010 (Colo. 1988); People v. Lybarger, 790 P.2d 855 (Colo. App. 1989); Woertman v. People, 804 P.2d 188 (Colo. 1991); People v. Schuett, 833 P.2d 44 (Colo. 1992). Where defendant did not object to use of photocopy, its use did not so undermine the fundamental fairness of trial as to cast serious doubt on the reliability of conviction. People v. Chavez, 764 P.2d 371 (Colo. App. 1988). Because defendant did not object to a jury instruction at trial the court's action is reviewed pursuant to (b) under a plain error standard, with a finding of error only if review of the entire record demonstrates a reasonable possibility that the improper instruction contributed to the defendant's conviction. People v. Blecha, 940 P.2d 1070 (Colo. App. 1996), aff'd, 962 P.2d 931 (Colo. 1998). The court committed harmless error in failing to give the jury cautionary hearsay instructions after each hearsay witnesses' testimony. Three hearsay witnesses testified in sequence, the court gave the cautionary instruction following the testimony of the last hearsay witness and during the general charge to the jury, and the hearsay testimony corroborated the testimony of other witnesses. People v. Valdez, 874 P.2d 415 (Colo. App. 1994.) If a defendant does not object to statements he feels are prejudicial, a plain error standard of review applies. People v. Pennese, 830 P.2d 1085 (Colo. App. 1991); People v. Mendez, 897 P.2d 868 (Colo. App. 1995); People v. Kerber, 64 P.3d 930 (Colo. App. 2002). No error where witness stated defendant was out of prison and that defendant had previously threatened him, where statements were part of the total picture surrounding the offense, the witness's description of defendant's threats were mentioned during defendant's cross-examination of witness, and defendant made no objections or mistrial motions. People v. Pennese, 830 P.2d 1085 (Colo. App. 1991). As long as a fundamental or substantial right has purportedly been violated. Although defendant's trial counsel did not make any contemporaneous objections nor raise the issue in his post-trial motion, an appellate court will consider, nevertheless, alleged error where it involves a fundamental right which has purportedly been violated. Hines v. People, 179 Colo. 4, 497 P.2d 1258 (1972). Even though defendant's counsel neither tendered an instruction on the presumption of innocence nor objected to the court's failure to instruct the jury on the presumption of innocence, because the failure to instruct on the presumption of innocence affects such a substantial right, the supreme court may take cognizance of the error pursuant to section (b). People v. Hill, 182 Colo. 253, 512 P.2d 257 (1973). To constitute reversible error, the introduction of the statement of aggravating factors which was not objected to at trial must affect the substantial rights of a defendant. People v. McKnight, 626 P.2d 678 (Colo. 1981). Whether a defendant has received effective assistance of counsel is a question concerning a fundamental right. Armstrong v.

People, 701 P.2d 17 (Colo. 1985). Which is prejudicial. An appellate court will consider issues not raised below where serious prejudicial error was made and justice requires the consideration. Larkin v. People, 177 Colo. 156, 493 P.2d 1 (1972). Effect of failure to object at trial. Where instructions used by the trial court failed to define the statutory terms, failure to object to the tendered instructions or raise any constitutional objection to the statute at the trial court level raises the standard of review to one of "plain error". People v. Cardenas, 42 Colo. App. 61, 592 P.2d 1348 (1979); People v. Campbell, 678 P.2d 1035 (Colo. App. 1983). Where the issue is raised for the first time on appeal, review is confined to a consideration of whether the error falls within the definition of plain error. People v. Barker, 180 Colo. 28, 501 P.2d 1041 (1972). Where a defendant failed to object to the adequacy of the jury instructions in his motion for a new trial, a judgment will not be reversed unless plain error occurred. People v. Frysig, 628 P.2d 1004 (Colo. 1981). Failure to make timely and sufficient objection at trial prevents consideration of issue on appeal unless it involves plain error. People v. Kruse, 839 P.2d 1 (Colo. 1992). Unless a prosecutor's misconduct is "glaringly or tremendously" improper, it is not plain error under section (b) where no objection to the behavior was raised. People v. Jensen, 55 P.3d 135 (Colo. App. 2001). And review limited when issue not cited in motion for new trial. Where defense counsel objected to the admission of certain evidence, but failed to cite its admission in his motion for a new trial, it may not be considered on appeal unless the introduction of that evidence constituted plain error. People v. Abbott, 638 P.2d 781 (Colo. 1981). Reversal justified where error contributed to conviction. Only when there is at least a reasonable possibility that the action claimed to be plain error contributed to the defendant's conviction can it justify reversal. People v. Aragon, 186 Colo. 91, 525 P.2d 1134 (1974); People v. Mills, 192 Colo. 260, 557 P.2d 1192 (1976). Unless there is a reasonable possibility that the alleged error contributed to defendant's conviction, reversal of the proceedings below is not required. People v. Miller, 37 Colo. App. 294, 549 P.2d 1092 (1976), aff'd, 193 Colo. 415, 566 P.2d 1059 (1977). Where the minds of an average jury would not have found the prosecution's case significantly less persuasive by the elimination of the error and the evidence of guilt of the defendant is overwhelming, a defendant is not entitled to reversal based on plain error. People v. Barker, 180 Colo. 28, 501 P.2d 1041 (1972). In order for the court to find plain error, there must be a reasonable possibility that an alleged erroneous instruction contributed to the defendant's conviction. The existence of this possibility must be determined by an examination of the particular facts of the case. People v. Dillon, 655 P.2d 841 (Colo. 1982). Plain error affects substantial rights of the accused, and the record must demonstrate a reasonable possibility that the alleged erroneous instruction contributed to defendant's conviction. People v. Cowden, 735 P.2d 199 (Colo. 1987); People v. Lybarger, 790 P.2d 855 (Colo. App. 1989). Plain error is present only if an appellate court, after reviewing the entire record, can say with fair assurance that the error so undermined the fundamental fairness of the trial itself as to cast serious doubt on the reliability of the judgment of conviction. People v. Fell, 832 P.2d 1015 (Colo. App. 1991). Deprivation of affirmative defense deemed plain error. The contention that a defendant has been deprived of an affirmative defense, if meritorious, is plain error. People v. Beebe, 38 Colo. App. 80, 557 P.2d 840 (1976). Improper testimony regarding the procedure for obtaining an arrest warrant and the prosecutor's mistaken statements that only defendant could claim self-defense sufficiently undermined confidence in the reliability of the judgment of conviction. These errors constituted plain error entitling defendant to a new trial. People v. Mullins, 104 P.3d 299 (Colo. App. 2004). To allege insufficiency of evidence as to indispensable element of a crime is to assert plain error. People v. Harris, 633 P.2d 1095 (Colo. App. 1981). Trial court's failure to submit instruction to defense counsel for review prior to reading the instruction to the jury is not plain error. People v. Martin, 670 P.2d 22 (Colo. App. 1983). Prosecutor's argument did not result in plain error. People v. Gilmore, 97 P.3d 123 (Colo. App. 2003); People v. Kendall, 174 P.3d 791 (Colo. App. 2007). "Plain error" rule must be read in harmony with Crim. P. 30, which provides that no party may assign as error the giving of an instruction to which he has not objected before the instructions are submitted to the jury. People v. Green, 178 Colo. 77, 495 P.2d 549 (1972); People v. Barker, 180 Colo. 28, 501 P.2d 1041 (1972); People v. Aragon, 186 Colo. 91, 525 P.2d 1134 (1974). Unless manifest prejudice or plain error. Where defendant does not object to the instruction given or tender any alternate instruction which might more adequately set forth the law, an assignment of error is not valid unless there is manifest prejudice amounting to plain error. People v. Bercillio, 179 Colo. 383, 500 P.2d 975 (1972). Because a defendant must make all objections he has to instructions prior to their submission to the jury, where the defendant failed to make any such objection prior to submission of the instructions, absent plain error, the court would not consider the defendant's arguments on review. People v. Tilley, 184 Colo. 424,

520 P.2d 1046 (1974). Where no specific objection was made prior to submission of instructions to the jury as required by Crim. P. 30, absent plain error, reviewing court will not consider these arguments on appeal. People v. Casey, 185 Colo. 58, 521 P.2d 1250 (1974). Where defendant only made a general objection to jury instructions, and failed to make a timely specific objection, supreme court on appeal will not consider argument by defendant that instructions were in error absent plain error. People v. O'Donnell, 184 Colo. 104, 518 P.2d 945 (1974). No prejudicial error if jury is adequately informed. Where the defendant objected to various instructions given to the jury by the trial court, but under the instructions as a whole the jury is adequately informed as to the law, there is no prejudicial error. People v. Lovato, 181 Colo. 99, 507 P.2d 860 (1973). Where instruction on trespass was given to jury in statutory language and instructions were, as a whole, adequate to inform jury of the law on these issues and defendant did not request or tender proposed instruction to define term "unlawfully", failure to instruct on that term did not rise to the level of plain error. People v. Wortham, 690 P.2d 876 (Colo. App. 1984). Prosecutor's comment that evidence of prior similar transactions between the sexual assault victim and the defendant, her father, explained the victim's response to two assaults and her failure to report them earlier is not improper considering the testimony of the victim and the limiting instructions given by the trial court regarding the proper use of the similar transaction evidence. People v. Fell, 832 P.2d 1015 (Colo. App. 1991). Doctrine of invited error precludes defendant from challenging jury instruction as prejudicial error since defendant approved and submitted comparable instruction to court. People v. Driggers, 812 P.2d 702 (Colo. App. 1991). Although failure to instruct on essential elements constitutes plain error. The trial court has a duty to properly instruct the jury on every issue presented, and the failure to do so with respect to the essential elements of the crime charged constitutes plain error. People v. Archuleta, 180 Colo. 156, 503 P.2d 346 (1972); People v. Hardin, 199 Colo. 229, 607 P.2d 1291 (1980); People v. Mattas, 645 P.2d 254 (Colo. 1982); People v. Williams, 707 P.2d 1023 (Colo. App. 1985). As does erroneous instruction. Where a given instruction permits the jury to convict without proof of essential element of the crime, there is plain error, and reversal is required. People v. Butcher, 180 Colo. 429, 506 P.2d 362 (1973). The giving of an instruction which allows the jury to find the defendant guilty upon a lesser degree of culpability than that required by the statute constitutes plain error. People v. Etchells, 646 P.2d 950 (Colo. App. 1982). Or inadequate instruction. Where a general instruction on specific intent does not particularly direct the jury's attention to defendant's theory that he could not have possessed the requisite specific intent, it is the duty of the court either to correct the tendered instruction or to give the substance of it in an instruction drafted by the court, and a court's refusal to give such an adequate instruction is error. Nora v. People, 176 Colo. 454, 491 P.2d 62 (1971). Under some circumstances, a court's failure to instruct sua sponte on intoxication may result in reversible error. People v. Mattas, 645 P.2d 254 (Colo. 1982). But not failure to instruct on lesser included offense. Failure of the court to instruct on a lesser included offense does not affect the substantial rights of defendant and is therefore not cognizable as plain error. People v. Chavez, 179 Colo. 316, 500 P.2d 365 (1972); People v. Sharpe, 183 Colo. 64, 514 P.2d 1138 (1973); People v. Brown, 677 P.2d 406 (Colo. App. 1983). Failure to instruct on element of "knowingly". The trial court's failure to include the element of "knowingly" in a second-degree kidnapping instruction is plain error. People v. Clark, 662 P.2d 1100 (Colo. App. 1982). It was not plain error for trial court to submit to the jury the "result" factor and omit the "conduct-and-circumstance" factor in the definitional instruction of "knowingly" in a first degree criminal trespass case because the instruction could neither mislead nor confuse the jury. People v. Wortham, 690 P.2d 876 (Colo. App. 1984). Failure to give definition of "attempt". The trial court's failure to include the definition of attempt found in the criminal attempt statute in instructions for the pertinent provisions of the second degree assault statute was not plain error. People v. Weller, 679 P.2d 1077 (Colo. 1984). Jury instruction on aggravated robbery did not constitute plain error as defendant was given notice by language in the information that he was being charged with both methods of committing crime even though instruction differed from language in the information. People v. Driggers, 812 P.2d 702 (Colo. App. 1991). Failure to give definition of "without lawful justification". Where this phrase appeared in second-degree kidnapping statute without further definition, and defendant made no claim of legal authority to transport nonconsenting victim, trial court's instruction to jury to give phrase "the common meaning that the words imply" was not plain error. People v. Schuett, 833 P.2d 44 (Colo. 1992). Trial court's failure to ascertain reasons for defendant's waiver of right to testify not plain error where defendant did not raise issue in his motion for a new trial and did not allege or present evidence that the waiver was not knowing, intelligent, or voluntary. People v. Wortham, 690 P.2d 876 (Colo. App. 1984). Failure to issue a contemporaneous limiting instruction. Failure of the court to issue a limiting instruction contemporaneously with the history of arrest testimony, which testimony related to a crime separate and unrelated to the crime for which defendant was being tried, did not constitute plain error. People v. White, 680 P.2d 1318 (Colo. App. 1984). Failure to instruct the jury on gender bias was not a "structural defect" or plain error requiring reversal of third degree sexual assault conviction where gender bias was not raised during the trial and the jury was instructed sympathy or prejudice should not influence its decision. People v. Johnson, 870 P.2d 571 (Colo. App. 1993). Although the general rule is that there may be no appellate review of issues not raised in a new trial motion, there is an exception for claims that the trial court committed plain error. People v. Ullerich, 680 P.2d 1306 (Colo. App. 1983). Where court presented the jury with irreconcilable statements about the requisite culpability for a securities fraud violation, a conviction cannot be permitted to rest on such an equivocal direction to the jury on one of the basic elements of the crime. People v. Riley, 708 P.2d 1359 (Colo. 1985). The cumulative effect of a proper jury instruction with improper jury instructions that contained erroneous statements of law which relegated to the jury the function of determining whether an affirmative defense was available in a case and which had the effect of relieving the prosecution of its burden of proof in regard to the affirmative defense was insufficient to dispel the potential harm created by the erroneous jury instructions and was, therefore, plain error. Lybarger v. People, 807 P.2d 570 (Colo. 1991). Joint operation instruction does not remove case from plain error rule. When the jury was told that specific intent applies to every element of aggravated robbery, that specific intent applies only to the intention to kill, maim, or wound, and that "knowingly" applies if the intent was to put the victim in fear of death or bodily injury, jury could not be expected to know what, if any, culpable mental state applied. People v. Pickering, 725 P.2d 5 (Colo. App. 1985). Error of constitutional dimension. Ordinarily, plain error requires reversal only if there is a reasonable possibility that it contributed to the defendant's conviction. However, if the asserted error is of constitutional dimension, reversal is required unless the court is convinced that the error was harmless beyond a reasonable doubt. Graham v. People, 705 P.2d 505 (Colo. 1985). An error in the admission of evidence, even if of constitutional dimension, does not require reversal of a criminal conviction if the error was harmless beyond a reasonable doubt. People v. Martinez, 83 P.3d 1174 (Colo. App. 2003). But admission of uncounseled statements by defendant may not be plain error. Fact that defendant's attorney was not notified that questioning of his client was going to take place did not make the admission of statements made by defendant during such questioning plain error since the record did not show that the interrogator knew that the defendant had an attorney, and the defendant took the stand and repeated his statements. People v. Pool, 185 Colo. 131, 522 P.2d 102 (1974). Trial court's actions cannot be considered as harmless error where the court's removal of the determination of the authority of a defendant charged with theft to borrow the victim's money from the province of the jury violated the defendant's sixth amendment right to a jury trial. People v. Gracey, 940 P.2d 1050 (Colo. App. 1996). In determining whether prosecutorial impropriety mandates a new trial, appellate courts are obliged to evaluate the severity and frequency of the misconduct, any curative measures taken to alleviate the misconduct, and the likelihood that the misconduct constituted a material factor leading to defendant's conviction. People v. Jones, 832 P.2d 1036 (Colo. App. 1991). Reversible error exists if there are grounds for believing that the jury was substantially prejudiced by improper conduct. Where the prosecutor's ill-advised and improper comments were so numerous and highly prejudicial, the defendant was deprived of a fair trial requiring that the judgment of conviction be reversed. People v. Jones, 832 P.2d 1036 (Colo. App. 1991). Prosecution's comments during closing argument did not rise to the level of reversible error where comments were small part of lengthy closing; prosecutor fairly summarized the evidence; prosecutor emphasized the jury's prerogative to make an independent determination of the facts; and trial court sustained defense counsel's objections and prosecutor withdrew her comments. People v. Griffith, 58 P.3d 1111 (Colo. App. 2002). Prosecutor's use of Burke quotation was an improper attempt to persuade jurors; however, the error was harmless as it was an isolated incident in an otherwise proper closing argument in which the prosecutor repeatedly urged the jury to apply the rules of law to the evidence adduced at trial. People v. Clemons, 89 P.3d 479 (Colo. App. 2003). The determination of whether a prosecutor's statements constitute inappropriate prosecutorial argument is generally a matter for the exercise of trial court discretion; however, if an appellate court concludes that prejudice created by a prosecutor's conduct was so great as to result in a miscarriage of justice, a new trial may be granted notwithstanding the trial court's failure to impose such sanction. Harris v. People, 888 P.2d 259 (Colo. 1995). A new trial is the appropriate remedy for the deprivation of the defendant's right to a fair trial where, in view of the prosecutor's repeated remarks, the temporal context of the trial, and the critical role of witness credibility in the case, there was substantial likelihood that the prosecutor's improper comments impermissibly prejudiced the defendant's right to have his guilt determined by an impartial jury applying applicable legal standards to facts found on an objective evaluation of the evidence. Harris v. People, 888 P.2d 259 (Colo. 1995). The sufficiency of evidence presented at trial will be considered on appeal when evaluating claims of prosecutorial misconduct. The conclusion that the prosecutor's comments, repeated over the course of the entire closing argument, were substantially prejudicial was compelled when the conflicting and inconclusive nature of the evidence presented at trial was taken into consideration. Harris v. People, 888 P.2d 259 (Colo. 1995). In determining whether prosecutor's improper statements so prejudiced the jury as to affect the fundamental fairness of the trial, the court shall consider the language used, the context in which the statements were made, and the strength of the evidence supporting the conviction. Domingo-Gomez v. People, 125 P.3d 1043 (Colo. 2005); Crider v. People, 186 P.3d 39 (Colo. 2008). In light of evidence demonstrating defendant's guilt, prosecutor's conduct was not flagrant or tremendously improper. Although prosecutor made improper statements implying that defendant had a bad character, evidence of the defendant's guilt was strong, defense counsel made no contemporaneous objections to the statements, and the statements were infrequent and a small part of prosecutor's argument. Therefore, the statements did not so undermine the trial's fundamental fairness as to cast doubt on the reliability of the judgment of conviction. People v. Cordova, __ P.3d __ (Colo. App. 2011). It is prosecutorial misconduct for an attorney to characterize a witness's testimony or his character for truthfulness with any form of the word "lie". A violation of this prohibition, although sanctionable in other ways, does not warrant reversal if it was harmless. Domingo-Gomez v. People, 125 P.3d 1043 (Colo. 2005); Crider v. People, 186 P.3d 39 (Colo. 2008). Review of jury instruction for constitutional error where such instruction was submitted by the defendant is barred by application of invited error doctrine. People v. Zapata, 779 P.2d 1307 (Colo. 1989). Failure to instruct jury as to presumption of innocence is plain error. People v. Aragon, 665 P.2d 137 (Colo. App. 1982). Instructions held not to constitute "plain error". People v. Otwell, 179 Colo. 119, 498 P.2d 956 (1972); People v. Majors, 179 Colo. 204, 499 P.2d 1200 (1972); People v. Buckner, 180 Colo. 65, 504 P.2d 669 (1972); People v. Eades, 187 Colo. 74, 528 P.2d 382 (1974). Instruction to the jury on the credibility of the witnesses, where the words "including the defendant" were crossed out but were not totally obliterated and could be deciphered by the jury, did not constitute plain error. People v. Miller, 37 Colo. App. 294, 549 P.2d 1092 (1976), aff'd, 193 Colo. 415, 566 P.2d 1059 (1977). Where the defendant is charged with aggravated robbery and conspiracy to commit aggravated robbery, and is not entitled to an instruction on theft, an error in a theft instruction is harmless. Graham v. People, 199 Colo. 439, 610 P.2d 494 (1980). Trial court's failure to instruct the jury that voluntary intoxication may apply to sexual assault on a child does not constitute plain error for there is doubt whether the issue is yet settled. People v. O'Connell, 134 P.3d 460 (Colo. App. 2005). Challenges to interpreter must be made. When an interpreter is necessary for the court to translate testimony and the defense makes no challenge to the interpreter's qualifications or competency, the doctrine of plain error may not be applied in motion for new trial. People v. Bercillio, 179 Colo. 383, 500 P.2d 975 (1972). As must challenge of medical expert, unless plain error. Where defendant failed to interpose a timely objection to the trial court's qualification of a prosecution witness as a medical expert, any error in this regard did not rise to the level of plain error and thus was not recognized on appeal. People v. Litsey, 192 Colo. 19, 555 P.2d 974 (1976). As well as objections to admonishment of defense counsel. Where the trial court recesses in the middle of the cross-examination and admonishes defense counsel in the presence of the jury to the effect that counsel should change his attitude, and defendant's counsel does not object to the recess or the admonishment, it is not of a level to be "plain error". People v. Lovato, 181 Colo. 99, 507 P.2d 860 (1973). Determination of whether the misconduct at trial was plain error turns not on the nature of the misconduct but on the impact of the misconduct upon the result. People v. Constant, 44 Colo. App. 544, 623 P.2d 63 (1980), rev'd on other grounds, 645 P.2d 843 (Colo. 1982). Prosecutorial misconduct provides a basis for reversal because of plain error only where there is a substantial likelihood that it affected the verdict or deprived a defendant of a fair and impartial trial. People v. Constant, 645 P.2d 843 (Colo. 1982). Prosecutor's statement in closing argument held not to be plain error as comment in context was not calculated or intended to direct attention to defendant's failure to testify in his own behalf. People v. Wieghard, 727 P.2d 383 (Colo. App. 1986). Prosecutor's remark not plain error where remark may have been invited by defense counsel, remark was tangential and could not have prejudiced defendant, and there was overwhelming evidence of defendant's guilt. People v. Joyce, 68 P.3d 521 (Colo. App. 2002). Although prosecutor's remark during summation that the defendant had lied during his testimony and allusions to defendant's friends' cocaine habit was inappropriate, it did not constitute plain error. The improper comments were isolated ones included in a lengthy summation and could not have affected the verdict. People v. Herr, 868 P.2d 1121 (Colo. App. 1993). The scope of final arguments rests in the sound discretion of the trial court and its ruling will not be disturbed on appeal in the absence of gross abuse of discretion resulting in prejudice and a denial of justice. People v. Pennese, 830 P.2d 1085 (Colo. App. 1991). Prosecutorial misconduct must be flagrantly improper to be classified as plain error. Prosecutor's comment that the evidence of similar transactions between the victim and her father explained the victim's response to the assaults and her failure to report them earlier was not error considering the testimony of the victim and the limiting instructions given by the trial court regarding the proper use of similar transactions evidence. People v. Fell, 832 P.2d 1015 (Colo. App. 1991). Prosecutor's characterization of defendant's statement held "plain error". The prosecutor's characterization in his summation of defendant's written pretrial statement as "riddled with lies" constituted plain error affecting defendant's substantial rights. People v. Trujillo, 624 P.2d 924 (Colo. App. 1980). As is exposure of handcuffed defendant. A denial of a fair trial occurs where a defendant appears before a jury in handcuffs when the exposure was unnecessary and prejudicial. People v. Rael, 199 Colo. 201, 612 P.2d 1095 (1980). As is improper admission of evidence of other offenses. Admission into evidence of offenses not alleged as basis of habitual criminality during the second phase of a bifurcated trial constitutes reversible error. People v. Lucero, 200 Colo. 335, 615 P.2d 660 (1980). The giving of a "time-fuse" instruction (which grants the jury a time limit to finish its deliberations, at the end of which the jury will be dismissed) constitutes plain error and requires reversal. Allen v. People, 660 P.2d 896 (Colo. 1983). Failure to provide transcript of prior mistrial is of such magnitude that it requires a new trial. People v. St. John, 668 P.2d 988 (Colo. App. 1983). Where enhancement of sentence for crime of violence is plain error. Where a defendant is convicted of first-degree murder, and the mittimus reads that he was found to have committed a "crime of violence", but the jury was not instructed on the elements of crime of violence nor given a separate verdict form or interrogatory as required, enhancement of sentence for having committed a crime of violence would be plain error. The cause must be remanded for correction of the mittimus to show conviction of first-degree murder only, and for imposition of sentence on that crime only. People v. Thrower, 670 P.2d 1251 (Colo. App. 1983). Fact that testimony of hospital employee regarding defendant's statements made while confined for sanity examination used to rebut defendant's self-defense theory was given in prosecution's case-in-chief rather than as rebuttal testimony did not constitute plain error. People v. Kruse, 839 P.2d 1 (Colo. 1992). Because the trial record contained significant evidence of defendant's guilt, any error by the trial court in admitting certain testimony was not plain error. People v. Mapps, 231 P.3d 5 (Colo. App. 2009). Testimony by the victim and police officer describing the robber does not constitute plain error. The evidence corroborated other properly admitted evidence and although arguably cumulative, did not have a tendency to confuse or inflame the jury's passions or undermine the fairness of the trial. People v. Boehmer, 872 P.2d 1320 (Colo. App. 1993). Allowing a jury unsupervised access to videotape and transcript of a drug transaction between the defendant and a police informant was not plain error. People v. Aponte, 867 P.2d 183 (Colo. App. 1993). Prejudicial error found. People v. Snook, 729 P.2d 1026 (Colo. App. 1986), aff'd, 745 P.2d 647 (Colo. 1987). Allowing defendant to stand trial in orange jump suit, which defendant described as prison garb, was not plain error. People v. Green, 759 P.2d 814 (Colo. App. 1988). Declaration of mistrial to correct error at trial. Zamora v. People, 175 Colo. 340, 487 P.2d 1116 (1971); Howe v. People, 178 Colo. 248, 496 P.2d 1040 (1972); People v. Medina, 185 Colo. 101, 521 P.2d 1257 (1974); People v. Lankford, 185 Colo. 445, 524 P.2d 1382 (1974); People v. Goff, 187 Colo. 103, 530 P.2d 514 (1974); People v. Rogers, 187 Colo. 128, 528 P.2d 1309 (1974); People v. Becker, 187 Colo. 344, 531 P.2d 386 (1975).

Rule 53 - Regulation of Conduct in the Courtroom

Conduct in the courtroom pertaining to the publication of judicial proceedings shall conform to Canon 3 of the Canons of Judicial Ethics, as adopted by the Supreme Court of Colorado.

Colo. R. Crim. P. 53

Rule 54 - Application and Exception

(a) Courts. These Rules apply to all criminal proceedings in all courts of record in the state of Colorado. These Rules do not apply to municipal ordinance and charter violations.

(b) Proceedings.

(1) Peace Bonds. These Rules do not alter the power of judges to hold for security of the peace and for good behavior as provided by law, but in such cases the procedure shall conform to these rules so far as they are applicable.

(2) Other Proceedings. These Rules are not applicable to extradition and rendition of fugitives; forfeiture of property for violation of a statute or the collection of fines and penalties; nor to any other special proceedings where a statutory procedure inconsistent with these Rules is provided.

(c) Application of Terms. "Law" includes statutes and judicial decisions. "Civil action" refers to a civil action in a court of record. "Oath" includes affirmations. "Prosecuting attorney" means the attorney general, a district attorney or his assistant or deputy or special prosecutor. The words "demurrer", "motion to quash", "plea in abatement", "plea in bar", and "special plea in bar", or words to the same effect in any statute, shall be construed to mean the motion raising a defense or objection provided in Rule 12.

(d) Numbering-Meaning of "No Colorado Rule". Insofar as practicable, the order and numbering of these Rules follows that of the Federal Rules of Criminal Procedure. In some instances, usually because of differences in judicial systems or of jurisdiction, there is no Colorado rule corresponding in number with an existing federal rule. In these instances to maintain the general numbering scheme, the phrase "No Colorado Rule" appears opposite the number for which there is a federal rule but not a Colorado rule. The phrase "No Colorado Rule" means only that there is no rule included in these Rules covering the subject of the federal rule bearing that number. The phrase does not imply either that there is or that there is not constitutional, statutory or case law in Colorado covering the subject of the corresponding federal rule.

Colo. R. Crim. P. 54

Annotation Rules of criminal procedure not applicable to extradition proceedings. Allowing full discovery in extradition proceedings would defeat the limited purpose of the habeas corpus hearing. Temen v. Barry, 695 P.2d 745 (Colo. 1984). Rules of criminal procedure govern all proceedings in criminal actions in courts of record. People ex rel Shinn v. District Court, 172 Colo. 23, 469 P.2d 732 (1970). But not trial de novo for violation of ordinance. The municipal court rules and not the rules of criminal procedure apply in a trial de novo in the county court for violation of a municipal ordinance. Rainwater v. County Court, 43 Colo. App. 477, 604 P.2d 1195 (1979). Rules of criminal procedure not applicable to extradition proceedings. Allowing full discovery in extradition proceedings would defeat the limited purpose of the habeas corpus hearing. Temen v. Barry, 695 P.2d 745 (Colo. 1984). Applied in People v. Brisbin, 175 Colo. 423, 488 P.2d 63 (1971); People v. Reliford, 39 Colo. App. 474, 568 P.2d 496 (1977).

Rule 55 - Records

(a)Register of actions (criminal docket). The clerk shall keep a record known as the register of actions and shall enter those items set forth below. The register of actions may be in any form or style prescribed by Chief Justice Directive or approved by the State Court Administrator. A register of actions shall be prepared for each case filed. The file number of each case shall be entered in the court case management system. All documents filed with the clerk, all process issued and returns made thereon, all costs, appearances, orders, verdicts, and judgments shall be noted chronologically in the register of actions. The entries shall be brief but shall show the date and title of each document filed, order or writ issued, data transfer submitted or received, and the substance of each order or judgment of the court and the returns showing execution of process. The notation of an order or judgment shall show the date the notation is made. The notation of the judgment in the register of actions shall constitute the entry of judgment.

(b)Criminal Record. Repealed effective September 4, 1974.

(c)Indices; Calendars. The clerk shall keep indices of all records. The clerk shall also keep as directed by the court, calendars of all hearings and all cases ready for trial, which shall distinguish trials to a jury from trials to the court. Indices and calendars may be in any form or style prescribed by Chief Justice Directive or approved by the State Court Administrator.

(d)Files. Repealed effective June 6, 2019.

(e)Reporter's Notes; Custody, Use, Ownership, Retention. For proceedings in district court, the practice and procedure concerning court reporter notes and electronic or mechanical recordings shall be as prescribed in Chief Justice Directive 05-03, Management Plan for Court Reporting and Recording Services. For proceedings in county court, that practice and procedure shall be as prescribed in C.R.C.P. 380.

(f)Retention and Disposition of Records. The clerk shall retain and dispose of all court records in accordance with the Colorado Judicial Department's records retention manual.

Colo. R. Crim. P. 55

Amended and adopted February 14, 2019, effective 2/14/2019; amended and adopted June 6, 2019, effective 6/6/2019.

Annotation Court of record has an affirmative duty to contemporaneously record all proceedings. Reconstruction of the record at a later time is not an adequate substitute for a contemporaneous record. Jones v. District Court, 780 P.2d 526 (Colo. 1989). Bench or side-bar conferences are not to be conducted off the record unless the parties so request or so consent. Jones v. District Court, 780 P.2d 526 (Colo. 1989). But a failure to record all trial proceedings will not always result in reversible error. Trial court's failure to record certain bench conferences and pretrial conference was harmless where defense counsel never objected to unrecorded proceedings, defendant cannot show how error prejudiced her, and there is sufficient information on the record to rule on appeal. People v. Pineda, 40 P.3d 60 (Colo. App. 2001). The court did not err by taking judicial notice of defendant's probation status after determining the status from the state computer system. Since § 13-1-119 and this rule expressly approve of records kept and maintained in a state computer system, the court may take judicial notice of the court records contained in the system. People v. Linares-Guzman, 195 P.3d 1130 (Colo. App. 2008).

Rule 55.1 - Public Access to Court Records in Criminal Cases

(a) Court records in criminal cases are presumed to be accessible to the public. Unless a court record or any part of a court record is inaccessible to the public pursuant to statute, rule, regulation, or Chief Justice Directive, the court may deny the public access to a court record or to any part of a court record only in compliance with this rule.

(1) Motion Requesting to Limit Public Access to Court Record Not Previously Filed. A party may file a motion requesting that the court limit public access to a court record not previously filed or to any part of such a court record by making it inaccessible to the public or by allowing only a redacted copy of it to be accessible to the public. The motion must be accompanied by the court record the moving party seeks to make inaccessible or partially inaccessible to the public, must be served on any opposing party, and must be identified on the publicly available Register of Actions as a motion to limit public access. An opposing party wishing to object to the motion must file a response within 14 days after service of the motion unless otherwise directed by the court. Upon receiving the motion, the clerk shall make the subject court record inaccessible to the public pending the court's resolution of the motion, except that if a party seeks to make inaccessible to the public only parts of the subject court record, then the party must also submit a redacted version of the court record with the motion and the clerk shall make the redacted version of the court record accessible to the public without undue delay. The clerk shall also make the motion and the response inaccessible to the public pending the court's resolution of the motion, except that, in its discretion, the court may order that the motion and the response, or redacted versions of the motion and the response, be accessible to the public during that timeframe.

(2) Motion Requesting to Limit Public Access to Court Record Previously Filed. A party may file a motion requesting that the court limit public access to a court record previously filed (including one not yet made accessible to the public) or to any part of such a court record by making it inaccessible to the public or by allowing only a redacted copy of it to be accessible to the public. The motion must identify by title and date of filing the court record the moving party seeks to make inaccessible or partially inaccessible to the public, must be served on any opposing party, and must be identified on the publicly available Register of Actions as a motion to limit public access. An opposing party wishing to object to the motion must file a response within 14 days after service of the motion unless otherwise directed by the court. Upon receiving the motion, the clerk shall make the subject court record inaccessible to the public pending the court's resolution of the motion, except that if a party seeks to make inaccessible to the public only parts of the subject court record, then the party must submit a redacted version of the court record with the motion and the clerk shall make the redacted version of the court record accessible to the public without undue delay. The clerk shall also make the motion and the response inaccessible to the public pending the court's resolution of the motion, except that, in its discretion, the court may order that the motion and the response, or redacted versions of the motion and the response, be accessible to the public during that timeframe.

(3) Title and Contents of Motion and Response. A motion to limit public access shall identify the court record or any part of the court record the moving party wishes to make inaccessible to the public, state the reasons for the request, and specify how long the information identified should remain inaccessible to the public. A response to a motion to limit public access shall state the reasons why the motion should be denied in whole or in part. The motion shall be titled, "Motion to Limit Public Access"; the response shall be titled, "Response to Motion to Limit Public Access."

(4) Orders Entered on Court's Own Motion. The court may, on its own motion, make a court record or other filing inaccessible to the public or order that only a redacted copy of it be accessible to the public. If the court does so, it must provide notice to the parties and the public via the publicly available Register of Actions and must also comply with paragraphs (a)(6), (a)(7), (a)(8), (a)(9), and (a)(10) of this rule. The clerk shall make the subject court record or filing inaccessible to the public pending the court's final decision, except that, in its discretion, the court may order a redacted version of the court record or filing accessible to the public during that timeframe. In its discretion, the court may hold a hearing in accordance with paragraph (a)(5) of this rule before ordering on its own motion a court record or any part of a court record inaccessible to the public.

(5) Hearing. The court may conduct a hearing on a motion to limit public access to a court record or to any part of a court record. Notice of the hearing shall be provided to the parties and the public via the publicly available Register of Actions. The court may close the hearing or part of the hearing if it finds that doing so is necessary to prevent the public from accessing the information that is the subject of the motion under consideration. If the court closes the hearing or part of the hearing, it shall enter appropriate protective orders regarding the transcript or recording of the proceeding and any evidence introduced during the hearing. Any such orders shall be modified or vacated if the court ultimately denies, in whole or in part, the request to limit public access.

(6) When Request Granted. The court shall not grant any request to limit public access to a court record or to any part of a court record, or enter an order on its own motion limiting such public access, unless it issues a written order in which it:

(I) specifically identifies one or more substantial interests served by making the court record inaccessible to the public or by allowing only a redacted copy of it to be accessible to the public;

(II) finds that no less restrictive means than making the record inaccessible to the public or allowing only a redacted copy of it to be accessible to the public exists to achieve or protect any substantial interests identified; and

(III) concludes that any substantial interests identified override the presumptive public access to the court record or to an unredacted copy of it.

(7) Duration of Order Granting Request. Any order limiting public access to a court record or to any part of a court record shall indicate a date or event certain by which the order will expire. That date or event shall be considered the order's expiration date or event.

(8) Public Access to Order Granting Request. The order limiting public access to a court record or to any part of a court record pursuant to this rule shall be accessible to the public, except that any information deemed inaccessible to the public under this rule shall be redacted from the order.

(9) Review of Order Granting Request. The court shall review any order limiting public access to a court record or to any part of a court record pursuant to this rule at the time of the expiration of the order or earlier upon motion of one of the parties. The court may postpone the expiration of such an order if, in a written order, it either determines that the findings previously made under paragraph (a)(6) of this rule continue to apply or makes new findings pursuant to paragraph (a)(6) of this rule justifying postponement of the expiration date or event. If the court postpones the expiration of the order, it must set a new expiration date or event.

(10) Limited Access to Original Court Record When Request Granted. If a court limits public access to a court record or to any part of a court record pursuant to this rule, only judges, court staff, parties to the case (and, if represented, their attorneys in that case), and other authorized Judicial Department staff shall have access to the original court record.

(11) When Request Denied. When denying a motion to limit public access to a court record or to any part of a court record under this rule, the court must ensure, without undue delay, that the public is given access to: the subject court record or the parts of that court record previously made temporarily inaccessible to the public pending resolution of the motion; the motion; any response; and, as to any hearing held, the transcript or recording of the proceeding and any evidence introduced during that proceeding.

Colo. R. Crim. P. 55.1

Amended and Adopted December 17, 2020, effective 5/10/2021.

Rule 56 - Courts and Clerks

(a) All Courts Deemed Open. All courts of record shall be deemed always open for the purpose of filing any proper paper, of issuing and returning process and of making motions and orders. The clerk's office with the clerk or a deputy in attendance shall be open during business hours on all days except Sundays, legal holidays and such other days as the courthouse of the particular court shall be closed as provided by federal or state statute.

(b) County Courts Away from County Seat. When a county court is held regularly at a location other than the county seat, the county judge shall designate by rule when such place shall be open for the transaction of court matters. The clerk's office, with the clerk or ex officio clerk or a deputy in attendance, shall be open during business hours on all days except Sundays, legal holidays, and such other days as the courthouse of the particular court shall be closed as provided by federal or state statute.

Colo. R. Crim. P. 56

Rule 57 - Rules of Court

(a) Rules of Courts of Record. All local court rules, including local county court procedures and standing orders having the effect of local court rules regarding the criminal courts, enacted before February 1, 1992, are hereby repealed. Each court, by a majority of its judges, may from time to time propose local court rules and amendments of the local court rules. A proposed local rule or amendment shall not be inconsistent with the Colorado Rules of Criminal Procedure or with any directive of the Supreme Court regarding the conduct of formal judicial proceedings in criminal courts. A proposed local rule or amendment shall not be effective until it is approved by the Supreme Court. To obtain approval, three copies of any proposed local rule or amendment shall be submitted to the Supreme Court through the office of the State Court Administrator. Reasonable uniformity of local court rules is required. Numbering and format of any local court rule shall be as prescribed by the Supreme Court. Numbering and format requirements are on file at the office of the State Court Administrator. Upon approval by the Supreme Court of the local rule or amendment, a copy shall be furnished to the office of the Judicial Administrator to the end that all rules as provided herein may be published promptly and that copies may be available to the public. The Supreme Court's approval of a local court rule or local procedure shall not preclude review of that rule or procedure under the law or circumstances of a particular case. Nothing in this rule is intended to affect the authority of a court to adopt internal administrative procedures not relating to the conduct of formal judicial proceedings as prescribed by the Colorado Rules of Criminal Procedure.

(b) Procedure Not Otherwise Specified. If no procedure is specifically prescribed by rule, the court may proceed in any lawful manner not inconsistent with these Rules of Criminal Procedure or with any directive of the Supreme Court regarding the conduct of formal judicial proceedings in the criminal courts, and shall look to the Rules of Civil Procedure and to the applicable law if no Rule of Criminal Procedure exists.

Colo. R. Crim. P. 57

Source: Entire rule amended January 9, 1992, effective 2/1/1992.

Annotation Applied in Sollitt v. District Court, 180 Colo. 114, 502 P.2d 1108 (1972).

Rule 58 - Forms

See the Appendix to Chapterнет 29 for illustrative forms.

Colo. R. Crim. P. 58

Rule 59 - Effective Date

These Rules, except as noted on specific rules, take effect on April 1, 1974. Amendments take effect on the date indicated. They govern all proceedings in criminal actions brought after they take effect and also all further proceedings in actions then pending.

Colo. R. Crim. P. 59

Annotation Applied in People v. Slender Wrap, Inc., 36 Colo. App. 11, 536 P.2d 850 (1975).

Rule 60 - Citation

These Rules may be known and cited as the "Colorado Rules of Criminal Procedure", or "Crim. P.".

Colo. R. Crim. P. 60

232

39812414R00128